PRAISE FOR *DAVID BALL ON DAMAGES 3*

"As is his custom, David Ball has brought his brilliance to bear once again to offer new and important insights into the evaluation and proof of damages in the third edition of *David Ball on Damages*. The most important aspect of the new edition is that it coalesces the timely and valuable wisdom of [the] Rules, Reptile, and Ball Damages methods and blends them seamlessly into techniques for influencing today's jurors. Once again, David's analytical skills are exceeded only by his ability to reduce the complex to simple, usable form. The book is a must read for trial lawyers."

—Howard L. Nations, Trial Lawyer Hall of Fame inductee, recipient of
the American Association for Justice Heavy Lifting Award

"David Ball's *Damages 3* is appropriately named. It has at least three times the information of the earlier editions. David is constantly in touch with hundreds of lawyers and trials in addition to ongoing focus group research. This new edition is an absolute must."

—Jude Basile, member of the Inner Circle of Advocates, president of the Trial Lawyers College

"It's hard to improve on a masterpiece like *Damages 2*, but *Damages 3* completely refines and improves the previous edition through teaching by example and by easy, step-by-step instructions with clear explanations. What you immediately notice about *Damages 3* is how clearly the principles are explained with new and improved techniques. In just one volume, David Ball has managed to bring together and refine the techniques of the Rules, Reptile, and Ball Damages methods. This book is a dramatic expansion of the previous edition. This updated and improved edition is a must."

—Paul Luvera, member of the Inner Circle of Advocates,
fellow of the American College of Trial Lawyers

"There are a few people whose arrival on the scene irrevocably changes it. 'Game changers.' From his first book on how stories need to be told in a courtroom, David Ball's commanding gifts of strategic analysis, audaciously original intelligence, penetrating understanding of the what/when/how of jurors' needs, [and] his investigations have changed how we speak to jurors (and to each other) on the subject of damages. If David Ball is reporting his latest research and results on how attorneys can help those who've suffered 'harms and losses' at the hands of others . . . read it."

—Joshua Karton, Communication Arts for the Professional, Gerry Spence
Trial Lawyers College, and California Western School of Law

"*David Ball on Damages*, 3rd edition, is a must have. It might be malpractice not to know this book."

—Robert T. Hall, author of *Grief and Loss,* former president
of the International Academy of Trial Lawyers

"*David Ball on Damages,* 3rd edition, is an invaluable source. Any trial lawyer who does not take the time to read this new edition is not adequately arming himself or herself to best represent their clients."

—Joseph A. Quinn, member of the Inner Circle of Trial Advocates, fellow of the International Academy of Trial Lawyers and the American College of Trial Lawyers

"*David Ball on Damages 3* is a must read for anyone seriously trying cases today. If you are still relying on *Damages 2,* you are out of date. *Damages 3* contains five years of additional research and incorporates lessons learned from *Reptile* and *Rules of the Road.* It is required reading."

—Bruce H. Stern, author of *Litigating Brain Injury Cases,* listed in *Best Lawyers in America* and *Who's Who in the Law*

"The third edition is essential reading and rereading before every trial and even pretrial proceedings."

—Ernie Teitel, fellow of the International Academy of Trial Lawyers, member of the American Board of Trial Advocates

"[*David Ball on Damages,* 3rd edition], is every plaintiff lawyer's bible."

—Jerome F. O'Neill, listed in *Best Lawyers in America,* member of the International Society of Barristers and the American Board of Trial Advocates

"Some works are timely; others are timeless. David Ball's *Damages 3* is both. The inimitable Dr. Ball has produced his best and latest work in *Damages 3*. Without learning the techniques and rules taught by *Damages 3,* you should not try a case. I used *Damages 3* in discovery in a recent case. The settlement was fifteen times higher than the offer before I was associated with the case. Almost the entire focus of my discovery was directed to [the] defendant's conduct, applying the rules and techniques taught in *Damages 3*."

—Guy R. Bucci, member of the American Association for Justice

"*David Ball on Damages,* 3rd edition, is essential for every plaintiffs' trial lawyer's toolbox. Not only has Ball moved his own work to the next level and refined it, but he has also expanded his vision to integrate all of the latest knowledge and cutting-edge techniques. And it's all in one book! Step by step, he explains how to do it and how to make it work for you. This third edition is the Rosetta stone of modern trial practice guides. Don't try another case without it."

—Thomas Penfield, adjunct professor of law, University of San Diego Law School; listed in *Best Lawyers in America*

David Ball
on
Damages

Third Edition

David Ball on Damages

Third Edition

David Ball, PhD

Trial Guides, LLC

Trial Guides, LLC, Portland, Oregon 97210

© 2013 Trial Guides, LLC

All Rights Reserved. Published 2013

TRIAL GUIDES and logo are registered trademarks of Trial Guides, LLC.

ISBN: 978-1-934833-84-1

Library of Congress Control Number: 2012947080

These materials, or any parts or portions thereof, may not be reproduced in any form, written or mechanical, or be programmed into any electronic storage or retrieval system, without the express written permission of Trial Guides, LLC, unless such copying is expressly permitted by federal copyright law. Please direct inquiries to:

Trial Guides, LLC
Attn: Permissions
2350 NW York Street
Portland, OR 97210
(800) 309-6845
www.trialguides.com

Printed and bound in the United States of America.

This book is printed on acid-free paper.

10 9 8 7 6 5 4 3 2 1

Dedication to the First Edition

As a trial consultant, I have worked on many hundreds of cases for a wide variety of trial attorneys on both sides of the aisle. The strategies in this book have as their source many of the good ideas from these attorneys, along with principles generated from years of research, focus groups, mock trials, and post-trial interviews with jurors, and the advice and strategies gleaned from trial consultants and attorneys with whom I have worked and taught CLE seminars across the country.

This book is dedicated to all those who will spot their ideas and strategies as the inspirations for these pages—especially Atlanta's Don C. Keenan, from whom I have borrowed the most. It is also dedicated to the National Jury Project's Susan Macpherson, who for years has provided me with enough wise guidance to deserve more gratitude than I can express; and to Raleigh attorney Donald H. Beskind, whose years of advice and friendship have shaped more things in my life than just this book.

I also dedicate this book to the insurance companies, chambers of commerce, and politicians whose methods of doing business inversely inspired this book.

David Ball, PhD

Contents

Publisher's Note xxix
Foreword to the Second Edition xxxi
Foreword to the Third Edition xxxiii
Preface xxxv
Acknowledgments for the First Edition. xxxvi
Acknowledgments for the Second Edition xxxvii
Acknowledgments for the Third Edition xxxviii
Introduction to the Second Edition, 2005 xl
Introduction to the Third Edition, 2010 xliii

Chapter One. Fundamentals

Introduction: The Poisoned Pool 1

Fundamental One: Juror Self-Protection 3

Fundamental Two: Proportion of Time on Harms and Losses. 4

Fundamental Three: You 6

Fundamental Four: Client's Point of View 7

    Isolation and Lack of Mobility 7

    Danger 7

    Learning the Harm 7

Fundamental Five: Defendant Conduct 10

    Rule Violations 10

        1) Applying the Rules 11

        2) The Umbrella Rule for Every Case: "Needless Danger" 12

        3) The Only Permissible Choice: The Safest. 12

    Defining Negligence as Outrageous 14

        "Ordinary" Care 15

        "Reasonable" Care 15

        Products Liability. 16

        "All the Other Kids Do It!" 16

- Egregious Conduct Does Not Stop with the Negligent Act 17
  - Harm upon Harm 18
  - Anger 18
  - Motivations 18
  - Defense Counsel 19
  - You 19
- Make Defendant Face Responsibility 20
- Last-Minute Stipulated Negligence 21
- Lack of Remorse (Crocodile Tears) 21
- Attacks on Your Client 22
- Malingering and Exaggeration of Symptoms 22

FUNDAMENTAL SIX: INADVERTENT WRONGDOING 23

FUNDAMENTAL SEVEN: WORTHWHILENESS OF MONEY 24
- Unclear Purpose 25
- Future Medical Inventions 25
- Money Not Necessary 25
- Getting Along Fine without Money 26
- Other Sources of Money 26
- Come Back for More 27

FUNDAMENTAL EIGHT: FIX, HELP, MAKE UP FOR 28
- To Fix 28
- To Help 29
  - Familiarity 29
  - Anchoring 29
  - Negative Anchoring 29
- To Balance (To Make Up For) 30
- Community Losses 31

FUNDAMENTAL NINE: DEGREE OF HARMS AND LOSSES 32

FUNDAMENTAL TEN: WHO GETS THE MONEY? 33
- Client Characteristics 33
  - Vignettes 33
- Stereotypes 33

    Negative Stereotypes 34

    Positive Stereotypes 34

Normal Behavior 35

    Avoiding the Harm 35

    Irrelevant Considerations 35

    In-Trial Impression 35

Client in Trial? 36

Client Preparation 36

Out-of-Court Behavior 37

    Driving 38

    What's Online? 38

Who *Really* Gets the Money? 39

Fighting Spirit 40

FUNDAMENTAL ELEVEN: IMPORTANCE 42

FUNDAMENTAL TWELVE: GOING HOME AFTERWARD 44

FUNDAMENTAL THIRTEEN: COMPROMISE KILLS 46

FUNDAMENTAL FOURTEEN: SEEN WORSE, BEEN WORSE 47

FUNDAMENTAL FIFTEEN: PEOPLE SHOULD PAY FOR THEIR OWN PROBLEMS 49

FUNDAMENTAL SIXTEEN: DIVINE PUNISHMENT ("GOD IS MY CO-JUROR") 50

FUNDAMENTAL SEVENTEEN: DON'T WANNA PUNISH THE DEFENDANT 51

CHAPTER TWO. NONECONOMIC DAMAGES

2-1 Obstacle 1: No Worthwhileness 53

2-2 Obstacle 2: No Way to Calculate 53

2-3 Obstacle 3: Can't Define "Compensation" 54

2-4 Obstacle 4: Defense Plea for Jury Nullification 55

2-5 Obstacle 5: Bad Comparison to Economic Damages 55

2-6 Obstacle 6: Why Pay Family to Be Caretakers? Why Pay
      for Professional Care When the Family Can Do It? 56

2-7 Obstacle 7: "Even If That's the Right Amount, It's Far Too Much
      for Any Individual" 58

CHAPTER THREE. RULES FOR JURORS: PREPONDERANCE; HARMS AND LOSSES ONLY

- 3-1 The Preponderance Template.................................61
  - 3-1-1 The Goal..62
  - 3-1-2 The Process..62
- 3-2 The Preponderance Formula..................................63
  - 3-2-1 Words..63
  - 3-2-2 Hands..63
- 3-3 Preponderance Template: Jury Voir Dire......................64
- 3-4 Preponderance Template: Opening (The Boilerplate Tag)......67
- 3-5 Preponderance Template in Plaintiff's Testimony.............68
- 3-6 Preponderance Template in Defense Testimony................69
- 3-7 Preponderance Template in Closing...........................69
  - 3-7-1 Teaching the Law...70
  - 3-7-2 Words, Words, Words....................................70
- 3-8 Preponderance Template: Conclusion.........................71
- 3-9 The Harms-and-Losses-*Only* Template........................71
- 3-10 Harms-and-Losses-*Only* Template: Jury Voir Dire...........72
- 3-11 Harms-and-Losses-*Only* Template: Opening.................74
- 3-12 Harms-and-Losses-*Only* Template: Testimony...............75
- 3-13 Harms-and-Losses-*Only* Template: Closing.................75

CHAPTER FOUR. WITH OR WITHOUT JURY VOIR DIRE

- 4-1 Voir Dire Limitations: Fight Them! No Voir Dire? Fight for It!.........79
  - 4-1-1 Sham Rehabilitation.....................................80
  - 4-1-2 Offer of Proof..81
- 4-2 Jurors' First Impression: Primacy and Persistence............82
  - 4-2-1 Primacy..82
  - 4-2-2 Persistence..82
- 4-3 How to Ask...83
  - 4-3-1 Seek Information with Every Question..................83
  - 4-3-2 Ask Open-Ended Questions..............................84
  - 4-3-3 Follow Up...85

4-4 Tort "Reform" 85
    4-4-1 The Essential Question 85
    4-4-2 Shallow or Deep Attitudes............................. 86
    4-4-3 Frivolous-Case Questions 87
    4-4-4 McDonald's Coffee 87
    4-4-5 Caveat on Tort-"Reformed" Jurors..................... 87
4-5 Noneconomic Damages: Spotting Problem Jurors 87
    4-5-1 Compare Demeanors 90
    4-5-2 No Advocacy... 90
    4-5-3 Short Version... 90
    4-5-4 "Poisoning" Other Jurors.............................. 91
    4-5-5 Promise to Explain How to Calculate Noneconomic Damages ... 91
4-6 Other Noneconomic Elements 92
4-7 Tolerance for Pain 93
4-8 Asking about (or Sneaking in) a Specific Figure in Voir Dire 93
4-9 Asking about Caps 93
4-10 Juror Demographics Affecting Damages 94
4-11 Personality Traits 95
    4-11-1 Optimist/Pessimist Scale 96
    4-11-2 Caretaker/Noncaretaker Scale 96
    4-11-3 Emotion/Non-Emotion Scale 98
        Extremes 99
        Initial Reaction to Case 99
    4-11-4 Insider/Dispossessed Scale........................... 99
    4-11-5 Content/Malcontent Scale............................. 100
        Focus-Group Learning 100
    4-11-6 Control/Not-in-Control Scale
        Ship Captain/Landlubber-Passenger Scale................... 101
4-12 Religion Matters 102
4-13 Inadvertence 102
4-14 Leaders 103
4-15 Child Witnesses.. 104

4-16 Paid Experts. 105
4-17 Multiple Survivors. 105
4-18 Harms Consultants 106
4-19 Harms and Losses Lists 106
4-20 Final Thoughts 109

CHAPTER FIVE. OPENING STATEMENT

5-1 Introduction 111
5-2 Your Standing with the Jury. 112
    5-2-1 Premature Advocacy 112
    5-2-2 Omission. 113
5-3 Structure 113
    5-3-1 Too Much Information 113
    5-3-2 Clarity. 114
5-4 The Template. 114
THE TEMPLATE. 117
5-5-1 Opening. Part I: Primary Rule(s) 119
5-5-2 Opening. Part II: Story of *What the Defendant Did*. 124
    Simple Chronological Sequence. 124
    Simultaneous Events 125
    Keep Track of Time Sequence 125
    Simple Present Tense 125
    Simple Short Sentences 125
    Defendant's Name. 125
    Active Voice. 126
    One Fact 126
    Sensory Input 126
    Move Forward in Time 126
    Events Only. 126
    Premature Advocacy. 127
    Other Things to Omit. 127
        Omit "Acts" of Omission. 127

    Omit Anything the Defendant Thought or Felt. 127
    Omit (For Now) Motive: Why the Defendant Did What He Did. . 128
Point of View. 128
    Camera Eyes and Ears 128
Subordinate Your Client 130
Don't Use Pronouns. 133
Telling the Story 133
    Set the Scene. 133
        When Does the Story Start? 134
        How Long?. 134
        Each Sentence Is Important 134
        End of Story 134
    The Next Thing the Defendant Did 135
    First Person Stories. 135

5-5-3 Opening. Part III. Who We Are Suing and Why:
The Safety Rules the Defendant(s) Violated. 138
    The Why-We're-Suing Paradigm 139
    "Failed to Follow" 144
    Expert Conclusions 144

5-5-4 Opening. Part IV: Undermine. What Is Wrong
with the Negligence Defenses?. 145
    How to Undermine 146
    Don't Miss Anything 148

5-5-5 Opening. Part V. Causation and Damages. 149
    A. Introduction to Harms and Losses. 149
    B. Mechanism of Harm
(How Did the Negligent Act Cause Each Injury?) 150
        Death Case 151
    C. Personal Consequences of Each Injury 152
        Undermining Defense Causation and Damages Contentions 152
        Malingering, Symptom Exaggeration, etc.. 154
    D. Fixes and Helps 154

    Minimum Life-Care Plan 154
    Life Expectancy 155
    Showing Longer Life Expectancy 156
    Geriatrics 157
    Case Manager 157
    Empirical Experience 157
    Attribution 157
    Future Care Costs v. Past Care Costs 158
    Language 158
    Who Gets the Money? 158
  E. What Cannot Be Fixed or Helped 158
    Base This on the Jury Instructions 159
    Interim Deprivation 159
        Plaintiff as "Normal" (Before) v. After 160
        Earlier Deficits 160
  5-5-6 Opening. Part VI: "Before" 161
  5-5-7 Opening. Part VII: What Can the Jury Do about It? 163
5-6 Damages-Only Case 164
  Part I. Primary Rules 164
  Part II. Story of What the Defendant Did 165
  Part III. Who We Are Suing and Why:
        The Safety Rules the Defendant(s) Violated 165
  Part IV. Undermine (What Is Wrong with the Negligence Defenses?) . . 166
  Part V. Causation and Damages 166
  Part VI. "Before" 166
  Part VII. "What Can the Jury Do about It?" 166
5-7 Loss of Personal Image 166
5-8 Beware the Unknown: What Jurors Don't Know Can Clobber You 166
  5-8-1 Seat Belts 166
  5-8-2 Stereotypes 167
5-9 Keep Jurors Listening 169
  5-9-1 Succinctness: The Lawyer's Challenge 170

 5-10 Fear of Not Understanding 171

 5-11 Motivations 172

 5-12 Loss of Consortium 173

 5-13 E-nun-ci-ate 173

 5-14 Stop the Bullet Points 174

 5-15 Dress Approachably 175

 5-16 Decorate Yourself Modestly and Moderately 175

   5-16-1 Men 175

   5-16-2 Women 175

 5-17 Length of Opening 175

 5-18 Eye Contact 176

 5-19 Movement 176

 5-20 Rehearse 176

   5-20-1 Notes 177

 5-21 Lighting 177

CHAPTER SIX. DIRECT EXAMINATION

 6-1 Mud and Gold (Less Mud = More Gold) 179

   6-1-1 Gold Standard for Inclusion 180

    Video 180

    Experts 180

   6-1-2 First Witness 180

 6-2 Controlling Your Witness on Direct ("~~What happened next?~~") 182

 6-3 Short Questions 183

 6-4 Don't Make Your Client a Whiner 183

 6-5 How Does that Make You Feel? 184

 6-6 Spouse 184

 6-7 Before and After Witnesses 185

 6-8 How Many? 185

 6-9 Stories 185

 6-10 Hollow Advocacy 186

 6-11 Witnesses as Sources of Worthwhileness 186

6-12 Sequence of Witnesses: Damages Witnesses...........................188
6-13 Children...188
6-14 Grief and Pain Counselors..188
6-15 Minimum Life-Care Plans (and Equivalents)..........................189
    6-15-1 Don't Rush Life-Care Plan Testimony......................189
    6-15-2 Show-and-Tell...190
    6-15-3 Edit the Plan...191
6-16 Using Liability Witnesses for Damages..............................191
6-17 Day-in-the-Life Videos...191
    6-17-1 "Staged!"...192
    6-17-2 Videographer..192
    6-17-3 Time Span...192
    6-17-4 Stranger in the House.....................................192
    6-17-5 Comfort...192
    6-17-6 Lighting..193
    6-17-7 Windows...193
    6-17-8 Sound...193
    6-17-9 Background..193
    6-17-10 Jurors Judge a Family Partly by the Family's Home........193
    6-17-11 Edit, then Shoot...194
    6-17-12 Settlement Conferences, Mediations.......................194
    6-17-13 Show a Day-in-the-Life Video That Is
            100 Percent Admissible..................................194
6-18 Should Your Client Be in Trial?....................................194
    6-18-1 Preparing the Jury for a Client Who Seems
           Less Harmed than She Is...............................196
6-19 Client In and Out of Trial...197
    6-19-1 Driving?..197
    6-19-2 Counsel (You)...198
6-20 The Best and Cheapest Experts: High-School Teachers................198
6-21 Paid Plaintiff's Experts...199
6-22 How to Use Experts...200

    1. Methodology 201

    2. Methodology Applied 203

    3. Methodology Misapplied by Defense 203

CHAPTER SEVEN. CROSS-EXAMINATION

7-1 Rules for Analysis 205

7-2 Hitchhiking: Use Defense Liability Experts for Damages 206

    7-2-1 When Hitchhiking, Be Friendly 207

7-3 Undermining Defense Life-Expectancy Estimates 209

7-4 Undermining Accusations of Malingering and
    Exaggeration of Symptoms 210

7-5 "Litigation Syndrome" and Other Bogusaria 211

7-6 Control 213

CHAPTER EIGHT. CLOSING

8-1 Overview 215

8-2 When to Write It 216

8-3 Make Jurors Listen 216

8-4 Teaching Your Favorable Jurors How To Win (*Arming* Them) 218

    8-4-1 The ABCs 218

    8-4-2 Cumulative ABCs 221

8-5 Keep on KISSING! 221

    8-5-1 Terms 221

    8-5-2 Details 221

    8-5-3 Time 222

8-6 Why Are You Saying That? 222

8-7 Help Jurors Respond to the Folks at Home 222

8-8 Essentials for Closing 223

    8-8-1 Structure 223

    8-8-2 First Words 223

    8-8-3 Who We Are Suing and Why: The Safety Rules
        the Defendant(s) Violated 224

    8-8-4 Undermining (Liability and Damages) 224

    8-8-5 Massaging the Negligence Instructions 225
    8-8-6 Massage the Harms Instructions 225
    8-8-7 Arguments. 225
    8-8-8 Story. 225
        First Person Story 226
        Other Story Methods 226
        Don't Be Tempted 226
8-9 Minimum Life-Care Plan in Closing. 227
    8-9-1 Life Expectancy. 228
    8-9-2 Senior Citizens and Life Expectancy 230
    8-9-3 Bottom-Line Figure. 231
8-10 Massaging the Jury Instructions and Questions 231
    8-10-1 How to Massage 232
    8-10-2 Misconceptions about Law 233
        Intervention 234
        Cause 234
        Breaking the Law. 234
        Omitting Compensation 234
8-11 Language. 235
8-12 Intangibles Argument: Ratio to Tangible Losses. 235
8-13 Holistic Damages 238
8-14 SCALES: Calculating the Intangible Amounts 238
        How Bad? (*e.g.*, How Much Does It Hurt?) 238
        How Long? 238
        How Interfering? (How Much Does It Prevent the
        Plaintiff from Doing?) 239
    8-14-1 Wrongful Death 241
    8-14-2 Lesser Harm 242
8-15 Admit Some Fault. 242
8-16 Comparative Fault: Double-Dipping. 243
8-17 Proportions: The Damages Circle 244
8-18 How Do You Decide on Appropriate Amounts? 244

8-19　Jurors' Weekends and Other Treasures..................245

8-20　The First Thing You Think 246

8-21　Two Futures................................246

8-22　Safety....................................247

8-23　Judo Law and "The Gift of Malingering" 247

  8-23-1　Videos Cause Harm 249

    Apply Judo Law...........................250

    The Dark Side—Stalking, Intimidation, Fear, and Shame........250

    Were They Seen?..........................251

8-24　Vague Language..............................251

  8-24-1　Nouns v. Pronouns 251

  8-24-2　Verbs.................................252

8-25　People Care v. Money Care 252

8-26　Closing: Quickies 253

  8-26-1　The Judge's Proportion of Time..................253

  8-26-2　Help Her Be Helpful Again....................253

  8-26-3　Law's Purpose; Jury's Purpose 254

  8-26-4　Taking Money from a Good Cause 254

  8-26-5　Too Much?............................254

Chapter Nine. Public Respect and Trust: Restore It and Deserve It

9-1　The Problem 255

9-2　The Foolproof Solution 257

9-3　Does It Work?...............................259

9-4　The Specifics 260

  9-4-1　2006—Oklahoma 261

  9-4-2　2006—Connecticut 262

  9-4-3　Years Ago—Midwest 262

  9-4-5　Web Sites 262

9-5　A Potpourri of Good Works 263

9-6　Rejecting Cases 266

9-7　Organizations 267

9-8 Show the World..268
9-9 Epilogue..269

SUPPLEMENTS

SUPPLEMENT A. JURY VOIR DIRE

A-1 The Law..272
    The Law Can Help...272
    The Law Can Help If You Know It.............................272
    The Law Can Help If You Use It..............................272
A-2 Rule #1..273
A-3 Open-Ended Questions.......................................273
    Why, What, How, Tell Me....................................274
    Limited Uses of Closed-Ended Questions.....................274
A-4 The All-Purpose Follow-Up Questions........................275
A-5 Demographics: The Error....................................278
A-6 The Worst Role Model: The Defense..........................279
A-7 Poisoning the Jury...280
A-8 Inoculation: Anticipating Defense Poison Questions.........280
    Defense Poison Questions...................................280
    To Win or Not to Win?......................................282
    "Tit for Tat?"...283
A-9 Inoculate..283
    How/When to Inoculate......................................283
    Gather Information...284
A-10 Creating Inoculation Questions............................284
    Malingering..285
    Not Telling Doctor Everything..............................285
    Consent Form...285
    Federal Standards..286
    Pain Exaggeration..286
A-11 Which Inoculation?..287

A-12	"Why Is She Asking About That?"	288
A-13	Home	289
A-14	Get the Whole Answer	289
A-15	Interrupting	289
A-16	Rewording	290
	Testimony	290
A-17	Get Them Talking	290
	Work History	294
	Other Good "Get 'Em Talking" Questions	294
	Lower the Barriers	295
	Word Questions in Ways that Lower the Bad Response Barrier	296
	Some People	297
	Other Dos and Don'ts	298
	Legalese	299
	The Really Silent Type: Non-Talking Prospective Jurors	299
	Practice	300
A-18	Enjoyment v. Control	301
A-19	Voir Dire: To See Speaking	301
	Rapport	302
A-20	Conditioning	302
A-21	When the Judge Stops You	302
A-22	Identifying Leaders	304
	Ask	304
	Look at Occupation	304
	Job Expertise	305
	Other Experiences and Activities	305
	Leadership Attributes	305
	Subtle Signs of a Leader	306
	Leadership Is a Comparative Quality	307
A-23	Depth of Attitude/Opinion/Belief	307
	Go Beneath the Words	308
	Caveat: Promises	308

A-24 The Last Six Questions 309

    First Three General Questions 309

    Jurors' Rights Questions 310

A-25 Challenging for Cause. 312

A-26 Pretrial Rehearsal. 315

A-27 Judge-Approved Questions; Judge-Conducted Voir Dire. 317

SUPPLEMENT B. STORY FOR OPENING STATEMENTS

B-1 Storytelling 319

    One Fact Per Sentence 320

    Present Tense 320

    Chronological Order 321

    Actions 321

        Actions Only. 322

        People Listen to Actions 323

        Move Forward in Time 323

        Short Sentences. 323

        Importance of Each Action 323

    Selectivity and Starting Point 325

    "Would Not Happen to Me" 327

SUPPLEMENT C. THE BALL OPENING: A GUIDED TEMPLATE

    I.   Primary rule(s) the defendant violated. 332

    II. Story of what the defendant did. 334

    III. Who are we suing and why?—The safety rules the defendant(s) violated. 340

        A. First rule-violating act. 340

        B. What's dangerous in general about violating this rule? 340

            B1. Tentacles of danger. 342

        C. How did the violation in this case cause harm?. 342

        D. What should the defendant have done instead? 344

        E. How would that have helped?. 344

        A. Second rule-violating act 344

    B. What's dangerous in general about violating this rule?...........346

        B1. Tentacles of danger................................346

    C. How did this violation cause harm?........................348

    D. What should she have done instead?......................348

    E. How would that have helped?...........................348

IV. Undermine negligence defenses.................................348

V. Causation and damages......................................350

    A. Introduction......................................350

    B. Mechanism of harm (How did the negligent act cause each injury?)...352

    C. Personal consequence of each injury.......................358

        Undermining a damages issue...........................364

VI. "Before."..368

VII. What can the jury do about it?................................370

Supplement D. Sample Opening

I. Primary rule(s) the defendant violated............................377

II. Story of *what the defendant did.*...............................377

III. Who we are suing and why: the safety rules the defendant(s) violated....378

    A. Rule-violating act. (i. What did she do? ii. How do we know she did it?)..378

    B. What's dangerous *in general* about violating this rule (and *who says so*)?...378

    C. How did violation cause harm in this case (and *who says so*)?.......378

    D. What should the defendant have done instead?................379

    E. How would that have helped (and *who says so*)?................379

IV. Undermine negligence defenses.................................379

V. Causation and damages......................................380

    A. Introduction to harms and losses..........................380

Supplement E. Differential Diagnosis in Med Mal Opening........381

Supplement F. Sample First-Person Story for Closing

Sympathy Bid...391

Mr. C—Mr. M—and Mr. F....................................393

SUPPLEMENT G. PITFALLS: A PRIMER FOR THE NEW LAWYER; A REMINDER FOR THE NOT-SO-NEW

The Words You Use	398
What You Do With Your Words	403
How to Keep Those Words Organized	404
Too Much Information	406
Too Much Repetition	408
How to Make It Memorable with Less Repetition	409
Honor Thy Jurors and Their Answers	409
Know Who Your Audience Is	414
Uncover What Your Audience May Find	415
Follow Where Your Audience Goes	416
A Flare for the Dramatic	417
Technological Overload	420
Who's That at the End of Your Table?	423
Setting the Mood	425
Reality Check	426

SUPPLEMENT H. VIRTUAL REALITY: HOW JURORS FINDING INFORMATION ONLINE CAN SWING YOUR CASE

What You Don't Know Might Kill You	429
Why You Should Do the Research	431
What You Should Research	431
When to Do the Research	432
Who Should Do the Research?	433
How Long Does It Take?	434
How Do You Do It?	434
Time	434
Internet Access and a Search Engine	434
A Way to Take Notes	435
Part A: Researching Topics of the Case	436
Getting Started	436

Time Involved	436
Step 1: List Every Topic or Item Relevant to the Case	436
Step 2: Go First to Sites that Seem Authoritative to Jurors	438
A. The Government and News Organizations	438
B. Associations and Professional Organizations	444
C. Companies Responsible for the Product or Service	446
D. Web Sites that Jurors May Think Are Authoritative, Whether They Actually Are or Not	447
Step 3: For Each Item, Conduct a Broad Search	447
A. What and How Much Information Is Available?	448
B. Who or What Is Providing the Information and Why?	448
Step 4: Narrow the Search by Following Leads Discovered during the Broader Search in Step 2	450
Step 5: Search Popular Sites that Jurors Will Go To	450
A. News Sites	450
B. YouTube	451
C. Wikipedia	452
D. Social Networking Sites Such as Facebook and MySpace	452
E. Local Government Web Sites	453
Step 6: Search Location-Specific Resources	453
A. Libraries	453
B. Historical Societies or Collections	454
C. Museums	454
D. Public Colleges and Universities	455
Step 7: Use Focus Groups to Pursue Topic-Specific Resources	456
Part B: Researching Individuals	456
Getting Started	456
Step 1: List Individuals Critical to the Case	457
Step 2: See If the Individual Has a Personal or Business Web Site	458
Step 3: Use a Search Engine to Do a Broad Search for the Individual's Name to See What Is Immediately Visible about that Person	460
A. Watch for People with the Same Name as the Individual You're Searching For	461

  B. Watch for Biases or Conflicts of Interest 461
Step 4: Search for Financial Information. 462
Step 5: Search for Criminal Records, Both State and Federal 464
  A Note on Online Criminal Background Check Services. 465
Step 6: Search for Political and Military Information 466
  Affiliation 466
  Contributions 466
  Military Experience 466
Step 7: Check Out YouTube and Social Sites like
  Facebook, MySpace, LinkedIn 467
Step 8: Try to Locate Religious Information 468
Step 9: Miscellaneous 469
  Licenses or Other Credentials 469
  A. Ratings and Popularity 470
  B. Publications. 471
  Feedback 472
  C. Soapbox or Informative. 473
  D. Work on Previous Cases 474
Start Researching!. 475
Addendum: What's *Actually* Online that Damages Your Argument. 475
How to Conduct a Simple Search. 476
  Searching Medical Sources. 477
  An Absence of Evidence. 477
  The Pyramid Effect 478
  Damaging Quotes Found. 478

SUPPLEMENT I. WHAT IS A DEFENSE EXPERT REALLY ALLOWED TO SAY?

Procedural Background and Facts. 483
Argument. 485
Conclusion. 504

INDEX 505

ABOUT THE AUTHOR. 529

Publisher's Note

This book is intended for practicing attorneys. This book does not offer legal advice and does not take the place of consultation with an attorney or other professional with appropriate expertise and experience.

Attorneys are strongly cautioned to evaluate the information, ideas, and opinions set forth in this book in light of their own research, experience, and judgment; to consult applicable rules, regulations, procedures, cases, and statutes (including those issued after the publication date of this book); and to make independent decisions about whether and how to apply such information, ideas, and opinions to a particular case.

Quotations from cases, pleadings, discovery, and other sources are for illustrative purposes only and may not be suitable for use in litigation in any particular case.

All references to the trademarks of third parties are strictly informational and for purposes of commentary. No sponsorship or endorsement by, or affiliation with, the trademark owners is claimed or implied by the author or publisher of this book.

The author and publisher disclaim any liability or responsibility for loss or damage resulting from the use of this book or the information, ideas, or opinions contained in this book.

Foreword to the Second Edition

Don C. Keenan

I am fortunate to have been associated with many large verdicts, and that is the light in which most people know me. But like every attorney, I have also tried my share of small cases. So I can report that *David Ball on Damages* will be useful to you whether you are trying to win a few thousand dollars for a client with only minor injuries, tens of millions of dollars for cases as large as those of the catastrophically injured children I now represent, or any figure in between. David explains why jurors give, why they do not, and how to motivate them to do the former instead of the latter. His book is one of the most useful trial advocacy books I know. It is certainly the best thing I have read on damages.

I wish I had had his book years ago when I started. I am grateful for it now. As I am sure you know, until now, there have been few if any helpful articles or books about damages, even though that is what we mainly need help with. Most of what I know I had to make up myself, and I am flattered David saw fit to include some of it. But there is far more in his book than what I already knew, and it is indispensable. David walks you in detail through voir dire, opening, testimony, and closing, providing step-by-step practical, effective, and innovative methods for pursuing damages.

David points us squarely at the goal we often lose sight of in the rush and blur of trial—that we are in trial solely to get money for our clients. Then he explains how to do it. He shows you how jurors view damages. Then he explains how to shape what they see.

David marries the practical to the theoretical. He avoids the kind of generalized advice we get so much of that sounds good, but does not really advise. He tells you what to do, why to do it, and exactly how.

Among his many innovations, David has even invented a way for you to teach jurors how to calculate intangible damages, an easy method that will surely become the standard approach and help you argue for intangibles as effectively as tangibles. His many such innovations are accompanied by necessary reminders of things we already know, but easily forget or let slide.

Those of us who have been athletes will appreciate the fact that David is like a great coach. He makes you the best player you can be. He will not let you settle for less out of yourself than you can achieve. He has told me that he assumes there is greatness in almost every one of us who works in front of juries, and he shows us how to tap into whatever greatness we are each blessed with. On every page, he teaches something new about pursuing damages. And by the end of the book, you will have learned a whole lot new about yourself.

I have worked with David in trial, so I have had the direct benefit of his insights. Now his book puts him at my elbow whenever I need him, whether he is here or not. Given the many reasons today's jurors have for not fairly compensating our clients, we all need David at our elbows with every case. Keep his book in easy reach. A cover-to-cover re-reading before each and every case will be your most valuable preparation time.

FOREWORD TO THE THIRD EDITION
Gary C. Johnson

Two decades ago, I went to an ATLA (now AAJ) advocacy college, where I met a new trial consultant named David Ball. Since then, I have watched his consulting, writing, and teaching change the world of trial advocacy. At that time, his background was in professional theater, and he had some unusual things to say. An instant decision (blink) was made to hire him to assist in a very difficult case. Naturally, this difficult case with David's help was a record verdict for its time and place.

David says I was the first attorney ever to hire him to consult on a case. So I now think of myself as the casting director who discovered Marlon Brando—or, maybe more appropriately given the forcefulness of David's work, Clint Eastwood. Though David looks a lot more like Woody Allen.

David and I learned a lot over the years as we worked together on everything from small ordinary cases to a case that resulted in one of the largest verdicts ever received in this country for an individual. As he sat alongside me in most of my important trials, I saw his damages concepts and other approaches develop in leaps and bounds, and I'm proud and lucky to have been the guinea pig among the first to field-test much of his work. He moved his work to a new level when he brought together attorneys Jim Fitzgerald, Don Keenan, and myself to participate with him in research to see if there was a way to deal with the devastation that had been created by tort "reform." The group expanded to include attorneys Rick Friedman and Charles Allen. Naturally, David's brilliant partner Artemis Malekpour was crucial in analyzing and interpreting the research material. The end result of David's initiative is the nation's signature methodology of trial advocacy—the Reptile. This method is defining the future of trial advocacy, turning much of the old advice on its ear, showing why much current "advice" is irrelevant, and explaining why the methods of past masters worked. It is now providing the guidance we need to put an end to the tort "reform" menace.

By now, with this third edition of *David Ball on Damages*, David has obviously become the most influential current voice in the field of plaintiff's advocacy, and quite possibly in its history. Good trial attorneys are a pragmatic lot: they use only what is useful, and they use David's ideas, approaches, books, seminars, and workshops in numbers far exceeding anyone else's. More good verdicts and settlements have been credited to the second edition of *David Ball on Damages* than to every other resource combined. If there are any trial attorneys left who do not heavily rely on David's work, they need to immediately immerse themselves in it.

This third edition is updated with another five years of David's research and experience. It is the only guide that integrates *David Ball on Damages*, *Rules of the Road* (Friedman and Malone), and *Reptile* (Ball and Keenan).

David Ball is the most intelligent person I have ever met. His grasp of social and emotional intelligence is without peer. This old theater hand is now our masterful, reliable guide. He's almost single-handedly led trial advocacy out of its dark ages and into a new world of advocacy that combines real science, real art, and real results. Most of all, he is my friend.

Preface

Over the past few years at my damages seminars, I have asked thousands of personal injury attorneys, "How many of you tell jurors that preponderance applies not only to liability, but also to verdict size?" Fewer than 2 percent raise their hands. Traditionally, plaintiff's attorneys have thought so little about damages that they have not mentioned the burden for decision making about money.

As a result, a common juror comment in deliberations is: "Well, I'm just not completely convinced that the verdict should be $_____. They didn't absolutely prove it." Not even the most favorable plaintiff's jurors argue with that, because they don't know that they should and they don't know how.

This failure is a perfect example of how attorneys ignore damages. Until this book's first edition in 2001, books, articles, CLE seminars, and law schools had little to say about damages persuasion—despite the fact that a plaintiff's injury attorney has no other purpose. Damages was treated like pornography—something to be ashamed of. Bogus theories sprang up: "Don't talk about damages until after you convince the jury of liability." "Don't mention a specific figure; leave it to the jurors." "Do liability witnesses first, then damages witnesses."

Every one, gifts to the defense. If you have not yet joined our damages revolution, I hope this book will enlist you now.

Caveat Number 1:	This is no cookbook. It's not a compendium of tricks. You need to understand the principles that underlie the methods. This will prepare you to best use the methods and develop more of your own.
Caveat Number 2:	Michigan trial consultant Eric Oliver points out that "It's not what you say, it's how you say it." When using the techniques in the chapters below, keep in mind that the way things are worded is important. It is not enough to learn just the concepts. The way you say them is crucial. The more closely you use the words I suggest, the more effective the techniques will be.

Acknowledgments for the First Edition

It is easy to go astray while sitting alone writing on a North Carolina porch. Among the patient guides who read what I wrote for the first edition and tried their best to keep me from straying too far were two remarkable trial consultants: Susan Macpherson (Minneapolis) and Eric Oliver (Canton, Michigan), and four exceptional trial attorneys: E. D. Gaskins Jr. (Raleigh), Thomas A. McNeely (Charlotte), the late Bruce D. Rasmussen (Charlottesville, Virginia), and Donald H. Beskind (Raleigh).

Katharine M. Wilson, one of the country's best professional technical writers, has read my writing with the patience of a saint and the acuity of a schoolmarm to tell me what needed to be better and how to make it so.

Susan Chapek took many long hours from her own writing to ensure that mine was better than I could do on my own and almost as good as hers.

ACKNOWLEDGMENTS FOR THE SECOND EDITION

Donald H. Beskind, Susan Chapek, Susan Macpherson, and Kate M. Wilson, all of whom have more than enough of their own work to do, have once again selflessly martyred many of their own hours in the cause of advising and correcting me on this edition. As with the first edition, they have made this a far better and more readable book. I thank them deeply. So should every reader who otherwise would have had to read my unvetted work, not always a pretty sight.

Jude Phillips, NITA's cover artist, has done it again: a perfect cover. You can tell a book by its cover when it's Jude's cover.

I also want to acknowledge the enormous contribution to our cause (and to my work) made by two of the best advocacy guides and teachers we have: Phoenix's David Wenner and Alabama's Greg Cusimano. Both are trial consultants as well as first-rate plaintiff's attorneys. Their coast-to-coast research into the real behavior of jurors has not only helped show many of the most important paths to traverse, but has also led to the widespread teaching of how to traverse them.

Artemis Malekpour, Esq., my valued and cherished consulting partner at Malekpour & Ball, has been a wellspring of this edition's most important new material.

Acknowledgments for the Third Edition

This edition far surpasses what I'd have been able to make it without the meticulous, wise, and beyond-the-call-of-duty input of my cherished companion, Susan Chapek Pochapsky. She guarded and bolstered the book's quality every step, every sentence, every thought of the way. She may have been somewhat less successful in protecting my sanity en route.

Attorneys Don Beskind (Raleigh, North Carolina, and Duke University), Don Keenan (Atlanta), and Ernie Teitel (Stamford, Connecticut) provided me with a level of expertise and input that only the finest lawyers can provide and only the most fortunate of writers get.

Kentucky's Gary Johnson has spent two decades demonstrating how brilliance and common sense require each other and ultimately are one and the same. Without Gary, *David Ball on Damages* would more appropriately be entitled *Just Another Trial Strategy Book*.

My senior partner Artemis Malekpour continues as the nation's most qualified trial consultant in applying and teaching this book's methods. And along with the National Jury Project's brilliant Susan Macpherson, she has helped make this book better with each succeeding edition.

Rick Friedman and Pat Malone have been of enormous help, forever having improved plaintiff's trial advocacy (and my work) with *Rules of the Road*. Rick's additional input to my thinking remains a constant challenge and inspiration.

I owe Duke University's Institute for Brain Sciences an unpayable debt. They've been allowing me to attend an endless number of seminars on the frontiers of the neurosciences and made it possible for me to pick the minds of some of the world's foremost neuroscientists.

I am indebted to many hundreds of complete strangers in shopping malls and other public places around the country, who for twenty years have granted me in-depth interviews about their attitudes and feelings—in return for no more than a lunch, dinner, or a drink or two.

Members of the Inner Circle of Advocates have long been generous with their input and support, showing me over and over that the best impulse of many of the best attorneys is to share the best of what they know. In particular, I (and the profession) am indebted to the willingness of Paul Luvera (Seattle) to share and inspire; and to the extraordinary Jim Fitzgerald (Cheyenne), a pillar of our tiny group that created Reptilian advocacy.

During all the years since this book's first edition was issued, AAJ's (née ATLA) Executive Vice President Anji Jesseramsing has done more than anyone else to provide it with the best of teaching and workshop platforms. Without her, the quality of plaintiff's advocacy would be nowhere near as good as it is. Nor would AAJ.

Mark Davis (Honolulu) provided some essential fast-turnaround advice for this edition. Chuck Zauzig (Woodbridge, Virginia) has remained a wellspring of great new ideas. Forensic Epidemiologist Michael Freeman (Oregon Health and Science University) has shown me a whole new world of trial weapons. Dorothy Clay Sims (Ocala, Florida) has given the defense bar's bottomless pit of lying "experts" a lot to worry about, ended the careers and made miserable the lives of many of those "experts," and helped me understand how to do both. Aaron DeShaw and Trial Guides have rapidly become the seminal purveyors of the most important of the new plaintiff's trial advocacy approaches, including much of my own work. Steven L. Langer (Valparaiso, Indiana) has provided me with years of input and essential admonitions that have heavily influenced this edition. Sonia Chaisson (Los Angeles) keeps me always aware that the best of advocacy can come from the best of human beings.

The late and beloved Howard Twiggs (Raleigh) was the first to launch my work from local to national, so I am ever grateful for his foresight—though others might call it one of his rare blunders.

Chris Conklin of Punch Buggy Design has provided cover art proving, in its simplicity and directness, that less is more. If only I could persuade every attorney that that's also the gold standard for trials!

Finally, I want to acknowledge you, the reader, in advance for your careful reading, study, and eventual mastery of this new edition. Without you, this nation would be in big trouble. So I'm grateful that you're taking the trouble to get better and better at what you do.

David Ball
Durham, NC
2010

Introduction to the Second Edition, 2005

If you leave the jurors alone on the topic of harm and damages, they will return the favor.

—David Ball

Since 2001, a revolution has taken place in the way good plaintiff's attorneys have been seeking damages. I'm proud to say this book's first edition flagshipped those changes.

But the times are still changing. Opposition tactics grow more sophisticated, and the public mood along with laws and rules grow more hostile. And tort "reform" grows like kudzu with an attitude. Staying a step ahead requires some leaps.

Those who thumbed ragged their copies of the first edition will see in this edition that we must begin in the same place: continuous awareness that the goal of going to trial is to get money for your client. Throughout the havoc of case preparation, harm and damages must remain uppermost in your mind and work—and stay there throughout trial.

Cut out and frame the motto on the next page. Hang it on your office wall with nothing near it. Read it aloud daily. And let it underlie all your trial preparation and execution.

> The *only* goal of trial is to get money for your client.
>
> —David A. Ball, PhD

Introduction to the Third Edition, 2010

I'm often asked: "David, your books and seminars are about damages *and* liability, so why call them just 'Damages'?" Good question. Answer: Because the way you do liability controls verdict size. This is truer than ever with the advent of this book's two companion volumes, essential for not only personal injury/wrongful death attorneys, but any plaintiff's attorney. Together, the essential trilogy arms you in ways the defense can do little about.

In addition to this book, the essential trilogy's companion volumes are:

Rules of the Road by Pat Malone and Rick Friedman (Trial Guides)

Reptile by David Ball and Don Keenan (Balloon Press)

It makes no difference which you read first, as long as you master all three.

To start the learning curve:

1. Read all three books. Highlight, underline, tab.

2. Before you begin litigating each new case, review all three books. This helps you re-absorb the material within the framework of the new case. When possible, do this even before filing the case.

3. Apply what you learn as precisely as you can. As with any valuable skill, doing it partway, or just "sort of" doing it "more or less," yields lesser results.

Along the way, seek out seminars, workshops, blogs, and Web sites that continue you on the road to mastering these techniques. American Association of Justice (AAJ) workshops along with ReptileKeenanBall.com seminars and workshops, and other resources, are available.

I don't just want readers. I want people who read and then proceed to do all it takes to become masters. Those are the lawyers who have done well over the decade since this book's first edition, and those are the lawyers who will do well over the next decade. The new decade will see unprecedented spending by the forces of tort "reform." If you master the essential trilogy and keep up with our continuing new developments, we will see you through in great shape.

This new edition of *David Ball on Damages* comes five years after the second edition. I hope you'll find that it contains five years' worth of good new advice.

David Ball
Durham, NC
2010

Chapter One

Fundamentals

You have to monitor your fundamentals constantly because the only thing that changes will be your attention to them. The fundamentals will never change.

— Michael Jordan, basketball player

INTRODUCTION: THE POISONED POOL

Jurors rarely deliberate about how badly the plaintiff was harmed. They mostly say things like this:

"A big verdict will drive up insurance prices."

"All that money will make lawyers rich and drive companies around here out of business."

"Why should one person get all that money?"

"Her health insurance probably paid for it."

"Her health insurance will continue to pay for it."

"No one deserves a windfall just because they got hurt."

"Money won't bring back the dead."

"You can't put a price on pain [death]."

"Money won't make the pain go away."

"Too much money will ruin his life."

"You know who'll be paying for this! [Us.]"

"I have pain, too, and no one paid me for it."

"My dad was killed when I was twelve; no one paid *me* for it."

"I have this huge jagged scar right here on my left butt, see? And my butt hurts every day! No one paid *me* for it."

These comments are some of the fruits of tort "reform," the multi-million-dollar fraud perpetrated by insurance companies, chambers of commerce, domestic (and more recently, better-funded international) corporations, and politicians. It has been the most potent jury-pool poisoning in American history. It has made more than a third of the population fear and hate you. There's a middle third almost as bad. And most of the "best" third tolerates, but does not like you. You have no strong friends to offset your zealous enemies.

The 2009–10 health-care "debate" made things worse: forces on both sides blame attorneys for the high cost of medical care. Even the most liberal of pundits—and President Obama—have swallowed the myth that medical lawsuits cause "defensive medicine." This "proves" to much of the population that *all* plaintiff's lawyers—not just med mal lawyers—are a serious threat.

I believe I have spoken in depth with more tort-"reformed" Americans than anyone else. This is why I can report that the techniques in this book, along with those in its two companion books, are bringing the blistering power of tort "reform" to an end.

So welcome to the plaintiff's revolution!

To join the revolution, first learn the fundamentals of juror decision making about money. That will launch you on the path of mastering the entire new advocacy.[1]

---

1. At the same time we fight tort "reform" in trial, we must also combat it in society and in the legislatures. This is more easily done that you may think. We don't need the wealth of the tort-"reform" forces. Nor should we or our organizations continue to emit embarrassingly self-serving "messages" and "communications" to "set the record straight." It's too late for that. By now, our "communications" and "messaging," when that's all we deploy, cause more harm. Luckily the news media rarely pick them up. Be sure to see chapter nine to learn about the practical methods—beyond the impotence of nothing but words and framings and announcements—that we need to employ to overcome the myths that turned public opinion against us.

FUNDAMENTAL ONE

JUROR SELF-PROTECTION

Put your own oxygen mask on before helping others.

—American Airlines

Protection of self and offspring is the unbeatable decision-making force, incapable of compromise. Without enlisting this force, you remain at the mercy of tort "reform," which itself is driven by that very force. Every case—no matter how small—offers jurors the opportunity to make their dangerous world safer. Controlling this force is *Reptile*'s[2] main topic. The methods presented in the chapters below enable you to make best use of *Reptile*.

---

2. DAVID BALL AND DON KEENAN (Balloon Press 2009).

Fundamental Two

Proportion of Time on Harms and Losses

> *. . . O, I have taken*
> *Too little care of this!*
>
> —Shakespeare, *King Lear*

A book, a play, a trial, a sermon, a TV show, or a movie is about *whatever it spends its time being about*. It can't be about what it spends little time on.

Shakespeare's *Hamlet* has about twenty seconds of dialogue that some English professors think shows Hamlet wanting sex with his mother. So they insist the play is about an Oedipus complex. Well, no. Even if that brief dialogue did show Hamlet wanting to have sex with his mom (it does not), the play would still not be about an Oedipus complex. An entire department of English professors stamping their feet and insisting that the play is about an Oedipus complex—as frightening as such a gathering might be—cannot change what the audience experiences: only a few seconds of anything even remotely related to Oedipus. The rest of the play's several hours is about revenge. So to the audience, the play is about revenge.

Similarly, an entire table of plaintiff's attorneys stamping their feet and insisting that their trial is about damages cannot make it so—unless they spend much of the trial time on damages.

A sprinkling of testimony about damages followed by a quick mention of damages in closing leaves the focus on liability. Jurors base their decisions on the information made available to them. So proportion your time well. For most cases, spend a third of your overall time on harms and losses. Half in your jury voir dire. A third in your opening. Lots of (brief) damages fact witnesses. Use every expert—on both sides—for damages, no matter why they were called (*see* section 7-2, p. 206, hitchhiking). And in most cases, spend at least a third of closing on damages.

> **Don't abbreviate liability,**
> **but don't skimp damages.**

Caveat: Don't stuff the trial with filler. This book will help you fill trial time—even during the defense case—with effective damages content.

Exception: In cases of minimal harms and losses, especially when using the methods outlined in *Reptile*, focus more heavily on liability, such as the violated safety rules. You still need enough damages time for jurors to allow[3] money. But when the seriousness of the negligence steeply outweighs the level of the harms and losses, you want jurors to focus on the dangers created by the defendant's kind of negligence.

---

3. Jurors don't "give" money. As Kentucky attorney Gary C. Johnson points out, they "allow" it. So that is how you should refer to it in trial.

Fundamental Three

You

I am what I am.

—Popeye

You better not be.

—Olive Oyl

Tort "reform" has convinced many jurors to try to defeat you—by making them believe that your greed and dishonesty endanger them *personally*.

When you fight this publicly or in trial by talking about justice, you convince such jurors that you are not only a personal danger, but a hypocrite, too. Their synonym for "attorney" is "greedy bastard."

You already know the obvious ways to deal with this: don't do anything that confirms the ugly stereotype. No expensive pens or jewelry in trial. Don't drive your Jaguar to trial. If you live in a small town, don't even own one. Send it to me.

Jurors notice *everything*, in and out of trial. They go online to look for more things to notice about you, as well as your case, your client, and all else they can find. (*See* Fundamental Ten, pp. 33*ff*.) So make sure you are in control of all that they notice—especially about you, and especially all the time and everywhere, not just in trial.

FUNDAMENTAL FOUR

CLIENT'S POINT OF VIEW

Try to see it my way.

—Paul McCartney, John Lennon

Jurors perceive the full weight of harm only when they walk in your client's shoes. That means subjectively, not from the outside.

Pay particular attention to the technique, illustrated in supplement F, of first-person narrative in closing argument. This can put jurors right into your client's shoes so they can comprehend the harms in the way your client feels them. (Just don't do it in opening!)

ISOLATION AND LACK OF MOBILITY

Lawyers customarily focus on physical pain as a major "noneconomic" harm. Of greater persuasive weight is your client's isolation from other people and his loss of mobility. The observer's brain actually experiences some of another person's feelings of isolation and lack of mobility, but not her physical pain. (*See Reptile* for more of what you need to know about isolation and mobility.)

DANGER

Look carefully for all the ways in which your client's injuries have placed him in danger. There's a lot wrong with being unable to walk, but among the worst is the inability to escape danger.

Brain damage is also lethally dangerous. A normal brain allows for a fast, safe decision of how to get out of a burning house. A damaged brain might not.

Showing dangers gives jurors a concrete understanding of what the harm has done—something they can identify with instead of just feel sorry about.

LEARNING THE HARM

Stamford, Connecticut, attorney Ernie Teitel, one of the northeast's premiere attorneys, advises that from the moment you take a case, start working with your medical and life-care-planning experts. When possible, a member of the trial team should completely take over this continuing responsibility so she can focus exclusively on damages without distraction. If you can't make this kind of personnel division, at least make gathering the damages information its own high-priority task.

And it is a wide-ranging task. You need to talk to neighbors, the dry cleaner, the minister, fellow churchgoers, the grocer, bus drivers, fellow carpoolers, acquaintances from the PTA and school yards—folks from every place your client frequented. The list will almost always be long. You'll get quotes as good as the one Ernie got from a dry cleaner: "Joe used to give me great stock market tips. Now he comes in and can't even count his change."

But all that is still not enough. You need to develop a personal and genuine emotional attachment to the reality and significance of your client's harms. You can't get that by sitting in your office, sending out investigators, making phone calls, listening to doctors, debriefing colleagues, and writing down answers to your questions. You must put yourself physically into your client's personal world. For days, not hours.

North Carolina attorney—and Duke's remarkable advocacy professor—Donald H. Beskind routinely spends a day or more in his clients' homes. This is not to talk business, but to learn and experience what it's like to be the client(s).

Ernie Teitel does the same. Don and Ernie see and hear things no one would have mentioned in an office interview or a few hours of discussion. *And they come to feel those things.* They get there by shedding their lawyer's skin and putting themselves into their client's skin.

In one case, Ernie learned his bedridden client's deepest secret terror: if some night there were a fire, her children would surely die trying to rescue her because she could not get out on her own. Ernie would never have learned so well-guarded a personal fear except within the intimacy of the home. More importantly, because Ernie heard it from his bedridden client in the very room in which she feared that her children would be killed, he felt its emotional power fully enough to convey it to a jury.

It's not an office matter. When it comes to the power of damages, not much is. Holding heart-to-hearts with your client and her family members, visiting the cemetery in wrongful death cases, trying on braces and using other necessary equipment yourself, spending quiet time with your client and her family, holding your client's hand through the pangs of searing pain—these are some of the ways you emotionally "learn" enough to put jurors into your client's shoes.

The most effective program that teaches how to walk in your client's shoes is Gerry Spence's Trial Lawyers College—not only the extended sessions, but even the abbreviated weekend sessions. You can also get individual assistance from a superb consultant: Joshua Karton. He consults out of Los Angeles, and a day or two with him can work wonders for your ability to convey harms and losses to a jury.

Do not underestimate the importance of this aspect of advocacy. Regardless of case size, you cannot do it well enough until you have made your client's harms part of your own experience. Even with nothing but a broken arm, until you feel what it's like to live with it, you can't make jurors feel it.

Fundamental Five

Defendant Conduct

When you do the things you shouldn't do
Peek-a-boo, I'm watchin' you!
—The Cadillacs, 1958

Kentucky's legendary Gary C. Johnson teaches that verdict size depends heavily on how bad the defendant's actions were. This is partly why you cannot separate liability from damages. Even with stipulated negligence, you'll see below that you can (and must) focus on defendant conduct.

Rule Violations

Our most useful way to show the egregiousness of the defendant's actions is to frame them as safety-rule violations.[4] No case is about its own topic (such as medicine, the nature of a product, the science, or the technology); **it is always about safety-rule violations**. Every case. Always. When jurors describe your case months later, if they do not say, "It was about some company [*or driver or doctor or whatever*] that violated safety rules," then—brutally but accurately put—you blew it.

So your main theme is safety rules. Your subthemes are safety rules. And everything you present should directly support your rules-violation case.

Why?

Because Americans—especially when they are jurors—easily forgive errors and misjudgments. They know that no matter how careful people are, inadvertence, mistake, or misjudgment is inevitable. To err is human. "Whoops" is one of life's most common events. By their own experiences, jurors know (and they are right) that there's no way to prevent "whoopses." You know it, too. So jurors are reluctant to punish or even blame anyone for them.

Besides, a high verdict can't reduce the number or severity of inadvertent acts. Result: a defense or low verdict.

In contrast, jurors find it worthwhile to blame and punish people who violate safety rules.

---

4. For complete guidance, *see* Rick Friedman & Patrick Malone, Rules of the Road (Trial Guides 2006). It is about every kind of case, not just highway cases.

Not coincidentally, that is also the most important part of tort law's public policy purpose: safety. Even when you cannot explicitly make that argument, it is so inherent to the birth of the justice system and the nature of a trial that when you present the case in terms of rules, jurors will figure it out for themselves.[5]

So never again say or even imply "accident" or "error" or "misjudgment" when referring to what the defendant did. "The trucker missing the red light" is inadvertence, which is useless. But jurors who won't allow much money for inadvertence will want to yank a physician's license for violating a safety rule.

Ignoring the distinction between inadvertence and safety-rule violation is among the most common causes of poor verdicts.

Loser argument: "The physician mistakenly diagnosed infection."

Winner argument: "The physician violated the patient-safety rule requiring the doctor to immediately treat or rule out every urgent danger."

Loser: "The defendant made the wrong judgment."

Winner: "The defendant made a judgment that needlessly endangered the patient." (It's generally better to avoid a theory of the case that involves judgment, unless you cannot avoid a "best judgment" instruction as a defense.)

Loser: "The trucker missed the light."

Winner: "The trucker violated the safety rule requiring him to look where he was going."

Every act of negligence violates some safety rule that the defense must agree with or make himself seem unacceptably dangerous or evasive.

What follows is a brief summary and adaptation of the Rules of the Road methodology you'll need for applying many of the methods in this book. (You still need to read *Rules of the Road*.)

1) Applying the Rules

Here are the requirements for each rule:

A) Defense must agree. You craft rules the defense must either agree with or seem dishonest or dangerous. As you'll see, this is a lot easier than it sounds.

---

5. *See* REPTILE, chapter six.

B) **Rule = what someone is or is not allowed to do.** "Driving drunk is dangerous" is not a rule. It does not tell us what someone can or cannot do. "No one is allowed to drive drunk" does, so it's a rule.

Similarly, "Safety is more important than profit" is not a rule. But it is easily turned into a rule with which the defendant must agree: "A company is not allowed to make profit more important than safety."

C) **Rules derive from** common sense, industry standards, policy guides, regulations, law, manuals, etc., ad infinitum.

D) **Must be a safety rule.** Violation of the rule must allow or increase danger.

E) **Plain English.** Just like everything else you say in trial.

F) **Crystal clear.** Just like everything else you say in trial.

2) The Umbrella Rule for Every Case: "Needless Danger"

"A [*doctor, manufacturer, driver, whatever*] is never allowed to needlessly endanger anyone."

Alternate wording:

"A [*doctor, manufacturer, driver, whatever*] is never allowed to make a choice that needlessly endangers anyone."

Always include the phrase "needlessly endangers." It makes the statement true, persuasive, and significant. Needless endangerment is the threshold, because **every needless endangerment is negligence, and every negligent act is needlessly dangerous**. There are no exceptions. Unless a rule prevents *needless* danger, violating the rule is not negligent.

Out of the umbrella rule flows every other rule in the case. So:

A physician must follow the rules of a differential diagnosis, or **she is needlessly endangering her patient.**

A manufacturing company must provide danger warnings, or **the company is needlessly endangering the public.**

A driver must maintain attention at all times, or **he needlessly endangers others on the road.**

3) The Only Permissible Choice: The Safest

Now for the best part:

Fundamentals

Once the defense agrees to the umbrella rule (no needless danger allowed), you have changed the playing field. Here's how. Follow the logic carefully:

a) Needless endangerment is *always* negligent or otherwise culpable. So:

   i) There's no such thing as ordinary care that needlessly endangers; if it does, it's not ordinary *care*.

   ii) There's no such thing as a standard of care that needlessly endangers; if it does, it's not a standard of *care*.

   iii) There's no such thing as a product fit for its intended use that needlessly endangers; if it does, it is not fit for its intended use.

So at defense depositions and in trial, ask defense witnesses, including the defendant, the umbrella question:

> "Mr. Taxi Driver, a driver is not allowed to needlessly endanger the public, is he?"

Insofar as he waffles, he alienates jurors, because jurors already know that the only acceptable answer is: "Of course not."

b) Whenever there are two available choices of how to accomplish *the same thing*, the second-safest choice—by definition—contains some danger that the first-safest does not. That makes the danger needless, since there is a safer choice. So:

> "Doctor [*or whatever*], when there are two available ways to accomplish the same benefit, if a physician chooses the more dangerous way, that would needlessly endanger the patient, right?"
>
> "Safer is better?"
>
> "So second safest is not enough."

The greater danger inherent in making the second-safest choice is *always* unnecessary. Unnecessary endangerment is negligence.

"Safe enough" does not count. Nothing is "safe enough" if it allows danger when a safer available (practical, at-hand, etc.) choice can achieve the identical benefit.[6]

In a defendant's view it may be "safe enough" for the doctor to get to the patient's room in an hour. But when it's safer—and possible—to get there in thirty minutes, taking an hour is negligent. It makes no difference what the defense says the standard of care is, because the overriding standard of

---

6. If there are shifting levels of benefit to the various choices of action, the situation becomes more complex. But most of the time, the benefit—to get to the other end of the road, to save the patient's life, to keep users safe—is identical for each available choice.

care is always to abide by a risk/benefit analysis safer to the patient—which is another way of saying "no needless danger." So even when the law allows "alternative choices," physicians cannot choose an alternative that needlessly endangers. It also falls well below the level of care every juror wants for herself and her family.

In a defendant's view it may be "safe enough" to put a warning in the manual only. But if it's safer to put that warning where a user will see it while using the product, then a warning only in the manual allows needless danger. And that equals negligent or otherwise culpable conduct.

So goodbye to most standard-of-care and other "it was safe enough" defenses. Neither the law nor the jury tolerates anyone choosing needless danger. How many patients would sit in a waiting room that has a wall sign reading:

This clinic needlessly endangers patients!

Who would sign a form seeking consent to "needless danger"?

Who would ride in a cab that had a sign reading:

This cab company and its driver needlessly endanger passengers and the public!

Who would buy a product that carried the warning:

This product needlessly endangers anyone who uses it!

Perhaps best of all, this approach couches all negligence as the result of an intentional choice.

DEFINING NEGLIGENCE AS OUTRAGEOUS

Here's another essential safety rule:

> The *more dangerous* something is, the more careful a [*doctor, manufacturer, driver, whatever*] must be. (For example, "The more dangerous driving is on ice, the more careful a driver must be." Or, "The more dangerous a surgery can be, the more careful the surgeon must be.")

Jurors rarely understand this axiom of negligence law, so even jurors who listen intently to the court's instructions make fundamental errors. For example, jurors can easily think that the driver of an eighteen-wheeler needs to be no more careful than the driver of a car. But an eighteen-wheeler is more dangerous—it can do a lot more harm—so it must be driven more carefully. Jurors will demand greater care once you get them to understand the law—and how needlessly dangerous its violation can be.

Fundamentals

The judge is usually powerless to convey the principle that greater danger requires greater safety. So it becomes your job. Do it by getting the defense to agree—as it must—that the more dangerous something is, the more careful one must be when doing it. It's not merely the law; it's common sense, the standard in every field and industry, and the foundation of all safety rules and safety training. So it is allowable testimony even when a judge does not want witnesses talking about the law. That means you can force the defense to admit it.

(Of course, care is a two-way street: it is also demanded of your client. However, *Reptile*'s methods turn it into a nonissue, since "reptilianized" jurors find little or no reason to factor in your client's carelessness. For more, see *Reptile*, p. 73.)

Here's a memorable analogy to explain that greater danger requires greater care: "If a snake handler walks through a crowd carrying a dead rattlesnake, it's not dangerous, so the handler need not be careful. But carrying a live rattlesnake through a crowd is very dangerous, so the handler must be very careful." That turns the rule into easily understood common sense. (I don't remember who I stole this analogy from, but thank you, whoever you are!)

"Ordinary" Care

Don't get caught in the common trap of misunderstanding the phrase "ordinary" care. "Ordinary" does not mean average or C+. Ordinary care is the level of care that the normally *careful* person uses in situations with a given level of danger. **A normally careful person or company—an "ordinarily" careful person or company—does not allow needless danger.**

"Reasonable" Care

No matter how tempting money or convenience or anything else might be, every person and company must be as careful as they "reasonably" can be to prevent a danger from causing harm. But be wary. Reasonable does not mean "moderate." It means "using reason": What does *reason* tell us the appropriate level of safety is for the circumstance?[7] Anything less is negligence.

---

7. *United States v. Carroll Towing Co.*, 59 F.2d 169 (2d Cir. 1947). Judge Learned Hand's decision established the "reasonable man" standard (the "Hand Rule") for both law and economics. It involves algebraic analysis of 1) the probability of a harmful outcome, 2) the degree of harm it could cause, and 3) the consequent level of care that must be taken. **It holds that the required level of care is that which helps keep the community safe, not merely that which the average person might want to exercise.**

Which is why there's no such thing as reasonable care that needlessly endangers.

Products Liability

When it is technologically and financially feasible to make a product safer, the maker must make it safer no matter how safe it already is. In other words, there is no such thing as a product fit for its purpose that needlessly endangers anyone.

"All the Other Kids Do It!"

The defense often argues that others are just as careless as the defendant was. "Lots of people carry live rattlesnakes the same way!" "Lots of doctors do it that way." "Lots of other SUVs roll over."

Makes no difference. When Ford says, "The Ford Explorer rolls over only as much as the Subaru," it is irrelevant unless Ford proves that the Subaru is safe. **Being as dangerous as something needlessly dangerous is not a defense to negligence.** Even where judges allow so ridiculous a defense, when you word it that way, jurors are not likely to put up with it.

Explain that no one—not Ford, not Toyota, not nobody—is allowed to needlessly endanger the public. If twenty other companies needlessly endanger the public, they are all negligent. If everyone allows needless danger, then everyone is negligent. In fact, when the defense offers such a bogus defense, you can empower the jury to make the world safer simply by means of a simple and proper compensation verdict in this case: "They're watching to see how far Durham County jurors will let a company go in needlessly endangering the public before making the company pay for the harm they did." This is not a punitive damages argument. It is a response to the defense's attempt to get off on the basis of being no more dangerous than everyone else—an attempt that should pass neither legal nor juror muster.

This expresses the public policy necessity of preventing a nation in which every vehicle rolls over because all the others do. Juries and even judges often miss this point.

"Everyone" speeds, but it's still negligent. Why? Because even when everyone else speeds, "prudent" drivers do not. No one being prudent or using reasonable or ordinary care speeds (i.e., needlessly endangers) just because others do. I cannot say, "I was going 85, but so was everyone else." Well, I can say it, but it does not excuse me.

When the defense talks about others who do the same bad act, it is relevant only if the defense proves that those others are prudent. The defense

Fundamentals

can never do this because, as you now know, prudent people and companies never allow or create needless danger.

EGREGIOUS CONDUCT DOES NOT STOP WITH THE NEGLIGENT ACT

Always find out what the defendant did afterward.

Did a trucker sit in his truck talking by cell phone to his boss and waiting for instructions while Jane was bleeding in the road? *Yes.* Did he go out in the rain to wave traffic away so Jane would not get run over again? *No.* Hold an umbrella over her? *No.* Help in any way? *No.* Call 911? Apologize?[8] Ask how Jane was afterward? *No, no,* and *no.* Those are examples of outrageous conduct. They make the plaintiff's suffering more real to jurors. And the plaintiff's awareness of these things exacerbates her suffering, so should be admissible for the purpose of damages. (After all, your client's failure to mitigate her harms would get into evidence; similarly, so should anything the defendant does to make those harms worse.)

In a hospital case, who showed up first in your client's room after the negligence? A social worker to help the family deal with what had happened? A doctor or nurse bringing solace or explanation? Or instead did the hospital's risk manager rush in to put a lid on things? Where was the doctor? What did she say when she realized what had happened? Did she disappear? Did the hospital hide anything? And for how long? Did it take discovery to get the truth for the family? (This is a primary reason many plaintiffs looked for a lawyer in the first place. It's often the only way to find out what happened.)

Look for the outrages. What machinations has the defense used to escape responsibility? Did the railway "lose" the speed records? *Outrageous.* Did the defense stipulate to liability the day before trial—as a trial tactic? *Outrageous.* (And it goes to your client's emotional suffering, so you should be able to get it in.) By denying responsibility all this time, did the defendant deprive your client of funds needed for his care and safety? (Be careful, though, not to open a collateral-source door.) Or make him worry he'd never get the money needed for his care? *Outrageous.* Is the defense now adding insult to injury by attacking your client's good name by saying he's lying, exaggerating his injuries, or malingering?

A defendant's refusal to accept responsibility (which means full compensation) adds to the plaintiff's suffering. Your client's pain and disability are bad enough, but are even harder to bear when the defendant says, "Not our fault" or "Your harm is meaningless to us."

---

8. Raleigh attorney and Duke law professor Don Beskind points out that many states now bar a doctor's apology from being admitted into evidence. Don suggests that you might be able to point out that a doctor did *not* apologize despite knowing it could do him no harm in court.

It's worse when the defense stipulates to fault, but still won't meet its responsibility. That says, "Yeah, we did it, and we don't care." It's even worse when they say that—and then blame the plaintiff for what happened!

Be thorough in your search for outrageous acts. Point out, for example, that the defendant's company representative at trial knows nothing about the case. "They didn't care then; they don't care now."

Harm upon Harm

A defendant's outrageous acts after the initial negligence constitute harm piled upon harm. Positioned correctly, those added harms can be seen as proximately caused by the initial negligence, so they might help you claim a higher verdict. When the defense wants to yank the child out of her mother's arms and send him to an institution far from family, it's piling harm upon harm.

Anger

Jurors who are angry at a defendant provide more money. Greater anger = more money. Jurors can become angry not only at a defendant's wrongdoing, but also at her pretrial and in-court behavior (lies, evasions, delay, refusal to accept responsibility, being more careful now about protecting her money than she was then about protecting people, etc.). Jurors get angry when a defendant corporation seems to not take the case seriously, such as when the defendant sends a representative who knows little about the case. (So consider calling that uninformed representative as an adverse witness in your case-in-chief before he has a chance to get comfortable or learn about the case from the proceedings. You might even call him first, if you are experienced enough to handle anything he says. If his ignorance angers jurors from the start, they may see the rest of the case through those anger lenses.)

Motivations

Go beneath the wrongdoing to show (or at least suggest) the defendant's motivations. Jurors are angered by negligence motivated by greed, dishonesty, hostility, corruption, callousness, laziness, or selfishness. Beyond angering the jurors, these things show jurors what drove the defendant to do what he did. Showing motivation makes it easier for jurors to believe that the defendant really did what you say he did.[9]

Make sure the motivations you offer are believable. When you say that a failure to warn was driven by the motivation to save a penny or two per $600 unit, it's hard to believe. Sure, you can multiply it out by the number of

---
9. *See* David Ball, Theater Tips & Strategies, 187 (NITA 2003).

units, but the total remains comparatively trivial. So jurors are unconvinced that the lack of label was due to a nefarious cause.

In reality, the choice to omit the warning label was likely driven by a far stronger motivation: manufacturers don't want warnings when competing products don't have them. If the Ajax mower has a warning, customers tend to buy another company's—one without the warning. Every warning is an added marketing demerit, so no manufacturer wants to be first with any of them. (This is why manufacturers don't care as much when the government forces everyone to add a warning label.)

Look for and find persuasive motivations for the defendant's behavior. They will convince jurors that the defendant did what you say he did.

Caveat: Do not raise a suggested motivation to the level of a "must-believe." For example, say in closing:

> We don't know whether the prison guard choked John because the guard was angry, or had been drinking, or was doing a favor for another prisoner, or had some other reason. And the guard won't tell us. But we know that for whatever reason, he choked John.

This conveys the possible motivations as suggestions, not must-believes, so jurors will use whichever they like—or none. But they won't decide that you should lose on the grounds that they disagree with the motivations you suggest. In other words, don't try to prove what you needn't prove.

Defense Counsel

Defense counsel can anger jurors. Questionable tactics, making too many objections that jurors find pointless, bullying a witness, and other such practices can lead some jurors to express their anger in verdict size.

You

For the same reasons, jurors can get angry at you. That can minimize the verdict. For example, being nasty or overbearing to a witness may feel good, but it is almost always a blunder. One of the country's otherwise finest plaintiff's attorneys regularly irritates jurors with his unrelenting, biting, often pointless sarcasm and anger on cross: he's unbearably rude. He gets great results because he makes up for his behavior with extraordinary work in other ways. But for him, as well as every other attorney, jurors who are repeatedly annoyed at counsel are less enthusiastic about making counsel happy. That great attorney could be doing even better.

You won't get a jury angry (except at you) by showing your own anger. Instead, show the facts that got you angry. With few exceptions, there is nothing as annoying and unpersuasive as an angry plaintiff's attorney.

F. Lee Bailey could read when his jurors were angry at the witness. I have watched him reflect that level of anger (not a jot more) in his own tone and behavior. He did not try to get jurors angry or angrier by acting in a way they were not already feeling. So always show less anger than you are certain the jury already has. That's the gold standard for your use of anger in trial.

Make Defendant Face Responsibility

Jurors tend to allow more money when they understand that the defendant is trying to use the trial to evade responsibility. Jurors know it is proper for a defendant to defend himself, but not to evade responsibility.

In closing, argue:

> It's fine to defend yourself when you've done nothing wrong. But when you're wrong, you are supposed to stand up and accept responsibility—not sidestep responsibility at the further expense of the person you hurt.
>
> First, Defendant Smith failed in his responsibility by not looking where he was driving. Then he refused to accept responsibility for more than two years, depriving John of the care he needed and forcing us to come to trial.[10] Now you have seen the defendant spend ten days in front of you trying to evade his responsibility—permanently.
>
> He does not want to fix, help, and make up for anything. He only wants to escape his responsibility. So it's up to you to determine how far someone can go in violating public safety rules and hurting members of the community before he is required to pay full and fair compensation.

You may want to add an aggressive ending:

> If you decide on less than full and fair compensation, then after you've announced your verdict, when you're walking through the parking lot to your car to go home, you'll see the defendant and his lawyers congratulating each other for having permanently escaped responsibility.[11]

---

10. Don't say this if it opens a collateral-source door.
11. If you are the one who suggested this to me, please let me know.

Last-Minute Stipulated Negligence

When a judge tries to bar evidence of the defendant's conduct after the injury, argue that the judge has grounds to do that only with respect to liability, not damages. Point out that the plaintiff's post-injury acts would be relevant if those acts constituted a failure to mitigate harms and losses. By the same token, a defendant's post-injury acts are relevant when those acts make any harms or losses worse. Then explain how the needlessly delayed admission of liability added to your client's emotional suffering. Your client will almost always be able to say this truthfully, as will any psychologist and even your client's physician. A defendant's delay in accepting responsibility creates real and unnecessary anguish—especially when all along the refusal has been groundless (as we see by the fact that the defense stipulated to liability despite having no new information).

Tell jurors:

> After two years, they finally admitted last night that they were negligent—even though they knew everything two years ago that they knew last night. So why did they wait? To wear John down so he'd walk away. Why did they finally admit it last night? Because they knew they had to face you this morning.
>
> Now they brag that they've admitted their responsibility. But taking responsibility is more than a legal maneuver.

Be on the alert for penalties a late stipulation might lead to. If the defense denied your request for admissions concerning negligence, only to admit it at the last minute, you may be entitled in some states to costs and attorney's fees.

For additional help with stipulated negligence, see *Reptile*, chapter twenty.

Lack of Remorse (Crocodile Tears)

Americans love remorse. A death-penalty jury is far more likely to give life than death when they see the murderer is remorseful. In the same way, civil jurors allow less money in the rare instances when they see the defendant is remorseful for her wrongdoing.

On the other hand, false remorse or a lack of remorse can anger jurors. Few defendants or their lawyers know how to be remorseful and defend their case at the same time.

Lack of remorse is easily found in defendant's post-injury behavior.

False remorse is easily shown by pointing out that if the remorse had been real, the defendant would have expressed it long before trial. If it had been real, the truck driver would not have stayed in his truck after the wreck talking to his boss; he'd have gotten out to help your client, visited him later in the hospital, or done something else that showed remorse. In closing, show that the defendant's last-minute "remorse" is a cynical maneuver—and that nothing is worse than fake remorse.

To lay the groundwork for showing that the remorse and responsibility implied by a last-minute stipulation are fake, in depositions ask:

"Are you sorry for what you did?"

"Are you saying you did nothing wrong?"

"Were you negligent?"

"Are you being unfairly accused?"

ATTACKS ON YOUR CLIENT

When the defense attacks your client in any way, argue that it is salt on the wound. First the obstetrician's negligence killed the baby, and now—to evade responsibility—the doctor blames Mom, knowing she'll forever have to live with having been accused on a permanent public record of killing her own infant.

MALINGERING AND EXAGGERATION OF SYMPTOMS

When the defense claims your client is malingering or exaggerating symptoms, point out that publicly branding her a liar is literally adding insult to injury. Jurors do not automatically see the malevolence or the destructiveness of such attacks. Emphasize it, so if jurors decide the defendant is liable, they will more likely make her pay full compensation. (*See* section 8-23, p. 247*ff*., "The Gift of Malingering.")[12]

---

12. Malingering or exaggeration implications are so common and usually so fraudulent that they deserve entire books. Fortunately there are two great ones: Rick Friedman's *Polarizing the Case* (Trial Guides) and Dorothy Sims's *Exposing Deceptive Defense Doctors* (James Publishing).

Fundamental Six

Inadvertent Wrongdoing

Baby, baby, baby, I didn't mean to do you wrong!

—Fifteen percent of all country songs

Mommy, I didn't mean to spill my milk.

*Then don't worry about it, dear. It's OK. It was an **accident**.*

—Mom teaching little girl to grow up into a terrible plaintiff's juror.

Many jurors believe that inadvertent error should be treated mildly or even forgiven: "Accidents, mistakes, errors, misjudgments—they happen, it's human, nothing can prevent them." Don't feed these *he-didn't-mean-to-hurt-her* jurors, or at best you can expect a smaller verdict or a lost case.

Do not allow the concept of inadvertence to get into trial, at least not through you. There's nothing inadvertent about choosing to violate a safety rule. Keep in mind that every act of negligence is the result of a choice to violate a safety rule. I have yet to hear of an exception. (*See* section 4-13, p. 102, and *Rules of the Road*.)

Jurors know you cannot make people stop making errors, mistakes, and misjudgments—so regardless of the harm the error caused, jurors are not strongly moved to allow a lot of money for it. But once jurors see that the negligence was a voluntary choice, they will see that in the future such choices can be prevented—and understand that full compensation will help make their own community safer. In fact, this is part of the public policy of tort law, so in most venues you can even argue it.

Rule of thumb: Refer to everything the defendant did as a choice, and never let it drop out of the framework of a violated safety rule.

Fundamental Seven

Worthwhileness of Money

Money is like manure; it's not worth a thing unless it's spread around encouraging young things to grow.

—Dolly Levi (Thornton Wilder's *The Matchmaker*)

For years, the National Jury Project and others have taught that jurors resist allowing money unless it will serve a worthwhile purpose. Arguments that your client "deserves" money or that money equals justice in themselves have little persuasive power. Jurors allow money for worthwhile purposes such as paying medical bills or providing for surviving children. Like shoppers, jurors want something for the money.

So what makes the expenditure worthwhile?

When a juror says, "Money can't bring back the dead" or "Money won't make the pain go away"—common in deliberations—that juror is arguing for a small verdict on the grounds that money can serve no purpose. "What's the point?" So the amounts allowed in wrongful death verdicts are usually smaller than those in injury verdicts in which money serves the purpose of, say, care. Unlike noneconomic damages, economic damages seem worthwhile.[13]

Money cannot help hopeless situations, so jurors tend not to allow money for them. Sometimes in your zeal to show how bad the harm is, you paint a totally bleak picture: unbearable and endless pain, no family, incapacity to do anything, no way to improve the situation. Result: No reason to allow money.

As soon as you take in each case, tune your antennae to anything that can be positioned as purpose or hope—especially hope that can be fulfilled or encouraged by means of a fair damages verdict.

Especially in cases with no permanent injury, many jurors have trouble understanding how money for noneconomic damages can be worthwhile. Money for last year's pain seems to serve no purpose.

---

13. Never use the phrase "economic damages." It sounds like it means "requiring no money."

Many of the techniques throughout this book help provide worthwhile purposes—beyond "justice"—for noneconomic damages. And the companion book *Reptile* shows you how to make it primary.

UNCLEAR PURPOSE

Jurors are reluctant to pay for treatment and care they do not understand. It is not enough for an expert merely to say, "He needs muscle therapy." Explain:

- What it is
- How it works
- Who does it
- Why it is needed
- How it will help
- And critically important: *What will happen if it is not provided*

Show videos of the therapy, photos of the clinic, a video or model of the muscles the therapy will strengthen, and visuals that show what will happen if the care is not provided (such as an atrophied muscle).

FUTURE MEDICAL INVENTIONS

Some jurors think medical science will eventually develop a cure for the "permanent" problem, so why pay for a lifetime with the permanent problem?

Turn this to your favor: Your experts should explain that if any "cure" is invented, it is not likely to be a complete cure, it will be painful and costly, and the minimum life-care plan (*see* section 6-15, pp. 189*ff*.) contains no money for it.

MONEY NOT NECESSARY

Jurors often think that some of the money you want is unnecessary.

For example, a life-care planner may specify a swimming pool for recreation and therapy. Even with explanation, it can seem an unnecessary frill when there's a city pool or YWCA nearby. That can make jurors suspicious of the whole minimum life-care plan. So with or without a minimum life-care plan, avoid asking for anything that jurors can interpret as frivolous or padding. It's not worth the risk of undermining the rest of the plan.

GETTING ALONG FINE WITHOUT MONEY

The defendants have been forcing your client to survive without money. Then they claim she is doing fine without money.

Even when the defense does not say this, some jurors think it on their own. So show that your client is not doing well without money. Do this during your opening, or it can color juror decision making throughout trial.

For example, jurors often think, "Her parents are taking care of her, aren't they? So she's fine as is." So you need to explain not only that this is unfair for the parents (a weak argument), but that it is dangerous to rely on them because 1) they're not trained, 2) they're not part of a group that can provide an immediate replacement if anything happens to them, 3) there are some kinds of care that cannot be done properly by a relative—such as causing the necessary level of pain that some kinds of physical therapy require, and 4) as the family caregivers get older, they won't be able to continue providing care—right when care needs will be increasing and getting more complex.

OTHER SOURCES OF MONEY

Jurors often assume that there are other sources of money: health insurance, social security, savings, workers' comp. "She was a teacher; they all have plenty of insurance." You need to offset this assumption in three ways:

First: Try to get into evidence that she has no source of money. Explain to the judge that it goes to suffering because, for example, she has been without the care and comfort that money could have provided. You just want to tell the jury, "She had no way to pay for the pain medications, so she could not get any."

Second: Explain to the jury that the community should not have to bear any of the cost of care for what the defendant has done. (Don't mention past care if it would open a collateral-source door.) In itself this is not all that powerful an argument, but within a "reptilian" context (*see Reptile*), it is bull's eye: A community (town, city, county, state, nation) has limited resources to care for people. When those resources are used to pay for what the defendant should pay for, everyone is deprived.

Third (and most important): Motivate and arm the jurors who will be on your side to enforce the law during deliberations—that the only money factors jurors are allowed to consider are the levels of harms and losses the defendant caused, not the outside-the-box factor of whether there might be other sources of money. (*See* section 8-4, p. 218.)

COME BACK FOR MORE

Some jurors think the plaintiff can come back for more money. On that basis they reduce the verdict.

Make sure jurors know this is Jane's only opportunity. Explain that she should not have to gamble on whether or not certain things will be provided if they are needed. The defendant put her in this position, so the defendant is the one who should be required to take any necessary gamble.

Fundamental Eight

Fix, Help, Make Up For

"Fix, help, and make up for" provides an effective framework for all your damages evidence and arguments. And it gives jurors a focused three-part structure for the jury's task:

1. *To* fix *what can be fixed*—some losses can be 100 percent fixed, such as repayment of medical bills or lost wages. (Point out that every cent of medical money goes to others—but again, don't open a collateral-source door.)

2. *To* help *what can be helped*—such as by paying for care that will help, but not cure; or for vocational courses to make a new career possible because Jane can no longer pursue the old one.

3. *To* make up for *(balance) what cannot be fixed or helped*—such as past pain or untreatable disabilities that won't get better.

To Fix

Money to fix serves a clear purpose, so jurors have the least trouble with it. Money can "fix" losses accrued due to the costs of care, treatment, and lost employment. Show jurors that 1) money *fixes* those losses, but 2) that all that money for care and treatment goes to others, not to your client, and 3) money for lost income just makes him even with where he'd have been if the defendant had not injured him in the first place. So money to fix is only one part of what a defendant must do to meet his responsibility for hurting a member of the community.

When jurors want to allow less money, they argue that income loss is just speculative: *How do we know he wouldn't have lost his job for some other reason?* Be especially wary of this in times of high unemployment. To offset this argument, show that his field of work is secure, or that the quality of his work made him the least likely to be fired, or whatever else you have that can show that he'd have kept his job. Also argue that the law says to provide money for the harm the negligence actually caused and not to take into account harm that something else only might have done.

To leapfrog it altogether, use the methods in *Reptile* so jurors will have no motive to minimize any part of the verdict.

TO HELP

Some harms and losses cannot be fixed; they can only be helped. Rehabilitation, for example, will strengthen the leg, but not restore it to its original state. The paraplegic can't walk again, but money for mobility aids will help her get around and keep her safe in emergencies. The dead cannot be brought back to life, but money will support the children.

> NB: Never use terms such as "economic" or "noneconomic" or "damages." They are legal jargon. Some attorneys misguidedly think there is some advantage to using the language of the instructions. This is a myth. Instead, legal terms are usually misunderstood in ways that hurt you—even if you explain them. Jurors don't learn much vocabulary during trial. During closing you will relate the nonlegal language with the legal. (*See* section 8-11, p. 235.)

Familiarity

Present the fixes and helps in ways familiar to jurors. Jurors allow money for a child because they are familiar with the financial needs of children. Carefully explain less familiar needs and try to find analogies familiar to the jurors. For example, some jurors may not easily provide for speech therapy unless you teach them what it is, why it is needed, how it will heal or help, *and what will happen without it*. So analogize to physical therapy, which helps people walk better, just as speech therapy helps them talk better.

Most people think "occupational therapy" is to help a person return to work. The term is particularly puzzling when you've told jurors that your client can never work again. *Result:* You get no money for rehabilitating the skills of daily living because jurors don't know that that's what you asked for.

Anchoring

In cases with significant economic damages, the economic total can serve as an anchor or benchmark for noneconomic damages: "John's pain is a far greater harm than just the million dollars in medical bills . . . ."

Negative Anchoring

With low economic damages, an economic-damages anchor can work against you. Low economic figures lead to low noneconomic figures. So if you have a realistic hope for high noneconomic damages, consider leaving out your low economic figures. Don't claim them. You don't want to lessen your chances of a $5 million verdict for the sake of only $45,000 in medicals or $6,585 for a funeral.

Sometimes you may have to show low economic damages for other purposes, such as meeting a threshold for an intentional inflicting of emotional distress claim. But nothing says you have to claim money for them. Similarly, you might want to show how little medical science was able to do about your client's condition; just don't claim money for those small expenses.

TO BALANCE (TO MAKE UP FOR)

Some harms—such as permanent injury and death—can be neither fixed nor helped. They can only be made up for. "To balance" is usually your largest damages request.

But on their own, jurors often withhold money for whatever cannot be fixed or helped. This kind of nullification has always been around, but tort "reform" has made it ubiquitous. Instead of talking about how much money it will take to follow the law, many jurors say, "If the pain can't be diminished, why pay for it?" "How can we put a price on it?" "It would just be a prize for getting hurt."

To offset this, show jurors why making up for such harms is the most important part of their job. Then teach them how to do it. As you will see in the chapters that follow, this trial-long task starts in jury voir dire (*see* chapter four) or, where lawyer-conducted voir dire is not allowed, in opening.

Reptile's community-safety approach provides worthwhile—indeed, essential—reasons to allow money for noneconomic damages.

No matter how you frame your appeal for noneconomic damages, in every case you must accomplish the following four steps:

1. In jury voir dire, identify and try to remove prospective jurors who will resist noneconomic damages. (*See* section 4-5, pp. 87*ff.*)

2. Teach seated jurors that making up for harm is required by law.

3. In voir dire (or opening, if you get no voir dire), promise that you will explain in closing how to figure out money for harms that cannot be fixed or helped (noneconomic damages, though you will not ever use that term). (*See* section 4-5-5, p. 91.) Do not say nonsense such as, "No one can help you figure out how to do it—not me, not the judge," etc. This is not only a false statement, but also makes noneconomic damages seem illegitimate. Worse, as National Jury Project's Susan Macpherson

points out, it gives jurors a convenient excuse not to grapple with noneconomic damages. Zero is an easy out.

4. In closing, show that time is an easily calculable component of all intangible losses. You can do this even where per diem arguments, which are not all that effective anyway, are barred. (*See* section 8-14, pp. *238ff.* and the noneconomic damages arguments in chapter two.) Get your client, family and friends, others who know her, and experts to figure out how much time your client has to spend "working for the defendant"—i.e., how much time does she lose to dealing with her injuries and disabilities? Brushing her teeth used to take two minutes; now it takes six. If she brushes twice a day, that's eight extra minutes a day times 365 days a year times life expectancy = a lot of hours for which she should be paid, including at time and a half when appropriate, and based on her old wage rate. Extend that into every minute she has to spend doing things—even resting—that she would not have had to do but for the harms the defendant caused.

Get time estimates from your client and experts. Have defense experts—including causation experts—corroborate that those are reasonable times with the kinds of injuries you are claiming.

Community Losses

When an injury has taken something away from a community, such as the good works your client used to do, the pleasure your client or his survivors used to get from those good works is usually compensable and often somewhat replaceable. Replaceable = fixable.

For example, your client has *lost the pleasure* of knowing that some elderly folks were eating well because she used to deliver meals to them. She *deeply worries* about those folks. She *misses their company*. That's three different emotional harms. Two can be *fixed*—turned off—if the jury simply allows money to hire folks to deliver those meals.

This shows that the defendant's violation of the safety rules has deprived the community of more than safety.

Fundamental Nine

Degree of Harms and Losses

The degree of harms and losses rarely drives an appropriate verdict. But your failure to provide a thorough harms and losses case can keep anything else from helping.

Unfortunately, many an attorney never learns enough about the harms and losses in a case to present them well or thoroughly. The first step—before worrying about how to present them—is to gather the information. Seek out the harms and losses at least as vigorously, concretely, and thoroughly as you pursue anything else in discovery.

I once asked an attorney for a complete list of the harms and losses in his wrongful death case. He gave me the following:

1. Death
2. Lost husband
3. Lost father

A guy dies and the whole loss takes five words!

Learn the full range and depth of harms and losses. Potential sources of that information include the client; people who know or knew him such as those who worked with him, live(d) near him, help(ed) him, or observe(d) him; and experts (whether or not they will testify, they can still be useful) such as social workers, pain counselors, grief counselors,[14] and others who work with victims of similar harms and losses. Consult books and Web sites that describe the full range of consequences of various injuries. Even your own earlier clients can help you better understand the consequences.

---

14. *See* Robert T. Hall & Mila Ruiz Tecala, Grief and Loss (Trial Guides, 2010).

Fundamental Ten

Who Gets the Money?

The way jurors feel about your client and how she comes across in trial are so important that you cannot gauge the value of your case in advance by comparing it to similar cases. No two clients are alike, so no two cases are alike. You must factor in—sometimes heavily—the impressions all parties make on the jury.

Client Characteristics

Jurors tend to withhold money from someone they see as a "bad" plaintiff, even when the "bad" is unrelated to the case. So when your client has down sides you can't keep out, maximize the good sides: having done good works, having accomplishments, working hard, being a dedicated parent, helping others, being honest, maintaining a stable home against the odds, etc. Kids turned out great? Good. Problems with kids? Good—just show how your client sticks by them and works (or worked) hard to help them turn out well. Client abused drugs? But then she worked hard to overcome it. Had brushes with the law? Yes, but once her daughter was born she reformed her life.

Jurors, as Don Beskind wisely teaches, love redemption stories.

Ask your client what she's most proud of. Interview friends, family, and employers.

Vignettes

The most effective way to present this kind of information is by means of witness vignettes—brief stories that illustrate the client's good qualities (*see* section 6-9, p. 185). Even when a client has no bad qualities, emphasizing the good ones is still important.

Stereotypes

Stereotypes can be your best friend or worst enemy.

Stereotypes are mental shortcuts created by a deeply inbred sophisticated neurological mechanism for information storage, instant retrieval, and near-permanent application. They are pre-logical—meaning that by the time you use logic to show that a stereotype (such as "fat people are lazy") is false, it's too late. Unless you have a few years and a strong will, you can't dislodge a stereotype—not even from your own brain.

Stereotyping is a defense mechanism. It drives—often on its own—a lot of decision making. Mostly without realizing it, we use stereotypes all the time. We prefer to think of ourselves as logical beings whose decisions are driven by conscious thinking. That's probably the falsest stereotype of all.

Negative Stereotypes

Some jurors will think your client is not worth investing in if she falls into a devalued stereotype (minority member, old person, immigrant, obese, foreigner, druggie, etc.). Judgments driven by stereotypes are lightning fast and set in stone.

The National Jury Project's Susan Macpherson (Minneapolis) is the go-to expert on dealing with stereotypes. She teaches you to show how your client is an *exception* to the stereotype. So if the stereotype's characteristics include 1) stupid, 2) lazy, and 3) unreliable, have witnesses show your client's 1) knowledge, 2) diligence, and 3) honesty. If jurors might stereotype your client as, say, a "welfare queen," list for yourself that stereotype's characteristics and then have witnesses show that she does not match those negatives. Do this subtly—just show the characteristics that don't match, but do not talk about welfare queens or their characteristics. (*See also Reptile*, chapter seven—codes.)

Positive Stereotypes

Positive stereotypes can help you almost as much as negative ones can hurt. Positive stereotypes provide one of the best ways to deal with negative ones. "Hardworking mom" is a readily recognizable, very positive stereotype. If you show that that's what your client is, jurors will think well of her. And "hardworking mom" is a powerful offset to the negative "lazy" stereotype attached to obese women.

Is your client someone who "works by the sweat of his brow"? Or does he have the characteristics of "salt of the earth"? Is he a "self-sacrificing parent"? Find out—not from your client, but from everyone who knows your client.

Once a juror assigns a stereotype to a client, the juror will believe that all the characteristics of that stereotype apply. (Obese = not only lazy, but also self-indulgent, greedy, smelly, uncaring, etc.) This mental mechanism can kill a verdict when the stereotype is bad and breathe life into your case when the stereotype is good. Think this through carefully when you have a client who can fall into any kind of stereotype, good or bad. It is often the most important factor in determining verdict size.

NORMAL BEHAVIOR

What was your client doing when she got hurt? Try to show that she was following her normal routine: "She did exactly what she had been doing at work every day for years." In contrast, show that the defendant's behavior was unusual.

Avoiding the Harm

Jurors often think that they'd have kept themselves safer than your client did. This is partly because random, unavoidable harm is frightening to jurors, so they persuade themselves that they'd have done something to avoid it. For an extreme example, after 9/11 many Americans said they'd never have taken a job working in buildings like the Twin Towers. This self-deceptive belief leads jurors to blame your client even when there's no contributory or comparative negligence claim: "I would not have done it that way"; "Dark or not, I'd have seen that black boulder in the road"; "My kid wouldn't have been using that kind of lawn mower"; "If I were sixty and my doc told me my prostate was fine, I'd say, 'OK, Doc, but I want a second opinion. Who can I get to do the test again?'" Such thoughts drive defense verdicts. At best, they drive down damages by making your client seem complicit in what happened.

Irrelevant Considerations

Some jurors find fault with things your client did that were neither wrong nor even relevant: "If you're going to live around here, you have to expect drivers like that." Even U.S. Supreme Court Justice Clarence Thomas has advised—in a case decision—that people who don't like the situation they live in (a town where the school strip-searches young girls) can avoid it by moving to another town. If a Supreme Court Justice can have such absurd thoughts, so can jurors.[15]

In-Trial Impression

Jury feelings about your client can be shaped by the demeanor and visual appearance of your client, his family, and his friends. Your co-counsel or paralegal must subtly but continually monitor that behavior. Facially acting out in response to defense testimony, snoozing, schmoozing, having too good a time, being too happy to see each other, staring at jurors, reading or texting during testimony, and other common behaviors can hurt you. Even crying!

---

15. *Safford Unified Sch. Dist. #1 v. Redding*, 129 S. Ct. 2633, 2656 (2009) (Thomas, J., concurring and dissenting).

Monitor these folks in the hallways and at lunch, too. Talk to your client's family and friends about appropriate behavior—not just in the courtroom, but in hallways, lavatories, parking lots, and driving to and from court. Even well-meaning people do the damnedest things, some of which can undermine the case. If you are not in 100 percent control of the impressions these folks make, make them stay home. Cases can be lost because of things they do that jurors see both in an out of the courthouse—things you will often never even know about.

Even when you are in control of these folks, strictly limit their number to two or three; others should be there only after they have just testified. More than that makes jurors think those people are vying for their cut of the verdict pie.

The only exception is when more people are necessary to provide the level of support your client needs. A good family turns out when one of their own is going through a difficult experience. But be sure to monitor them constantly.

Some attorneys resist changing how a plaintiff dresses or does her hair or makeup. They fear that the defense will call attention to the changes. Make the changes anyway. Your client is your most emphatic visual exhibit. Defense counsel's snide remarks about changed appearance are momentary; your client's appearance is stage center throughout.

(If the defense attorney does refer to the change, respond that the case is so important that your client wanted to look her best. I learned this from the inspirational attorney Rikki Klieman, who learned it from a client who said it—spontaneously—on the stand. And in some situations you can point out that your client has changed her appearance to try to offset the visible harm the defendant did to her—such as scarring or an awkward-looking brace.)

CLIENT IN TRIAL?

In many cases, your client should rarely or never come to court (*see* section 6-18, pp. 194*ff*.). This is especially true when your client looks to be in better condition than she actually is, as brain-damaged clients, for example, often do.

No severely injured client should be there throughout trial. It cannot possibly help you, and in many unpredictable ways can hurt a lot.

CLIENT PREPARATION

Some kinds of problems require competent client preparation—not only for trial, but as importantly for deposition. Few attorneys know how to do it. It is antithetical to the normal skill set. Since good client preparation is essential to every case, you need to learn how to do it.

Here are three ways. You need all three.

First, read what the specialists have written. By far the best approach to client preparation is Don Keenan's chapter in *Reptile* (chapter seventeen) as well as his instructional video (at ReptileKeenanBall.com). You can learn to use Don's method to great effect.

Second, see chapter two in *Theater Tips and Strategies for Jury Trials*.[16]

Third, consider using a specialist to help prepare your client.[17] This will not only result in a client doing far better in testimony, but show you firsthand how to go about the process. (If you use a specialist, be certain to have her help your client understand how to answer questions about the preparation. It rarely comes up, but it can. In fact, ask the specialist in advance how she helps the client handle such questions. If she has no good answer, don't hire her.)

The vast majority of attorneys relegate client preparation to low priority: an hour or two of rushed work just before trial, admonitions of "Don't do this! Don't do that! And for God's sake, if you say X, you will lose the case for us!" A client unprepared to be clear, confident, and eager to testify can undermine your case in ways you might never be aware of—even as they unfold in front of you. And there's nothing that can take a verdict down like a client who has not been properly prepared. It is well worth your trouble to master this difficult area.

There is no client who cannot be improved: made clearer, more credible, more confident, less susceptible to cross-exam tactics. But many lawyers don't know how.

OUT-OF-COURT BEHAVIOR

Constantly remind your client and her family and friends that they are on display from the time they leave their homes in the morning until returning home at night—even when they are nowhere near the courthouse and even on weekends. You never know when a juror is around. Jurors will even drive by the house to check it out, so your client must not be out there shoveling snow if there's a bad-back claim. She must not smoke where anyone can see, regardless of the nature of the claim. Smoking will turn some jurors against her, even when smoking has nothing to do with anything.

---

16. DAVID BALL, THEATER TIPS AND STRATEGIES FOR JURY TRIALS (NITA 2003).
17. Joshua Karton in Los Angeles; Gillian Drake in Chevy Chase, Maryland.

Driving

This can be difficult to enforce, but *your client must not be driving if her claim includes anything that could make driving dangerous.*

Arguing that "driving is the only thing she has left" is a pathetic excuse for allowing your client to be a public menace. Jurors don't want to help plaintiffs who endanger the public, and who can blame them? (This is common in brain-damage cases, where brain damage has rendered the client dangerous to herself and others because she cannot make decisions in emergencies—yet she's driving!)

What's Online?

Before accepting a case, and again before trial, find everything a thorough search can possibly find online about your client and the family—or that can be mistaken for being about them. How you deal with what you find will depend on what you find. But not knowing about it can result in your losing your case. It can even damage your own reputation ("local attorney argues millions for child-molester").

Pay particular attention to social and business networking sites (Facebook, LinkedIn) as well as to sites where clients might have posted their injuries, such as CaringBridge.org.

Jurors will even look up your client's children on Facebook and other social networking sites. They'll look up your kids, too. We no longer live in a private world. For better or worse, the "community" is back the way small villages were in the early days of American jurisprudence—everyone knows everything, including a lot of things that are unflattering or just plain wrong. So you better know what the "neighbors" are thinking and why. And you better see what's out there that you can get rid of before trial.

This goes beyond your client. Many jurors Google the parties and families, as well as the lawyers and their firms, the experts and fact witnesses, the judge, topics of fact and expert testimony, the law, your marketing Web site (such as your counterproductive site that brags about your track record, implying that you know how to play the system to win lots of cases), professional organizations to which you or your client may (or may not) belong, and whatever else is out there, correct or incorrect. Even political contributions! Google Earth can show your house (or your client's house), along with its four-car garage and Olympic-size swimming pool. If you don't know what's out there, you don't know what the jurors might be thinking . . . so you don't even try to do anything about it. The most common result: you lose the case and never know why.

For example, even if defense counsel has not found it, chances are high that the jurors will know that your expert belongs to the same advocacy group you do. It's amazing how many otherwise smart attorneys hire such experts! To jurors, it's as sleazy as you can get.

So learn what's out there, and fix what can be fixed. Avoid the traps. And keep all this in mind when you (or your family or client or client's family) post anything online, put up a Web site, or donate to anything that can be publicly reported.

In one case, a juror found a plaintiff's expert's Web site that promised he'd make sure you win even when the facts are against you. To this day that attorney believes he lost for other reasons.

In another case, a Wikipedia entry agreed more with the defense expert than with the plaintiff's. Jurors took Wikipedia to be a neutral voice, so decided in favor of the defense. This was an avoidable loss because the plaintiff's expert could easily have shown what was wrong with what Wikipedia said, but plaintiff's counsel had not done her online homework.

Finally: You can count on the defense (including the insurance companies and various corporations and interest groups) to make things even worse by planting bogus information for jurors to see. Kinda disgusting, but it's being done, and you need to know about it.

Be sure to see Supplement H, "Virtual Reality," to gain control of this dangerous and ubiquitous new problem.

Who *Really* Gets the Money?

Jurors worry about money getting into the wrong hands. They might agree that the injured child needs treatment, but they think Dad might grab the money and run. Or that Mom and Dad could get run over by a bus, leaving Uncle Benny to grab the money and run. Or that you will grab the money and run—a concern created not solely by the forces of tort "reform," but by the handful of attorneys who did grab fistfuls of money and run. Jurors want to know that the money will go where it's supposed to. Otherwise they can suspect it will go to a nonworthwhile use.

For every case potentially involving a significant verdict for a child, establish a trust account so jurors know the money will go for its intended *worthwhile* purposes. If possible, name the trust holder as a plaintiff: *First National Bank and Bobby Smith v. Acme Trucking*. Make sure you do this in the way permitted by your jurisdiction. This allows the trust officer to testify to how the money will be controlled for Bobby's benefit. (Given the banking industry's recent history, have the trust officer describe how your client's money is protected no matter what happens to the institution.)

You can accomplish the same thing with an appropriate guardian or conservator.

Not as effective, but adequate, is to explain or have the judge explain that the court will control the money. If the defense or the judge balks at allowing jurors to hear this, argue that the consequences of not doing so would be prejudicial solely to the child. Point out that the only reason the defense would argue against it is that they know it would be prejudicial against the child to hide the fact that the money is being protected. And there is nothing prejudicial to the defense in revealing it.

With adults as well, jurors often keep verdicts low out of worry over who will really get the money. Will the quadriplegic's attractive young wife grab it and run? Consider carefully what factors might make the jury think this way and offset them—for example, by showing the selfless devotion of the attractive young wife.

FIGHTING SPIRIT

Rather than focusing on how injuries have burdened your client, we advise attorneys to focus on how their clients have striven to overcome their injuries. Don't say, "Despite all that therapy, she can't walk a hundred feet on her own." Say, "After months of hard work, she can now walk a hundred feet on her own!" So she's no quitter. Jurors allow verdict money when a plaintiff keeps fighting no matter how hard or hopeless it is. Americans love a fighting spirit that refuses to give in.

If the harm is all in the past, show how your client strove and prevailed. If the harm is continuing, counsel your client to engage *right away* in activities that are as optimistic and hopeful as possible and show a continuing refusal to give in. If the client cannot work, perhaps she can volunteer a few hours a week. If she cannot get out of the house, maybe she can use e-mail and the Internet to stay in touch with people and the world in general. She might even be able to do something constructive and helpful on the Internet—such as helping others get through similar difficulties.[18] Counseling your client to strive in such ways will not only motivate jurors to allow money; it will also improve the quality of your client's life—which is, after all, the primary goal.

---

18. But caution your client not to counsel others on how to get an attorney to get money. Jurors might see it. And if your client has a Web site, check to be sure it's OK for the jurors to see.

Be sure your client does not fall into the opposite kinds of behavior, such as not getting treatment, missing therapy sessions, or quitting rehabilitation. That's a gift to the defense. If your client has done those things, explain why. Not enough money can be a great explanation, if it's true.

Even with a minor injury, show how your client tried to cope and overcome instead of lying down and waiting to get better. (Just be careful not to turn this into her harming herself by trying to do too much too soon.)

Fundamental Eleven

Importance

How far that little candle throws his beams! So shines a good deed in a naughty world.

—Shakespeare, *The Merchant of Venice*

Even the smallest person can change the course of the future.

—J.R.R. Tolkien, *The Fellowship of the Ring*

People have a deep need to feel they are part of something important or that they'll be seen as having been part of something important. When jurors think a particular verdict will give them importance, it can drive their decision making.

Every case, even the smallest, can be positioned to make jurors feel important by providing a full plaintiff's verdict.

The reverse is at work when tort "reform" takes over a decision. Tort-"reformed" jurors believe that each plaintiff's verdict—even in a small case—is a menace to the community. Their sense of importance comes from "protecting" the community by means of a defense verdict. You have to turn the tables by showing that any importance attaching to a defense verdict will pale in comparison to a full verdict for the plaintiff. This can be done even in the smallest of cases (*see Reptile*, chapter nineteen, "small" cases).

Here's how it works in large cases.

In a 1992 gas-well negligence case, Kentucky attorney Gary C. Johnson started jury voir dire by saying:

> Folks, before I start my usual questions, there's something I've got to ask first. This case is likely to be the most important case you ever heard about. It may permanently change how things are done across the state, even across the country. It may change how outside corporations operate in Kentucky and how we live here. There will probably be media coverage. Some reporters may try to talk to you after trial to find out why you decided the way you did. Now, you don't have to talk to them, you can

say no—but some people don't want to be put in that position. And some people are uncomfortable being on a jury whose verdict could have such an important effect. So tell me this, and let me start with Mr. Jones here: How do you feel about being in a position like that?

This is a legitimate information-seeking voir dire question. You need to find out how jurors feel about this, because importance-avoiding or limelight-avoiding jurors may keep a verdict low so they do not have to be part of such a situation.

But beyond gaining information, the question also aligns what you want (a large verdict) with what most jurors want (importance). As trial progresses and jurors come to understand what is at stake, they realize they can get what they want (their importance, their fifteen minutes of fame, or the chance to do something important) only by deciding on a full plaintiff's verdict.

When Gary Johnson asked that question, almost everyone—possibly excepting the defense attorneys—was suddenly eager to be on the jury. Prospective jurors who had earlier written five reasons why they could not possibly serve bounded into the jury box the instant their names were called, proud and primed and eager to serve. The judge asked one: "What about these problems you mentioned on the questionnaire?"

"Oh, I took care of all that. No problem." Actually, he had not. He just wanted to be on that jury.

Most jurors who were dismissed were crushed. They wanted to be part of something important. They wanted to do something important. They wanted to be interviewed on TV.

At the end of voir dire, Gary asked again, "Well, folks, now that you've had some time to think about it, is there anybody who thinks they'd be uncomfortable on a jury that could be so important?" They all waved that off as a ridiculous possibility.

Over the course of trial, Johnson made sure the jurors understood that a large verdict was necessary to make it an important trial. So the jurors got the importance they wanted, and the client got a full and fair verdict. The only unhappy ones were the out-of-state company that had poisoned the groundwater all over eastern Kentucky and their lawyers—none of whom left the courthouse feeling very important.

Fundamental Twelve

Going Home Afterward

You can *go home again.*

—Thomas Fox

As some jurors draw closer to making a real decision, they start worrying about how people they know will react to that decision. A hospital secretary may start to worry that her colleagues and bosses, who resent lawsuits and plaintiff's attorneys, will resent and punish her for being on a jury that has allowed a large verdict—even on a non-medical case.

Such jurors often push for a defense verdict to avoid having to deal with the money problem. This is particularly true when the harm is so great that a verdict would be large if the jury decides the defendant is liable.

In voir dire, find out who the juror goes home or back to work to. Might those people disapprove if this juror decides on a large verdict? For example, a juror whose wife runs a business that needs a lot of insurance can be a bad choice. Even if the juror does not think that large verdicts raise insurance rates, his wife might—and she, not you, will be there after the case is over. And no matter what a nurse's mother says, she's not likely to be your kind of juror in a med mal case.

Ask jurors how lawsuits have affected the businesses or fields they work in and how people at work and with whom they spend their spare time feel about lawsuits.

Focus groups, while helpful in many ways, cannot show how much this kind of thinking will affect your case. This is because focus jurors, unlike real jurors in open court, know that no one at work or home will know the outcome, so they do not worry about negative reactions. Real jurors feel exposed because the verdict will be public.

The National Jury Project's Susan Macpherson suggests this remedy: Tell jurors that they can say to their friends, "Over the course of trial, I became an expert. The case was very complex, but I know if you'd heard all that I heard over the past four weeks, you'd have made the same decision."

It is never enough to say that jurors who will go home to problematic friends (or any other kinds of unfavorable jurors) have to be removed in jury selection. Of course you should try, but it is rarely possible to be thorough, and often you don't have enough jury selection time to do it at all. Michigan trial consultant Eric Oliver has long advised that you should do the best you can in de-selecting jurors, and then assume that the worst ones snuck by and are now seated. They're not likely to sneak by with Eric doing the selecting, but you still need to assume it.

Fundamental Thirteen

Compromise Kills

All compromise is based on give and take, but there can be no give and take on fundamentals. Any compromise on mere fundamentals is a surrender. For it is all give and no take.

—Ghandi

Jurors who are only mildly supportive of liability often try to lower the verdict size. In a jurisdiction requiring unanimity, one such juror can lower the verdict significantly. She is in a powerful negotiating position because the others know if they insist on too large a verdict, she can reverse her liability vote and there will be no money. In a jurisdiction that does not require unanimity, just two or three jurors can do the same thing.

But this is no two-way street. Eleven high-money jurors have little power against a low-rolling minority of one. To achieve liability at all, they are forced to compromise way down on money.

This is one reason why you must substantiate a high figure. Turning your life-care plan into a *minimum* life-care plan (*see* section 6-15, pp. 189*ff.*), arguing for life expectancy well beyond the official tables (*see* section 8-9-1, p. 228), and the wide variety of other techniques in this book will help you accomplish that.

The power of the low-balling juror also reinforces the value and necessity of the trial methods covered in *Reptile*.

Fundamental Fourteen

Seen Worse, Been Worse

Familiarity breeds contempt.

—Aesop

Jurors gauge harms through the lenses of what they are familiar with in real life. This can hurt you, especially when the juror knows someone with injuries as serious as your client's, yet who seems to get along without the money you say your client needs.

Further, jurors who know people with harms similar to your client's will probably be less shocked by your client's harm: "My uncle is blind, and he manages well." That takes away a juror's motivation to allow much money. Jurors notice how well people they know *seem* to cope. But jurors are often unaware of the real difficulties. They see the smile on someone's face, but not the pain inside. "My uncle had trouble when he first went blind, but now he gets along pretty well." No, he doesn't get along pretty well; he's blind. He just doesn't wear his heart on his sleeve.

Consider using an expert who can explain how most badly injured people hide their worst internal pain even from people who know them best—as your client is doing. A good expert can explain this in a way that will have such a juror nodding with recognition.

What about jurors who themselves are disabled or are victims of serious injuries or disabilities? For a number of reasons, most jurors who have been badly injured or disabled turn out to be unfavorable for plaintiffs. Most such jurors secretly blame themselves for what happened to them ("if only I'd…"), and they transfer that blame to your client ("she should have…"). That, of course, steeply drives down verdicts and even results in no-negligence decisions.

Nonetheless, the defense usually strikes such jurors. The defense knows that occasionally such a juror can lead the way to an enormous verdict, a defense attorney's worst personal nightmare. They do not want to take that chance, despite the odds against it.

And because of the odds against it, you should not take that chance, either. But in strike situations in which you and the defense alternately announce your strikes, try to save one by placing this kind of juror last on your strike list. The defense is likely to strike him first.

Finally: Be careful with potential jurors—such as rehabilitation therapists—who work with badly injured or disabled people. Someone who daily sees severe injuries, disabilities, and pain can view your client's problems as minor by comparison.

FUNDAMENTAL FIFTEEN

PEOPLE SHOULD PAY FOR THEIR OWN PROBLEMS

God helps those who help themselves. Leave the rest of us out of it.

—Mock trial juror

Some jurors believe people should pay for their own problems, no matter who caused the problems. These "play-the-hand-you're-dealt" jurors want your client's life to be a gamble—when something bad happens, "that's the breaks and it's up to you to suffer through." They also feel that human beings should not be expected to take care of each other. Often life has given them good reason to feel this way.

One way around this is to show jurors the financial and community-safety costs of allowing the defendant to walk away free. As *Reptile* explains, when the defendant walks free, it encourages still more dangerous behavior at the expense of the community's financial resources and safety.

Some jurors may have overcome other kinds of serious difficulties without help. For example, recovering alcoholics may have had AA support, but had to conquer their demons on their own. These "I managed!" jurors tend to demand the same of others. So show those jurors how extraordinarily your client tried/tries to overcome what happened to her. They—and most other jurors—can be moved to compensate that heroic effort more than the injury itself.

Susan Macpherson observes that some jurors will think the plaintiff should be forced to struggle to get by with little money on the grounds that it builds character and strength. Such tough-love jurors think that handing someone tons of money creates more disability. "Better to have to make their way without it." So show that they need financial help so they can make something of the character and strength they already have.

Fundamental Sixteen

Divine Punishment ("God Is My Co-Juror")

Do nothing till you hear from Me.

—God

"It's God's will!"

Some jurors believe that serious illness or injury is likely the result of unrelated wrongs the victim committed earlier in life: "If he got hurt like that, there had to be a reason for it. There always is." This is another of those beliefs some people cling to; it makes them feel safe—until, of course, something bad happens to them.

Consequently, such jurors can believe that giving verdict money would be contrary to God's plan. Try to spot these jurors in jury voir dire, but always assume some have slipped through.

One way to deal with them is handily provided by Scriptures, which you can—and should—use even where explicit use of them is banned or you are afraid of offending other jurors. (*See* chapter fourteen in *Reptile*.) For example, "We are all taught that even the least among us deserves justice" has biblical overtones, but does not offend anyone.

Fundamental Seventeen

Don't Wanna Punish the Defendant

Let the punishment fit the crime and this was no crime.

—Iago in *Othello,* VI, 3

Many jurors believe that any verdict beyond medical and lost income expenses is "punitive."

Make jurors understand that none of the money is intended to punish; it is only intended to fix what can be fixed, help what can be helped, and make up for what cannot be fixed or helped. Describe "punishment" as money that goes beyond the costs of fixing/helping/making up for.

Use an analogy: When a child breaks a window, making him pay the cost of the window out of his allowance is not punishment; it's just making things right for whoever owns the window. "Punishment" would be something different, such as "Go to your room!"

Also, explain to jurors that no one is going to jail, no licenses will be revoked, and no one will lose his career. This is especially important with medical defendants.

Point out that an undercompensating verdict would punish your client for what the defendant did.

Chapter Two

Noneconomic Damages[1]

This chapter is about some principal obstacles to fair noneconomic damages—the kind of damages jurors usually have trouble with.

2-1 Obstacle 1: No Worthwhileness

Jurors rarely see the purpose of money for noneconomic damages. For one of this book's many ways of overcoming this obstacle, see p. 31.

2-2 Obstacle 2: No Way to Calculate

Jurors don't know how to figure out the amount. Gimmicks (such as a per diem argument) can help some individual jurors, but your favorable jurors need more to be able to persuade jurors who want to give less.

Here's a common introduction to calculating noneconomic damages. It happens in jury voir dire:

Prospective juror: I wouldn't know how to figure out how much money there should be for pain.

Counsel: (*giving the worst possible response*) Well, you know, I can't tell you how to do it. Nobody can, not even Her Honor. You're just supposed to use your own life experiences and your common sense.

But no life experiences prepare a juror for anything like this. Nor does common sense. If you cannot explain how to do it, and if neither the judge nor anyone else can, jurors conclude that (1) it can't be done right, and (2) since no one knows how to do it right, it should not be done.

So you must teach jurors exactly how to figure out the noneconomic damages figure. The dialogue above should go like this:

---

1. Sorry for the repetition, but please remember never to use the term "noneconomic damages" in front of a jury. You may see this reminder in yet another footnote.

Prospective juror:	I wouldn't know how to figure out how much money there should be for pain.
Counsel:	(*giving the best possible response*) Don't worry about that; we'll make sure you know how by the time you have to do it. Right now, I'm just asking you this: Some people—even when they know how to calculate the amount—don't think it's right to allow money for pain. Other people are OK with it. I'm just asking which you're closer to.

And no matter their answer, follow up with "Please tell me about that." (See more about this voir dire technique in chapter four [section 4-3-2, p. 84]. And see how to teach jurors to "calculate" noneconomic damages in "Scales," section 8-14, p. 238.)

2-3 Obstacle 3: Can't Define "Compensation"

Jurors don't know what "compensation" means. Reward? Entitlement? Happy money? Punishment for the defendant?

You make matters worse by saying anything like, "We submit the figure should be $_____." This ghastly piece of legalese cannot help or guide even your most favorable juror. The fact that you "submit" it actually makes it suspect and undermines—if not kills—the ability of your favorable jurors to argue for it in deliberations.

And when you offer no noneconomic figure at all, you leave your favorable jurors with no guidance, so don't be surprised when they don't deliver. Even in venues where you cannot ask for a specific figure, you can and must tell jurors how to arrive at one. (*See, e.g.*, p. 238, section 8-14, "Scales.")

So find a good way to explain exactly what compensation means. It means the "fair-trade value" of the harms—the level of money it takes to equal the level of harm. Explain that this is the oldest way we have of valuing anything. When great-grandpa bought a cow in exchange for five goats, five goats were the fair-trade value of the cow. So when you buy a heifer today for $1,400, that's the fair-market value of the cow. It's the same with harms in a case—how much money equals the value of the harms?

Jurors must also understand that compensation does not mean "reward," like a lollipop to a kid with a bruised knee. This is one reason you must never use the word "award"—that word is legalese, which many jurors take to mean "reward." "Reward" means prize, and jurors don't give prizes.

Noneconomic Damages

Remember this: insofar as you allow jurors to start deliberations with misconceptions about what "compensate" means, they will use those misconceptions to your client's disadvantage.

2-4 Obstacle 4: Defense Plea for Jury Nullification

Defense attorneys often make wildly improper arguments. For example, some argue, "All that money for pain and suffering can do no good because it won't make the pain or suffering go away." This begs for nullification. Even in venues where nullification is allowed, counsel cannot ask for it.

It's a request for nullification because "making the pain go away" is not relevant to deciding how much pain compensation should be allowed. Money for anything that can make pain go away is economic, not noneconomic. Money to compensate for the pain itself is for pain that could not or cannot be made to disappear. Arguing otherwise misleads the jury. As a plea for nullification, it should not be allowed.

For this and other improper defense arguments, make sure you routinely file objections in limine, supported by law and public policy. If you lose the motion, object again during trial. The judge might change her mind. If not, you might be able to make good law on appeal.

Defense attorneys also frequently use tort-"reform"-based arguments: that big verdicts hurt the economy, enrich lawyers, etc. This is improper for a variety of reasons. Deal with it in limine. If you let the defense give the argument in closing before you object, you invite disaster: a misguided or biased judge will overrule the objection. And even if the judge sustains, a curative instruction won't unring the bell.

If you lose such motions in limine, be extra careful to make sure the jurors understand the law—preferably as early as voir dire (*see* chapter three) and certainly in closing (*see* p. 225, Essentials for Closing—Massaging).

2-5 Obstacle 5: Bad Comparison to Economic Damages

Jurors tend toward noneconomic verdicts that are some proportion, fraction, multiple, or equivalent of the economic damages figure.

So if medical bills and lost wages are $125,000, jurors are likely to argue that the plaintiff should get *half* that amount, or *double* (once in a while), or that amount exactly, or "just a little more" or "not as much as." This is because they seize on anything tangible as an anchor to help them "calculate" the intangible—even when there is no relationship between the two.

This makes your economic damages figure extraordinarily important—and, sometimes, extraordinarily dangerous. In a case with $125,000 in economic damages, jurors are likely to add no more than a few hundred thousand for noneconomic damages. With identical noneconomic harms, $2,000,000 in economic losses is almost sure to result in a far greater noneconomic verdict than just a few hundred thousand.

This is true especially in venues that don't allow you to specify noneconomic figures. In many such venues, you can call the noneconomic damages "the greatest harm in the case." Point out that the money for future medical care all goes to other people to help take care of John—John never gets a cent of it, and the money for lost wages only makes John even with where he'd have been if the wrongdoing had never happened. So none of that money makes up for the biggest losses, the harm to John himself. That argument gets jurors to compare "biggest" to the smaller anchor of the economic amount.

2-6 Obstacle 6: Why Pay Family to Be Caretakers? Why Pay for Professional Care When the Family Can Do It?

Money for the family for its caretaking is often hard to get: "People marry for better or worse; loving kindred gladly help"; "Money has nothing to do with it—that's how families express their love." Such beliefs lead some jurors to withhold money for professional care.

As Susan Macpherson teaches, start by identifying prospective jurors who are or have been caretakers. Some who care for, say, elderly parents understand what it does to the caretaker's life—but they think that this is what everyone should do, including your client's family. Others think that caretaking is a living hell forced on them. And most jurors resist helping a plaintiff who has the same problem they do.

Jurors not already serving as caretakers may be likely to do so in the future, so ask what their thinking is at this point.

To overcome the mindset that leads jurors to expect your client's family to be the caretakers—and to do it for free—show four things:

1. *Forcing the family to provide care for harms the defendant caused is unfair.* The family does not begrudge doing it and will do it as long as necessary. But the defendant's responsibility is to relieve the family of that burden and return the family to being family members, not permanent caregivers.

    Usually, the injured plaintiff is deeply disturbed, depressed, and plagued by guilt because his family is trapped into having to take care of him. This is one way in which the defendant's lack of responsibility has piled harm upon the original harm (*see* Fundamental Five, p. 18). The proper verdict can 100 percent fix this part of the harm.

If your client is unaware of the care his family is providing (because, say, he's in a coma or has severe brain damage), make it clear that it's not family members who are asking for money for their work. It is you, as the protector of their legal rights, who is asking because you are required to do all that the law allows to help them.

Consortium: The brilliant Los Angeles attorney R. Rex Parris teaches that in states that allow it, you should pursue your consortium claim as a separate case with its own separate trial. In states where you must do both in one trial, consider assigning one attorney to everything having to do with the principal plaintiff's case and a separate attorney to the spouse's consortium case. Overlap as little as possible. This separation keeps the principal case from overshadowing the consortium claim and minimizing the consortium verdict. The separation also highlights both sets of harms, potentially increasing the size of both verdicts.

2. *Show that family-provided care diminishes a husband-wife (or whatever) relationship into a care giver-patient relationship.* Show how the specifics of the care (such as help with toileting) limits and destroys many normal family relationships. A good social worker or marriage counselor is well worth the cost of providing testimony about this. And you must not be delicate about delineating the distasteful tasks. You need not be graphic, but you must provide enough information—starting no later than opening—for the jurors to know that someone has to wipe someone else's butt.

3. *Show that family-provided care is neither safe nor good, no matter how hard the family tries.* Trained helpers provide better and safer care. Even when a family member happens to be a professional caregiver, an expert or treating physician or therapist can explain why non-family care is always preferable. In part, this is because an outsider's objectivity is unimpeded by emotional attachments. Give examples of why this is important. For instance, a family member can be reluctant to put the patient through enough discomfort during home physical therapy to reap the therapy's benefits. This is because the family member, even when a professional, is less likely than an outsider caregiver's employees to have the emotional fortitude or personal authority to push the patient to do what needs to be done. This is true even for physicians, which is partly why they do not treat their own family members.

Focus on replacing the family's amateur care with that of paid caretakers—trained to deal with specific issues, if that's what's needed.

Norfolk, Virginia, lawyer Jeffrey Breit effectively tells juries that professionals are trained to spot problems that untrained family cannot, such as early signs of bed sores. By the time a family member recognizes the problem, it can be too late. So allowing family to continue as caretakers unnecessarily endangers your client. This is particularly powerful because jurors do not consider safety a frill.

Showing that better care is needed than the family can provide also undermines the common defense-juror argument: "The plaintiff has been getting along fine until now without all that money, so why allow so much now?"

4. *Get the focus off asking for money to pay the family.* Many jurors find it offensive that a wife, for example, would ask for money to care for her husband. Explain—in opening—that you are citing the family's number of hours and the value of those hours only so the jury can understand the enormity of the job involved in caring for anyone with these injuries. Then explain that the family members are not asking to be paid; it's you who are protecting their rights, and your client feels badly at this intrusion.

Lost services. Jurors' resistance diminishes when you show that someone was actually hired and paid. And those amounts provide anchors for the cost of future services. In many jurisdictions, you can claim "loss of services." Because they can be time- and market-based, you can easily valuate any services around the home that your client usually did, but could not or cannot do now. Dad used to mow the lawn and paint the garage, but now someone else has to do it. An economist can attach a figure to these tasks, or anyone in the family can total the hours and multiply by the customary local hourly wages for such tasks or show payment receipts.

When the family has had no money to pay for these services, things may have fallen into disrepair. This adds to the money you can claim—first for the value of the lost services, and second for the plaintiff's distress that his family had to endure living in the midst of disrepair.

2-7 OBSTACLE 7: "EVEN IF THAT'S THE RIGHT AMOUNT, IT'S FAR TOO MUCH FOR ANY INDIVIDUAL"

Sometimes you can find unique and worthwhile uses for money. For example, the family of a daughter killed in a traffic accident might find solace in starting, and raising money for, a charitable foundation named for their daughter. The foundation would serve the purpose of finding better ways to

Noneconomic Damages

teach traffic safety "so that her death will mean something." Since the concept of the foundation provides a way to ameliorate the emotional pain, it should be legitimate damages evidence.

In voir dire:

> "Who here has ever heard of the Sally France Smith Road Safety Foundation?"

In testimony:

> Q: Mrs. Smith, how have you been trying to come to terms with the death of your daughter?
>
> A: Well, it has helped that we've started a road safety foundation we're raising money for; that will help if we can raise enough money for it to make a difference.

Giving jurors this kind of worthwhile purpose for money helps overcome many reasons they have for withholding it.

Of course, the most valuable use of this approach is that it genuinely removes some of the family's anguish and reshapes that emotional energy into something that will help the community. So this may be one of the most valuable suggestions you ever make for your client, and it's a Reptilian bull's eye (*see Reptile*).

Connecticut's Ernie Teitel teaches that the establishment of a foundation is necessary in every significant case—and that it gets into evidence for a variety of reasons. For example, the defense usually suggests that your client is driven by wanting to get rich. You are entitled to show that that's false; your client wants to instead assuage his loss by being able to help others.

Chapter Three

Rules for Jurors: Preponderance; Harms and Losses Only

Two of your biggest problems:

1. Most jurors refuse to make decisions based on preponderance of the evidence.
2. Many jurors base their money decisions on improper factors.

Jury instructions have virtually no effect in solving either problem (or much else), even when the instructions are in plain English. Unless you are barred from doing so, it is up to you alone to solve these problems.

You solve them by extending your use of the "rules" beyond defendant conduct (*see* chapter one, Fundamental Five, p. 10) and into the realm of juror requirements. Do this without straying from the guidelines below (rules *you* have to follow).

3-1 The Preponderance Template[1]

Almost all jurors expect you to prove your case beyond a reasonable doubt. You can't change that merely by explaining preponderance. Nor can the judge. But when you turn preponderance into a working theme throughout trial, jurors will use it. Accomplishing this is probably even more important than you think. Throughout your career, you'd probably have won most of the cases you lost if the jurors had based their decisions on preponderance. So you really have no more important task than to master and use this template. Omit nothing, add nothing, change nothing—unless forced to.

Most attorneys pay so little attention to their very minimal burden of proof that they don't even mention to jurors that it applies to decision making not only about liability, but money as well. It is time to change the situation.

---

[1]. The material on preponderance is adapted from David Ball, *Making Preponderance Work*, Trial Magazine, March 2008, by permission.

3-1-1 The Goal

In deliberations, when a defense-oriented juror says, "I'm just not *sure*," you want the other jurors to insist, "We're not here to be sure. We're just here to say whether the plaintiff is more likely right than wrong. If you won't go along with that, let's get the judge." Favorable jurors you have armed to say that are not likely to fold on you.

3-1-2 The Process

All through trial, not just in voir dire and closing, keep the concept of "more likely right than wrong" in front of the jurors. It must be the lens through which jurors see and gauge all your evidence—not in retrospect, *but as it comes in.*

When you explain preponderance merely in voir dire or opening, it has little effect on how jurors hear the evidence. So even when you repeat it in closing, it's too late. No one can go back and reapply a standard they didn't apply while the evidence was coming in. The brain does not work backward. You can't even rattle off your own Social Security or phone number backward.

You must ensure that jurors keep preponderance in mind throughout trial. Otherwise you will suffer the consequences of the juror's standard of near-certainty.

As with any important skill, following the template is easy—*if* you practice until you master it.

It starts in jury selection. If you don't get to conduct your own jury selection, the template will still work if you begin using it in opening. (But you must not leave it out of voir dire when voir dire is available.) Weave the template theme into every available element of trial, or it weakens.

NB: Because this template works so well, don't use it when there's a dangerous affirmative defense. Is lowering the burden for your side worth lowering it to the advantage of the defense as well?

NB2: Don't try to justify the doctrine of preponderance. As far as I know, there's no way to do it that makes it seem right to jurors. It makes even less sense to jurors than why an innocent person needs the benefit of the Fifth Amendment. So don't get them thinking about why preponderance is the rule; just present it as the rule. The explanation that we reserve the higher burden for when a person's liberty is at stake strikes many jurors as backward. They'd rather imprison a criminal defendant than make a civil defendant—whom they see as a "victim"—pay money. After all, the United States imprisons more people than any other country on earth. So don't bring up the comparison to criminal cases.[2]

3-2 THE PREPONDERANCE FORMULA

You will use a combination of words and gesture every time you talk about preponderance during trial.

3-2-1 Words

The words are always: "More likely right than wrong." Use those exact words. Don't mess with them. "More likely right than wrong" is the clearest possible expression of preponderance.

Use different words only if the judge thinks that "more likely right than wrong" does not reflect the law. In that situation, simply find a different plain-English wording she can accept.

Don't use the words "preponderance" or "burden," or phrases such as "greater weight of the evidence" until closing, when you will connect the by-then familiar concept of "more likely right than wrong" to the language of the law. The primary principle of all good teaching is *concept first, then vocabulary*. The other way round (strange terms first) makes the listener tense up so that the learning gets harder and often does not even occur. Further, many jurors neither like nor understand legalese and can be suspicious of you when you use it. They'll also regard you as arrogant and even comical. Plain English is a great invention, so simply say, "More likely right than wrong." It's clear. And clarity is your friend. Sounding like a lawyer—anytime—is like putting your worst foot forward and then stomping it with your other foot.

3-2-2 Hands

As you say "more likely right than wrong," position your hands side by side and close together, palms up, at waist level. Right hand should be half an inch higher than left.

Do this every time you say "more likely right than wrong" for the rest of trial. This will be often. Result: Jurors will use that exact hand language on your behalf in deliberations. The judge will probably do it when reading the jury instructions. Sometimes even defense counsel helps out by doing it in closing, though who knows why?

---

2. If the judge does not allow you to use the Preponderance Template in voir dire, when asking whatever little you *are* allowed about preponderance you will need to use the comparison to "beyond reasonable doubt."

3-3 Preponderance Template: Jury Voir Dire

NB: As you'll see, this Preponderance Template is an easy way to remove jurors for cause. So don't use it until you're far enough into voir dire to know which jurors you really want excused. Some who won't go along with preponderance might be good in other ways, so don't decide solely on the issue of preponderance—though give it a lot of weight.

That said, jurors who have trouble with preponderance are likely to be tort "reformed." That does not mean they've ever thought about preponderance; hardly anyone ever has. But once they hear about it, tort-"reformed" jurors dislike it: "These damned plaintiff's lawyers don't even need to *prove* anything!"

Step I. At the appropriate time in jury voir dire, say this:

> In trials like this, jurors make their decisions on the basis of whether my side is more likely right than wrong. [*use hands*]

It is important to say "in trials like this" and not "in this trial" so jurors understand that the rule *always* applies.

Step II. Then say:

> Some folks think more likely right than wrong [*use hands*] is not fair because it makes things a little too easy on my side and a little too hard on the defense, because my side doesn't really have to prove anything.[3]
>
> Other folks feel that it [*hands*] is OK.
>
> So, Ms. Juror, are you a little closer to the people who think it's a little unfair, too easy for my side? Or are you a little closer to folks who think it's OK?[4]

Don't ask, "Which side do you agree with?" That's hard for jurors to do, so it suppresses responses you need to hear. On every topic, not just preponderance, jurors respond more easily to "Which folks are you *a little closer to*?"

---

3. This is one of only two times you will use the word "prove" or "proof." At all other times, use the word "show." When you say "proof," jurors think you mean absolute proof. That leads them to decide on the basis of absolute or nearly absolute proof, no matter what you say about preponderance.
4. When you must question the group before asking individual follow-up questions, ask: "How many of you are a little closer to the folks who feel that 'more likely right than wrong' [*hands*] might be a little unfair, a little too easy on my side?" Then: "And how many of you might be a little closer to the folks who think it's OK?" Then: "And how many of you think you might be somewhere in the middle?" Follow up individually.

When the juror responds, ask her the all-purpose follow-up question: "Please tell me about that."[5]

Don't lead. Don't even suggest a specific follow-up topic, such as, "What makes you think like that?" The only follow-up question to ask is the wide-open "Please tell me about that." And after the juror tells you about that, ask, "Please tell me more about that." If you have time, ask Ms. Juror that same question until she has no more to say. (*See* supplement A, p. 275.)

This starts a powerful process that accomplishes three essentials:

Gets lots of cause dismissals. Many jurors won't agree to decide on the basis of 80 or 70 or 60 percent certainty, so they are easy to remove for cause.

Exposes tort-"reformed" jurors. Jurors uncomfortable with preponderance are usually (not always) tort-"reformed" jurors.

Initiates the "more likely right than wrong" theme as the lens through which jurors will view each new piece of evidence.

Step III. After the jurors all have their say, say this:

> I had to ask about this because in this case you will be *required* to make all your decisions on the basis of whether we're more likely right or wrong. [*hands*]
>
> We expect to show you far more. But by the end of trial, even if someone thinks we're just *slightly* more right than wrong [*hands*] on a question, you'll have to decide that question in our favor.
>
> You can have all the doubts you want on both sides. But when you weigh them all out, if you think we're more likely right than wrong, even by a little bit, then the law says you must decide in our favor.

Don't chicken out and omit the next four words; they're the most important part.

> *Mr. Defense Attorney agrees* that you have to base all your decisions on whether our side is more likely right than wrong. [*hands*] And Her Honor will tell you that more likely right than wrong [*hands*] is the law you must follow.

Preponderance becomes the operative rule only when jurors hear that your opposition—not merely the judge—agrees with it.

---

5. "Tell me about that" is your all-purpose follow-up question. You should use it virtually all of the time.

Then say:

> So, Mr. X [*choose a juror who earlier had trouble with preponderance*], what trouble would you have, even a little, making your decisions on the basis of whether we're more likely right than wrong [*hands*], not total proof?[6]

To pursue cause dismissals, urge jurors along by asking if they could decide questions in a trial if they're less than 100 percent sure. If they say yes, ask:

"How would you be with 90 percent?"

If a juror says, "That's OK," drop down:

"80?"

"How about 70 percent?"

You'll get to their minimum, and whatever that is, it won't be legal. Ask them why it's important for them to go no lower. Then: "Tell me more." The more they nail themselves down by talking about it, the harder they'll be for anyone to rehabilitate. In this way, attorneys have sometimes removed for cause most of the entire panel! After all, 60 percent—which is lower than many jurors will go—is still higher than preponderance. So if the juror would have difficulty going below 60 percent, or even below 52 percent, he should not serve.[7]

This will probably lead to more cause dismissals than you've ever had.[8]

And with or without cause dismissals, by having taught the jurors what preponderance is and that the defense agrees with it, you're well on your way to a preponderance-based verdict.

Step IV. Jurors' Rights Questions. Your final three voir dire questions—about jurors' rights—will reinforce the Preponderance Template, as well as the Harms-and-Losses-*Only* Template below. These jurors' rights questions are adapted from those I first learned from the brilliant California attorney and trial consultant, Dr. Sunwolf, and were further augmented with help from innovative Virginia attorney Chuck Zauzig.

> Folks, jurors have certain rights. It's important to both sides in this case, and to the judge, that you use these rights when necessary. So I need to ask you about them.

---

[6]. This is the second and last time to use the word "proof."
[7]. Show the judge *Wainwright v. Witt*, 469 U.S. 412 (1985). Its first holding is that prospective jurors must be excused if their views could substantially impair their ability to perform their function as jurors; the impairment need not be shown with unmistakable clarity. Tell the judge you simply want jurors who will follow the judge's instructions, which research has shown many jurors will not do.
[8]. For a good method for pursuing cause challenges, see supplement A.

> First, you have the right to hear all the testimony. So if you don't hear something a witness says, will you all be comfortable raising your hand and telling the judge, "Your Honor, I did not hear what the witness said. Could you ask her to repeat it?"

Then:

> Second, and even more important, you have the right to know that you and every other juror clearly and correctly understands the law and follows it.
>
> You have the right to know that you are on a jury in which every juror is following the law you took an oath to follow.
>
> No one—not me, not Mr. Defense attorney, not even Her Honor—has the right to make you go home afterward having been part of a jury decision that was made by violating the law. You have the right to keep it from happening.
>
> So during deliberations, if anyone is refusing to follow the law the judge gives you, will you all be comfortable asking your foreperson to knock on the door and tell the bailiff you need the judge to come talk to a juror who won't follow the law?[9]
>
> And finally, can we count on you yourself to stay strictly within the law when you're making your decisions so we won't get into that situation?

Never omit these questions. We want jurors to follow the law. These questions are a crucial part of your making them do that.

If this kind of questioning is new for you, run a practice session with half a dozen strangers the evening before trial. You want to be comfortable, not tentative, when asking these questions of real jurors.

3-4 PREPONDERANCE TEMPLATE: OPENING (THE BOILERPLATE TAG)

In opening statement, continue to reinforce your "more likely right than wrong" theme. You want to attach "more likely right than wrong" like a boilerplate tag to each piece of important evidence. So from time to time, cite what a witness will say and include this theme. For example:

---

[9]. Some judges won't allow this. In that situation ask, "So during deliberations, if anyone is refusing to follow the law the judge gives you, will you all be comfortable working as a group to get that juror to follow the law?"

> Heather Witness will tell us the light was green. She'll also tell us she's more likely right than wrong [*hands*] when she says the light was green—and that beyond that, she's sure.

Don't do this for everything, just for your key points.

When referring to expert witness testimony, say:

> Dr. Expert will tell us that her conclusion is more likely right than wrong. [*hands*] She'll also explain that beyond that, her conclusion lies within a reasonable degree of medical [*or engineering or whatever her field is*] certainty—and that beyond that, she's certain.

In situations where you can't start to establish the Preponderance Template in voir dire, attaching the boilerplate tag throughout opening and testimony will suffice.

3-5 Preponderance Template in Plaintiff's Testimony

A theme is a theme only if it is continuously maintained. So during testimony, continuously do what you promised in opening:

> Q: Ms. Witness, when you say the light was green, are you more likely right than wrong [*hands*] about that?
>
> A: Yes.
>
> Q: And beyond that, are you certain?
>
> A: Of course.

And:

> Q: Mr. Engineer, when you say that the van was going thirty-four miles an hour, are you more likely right than wrong [*hands*] about that?
>
> A: Yes.
>
> Q: And beyond that, does your conclusion lie within a reasonable degree of engineering certainty?
>
> A: Yes.
>
> Q: And beyond that, are you certain?
>
> A: Yes.

Your frequent repetition of "more likely right than wrong"—like a yellow sticky-note on every important point of evidence—continually reminds jurors that preponderance is the requirement.

Every so often, start a question by direct reference to the jury's task:

> Mr. Beckett, these folks [*the jury*] have to decide whether we are more likely right than wrong. [*hands*] So when you say you waited six hours, are you more likely right than wrong [*hands*] about that?

Most judges have no problem with that first sentence. So when you can, use it early in the testimony of each witness.

In these simple ways, you keep the jurors' judgments focused on preponderance throughout your case-in-chief and rebuttal phase.

3-6 PREPONDERANCE TEMPLATE IN DEFENSE TESTIMONY

You can also work the Preponderance Template into defense testimony:

> Q: Are you saying it's more likely than not [*hands*] that she's lying about how much she hurts?
>
> Q: You have no basis, do you, for saying she's more likely lying than telling the truth?[10]

And work it into your objections:

> Your Honor, that's speculation, so the jury cannot use it in deciding whether we are more likely right than wrong. [*hands*]

Consider asking the judge to instruct the jury that they are not allowed to use speculation in deciding whether the plaintiff is more likely right than wrong.

You want the "more likely than not" + *hands* to pop up often. Out of sight, out of juror's mind.

3-7 PREPONDERANCE TEMPLATE IN CLOSING

In general, your most important task in closing—even more important than persuasion—is to arm the jurors favorable to your side with the weapons they need to go into deliberations and fight on your behalf. It does little good to persuade jurors if you have not also armed them. (*See* chapter eight on closing.)

---

10. *See* Rick Friedman's *Polarizing the Case* (Trial Guides 2007) for many other ways to attack defense implications of malingering, exaggeration, etc. *See also* Dorothy Sims's *Exposing Deceptive Defense Doctors* (James Publishing 2009).

The following shows you how to arm jurors to make sure they use—and insist that others use—preponderance in deliberations.

3-7-1 Teaching the Law

In closing, you need to teach law. (See chapter eight.)

Via large, clear slides or boards, show the essential fragment of the jury instruction on preponderance. Face the jury with the instruction behind you and recite the fragment from memory. You want the jurors to see that you know the law without having to look at it. Then say:

> This just means what we have been saying throughout trial: Are we more likely right than wrong? [*hands*]
>
> We have shown we are far more than just more likely right. [*Raise one hand as high as you can.*] But the law says that even if someone thinks we're only a little more likely right than wrong [*hands*]—even by the smallest amount—you still have to answer the question our way. You can have all the doubts you want on both sides as long as when you come down to it, you think we are more likely right. [*hands*]
>
> Remember that Mr. Defense Attorney *agrees* that more likely right than wrong is the way you must decide. And after I sit down, Her Honor will officially instruct you that more likely right than wrong is the law you must follow.

3-7-2 Words, Words, Words

The most important part of arming jurors is to provide the exact words and phrases they will need to advocate for you in deliberations. Provide simple, plain-English, ten-to-fifteen-word "boil-downs"—shorthand versions—of each crucial point in the case.[11] Make sure your favorable jurors can comfortably use these words, phrases, and boil-downs. Use no legalese, no complex sentences or ideas, no big words, no technical language. Use simple phrases and short sentences. You'll say:

> Folks, during deliberations, if anyone says *ABC*, remind them that *XYZ*.

Do this for every important point in the case. Here's how it works with preponderance:

---

11. I learned this key point of advocacy from Susan Macpherson, who had the good sense to see that I had the bad sense not to have figured it out.

> Over the course of deliberations, if anyone says they're just not sure [*that's the ABC*], remind them that you don't have to be here for weeks trying to be sure. All you have to do is follow the law: are we more likely right than wrong? [*That's the XYZ.*] Even by just a little.

Then explain what jurors should do if one of them won't go along with the law:

> After you explain it, if a juror still won't go along with more likely right than wrong, tell your foreperson to reread instruction number five out loud.

If the instructions are not sent into deliberations, say instead:

> After you explain it, if a juror still won't go along with more likely right than wrong, tell your foreperson that the judge needs to re-read instruction number five to the jury.

Now here's the enforcer:

> If that juror is still not willing to use more likely right than wrong [*hands*], ask your foreperson to knock on the door and tell the bailiff that you need the judge to come talk to a juror who is refusing to obey her instructions.[12]

3-8 Preponderance Template: Conclusion

If you meticulously follow the Preponderance Template, jurors—even tort-"reformed" jurors—will use preponderance.

Finally, remember to tell jurors that "more likely than not" applies to their decision making about money, not just liability.

3-9 The Harms-and-Losses-*Only* Template

Just as the Preponderance Template gets jurors to follow the law on the burden, so does the Harms-and-Losses-*Only* Template get jurors to factor out illegal considerations when deciding money.

Many jurors would follow the law if they knew it, but instead they unwittingly minimize verdicts by violating the law. And some jurors who know the

---

12. After the final jury instructions have been given, some judges, if asked, will be willing to say: "Over the course of deliberations, if any juror is disregarding my instructions, your foreperson must tell me. If the foreperson does not do that, it is the duty of every other juror to do so." If the judge is reluctant, point out that nothing is more important than jurors understanding and following her instructions and that we are in an era when jurors routinely ignore them. Add that any defense argument against this statement has to be based only on their desire for jurors to not follow the law, which makes the statement even more important.

law do the same. You can prevent both by means of the Harms-and-Losses-*Only* Template. It works the same as the Preponderance Template.

Tort "reform" has led jurors to incorporate into their decision making such factors as raising insurance rates, harming the economy, hurting the defendant, and other illegal factors. This is a principal reason that mediocre defense attorneys easily keep verdicts low. It's not their skill; it's tort-"reform's" poison.

When jurors follow the law, verdicts go up.

The judge, her instructions, and the defense attorney fall all over themselves telling jurors to factor out sympathy for the plaintiff, but say nothing about factoring out many other equally improper things that diminish verdicts. So it's up to you. Which is why we have the Harms-and-Losses-*Only* Template.

3-10 Harms-and-Losses-*Only* Template: Jury Voir Dire

Explain in voir dire that jurors are going to have to figure out (not "decide," but "figure out") the size of the verdict:

> When figuring this out, some folks feel that juries should consider only the amount of harm. Others feel it's important to consider other things, such as sympathy, or the fact that money cannot make the pain go away, or who it was that got hurt, or the fact that enough money to equal the harm might make prices go up for things or services we all have to buy, or whether enough money would be too much for one person, or might seem like a windfall—or other things besides the harms and losses caused by the defendant.
>
> Mr. Juror, do you think you might be a little closer to folks who'd base their verdict amount only on the amount of harms and losses? Or are you a little closer to folks who think it's important to take other things into account? [*Or*, "How many of you are a little closer to . . . ." etc.]

Whatever they say—especially if they want to include considerations other than harms and losses—respond with: "Tell me about that." When they finish, say, "Tell me more," or as Michigan trial consultant Eric Oliver suggests, "What else?" Either way, keep the juror talking on this topic as long as you can. The more they say, the more likely you can get rid of them for cause.

Generally, jurors who respond by saying, "It depends on the case," are probably not jurors you want. Follow up to find out: "Tell me more." If they never manage to clarify what they mean, chances are high they have something to hide and you do not want them.

Let jurors who want to consider factors other than harms and losses talk about each factor they want to consider. Get them to explain why they think it is proper or fair to consider it. Do not try to talk them out of it, or you will cement it in place for that juror and convince others who agree to keep quiet about it.

Common improper factors include:

- whether the money would do any good;
- whether there's insurance;
- whether it might harm a profession or business;
- whether it might raise insurance rates or other prices;
- whether the defendant can afford it;
- whether it seems too much for one person;
- whether it might be a windfall;
- whether all that money could harm the plaintiff (as lottery winnings often do);
- whether it might change (i.e., improve) the plaintiff's lifestyle;
- how convinced the juror is that the defendant was negligent (less money if he thinks you proved negligence by, say, only 60 percent).

Don't worry about suggesting anything they would not have thought of or letting them talk about these things in front of the other jurors. While this questioning might be better at the bench, judges rarely allow it—and jurors do not poison each other's incoming attitudes. Your job is to find out who will have the most trouble factoring out improper money considerations. Even if jurors did poison each other, better they do it in voir dire than in deliberations. So get jurors talking freely, and you will hear the information you need on which to base peremptory and cause challenges.

Often jurors will quickly learn that the "correct" answer is "harms and losses only." That doesn't mean they'll all abide by it, so you'll need other questions later in voir dire (*see* chapter four). But even then there's no way to fully cleanse the jury of this problem, which is why this template is so important—it gets the jurors on your side to enforce the harms-and-losses-only law in deliberations.

Once you have all the voir dire information you are likely to get from every juror on this topic, tell them what they are supposed to do. And find out who might have trouble doing it:

> I asked about that because everyone here—me, Mr. Defense Attorney, and Judge Wagner—all agree that you must figure out your dollar verdict based *only* on the amount of harms and losses the defendant caused.
>
> Now knowing that, who might have even a little trouble factoring out everything except the harms and losses? Mr. Williams?

Aside from learning important things about the prospective jurors, the questioning effectively sets up your harms-and-losses-*only* theme. Combined with the jurors' rights questions (*Step IV, p. 66*), you're on your way to a jury that is likely to factor out most tort-"reform" considerations from their money decisions. This happens because, as with the Preponderance Template, your favorable jurors will fully understand the law and know how to enforce it.

3-11 HARMS-AND-LOSSES-*ONLY* TEMPLATE: OPENING

Later in this book, you will see how to best structure your opening (chapter five and supplement C). The structure easily incorporates your Harms-and-Losses-*Only* Template. If you can't start it in jury selection, it will still work by starting it in opening.[13] Either way, work it into the beginning of the damages part of your opening:

> Your verdict form will ask how much money the verdict should be. When figuring that out, the only thing you are allowed to take into account is the level of the harms and losses the defendant caused. Nothing else. No outside reasons. For example, we're not showing you the losses and harms to get your sympathy. The time for sympathy is long over. We're here for the money it will take to make up for the harms and losses the truck driver caused. And those harms and losses are the only things you can use for figuring that out.

In addition, use the phrase "harms and losses" at every opportunity: *e.g.*, "The fourth of the harms and losses the driver caused was . . . ." And find other opportunities to use "harms and losses only" whenever you can. Use it like a brand.

---

13. Again, remember that you must not leave it out of voir dire when voir dire is available. You have to weave this into every available element of trial.

3-12 HARMS-AND-LOSSES-*ONLY* TEMPLATE: TESTIMONY

Simply work the theme in often enough to make sure it's always in the jurors' minds.

> Good morning, Mrs. Smith. Will you be able to talk to us today about the harms and losses to your husband?

If the judge allows, from time to time word it this way:

> These folks have to make some decisions based only on John's harms and losses. Will you be able to help us with that today?

3-13 HARMS-AND-LOSSES-*ONLY* TEMPLATE: CLOSING

Chapter eight on closing explains how to "massage" the jury instructions. Make sure jurors understand what compensation is—and what it is not.

Compensation is—*exclusively*—the amount of money that equals the amount of harms and losses the defendant caused.

As with the Preponderance Template, show the essential fragment of the jury instruction on damages. Explain each element of damages. (Be sure to emphasize that jurors are not allowed to leave any out.) Then say:

> And that's all. Those are the harms and losses. The harms and losses the defendant caused are the only measure of compensation.
>
> So what does "compensate" mean?
>
> Now, this is the most important topic in the case, so I'm required to go through it even though I think you probably already know it.
>
> Compensate means balance the scales. [*Use your hands, palms up and about two feet apart.*]
>
> Compensate means that you match the amount of money with each of the harms and losses as John feels them.
>
> Compensation means the *fair-trade value* of the harms and losses.
>
> Now, it's even more important what compensation does *not* mean. What you cannot factor in—such as sympathy. You are allowed to feel sympathy, of course. But you cannot raise a verdict just because you feel sympathy for the plaintiff. That's an outside reason.

Nor can you lower a verdict because you feel sorry for a defendant. That's an outside reason, too.[14]

The law uses a confusing word for your verdict: the law calls it an "award." To normal people, an "award" means a prize. To the law, it means compensation for harms and losses. It's not a consolation prize. Making it a consolation prize would be an outside reason.

There are other outside reasons. Juries have to avoid them all. Let me explain them this way. Let's say a person works his forty-hour week. His work goes into the scale on this side. [*hands*] The longer he works, the heavier the scale and the lower it goes. [*hands*] If he works a few hours overtime, the scale gets even heavier.

Now the boss pays the worker. The boss *compensates* him. That means *balances* the hours of work with money. *Equalizes*. Fair amount for that number of hours.

Boss pays too little, the worker is *under*-compensated [*hands*], or underpaid.

Boss pays too much, the worker is *over*-compensated [*hands*], or overpaid.

Compensation means perfect balance. [*hands*] Work. Money.

Now here's the *outside reasons* part.

The boss can't decide, "Well, I'll give him less money because his living expenses are low, so he doesn't need the full amount. It won't do him any good." That's an outside reason. It makes no difference whether or not the money will do the worker any good. The boss can think about that all he wants, but he can't let it affect the amount he pays.

Just like juries. If a juror thinks, "John doesn't need all that money, so we should allow less money than the fair-trade value of the harms and losses." Not allowed.

Another example. The boss cannot say, "Paying the full amount will raise prices of things we all have to buy, so I'll pay less." Outside reason.

---

14. Note the language: "*a* plaintiff," "*a* defendant," etc. When explaining rules of any kind, you want to generalize to all cases, not delimit to your present case. That gives every kind of rule more authority.

Same with juries. So you might have to keep reminding each other about this.

Another example: The boss cannot say, "I really don't like John, so he gets less this week." Makes no difference if the boss likes him. Same with juries: whether someone likes or hates a plaintiff is not allowed to affect the amount of money.

During deliberations, if a juror uses an outside reason—such as "that much money will drive up prices of things we all have to buy"—remind that juror that that's an outside reason. It is not allowed. If that juror insists, read this instruction aloud again. If that does not work, let the judge know that there's a juror who won't follow the judge's law.

This threat of bringing in the judge to correct a wayward juror is an extremely effective way to arm your favorable jurors.[15]

You already know that your most important sworn duty is to follow the law. No one in this room has the right to make you go home having been on a jury that did not follow the law. No one has the right to put that on your conscience.

So if anyone says, "It's more money than anyone needs," or "She's getting along fine right now without all that money, so why give her more?" or "You can't put a price on pain, so let's put a low price on it," remind them: no outside reasons.

"He probably has some way to pay all those bills" is an outside reason—so even if he did, **and John does not**, it must not affect the verdict amount. "It won't make the pain go away [*or "It won't bring the dead back to life"*] is an outside reason that has nothing to do with weighing the amount of harms and losses.

"He never would have made that much money, so why should he get it now?" is an outside reason. Against the law to use. It has nothing to do with the weight of the harms and losses the defendant caused.[16]

As a juror, even if you're not the foreperson, you have control. You can protect yourself from having been on a jury that did not follow the law—you'll have the instructions the judge will

---

15. Caveat: Not all judges or venues (e.g., New Jersey) allow this. But it's extremely effective, so don't omit it just because you're not sure. Find out.
16. If "outside reasons" came into evidence for purposes other than deciding damages, explain to jurors the limited purpose they came in for and remind them that those "outside reasons" cannot be used to decide money. You might also get a limiting instruction to that effect.

give you, and you have the right to call the judge when another juror is violating the law.

As with the Preponderance Template, you get jurors to follow and enforce the law by:

1. Assuring that they understand the law you need them to get right;
2. Motivating them to follow and enforce it;
3. Providing the tools for enforcement.

Doing these things for preponderance and damages will always be among your most important tasks. If you do not do them, the jurors will certainly not do them for you, so they won't follow the laws you most need them to follow.

Chapter Four

With or Without Jury Voir Dire

Even if you get little or no voir dire, many of this chapter's principles are essential for other elements of trial. Don't skip them.

Additional guidance with jury selection can be found in supplement A.

4-1 Voir Dire Limitations: Fight Them! No Voir Dire? Fight for It!

In personal injury and wrongful death cases, limitations to jury selection usually hurt our side, not the defense. This is because our side, not the defense, has to deal with many powerful juror biases, mostly created by tort "reform." In a minimized voir dire, we are more likely than the defense to miss harmful biases. This is because there are comparatively few anti-defense biases. So the defense gains a significant advantage from voir dire limitations that diminish your ability to learn about jurors.

When you take those limitations lying down, you cheat your client.

Many courts allow all of this chapter's jury voir dire strategies and questions. Some courts allow most, others at least a few. But in every venue, the judge should do everything possible to seat jurors who can be fair to all sides. Limiting your questions and follow-ups, or your time to ask them, makes seating a fair jury unlikely, if not impossible. So you must always come armed with legitimate grounds on which to argue for the removal of such limitations. (*See* p. 81 for published resources to help with this.)

You should also have jury voir dire placed on the record. In most venues, if you have expended all your peremptories, every debatable but denied cause challenge becomes a separate point of appeal.[1]

For example, a thirty-minute limit on voir dire is, even in the word's strictest legal sense, "onerous"—its time-saving advantages are vastly outweighed by the cost of diminishing the chances of seating a fair jury. The fact that the judge doesn't care about a fair jury does not change the fact that your venue's law does. Onerous is onerous.

---
1. You may also have had to ask for and been denied extra peremptories.

4-1-1 Sham Rehabilitation

One particularly harmful and common court practice—one based either on ignorance or just not giving a damn—is for the judge or opposing counsel to "rehabilitate" jurors by means of leading questions. Not every venue allows this; in Virginia, for example, it's reversible error for the judge to use leading questions ("Will you follow the law?") to rehabilitate. Rehabilitation—especially by means of leading questions—is harmful not only because it results in seating unfair jurors. It also demonstrates to everyone in the courtroom—including prospective jurors—that the entire process (not only voir dire, but the whole trial, and even the system) is a sham, with the judge as the shammer-in-chief pretending that maneuvering and intimidating jurors results in true answers. When an obviously biased juror says, "Yes, I can be fair and follow your instructions," everyone but the judge sees through it. So when the judge accepts it, the prospective jurors conclude that the judge is either dishonest or naïve or that the system is bogus.

A judge who thinks he can "rehabilitate" with leading questions is like a physical therapist using fairy dust to turn a quadriplegic into a marathon runner.

Jurors don't respect such judges. Worse, it makes jurors—especially the "rehabilitated" jurors—less likely to follow the judge's jury instructions. But the judge is happy because the jury pretends to respect him. Well, the jurors are laughing—if not sneering—behind his back.

Similarly, when the judge says he wants fair jurors and then, for example, forces you to limit voir dire to thirty minutes, jurors find the judge either hypocritical or stupid.

The situation is severely exacerbated when jurors see that same judge spend far more than thirty minutes deciding comparatively minor points to protect himself on appeal—but won't spend more than thirty minutes to protect the judicial system by making it possible to assemble a fair jury.

So when faced with time limitations, barriers to important voir dire questions, rehabilitation via leading questions by court or opposing counsel, or anything else that minimizes the chances of seating a fair jury, your job is to help the judge maintain respect for himself and the system.

Lawyers often tell me, "Oh, you don't know our judges around here." But we (the trial consulting profession) do know them. We find that well-crafted motions for voir-dire improvements—motions based solidly on law and public policy, including the public policy of maintaining respect for the judicial system—succeed in gaining some level of improvement more than a third of the time. That's a high enough proportion to make it worth trying every time.

If you don't wait until the last moment, most judges will at least consider—without rancor—well-written, well-reasoned, well-researched motions for voir dire improvements: Two hours instead of one for questioning, a written questionnaire, attorney-conducted voir dire (or at least attorney-conducted follow-ups to the judge's initial questions), more of your questions being allowed, more and better follow-ups.

Your failure to seek necessary improvements cheats your client. The failure often stems from your being too busy just before trial. But what's higher priority than getting rid of problem jurors?

There are many ways to seek voir dire improvements. For example, make your motions narrowly specific to your particular case. This allows the judge to accept a motion without having to explain why he won't the next time someone asks.

For many experience-proven suggestions on seeking improvements, as well as for sample motions and lists of where certain improvements have been granted, see:

Jurywork (Westgroup)

Jury Trial Innovations (National Center for State Courts)

Blue's Guide to Jury Selection (Thomson/West)

These books are worth reading for many reasons, not just jury selection. Also see the ABA's *Principles for Juries & Jury Trials*, principle 11 (www.americanbar.org/content/dam/aba/migrated/juryprojectstandards/principles.authcheckdam.pdf).

Some appellate decisions have created major improvements in jury selection.[2] So when the judge rules against you in trial in a way that interferes with your ability to try your case before a fair jury, consider that part of your grounds for appeal.

4-1-2 Offer of Proof

Every decision a judge makes can be subject to appellate review. For appellate judges to review a judge's jury voir dire decision, they need to know whether something you wanted to do in jury voir dire would have resulted in something you had the right to elicit. An offer of proof traditionally relates to evidence. But when a judge won't let you ask particular (or enough) jury voir dire questions, or to follow them up, you should have the right to show

---

2. *See, e.g., Pellicer v. St. Barnabas Hospital*, 974 A.2d 1070 (2008). This case establishes the necessity of asking a juror certain kinds of questions outside the hearing of other jurors. While the New Jersey Supreme Court used this finding to help overturn an eight-figure medical malpractice case, the result is an important jury-selection improvement.

the appellate court what the questions would have been and possibly even demonstrate by a "voir dire-voir dire" what the answers would have been.

So when a judge stops you from asking a jury voir dire question that does not automatically violate the law, request an offer of proof.

Do the same with a judge's refusal to allow a written questionnaire. It makes no difference whether the defense agrees there should be a questionnaire. You have the right to a fair jury no matter what the defense wants. Judges have wide discretion in voir dire, but they should not have the right to interfere with seating a fair jury.

4-2 Jurors' First Impression: Primacy and Persistence

What you ask in jury voir dire creates some initial impressions of the case. This is largely due to two psychological mechanisms: ***primacy*** and ***persistence***.

4-2-1 Primacy

Primacy, as important as it is to trial advocacy, is almost always taught to lawyers incorrectly. "Primacy" does not mean that "people best remember, or are most affected by, what they hear first." This is accurate only in very short presentations, such as a brief paragraph.

In anything longer, placing something first—all else being equal—makes it *less* noticed, *less* memorable, and *less* effective. Primacy is actually something far more significant. It means that **people tend to continue believing whatever they already believe**. That's why it's harder to change someone's existing belief about a topic than it is to create a new belief in someone with no pre-existing belief about it.

As a result, logical and fact-based arguments almost never change our strongest beliefs. Belief = momentum.

The stronger the belief, the stronger the momentum, because once a person believes something, his belief colors how he hears everything relevant that follows. That coloring reinforces his initial belief, making it stronger—and the cycle goes on and on.

4-2-2 Persistence

Persistence is the main mechanism by which primacy works. Persistence is the brain's hard-wired tendency to process new information in ways that support what we already believe. When we encounter new, nonsupporting information, we distort it into something that supports our existing belief. Or we give it very little weight. Or we simply ignore it.

Jurors do this all the time. So do you. We all do. People who believed O. J. Simpson guilty "knew" that when they saw the glove display, it proved his guilt 100 percent. People who believed him innocent equally "knew" that when they saw the glove display, it proved his innocence 100 percent. This is primacy and persistence at work.

What does this have to do with voir dire?

By the end of most voir dires, jurors have started developing beliefs as to what the trial is about. You want that to be harms and losses, not liability. This is because you want the juror's mind to be on harms and losses as early as possible.

If your questions make jurors think the case is mainly about liability—if that's their primacy of belief—then liability evidence takes on great importance to them. So that's where they focus. But you want them to focus on the harms and losses so they can see them as representative of community dangers. That's a very different primacy of belief, and it's up to you to establish it.

So half of your voir dire should be spent asking questions about damages. And most of your opening's second half should be about harms and losses. That establishes a primacy of belief that the trial is about harms and losses. And *persistence* of belief will help keep juror attention there.

This seems like a small point, but it has a large effect. If trial is stopped at the end of voir dire or opening and jurors are asked, "OK, folks, what do you think the trial is about," if they respond, "It's about whether the truck driver went through the red light," you have not done your job.

We don't usually stop trials. But when the juror goes home at the end of the first day, what does she tell her spouse—in one short sentence—that the case is about? Whether a truck driver ran a red light? Or how badly someone was hurt? You need to be in total control of the answer. So whether you have thirty minutes or two weeks for voir dire, a third to half should be spent on harm and damages.

Among other uses, the methods in this chapter and the next show you how to inculcate primacy of belief in a way that the mechanism of persistence works for and not against you.

4-3 How to Ask

4-3-1 Seek Information with Every Question

Good voir dire questions mainly gather information, and secondarily—if subtly done—can shape a juror's thinking about the case. Bad voir dire questions try only to shape the juror's thinking. This easily arouses juror resentment. The defense can get away with it; you can't.

4-3-2 Ask Open-Ended Questions

Some decades ago, the National Jury Project's Diane Wiley (Minneapolis) pioneered the use of open-ended questions for voir dire. Open-ended questions are those that cannot be answered in a word or phrase. The closed-ended "Will you be able to award money for pain and suffering?" gets only a yes or no. That often masks the real answer; but even if accurate, it provides little information.

So ask open-ended questions such as, "What trouble would you have allowing[3] money in your verdict for pain and suffering?"

If you are required to ask a group question before individual questions, you are pretty much stuck with a preliminary closed-ended question such as, "Who here has—or knows anyone who has—ever been seriously injured?" or "Who here thinks—or knows anyone who thinks—that lawsuits are causing problems these days?" In response, hands go up. Now you can start your open-ended, individual juror questioning of each juror whose hand went up.

Design your group questions to get as many hands raised as possible. So don't ask, "Who here will be unable to consider money for pain and suffering?" Even many of the anti-pain-and-suffering jurors who understand such a bafflingly worded question will sit on their hands. The question creates its own barrier—few people are comfortable admitting to an answer that is not the "acceptable" one. You have to cajole it out of them. So for the group question, ask, for example:

> Many folks have some trouble allowing money for pain and suffering[4] because it doesn't make the pain and suffering go away. Other folks think money for pain and suffering is OK. How many of you are *a little closer* to the folks who think money for pain and suffering is OK? [*Hands go up.*] And how many of you are a little closer to the folks who think there's no point because, say, it doesn't make the pain go away, or for some other reason? [*Hands go up.*] How many of you are in the middle or just not sure? [*Hands go up.*]

---

3. Again, don't use the word "award." It sounds like a prize. Gary Johnson teaches to use the word "allow."
4. "Pain and suffering" are tort-"reform" buzzwords. So the only time to use them is in voir dire to lower the barrier to bad responses.

Then:

> Mr. Smith, I didn't see your hand go up. Which group are you a *little closer* to? A *little closer* to people who think money for pain and suffering is OK? Or to folks who think there's no point to it?

Saying "many folks" or "some folks" lets jurors feel that either answer is acceptable. And "which are you a little closer to?" means jurors don't have to polarize themselves. That's more comfortable than having to take a firm stand—especially about things the juror probably has never thought much about, such as money for pain and suffering.[5] "I guess I'm about in the middle" is easy for them to say, and it's enough for you to get them talking, if you follow up.

4-3-3 Follow Up

A juror's first response almost never gives you useful information. Only by the second or third follow-up question do you start to learn anything. So after everyone in the group has indicated which folks he or she is closer to, you can individually question everyone. Ask each juror the all-purpose follow-up question: "Mr. Jones, *please tell me about that.*"

Then listen. Don't interrupt. Don't argue. Let them talk. Be nothing but an ear! Don't even take notes. Let someone at your table do that. When the juror finishes his answer, say, "Thanks, now please tell me a little more about that." And do that for as long as the juror has new things to say.

4-4 TORT "REFORM"

> *This section applies only when you are not "reptilianizing" your case. When you skillfully and thoroughly "reptilianize," most tort-"reformed" jurors are actually good for you. See section 4-4-5, p. 87.*

4-4-1 The Essential Question

When you have time to ask only one voir dire question, it should be about tort "reform." You can safely (if that's the word) assume a third of every jury pool is severely tort "reformed," that the middle third can swing either way

---

5. Sometimes an impatient judge will say, "Counsel, just ask if they can follow the law." Show the judge the case or law that says you are to use your peremptories based on information you gather in voir dire. And explain that "following the law" goes not to peremptories, but to cause dismissals.

on tort "reform," and that the rest don't have much of an opinion either way. In other words, there are no great folks to offset the terrible folks. So the matter of tort-"reformed" jurors is probably your most important concern in every case.

Ask jurors how they feel about lawsuits and tort "reform." Then get out of the way, and let them talk. When they stop talking, follow up. You're looking for those who most strongly express their tort-"reform" opinions.

4-4-2 Shallow or Deep Attitudes

The jurors' words alone aren't enough. Tone, demeanor, and attitude help you distinguish between a juror's shallow or short-term hostile opinions (which aren't necessarily dangerous for you) and his deep-seated hostile attitudes (which are). The more you get a juror to talk ("tell me more about that"), the more obvious the difference will be.

And remember, some of the most severely tort-"reformed" jurors are extremely likeable people, so you might think you can reach them. But you don't want a likable, strongly tort-"reformed" juror—because jurors will like her, too, and be more likely to follow her lead. (*See* p. 103, section 4-14, "Leaders.")

Work every tort-"reformed" juror carefully for a cause challenge. (*See* supplement A, p. 312.) Failing that, put them high on your list of likely peremptories.

As with every topic, start to ask about tort "reform" by **making sure the jurors understand the topic**. Most jurors don't know what the term "tort 'reform'" means, even when they think they do. So without at all revealing your own feelings by means of your words, tone, or demeanor, explain it:

> I need to ask how you feel about lawsuits. Many folks on TV and in government, and on the Web and in newspapers, are concerned with what they call "tort reform": too many lawsuits, frivolous lawsuits, big verdicts, runaway juries, greedy lawyers, greedy clients, and verdicts making prices go up and driving away jobs and doctors.
>
> As a result, some folks think that the court system needs changes. Others think things are OK as they are. Which folks are you a little closer to? [Or, "How many of you are closer to the folks who think we need some changes?" "Who's closer to folks who think things are OK as they are?" "Who's in the middle?"]

As they answer, ask: "Please tell me more about that." You'll soon start to hear what they have on their minds.

Resist showing even the slightest disagreement. Never try to change their minds. You can't. And don't say, "If I show you that this case is different, will you . . . ?" That's turning from questioner into advocate, which *you must not do*—even a little bit—at this point. It will drive them deeper against you.

If you try to change a particular juror's mind, you will drive the opinions of other jurors underground—and end up seating some of the worst possible jurors.

4-4-3 Frivolous-Case Questions

Asking the jury if they hate frivolous cases and then raising your own hand to show that you, too, dislike frivolous cases, is a shallow, amateurish gimmick. It makes you seem hypocritical.

4-4-4 McDonald's Coffee

Don't try to convince prospective jurors that the McDonald's coffee case was legitimate![6] You'll alienate some of them and succeed only in convincing them that you're a jerk. They'll pretend to be swayed by your great explanation, then go home and tell their friends that they sorta liked you until you actually tried to tell them the McDonald's verdict was deserved—at which point they stopped trusting you and your sanity.

And certainly don't say that you disagree with the McDonald's coffee verdict, because some jurors know it was a fair verdict and will see that you are shamming.

In brief: When McDonald's or any other verdict or topic comes up, do nothing but ask questions about it. Make no comments. Take no sides.

4-4-5 Caveat on Tort-"Reformed" Jurors

The research team that developed and continues advancing the Reptilian approach to trial advocacy has seen extensive and persuasive evidence that well-applied Reptilian techniques turn jury selection on its head. This anti-intuitive probability is a game-changer. **This does not mean you should start seating tort-"reformed" jurors; you first need to master the Reptilian approach to advocacy**, which you should be doing anyway.

4-5 NONECONOMIC DAMAGES: SPOTTING PROBLEM JURORS

The following two-part question spots jurors with problems in allowing noneconomic damages.

---

[6]. There's a well-intentioned documentary film that tries to justify the McDonald's verdict. Don't refer to that film. If a juror brings it up, don't side with or against it.

First: Ask about medical care, the most tangible kind of economic loss:

> Ms. Juror, in cases like this, jurors get to see the costs of the medical care. So if you were a juror in this kind of case, and you decided that someone's negligence hurt a person and caused the need for those medical bills, what trouble would you have—even if a little—allowing money in your verdict for the medical costs?

(Be careful that your wording does not open the door to collateral sources.)

If possible, ask that question, and those that follow, of each individual juror rather than as a group question.

Please note six things about this question:

1. **It is not about *this* case.** So you are not "staking out" jurors. You are instead trying to get at a general attitude that commonly hurts plaintiff's cases.
2. **It asks about the most concrete kind of economic loss.**
3. **It does not use the word "award."**
4. **It's open-ended:** "What trouble would you have . . . ?" not "Would you have trouble . . . ?"
5. **Its wording assumes that the juror will have problems.** "What trouble *would you have* . . . ?" This makes the juror feel that it's OK to have some problems, so she'll more easily talk about them.
6. **It asks about even little problems, not just major ones.** This lowers the threshold to getting the bad answers you need to hear. Other than in the end-stages of pursuing a challenge for cause, never ask anything like: "Would you have a *really hard time* doing such and such?" Instead, ask: "What trouble would you have—*even if a little*—doing such and such?"

However the juror answers, try to get her talking. For example,

> A: I'd have no trouble with it.

Virtually every juror will respond that she'll have no trouble. But you're not looking just for the answer. You're looking for a **baseline**: *How does the juror come across when telling the truth?* Focus carefully on her word choice and on her vocal and physical demeanor: tone, body position, where she's looking as she answers, etc. You'll compare this baseline to the way she answers your later questions about money for, say, pain.

If you're not sensitive to subtle changes in demeanor and tone, bring someone to trial who is—a partner, a paralegal, a consultant, your teenager. It need not be anyone involved in law. Just find someone good at reading people and give her this section to read so she knows what you're looking for.

The *second* part of this technique goes to the opposite extreme: ask not about medical costs, but about pain, an intangible harm.

> Ms. Juror, in cases like this, jurors hear about physical pain and are asked how much money to allow for it.
>
> I don't mean money for pain medications or therapy. Those are other categories. Right now I just mean money for the fact that someone is having pain.
>
> Some folks have trouble allowing money for pain—and others are OK with it. Which are you a little closer to?

You might want to lower the threshold to the bad answer even more by asking it this way:

> Some folks—like my own mother, for example—have trouble allowing money for pain because money does not make pain go away. Others are OK with it. Which are you a little closer to?

You get to use your mother for only one voir dire question per trial.

Some jurors may be more responsive to this kind of wording:

> Some folks have some philosophical, moral, or other reasons for not allowing money for pain. Others are OK with it. Which are you closer to?

However you ask it, follow up their response with, "Tell me about that."

In a wrongful death case with no pain, substitute whichever element is the least tangible element of harm.

Note that the question **lowers the threshold to the bad answer**. It does not mention the law, what the judge will say about it, or what jurors are supposed to do. This is crucial. With any jury voir dire question, when you turn advocate and start preaching law—such as by saying, "Mr. Juror, the judge will tell you that the law of this state says that pain and suffering are to be compensated . . . ."— you bury information about the jurors instead of unearthing it. Few jurors will say, "Well, Mr. Lawyer, screw the law! Screw the state! Screw the judge! I won't allow money for pain!" A juror who would never allow a dime for pain will usually still want to be seen as law abiding. So you get no information from her, lose the chance of a cause dismissal, and might not even know you need to consider her for a peremptory.

Instead, keep the barriers to bad answers low. Encourage bad answers.

4-5-1 Compare Demeanors

In answering the pain question, a juror who was comfortable with medical costs but not pain is likely to be a problem juror. But when a juror says he's fine with money for pain, this is where your teenage daughter (or your own sensitivity to demeanor and tone) comes in. Regardless of the words in the answer, a juror's tone or demeanor that is substantially different from her tone or demeanor during her medical-costs answer may be displaying a red flag.

For example, a juror's medical answer might be a firm, "Medical expenses? Well, sure, no problem!" But with the same words, the pain response might be a tentative: "Pain and suffering . . . ? Well . . . hmmmm . . . sure . . . no problem . . . ." Same words. Different vocal demeanor. That's a red flag!

Or a juror might nod agreeably and comfortably when talking about medical money, but when talking about money for pain, she might shift and look away or change in other ways.

Be particularly wary of jurors who sidestep the pain question by saying something such as, "I would have to know more." You did not ask anything that requires them to know more. They did not ask for more regarding medical expenses. So when they say, "I'd need more information," it's a red flag. Follow up with "Tell me about that," and finally, "What kinds of information would create greater problems for you in allowing money for pain?" and "What kinds of information would make it easier?"

Generally, a juror who says, "I'd need to know more," is likely trying to hide something. Put that juror high on your list of possible strikes.

4-5-2 No Advocacy

Resist the temptation to argue or explain. And don't load these bias-seeking questions with information-giving facts: "In addition to the past medical costs there will be a lot of medical costs in the future, too. So . . . ." Your *only* goal with the questions in this section is to spot jurors who will have problems allowing noneconomic damages. Anything else at this point—such as trying to educate jurors as to the extent of the claims—will mislead and interfere.

4-5-3 Short Version

When you haven't got time to ask everything this section suggests, you can do the whole thing with just the second question—the one about pain. You sacrifice the valuable advantage of learning the juror's baseline, but you can still spot jurors with problems allowing noneconomic damages.

4-5-4 "Poisoning" Other Jurors

Don't fret about poisoning jurors by saying such things as "your mother is against money for pain and suffering," or that preponderance might not be fair (*see* section 3-2, p. 63*ff.*). You won't change their attitudes.

Nor need you worry about letting jurors hear bad answers from other jurors. Jurors in jury selection don't influence each other's attitudes. They do not think, "Oh my goodness, I've been wrong all these years. I'm so glad this delightfully helpful juror has made me see the error of my ways." Bad attitudes do not poison good attitudes in voir dire (or vice-versa). Bad attitudes poison only deliberations.

The information jurors glean from your information-seeking questions can affect juror thinking about the case—mainly, what the case is about. And information a juror may mention that won't be in evidence can have an effect ("Yes, I knew your client from reform school"). But exposing jurors to the bad attitudes of other jurors is not dangerous.

Even if it were, you're better off uncovering it in voir dire than letting it lie dormant like a land mine until it explodes in deliberations.

4-5-5 Promise to Explain How to Calculate Noneconomic Damages

In answering your pain or other noneconomic-damages question, some jurors will say, "I wouldn't know how to put a price on it." This does not necessarily mean they're bad jurors for you. It just means they don't know how to figure out the money.

As noted above, when jurors say they don't know how, plaintiff's attorneys usually give the worst possible answer: "No one can tell you how to arrive at an amount of money for pain. I cannot tell you. The judge cannot. No one can. You just have to use your own good common sense and your best judgment." When you say that, jurors hear this: "It's impossible to do it right, so we don't have to do it and probably should not—and if we do it, keep it low. And just guess. No need to listen to all this stuff about the harms and losses."

So never say, "No one can tell you how to do it."

Instead, when a juror says she would not know how to decide how much, tell her, "I'm not asking if you know how to do it; that will be covered later in the trial. (*See* p. 238*ff.*, section 8-14, "Scales.") All I'm asking now is whether you're closer to the folks who would not want to do it even if they knew how or closer to folks who'd be OK with it."

4-6   OTHER NONECONOMIC ELEMENTS

If you have enough time after asking the questions in the preceding section, go on to ask similar questions about the other noneconomic damages elements. This is especially important with the kinds of elements that tend to appear in wrongful death cases.

Ask jurors about their experiences and situations (and those of people they know well) with each item. "What kinds of *guidance* do you still provide to your adult children?" Or, "How do you rely on your parents for *advice* or *guidance*?") This helps you determine whether a juror has reason to value that loss element.

And during the process, the jurors start to learn what those elements are, start to relate them to their own memories and experiences, and are sensitized to them as they come up in trial.

The multiplicity of line-item damage elements helps arm your favorable jurors with bargaining chips in deliberations. A defense-leaning juror can get the satisfaction of making the others allow zero for one element in return for allowing money for others. ("OK, $50,000 for lost advice, but not a nickel for loss of services.")

In many jurisdictions, wrongful death damages include loss of:

Services	Companionship	Care
Protection	Comfort	Guidance
Assistance	Kindly offices	Advice
Society		

Great list. But plaintiff's attorneys usually rattle it off so fast (if they even bother with it) that it sounds like one mucously amorphous gob: "Loss-of-services-protection-care-assistance-society-companionship-comfort-guidance-kindly-offices-and-advice . . . whew!" This turns your line items list into mush.

So make each item separate from all the others.

There are also separate elements of loss for living clients: physical pain, emotional suffering, loss of use of body parts, etc.[7]

The process of getting jurors to focus on each line item for its own value starts with doing it yourself during your earliest exploration of the case. Think about what each element means. What's the difference between "advice" and "guidance"? How does that difference apply to the losses in your case? Do an exhaustive study of both in your case. And never assume you know what those losses were. You need concrete, story-based illustrations of the depth of each of those losses. (*See* section 6-9, p. 185.)

Here's what to do in voir dire to get jurors to focus on every noneconomic (or unfamiliar economic) element:

1. Name and explain the element (such as loss of services).

2. Ask who has known anyone or have themselves experienced such a loss (such as services from an injured or ill family member). If a juror responds yes, follow up.

3. After questioning every juror on this element, explain the next element, including how each differs from the other, such as advice versus guidance, or loss of services versus loss of protection.

4-7 Tolerance for Pain

Ask about each juror's pain tolerance. Jurors who think or claim they have a high pain threshold are less likely to allow much money for pain.

And ask jurors about the worst pain they've ever had: what caused it, what it was like, and how bad it was. Use their answers for comparisons later in trial.

4-8 Asking about (or Sneaking in) a Specific Figure in Voir Dire

Don't. It used to be a good idea. Now it's a terrible idea.

Wait until the end of opening. In voir dire these days, it will create resistance.

4-9 Asking about Caps

When you ask about caps, jurors' answers no longer predict the size of verdict they will allow. Instead, try to let the subject of caps come up on its own while you are asking about tort "reform." When a juror brings up caps on her own, she'll probably be a problem juror.

---

7. If one of your damages elements is hedonistic losses, don't use the word "hedonistic" until you explain that element in closing. In the real world, "hedonistic" means self-indulgent—and some jurors think it means promiscuity. Use plain English: "The normal pleasures of life."

A juror who has not thought much about caps is probably not bad for you. But even many who have thought about them and believe in them can shed that belief when they hear what happened to your client.

4-10 Juror Demographics Affecting Damages

> For the vast majority of cases, you cannot select a jury on the basis of demographics. Members of any particular demographic group (age, race, nationality, religion, vocation, sex, income level, etc.) are not similar enough to each other for you to use their grouping as a marker for jury selection. When you think you can, you are falling into the cognitive trap that underlies racism.

Demographic jury selection is easy and tempting. But it does not work. Demographic groupings can work for marketing when based on enormous banks of data—and to be useful in marketing, demographics need to show only mild tendencies, as low as 5 or 10 percent. Fine in marketing, not jury selection.

Black people do not all have similar attitudes on any topic, nor make the same decisions. Nor do old people, Asians, young men, older women, GenXers, Baby Boomers, any other kind of generational "cohort," rich people, bald guys, or any other demographic group. In the absence of extensive research on your specific case, choosing jurors on the basis of demographics is almost always nuts. It most often will lead you astray.

Be especially careful not to fall into the "age cohort" trap. Despite some general and sporadic similarities among people of particular age ranges, you cannot gauge any individual even roughly on that basis. The only people who think everyone in an age cohort (or any other demographic group) is similar are people who do not belong to that cohort.

After all, how similar are you to everyone else in any demographic group you belong to?

Batson[8] and its progeny did you a favor. Both legally and in terms of effective strategy, you need demographic-neutral criteria for jury selection.

---

8. *Batson v. Kentucky,* 476 U.S. 79 (1986).

If choosing jurors by demographic grouping worked, every trial consultant would insist you do it. But the good ones do not. In fact, that's one of the quickest ways to spot a bad one.

All of that said, however, there is one good use for demographic groupings: they help you identify tendencies to share some experiences. For example, poor people are more likely to have had difficulty getting medical services. But not every poor person. You still need to ask. But demographic groupings can tell you who it's most important to ask. And even if an individual has had that experience, you can't conclude much about how it might affect his decision making without individual questioning.

For example, given the overwhelming number of African American jurors who have had direct or near-direct experience with significant police misconduct, did the O. J. Simpson prosecutors in Los Angeles invite loss by working so hard to seat an all-African American jury? Of course. Is there a population group in America with greater reason to *personally* understand and sympathize with the principal defense of police misconduct?

But even so, the defense had the good sense to question every African American juror in order to be certain that he or she had experienced or knew someone who had experienced police misconduct—*and* resented it. (Never assume a juror will react to an experience or use it in trial the way you think she will. There are wide variations even to extreme experiences.)

So yes, you can use demographic groupings—*if* you know why that grouping would make a difference in your specific case. But the generalized use of demographics is lazy and dangerous.

4-11 Personality Traits

Certain personality traits are far more useful than any demographics. These personality traits can especially affect how much verdict money a juror will allow. So during voir dire, try to discover where each prospective juror falls on each of the following six continua:

Optimist/Pessimist scale

Caretaker/Noncaretaker scale

Emotion/Non-Emotion scale

Insider/Dispossessed scale

Content/Malcontent scale

In Control/Not-in-Control scale

These scales are detailed in the next six sections.

4-11-1 Optimist/Pessimist Scale

Optimists more readily allow money than pessimists. This is because optimists are more likely to think that money can do some worthwhile good. (Remember the importance of juror perception of the worthwhileness of money; *see* Fundamental Seven, p. 24.) You can see where a juror lies on the Optimist/Pessimist scale by her answers throughout voir dire. When a juror mentions any problem or bad situation, ask how she feels it is likely to work out and why.

See if there is a difference between the juror's background/training/experience as opposed to what she is actually doing. A PhD waiting tables could well be more embittered than optimistic.

Ask if the juror feels she has done better in life than she'd initially thought she would or whether some things held her back. Ask how she feels about her future: Are things likely to get better for her? Stay about the same? Get worse? Ask what she'd like to do next and if she thinks she'll get to do it. And follow up: "Tell me about that."

Sometimes such questions can relate to current topics. In an economic downturn, some jurors can become pessimistic: despite all their hard work, they've lost their home and can't pay the kids' tuition.

Ask how jurors feel their children will do as the years go on: Better than the parents? Worse? "Tell me about that."

4-11-2 Caretaker/Noncaretaker Scale

Caretakers more readily allow verdict money than do noncaretakers. Caretakers feel it is right to help *strangers* who need help. Caretakers get satisfaction out of helping.

"Caretaker" in this sense means an attitude, not a forced situation. Someone forced to care for a family member, or working in a caretaking job, may or may not be a caretaker in spirit.

Noncaretakers often believe—or make themselves believe—that it's better for people to take care of themselves than be taken care of; that people should be self-sufficient; that each person is responsible for himself, so others should not be expected to help shoulder his burdens; that life is a gamble, and you have to play the hand you're dealt without relying on others; or that people are usually partly at fault for their own problems, and so do not deserve help.

In voir dire, you can distinguish caretakers from noncaretakers in several ways. Some of these ways also give you other useful information.

For example, ask jurors what they think are the most important values to teach children. Jurors who respond with values aimed at taking care of other people (such as "help those less fortunate") are likely to be caretakers themselves. Jurors who focus on values like "be strong" or "be self-reliant" may be noncaretakers. Follow up by asking why they name the values they do, and how they put them into practice.

Another example: Explain that you understand that most people don't have time to do much for others outside their families, but you'd like to know: "Who here is involved in things intended to help other people—people outside your own family?"

Ask what organizations and clubs jurors belong(ed) to and where they do (or did) volunteer work—and why. A person who belongs to a garden club, a bridge club, and a book club may or may not be a caretaker. A person who volunteers for Meals on Wheels is probably a caretaker. If a juror mentions a group or club that is not obviously care-oriented, or if you do not know the group, ask its purpose, what's the juror's involvement, and why. A response such as, "We get together at Kiwanis for lunch to catch up with old friends" is very different from "We raise money for the hospital." The group may serve both purposes, but the way a juror describes it can tell you why she's in it.

If a juror used to do charitable or volunteer work, but no longer does, ask why she stopped and what would make her go back.

Find out which charities the jurors support. Do they send money only to their alma mater or also to the local soup kitchen? And ask: "If someone offers to send money to the charity of your choice, which would you choose?" And follow up: "What do you like about that one?"

Since it is useful to spot leaders (*see* p. 103 section 4-14), find out which jurors are officers in their groups or clubs and be on the lookout for any such groups that are caretaking in nature (do they build hospitals or do they build stock-market accounts?).

Ask about activities outside work: "What do you do evenings after work?" and "What do you do Saturdays?" and "What do you do Sundays?" Follow up. If a juror says he spends Sunday afternoons in church, say, "Tell me about that." Look for caretaking activities—things jurors do to help other people. (However, be wary. Some church folks care for others, but are really interested in furthering the goals of their church, or their own chances of getting into heaven, or just being seen as a good person. Self-serving caretakers are not on the good end of the caretaking scale.)

An excellent voir dire question that separates caretakers from noncaretakers (and good plaintiff's jurors from bad): "What should be done about the homeless?" The noncaretaker's knee-jerk reaction is something like, "Get them to work." The caretaker's knee-jerk response, at least partly, is to help them. Most people answer somewhere between, so note which way they lean—and follow up.

The goal is to discover whether or not each particular juror will be affected by a stranger's problems and be motivated to help.

To field objections to caretaker questions, explain to the judge that many jurors are reluctant to help others, and so are less likely to compensate fully and fairly. Explain that jurors whose attitudes and activities reveal a willingness to help those in need are more likely to use nothing but the evidence as the basis for their verdict, rather than incorporate their reluctance to help despite the evidence. Remind the judge that a juror's reluctance to help others does not have to rise to the level of a cause dismissal for it to be relevant to a peremptory challenge.

4-11-3 Emotion/Non-Emotion Scale

Jurors who are comfortable with their own and others' emotions as a palpable and normal part of living and decision making tend to see emotional harm as worthy of compensation. Such jurors are likely to see that emotional harm is a component (sometimes the primary one) of almost all intangible harms: sadness, feelings of loss, worry, anxiety, fear, frustration, despair, loneliness, etc.

Jurors less at home with emotion tend to dismiss or not recognize emotional harms, so are less likely to compensate for them.

Recent neuroscience research has shown the importance of the emotions as a memory and processing system that is intimately involved with almost all important decisions we make—even when we think we are being purely logical. Some people deny or try to suppress that. So they resist anything that smacks of emotion (even though, ironically, the tendency to do that is almost purely emotional!).

The distinction between jurors who incorporate emotion and those who resist it can be difficult to determine in an abbreviated voir dire. One useful marker is whether a juror involves emotion in the way he answers your voir dire questions. Does he base his thinking and responses mainly on logic? Or does he incorporate emotion? Are all his reactions centered on logic and practicality? Or does feeling play a role? Don Beskind listens for a useful distinguishing factor: Does the juror sound like a newspaper—just the facts? Or more like a novelist, especially with respect to feelings?

Listen for how each juror talks about and feels about his experiences as he speaks throughout voir dire. Phrases such as "I feel . . ." or "You could see the emotion in their faces" can reveal a comfort in taking emotions into account.

Many jurors are surrounded by strong emotions in their jobs—such as hospital workers. Find out how it has affected them. Have they become hardened to those emotions? Or have they remained open to the impact of those emotions? A juror who is, say, an emergency room attendant may be highly sensitive to the kind of suffering your client has undergone. Or he may be hardened to it. (Even if he's open to it, he may find your client's emotional suffering minor in comparison to what he sees regularly at work—so this may not be a good juror for you.)

Extremes

One of the many pieces of advice I got long ago from the National Jury Project's Susan Macpherson—and that years of experience has long since proven correct—is that you need to distinguish between jurors who incorporate emotion into their decision making and those who are simply very emotional in how they talk and act. The latter group can be unpredictably dangerous, because there's no telling to what or which side their extravagant emotions might attach. Fortunately, the defense usually strikes that kind of juror.

Initial Reaction to Case

Many judges give a brief case overview before jury selection. And some judges ask you to give a five-minute "mini-opening" before jury selection. If you are forced to do this, do it without *implying any blame*. That can be tricky but it is essential.

Connecticut's Ernie Teitel suggests that when the jurors are listening to the brief overview—be it from judge or counsel—you have someone carefully watch and note each juror's reactions.

And in voir dire, ask each juror: "**When you first heard about this case, what was your reaction?** What were you thinking?"

4-11-4 Insider/Dispossessed Scale

Jurors with no stake in the establishment can tend to allow more money than do jurors whose lives are integrally involved with the establishment or who aspire to such an involvement.

The dispossessed, the renegade, and others who stand outside society's mainstream are less likely to feel threatened by the impact of large verdicts on prices and insurance rates or by other supposedly harmful effects to society of a large verdict. Even if they believe in such harmful effects, such jurors have less reason to care about them. (But be careful; they might also be pessimistic as a result of having been unable to become part of the establishment, and pessimism does not usually make for a favorable plaintiff's juror. *See* section 4-11-1, p. 96.)

And when you are working with a Reptilian approach, they may care a lot less about the well being of the community.

Outsiders tend to have an easier time deciding against an authority or establishment figure, such as a doctor or corporate leader. This does not mean that every such prospective juror is an automatic good choice. View each juror's outsider characteristics in the light of everything else you can learn about him or her. For example, some outsiders are outsiders because they don't care about anyone but themselves—a bad characteristic for our side.

And be wary of the kind of outsider who seems ready to fight whatever anyone around him says. He'll fight a large verdict solely on the grounds that the other jurors want it. While any kind of divisive personality can hurt you on a jury, the one who fights for the sake of a fight is particularly dangerous.

4-11-5 Content/Malcontent Scale

Jurors contented with their lot in life can go either way in any case. But jurors who are discontented with life due to the hand they have been dealt are not likely to worry about what has been handed to your client. Similar to some pessimists, a person living in what he perceives to be a highly successful, happy society—and who is bitter about how his own life is turning out—may well have little sympathy for anyone but himself. He's likely to believe that he did not deserve the raw deal his life has been and sees no reason to provide much help to someone else who has gotten a raw deal.

Focus-Group Learning

When you do focus groups—which you always can and must, even in "routine" or "smaller" cases—try to spot the negative characteristics of the focus-group jurors, such as discontent, *before* your focus-group jurors start talking about the case. Then watch carefully to see if 1) you were right about which jurors had the negative characteristics, and 2) whether and how their negative characteristic(s) affects their decision making.[9]

This is among the best ways to sharpen your jury-selection skills.

4-11-6 Control/Not-in-Control Scale
Ship Captain/Landlubber-Passenger Scale

Some people believe they can keep themselves safe from the dangerous (or otherwise negative) forces around them. At the other end of the scale are people who feel they cannot. Those who think they can keep themselves safe will likely have trouble sympathizing with a plaintiff and so be less likely to properly compensate. (This is not about whether a person actually has control; it's about how much in control the person *feels*.)

The experienced captain of a ship feels capable of navigating through the storm. We landlubber passengers have to trust him. Does each particular juror go through life feeling more like the captain or the passengers?

And do the necessarily reliant passengers worry about being in that position of dependence? Or do they think that if necessary they could swim to shore? So:

> Q: Some folks feel they're pretty capable *on their own* of keeping themselves and their family safe. Others feel they have to depend on others. Which group are you a little closer to?

Then:

> Q: Are you OK with that? [i.e., their situation of either having to take care of themselves or being reliant on others.]
>
> A: "Sure," says the in-control juror. "I drive defensively, I've got fast reflexes, I know what I'm doing on the road."

Or,

> A: "I hate it," says the juror on the other end of the scale. "Having to depend on people I don't even know scares me to death."

---

[9]. The kind of jury research (focus group) that best prepares you for trial is a *deliberations* focus group, not a discussion, debriefing, or "unpacking" group—all of which are useful to guide discovery and early thinking, but are not thorough enough for reliable trial preparation. *See* DEBRA MILLER, ARTEMIS MALEKPOUR, & DAVID BALL, FOCUS GROUPS: HOW TO DO YOUR OWN JURY RESEARCH (Trial Guides DVD).

Take this measure for different specific situations: highway, neighborhood safety, finding safe medical care, etc. Otherwise you can be misled when an ordinarily high-control person says he's scared of traffic; it might be because he doesn't drive much, while in other situations he feels perfectly able to protect himself.

But be careful with this. You may accurately decide that the unmarried inner-city mom thinks she can't control the dangerous forces that surround her children. But she also may feel powerful enough to protect her children anyway. "It's not safe in crowds—so I just make sure I've always got my hand on my child's head." Such a juror might have little sympathy for any parent who did not exercise that much care.

Jurors who generally feel they have to rely on "those in control" will make higher demands on people in control—such as the defendants—than will jurors who feel they can provide safety without being dependent on those in control. The latter can blame your client for having been the same way.

4-12 RELIGION MATTERS

While some religious fundamentalists can be good plaintiff's jurors, many believe that calamity is probably the consequence of earlier wrongdoing or that God decrees all things—so a lawsuit is a challenge to God's will. They can also believe that "decent" people—or "good Christians"—do not sue each other. In voir dire, ask about these issues.

Some jurors take comfort in thinking that God is in control to the extent that "If I behave well, I'll never get hurt." And conversely, "The plaintiff was hurt, so she must have behaved badly earlier in life—so it was her own fault." Such a juror is unlikely to give up these comforting beliefs as she would have to do in order to allow your client much money.

Fortunately, some religious fundamentalists—by no means all—believe that God wants them to be honest. This gives you some chance of spotting them and removing them for cause. But many have an elaborate rationale for dishonesty when used in the service of what they think God wants (such as "God must want me to get on this jury to keep the plaintiff from getting money").

Please see chapter fourteen in *Reptile* to see how you can work with such religious folks on their own turf.

4-13 INADVERTENCE

The law holds defendants responsible for unintentional wrongs. But many jurors reduce verdict size—and sometimes even decide on no liability—when they see the wrongdoing as inadvertent: "The truck driver didn't hurt him on purpose," or "The doctor didn't cut the wrong blood vessel on purpose."

A focus-group juror once said, "The machine operator was careless and stupid, and he killed the guy. But it wasn't negligence." This juror had been told that negligence meant the failure to be careful. But he would not give up his notion that it meant "on purpose."

It makes sense. From childhood on, we are taught by example that no one gets punished for doing something wrong "not on purpose." Little Sally cries, "Mommy, Mommy, Billy knocked me down!" And Mommy, ruining little Sally as a future plaintiff's juror, says: "I'm sure he didn't do it on purpose, dear. It was just an accident." Sally is still on the ground. Her knee is still scraped. She is still hurting, angry, and upset. But Mommy does nothing to Billy because Billy did not do it on purpose. "Just an accident." In fact, Mommy probably even consoles little Billy to keep him from feeling bad about what happened.

The lesson learned at Mommy's knee? **It is not fair to punish inadvertence.** "It was an accident" and "I didn't mean it!" carries us from spilling milk in kindergarten to the rest of what we do in school, career, and family life. So expect it from jurors.

Jurors who believe that inadvertent harm should be compensated less will sometimes oppose you on liability—and often on intangible damages. It used to be important to identify and remove those jurors. But by means of techniques you'll learn in *Rules of the Road* and *Reptile*, you'll be able to show that, regardless of the case, there is nothing inadvertent about the negligence. Our Reptilian research has shown that once a defendant's act is framed as a choice to violate a safety rule, almost all jurors stop giving it the good old "inadvertence" pass.

In brief, never use words that imply inadvertence, such as "accident" or "mishap" or even "misjudgment." There is no such thing as negligence that did not violate a safety rule. The driver may have accidentally hit your client, but there was nothing inadvertent about the driver breaking the safety rule that required him to look where he was going and see what was there to be seen.

4-14 LEADERS

Leaders are jurors with the persuasive skills, charisma, or other qualities that can influence other jurors during decision making. Leaders who are against you can be lethal. Leaders who are for you can lead the jury to your side and to a high verdict.

Be extremely careful in seating any leader. If you have any doubts about which way a strong leader is likely to go, *do not gamble*. You can win and even do well without a strong leader on your side, but it can be impossible to win or get much money with a strong leader against you. Persuasive leaders can change the minds of three or four jurors within just a few moments, after which the other jurors follow. So when evaluating leaders in voir dire, **get rid of them unless you are *sure* they will be with you.** (*See* section A-22, pp. 304*ff*, on how to identify and evaluate potential leaders.)

Caveat majeure: The fact that a juror—leader or otherwise—seems to like you **does not mean he or she will support you.** Connecticut's Ernie Teitel wisely observes that some jurors will like you because you are brave for pursuing an "impossible case." And they will vote against what they consider your impossible case: "I knew he had a losing cause, and I thought he was great for pursuing it—I'd hire him anytime to be my lawyer!—but he still had a losing case!"

4-15 CHILD WITNESSES

Sometimes your most effective harms witness will be a child, such as your client's young son or daughter. Sometimes the client will be a child, and under some circumstances that child could be a good witness.

But some jurors have problems with your bringing a child into court. Such jurors may resent you if they think you are doing it to get sympathy at the expense of the child, whom they believe should not be subjected to the courtroom.

In voir dire, you can do three things to deal with this problem:

First, learn who these jurors are.

Second, explain why you have to bring in the child.

Third, determine if the explanation is sufficient for each juror.

So:

> Mrs. Jones, you'll be asked to figure out how much money it will take to fix the harms that can be fixed, to help the harms that can be helped, and to make up for the harms that cannot be fixed or helped. To do that, you'll need to know the harms. So we bring in witnesses to tell you what they've seen.
>
> In some cases, one of those witnesses could be a young child. Seven, eight, nine years old. But even when that seems necessary, some folks are against it. They feel children should never be part of anything like this. Others are OK with it. Which are you a little closer to?

And follow up with "Please tell me about that."

When you must use a child witness, sit down with the child in her home. She should never see the inside of your office. Spend a lot of time with her. "What's your favorite thing that reminds you of Daddy?" Don't even try this in your office. In fact, don't try it yourself if you have anyone in your firm that has better rapport with kids than you do.

Remember that good questioning can be cathartic for the child. But bad questioning—without a close eye for the child's well-being—can make you as destructive of the child as was the defendant.

In voir dire, learn what you can about the jurors' own kids: under what circumstances would they let them testify in trial? You'll be surprised.

4-16 PAID EXPERTS

Some jurors will not believe paid testimony. You need to find out who they are. Such a juror is not an equal disadvantage to both sides. You have the burden. If a juror believes no experts on either side, it is no draw—it hurts your side. Pointing this out can help you convince the judge to dismiss such jurors for cause.

Such jurors tend to be bad plaintiff's jurors for other reasons. They can feel that lawsuits are frivolous and that plaintiff's attorneys buy dishonest testimony to make themselves and their clients rich. Jurors who think (often accurately) that plaintiff's attorneys have been paying legislators to vote against tort "reform" can feel that plaintiff's attorneys are the ones most likely to pay experts to provide favorable opinions.

4-17 MULTIPLE SURVIVORS

In a wrongful death case with multiple survivors entitled to seek damages, ask prospective jurors how they feel about compensating several people for the death of one person.

> Some folks feel that each survivor should be compensated for what he or she individually lost. Other folks feel the verdict should be the same whether there's one survivor or five. How do you feel about that, Mr. Jones?

And follow up.

This helps reveal jurors unlikely to compensate multiple survivors. And it starts the process of arming your favorable jurors to argue for you in deliberations that the jury must compensate each survivor's losses. You want jurors aware of this as early as possible.

4-18 Harms Consultants

Consult experts in fields related to your client's kinds of harm. These experts may or may not become witnesses. You can use them to provide you with ways of better understanding the scope of the harms and how to explain those harms to jurors. Or you can bring them in to testify.

For example, Virginia attorney Robert T. Hall advises that in wrongful death cases you need a grief counselor to study and report on the kinds of harms there have been to the surviving family and what those harms will be as time goes on. (*See* section 6-14, p. 188.)[10]

Physicians and therapists who are pain specialists can help you show jurors the full range of pain's consequences—not just that "it hurts." Social workers, physicians, therapists, mental health care specialists, and others can help you find and explain to jurors the consequences of every kind of mental, emotional, and physical injury. For just one example, it would take a good counselor to come up with "Think what happens when a paralyzed person has a terrifying nightmare." Can't even roll over and pull the covers over his head.

In cases of permanent harm with long-term care consequences, use a geriatric disability specialist, such as a physician or social worker, who will know how your client's injuries will affect him and what kinds of care he will need as he goes into old age. Jurors usually think that if you take care of current problems, things will get better in time. You need to show that things will actually get worse over time so that your client will require more care—and that the consequences of not getting proper care now will grow more and more serious as your client ages.

Select counselors and specialists who can provide portraits of the plight of the harmed—but not one of those hyper-sympathetic semi-hysterics likely at any minute to lovingly break into group hand-holding. You want a clinical report of human suffering, not a soap opera and "Kumbaya."

4-19 Harms and Losses Lists

Here's how to teach jurors the harms in your case without you falling into the trap of premature advocacy (*see* section 5-2-1, p. 112).

- List for yourself every single harm and loss in the case.

---

10. *See also* Robert Hall & Mila Ruiz Tecala, Grief and Loss: Identifying and Proving Damages in Wrongful Death Cases (Trial Guides 2010).

- List how each harm happened: What crushed the bone? What stopped the oxygen? What twisted the neck?
- List for yourself the physical consequences of each harm.
- List—in detail—the economic consequences of each harm.
- List—in detail—the quality of life consequences of each harm.
- List—in detail—all the fixes and helps.

If you do this well, the list will usually be long.

The last thing in voir dire before the jurors' rights questions (*see* p. 66, Step IV), ask questions about as many of your listed items as you have time for.

This gathers information you need for selection. It gets your harms/losses case in front of the jury early—with no advocacy. And if your case is bifurcated with damages in phase two, these questions get your harms and losses into the jurors' minds before you even start phase one.

The Harms and Losses Lists lay out your harms/losses case without relating it to your client, which is the only safe way to do it in voir dire. So do not say, "My client had a broken arm; who here knows anyone who's had a broken arm?" Leave your client out. Instead:

> Q: Who here knows anyone well—including themselves—who has been hit by a car?
>
> Q: Who here knows anyone well—including themselves—who has lost some income because he or she was physically unable to work?

When a hand goes up, ask, "Please tell me about it."

You are trying to spot jurors who don't attach much importance to that particular kind of harm, as in, "Yeah, they said she had some brain damage but she seemed fine and gets along now with no problems."

Ask jurors who have experienced any of the harms to tell you about it. Get them to tell you how it happened, whose fault it was, how bad it was, how long it lasted, and how they (or the harmed person) felt about it. But start by just asking them to tell you about it.

> Q: Who here has—or knows anyone who has—ever had to be in a wheelchair for any length of time?

Juror Berger raises her hand.

> Q: Tell me about that, please.

A: Well, my uncle broke both legs, so they had him in a wheelchair for a few months.

Q: Please tell me about that.

A: He wasn't happy about it at first. But after a few weeks he was fine. Didn't have to go to work, spent the whole time fishing except when he was home with his buddies drinking beer and playing poker. I never saw a happier man, actually. I think he was sad to get up and have to walk again.

Probably not the juror you want if part of your client's problem is being confined to a wheelchair.

It's best not to group multiple items from your list into one question, but if your time is limited you may have to. Combine, say, broken arm, broken leg, and broken rib into "broken bones." As you ask follow-up questions, jurors will get specific: "Grandpa Dylan had to stop working the farm for a few weeks." Since you are trying to find out whether or not a juror regards the harm as serious, ask: "How did Grandpa Dylan feel about that?" The juror might answer: "Hated it. He couldn't pay his mortgage that month." Or he might say, "Loved it! Got a few days off and went fishing." If the latter, this juror might not think the harm to your client was such a bad thing.

A surprising number of jurors see some kinds of serious harm as relatively insignificant. This is partly why jurors who know people with harms similar to those in your case can be bad for you. They've seen how Uncle Joe *seemed* to cope well and cheerfully with his harm. But that's often because Uncle Joe kept his suffering to himself. The juror who doesn't know that can think, "If being in a wheelchair didn't bother Uncle Joe, why should it bother this guy?" And worse: "Uncle Joe got along fine," the juror may say in deliberations, "so this plaintiff's got to be lying about not being able to work."

When a juror has reason for undervaluing the important harms in your case, he can be bad for liability as well. A juror who thinks Uncle Joe coped easily with his broken leg can think that broken legs are no big deal. She can think you're exaggerating your client's problems. That undermines your credibility with that juror and can poison how she perceives your entire case, not just damages.

Be careful not to relate the harms-lists questions to your client, such as by asking, "John, here, has a broken leg; who here knows anyone who's had a broken leg?" That turns you into an advocate dangerously early. The jurors will figure out the connections to your client for themselves. So ask your harms questions as a genuine attempt to get information from the jurors, not to try to show how badly your client was hurt. This lets you present your damages case in voir dire without arousing juror resistance—even from the tort "reformers."

4-20 FINAL THOUGHTS

See supplement A for important additional guidance on conducting voir dire. And always conclude voir dire with the juror's rights questions. (*See* p. 66, Step IV.)

Finally, avoid the common error of waiting until the last minute to prepare voir dire. Useful voir dire questions take careful preparation and practice. The closer you get to trial, the less time you'll have to do it right.

Chapter Five

Opening Statement

__Premature Advocacy__: "Inability to control one's advocacy urge long enough to avoid a disappointing outcome."

5-1 Introduction

Jurors rarely make up their minds by the end of opening.[1] But even sooner, they start leaning one way or the other—even when they do not realize it. That lean creates a primacy of belief (*see* section 4-2-1, pp. 82*ff*.) that can color how they receive and process everything else in trial: what they pay attention to and what they ignore; what they consider, remember, throw out, use; how they interpret, distort, and weigh each argument, opinion, witness, and piece of evidence; and, ultimately, what they will do in deliberations.

So by end of opening they have not made up their minds. But they have established the groundwork that will eventually lead them to a decision. That groundwork can be dislodged, but not easily.

That means you need tight control of what jurors come to believe in opening. You want to be ahead, not behind, by the time you call your first witness.

This chapter's template for opening—if you adhere closely—will give you that tight control.

More good news: Once you've used this opening statement template a few times, you'll find yourself writing your openings in a third of the time you do now. You'll barely need notes to deliver it. And if you ever have to prepare an opening on the spur of the moment, you'll be able to. Your muddy and

---

1. Many otherwise fine trial advocacy teachers think that "reliable research" shows that most jurors decide the case by the end of opening. But the research to which they refer—*The American Jury* by Harry Kalven Jr. and Hans Zeisel (1966)—says no such thing. Its authors have forcefully denied that their research showed any such thing or that they saw anything to even suggest it.

meandering stream-of-consciousness will be replaced by the straight, clear arrow of structure.

5-2 Your Standing with the Jury

At start of opening, plaintiff's attorneys have no credibility with many jurors. No matter how well you did in jury selection, you must assume that many of the seated jurors come in with a strong primacy of belief: that you (not the defense) will exaggerate and lie. Until you're well into opening, your credible looks and tones can't suddenly wipe out decades of multi-million-dollar tort-"reform" campaigns. "Sure," say the jurors, "he looks credible. That's a *trick* they learn in law school!"

So you must strictly avoid placing your credibility on the table until well into opening. Don't ask jurors to trust you before you've earned their trust. Until then, advocacy is risky even with jurors who aren't suspicious of you. **When you start advocacy too soon, every juror is likely to push back—sometimes permanently.**

Your early role is to *inform, not advocate.* Connecticut's Ernie Teitel points out that this is like the difference between the iconic newsman Walter Cronkite—the bearer of facts—and our current news pundits, who give not facts but opinions. You must be Cronkite. If you're too young to know who Cronkite was, ask the nearest older person.

An early attack on what the defendant did *feels* good. You may think it's working. But even when the jury appears to approve, early attacks work against you—especially with those jurors you most need to worry about.

Who would ever have thought that starting with, "Good morning. This is a case about a careless driver" could cost you the case? Yet it can—by making jurors consciously weigh your credibility while they still think you have none. So all they can conclude is that neither you nor what you just said are credible. That can be close to impossible for you to reverse for the duration of trial.

5-2-1 Premature Advocacy

Premature Advocacy occurs when you imply—even subtly, even by tone much less words—any criticism of the defendant before Part III of opening.

5-2-2 Omission

The mention of any omission by the defendant is criticism. "The driver did not turn the wheel" is advocacy. Delay it until Part III of opening, when it starts to be safe to advocate. NEVER before.

Never.

No matter what: NEVER.

Jurors don't want you to tell them what to think. Doing so undermines—rather than builds—trust. **Jurors want to hear what someone did, not what you think about it.** They want to arrive at their own conclusions as to whether it was OK or not.

So until you get to Part III, pretend you went to journalism school, not law school.

5-3 STRUCTURE

Why structure? Some old hands think, "Hell, I'll just get up and look 'em in the eye and tell 'em the case. I know my case well enough." Or, "I'll just look 'em in the eye and tell 'em the important stuff!" But when you look 'em in the eye, they're not looking back. They're staring blankly as you wander on.

Whatever you know best is the hardest to teach. That's because of the difficulty—especially extemporaneously—of seeing what you know through the eyes of someone who doesn't. You saw that in law school: smart professors who knew their subject well, but could not convey it clearly to those who knew nothing about it. Don't do that to your jury. Your easy job is to know your case. The hard part is to communicate it. Your most important tool to do this in opening—*structure*.

So stick strictly and exclusively to the structure of this chapter's opening template. None of it is arbitrary. Neither add to nor alter it. It has been extensively and meticulously tested, evaluated, crash tested, field tested, and refined for more than a decade. Used right, it conveys the greatest possible amount of information in the most persuasive possible way. **It forces you to sequence everything in the way that creates the least juror resistance and the greatest juror comfort to each new thing you say.** It optimizes the ability of jurors to listen to, process, and remember each new piece of information.

5-3-1 Too Much Information

One reason to follow the template closely is that the template prevents TMI. TMI means *Too Much Information* for jurors to absorb.

Atlanta's Don Keenan, my close friend and my co-author of *Reptile*—and one of the country's top attorneys—says lawyers know too much. Over the course of discovery, you learn too much to convey. You must sort what jurors need from what they don't. The more you include in trial—especially in opening—that jurors don't need, the less your needed information will help you.

Sadly, many attorneys don't sort. Instead, they information-dump. When you information-dump jurors, they dump back. But rather than dumping information, they dump you.

Unfortunately, you are *trained* to information-dump. Your trainers taught you that *information* persuades judges and jurors. Major wrong.

Treat information as if you're the world's tightest miser—and every little piece of information is a gold nugget. Give jurors the fewest possible nuggets. And before giving one, chisel it down to the smallest usable sliver.

Less is more. In every case. In every opening. In every witness exam. In every closing. Wheat, please; not chaff. Don't give a bowl of stew to someone who wants only peas. Give them a bowl of peas. If someone asks you what time it is, tell them the time—not what kind of watch you have and who gave it to you.

The amount of information you think you need is probably double or triple what you should provide. This chapter's template helps you control yourself.

5-3-2 Clarity

Because you speak to listeners who can say nothing back, you can never be sure that you're getting through or being clear. The opening template, based in part on how scriptwriters deal with nontalking audiences, takes care of that.

It's also adapted from what I learned twenty years ago from one of the National Jury Project's brilliant trial strategy pioneers, Diane Wiley. In the years since, I've incorporated many newer things into the template, including my ongoing damages developments, as well as Rules of the Road and Polarizing the Case techniques from the books of those titles—and, most recently, the revolutionary Reptilian approaches.

5-4 THE TEMPLATE

This template works so well that immediately following it, many cases settle. The more you use the template, the better it will serve you.

You won't quickly master it. You can only learn it layer by layer. Steve Langer, the remarkable Indiana attorney, cautions that you can't go the whole way at first and that it takes time—sometimes a long time—to get there.

Defense attorneys have reported how much they hate having to open after plaintiff's counsel has used this template. Every time I hear this, I smile. As the great ancient Greek logician Stompicles taught, "Don't get mad. Get even." This chapter's template is a series of razor-edged weapons to help you get even.

Almost every departure from the template makes it harder to get the jurors where you need them. This sounds narrow and dogmatic, but it's true. As with the application of any straight-edged razor, only a slight deviation can turn a clean shave into a bloody mess.

The template's skeletal outline is on page 117. Below that, each part is explained.

THE TEMPLATE

I. **Primary rule(s) the defendant violated**

II. **Story of *what the defendant did***

III. **Who we are suing and why: the safety rules the defendant(s) violated** *(From here on, cite experts and other witnesses for everything you say. Make yourself the messenger, not the source.)*

   A. What was the rule-violating act?

   B. Without referring to your specific case, tell us what's dangerous *in general* about violating this rule.

   C. How did the defendant's violation of this rule cause harm in this case?

   D. What should the defendant have done instead of violating the rule?

   E. How would that have helped?

IV. **Undermine negligence defenses**

V. **Causation and damages**

   A. Introduction to harms and losses.

   B. Mechanism of harm. (How did the negligent act cause each injury?)

   C. Personal consequences of each injury.

   D. Fixes and helps (treatments, etc.).

   E. What cannot be fixed or helped.

VI. **"Before"**

VII. **What can the jury do about it?**

5-5-1 Opening. Part I: Primary Rule(s)

Start where jurors want you to start. Find the place where people want to start when beginning any unfamiliar task. When your child comes home with a new board game, you open the box, spread the pieces, and ask, "How do we do this? What are the *rules*?"

"What are the rules?" is always the first question. It's the brain's new-task default question.

Until jurors know a major rule or two, they don't know what to do with any of the rest of the information you give them. The rule tells them.

The rule also tells them how to play and what to pay attention to. Jurors use the major rule(s) as their trusty guide. Every negligent act constitutes a safety-rule violation, so that safety rule is the first guide you want them to have.

Starting with *anything* but the rule—except "Good morning"—is like swinging at and missing an easy pitch.

What kind of rule should you start opening with? Here's a perfect beginning [// = brief pause for clarity]:

Good morning. //

[That's enough chatter. Now go straight to the rule:]

A driver //

is required //

to watch the road //

and see what's there to be seen. //

If the driver does not, //

even for an instant, //

and as a result hurts someone, //

the driver is responsible for the harm. //

[Here's your transition to Part II of your opening:]

Now let me tell you the story[2] of what happened in this case.

---

2. A myth afloat in advocacy-teaching circles is that the word "story" makes jurors feel that you're telling them fiction. The myth is absolutely wrong. In nonfiction contexts, "story" clearly and instantly means "true story." No one is ever confused, anymore than they are confused by any word that carries different meanings in different contexts. (So in court, "In this *case*" does not mean "In this *box*." It never even occurs to anyone in court that it could mean box—not even when there are dozens of boxes around.) "News story," "Gospel story," "The Story of Lewis and Clark" versus "Story of the Three Little Bears." In opening,

Even if the defendant violated a dozen rules, choose only one or two principal rules for Part I of opening. You'll talk about the others later. For now, select the rule or two that will best guide jurors as they listen to the upcoming story of what the defendant did.

The pauses (//)—not too long, but distinct—are essential. Without pauses, jurors can't follow even the simplest of rules. **When jurors hear anything for the first time, phrases not separated by pauses wash over them** like this:

Adriverhastowatchtheroadandseewhat'stheretobeseen.Ifhedoesnotevenforamomentandasaresulthurtssomeonethedriverisresponsiblefortheharm.

Here's a slight expansion of Part I's rules:

Good morning. //

A manufacturer //

> is never allowed //

> to needlessly endanger the public. //

If he does //

> and as a result someone is hurt, //

> the manufacturer is responsible for the harm.//

A manufacturer //

> is never allowed //

> to conceal a danger they know about //

> in their product, //

> because concealing the danger //

> would needlessly endanger the public. //

Now let me tell you the story of what happened in this case.

---

you want to say that you're going to tell a story because the brain is wired to relax and pay attention when we hear we're about to be told a story. We lean forward. We open our ears. We let everything else drift to the bottom of our consciousness. *We settle uncritically into your hands*, listening to our favorite thing: a storyteller. The brain's dopamine flow increases. And not a single juror will think that what you're saying is meant to be fiction. Not once, not ever.

Make no accusations (no **Premature Advocacy**). You do not say or imply that anyone did anything wrong. Nonetheless, the jurors now "know" that someone did something wrong that hurt someone else. So in Part II, as you tell the story of what the defendant did, jurors will spot the violation *for themselves*.

Here's another example (without pause markers, since by now you know them).

Good morning.

A public facility of any kind—

> such as a movie theater, or shopping mall, or school, or any other kind—

must never expose its visitors

to needless danger.

If it does,

> and as a result someone is hurt,

the facility is responsible for the harm.

The public facility

> must do everything that can be done

to protect the public

from preventable outside crime.

If it does not and as a result someone is hurt,

the facility is responsible for the harm.

Now let me tell you the story of what happened in this case.

If a judge thinks this is too close to talking about the law, point out that witnesses—including defense witnesses—will testify (or already have testified in depositions) in these very words. (See *Rules of the Road* and *Reptile* to learn how to get defense witnesses, even the defendant, to do this.) So since the rules are evidence, you can say them in opening—even in damages-only cases (*see* p. 161).[3]

If a rule is not a common-sense truth, refer to the experts (on both sides) who support it:

> Good morning.
>
> A police officer is never allowed to needlessly endanger anyone.
>
> Experts from the Indiana Police Training Center,
>
> along with every police officer who will testify,
>
>> will agree that a police officer is not allowed to use more force than necessary,
>
> not even when making an arrest.
>
> This is because using more force than necessary can needlessly endanger people,
>
> which everyone agrees is never allowed.[4]
>
> They will also agree that when a police officer uses more force than necessary,
>
> and as a result injures someone,
>
> the officer is responsible for the harm.
>
> Now let me tell you the story of what happened in this case.

In every kind of case, no matter how complex or how many rules were broken, you must select the most important one or two for Part I of opening. In exceptional circumstances a third rule may be necessary. If you give more, the juror will remember none of them as you tell the upcoming story.

---

3. If you persuade the judge to provide pre-instruction on the law, you'll have an easier time connecting the rules to the law, and you will also make yourself the guide to the law as trial progresses. In addition, once a judge has pre-instructed, she will likely be less concerned about how you word it. To help you persuade the judge to pre-instruct, see Principle 6(C)(1) of the ABA's *American Jury Project* report:
> The court should give preliminary instructions directly following empanelment of the jury that explain . . . basic relevant legal principles, including the elements of the charge and claims and definitions of unfamiliar legal terms.

www.americanbar.org/content/dam/aba/migrated/juryprojectstandards/principles.authcheckdam.pdf.

4. Yes, you can and will get every police officer in the case to admit to this rule. They cannot deny it without violating the law and their own policy requirements.

In a very few kinds of cases, the rules section will be longer. For example, in failure to diagnose cases, the major rule is the requirement to do a full and proper differential diagnosis. (*See* supplement E, p. 381.) Even then, the explanation must quickly boil down to a simply-stated rule.

> **As with every section of this structured opening, be certain that you do not pollute this section. "Pollution" means saying *anything* other than what the section calls for, no matter how much you think you need it. As this structure proceeds, it holds everything you need, so don't defeat its effectiveness by injecting something where it does not belong.**

Here are errors attorneys often make in this first section:

1. Using legal language.

2. Using the exact language of a policy or guideline or law instead of clarifying it into simple, plain English.

3. Giving too many rules (two is best; three the maximum).

4. Using too many words. Conciseness = clarity, and vice-versa. State each rule in one sentence. You'll get to say more later. More now can destroy the rule's main benefit: guiding jurors to the point of the upcoming story.

5. Trying to advocate too soon, by criticizing the defendant in any way or even just using an accusatory tone.

6. Preceding the rules with anything more than "Good morning." Say *nothing else* before the opening rule, especially such blather as "Nothing I have to say is evidence," or "Thank you for being here," or "I am privileged to represent Sally Smith." Especially don't say, "Opening is like a road map." Jurors won't think, "Oh boy! A road map! Golly, I can't wait!" Don't waste your precious first moments.

7. Preaching instead of teaching.

8. Dealing with your case weaknesses. Talk about them later (in Part IV of opening, undermining the opposition). Doing it sooner makes jurors think the case is about its weaknesses, and they'll never stop focusing on them.

Part I's rule(s) initiate your layer-by-layer teaching of your case. The rules relax jurors into their task. You have implicitly given the jurors an irresistible task: to find the bad act. So in the upcoming story, they will find it—because you've pointed them right to it without making any accusations. They'll get to your conclusions on their own—which is the gold standard of persuasion.

So don't muck it up. Do exactly as Part I instructs. No more, no less.

5-5-2 OPENING. PART II: STORY OF *WHAT THE DEFENDANT DID*

Once jurors know Part I's rule(s), they're primed to hear the story of *what the defendant did*. That story must be simple, immediate, and indelible.

And it must contain nothing to distract jurors from seeing what the defendant did.

You need not be a gifted storyteller. Just learn the guidelines below, stick to them, and practice them over and over.

Start with absolute **KISS: Keep It Simple, Storyteller**.

Simple Chronological Sequence

The first necessity of keeping it simple: **pure chronological order**. Forget every variation. No "V" structures, such as, "Let's leave Sally in her car at noon and go back to ten that morning at Joe's Tavern." No flashbacks, no jumping back and forth in time *at all*.

This is because **you cannot be maximally (or even adequately) clear with any order but chronological**. No writer has ever been. The brain's *only* frame for processing events is a chronological frame. If you doubt that, try saying your social security number backward without having to think hard. Or scramble as few as two or three letters of the alphabet and then try to say it aloud and fast—such as "A B C D E F G H I K J M L N P Q R S T U V W X Y Z." Go ahead, look away from the page and see what happens when you try to say that fast and loud. In fact, you will have trouble saying it aloud and fast even with your eyes following it on the page—because chronological order is the brain's imperative.

Simple chronological order = KISS. Any other order interferes, usually severely.[5]

---

5. In analyzing your case for yourself, and in your closing to help jurors understand causation, you can use a technique called "Backward Analysis," the standard tool for theater and films (i.e., story) script analysis. *See* DAVID BALL, THEATER TIPS AND STRATEGIES FOR JURY TRIALS, 3d, 171 (NITA 2003). *See also* DAVID BALL, BACKWARD AND FORWARDS (Univ. of So. Ill. Press 1983).

Simultaneous Events

When two defendants have done different things at the same time, first tell us about one, and then say, "At the same time . . ." to introduce the other. Jumping from one defendant to the other is clear. Jumbling the time sequence is not.

Keep Track of Time Sequence

When you say, "On June 17th, the doctor . . ." and then go on to say what he did on that day, don't start the next part of the story with the date, such as: "On June 23rd . . . ." Jurors won't remember the previous date to compare it to. Instead, provide the comparison: "Six days later . . . ." That way, jurors know where they are in time.

Further: Place the time-tag at the start of the sentence.

Bad: "Dr. Brown sees the patient six days later."

Good: "Six days later, Dr. Brown sees the patient."

Develop this as a habit you always use—especially in testimony:

Bad: "Doctor, when you got to the house on January 17, what did you . . . ."

Good: "Doctor, on January 17, when you got to the house, what did you . . . ."

This keeps time sequence clear.

Simple Present Tense

Neuroscience has recently shown what theater has known for 2,500 years: more of the brain listens to a present-tense narrative than a past tense narrative. "I drove to New York" is past tense. "I drive to New York" is present tense. If you have trouble telling stories in the present tense, ask a librarian to recommend a good novel written in present tense. By the time you're a few pages in, you'll be able to do it. Present tense = more intensive listening.

And, of course, more intensive listening ==> **KISS**.

Simple Short Sentences

No compound or complex sentences. No long sentences.

Defendant's Name

Start every sentence with the defendant's name as the grammatical subject.

Active Voice

Continue the sentence with an active, not passive, verb. "Dr. Jones [*subject*] looks [*active verb*] into a microscope." "Ford *sells* the car." Not "The microscope is looked into by Dr. Jones," or "The car is sold by Ford."

One Fact

And as you do with effective cross-examination: **one fact per sentence**.

Sensory Input

To a limited extent, include a specific kind of information in your story—a morsel or two of sensory input strengthens the story's immediacy. Color, smell, sound, texture, touch, taste. Smell, for example, is our most primitive and protective sense, so we remember smells.

Don't force sensory input; use it in a natural, unobtrusive way.

The driver gets out of his *white* truck.

He hears *sirens* coming.

He *smells* rubber burning.

He *tastes* fumes on his tongue.

Move Forward in Time

Every sentence must be exclusively about what the defendant did that moves the story forward in time ("Dr. Barnes leaves the room"; "Joe Smith drives"; "Mrs. Ranhosky wakes up").

Events Only

Nothing but what the defendant did.

Beyond the above, include only an absolute minimum of embedded information: "Joe Smith is driving a new green Ford Explorer" embeds into the action some information (the vehicle is new, a Ford, and an Explorer). That's the upper limit. And do it only once every dozen or more sentences. **Jurors remember events—acts—and not information.** In fact, information takes the attention off the events, so the jurors end up hearing and remembering neither.

Opening Statement

Information bad. Events (actions) good.

Don't cram in that the car "weighed 4,100 pounds and had no traction control, a system invented in 1997 that adjusts for road friction in certain conditions; 'friction' means . . . ." That information might be important to the case, but it will kill Part II of opening.

Why? Because there is a relationship between the structure of the brain and the structure of an events story. The brain is built to house events stories. Once an events story is embedded, it houses information added later—*if* you complete the story of the events before you try to move information in.

So save that information until Part III. (And even in Part III you'll need far less information than you may think.)

Premature Advocacy

Your story must not seem to try to persuade. You still don't have standing with jurors to advocate, not even subtly or in tiny ways. **Let the events speak for themselves—so jurors can think for themselves.**

As with information, injecting advocacy into your story of what the defendant did throws both the story and you into doubt and weakens your later advocacy.

Other Things to Omit

Omit "Acts" of Omission

"The story of what the defendant did" does not include what the defendant did *not* do. Including an act of omission ("the driver did not look at the road") is an accusation. No accusations allowed in the story!

You can include an act of omission if you can frame it as what the defendant did *instead*. So instead of giving an omission—*e.g.*, the defendant did not slow down—reveal it this way:

> At 6:00 p.m. the Acme Truck driver *is driving* 75 miles per hour.
>
> The Acme driver *sees* the speed limit sign.
>
> He *sees* that it says 60.
>
> He *continues driving* 75.

The difference may seem tiny, but it's huge: you show jurors only the acts so that they, not you, conclude that the driver chose not to slow down.

Omit Anything the Defendant Thought or Felt

In fact, omit everything that a video camera would not see and hear. It can't hear thinking or feeling.

Omit (for Now) Motive: Why the Defendant Did What He Did

The camera can't see motive either. Let jurors figure out motive on their own, because they'll believe themselves more than they will you. Your story leads them to fill in motive for themselves—*e.g.*, "He looks at his watch and steps on the gas." You don't say he's in a hurry, but it's clear.

For the same reason, omit what was wrong with what the defendant did. Jurors will spot the rule violation for themselves.

You'll easily and effectively fill the jurors in later on anything they don't figure out now on their own. Meantime, **keep the story clear and pure: just show us the documentary film of what the defendant did—without a single word of commentary.**

Point of View

Camera Eyes and Ears

Show **only what a video camera would have seen and heard**. Video cameras don't think, analyze, accuse, or infer. They don't read minds. They don't know someone is hungry or angry or in a hurry. They just see someone eating or shouting or going fast.

So limit what you say to nothing more than what a sound movie would record.

Video cameras don't see or hear that someone is drunk; they just see some staggering and hear some slurred speech.

Video cameras draw no conclusions. That's the viewer's job.

The video camera can see someone is reading, and even what she's reading. The camera cannot see whether the reader likes what she's reading. It sees a smile which—unlike the camera—we can interpret.

Example:

Mr. Jones, *worrying about being late for work*, speeds up to 65.

Take out the phrase about worrying—it can't be seen or heard. Instead, tell us what can be seen and heard that will lead us to the same conclusion:

Mr. Jones *is driving* to work.

> Mr. Jones *sees* a clock on a billboard.
>
> He *sees* that it says 8:55.
>
> He *presses down* on the gas.

See? We figured it out! Ourselves! We don't need you—still the least-trusted person in the room—to figure it out for us.

And when the tort-"reformed" jurors figure it out themselves, they don't question it—or you. You have not plopped into Premature Advocacy. You're just telling us what the video camera saw.

This works the same way even with the most complex matters. When jurors know the rule from Part I and you strip Part II's story of excess information, **the rule remains clear in their uncluttered minds. So they almost always spot the violation as you tell the story.**

Example:

Rule: "A surgeon must not cut anything unless he can see it and know for certain it's what he means to cut." You need not explain any medicine for jurors to understand the negligence. In light of that rule, here's how the story of what the surgeon *did* becomes accusatory *without your making the accusation:*

> Dr. Bladem sees the uterus wall.
>
> He sees the wall is covering his blade from sight.
>
> Dr. Bladem uses his blade to cut something behind the wall.

You've let the story do the work.

Joshua Karton is his generation's most gifted and accomplished advocacy trainer, despite stiff competition for that distinction. He teaches that during the story, your ultimate goal is to make the juror desperately want to reach out just before the destructive act and yell, "No! Stop! Don't do that!"

We've just done that with the cutting example. The juror knows from the Part I rule that a surgeon must not cut what he can't see. Then:

> Dr. Bladem sees the wall of the uterus covering his blade from sight.

The juror easily figures it out: the surgeon a) can't see his blade, so b) can't see what it's about to cut. The juror heard the rule just a little while ago, uncluttered by information or accusations. So almost reflexively he thinks, "No! Don't cut what you can't see! What the hell is wrong with you?" The juror is damning the surgeon before even knowing what harm the cut did. And without knowing an iota of medicine or even why the surgeon was doing the surgery.

Jeez, counsel. What more could you want within the first few minutes of your opening?

So don't blow it. Don't shove Too Much Information into the story—such as the purpose of the surgery, the structure and description of the anatomy, the medical technology of the operation, or all those useless medical terms.

Just cut to the chase: from rule to what the defendant did, taking us quickly to the destructive act. **Result:** jurors will actually be hungry to hear the rest of your information later. And they will find your later explicit accusations delicious, not suspicious.

Subordinate Your Client

Minimize mention of your client. The case is about what the defendant did, not about your client. When possible, leave your client entirely out of the story until the point at which the defendant hurts him. If your client must be in the story earlier, position him as a *passive receiver of what the defendant did.*

I know you are eager to personalize your client and make the jury feel his pain. Well, the defense is even more eager for you to do that. Do not oblige them. Jurors believe they're here to decide who did something wrong. To do that, they will start by using whatever information they get. If that information is about your client, jurors will start to blame your client—even if your client did nothing wrong, and even if the defense is never going to claim he did.

So never say:

> John Howard [*plaintiff*] sees that a mole on his neck is getting larger.
>
> John goes to a dermatologist.
>
> John shows the dermatologist the mole.

By now, some jurors are already blaming John and may never stop. Can you figure out how before looking down at the footnote?[6]

Never underestimate the drive and imagination that a tort-"reformed" juror will use to find ways to blame your client. That's because, as *Reptile* explains, anything a tort-"reformed" juror can find (or twist) to blame your client helps the juror feel that he's protecting himself from the survival-level threat you and lawsuits represent to him. (See *Reptile*, chapter three.)

---

6. They are thinking, "John probably waited too long before going to the dermatologist." So John's case has already taken a nosedive.

The more you subordinate your client, the less the jurors will think about blaming her. That means they remain more open to seeing why they should blame the defendant. That's why the story in Part II is solely about what the *defendant* did. Don't let the jurors dwell on your client until much later in opening.

Don't even use your client's name in the story. So:

Dr. Harvey sees a patient.

Dr. Harvey examines a mole on the patient's neck.

Subordinate everyone else, too. Keep attention solely on the defendant. So if you're suing—among others—Dr. Harvey, use his name. If you're suing the doctor's employer, but not the doctor himself, refer to the doctor as "Memorial Hospital's doctor"; don't use the doctor's name in the story.

Example:

A premises liability case—three men beat an elderly couple in the couple's motel room. You're suing the motel.

Do not start the story this way:

Two a.m., January 12, 2009.

Three Central Prison inmates shoot a prison guard in the head.

The prisoners escape over the prison wall.

The prisoners run.

The prisoners get to an intersection.

The prisoners surround a gray Buick.

The prisoners pull the driver out.

The prisoners shoot her in the chest and abdomen.

The prisoners drive off in her Buick.

The prisoners lose their pursuers.

The prisoners park behind the C'mon Inn Motel.

The prisoners shove open the door to Room 123.

The prisoners demand money from the couple inside.

One prisoner beats John while . . . .

Good storytelling. The jury will listen, remember, and get the full horror of what the prisoners did. But this case is about the motel owner who installed flimsy locks and never told guests of recent break-ins. If you start with the story as narrated above, by the time you get to what the motel owner did, the jurors will be irrevocably furious with and totally blaming the escapees.

You'll have created your own competition.

So instead, tell this story:

> Let me take you back to November 14th, 2008.
>
> The owner of the C'mon Inn Motel opens a letter from the police department.
>
> The motel owner reads that there have been fourteen recent break-ins in the area.
>
> A week later, November 21st, the motel owner goes to Home Depot.
>
> The motel owner looks at a selection of door locks.
>
> The motel owner looks at $12.00 locks.
>
> The motel owner looks at $6.00 locks.
>
> The motel owner looks at $4.95 locks.
>
> The motel owner buys twenty-six $3.00 locks.
>
> Two months later, nine in the evening.
>
> The motel owner is working at the check-in desk.
>
> The motel owner tells an elderly couple, "Yes, our sign out front is true, this motel is absolutely safe. Nothing to worry about."
>
> The motel owner checks them in.
>
> Six hours later, three in the morning:
>
> The motel owner hears screams from a guest room.

Guess who the jury is blaming at this point? They don't yet even know who the victims are or what is making them scream. But the jury is already blaming the defendant.

This approach is a far cry from the usual opening that starts with the elderly couple—your clients—leaving for their anniversary trip, traveling all day, etc. Jurors don't need to be distracted by any of that. **An effective story leaves jurors with *nothing* on their minds except what the defendant did—and especially *not* with your clients in mind.**

Please write this in big letters on the surface of the desk where you write your openings:

An effective story leaves jurors with *nothing* on their minds except what the defendant did.

All the rest comes later, after primacy of belief has settled in the way you want it to: that the case is about what the defendant did.

Don't Use Pronouns

For many reasons, pronouns in opening and closing are bad. Use the defendant's name or title: "Dr. Smith" or "the doctor." With every mention, your client is *merely* "the patient," "the pedestrian," "the homeowner." Never "she" or "he." "I once knew two guys who got in a terrible fight. One pulled a knife and stabbed the other guy and then dropped the knife in front of the other guy. So he picked up the knife and stabbed him and a cop came and arrested him, and boy was he angry!"

Telling the Story

Set the Scene

Start your story by saying, "*Let me take you back to* _____." Then, in a few short phrases, set the scene.

Let me take you back to October 12th, 2008.

[*I hope that will be the last time you tell us the year. Many lawyers love repeating the year over and over, like a deranged calendar clock. Quit it.*]

Hennepin Avenue, downtown Minneapolis.

Clear weather, dry street.

Smell of snow in the air.

Two in the afternoon.

Acme truck driver John Smith is driving his steel-blue tractor-trailer.

Acme driver Smith comes west over the Hennepin Avenue Bridge.

Acme driver Smith looks down at his GPS map.

Setting the scene pulls the juror right into the story.

When Does the Story Start?

It starts with the first thing a defendant did that led to the harm. That can be thirty seconds in advance or thirty years. From then on, include only what we need to know to make the journey to the harmful act. So:

> Let me take you back to winter 1997.
>
> Headquarters of Acme Trucking.
>
> Vermont.
>
> The President's office.
>
> Nine in the morning.
>
> Acme's President, Alan Acme, starts a staff meeting.
>
> Mr. Acme says . . . .

Now tell the story of the company making the decision to amend its hiring and training policies.

Then take us step by necessary step to the driver coming west into downtown Minneapolis. You may have to skip a decade, which is fine:

> Now let me take you up to 2009 . . . .

How Long?

Some stories are a few sentences long. Others, twenty minutes. Some, much longer. But remember: less is always more. Less = KISS. Tell us just what we need to know to have an overview of what the defendant did.

Each Sentence Is Important

In telling the story, give each sentence its own importance. Do not subordinate or rush through a sentence to get to a more important sentence coming up. When you do that, jurors start listening carelessly, because they know by your own subordination that only some of what you say is important.

End of Story

After the harm is done, add a two- or three-sentence overview report of what happened to your client. This is when you *first* use your client's name.

Examples:

> The pedestrian—Jonathan Smith—was thrown against the concrete wall. The wall bounced him back onto the highway.

He ended up with seven broken bones and permanent brain damage.

Or,

John's knees were broken, and they'll never properly heal.

Or,

Jack was killed.

Or,

Allison's neck was injured and took a year and a half to get better.

Save the rest of the harm for later, Part V.

The Next Thing the Defendant Did

Carefully research so that you know everything that happened right after your client was hurt. For example:

A passing motorist calls 911.

Another passing motorist rushes to Jane's side.

He waves traffic away from her.

Meantime the Acme driver sits in his truck talking with his boss on his cell phone.

In a med mal case, did the hospital immediately send in a social worker to help the family deal with what had happened? Or instead did the hospital send in a risk manager?

Remember—still no advocacy. Report these after-acts in Cronkite-journalist, *non*-advocate mode. Just say what the defendant did.

First Person Stories

Some trial advocacy teachers tell you to tell your opening story in the first person—*I* instead of *he*. But don't do it in opening; save it for closing. While first-person stories can sometimes work in opening, they more often backfire in a big way. To cynical, tort-"reformed" jurors, a first-person story *in opening*—before you've earned the standing to be trusted—comes across as a manipulative trick. Jurors can resent it, and for the rest of trial they will carry the primacy of belief (*see* section 4-2-1, pp. 82*ff.*) that you are manipulative.

Moreover, since your opening story should be the story only of what the *defendant* did, you'd have to tell the *defendant's* story in the first person. That lands you on objectionable ground: you have no evidence of his internal point of view. You'd be putting words in his mouth and thoughts into his head.

Besides, why give the defendant's point of view?

Finally, it is difficult to confine a first-person story solely to what is seen and heard, as you must with your opening story. You'd have to detour into what the first person thinks and feels—which is conjectural and conclusive, neither of which you want in your opening story.

That said, however, first-person storytelling can be terrific in closing *when done properly*. (*See* supplement F, pp. 391*ff.*) I think I first taught this in 1973 at the University of Minnesota Law School. The best place I know of to learn this method now is Spence's Trial Lawyers College (even the weekend sessions around the country), though we may differ on the prudence of using the technique in opening.

OPENING, PARTS I AND II—EXAMPLE

Here is an example of rule + story. (The // marks are pauses.)

Good morning. //

A driver has to watch the road //

and see what's there to be seen. //

If a driver does not, //

and as a result hurts someone, //

the driver is responsible for the harm. //

Now let me tell you the story of what happened in this case. //

Let me take you back to December 12th, 2008. //

Interstate Highway 85 in Durham. //

Wet road. Rain and wind. //

Just past midnight. //

Acme Company truck driver Howard Littlejohn is driving south //

in his eighteen-wheeler tractor trailer. //

The Acme driver passes the Gregson Street Exit. //

The Acme driver pushes in his cigarette lighter. //

Acme's driver feels around the seat for cigarettes. //

Acme's driver leans down to feel around on the floor. //

He finds his cigarettes. //

Acme's driver sits up with his pack of cigarettes in his hand. //

Acme's driver looks back at the road. //

Acme's driver sees his truck has drifted partly onto the shoulder. //

Acme's driver sees a red flare in front of him on the shoulder. //

Acme's driver sees a disabled pickup truck beyond the flare. //

Acme's driver sees someone changing a tire on the right side of the pickup truck. //

Acme's driver swerves left. //

> The Acme driver's front right bumper clips the pickup truck. //
>
> The Acme truck's impact knocks the pickup into the man changing the tire. //
>
> The man changing the tire is Jim Franklin. //
>
> The impact breaks Jim's neck, leaving him permanently paralyzed from the neck down. //
>
> As Jim lies on the pavement, Acme's driver is sitting in his truck talking to his boss on the phone.

5-5-3 Opening. Part III. Who We Are Suing and Why: The Safety Rules the Defendant(s) Violated

The start of advocacy.

First, explain *who* you are suing. It's amazing how often this is left out!

We are suing truck driver Ed Littlejohn for three reasons.

We are suing his employer, Acme Trucking, for two reasons.

You finally get to point fingers of blame! You've achieved immunity from **Premature Advocacy**. If until now you have allowed jurors to come to their own conclusions, not yours, you have earned the privilege and standing of being an advocate. You get that not from your law degree, but from avoiding Premature Advocacy in Parts I and II.

Just do the transformation gradually.

And keep control! Don't yet strip bare nekked and jump into stream-of-consciousness, not during this crucial part of opening. Instead, adhere to Part III's five-part "Why-We're-Suing" paradigm. It's easy.

Run all five parts of the paradigm in their full sequence for *each* violation by *each* defendant. (Remember that every act of negligence is, by definition, the violation of a safety rule. *See* Fundamental Five, pp. 10*ff.*)

The Why-We're-Suing Paradigm

  A. What was the rule-violating act?

   i. Tell us the rule and how the act violated it. (No need for present tense.)

   ii. Tell us how you know the defendant did that act.

  B. Without referring to your specific case, tell us what's dangerous *in general* about violating this rule and who says so.

   i. Unless it is a common-sense rule (such as that drivers have to look where they're going), tell us who says the rule is a rule: your experts. And if you did your job in discovery, the defendant and her experts will have already agreed it's a rule. So will fact witnesses on both sides. (*See Rules of the Road* and chapter six of *Reptile*.)

   ii. Tell how the rule protects people (what makes violating the rule dangerous?)—and who says so.

   iii. Tell what your experts will explain about how the rule works and how violation endangers. Use analogous situations very different from your case. Explanation by analogy is always acceptable and almost always an excellent way to explain anything. For example, the inner-city movie theater's premises-safety rules violation is identical to rules for suburban schools and malls. The ob-gyn's violation of the safety-rules within a differential diagnosis (such as "must rule out, not guess out") is best illustrated by analogy to other medical situations—such as chest pains in an elderly patient in an emergency room. The analogy's purpose is twofold: 1) for the jury to clearly understand the rule and the danger of violating it, and 2) for the jury to see that the rule applies to their own circumstances, not just to someone who was in your client's position. (Again, this is fully explained in *Reptile*.) You can do this with every kind of negligent act, though at first you may need assistance.

   iv. Show how dangerous it is to violate the particular rule. This is determined not by the harm it did in your case, but by a) the maximum harm it could have done, and b) how often it causes harm. These are the major factors that every safety commission takes into account. A driver driving 12 mph who looks away from the road and hits your client stopped at a light does not sound like much of a menace. But that particular violation injures and kills thousands every year, so is extraordinarily dangerous. And how serious is it? Well, a driver missed seeing a three-thousand-pound vehicle with bright red taillights; he certainly would have missed a group of four or five children in the crosswalk. That's the violation's measure of danger.

C. How did the defendant's violation of this rule cause harm in this case?

   i. Explain what the defendant did that violated the rule.

   ii. Explain how violating the rule caused the harm (not medical causation, but how the violation caused the injurious event). Explain how you or your experts know. (An expert's conclusion—here or on the stand—is useless until the jurors understand that basis for the conclusion. *See* section 6-22, p. 200.)

D. What should the defendant have done instead of violating the rule?

   i. Specify the act that would have constituted obeying the rule. Jurors tend to give more money when the defendant could easily have avoided the wrongdoing. When avoiding the wrongdoing seems hard or complicated—or even difficult to understand—jurors give less. So show how easy and simple it would have been for the defendant to have done the right thing. Make jurors feel that they themselves could easily have done the right thing in the defendant's place. This is where you must use extremely simple language: "Stick the label here." "Follow this rule." "Give the test before the drug." "Look what you're doing."

   ii. Explain how you know.

E. How would that have helped? (Cite experts, unless it is common sense.)

OPENING, PART III—EXAMPLE[7]

Introduction:

> We are suing Acme's driver, Howard Littlejohn, as well as Acme itself. Acme operates 3,274 tractor-trailer eighteen-wheelers in every state from coast to coast.

A. *What was the rule-violating act?*

  i. *Tell us the rule and how the act violated it. (No need for present tense.)*

  > The first reason we're suing Acme's driver is that he violated [or *"chose to violate"*] the safety rule requiring drivers to have their brakes checked every twenty-four hours of operation.

  ii. *Tell us how you know the defendant did that act.*

  > Mr. Littlejohn's log records and Acme's shop records show that Mr. Littlejohn let more than fifty hours go by before having the Acme truck's brakes checked.

B. *Without referring to your specific case, tell us what's dangerous in general about violating this rule and who says so.*

  i. *Unless it is a common-sense rule, tell us who says the rule is a rule: your experts.*

  > Federal regulations require interstate truck drivers to have their brakes checked every twenty-four hours of operation. Ezra Harrington, director of the Northeastern Trucking Safety Association, will tell us that every fifteen hours is more advisable to keep from needlessly endangering the public. He will also explain that his conclusion is more likely right than wrong [*hands*]—and that beyond that, he's certain. [*See* section 3-2-2, p. 63.] Acme Trucking's own president, Owen Wheeler, will admit to us that all interstate trucking companies must follow the federal regulations.

---

7. Please note that this and other examples in this book are not intended to provide guidance about what the rules applicable to certain cases might be. The examples are strictly to demonstrate methodologies.

ii. *Tell how the rule protects people (what makes violating the rule dangerous?) and who says so.*

> When a driver does not have his brakes checked every twenty-four hours, the odds skyrocket that one or more of his brakes will fail. Truck safety expert Harrington will explain that if this happens in an emergency stopping situation when the driver needs fast and full braking, the failed brake will diminish the truck's stopping ability *and* send the truck out of control. Again, Dr. Harrington will say that this conclusion is more likely right than wrong [*hands*], and that beyond that he's certain—the truck goes out of control because when brakes stop one side's wheels better than the other side's wheel, the truck veers out of control.

iii. *Tell what your experts will explain about how the rule works and how violation endangers. Use analogies to other situations.*

> Dr. Harrington will also explain that this is why all mechanical equipment—anything that human beings manufacture—can break or wear out if not inspected and repaired at proper intervals. For example, he'll tell us that allowing a gas furnace in a school or home to go uninspected longer than allowed can lead to a leak that can kill everyone in the building. So no one should ever exceed the recommended time between safety inspections for *anything*— because it needlessly endangers people.[8] Everything wears out, and that often turns equipment needlessly dangerous.

iv. *Show how dangerous it is to violate the particular rule.*

> Uninspected equipment is the third-largest cause of death and serious injury in America. In

---

8. This is called "spreading the tentacles of danger." It's one of the most important parts of opening. Another example: the prison guard who illegally beats a prisoner is also violating the very rule that protects our kids from predator-teachers or rage-driven teachers in school, protects our senior citizens in rest homes, etc. You want to show the dangers we are all in when the specific safety rules are violated. You need not preach community safety; just use analogies that get the jurors to see the point for themselves.

every situation, the operator and the owner are responsible for making sure the equipment is inspected. Yet most of the people killed or hurt by uninspected equipment are members of the public, not the operators or owners.

C. *How did the defendant's violation of this rule cause harm in this case?*

  i. *Explain what the defendant did that violated the rule.*

  Instead of driving into any of the inspection centers along his route, Acme's driver continued without stopping—so he'd get to his destination earlier. Here is his driver's log. [*show*] You can see that there are no stops in the fifty hours of operation leading up to the wreck. Here is the truck's blackbox printout, showing the same thing.

  ii. *Explain how violating the rule caused the harm. Explain how you know.*

  We asked Dr. Eliot Klizan to look at what happened. He'll explain that when the Acme driver had to slam on his brakes, the bad brake in the left front wheel did not work. So the right side of the truck slowed sooner than the left, sending the truck sharply to the right and out of control. He'll show us a neat little demonstration of how that happens. He'll explain that he's not only more likely right than wrong [*hands*] about this, but 100 percent accurate.

D. *What should the defendant have done instead of violating the rule?*

  i. *Specify the act that would have constituted obeying the rule.*

  Acme's driver was required to have the brakes checked, as the safety rule and federal regulations demand.

  ii. *Explain how you know.*

  Everyone in the case will admit that if the brakes had been checked, the problem would have been found and fixed. That's the purpose

> of safety inspections at the proper times.
>
> E. *How would that have helped? (Cite experts, unless it is common sense.)*
>
> > If the brakes problem had been found and fixed, the truck would not have swerved, so the truck would not have veered into John's car in the next lane.
>
> Then do it all again for the next reason you are suing the driver:
>
> > The second reason we're suing Acme's driver is that he violated [*or "chose to violate"*] the safety rule that requires him to keep his eyes on the road at all times and to see what is there to be seen.
>
> *Etc.*

Here's the final reason you are suing:

> The final reason we're suing is that the defendants refuse to provide full and fair compensation for what they did. So we're forced to bring them to trial.

This does not refer to negotiations. It is simply a statement of fact.

"Failed to Follow"

Don't say that someone "failed to follow" the rule. Say they "violated" or "chose to violate" the rule. A rule violation is always intentional. Jurors forgive failure, but not an intentional violation. If you trace back the reason for an apparently inadvertent violation (accidentally letting the mind wander), you will always find that it was a matter of choice (choosing not to maintain control of one's attention).

Expert Conclusions

When citing an expert's conclusion in this or any other section of opening, explain its basis. Be brief, but complete. Never just say, "Dr. Barnes will tell you that if Dr. Larson had spotted the cancer in time, Sally would have lived." Explain *how Dr. Barnes knows:*

Dr. Barnes will show us medical textbook diagrams of how fast this kind of tumor grows. He'll explain that we know its size when Sally died. And we know its growth rate. So working backward, we can calculate that when Dr. Larson saw it in 2007, it was big enough to see, but small enough to have been removed before the cancer spread. He'll do the calculation for us. And every doctor on both sides of this case will testify that this kind of tumor does no harm if it's taken out before it spreads.

Never call *your* expert's conclusion an "opinion." And never call the defense opinion witness an expert. We have experts who have conclusions. The defense has opinion witnesses who have opinions.

5-5-4 OPENING. PART IV: UNDERMINE. WHAT IS WRONG WITH THE NEGLIGENCE DEFENSES?

This is where you provide your side of every defense negligence contention. (Undermining causation and damages defenses comes later.) Any defenses that jurors hear first from the defense will instantly take on an aura of truth.[9]

When the first a juror hears about a defense point is from the defense, the juror will conclude that you hid it. That makes you dishonest. So with rare exception, everything you do not want the jury to believe should be covered in this section.

Moreover, if the defense surprises you with an important contention you did not anticipate, do all you can to dispose of it as early as possible in testimony. If you don't, it can undermine everything your witnesses say, even on other topics. An important defense contention can offer jurors an easy way to decide the case; if they take that way, they'll barely listen to testimony from your side. So when a defense contention surprises you in the defense opening, it may merit altering your witness order to allow you to attack it as soon as possible. Otherwise, by the time you get to it, it can be too late. Fixing a leak after a ship is half full of water does not empty out the water.

Caveat 1: **Do not breathe a word of your undermining topics earlier than Part IV of opening.** Jurors first need your entire affirmative negligence case under their belts.

---

9. In fact, some "just plain facts" that can hurt you also need to be undermined in your opening. For example, you can be miles in front by the end of your opening—but when your client is an illegal immigrant, or smokes, or uses street drugs, common survival instincts take over and you will be losing with the first sixty seconds of the defense opening when jurors learn about the unsavory fact. This is less likely to happen if you deal with it in your opening. (*See* section 5-8-2, p. 167, for how to deal with such problems.)

Caveat 2: **Do not use the undermining section to reprise affirmative points from Part III.** Just tell us what's wrong with the points you are undermining. No need to say, "One of the things we had to determine was whether what we said before is accurate."

Caveat 3: **Don't just tell us why your experts are right about each undermined point.** You must also tell us *why the defense is wrong:* What's wrong with their analytic process or facts? But do this without discussing what the defense is going to say. You want to show that you dealt with this possibility before the defense brought it up. So say something like "For anyone to think there was an earlier back problem, he'd have to ignore *X* information and leave out the *Y* part of the required analysis procedure."

How to Undermine

Never say: "You will hear the defense tell you *X*, but . . . ."

That wording is dead wrong. It makes jurors believe that you needed the help of the defense to figure out the problems in your case, and now you have to desperately dream up ways around those problems. If that happens, some jurors will wonder whether you'd have taken the case in the first place if you'd been thorough and smart enough to discover its problems yourself.

So instead of saying, "You'll hear the defense tell you . . . ," explain that you took the initiative: that *before deciding to come to trial,* you considered and researched all the possibilities.

Here's how:

First*, say:*

> Before we decided to come to trial, several things had to be determined.

Second*, state a negligence contention to undermine and explain why it was important to the case:*

> For example, was there ice on the road that afternoon? Because if there was, it would explain why the Acme truck hit John. So we would not be suing Acme. So it had to be determined whether there was ice.

This shows that you took the initiative to investigate. It makes your conclusion credible. And it keeps you from seeming defensive.

Caveat. Don't raise a nonpivotal defense contention to a pivotal level. Once you say ". . . there'd be no reason for us to come to trial," you make the issue case-pivotal—even if it is not. So say "no reason for us to come to trial" only when the issue is actually pivotal. When it is less, say something like:

Because ice would have been one reason the Acme driver hit John.

Third, *explain what you did to determine the truth.* Cite fact witnesses, experts, and whatever else you have. (Continue to refrain from mentioning the defense. Sound like you dealt with this before the defense got involved.)

> So we asked the two motorists who stopped, as well as the state troopers and both EMT workers on the ambulance crew. All six will be here to tell us there was no ice. We also contacted the National Weather Bureau, and they're sending a meteorologist to bring temperature charts here that show it never went below 35 degrees, much too warm for ice.

Fourth, *explain what the result means:*

> That's how it was determined there was no ice, so we could come to trial.

Sometimes there is only one defense negligence contention. Usually there are more, sometimes many more. Undermine them all.

The test of how well you did this is whether the defense attorney will appear awkward talking about them in her opening. If not, you have not done your job.

Caveat majeure. Remember that it is never enough to just say why your experts are right. You have to explain what is wrong with the defense conclusion. So:

> ***Not enough:*** We asked our expert, Dr. Oshyaramon, whether the truck could have slid on the ice. He said no, it was too warm that day. He'll show us that the weather records from every weather station within fifty miles shows temperatures well above freezing.

This does not help you when the defense contends that wind sweeping over a puddle on a thirty-five-degree day can, by increasing the evaporation rate, cool the water enough to freeze it. If you don't deal directly with that point, you fail to undermine. So you must explain.

> To make sure there could have been no ice, *it had to be determined* whether there was enough wind to increase the evaporation rate of the water. This is because evaporation can cool water, sometimes enough to freeze it. So we asked our weather expert. He told us, as he'll testify later, that there was almost no wind—and even if there had been, it would have to

have been blowing at more than 100 miles per hour that day to increase evaporation enough to freeze the water.[10]

Don't Miss Anything

Some of the most potent defenses are those the defense will not use. For example: "The plaintiff shoulda got a second opinion!" That's a hard one for the defense to proffer, but is still dangerous for you, because jurors will come up with it on their own. So you have to undermine it.

> Another thing that had to be determined was whether Sally should have gotten a second opinion. So we asked four doctors if Sally had been in a situation where they'd advise a second opinion, and they all said no—that second opinions are reserved for something such as when a doctor advises surgery, not for when a doctor says the tests show no cancer.

Sometimes the defense will make absurd claims that fly in the face of the law. For example, they will say that your med-mal client signed a consent form, so his family should not be here suing. "He accepted the risk of death!" Jurors accept this outrageous but common defense point because it's simple. They come up with it on their own even when the defense never mentions it. So you have to deal with it in opening.

> One of the things we had to determine had to do with the consent form that John signed. It said he accepted the risk of death. So it had to be determined if that meant the doctors cannot be held responsible. So we asked the doctors themselves: "Are you ever allowed to ask a patient to consent to the risk of death by your negligence?" We also asked the woman who runs the hospital. And we asked our expert on hospital administration. All of them explained exactly what every lawyer—including Mr. Defense Attorney—learned in law school: that an agreement asking a patient to accept the risk of death by negligence is an illegal agreement and would also violate basic medical ethics. They all explained that a consent form is only about *unavoidable* harm. So if a doctor's negligence—which is always avoidable if the doctor follows the patient safety rules—causes an avoidable death, the doctor has agreed in advance that he will be responsible for the death and not blame the patient.

---

10. Again, I am not offering this "science" as real. It is for illustration only.

5-5-5 Opening. Part V. Causation and Damages

In terms of time, you're about 75 percent through opening.

The Opening Template's first four parts prepare jurors to accept Part V: causation and damages. Don't jump the gun. By the time you get here, jurors see that the kind of thing the defendant did represents a community danger. They'll want to minimize that danger. Part V gives jurors the way to do that: simply force the defendant to pay full and fair compensation (but don't yet use those words with the jury).

The damages part of opening—as well as the damages part of your entire case—is not about throwing tons of harms and losses at the jury and hoping it sticks.

A. Introduction to harms and losses: Explain why you're talking about harms and losses. It's obvious to you, but not always to jurors.

B. Mechanism of harm (how did the negligent act cause each injury?): Explain step-by-step how the negligence damaged your client's body and mind (mechanism of harm).

C. Personal consequences of each injury: Show how those damages intrude(d) on your client's life.

D. Fixes and helps (treatments, etc.): Detail the necessary fixes and helps, and what your client has gone through and goes through for their sake. Surgery, for example, adds to the harm because it hurts.

E. What cannot be fixed or helped.

A. Introduction to Harms and Losses

So start by explaining—even if you explained in voir dire—why you are required to tell them about the losses and harms.

> Your verdict form will ask how much money you will allow in the verdict.
>
> To figure it out, you can take into account only one thing: the level of the harms and losses the defendant caused. Nothing else.
>
> Mr. Defense Attorney agrees. At the end of trial, Judge Maxim will tell you it's the law: harms and losses only.
>
> Everything else is outside the box.
>
> So I need to show you those losses and harms . . . and how severe they were. You need to know this as the basis for your decisions.

> I'm not showing you the harms and losses to get your sympathy. Sympathy is outside the box. You can feel sympathy, of course—but you cannot factor it into your decision making. Same with anything else outside the box: you can think it or feel it, but you cannot let it affect your verdict.
>
> So during trial, here's what you'll hear about the harms and losses . . . .

This reinforces (or without jury voir dire, it establishes) your harms-and-losses-*only* theme (*see* section 3-10, pp. 72*ff.*).

It also tells jurors why you're showing harms and losses. If you don't, some jurors will think you're talking about harms and losses to get sympathy and move them to help you win liability.

B. Mechanism of Harm (How Did the Negligent Act Cause Each Injury?)

Mechanism of harm establishes causation and harm simultaneously. Each supports and reinforces the other.

Tone: clinical.

Explanations: simple.

Language: no medical or other technical terms.

"Step-by-step" means to show how each domino falls into the next domino. Start with the negligent act and explain how each domino pushes over the next—all the way up to each of the physical damages to your client's body.

Did a rear-end collision cause brain damage? Then take us domino-by-domino from the negligent act impact to brain damage.[11]

Don't turn this into a physics or medical course. But don't leave any domino gaps.

This is your causation chain. The defense wants the causation chain to be hidden inside a mysterious black box. You need to rip away the sides of the box and shine a light on those dominoes.

As you run through the dominoes, leave your client out of it. Just describe *in general* the domino mechanism by which, say, an impact forces itself through layer after layer of skin, then bone, etc. Explain the progress of the undiagnosed cancer a) growing into adjacent tissue b) from where it migrates into the lymph system and c) then is carried by fluids, to be d) planted in the lung, where it e) grows and f) interferes with how the lung works.

---

11. Do not rely on the accuracy of these sample steps; I use them solely to illustrate the method.

Explain how the force of the rear-end collision is transferred step-by-step through parts of the car—so that we see how it gets to a driver's neck. (A good high-school physics teacher can provide inexpensive and extraordinarily credible expert testimony about this process, and even create a "Mr. Science" exhibit to demonstrate; *see* section 6-20, p. 198.)

It's the same process for every kind of case. Here's how the dominoes 1) stay simple, 2) leave the client out, and 3) require no medical or technical terms in a medical case:

a) Dr. Cuttem cuts blood vessel

b) –> bleeding

c) –> less blood in circulation system

d) –> lower blood pressure

e) –> not enough pressure to get enough blood to brain cells

f) –> etc.

Use simple line-drawing slides or boards. There is hardly ever any reason to use elaborate, expensive graphics. Simplicity is always best, especially with exhibits.

Death Case

Take us step-by-step from the "insult" (but never use that word in trial) to the ultimate cause of death. Then go step-by-step from the death to the survivor's harms and losses caused by the death.

Your dominoes must traverse the space from the negligent act(s) to each harm. The defense wants that black-boxed so they can beat you on causation. So you need to show the dominoes in opening. By testimony it's too late, because jurors who think you have no causation don't bother to listen to your case.

The dominoes solidify causation.

They also let jurors go through the severity of the injury *as it happened*.

And within the template, they help position the injuries as emblematic of the harm that violations of the rules can cause to *anyone*. (*See Reptile*.)

C. Personal Consequences of Each Injury

This is where you put the jurors into your client's shoes. This is easy to do without violating any Golden Rule prohibitions.

Start by using the dominoes to show the process from physical harms to all the rest—everything that has affected your client's life. That shows, say, how the negligence led to dead brain cells and then to a ruined memory. Now show how that ruined memory hurts your client's life. Or you have just shown us how the negligence led to broken bones, pain, and inability to walk. Now show us those things intruding on your client's life.

This is where things get personal and specific. You can't be a lawyer reciting deficits you know nothing about, except as facts. You have to make yourself deeply and personally involved with your client so you can tell his story, not just narrate a report. Do you know what broken bones feel like? What they do to your everyday, moment-to-moment life?

Have you spent plenty of time with your client to feel close to his harms? Have you asked him and his family to educate you—and in their home, not your office? If not, you aren't ready to talk about your client's harms to a jury. You are, after all, a personal *injury* lawyer. So you must know and empathize with injury. You cannot convey the enormity of harm to a jury when it's just an intellectual concept to you. (*See* Fundamental Four, pp. 7*ff.*)

Connecticut's Ernie Teitel advises that you spend days in, say, the kitchen: the center place of home life where you can learn about your client's family. Make yourself part of the day's routine so you can be the champion of people you are part of. You have no higher calling.

This short section of opening demands a lot of you. You must become a comprehensive expert on the life consequences of your client's injuries. Don't pull out all the stops in opening, but do lay the groundwork for testimony and closing. The consequences to your client's life are the living consequences of the defendant's safety-rule violations. That gives jurors their impetus to complete the equation.

For that to happen, you must be personally as invested in, and as expert about, the intrusions on your client's life as you are about the violations.

Undermining Defense Causation and Damages Contentions

As you come to each point, undermine any causation defenses in the same way you undermined negligence defenses:

> Before coming to trial, it had to be determined that the problems with John's spine did not come from something before the wreck.

To find out, we asked Dr. Upland, his personal physician, who will explain that . . . .

And here's how he knows he's right . . . .

Support your conclusions. Conclusions alone are not worth the air it takes to speak them—until you explain why they're true.

Remember that when undermining, it's never enough to explain only the favorable conclusions of your experts; you have to explain **what is wrong with the reasoning—the step-by-step dominoes—of the other side's experts:** where did the defense expert go astray in following the required analytic steps to get to a valid conclusion? (*See* section 7-1, pp. 205*ff.*)

As with undermining the defense's points about negligence, attack the defense "expert" in a way that does not mention the defense or its witnesses or even hint that they know about that defense. So again: "In order for anyone to come to the conclusion that there was an earlier back problem, they'd have to ignore *X* information and leave out the *Y* part of the required analysis procedure."

Your experts, or a nonwitness medical consultant, can tell you the steps necessary to go from evidence to medical conclusions. This will tell you what to probe for in depositions of the defense medical "experts." The goal is to find the required steps the defense omitted or did wrong. Get your expert or consultant to explain each step and what happens when that step is omitted or done wrong—and then show that that's exactly what the defense "expert" did. (Do the same for your earlier negligence undermining of every kind of defense "expert.")

Example: In any medical analysis, the first required step is for the expert to put himself in a neutral frame of mind. Step two: gather all available information. Defense medical experts often don't do step one—and many times they don't even do step two, including when they bill for step two! (That's part of their nifty sub-rosa deal with the insurance company.)

Tell the jurors that your expert will explain the following:

1. The rule that says to **gather all available information;**

2. **Why** that rule exists;

3. **Who says** it's a rule;

4. How violating the rule also **violates necessary clinical or medical research or analysis requirements;**

5. In general, how violating that rule **results in incorrect results;**

6. And how violating that rule **resulted in the specific incorrect results in this case.**

Of particular use in learning to do this is Dorothy Sims's *Exposing Deceptive Defense Doctors* (James Publishing).

Malingering, Symptom Exaggeration, etc.

When you must fight implications (or outright accusations) of malingering, symptom exaggeration, "litigation syndrome," and other such junk-science detritus, Sims's book will be of great help. So will Rick Friedman's masterful *Polarizing the Case*.

By adding *Reptile* to the mix, you'll have the techniques to show (without necessarily being explicit about it) that the defense's **very manner of defending the case creates a public menace, which the jurors can squelch** merely by means of a fair compensation verdict.

D. Fixes and Helps

Cover all past/present/future care, therapy, and other measures necessary to restoring as much of the plaintiff's functioning and normal emotional state as possible—life-care plans, medical bills, doctor's reports and orders, safety necessities (people with broken legs can't run from fires, so need someone with them at night), etc.

When appropriate, explain why your client's current (uncompensated) situation cannot provide adequate care, comfort, and safety. For example, cite your expert's explanation of how the family does not have the training to provide a decent level of care, safety, and comfort. Cite the wife's worries about this. And tell stories of bad things that have already happened that would not have happened if there'd been trained people in place.

Minimum Life-Care Plan

A life-care plan is invaluable. With no formal life-care plan, make your own list. Explain each particular harm that money will fix or help.

Ask your life-care expert for a *minimum* life-care plan. This does not mean the expert should remove anything. It simply means she should be able to explain (as you will in opening) that a *minimum life-care plan provides the* **minimum** *humane level of care, comfort, and safety.* This lets you argue that "two or three times the cost of the minimum life-care plan could be spent on the *best* care, comfort, and safety." Give examples of what is not covered: "If in ten years the Mayo Clinic discovers a way to help Jack walk again, the cost is not in the minimum life-care plan."

Never call the plan a "life-care plan." Throughout trial, call it the "*minimum* life-care plan." If your life-care expert can't or won't do the same, don't use her again. And warn your colleagues not to.

Pay particular attention to safety. Jurors can be quite willing to go beyond the minimum life-care plan to provide better safety. You can lead jurors to allow money for good alarm systems, nighttime attendant care, and conservative medical monitoring, even when these things are not in the minimum life-care plan.

"Minimum life-care plan" turns your life-care figure into a floor. (*See also* section 6-15, p. 189, and section 8-9, p. 227.)

> **BLACK-BOX WARNING**
>
> Never use a life-care planner who sells the services she proposes in her plan. Unless the defense and the jurors are asleep, such a life-care planner's obvious financial motive undermines her credibility. You wouldn't believe her yourself.

Life Expectancy

One of the most disgusting of defense tactics is the gruesome claim that "Well, hell, the harm is so bad that this pestering plaintiff is gonna die soon anyway, thank God, so don't provide care for too long." Defense attorneys make this argument as if there is no Hell, making the rest of us hope there is. Such a claim is absurd from a public policy point of view, because it encourages people and companies to hurt their victims not just a little, but badly enough to kill them within a few years.

But the claim is really a confession by the defense that they shortened your client's life. This is compensable in almost every venue. (Where it is not, use the claim as an exacerbation of emotional suffering: what makes a person suffer more than a prediction of early death?) So when the defense does its nasty dance to show lower life expectancy because of the very thing the defendant caused, use the defense numbers and their estimate of premature death as the basis for claiming additional money.

And in closing, argue that the money *should far exceed the costs of caring for the person for those same years.* "Which is worse? Having to pay for care? Or having to think every day about losing all those years and then actually losing them?"

Showing Longer Life Expectancy

In opening, explain that many people in your client's population group will live longer than the figure on the official tables. In fact, statistically, more than half the people in your client's group will live longer, many a lot longer. Use a simple spreadsheet exhibit to show how many in your client's group will live longer than the average. This gives you preponderance: your client is more likely than not to live longer. So you get to argue for more than the minimum life-care figure on which your life-care expert based life expectancy.

Even if fewer than half of your client's group live longer, you still get preponderance. Your client is worried *right now* about **what happens when he outlives his life-care money** if it runs out at that "expectancy" age, the very age when he'll be least able to get along without any money. This nightmarish worry turns even a less-than-50-percent chance of longer life into a beyond-reasonable-doubt worry about what happens if he beats the average.

His worry can be removed by providing the amount of money it will take to remove it. In other words, this harm can be fixed if jurors provide money for many years beyond average life expectancy.

Once someone lives to her life expectancy, which most people do, she has a *better than even* chance of living another X years. When she gets to that extra X years, as most people do, she has a *better than even* chance of living another X years. And so on.

Have your planner show a chart of how many people are expected to live an additional three years, six years, nine years, etc.

And have your minimum life-care planner or your economist provide care-cost figures for each additional three-year period.[12]

As California's great consultant Rodney Jew asks, "What happens when the money runs out?" **So make sure the jury knows.** In opening, explain what your life-care expert will say about what will happen when the money runs out. Or at least make it clear that once it runs out there will be no more care; then review the awful details in closing.

---

12. When using an economist, remember that 1) most Americans are economically illiterate, and 2) few Americans care or trust what economists do. During the 2009 economic crisis, the economists were wrong, irrelevant, quibbling, and useless. So many jurors regard economic predictions as less reliable than next month's weather forecast. Solution? Your life-care planner should be the one who says what things will cost, and your economist should merely validate it. The more an economist talks, the less some jurors believe him.

Geriatrics

Your minimum life-care planner should enlist a geriatric medical specialist who knows the increasing special needs of the aged. Health-care providers who are untrained and inexperienced in geriatric needs will miss most of a minimum life-care plan's requirements for the later years. And many jurors think that even the worst needs and problems diminish over time. So you need a geriatric specialist to show that your client's needs will dramatically increase, her plight will worsen as she ages, and she will never "get used to" her situation—because each time she gets used to it, things will get worse.

For the aging person who is injured, things often can get worse over a series of dramatic downward plateaus. Nongeriatricians don't usually know about this. So even with a young client whose injuries are permanent, you need a physician or a social worker who specializes in geriatrics to explain how things will get worse as the years pass—far beyond just what the normal processes of aging would have caused.

Case Manager

If there's a case manager in the life-care plan, make sure the jury understands why. A good case manager is not merely a clerk who arranges appointments, though that's usually how life-care planners explain it. **The major factor is safety:** a case manager has the expertise to spot risks and dangers in time to prevent or minimize them. Give examples.

Don't allow your planner or any other witness to nominate herself for the job of case manager. Jurors (and everyone else with a brain) see this as financially motivating every word the life-care planner utters. Your life-care planner must gain nothing from the verdict. This may seem like a no-brainer, but it happens frequently. It hurts cases and exacerbates the bad reputation of plaintiff's lawyers.

Empirical Experience

Your planner needs experience in following up her earlier life-care plans to see how things have worked. Delineate this experience in opening: how your life-care planner has monitored her earlier plans over a long period of time to see if they were correct (were those things really needed?). Give many examples. Otherwise she's working on theories, not experience. A life-care planner too young to have done this is still too young to be your life-care planner.

Attribution

Attribute to others, such as treating or expert physicians, all you say about each harm, fix, and help. In opening, never ask jurors to take your word for anything. Many jurors think your substantial cut of the verdict motivates you to exaggerate harms and costs. So do not say that Mary needs pills costing $1,000. Say instead that her *physician says* she needs them. Don't say she lost wage money; say, "The *wage records* show that . . . ."

As trial progresses, be careful not to shorthand these things into your own assertions. Throughout trial, position yourself as the messenger, not the source.

Future Care Costs v. Past Care Costs

Be careful with the common situation in which annual future care will cost more than annual past care. Explain, for example, that past costs are low because the family had no money for proper care—which is why you're in court. Or that medical costs were low because there was only so much that medical science could do—but as a result, future care costs will be high. Otherwise jurors will use what was spent in the past as a basis for what is needed in the future.

Language

Here and elsewhere, do not use language that can be interpreted as exaggerated. Hyperbolic language undermines credibility. I recently heard a lawyer ask a jury to compensate his client for the "*tragedy* of her broken leg"! What then do we call *Hamlet*?

Understate. Allow the facts, not hyperbole, to do the intensifying.

Who Gets the Money?

Explain that the money goes to pay other people for John's care, treatment, medications, and equipment. Even lost wages compensation will only make John even with where he would have been if this had not happened. (But open no doors to collateral sources.)

E. What Cannot Be Fixed or Helped

"None of this money makes up for the greatest part of the damage: what this did to John himself, his life." Show the distinction: Paying for surgery for a broken arm is one kind of required compensation; money to make up for John's pain is another.

Base This on the Jury Instructions

Jury instructions often detail intangible losses more specifically than merely "pain" or "suffering" or "death." They often include "loss of use of a body part," "inconvenience," "humiliation," etc. In death cases, the instructions often list loss of services, advice, kindly offices, guidance, companionship, etc. Make specific use of each one.

Even if your instructions have no such items, get lists from other jurisdictions. "Loss of use of a body part" and "humiliation," whether in your instructions or from the next state, are useful in detailing the various kinds of suffering.

Do not bunch the losses or rush through them. Make each a separate item. With each, do two things.

First, explain each one separately and clearly: "Humiliation means deep embarrassment, or feeling disgraced, disparaged, or reviled."

Second, relate it to this case:

> Sally's therapist says Sally feels that way a lot. In restaurants, she can't help seeing that people are staring at her. She can't help thinking she repulses them, that they want her to leave so she won't ruin their lunch. She thinks they talk about her when she leaves. And often she's right. That gets inside you. You never get used to it. It never goes away. You want to run and hide. That's what the law means by humiliation.

Follow that immediately—or at least in testimony—with a mini-vignette of one or two such instances.

In closing, each such intangible loss will become a separate line item in your request for money. So in opening, start the process by showing each intangible harm. Focus on the human content of each item. Loss of guidance? "It would have been John's job as a dad to teach John Jr. how to ride a bike and in another few years to talk to him about girls." **But don't worry about the legal terminology of the elements until closing.**

Interim Deprivation

The defendant's refusal to admit responsibility has forced your client to get along without the fixes and helps that could have made her life safer and more bearable. So your client has had to endure months and years of unnecessary extra pain, danger, significant inconvenience, and discomfort. There may even have been a fix—such as timely physical therapy—that would have worked earlier, but now it's too late.

All of that adds to the harm. It should be compensable. After all, a plaintiff's failure to meliorate the harm is admissible to diminish the verdict. By the same token, the defendant's exacerbation should be equally admissible.

So show everything your client has been forced to go through because of the absence of funds that a decent defendant would have provided. This is especially effective when the defense stipulates to liability at the last minute and then whines to the jury about how "responsible" they are being. "Responsible" means admitting you did something wrong and then doing everything necessary to fix, help, and make up for it. Anything less is not responsibility. (*See Reptile*, p. 238, "Repentance.")

Plaintiff as "Normal" (Before) v. After

Use the same chart you will use in testimony: a simple, double-column chart with previous problems in the left ("Before") column, and new problems and aggravations[13] in the right ("After") column. Starting in opening, emphasize that you seek no money for the left column. As you talk through each "After" item, cite your experts' or treating doctors'[14] explanations of how they know the defendant caused it. Refer back to your earlier explanations of the mechanism of how it happened.

Before	**After**
No disability	Disabling back pain
Temporary back pain	Permanent back pain
Worked 3/4 time	Can't work
No meds required	Heavy meds required

Earlier Deficits

When the defense is going to claim that your client had some of the problems before (never use the word "prior"), use this part of opening to distinguish clearly and frankly between earlier problems and those the defendant caused or worsened. Emphatically make clear that you are seeking money only for harm the defendant caused, not for anything from before.

---

13. Do not say "aggravate." To most people it means "annoy," not "worsen." So instead of "it aggravated her back pain," say, "It made her back pain worse." If "aggravate" is in the jury instructions, wait until closing to say it, when you explain what the instructions mean. Don't use any legal words until then—and even then only when essential.

14. "Treating doctors" is another term unfamiliar to many jurors. Say instead, "John's own doctors."

Where there are grey areas (i.e., no one can tell or there is strong evidence both ways), tell jurors not to provide money for those "grey" areas unless the defendant "more likely than not" caused them. This adds to your credibility, bolsters your preponderance theme (*see* section 3-2, p. 63*ff.*), and makes jurors feel better about your client.

5-5-6 OPENING. PART VI: "BEFORE"

This is where you first tell us about your client as she was before the defendant hurt her, or where you first tell us about your client and his family before the defendant killed him. Don't do *any of it* earlier, not even "John, father of three . . . ." This is where it will have the most effect.

This may seem backward to you, and it is. And yes, within any story you must use chronological order (*see* section 5-5-2, p. 124). But this is the important exception. We learn it from the greatest dramatists in history. They made their sad stories far more powerful by letting the audience know the catastrophic outcome *before* they show the happy parts of the character's life. Shakespeare, for example, not only labeled tragedies as tragedies (so that we'd know everyone was going to end up dead), but often had an actor come on before the play to tell us there'll be a tragic ending:

ROMEO and JULIET

Prologue

Two households, both alike in dignity,
In fair Verona where we lay our scene,
From ancient grudge break to new mutiny,
Where civil blood makes civil hands unclean.

From forth the fatal loins of these two foes
A pair of star-cross'd lovers take their life;
Whose misadventured piteous overthrows
Do with their death bury their parents' strife.

The fearful passage of their death-mark'd love,
And the continuance of their parents' rage,
Which, but **their children's end,** nought could remove,
Is now the two hours' traffic of our stage. . . .

Why would Shakespeare give away the ending?

For the same reason that he, as well as the great Greek playwrights, used old stories everyone already knew—including the ending. The happiest moments in a play or movie take on an aura of almost unbearable tragedy when we watch them already knowing the bad outcome. *Romeo and Juliet* contains one of the loveliest "lovers meeting" scenes of all time. Romeo turns and sees Juliet for the first time! She turns and sees him for the first time! They gaze awestruck! Lovestruck! Across a crowded room! Everyone in the audience thrills as they feel again the amazing power of young love. It's wonderful, exciting, all the enchantment of youth and young love and promise for the future and . . . then . . . you . . . suddenly remember that the happy couple will soon be dead.

The sadness and sense of loss are overpowering.

The same thing happens whenever you re-watch your favorite love-story-with-tragic-ending movie, because the terrible outcome is firmly in your mind as you watch the earlier, happy moments—now all framed by the bad outcome. It's one of the world's oldest and strongest dramatic techniques.

It's no different in an opening statement. Don't default to the usual "before and after." It carries virtually no impact to tell us early that "Brooke was a really good mother to her three children." Actually, that kind of soulless, cloying, abstract statement is of no use anywhere in trial. But even great little vignettes of Brooke being a great mom carry almost no impact when they come before we know the results of what the defendant did to her. When the jurors have no frame of loss to put the earlier life into, the "before" comes across as hollow—an ineffective appeal for sympathy.

One case had a splendid "before" video of a client whose "after" status was quadriplegia. In preparing a settlement video, the attorneys told the editor to start the video with that "before" clip: backyard on a bright summer day, mottled shadowing on the lawn of beautiful trees, Dad passing a little foam football to his five-year old. The clip almost seemed slow motion, though it was not. Dad tosses the ball; the little boy, eyes wide, stretches out his hands and fingers, grabs the ball out of the summer air; he bobbles the ball, he grabs it to his chest, he nearly drops it, but at the last instant he saves it and starts laughing in delight; Dad runs across the yard, picks him up, swings him round and round.

A lovely, lovely showing of a dad–little boy moment that told the whole story of their lives together.

Focus-group response: "Kind of hokie."[15]

---

15. Never show any video without first focus-group testing it.

The videographer moved the football scene to the end of the video. So first we saw how badly Dad was hurt, the necessities of caring for him: toileting him, moving him. We saw one shot of the little boy having to carry his younger brother's bathroom booster step into Dad's room to stand on, so Dad could see him—because the boy was not tall enough for Dad to see without Dad turning his head, which Dad could not do.

Then, at the very end: the backyard football shot. Firmly in the grip of all the horror they'd just seen, "OK" and "hokey" went to "Ohhhh my God . . ." and tears—because the viewers were now feeling the full depth of the profound loss.

Aside from being a powerful way to show your client's life before the defendant hurt him, the "before comes after" sequence makes it seem less like shallow advocacy and more like real life.

Start Part VI by explaining why it's important:

> I'm going to tell you what Brent was like before any of this [i.e., Part V] happened.

This is where you tell us about your client before he was hurt. Include some vignettes to illustrate the abstractions: not just that he had a lot of energy but a brief story that illustrates it. Base the "before" on the testimony of numerous fact witnesses. (*See* section 6-7, p. 185.)

Then:

5-5-7 OPENING. PART VII: WHAT CAN THE JURY DO ABOUT IT?

You're now at a delicate intersection. Choose your words carefully. For example:

> From beginning to end, everything I show you in trial is for you to see what caused John's harms and losses, and how much money it will take to fix, help, and make up for them. By the end of trial, you'll see why the evidence **makes this the kind of case**[16] in which I will have to come back later and ask for an amount that right now will sound really high—but which you'll later see is the proper one for this kind of case.

That amount will be $_____.

Thank you.

Then sit down. Shh! Not another word. Anything else you say will detract.

---

16. Above all, do not alter the specific words "this kind of case." They might be the most important words you ever say.

If you are not allowed to specify a figure for noneconomic damages, say:

> It will take $_____ to pay others for John's medical care, and $_____ to get John even with what he'd have earned if he'd not been hurt. That totals $_____ + _____. But that's **the smallest part of this kind of case.** The far larger part is what this did to John himself: his life. That will call for adding a far larger amount to the $_____ + _____.

If you are not allowed to proportionalize, you can probably still do it with your hand—palm down and well lower than your waist—to signify the $_____ + _____ figure, and around your full height for the total.

With or without using your hand that way, say this:

> It will take $_____ to pay others for John's medical care, and $_____ to get John even with what he'd have earned if he'd not been hurt. That totals $_____ + _____. In cases like this, those figures are the complete fixes: they completely take care of the bills; they retrieve the income. Then you look at the rest: all that can't be fixed or helped: what this has done to John's life. **In this kind of case,** that's the most serious part. Once you've seen the evidence, you'll know what to do.

Whichever ending you use, when you're done say "thank you" and sit down. No big finish. Keep things rational at this point, not emotional.

There's a long-standing debate over whether to give a dollar figure in opening. The answer is yes. Jurors want guidance. Give them that guidance when it will do you the most good: *before* your case-in-chief. You want your figure anchored in their heads while, not after, the jurors are hearing what the defendant did wrong, how he caused harm, and how bad the harm was.

5-6 DAMAGES-ONLY CASE[17]

With minor adjustments, the same structure for opening—minus whatever won't be admissible—works well for a damages-only case. Here's how:

Part I. Primary Rules

No advocacy.

Focus the rule on money:

---

[17]. For additional help with damages-only cases, please see chapter twenty of *Reptile*.

When a truck driver's negligence harms a pedestrian, the pedestrian is entitled to an amount of money equal to the level of the harm. Now let me tell you about the harm in this case.

Part II. Story of What the Defendant Did

No advocacy.

Tell as much of the negligence story as allowed. Argue to get in as much as possible. Explain to the judge that part of the emotional harm is your client's vivid, painful memory of what happened. The traumatic memory of the defendant's truck careening at her across the median is causing her emotional harm now, so that memory goes to damages.

Part III. Who We Are Suing and Why: The Safety Rules the Defendant(s) Violated

Start of advocacy.

Again, include all you can get in. Try to cover each thing the defendant did wrong, why it was wrong, how it caused harm, what the defendant should have done, how easy that would have been, and how that would have prevented the harm. These elements should get in because each of your client's harms is exacerbated by her knowing about the very simple safety rules the defendant so needlessly violated. Your client will tell you this, as will any psychologist or similar kind of therapist. Knowledge of how easily the defendant could have followed the rules makes the pain harder to bear.

When possible, part of your story of what the defendant did should include the defendant's denial of negligence until the eve of trial—when they stipulated despite having no information they did not have in the first place.

Last-minute stipulation is relevant to damages because it causes additional harm:

> For three years, Jane had to live with the knowledge that she was stopped at a light and hit from behind—yet they denied doing anything wrong and refused to meet any responsibility. That makes things a lot worse for anyone. **It increased her worry** that she'd never get the money she needs to take care of herself. And they did it just to scare her into walking away from her case. Only when they knew you were coming did they decide to try to look as if they were exercising some responsibility—far too late to do anyone any good but themselves.

Remember, the defense can diminish damages by showing your client's failure to mitigate them. So you should be allowed to show how the defendant's last-minute stipulation exacerbated them.

Part IV. Undermine (What Is Wrong with the Negligence Defenses?)

This is usually not necessary for a damages-only case. You'll undermine the causation and damages defense points in the next section.

Part V. Causation and Damages

Same as with a regular case.

Part VI. "Before"

Same as with a regular case.

Part VII. "What Can the Jury Do about It?"

Same as with a regular case.

5-7 LOSS OF PERSONAL IMAGE

An often ignored loss has to do with your client's self-image. North Carolina's William O. Faison explains that the discrepancy between your client's self-image and the actuality now forced on her is a profound loss and always a source of mental suffering. Her lifelong self-image, until now, has not been that of a woman whose face is scarred or whose hand is useless. Inside she still thinks of herself as a normal-looking person who can do things with her hands. So every time she looks and sees what she really is, or tries to use her hand, it wrenches her apart.

We begin constructing our personal self-image when we are very young. We layer it in piece by piece over decades. It becomes the foundation for the way we see ourselves in relation to ourselves and to the world. (Pain and disability counselors can help identify and describe the loss of personal image and its consequences.)

5-8 BEWARE THE UNKNOWN: WHAT JURORS DON'T KNOW CAN CLOBBER YOU

5-8-1 Seat Belts

If your client was not wearing her seat belt, and the law says it's inadmissible, your careless client is somewhat protected.

But more frequently, that law disadvantages your careful clients. Artemis Malekpour, our firm's senior case consultant, reports that at the start of wreck cases when we ask if the client was belted, the attorney often tells us, "It makes no difference; it doesn't get in." But even without getting in, it gets in.

This is because jurors who hear nothing about a belt tend to default to "no belt."

Years ago, the eagerness of safety proponents to institute seat-belt laws led to compromise: "OK, give us seat-belt laws, and in return we'll agree they won't be evidence." Result: jurors do their own human factors and biomechanical analysis, an error-plagued "science" even when "experts" do it. So jurors erroneously conclude: "She couldn't have hit her head if she'd worn her seat belt. I'm not rewarding anyone who wasn't wearing a seat belt."

So don't underestimate the importance of getting belt use in.

Suggestions:

- Make sure your state's law bars mention of belt use, not just lack of use.

- If the defense is blaming your client for causing the wreck, they're saying she was careless—so seat-belt use should be admissible rebuttal that she was a safe driver.

- To show how the wreck caused injuries, the belt mark on your client's chest should be admissible.

5-8-2 Stereotypes

What jurors don't know can clobber you in other ways. Among the most common are the negative stereotypes that can apply to a client, witness, or you: the "welfare mom," the immigrant (legal or not), the "fat lady," the rich guy, etc.

Even with no supporting information, many jurors will assume that the stereotype's bad characteristics fully (and sometimes especially) apply to your client. Even jurors who regard themselves as totally unbiased commonly do this. In fact, such jurors can be among the most dangerous: they are difficult to ferret out in jury selection, and they are blithely unaware of how completely they are integrating their stereotype-based conclusions into their decision making.

In a recent med-mal mock trial, at the end of the plaintiff's presentation, twenty-two of twenty-five jurors heavily favored the plaintiff. But thirty seconds into the defense presentation they almost all turned against the plaintiff. Why? They learned she was an undocumented alien—you know, the kind of person

Jesus and the Talmud and the Koran insist we protect. God notwithstanding, the jurors automatically assumed (as we heard them say in deliberations) that 1) this case was a scheme the plaintiff had cooked up to sneak some money, 2) she would do anything to get "our" money, 3) it's hard for "them" to get money legally because they don't learn English, etc. For those jurors, each piece of the stereotype was highly though improperly probative, even with no evidence or defense claim that any of these things attached to her.

(The plaintiff's baby, having been born here, was a U.S. citizen—which some jurors refer to as "stealing" a citizenship!)

The National Jury Project's Susan Macpherson long ago taught me how to deal with stereotypes:

1. Make sure you spot the possible stereotype(s) that could attach to your client. "Illegal alien" is easy to spot. But you can easily miss something such as "uncaring businessman" or "spoiled rich kid." Your client may be neither of those things, but jurors might think he is.

2. List each negative association that applies to that stereotype as well as any positive associations that could be twisted into something bad. (Young Asians are commonly thought to be very smart, but that attribution can do harm in trial: "Anyone that smart knows how to lie.") Do some research to be sure you have listed every potential association; don't assume you know them all. One good source—your client and others who are frequent victims of the stereotype's use.

3. Find as many things as you can in your client's story that illustrate exceptions to the stereotype's characteristics. Work those exceptions into your opening, Part VI.

Here's how it works:

1. Client's stereotype:

    Morbidly obese woman

2. Characteristics of that stereotype (partial list):

    Lazy

    Greedy

    Sloppy

    Smelly

Inconsiderate of others

Stupid

3. Show the exceptions to each characteristic. Don't just do this in the abstract. Use vignettes that show the exception in action.

In opening, in the "before" section, provide the little vignettes that jurors will hear more of in testimony: stories of your client's energy that show her long, hardworking hours, active hobbies, lots of walking, volunteer work requiring physical energy, etc. Do not rebut presumed characteristics merely by means of abstracts, such as "she's very energetic." That's useless and can make matters worse. Jurors need illustrations and specifics: "Every afternoon she and her daughter used to walk the mile and a half to the grocery store . . . ." and "Her daughter will tell us about the time they took the long way to see a friend's flower garden, when they . . . ."

Show vignettes and specifics illustrating all she does (or did) to share with and help others.

If she is either sloppy or smelly, overcome your discomfort and have a gentle but frank talk with her: how to dress—and even sit—in trial. If she smells bad, you will hate having to have this conversation, but you (or whoever in your office has the closest relationship with her) must do it. Smell can derive from a hygiene problem, or medication, or some other source. In the kindest way, find the source and deal with it. You might not only solve a problem for trial, but provide the kind of help no one has ever dared give her before; this can have a great effect on the quality of her life.

If you ignore such problems because of your own discomfort, they will confirm jurors' other stereotype assumptions—such as laziness or stupidity or dishonesty—even when they don't exist.

As Susan Macpherson teaches, you can't change a biased juror's stereotypical view of a group. But you can show that *your client is an exception.*

Caveat: Be careful not to validate the stereotype—such as by saying, "She's not like all those other illegal immigrants." Don't mention the stereotype. Just show the characteristics that contradict it.

5-9 Keep Jurors Listening

With or without stipulations, the final parts of opening are about harm and money, so you want jurors listening intently.

Do nothing before then to diminish their listening.

Late in opening, feeling jurors growing restless, you might be tempted to speed up or skim. You should, of course, be sensitive to jurors' restlessness. But the solution is not to omit things, nor to speed up or skim, because it makes jurors feel that what you are saying is unimportant.

Instead, slow down and speak more directly, conveying the impression that this is your most important topic. Take a step closer. Speak more quietly (but articulate *very* clearly or some won't hear you). Tell them this is your most important topic. Emphasize that they particularly need to know what you are now going to talk about.

5-9-1 Succinctness: The Lawyer's Challenge

Almost everyone who went to law school is, to put it kindly, succinctness-challenged. To keep jurors listening through the end of your opening, you must overcome this. No need to talk fast—in fact that's almost always a poor choice—but learn to be succinct.

Practice your opening out loud a number of times, each time paying close attention to, among other things, speaking concisely. And *talk less.*

You can do that by simply correcting five bad habits from law school:

1. Stop using too many words to make each point. In the nineteenth century, lawyers were paid by the word, just like novelists were. So books ended up ridiculously long, and by the ends of openings jurors were dying of old age. These days, assume that you have to pay extra for each unnecessary word.

2. Stop repeating obvious or unnecessary information. "At approximately 8:45 p.m. late in the evening of October the twelfth, in the year nineteen-hundred and ninety-seven . . ." translates to: "8:45 p.m. October 12, 1997." **And it need be said just once.** After that, just say: "That night . . . ."

    A former juror told me that halfway through trial she started keeping track of how many times "the idiot" repeated the entire date: more than 100. "Because he's an idiot," she said. "He should be locked in a cellar."

3. Beware the passive voice! It uses more words than necessary and is less effective and interesting than the active voice. The passive "The car was hit by the truck" is 40 percent longer and 100 percent less emphatic than the active "The truck hit the car." "The truck hit the car" is five direct, effective words instead of seven boring, indirect, "legal speak" words.

However, because the passive voice is less emphatic, you might want to use it when referring to anything your client did wrong.[18]

4. Do not give speeches. Talk to jurors the way you talk in real life. Speeches entail a formality of demeanor and tone that inspires not awe, but mistrust, boredom, and laughter.

5. Never be satisfied with semi-clarity in place of crystal clarity. Express your points clearly enough to be understood by every juror *the first time*. That way you won't have to repeat yourself to make your point more clearly.

Repetition, passive voice, speeches, lack of clarity, too many words: conquer these problems and jurors will still be listening when you get to your opening's money parts. In fact, jurors will listen to you carefully throughout trial and listen willingly in closing instead of thinking, "Is he *ever* gonna shuddup?"

5-10 Fear of Not Understanding

Even in "simple" cases, many jurors fear they will never be able to understand enough to make a decision. The National Jury Project's Susan Macpherson advises that you assure jurors early in opening (if not in voir dire) that you will make everything clear. Then do so.

Don't promise clarity and then emit a lot of "Corpus Colossums."

Demonstrate in all you say (and all that you elicit in your direct exams) that **you are the jurors' constant provider of clarity**. If you establish yourself that way early, jurors will more likely be listening intently as you get to the important damages parts at the end of opening and when you get to closing.

Clarity is especially important when evidence or the instructions are complex or unfamiliar to everyday experience. For example, some jury instructions make the assignment and computation of damages or the assignment of fault sound impossibly complex or vague. You be the clarity guide.

Think of this as an opportunity to create rapport with jurors. Rapport does not come from smiling and pretending you like them and are like them. **Rapport comes from helping people—such as by being the one who helps them understand all the hard stuff.**

---

18. One reason you may "instinctively" think the passive voice belongs in trial is that you hear defense attorneys use it all the time to de-emphasize what their clients did. Don't cooperate. Shove their client's acts into active voice. And pick someone more useful to imitate than defense attorneys. Their needs are very different.

Remember that you cannot be clear when you use technical, medical, or legal language. When jurors do not clearly understand, say, the simple steps of the surgery, they'll think it was complicated and difficult. This tells them that a bad outcome was hard to avoid.

5-11 MOTIVATIONS

Motivations are the foundation of belief. Say that sentence aloud a few times every day.

By far, the most persuasive way to convince jurors that someone did what you claim is to show the motivations that drove her to do it.

So it is never enough to say that the radiologist read the x-ray too fast. Many jurors won't quite believe a doctor would do such a thing. "Why would someone who cared about helping people, who cared enough to go to all those years of medical school, who cared enough to study hard, who cared enough to invest years and lots of money, suddenly speed dangerously through reading an x-ray?" In this way their inferred motive of "caring" can make them decide the doctor did nothing wrong.

So suggest a different motivation: he had a dinner meeting at 6:00 p.m. and did not want to be late. So he was *motivated* to speed through his work. That makes it easier for jurors to believe he did what you say he did.

Similarly, do not merely claim the driver was speeding. When possible, show motivation—why he was in a hurry to get where he was going.

Did a manufacturer choose not to put a warning label on the chemistry set? Why? Not to save the minuscule cost of the warning label; that's not very convincing. Instead, suggest that the manufacturer was motivated by the fear that a warning label would send most parents off to buy the competitor's chemistry set.

Money, of course, is one of the most common motivations for wrongdoing. The nurse had to work too fast because the hospital did not hire enough nurses—because the hospital wanted to save money.

The van was overweight because more weight ==> more freight transported ==> more income.

The truck driver did not slow down because slowing down wastes gas.

Introduce the motivations in opening or (when possible) by means of jury voir dire questions:

> *Who here knows anyone who hates to slow down because it uses extra gas to get back up to speed?*

Know anyone who's overworked because their employer should have more people working there?

Look for motivations during discovery. Find out where the defendant doctor was planning to go after the surgery. Did the trucking company give a bonus to drivers who used less gas? Search for clues. You need no absolute proof, you only need suggestions. So in closing: "We don't know why the doctor sped through the x-rays. Was it because of his daughter's birthday party that night? Or was he just tired that day? We don't know, and he's not telling." In this way, you needn't raise a motivation to the level of "must prove." It need be only a plausible suggestion—always a fair inference.

5-12 Loss of Consortium (also see p. 57)

Many jurors believe a spouse signs on "for better or for worse." When they hear your consortium claim, they wonder whether the spouse read the big print in the marriage contract. So never present consortium as subordinate to the "main" case. You might even find ways to make it bigger. Positioning a consortium claim as an afterthought or addendum often results in very little money.

Instead, from opening through the end of trial, position the harm to the spouse (or whomever) as among the most important harms in the case. For example, you can show the harm to Mr. Plaintiff as seen through his spouse's eyes. Instead of just showing how awful it is to be paralyzed, show how awful it is for the spouse to have to lug the poor guy in and out of bed and take care of his toileting, etc. That shows all the harms to the husband from the poor spouse's viewpoint, magnifying the harm to both.

And always focus on one of the greatest harms to the injured person: his anguished awareness of what the injury has done to his spouse.

5-13 E-nun-ci-ate

In our age of iPods and battle veterans, many jurors, even young ones, don't hear poorly enunciated speech, especially in the acoustics of most courtrooms. So speak distinctly. "Can't you," not "cantchu."

Volume alone does not make your words more understandable. In fact, clear enunciation can usually be heard even at low volume. For that reason, when Laurence Olivier whispered, they could hear him in the back row of the balcony.

The speech teacher at a local university theater department can give you easy exercises to help you better enunciate.

Speaking quietly from time to time can provide emphasis—but not if jurors can't hear you. But they'll always hear you if you enunciate clearly.

5-14 STOP THE BULLET POINTS

Now how can I say this without screeching?

I can't.

STOP THE DAMNED BULLET POINTS!

1. Bullet points have some effective uses, but NEVER to introduce new topics. They diminish your humanity, your capacity to teach and persuade, how interesting you are, and your general worthwhileness as a human being.

2. It's OK to show a bullet point *after* you have explained the point. But not before. When you show a bullet point and *then* talk about the point, people don't hear what you say. They read the bullet point and think they already understand your entire point, so they don't listen. Instead, they numbly stare like zombies at the bullet point while you are talking. Or they check their e-mail. (Yes, even jurors. You'd be amazed what they get away with in the second row.)

3. Many corporations now ban bullet points because they constitute a near-blockade to communication, thinking, and retention.

4. If this kind of bullet-point usage worked, TV commercials would use them all the time. They never do except for local commercials made by local producers who will, deservedly, remain forever local. Competent people who create TV commercials know a lot more about communication than trial lawyers, so take their lead.

5. A trial is a human event. You are a human. Bullet points are not.

6. You must become our *leader*. Leaders do not use bullet points to explain new things! Leaders do not let people stare at bullet points instead of the leader.

    You know who uses bullet points before explaining? Law professors. The boring ones.

7. If Satan used bullet points to introduce new topics intended to persuade folks to sin, Hell would be empty.

5-15 Dress Approachably

Donate your black and dark blue suits and dresses to charity or save them for funerals or when you're acting the part of a lawyer in a play. Blue and black suits are "power costumes" that place you squarely into the negative stereotype of trial lawyer. Jurors relate to you better when you can be secure enough to seem approachable, not powerful. So wear browns, olive greens, grays, whatever you want—but no dark blue or black.

These are not quite case-pivotal points. But they do make a difference.

5-16 Decorate Yourself Modestly and Moderately

Very few plaintiff's attorneys can get away with Rolex watches or the like. Or expensive pens. Or, to quote Orenthal James Simpson, "those ugly-ass" high-class shoes.

5-16-1 Men

No expensive haircuts.

And guys, listen up to an old bald guy: **Lose the toupee.** Leave it home to scare the cat. If you're still at that pathetic comb-over stage, stop it. When jurors spot toupees or comb-overs (and they *always* do), they conclude that if you can't be honest about the natural act of going bald, you are certainly not going to be honest about what you say to get a ton of money. (And, Slick, they laugh about you in the jury room.)

5-16-2 Women

Minimal and simple jewelry and other accouterments. If your engagement ring is an eye-popper, in trial wear a surrogate. Or find a fiancé with less money. And while no formal research backs this up, don't change hair style or color during trial.

5-17 Length of Opening

Jurors listen for as long as they think they need what you are saying. As soon as they think they don't, they stop listening.

So never say anything unless it's clear to jurors why they need it.

Total time is beside the point. The important thing is to say no more than necessary about each point.

Claims that modern Americans have short attention spans do not match experience. Social "scientists" and others who say that modern attention spans are shorter than before have missed the reason: what they themselves say is darned boring. When something is useful or interesting or entertaining, people—even young ones—listen for as long as it takes. They read and watch movies, plays, concerts, and sporting events for hours on end without their attention dissipating.

So the question is not how long your opening should be, but *how long it continues to provide what jurors understand to be necessary to their work*. Not what *you* think is necessary, but what *they* think is necessary. That's the measure of how long an opening or closing or examination should last. You can find this out in focus groups or by giving your opening to a few people—strangers, preferably—at a time. Watch them, and their reactions will tell you when enough is enough. And afterward ask them how much they think they did not need to hear.

5-18 Eye Contact

In opening, don't say anything unless you have eye contact with one of the jurors. Move your eye contact from juror to juror frequently; no one likes your staring at them. And while words are coming out of your mouth, do not look at the floor or the wall or your notes. Make contact with jurors, not inanimate objects.[19]

5-19 Movement

Stand in one place and talk to the jurors. Move when there's reason to. Jurors are discomfited when counsel bobbles back and forth as if he needs a bathroom pass.

If you have trouble standing in one place and not rocking around or dancing, or if you constantly shift your weight from one leg to the other, practice your opening once or twice wearing just one shoe. Make a video recording of it. Show it to your kids. Their hoots of derision will cure you.

5-20 Rehearse

Rehearse your opening often and over a period of at least a week.

But not in front of a mirror. Video yourself so you can watch later and take notes for improvement. Rehearsing in front of a mirror allows you to make subconscious adjustments as you go that you won't make without the mirror. So you miss some problems.

For best results, rehearse in front of "juries" of people you don't know and who are not in the legal profession. At some of these sessions, first run your

---

19. *See* David Ball, Theater Tips and Strategies, 4 (NITA 2003).

jury voir dire, and then do your opening. Get their reactions afterward. Try to do the last session the night before trial. You'll be amazed how much better you'll feel and do as you get started in trial.

5-20-1 Notes

Do not memorize or you'll sound memorized, which means fake. Nor should you read your opening. Speak from skeletal notes typed large enough to see when you glance at them from a few feet away.

Remember that it's harder to read your notes when they are all in capital letters.

Once you have used this chapter's opening template for a number of openings, you may well find that you no longer need any notes at all to deliver your opening. Amazing, but true.

5-21 LIGHTING

During your opening (or closing), if the blinds are open behind the jury, shut them before the jury gets into the room so you can see the jurors and not just their silhouettes.

For the same reason, if the blinds are open behind you, shut them.

You can always open them later just before the defense gets up to talk.

Chapter Six

Direct Examination

6-1 Mud and Gold (Less Mud = More Gold)

A sure way to kill the momentum of a great opening is to leave unnecessary information in your direct examinations.

Hone all direct testimony down to its essentials, and that is almost always a lot less than you think.

How do you decide what you don't need?

Here's the standard:

Does the juror *need it* for deciding anything on the verdict form?

Not "sort of, I guess" need it. Not "it fills everything in for them." Not "the more they know, the better." You need to define exactly how the juror *needs it* for deciding something on the verdict form.

For example, jurors might need to know that the ABS braking system kept the tires from leaving skid marks: "There were no skid marks because the car had ABS brakes. ABS prevents skidding, which means no skid marks." Unless the defense is going to claim that ABS does not prevent skid marks, you do not need—**so you must omit**—"ABS is a computer-controlled system developed in the late 1980s to provide control in an emergency stopping situation." That's TMI, and TMI kills. (*See* section 5-3-1, p. 113.)

Another example: jurors in medical cases need hardly any medical information. They don't decide negligence your way on the basis of medicine **except insofar as the medicine explains why a rule is a rule** (*see* section 5-5-1, pp. 119*ff.* on rules). Beyond that, too much medical (or any other kind of) information creates needless complexity. "Needless complexity" is a redundant phrase, because complexity in trial is always needless—and lethal. Complexity in trial—which is largely the result of counsel's inability to extract the essentials from the morass of information—keeps jurors from being able to figure things out.

Nothing wrong with that—except for the side with the burden.

For causation, you might need a little more medicine than for negligence. But even then, the battle is not about details of the medicine. It is about why the defense causation witnesses are wrong and yours are right. And that's usually about medical rules of analysis (*see* section 7-1, p. 205).

6-1-1 Gold Standard for Inclusion

With medical or any other kind of information, if a juror can use it to argue down another juror in deliberations, include it. Otherwise, exclude it.

I see too many "warm-ups" at the start of testimony—three or four minutes of useless questions and answers. There's no better way to get jurors bored with your witness. And once they're bored, they stop listening.

I also see the results of too many lazy preparations. You need to know everything the witness has to say so you don't have to waste trial time digging around for what you need.

In other words, direct exam means getting to the point and not asking a single question that elicits anything that is not directly to the point.

When you start asking off-course questions aimed at, say, giving the jury some "background," you're asking for trouble. Jurors neither need nor want background.

Video

Direct exam on video must be even shorter. Remove everything you don't need, especially at the start. On video, you need to make your important points within the first ten or twelve minutes or the jury will barely hear them. Video testimony is almost always unbearably boring.

Experts

You spent lots of time and money gathering everything your experts have to say. So it's easy to think the jury needs it all, too. They don't. They need hardly any of it. As with all else, LESS IS MORE. To undermine a terrific expert, just have him say more than the essential minimum.

In brief: In preparing for witness examination, you need to spend as much effort deciding what you should not ask as on what you should ask.

6-1-2 First Witness

Your first witness should come as close as possible to meeting the four criteria:

1. *Provides overview.* She should be able to tell some significant part (not necessarily the largest part) of the overall story: either what the defendant did or the results of what the defendant did. Unless the defense opening made effective headway in showing that your client did something wrong, your first witness should not talk about what your client did. Lead off with what the defendant did. Your second witness can talk about how that violated safety rules.

   For example, your first witness can have seen the defendant truck driver following your client's car only a few feet behind. And witness #2 can be an expert, explaining why following too close violates a rule that is far more important for large trucks than cars.

2. *Introduces the harm.* Your first witness should be able to speak at least a little to the harm that was done—such as seeing how hard the car hit your client or hearing his screaming.

3. *No stake in outcome.* Your first witnesses should have no stake in the outcome.

4. *Cross-proof.* Your first witness *must* be cross-proof. Your opponent's cross-examination of your first witness is the first time jurors see your case tested in cross-examination, the crucible of truth. Jurors are primed to create their first belief about your credibility. Your longer-term trustworthiness is on the line.

   If your witness holds up under cross, the jurors' initial belief will be that you are credible. If the cross-exam shows holes in your claims, the jurors' initial belief will be that you are not altogether credible. Due to primacy (*see* section 4-2-1, pp. 82*ff.*), that initial belief will linger and even strengthen throughout trial. It can diminish all you say and present. So no matter how much of an overview of your case a witness can provide, do not use her first if she can be impeached in any significant way.

   The ideal first witness is one whom you know the defense will try hard—and fail—to undermine in cross. Next best is simply one who has nothing to be crossed about. Worst: Anyone even mildly impeachable. In a first witness, that's enough to inject permanent doubt into your case.

6-2 Controlling Your Witness on Direct ("~~What happened next?~~")

Years ago, Court-TV anchor and inspirational attorney Rikki Klieman taught me a profoundly simple way to keep your direct exam witnesses from running off ad infinitum and endangering the focus of their testimony.

Here's the unfortunately common direct exam:

> Q: What did the truck do?
>
> A: Went through the red light.
>
> Q: **What happened next?**

You wanted the witness to focus on: "He hit the blue car." You wanted to follow up with: "Had the blue car blown its horn?" But that point gets buried as the witness charges ahead:

> A: [*off and running*] He hit the blue car, and it bounced over on its side, and then everyone was screaming until the ambulance came, but the police got there first, and they were bleeding all over the place and . . .

This mess happened because you asked, "What happened next?" **Don't ever ask that question again.**

Instead:

> Q: What did the truck do?
>
> A: Went through the red light.
>
> Q: **After the truck went through the red light, what was the first thing that happened?**

This wording gets the witness to provide *only* the information you want.

> A: The truck hit the blue car.

And if the witness leaves something out, ask:

> Q: What happened between the time the truck ran the light and when it hit the car?
>
> A: Oh. The blue car blew its horn.

By specifying the exact instant that you want your witness to talk about, you control direct without seeming to. And the more you control direct, the better you can limit it to the essentials of what the jurors need to know.[1]

---

[1] **"What, if anything . . .?"** One of the most cloying, unnecessary lawyer-phrases is "What, if anything . . . ." As in "What, if anything, did you see next?" This is never any reason for this

6-3 SHORT QUESTIONS

The best direct exam questions, like good cross-exam questions, are short! The longer your question, the less impact the answer will have. If you can't ask your direct exam question in a dozen words or so, you haven't thought it through.

6-4 DON'T MAKE YOUR CLIENT A WHINER

Try not to use your client as a main source of testimony about harms or he'll seem like a whiner, even if he does not whine. Jurors don't like people complaining about their own problems—no matter how justified.

Sometimes you can be lucky and your client will do a good, nonwhining job. But that's rare. You increase the odds by properly preparing your client, but few lawyers do so. The best guidance on this topic comes from Don Keenan (*see Reptile*, chapter seventeen, as well as *Reptile Witness Preparation DVD* from ReptileKeenanBall.com.) But even with a well-prepared client, the more you have others talk about the harms to him, the better.

Ideally, your client should talk about how he transcends or transcended his harms. Americans love fighters, not whiners. So, "She can walk as much as a hundred feet" is stronger than "She can walk only a hundred feet." The legendary Moe Levine, a powerful voice of good sense in the courtroom, advised lawyers to talk less about what their client *lost* and more about what she still has. Your client (and others) can effectively talk about this. It shows her will to fight rather than give up. It is, even in the lowliest of human beings, a kind of leadership charisma that we all admire.

When there is permanent harm that seriously interferes with how your client lives her life, ask her what her long-term plans had been before she was hurt. Then ask her how she is pursuing the fragment of those plans she is still able to pursue. This shows her to be unwilling to give up.

---

awkward, pretentious phrase. "What, if anything, is your name?" is no sillier than "What, if anything, did you see next?"

6-5 How Does that Make You Feel?

Jurors cringe when you ask your client how she feels about her lost plans or injuries. If you need your client to explain how she feels about the loss, then you have done badly at describing the loss.

> Q: How do you feel at not being able to become a nurse?
>
> A: Bad.
>
> Q: Why?
>
> A: Because I wanted to become a nurse.

On that basis you're gonna ask for money? Good luck.

Instead:

> Q: Why did you want to become a nurse?
>
> A: I wanted to help people.
>
> Q: Tell us about that.
>
> A: My parents taught me that the highest calling was to help others.

Later, ask her mom why being a nurse was so important to your client. Mom says:

> Lots of reasons. Mainly, her dad would have died in Vietnam if someone had not helped him. So from the day her dad came home, he preached helping others. She wanted to do that by being a nurse. Now she can't, and I know she feels like she's letting her dad down.

Now the case is not just about your client feeling "bad." It's deeper, sadder, and realer. And your client was not the one to talk about it, so she's no whiner. There is something admirable and worthwhile about her. So to jurors, money for her will be more worthwhile than for a whiner.

6-6 Spouse

Testimony from the spouse can be helpful, often essential. But the spouse has an obvious interest in how the case turns out. You need others to corroborate who stand to gain nothing from the verdict. This can include neighbors, co-workers, friends, clergy, and anyone else in a position to know the situation. Look for those who know the harm and can best communicate it. The easy or obvious choice is not always the best. Audition your possibilities.

6-7 Before and After Witnesses

You need witnesses who can describe your client in his pre-injury state, and witnesses for after the injury. Sometimes one person can do both; often, you will have different witnesses for each.

Too often, attorneys tell me they "couldn't find any of those witnesses who have nothing to gain by a good verdict." This means, "I didn't look very hard." **These are must-have witnesses.**

6-8 How Many?

In most cases, use no fewer harms witnesses than liability witnesses. Three or four is OK for a small case. In larger or longer cases, use ten or fifteen. Different people see different things about the situation, so no need for this to be repetitious. Keep their examinations brief; you are building a mosaic of different points from each witness. Three hours filled by fifteen such witnesses is more credible and effective than three hours filled by one or two witnesses.

Exception: If you are working with a Reptilian approach where the harms are not very great, your main focus should be on how the kinds of rules-breaking the defendant committed are dangerous. And diminish the focus on the harms. (*See Reptile*, chapter nineteen.)

6-9 Stories

Good harms testimony is story-based. A witness who merely reports abstractly or in generalized conclusions ("She can't do much any more" or "She's unhappy now") is hardly worth having.

So when a witness says, "She had incredible energy before; now she's tired all the time," take him the next step: "Can you give us an example of her incredible energy?" and "What have you seen since she was hurt that shows she's always tired now?"

Jurors remember mini-stories:

> We'd all go shopping, and she'd make me go into every store in the mall. During Christmas shopping the year before she got hurt, her sisters and me and the kids finally just dropped our packages and collapsed and couldn't move. She kept right on going. The kids called her our Energizer shopping bunny. But last week I took her to the mall. She was so wiped out from just getting there that she could only sit on a bench with her head drooped over while I shopped.

The defense can't wipe out that mini-story or diminish its effectiveness.

In venues where wrongful death claims include losses to survivors, your witnesses should tell mini-stories illustrating the differences in the family before and after the death. The jurors already know the general kind of loss any surviving family undergoes; you need mini-stories for specifics.

In death or severe-injury cases, one effective kind of mini-story is for each affected person to describe where she was and what she was doing when she first heard what happened—and what she did right after.

North Carolina attorney Don Beskind suggests getting family members to talk about your client's past role in specific family events, such as decorating the tree or carving the turkey—and tell a mini-story of what happened the first time your client could not do that or was no longer alive to do it.

Loss of life's treasures is not about losing unusual things. Loss of everyday, mundane things is more important. But it takes a story form to give power to anything mundane.

6-10 Hollow Advocacy

Among the hollowest of advocacy moments can be when counsel says, in opening, that his client has lost one of her great pleasures—say, gardening. The moment is hollow when counsel clearly has no idea what gardening is about or how anyone could possibly love it. He barely knows where it is done.

Talking about the gravity of a loss does not gain power just because you say it forcefully. *You have to know and feel what you are talking about.* If you don't know—from experience—how and why people cherish gardening (or whatever), go find out. Ask half a dozen people to tell you about it. Go to the garden with one of them and ask them to tell you what they've done there.

Your hollow mouthing of losses can profoundly undermine their value to the jury. And it makes you kind of hypocritical, which can turn even the friendliest of jurors into enemies. So if you don't deeply know what you're talking about, either find out or don't talk about it.

6-11 Witnesses as Sources of Worthwhileness

Use direct to suggest worthwhile uses for money. (*See* Fundamental Seven, p. 24.)

Ask everyone who knows the situation—your client, potential witnesses, and even others who may not actually testify—what good money might do beyond paying care and living expenses. While most answers will not be useful, some will be persuasive.

I asked the neighbor of a West Virginia quadriplegic plaintiff the following question: "He'll never heal, so what's the point of money beyond care and living expenses?" This neighbor was not going to be a witness; all he knew about the case was that the plaintiff was paralyzed. But he had an answer:

> Eddie loved hunting. He never shot anything, I don't think, but he loved those woods. Now he's stuck inside this city apartment forever. If he had some money, his wife could buy a mountain place where she could wheel him onto the back porch every day, and he'd at least be back out in the woods he loves.

Few jurors would turn a deaf ear to that.

A New Jersey plaintiff had reflex sympathy dystrophy in her arm. The slightest touch was excruciating. I asked her, "What good can money do you? Your pain won't go away."

She said:

> I miss my grandchildren. They live out West. They're too young to fly to see me, so I have to go there. But I never know from one day to the next when I'll be well enough to fly. So I can't get cheap advance-purchase tickets any more. Even if I could, the aisles on the plane are so narrow that I can't take the chance that the stewardess might bump my arm as she goes by. Or whoever's sitting next to me could accidentally do it. It's too painful, and it happens all the time. If I had enough money for a wider seat up front, and if I didn't need an advance purchase cheap ticket but could buy the ticket on a day when I felt well enough to travel that day instead of having to guess weeks in advance, I could go see my grandchildren.

All by itself, this will not get you a huge verdict. But a few things like this can give a large intangibles damages request some worthwhile substance. The more you show how money can help—beyond providing care and replacing lost income—the more you are likely to get.

Spend time with family members. At first they will usually have few suggestions, but after some discussion they'll likely start to think of things: "My husband lies awake. I ask what's wrong; he says he's worrying about how to pay for the kids' college now that he can't work anymore."

No element of damages goes to paying the kids' tuition. But because the husband's worry is a consequence of the wrongdoing, you can show what he is worried about. You can argue in closing that therapy cannot fix this particular harm—his worrying—but that the jury can fix it with money. Money to remove worry is worthwhile. So jurors are likely to include it in their verdict.

It can take creativity to get some of these ideas into evidence, but you can almost always do it. It is worth doing, because they show how money for your client is worthwhile.

6-12 Sequence of Witnesses: Damages Witnesses

If your opening did its job (*see* chapter five), you need not clump all your damages witnesses at the end of your case-in-chief. Instead, keep harm and money on the jurors' minds throughout your case-in-chief—alternate between loss/harm/money witnesses and liability witnesses.

6-13 Children

Children, even small children, are sometimes good witnesses to a plaintiff's losses. This can make for effective testimony. But some jurors will have problems with your bringing a child to court.

Be careful not to appear to be exploiting the child or to be putting the child through anything jurors might construe as hurtful or harmful. Treat that child in court as if she were your own and you were an excellent, gentle parent.

In some venues, wrongful death losses include, or are limited to, the dead person's losses. Connecticut's Ernie Teitel advises that in such a situation, it can be especially useful to bring in the deceased's children—but not to have them speak of their losses. Instead, have them describe, in an upbeat way, what their lives are like: what they do at school, in sports, in clubs; what their achievements have been; what their future plans are—because these are some of the most valuable things the deceased has missed out on. This can be excellent testimony because you can keep it entirely upbeat and positive, and that makes the losses more excruciating.

This is far more powerful than the attorney mouthing shallowness like, "He'll never see his daughter's graduation or her marriage or . . . ."

6-14 Grief and Pain Counselors[2]

Grief counselors, disability counselors, pain counselors and specialists, and other counselors and therapists who specialize in the emotional, psychological, and other consequences of suffering and loss can be excellent sources for information to help your damages case.

---

2. *See* Robert Hall & Mila Ruiz Tecala, Grief and Loss: Identifying and Proving Damages in Wrongful Death Cases (Trial Guides 2010).

By studying your case, these experts can find and explain the hidden harms and provide insights into the injury's worst consequences: the pain, the emotional suffering, the grieving, the long-term consequences, and how things will get worse instead of better. These experts provide information you cannot get from your clients, their acquaintances, other experts or treating physicians, or your own analysis. This information is often central to the jury's calculation of damages.

Merely saying, "It's ten on a scale of ten" no more describes pain than "dinner was good" describes dinner. Jurors need more.

You can use pain or grieving counselors as witnesses or just as a pretrial resource to educate you. Either way, they add professional and scientific authority—and thus tangibleness—to the subject of intangible losses. They can also help you understand how to best communicate the severity of your client's problems.

6-15 MINIMUM LIFE-CARE PLANS (AND EQUIVALENTS)

Jurors usually base their noneconomic damages amount in large part on the economic amount. Using the economic amount as a benchmark, they discuss noneconomics as some proportion of that amount. So the higher, the more concrete, and the more persuasive your economic damages figure is, the more money you are likely to get for noneconomics as well. (The reverse is also true: a low economic figure can drag down the noneconomic figure. *See* section 2-5, p. 55.)

One of your most important damages figures can be the minimum life-care plan or an equivalent list. (In cases with no life-care plan, you can assemble a list: everything the treating physicians say will be—or was—necessary or helpful to treat and care for your client.)

Aside from helping you get more money, care lists help show the extent of the harm.

The suggestions below assume the presence of a full-blown life-care plan. With a less formal list, you can use many of the same strategies.

6-15-1 Don't Rush Life-Care Plan Testimony

The defense hopes you will. The defense prefers you to leave the jury with only a vague idea of the plan's content. This almost always results in jurors considering the life-care plan in the same way they think about noneconomic damages: fuzzy stuff to be bargained over, a kind of prize for the plaintiff instead of a necessity. So jurors compromise on its size.

Jurors tend to fight for giving the full amount of a life-care plan when they understand everything in it and know what happens if your client doesn't get each particular care item. This means that for each key item, your expert must explain:

1. What it's for.
2. When it was invented, and why (how widespread and serious a problem it solved).
3. How it works.
4. Why your client needs it.
5. How much it costs (per each and over the term of the plan) and why there's no cheaper substitute.
6. **What happens if the plaintiff does not get it** (focus on medical and safety consequences).

Treat each important item on the life-care plan as a separate issue to be proven.

You might want to explain in voir dire or opening that this section of trial will take a while because so much is needed to take care of your client—and the jurors need to know about all of it in order to figure out how much money to provide. Build that same point into an early question to your minimum life-care planner: "These folks have to figure out what Sally needs and how much money to provide for it, so let me start by asking you . . . ."

Your life-care planner can be an important centerpiece. Put her on for the better part of a day. In long trials, continue her direct into a second day. Don't let her testimony get buried.

6-15-2 Show-and-Tell

Turn your life-care planner's testimony into a show-and-tell. That keeps her testimony interesting and makes each of the care needs more concrete to the jury. Have her bring things to court—the leg braces, the special dinnerware, the Velcro fasteners for clothing, the urinary catheter, etc. Pass these things around the jury. Rub them with alcohol pads beforehand so that jurors will be comfortable handling them and the room will smell like a clinic.

Have your life-care planner teach the jury what these things are for—especially how they are used. Have her show videos of the kinds of therapy in her plan. Show a video tour of the rehabilitation center.

Lazy life-care planners bring a catalogue of the necessary items. That's not good enough. A good life-care planner probably needs to drive a large van to haul all her stuff.

6-15-3 Edit the Plan

Before presenting a minimum life-care plan, edit carefully. Omit anything that might seem unnecessary or frivolous. Even if there is good reason for that swimming pool, you might be better off getting rid of it. It can undermine the rest of the plan's validity. You want jurors to have total confidence in everything in the plan. Otherwise they can easily compromise the full figure way below the items they don't think are necessary.

For the same reason, make sure the plan's prices seem reasonable. Some items are expensive only when purchased from a medical supply house. That $350 canvas chair might cost $19.95 in a regular store. A minimum life-care plan with seemingly overpriced items undermines juror confidence in your entire damages case and even in your liability case. So scrutinize for reasonable prices. Your planner is the planning expert, but you are the jury expert.

Please see section 8-9, p. 227*ff*, on how to bring your plan home in closing. It's an essential ingredient.

6-16 USING LIABILITY WITNESSES FOR DAMAGES

One of the dangers of fighting a difficult liability case is that jurors can go for hours, days, and sometimes weeks without hearing about harm or money. This undermines your pursuit of one of the basic principles of damages: time proportion. Out of sight, out of mind. Using your liability experts for damages is one effective way to offset that problem.

Your liability expert who testifies about why the light pole's location was dangerous can provide statistics about the number and nature of severe injuries such placement has caused.

If your expert physician who testifies about standard of care can explain why that particular standard of care exists and the kind of harm it is intended to prevent, he can probably talk about the mechanism of the injury that results from the violation (because that's the kind of injury the standard was designed to prevent).

6-17 DAY-IN-THE-LIFE VIDEOS

Day-in-the-life videos are effective when they focus on the obstacles your client has to (or had to) face. But beware. Jurors' most common reaction to most day-in-the-life videos is something like: "He's *not as bad* as I expected from what they said." Result: lower verdict. So always test your day-in-the-life video with a focus group to see its effect. Skip this and you risk turning your costly video into a far more costly blunder.

6-17-1 "Staged!"

Don't show anything in a day-in-the-life that looks staged. One video showed a woman who had had the use of only one arm for two years struggling to open a jar of peanut butter. She tried several maneuvers that failed. Finally she discovered a way to do it. The camera "caught" it all.

"Obviously staged!" crowed the jurors. And they were right. Obviously the woman did not actually discover how to open peanut butter while the camera just happened to be there and running. This undermined the jurors' confidence in the video, the client's injuries, the attorney, and the case.

6-17-2 Videographer

A human being does not develop into a videographer just by owning a video camera. Before hiring someone who calls himself a videographer, look at samples of his work. Make sure he knows the basics—such as how to expose properly so that faces are easily visible. And make sure he knows the *feel* of a day-in-the-life video: emphasis on the obstacles, the pain, the difficult measures necessary to get through the day. He also needs to know the enormous difference between showing facts and fishing for sympathy. And he needs to know how to convey all of this in ten minutes or less.

6-17-3 Time Span

Videographers are often too literal about what "day-in-the-life" means. It need not end at the end of the day if there are night problems.

6-17-4 Stranger in the House

Before starting to shoot, the videographer should have spent a good amount of informal, relaxed time getting to know the client and family and letting them get to know him. Otherwise the resulting video can show your folks at their worst.

6-17-5 Comfort

Many people—especially older people—are uncomfortable on camera. So it is best to shoot over the course of two or three days. (But don't shoot too much; *see* Edit, *then* Shoot below.)

6-17-6 Lighting

Avoid extra lighting unless absolutely necessary. Good video cameras produce good results even in low light, especially with a videographer who knows how to take advantage of existing natural and artificial light that is already part of the room. And if some of the shots are somewhat underlit, that adds to their veracity as long as we can see what is going on.

6-17-7 Windows

A videographer who puts his subjects between the camera and a bright window or other bright light source will produce useless silhouettes, not striking images. A competent videographer never does this. Look for this danger sign when you view a videographer's sample work before hiring.

6-17-8 Sound

If you're allowed sound in your video, it can be effective—or it can undermine you. When watching the finished product, listen carefully to make sure the sound helps. Dad cursing at the kids in the next room while mom lovingly helps the disabled child may not be the family image you wish to convey.

6-17-9 Background

Be careful what your video shows in the background or periphery. The injured child can be getting rehabilitative therapy in the living room on an exercise mat. Very effective—unless the exercise mat is in front of the family's seventy-inch TV, evidence that the last thing this family needs is money. (Especially with the Jaguar in the driveway outside the picture window.)

And regardless of the TV's size, turn it off. Even if people are watching one in the next room, turn it off. Or have the volume at such a low level—too low to understand—that it seems like part of the daily routine. You don't want jurors paying more attention to what the family watches on TV than to your client.

6-17-10 Jurors Judge a Family Partly by the Family's Home

Make sure what the jurors see of the home on the video conveys the impression you want. You need not show abject poverty. But if your day-in-the-life video shows an extravagant lifestyle—like that seventy-inch TV—jurors will conclude that this family needs no money to take care of Junior. Instead, have your videographer focus on elements that show a caring home and normal lifestyle. This is especially important when you are fighting for home care while the defense wants the jury to settle for institutional care.

6-17-11 Edit, then Shoot

Ernie Teitel cautions that you should plan carefully *before* you start shooting the day-in-the-life video so there is hardly any excess video you have to turn over to the defense. In other words, *advance edit*. A five-minute video is almost always enough, so try to do it without shooting much more than those five minutes.

6-17-12 Settlement Conferences, Mediations

A reliable day-in-the-life video (one that has been tested in front of lay strangers) can be powerful at a settlement conference—especially if the defendant and not just the defense attorneys and insurance adjusters are there. In fact, if the defendant has control over settlement, you should *demand* that he be there so he can feel the impact of your settlement presentation and not just leave it to his lawyers and the insurance company, whose concerns are usually not the same as the defendant's.[3]

6-17-13 Show a Day-in-the-Life Video That Is 100 Percent Admissible

Your settlement video can go farther, to some extent, but the day-in-the-life should be a realistic threat.

In mediation conferences, whether showing a day-in-the-life or a mediation video, ixnay on the drippy, sappy, sentimental announcers and soft-focus views and emotional cross-fades and all the other soap-opera gimmicks! Especially get rid of the syrupy music. That stuff fools no one.

6-18 SHOULD YOUR CLIENT BE IN TRIAL?

One of the long-taught "basics" of trial advocacy is that your client should be present during trial. But reconsider. Instead of a "client-in-trial" default, start with a "*no*-client-in-trial" default. Then see if you can come up with good reasons why she should be there.

Be particularly careful when your client looks better than she really is—as is the case with most clients with brain damage and other kinds of invisible or barely visible problems. In those circumstances, it is probably best that your client never enter the courthouse. Verdicts almost always go down when jurors see such clients.

For example, your brain-damaged client can do OK on the stand and even withstand a forceful cross, despite your claim that she cannot think or remember well enough to keep a job. Jurors say, "She looks great, and

---

3. For essential guidance on how to approach settlement conferences, ADR, and mediations, see *Reptile*, chapter sixteen.

she remembered all that stuff on direct, and she handled cross-examination better than I could. Her attorney and those 'experts' must be lying about brain damage."

Even if your client never takes the stand, she's going to look just fine sitting at your table, possibly taking notes, talking during recesses, looking happy, seeming normal in every way. That can have an enormous effect on your verdict.

In deciding whether or not (or how much) your client should be in trial, don't worry that the jury will "expect" her to be there or that they'll think her absence means she does not care about her case. Explain that her doctors and family say it's better for her not to be in trial and be forced to relive everything all over again. Jurors will not fault her absence. Rarely will one think, "I have to be here so why isn't she?"

Keeping your client out of trial seems counterintuitive. But we know it's effective if only because when the defense finds out, they try to get the judge to force her to be there. The defense knows how powerfully your client's "OK" appearance works against her. They want jurors to see that she looks and sounds normal—even though how she looks and sounds is a deceptive measure of her harm.

Some judges approve defense motions or subpoenas to force your client to be there. Be prepared to fight.

Show that there's nothing probative about her being there—that her presence provides only a visual impression that not even an expert can correctly evaluate, and that can only mislead a layperson.

Point out that the only possible reason the defense wants her there is precisely so the jurors will be misled.

Point out (by means of an expert affidavit) that there is no reasonable way that anyone—especially not a layperson—can gauge by your client's appearance whether or not she is as harmed as her doctors say she is. In other words, how she looks is a scientifically invalid determinant.

Point out (by means of expert affidavit) that it would be malpractice for a medical professional to arrive at *any* opinions one way or the other based on how she looks and that how she looks offers no clue one way or the other *even when considered in light of other information.*

Argue that the defense has no right to inflict more harm on your client for no legitimate purpose. Forcing her to be in trial will make her relive the trauma, hear and dwell on how hopeless her condition is, and undergo needless public humiliation. Submit affidavits from her doctors affirming the harm her being there will cause her. Such harms could be considered the costs of litigation when they are legitimate to the process—but the way she looks is not any legitimate part of any process.

Unless your client is needed for testimony, her presence or absence should be none of the defense's business, and none of the judge's, either. Even if the judge decides that how she looks is probative, just as with every other kind of evidence it's no less probative if she's there just for a few minutes—so there's no cause for her to be there throughout trial. If how she looks is probative, the defense can put it on the stand, not keep it on display throughout trial. (It's no different from your having to take down your exhibits when you're not using them.)

Some years ago, a judge forced a five-year-old paralyzed little girl to be present throughout the entire trial. If there's a judge heaven and a judge hell, I have no doubt which will house that particular creep.

6-18-1 Preparing the Jury for a Client Who Seems Less Harmed than She Is

If the defense subpoenas your client to testify or is going to show her video deposition, or if you decide to have her appear in court, or if the judge forces her to be there, have your experts explain to the jury *in advance* why she seems to be so much better than she really is.

Do not position this in a defensive way, but as a serious harm in itself. A person with brain damage or other harm that cannot be seen is constantly thrust into situations she cannot handle. The expectations people place on her—that she's normal and can do normal things—often result in painfully humiliating situations. People don't expect a person missing a leg to walk or run, because they can see that the leg is missing. But people routinely expect a person missing millions of brain cells to think normally because they cannot see that the cells are missing. This is a large reason why brain-damaged people slowly withdraw from society. They're in constant fear of being humiliated because they can't do commonplace things like remember how to get home from downtown.

Treat this humiliation and the enforced isolation it leads to as the compensable harm it is. For example, have your experts explain why someone with brain damage can look good and talk cogently, how that leads to enforced isolation, and how enforced isolation can be one of the worst effects of brain damage or almost any other kind of serious condition. Explaining all this *before the jury sees and hears your client* turns your client's later testimony and how she looks into an effective illustration of your expert's explanation. It turns your client into a demonstrative exhibit that helps instead of hurts.

Still, you don't want such a client in front of the jury any longer than necessary.

And of course, even if your client is never in the courthouse, you should still claim compensation for this kind of harm. Isolation and the inability to move freely in one's community really are among the worst of harms.

6-19 CLIENT IN AND OUT OF TRIAL

All the world's a stage—and jurors are the ubiquitous audience. Instruct your client that from the week before trial until the verdict is in, he must assume that every time he goes out of his house jurors will see him. Smoking, drinking, rudeness, or anything else you would not want jurors to see in trial should be strictly avoided in public at all times—even in the next state, and no matter the time.

Obviously—or perhaps it's not so obvious, judging by some of the things we've seen—this especially includes trying to do things you are claiming he cannot do.

6-19-1 *Driving?*

Are you claiming deficits for your client that would make him a dangerous driver? Lack of decision-making ability in an emergency? Poor eyesight? Yet he's driving? That makes him selfish and uncaring of others.

It will be bad enough for jurors to *hear* that he's still driving. So make him stop. But if jurors actually see him behind the wheel, the reaction can range from disgust to anger: he's either a fraud or a danger to the entire community. Jurors love neither.

Often the client's family will say, "But driving is the only freedom he has left!" So what? No one cares; your client is a menace to the community. "If we give him money he'll express his damned freedom by buying a Corvette! Uh-uh. Not in *my* town!"

So get your client's driver's license and keys away from him. Failing that, hire someone to steal the car or slash the tires. (I think I am kidding.)

6-19-2 Counsel (You)

You, too, must be careful how you behave outside the courtroom. Assume there's a juror in every car you see. That includes the jerk who just cut in front of you and slowed down.

For the duration of trial, wave motorists into your lane of traffic, don't steal anyone's parking space, and in every other way pretend to be a mature and generous adult. And unless you live within the relative anonymity of a big city, be that way all the time.

6-20 THE BEST AND CHEAPEST EXPERTS: HIGH-SCHOOL TEACHERS

Every community has a supply of first-rate expert witnesses—high-school teachers—who can testify as experts on many topics. Explore this resource especially (but not exclusively) for smaller cases where you have no money to bring in the usual high-priced array. For between $50 and $100 an hour you can often solve some of the biggest problems in your case.

For example, the defendant hit the rear of your client's car at only nine miles per hour. No dents. So jurors will say things like "My Uncle Benny's car rolled over three times, it was flattened to a pancake, and Uncle Benny walked out just fine. So how can someone be hurt as bad as this lawyer claims in a car that's got hardly a dent?"

The defense lawyer will say the same thing if you don't move to prevent him from making scientific conclusions on the basis of no scientific evidence. An inference from evidence is not allowed if it is a scientific conclusion that has not been offered in evidence by an expert—especially when it is junk science. It should not be up to the jury to decide if no dents means no injury unless an expert has provided legitimate science.

If you had the money to bring in an accident reconstructionist or a physicist, you could convince jurors that this little no-dent rear-ender can result in plenty of injury. You could bring in a forensic epidemiologist to show how frequently it happens. But when the case can't afford it, you can't do it. Result? You win liability and get a verdict of a dollar or two.

So what can you do?

Use a high-school teacher. All he has to do is explain (and perhaps demonstrate) a principle or a process. Good high-school teachers know how to relate to the people they are teaching. They bring with them more credibility—especially locally—than many professional witnesses. And high-school teachers are often more cooperative and easier to work with.

Good high-school teachers are experts at teaching complex concepts to people who know nothing about them and don't particularly want to learn. They are usually better at this than the high-priced experts. And most are certainly more credible. Who ya gonna believe—the local high-school teacher you entrust your kids to? Or the high-priced gouger you have to import?

A well-selected local high-school physics teacher can explain how a nine-mile-an-hour impact can leave barely a dent on the car, but still injure people inside. "You would never put your hand between those cars as they hit. There's too much force. Now, that force has to go someplace. It can't just disappear. Much of it goes into abruptly shoving the car forward. The less dent, the more forcefully it shoves the car forward, because making a dent would absorb more of the energy. So a smaller dent means the shove forward was stronger. So strong it can bounce a head back and forth hard enough to damage anyone's neck. Here, look at this." And he shows his Mr. Wizard demonstration.

What Mr. Wizard demonstration? For a few hundred dollars, the teacher can devise and build a Mr. Wizard demonstration of how the force of impact goes from the back bumper to moving your client's neck. Such a show-and-tell demonstration makes it easier for jurors to believe that a low-speed rear impact can injure the driver.

You'll use that Mr. Wizard demonstration along with this high-school teacher in case after case—for a fraction of the cost of far less persuasive "professionals."

Or bring in the high-school driver's ed teacher, who teaches his students how many people are thrown out of work and into severe pain every year by those low-speed collisions. These are the facts that trump the defense claims that "no one gets hurt at such a slow speed."

Closing: "Don't you think if the defense could have found even one qualified teacher anywhere in the country to come say that no one gets hurt in a nine-mile-per-hour crash, they'd have done it?"

6-21 Paid Plaintiff's Experts

When the defense asks how much your expensive (or inexpensive) expert is being paid, the defense's sole purpose is to impeach your expert by attacking her motive for testifying. This should open the door to you showing your expert's real motives.

So on redirect, ask your expert about her real motives—motives such as:

> With 650 people a day dying in hospitals from negligence, those of us doctors who care about good medicine participate in trials like this—when we are certain that medical negligence caused the harm.

Or,

> I know how they design cars in Detroit; I worked there twenty-five years. Too much of it is careless and purely profit driven, and so it kills too many people. So when I see a case like this, where someone was killed because of that kind of thing, I want to help a jury set things right.

Such motivation can also explain why this expert testifies so often for plaintiffs: "The companies don't need me. They already know what they're doing wrong."

The key is that the defense opened the door to your expert explaining her real motives—regardless of the usual admissibility of those motives.

6-22 How to Use Experts

(Show this section to your expert.)

In itself, an expert's conclusion is usually not worth much to you. Nor is her sensational CV. Even taken together, conclusions plus credentials are far less persuasive than you may think. The defense often gets away with inferior experts because the defense merely needs to sow some seeds of doubt. We actually have to prove things.

So we need a lot more than conclusions and credentials.

Your expert must explain the **step-by-step process of analysis required to come to a valid conclusion**. In other words, there are rules—steps—by which an expert must do her analysis. This is her required methodology. You need an expert who knows and can clearly explain those step-by-step rules in lay terms, apply them to the case, and then use them to explain what's wrong with the defense claims.

For example, the first required rule/step in almost every kind of expert analysis is to **adopt a neutral stance**.

Rule/step two is to gather all the available information.

Rule/step three is to validate the accuracy of the information.

From there on the rules/steps vary according to the expert's field and the particular task to be accomplished. For example, rule/step four might be to enlist relevant textual or consult-level input.

Without knowing all the rules/steps the expert must follow, why they are necessary, how they are accomplished in this case, *and how the defense expert failed to follow one or more of them*, jurors have no secure way of weighing your experts against the defense's. So jurors resort to irrelevant measures ("I liked him better") or, more often, ignore both sides' experts. Since you have the burden and most of the worst juror biases, you must give jurors the way to favor your expert. In this situation, credentials border on useless. You need the step-by-step process of analysis (the rules of the expert's road) from raw fact through to conclusion.

Here's the testimony sequence:

1. Methodology

Have your expert explain her methodology—her step-by-step process for analyzing cases like this in general, not just for this particular case. This anchors her expertise and methodology.

Her explanation must be clear enough for a juror to instantly learn well enough to take home to his very average fourteen-year-old kid. An expert who cannot be that clear should not be allowed on the stand.

Your expert should explain why each step is important:

- What good does the step do?
- How would omitting that step or doing it badly invalidate a conclusion? (For example, why is it dangerous to begin analysis without the required first step of starting from a neutral stance? Isn't science science? How does starting from a biased stance affect scientific conclusions? And what can go wrong when the expert does not gather all the available information?)

The expert should provide examples—not related to the case, but rather analogies for purposes of explanation—of what goes wrong when someone omits or improperly executes a step and what kind of wrong conclusion it can lead to (such as the defense "expert's" opinion!).

Your expert should also explain how each step has been established in the field and provide any other validation for it (standard of care, scientific method, etc.).

So the first thing for your expert to prove is *how her job must be done*, why it must be done that way, and that when someone does the job wrong, the result will be wrong.

If your expert does this in plain English, concisely, without condescension, and with the presentation style of a caring teacher, jurors will enjoy it. And they will quickly come to like their teacher.

Once jurors understand why each rule/step must be followed, the defense "expert" will later either have to agree or look bad. It's Friedman's and Malone's *Rules of the Road*—but applied to experts instead of defendants.

And as *Reptile* teaches, an "expert" who ignores the rules of her own discipline to help a defendant get away with negligence amounts to a community menace.

This means the process begins in discovery. Meet with your expert early so she can teach you the rules/steps soon enough for you to find out before trial how well the defense expert followed them. This allows you to ask the defense expert such questions as:

Q: What was your first step?

He probably won't know that it's the expert putting himself in a neutral frame of mind. So when you tell him, ask him if he agrees it's necessary. Then:

Q: So before starting your analysis, what did you do to place yourself in a neutral frame of mind?

Q: What precautions did you take to make sure your analysis would be neutral?

Q: Even though you would have been hired for today only if you gave the defense the answer they wanted?

Q: And you are paid more for testifying in trial than for reviewing the case in your office?

Do the same with each of the other rules/steps.

Your expert's methodology is your best way to show why your expert is right and the defense expert is wrong. It transforms the battle of conclusions into a battle of who did it right and who did it wrong.

Did the defendant's expert gather and look at *all* the available information—or only information that would allow him to get to the defense's conclusion? After all, your expert has taught the jury this rule: "When trying to decide a cause of harm, a doctor [*or whatever*] must gather and look at all the available information." It is often easy to show that the defense expert did not gather or look at all the available information. (Be sure yours has!)

It's a great one-two punch: treat your expert's methodology as a specific issue in question and prove its necessity and validity beyond the shadow of a doubt. Then show how the defense expert violated the rules of that methodology.

As with establishing any kind of rule, start by validating the methodology rules without referring to your specific case. Always begin by showing the rules to be true beyond the narrow conditions of your particular case.

2. Methodology Applied

Only after your expert has explained each methodology rule independent of this case, have her fill in *how she used each rule/step on the facts of this case*. Have her take the jury on the step-by-step journey from raw facts to conclusion. When a jury understands the rules/steps, and then can plug in to each step what your expert did, doubt does not much enter their minds. This is because they are learning how to do the analysis for themselves, not simply being asked to take someone's word for it.

As your expert is explaining how she accomplished each step and how that made her ready to take the next step, jurors are likely to be convinced she's got the correct conclusions even before she says what her conclusions are. That's almost impossible for the defense to turn around.

3. Methodology Misapplied by Defense

Finally, have your expert show how **the only way to arrive at the defense's opinion would be to violate or improperly execute one or more of the rules/steps**. A good expert should be able to pinpoint where the defense "expert" went wrong and how that was the only way to come to the defense's favored conclusion.

Add some authoritative texts supporting the necessity of following the rules/steps and the defense will have a frustrating time trying to dislodge your expert's testimony. Some jurors will even feel the defense is trying to cheat them.

Chapter Seven

Cross-Examination

7-1 Rules for Analysis

I've placed this section at the start of this chapter because this section is the chapter's most important. Don't let its brevity make you ignore it.

Your only reliable tool for undermining defense experts is to show *how they violated or ignored certain required steps* in arriving at their opinions. See section 6-22, p. 200*ff*, on how to establish, develop, and verify these steps, and what to do with them during direct.

When you show that a defense expert did not properly follow all required steps, you undermine the defense expert's opinions by showing 1) how she didn't do her required job, and 2) that her failure was necessary for her to get to her opinion. So you win the battle of the experts. And you have a great argument in closing:

> If the defense could have found even one [*doctor, engineer, economist, whatever*] anywhere in the world who could follow the rules of his own profession and still come to the conclusion the defense wanted, the defense would have had him here!

When there's no clear way for jurors to choose between which side's expert to believe, juror biases take over—most of which are against you, so even the least effective defense expert often and easily holds sway.

Credentials have surprisingly little to do with the battle: Your expert's credentials may work against you when they are unusually weak, but rarely help when strong. In deliberations, credentials—of either side's experts—are rarely discussed or even thought about.

To use the "Rules for Analysis" approach, your expert's key task is to testify about why his defense counterpart is wrong. The sine qua non is for your expert to show and explain what the defense expert omitted or did wrong. During the defense case, that will be central to your crosses. Otherwise, even your most effective attempts to cross defense experts will do little to dislodge their opinions.

One of the best ways to make a defense expert's conclusions *more* credible is to try, then fail to impeach. But you won't fail when you show that the defense expert ignored or misused a required step—as long your expert has earlier taught the jury the importance of that step.

Use the "Rules for Analysis" the same way you use rules for defendant conduct. (*See* Fundamental Five, p. 10, as well as *Rules of the Road*.)

7-2 Hitchhiking: Use Defense Liability Experts for Damages

The defense case often pushes your harms case out of the spotlight. Don't let it. Keep the jurors thinking about harm. Hitchhiking helps you do that.

"Hitchhiking" is the subversion of defense negligence and causation opinion witnesses into plaintiff's damages *experts*.

> Q: Doctor, John's brain damage is minor?
>
> A: Very minor.
>
> Q: Not enough to cause severe depression?
>
> A: Not at all.
>
> Q: You have the experience to know?
>
> A: I do.
>
> Q: You have patients with depression?
>
> A: Of course.
>
> Q: Severe?
>
> A: Yes.
>
> Q: So severe nothing can help?
>
> A: I have patients like that.
>
> Q: Who aren't going to get better?
>
> A: Correct.
>
> Q: They can never hold a job again?
>
> A: Correct.
>
> Q: You understand why their severe depression keeps them from working?
>
> A: Of course.
>
> Q: For example, because X?

A: Yes.

Q: And Y?

A: Yes.

Q: And Z?

A: Yes.

And so forth. You have just added a damages expert—on the defense's tab.

This works in many situations. A defense expert testifies that your client's back problem is from a previous condition. Before—or instead of—battling that, explain through him what makes a back problem so painful, disabling, and permanent. Sure, a defense expert can claim that the defendant did not cause your client's bad back—but to defend her own expertise, she has to agree that the kind of bad back you're claiming can incapacitate and hurt. You can get her to detail how bad it can be, why it can be permanent, how it will get worse as the years go by, what that will mean, and how it can be absolutely real. After all, if she does not know those things, then she can hardly be a credible expert.

So hitchhike! She's gotta pick you up. And it's a great ride.

You can do this with almost every defense liability witness.

7-2-1 When Hitchhiking, Be Friendly

The witness is on your side for the above, and you want that to be apparent to the jurors.

Do the same thing for a client whose brain damage does not show on imaging. By challenging the expert's qualifications to know about such things, you can get her to tell the jury that she is helping to create treatment and rehab plans for some of her patients whose imaging shows nothing.

Or does she send patients home and say, "You're fine," when nothing shows up on the imaging—even though doing so would violate the standard of care for failing to make proper use of the differential diagnosis?

Hitchhiking is extremely valuable with maladies some jurors have trouble believing in. For example, some jurors, especially older ones, think that depression is voluntary—that anyone can get rid of it just by "cheering up." So in a medical case, a defense standard-of-care expert would have to admit that depression is real, that his own patients who complain of depression really have it, that it is involuntary, that it can be incapacitating, that many depression patients can never be cured, that you cannot look at a person and see it, that it can be more painful and debilitating than physical pain, etc.

So use this defense witness to make depression and its terrible consequences real for your jurors.

Defense will object: "This is not what he's here to testify about!" But this is cross-examination. You're trying to test whether this expert really knows anything about this kind of problem. It's fair game.

The only thing the defense expert will not admit is that this kind of problem happened to your client—but he wasn't going to admit that anyway. (Though you can show it by means of this chapter's first section.)

Be sure to hitchhike before attacking the defense expert's liability opinions. Don't undermine his credibility before you get him to talk about your harms.

Examples:

Q: You've had patients with _____, yes?

Q: Sometimes there was nothing you could do to make it any better, right?

Q: Some had to stop working, right?

Q: Some never got back to work?

Q: Why not?

* * *

Q: Doctor, have you ever changed the diaper on a twenty-year old?

Q: Know anyone who has?

Q: Why does she have to?

* * *

Q: Doctor, depression can be real, yes?

Q: Patients cannot get rid of it just by wishing, can they?

Q: Or deciding to "cheer up"?

Q: Doctor, you treat patients with depression?

Q: Some of them dozens of times?

Q: More than that?

Q: Some for years?

Q: How much does it cost per visit?

Q: Why don't they get better?

Q: Why not just tell them to "go home and cheer up"?

* * *

Q: A blade that flies off the shaft could hurt someone?

Q: Could hit them in the face?

Q: Could cut to the bone?

Q: Blind a person?

* * *

Q: An electrical explosion could hurt someone?

Q: Burn through the skin?

Q: All three layers of skin?

Here's a mental exercise to help you make the best use of defense witnesses. Ask yourself how you would present your entire case if you were to have no case-in-chief, but only cross-examination of defense witnesses. See how much you can get in. In some cases, you will be able to show that every fact and assertion in your case is corroborated by one or another of the defense witnesses.

In trial, do your case-in-chief in the normal way—but in closing, point out that you could have done without your own witnesses because the defense did it all for you. Then take the jurors through every link of your case citing *only* the defense witnesses.

Hitchhiking can get you a long way. But like hitchhiking on the highway, it can be dangerous unless you carefully prepare. A well-armed highway hitchhiker will safely get where he's going. The same is true in trial.

Hitchhiking gathers evidence in a powerful and interesting way. It keeps jurors' minds on harm and damages during the defense's liability case. Like highway hitchhiking, it's free. Unlike highway hitchhiking, you don't even have to say thanks.

7-3 UNDERMINING DEFENSE LIFE-EXPECTANCY ESTIMATES

Life-expectancy estimates from the defense are often based on junk science or no science at all. They are partisan-based, not scientific. When a defense expert says your client will live until, say, thirty-five instead of eighty-two, ask the expert if he will pay for her care for each additional year she lives past thirty-five. Ask him if he'll sign an agreement to that effect; after all, he's asking the jury to force your client to take that gamble. This shows he's not so sure his conclusion is correct. Be prepared for an objection, although the defense will not quite know any grounds. The judge may sustain it anyway—but he should not, and you've already made your point.

In closing, point out that if anyone should be forced to gamble, it's the defendant who put your client in this position.

No one can predict when anyone will die. Doctors can be somewhat accurate with an acute situation in which death is days or weeks away. But when it is a matter of years, doctors can only guess. So object to the defense guess coming in. It is junk science, it uses and calls for speculation, and it rests on a misuse of statistical data. Disease process does not reliably predict mortality; in many situations, it can be wrong by decades.

Even when the statute requires you to establish life expectancy, an epidemiologist can explain why the official tables cannot be used to predict how long your client will live. Hardly anyone dies on the date the chart says. They all die off schedule, durn 'em! So how can jurors use life expectancy as a basis for anything?

In jury voir dire, ask jurors who they have known or heard of who outlived what the doctors predicted. Ask each juror why she thinks that happened.

7-4 UNDERMINING ACCUSATIONS OF MALINGERING AND EXAGGERATION OF SYMPTOMS

No physician has a scientific way to say to a reasonable degree of medical certainty that someone is faking or exaggerating. It really cannot be done. So on cross, probe the "science" behind what such a physician is saying. There is none. A patient can be in dire pain with no objective verification or measurement. Calling her a malingerer or exaggerator is no more than guesswork—or as with most defense doctors who do it, conscious prostitution.[1]

Invite the defense witness propounding malingering or exaggeration to explain the science backing up his claims. Have your own experts give you the information in advance to help you show on cross that the defense claims derive from partisan guessing, not science.

---

1. If your client is not very credible, try to have junk-science testimony barred. Virginia attorney Roger Creager has had success doing this. (*See* supplement I.) Oregon forensic epidemiologist Michael Freeman has a great record of getting judges to bar such testimony. *Polarizing the Case* teaches you Rick Friedman's powerful approach against such bogus testimony. Dorothy Sims's *Exposing Deceptive Defense Doctors* was to be called *Sworn to Lie*, but her otherwise excellent publisher chickened out. Still, her book—along with Friedman's—are the bibles of how to impeach the plenitude of doctors who sell their calling at an hourly rate.

If your client is credible, do not try to bar defense testimony on malingering, exaggeration, or any other topic that makes your client out to be lying. When you have a credible client, such testimony can be a gift. (*See* section 8-23, p. 247. *See also* Rick Friedman's *Polarizing the Case*.)

7-5 "Litigation Syndrome" and Other Bogusaria[2]

The defense may claim your client has "litigation syndrome" or some such malady. But only unicorns can get it. The defense expert will explain that it's an unconscious (and thus not dishonest) syndrome in which your client is under the delusion that her problems still exist when they no longer do.

"Litigation syndrome," or whatever else it is called (the nomenclature of Bogusarian maladies has not yet been regularized), is so called because the defense claims it will end when the case ends. When suffering from "litigation syndrome," the litigation apparently so focuses the litigant on her injuries that the injuries have lasted this long and even gotten worse only because there's a case going on. "Otherwise she'd be cured, yes, indeed!"

Maybe it's possible. So's the Loch Ness monster. Yet it's enormously prejudicial. (I guess the Loch Ness monster is prejudicial, too.) A responsible judge will ask for its scientific basis and find there is none. "Litigation syndrome" is an invented malady no one has ever had. It is a diagnosis used nowhere in medicine except for purposes of courtroom defense for pay. No decent treating physician tells a patient, "Oh, your signs and symptoms are just *litigation syndrome;* you'll be fine when the case ends." That would, after all, violate a physician's duty to do a differential diagnosis.

If a defense expert claims "litigation syndrome," **ask how he would deal with such a patient in his clinic**. Would he medically rule out every other reasonable possibility before sending her home with a pat on her "litigation-syndromed" head? Or would he leap to a diagnosis of litigation syndrome and ignore every other reasonable possibility? (That is, would he do the required differential diagnosis—or commit malpractice?)

Then ask what he has done to rule out the other possibilities in *this* case. This is the only kind of science a doctor is allowed to practice. Prepare the jury for this by having your own medical expert explain what a differential diagnosis is, what "rule out" means, and thus why such a "diagnosis" would be malpractice in a clinic. (*See* supplement E, p. 381.)

---

2. "Bogusaria" /bo-gus-a-*ri*-a (abbreviated BS and rhymes with diarrhea) is the category of medical maladies that exist only for the purposes of defense testimony. It is apparently admissible.

Carefully trace this defense expert's testimony from other trials. How often has he testified identically? **How often has he followed up to see if any plaintiffs actually got better after the case ended?** If he has not done that, it means he has not gathered all the available information about how accurate his predictions are. You might want to follow this up yourself: **if the defense doctor has a long record of saying that plaintiffs will get better, how often has he been wrong?**

In these days of tort "reform," some physicians feel justified in offering scientifically and medically fraudulent opinions. These physicians feel under siege by trial attorneys, so to them, "All's fair in love and war." Result: they readily and self-righteously lie on the stand. Of course, along the way they make a fortune doing it. That's why you need to track down their testimony in other trials and check out its validity in retrospect.

When you have unmasked one of these experts, do not keep it a secret. Make sure every other plaintiff's attorney learns how you did it—so that that doctor can never lie about another plaintiff.

It's not enough to attack an opinion. It's not enough to show that the doctor always testifies for the defense. Instead, you should also show that he gives exactly the same testimony. Show how his testimony does not square with the truth—that plaintiffs did not suddenly lose their symptoms when the trial ended or children did not die in the four years he predicted.

When the defense expert uses tests to support his opinions, have your experts dissect and debunk how he ran them and analyzed or scored them. Show how the defense expert routinely and intentionally tilts the results to favor the defense.

Do not approach this kind of testimony as if it is just a difference of opinion. While you might not always be able to make the charge in court, you must constantly remind yourself that it is flat-out lying. The defense doctor finds this a good way to make a great living. Sufficient research into how he gets to his opinions often unearths dishonest methods.

In trial, be polite to these snakes (let the facts you unearth speak for themselves), but conduct your behind-the-scenes work with all the aggressiveness with which you'd impeach a jailhouse snitch. You're dealing with criminals in white coats.

Ninety-nine percent of physicians are honest and would never stoop to such testimony. That's why those who do stoop make such good money. Being rare, they're in demand—or they're new at it and would like to become in demand.

7-6 CONTROL

Everyone teaches—correctly—that on cross, it is important to keep the witness under your control. But they usually leave out a crucial warning: When you are controlling a witness, *your control must not be apparent to the jury.* Visible control hurts you. Many people believe "lawyers can get you to say anything!" and your visible efforts at control confirm their belief.

When jurors can see that you're controlling the witness, they give the witnesses responses less weight; after all, you used power and tricks right in front of them. Some will think, "Jeez, I hope no lawyer ever gets to make me say what she wants me to instead of what I want to."

Visible control of witnesses gives opposition jurors a powerful deliberations argument: "I know what the witness admitted, but the lawyer forced him to admit it; the lawyer never let the guy say what he wanted to. That's what lawyers do."

So your control must be invisible. Unfortunately, many lawyers spotlight it—for example, by the blunder of visibly taking pleasure in points they score on cross. You have to leave your ego at home. Brag later, not visibly in front of the jury.

And don't show a single macho or competitive impulse.

During cross-exams, you are seen as the power figure and the witness is seen as being at the mercy of your situational power. Don't abuse your power. Don't even appear to exercise it.

Invisible control means:

- Don't bully.
- Don't be sarcastic or rude in any other way. For example, when a witness finally gives you the answer they have been avoiding, don't sarcastically say, "Thank you!"
- Try not to interrupt except when absolutely necessary.
- Use control methods that are not apparent.
- Don't show off.
- Stay nice. Not just respectful, but appropriately nice. ("No!" said one attorney. "I don't want jurors to see me acting nicely with the doctor who killed my client." That would be good thinking—if it didn't undermine your cross-exam.)

As Duke's Don Beskind teaches, one of the best ways to control invisibly is by means of relaxed, brief, one-fact-per-question cross-exam questions.

When asked *without* a forceful or angry tone, they don't seem to control—but they do.

> *You were in the house?*
>
> *In January?*
>
> *On the twenty-ninth?*
>
> *Daytime?*
>
> *In the living room?*
>
> *The television was there?*
>
> *You saw it?*
>
> *You were in the house again?*
>
> *In August?*
>
> *Middle of the month?*
>
> *Daytime?*
>
> *In the living room?*
>
> *You saw the TV?*
>
> *Because it was gone?*

Tone is crucial: relaxed, not hurrying, no pressure. Sound like you're cordially agreeing in advance with the "yes" the witness is going to give you.

An additional advantage of invisible control is that it puts the witness off guard. Instead of making him defensive and very careful, he lets down his guard. So even when you cut off his head, do it pleasantly.

Chapter Eight

Closing

8-1 Overview

A closing must do many things. Each is numbered according to its importance:

    ___1. Arm jurors

    ___1. Focus on rules

        ___1. As they apply to the defendant (*see* sections 5-5-1, p. 119, and 5-5-3, p. 138)

        ___1. As they apply to defense experts (*see* section 7-1, p. 205)

        ___1. As they apply to jurors (*see* chapter three)

    ___1. Explain the law

    ___1. Apply the facts to law (show how evidence "proves" the important instructions your way; *see* section 8-10-1, p. 232)

    ___1. Avoid details

    ___1. Avoid "marshaling" the evidence (*see* below)

        ___1. Show how facts prove each of your reasons for suing (*see* pp. 114*ff.*, section 5-4, "Template for Opening")

        ___1. Show how facts prove each of your negligence undermining points (*see* section 8-8-4, p. 224)

    ___1. Avoid anything that can harden defense jurors against you (such as saying, "It's ridiculous to think that . . ." when a defense juror might be thinking it)

    ___1. Avoid falling back on old ways of doing closing

Under no circumstances should you simply "marshal the evidence." It's the best way to keep jurors from listening. And it's insulting to review everything as if the jurors have not been there the whole time.

Instead of marshaling evidence, use it as described on p. 233 to teach your favorable jurors how to use it in deliberations. Otherwise even jurors who seem to be listening won't be. We all learn by second grade how to pretend to listen.

8-2 When to Write It

Responsible advocacy requires you to write both your opening and closing long before trial and then revise as things progress. There are several reasons for this.

First, on the eve of trial the defense will be wasting your time with useless motions, and you'll be busy with a dozen other things as well. Your opening is too important to cram into that busy time; do it at your leisure well in advance.

Second, if you wait until the end of trial to write your closing, you'll usually be too tired to do your best.

Third, having written full drafts of both opening and closing in advance helps you organize your case in your mind. It also keeps you on focus as trial progresses. **So skim your opening and closing every morning before trial.**

Fourth, when you've written your closing in advance, you needn't take as many notes during trial about points to put in your closing; they'll mostly be there already. (By the way, whenever you take a note, some jurors see you—and it alerts them that you think there's a problem with your case, even when that's not what the note is about. So when you take a note, do it a few moments after its impetus came up—and do it subtly.)

Fifth, knowing that your closing is written and requires only minor adjustments will bolster your confidence and comfort throughout trial.

When you work with co-counsel or a trial consultant, writing opening and closing in advance is the best way to be certain you are both on the same wavelength.

8-3 Make Jurors Listen

They would not listen, they're not listening still.

Perhaps they never will....

—Don McLean, "Vincent (Starry Starry Night)"

It's hard to face this, but jurors don't automatically pay attention just because you are talking. It's quite the opposite. Especially in closings, jurors usually hear and absorb remarkably little. They look rapt, but mostly they are not hearing a word you say.

Jurors tend not to listen carefully to closing because most—more than 90 percent—think they've made up their minds, so they have no need for anything you have to say. Even the few still trying to make up their minds stop listening as soon as you start rehashing what they already know.

So your first task is to get them listening. You can do this by saying:

> Folks, in a little while you'll go into the deliberation room, and you'll have three jobs.[1]

That surprises them into listening—for a moment—because they think they have only one job.

Now that you have their attention for a moment, give them reason to listen longer. The third job does that (italics below):

> One of your jobs is to answer the questions the judge gives you.
>
> Your second job is to make sure everyone on the jury carefully follows the law the judge gives you.
>
> And third, before you answer any questions, *you'll have to explain to each other why you feel the way you do about each question.*
>
> *So for the next ___ minutes, I'd like to give you some ways to do that.*

This taps into the juror fear of speaking in front of a group of people they don't know well.

Fearful or not, your favorable jurors will listen because they want the help you just offered. And jurors leaning against you will want to hear what they'll have to contend with in deliberations.

So everyone is listening. Now all you have to do is say things that keep them listening. That mainly means arming your favorable jurors to go into deliberations and do what you need them to do. Deciding you should win is merely the beginning. Knowing how to win for you is the goal.

---

1. It used to be two until Virginia attorney Chuck Zauzig brilliantly added the middle one.

8-4 Teaching Your Favorable Jurors How To Win (*Arming* Them)

Few jurors (under one in twelve, on average) change their minds during closings—or even move much in any direction. So you have a more important task in closing than mere persuasion. Your ultimate goal in trial—especially in closing—is to arm your persuaded jurors, whoever they may be, to go into deliberations and win for you. Your favorable jurors are far more able than you to sway unfavorable jurors your way.

In other words, *you* can't win your case. But your favorable jurors can win it for you. If they know how.

Look at it this way: You went to a great deal of time, effort, and analysis to figure out how to persuade them—and they were the *easy* jurors! Now you must do even better in teaching the easy jurors how to persuade the hard jurors. Too many attorneys waste all their closing time persuading jurors who are already persuaded instead of teaching the persuaded jurors how to persuade the as-yet unpersuaded. This is among the most common causes of bad verdicts.

8-4-1 The ABCs

While you must arm jurors throughout trial, in closing you must explicitly teach the *exact words to say*, not just concepts. Here's the paradigm:

> During deliberations, if someone says *XYZ*, remind them that *ABC*.

Here's an example:

> If someone says **Jamie had back pain** before [*that's the XYZ*], remind them that **"We're not suing for the pain he had before"** [*that's the ABC*].

For every important point—factual, legal, and anything else—you need to identify every defense *XYZ* and provide a *short, plain-English ABC*. By closing, jurors already understand the evidence, so they need only reminders. You provide those reminders with your *ABCs*—the easy ways for them to say each point.

Why? Because jurors who know how to say something will be far more likely to say it. And once they say it, they will be far more likely to stick to it.

In most trials, jurors who fought for the losing side say, "I had to fold because I didn't know how to explain my point of view."

Your *ABCs* are so important that when providing them, you might want to say, "You may want to write this down."

> **NOTES**
>
> Because teaching and arming jurors is so important, always push hard for jurors to be allowed to take notes—not just in closing, but throughout trial. You have the burden, so the jurors' failure to retain information hurts you more than it hurts the defense. And it has been longer since jurors heard your side's testimony. Point out to the note-recalcitrant judge that 1) there are no lawyers who would have passed law school classes without taking notes, 2) for many people, learning is enhanced by notes because it helps keep the evidence organized in their minds, and 3) **the most important requirement of trial is for jurors to hear *and retain* the evidence.** Many people can neither listen well nor learn at their best without taking notes.
>
> Argue that disallowing notes dumbs down the jury.
>
> Some judges fall for the unsupported myth that jurors with notes carry more weight in deliberations than do other jurors. Ask a good plaintiff's trial consultant to provide you with an affidavit that counters this mistaken belief. And once you've got the affidavit, post it on your Listserv for others to use.
>
> If your note-barring judge likes to send a copy of the jury instructions into deliberations, point out the contradiction: the judge is afraid they'll forget his instructions but not your evidence.
>
> If a judge refuses and you lose the case—particularly a complex case in which a verdict your way would have required jurors to retain complex or copious evidence—consider raising the issue on appeal. Many things are within a judge's discretion, but interfering with a juror's ability to understand and remember evidence is not one of them.

Jurors who switch from plaintiff to defense during deliberations often tell us later, "I knew I was right to support the plaintiff, but I didn't know what to say or how to say it to support my position." So eventually they have no option but to cave in. Tell them what to say in order to support your side, and try to get the judge to allow them to write it down. But even without notes, you still need to arm.

It is *always* counsel's fault when jurors don't know *exactly* what to say on each pivotal point. Your most important duty is to train jurors the way a coach trains athletes: "Here's what to do when you're out there and I can't help you: *When XYZ comes up, you say ABC.*"

Your *ABC* will be **no more than fifteen or twenty words**, preferably fewer.

It will be in the **plainest English**.

Well-armed favorable jurors are confident in speaking their minds in deliberations. And when other favorable jurors hear each other, especially early in deliberations, they unify and make each other more resolute. That creates a hard-to-beat group momentum.

A juror who does *not* speak backs down easily. This is because it's very easy to back down when you haven't taken a "public" stand; there's no social price to pay. So, as the National Jury Project's Susan Macpherson advises, boil down each important point:

> If someone says Dr. Fischer did the best he could, remind them that Dr. Fischer violated the rule that a surgeon must never cut without looking.

Don't re-explain the whole point. Jurors already know it. They never need to hear: "On September 17, 2008, at 4:20 p.m. in the afternoon in the operating room in Granville Hospital in Oxford, North Carolina, Western Hemisphere, Dr. Ulysses Moses Giordano, a surgeon who had had privileges to work in that hospital since June 3, 1998, operated on thirty-eight-year-old John Lawrence Smith, and . . . ." Once jurors stop listening, getting them all the way back is hard.

> If a juror says that [XYZ] the company didn't mean to hurt anyone, remind that juror that [ABC] *the company intentionally violated its own safety rules.*

You may want to say the *ABC* twice.

Keep the language simple and concise. No juror will say anything in deliberations like: "The proportionality of compensable damages is the physical pain deriving from the defendant driver's negligent operation of a motor vehicle at approximately 8:30 p.m. on the evening of January 21, 2009." No one will listen to you talk like that in closing (or any other time). No juror will use those words in deliberations.

But they'll use "*Pain is the worst harm in the case.*"

When jurors are writing down your *ABC*, give them time to finish.

8-4-2 Cumulative ABCs

As you introduce each *ABC*, put it on a board or slide, and leave it up after you say it. When you come to the next *ABC*, add it to the earlier slide or board. That way you end up with a display of all the *ABCs*. This is important because it allows your note-taking (*see* p. 219) jurors to get them all down. To do this you may need multiple boards or projections displayed at the same time. But you will find that most cases need surprisingly few *ABCs*. (If you've done *well-run* focused groups, you will know most of those *ABCs* in advance.[2])

Your *ABCs* are the next best thing to being in deliberations yourself. Often better.

8-5 Keep on KISSING!

In closing, many lawyers who have kept things clear and simple throughout trial suddenly transform into monsters of complexity, drowning themselves—and the jury—in details. We call this the Jekyll-to-Hyde syndrome. Don't turn your accessible and familiar case into a strange case of Jekyll and Hyde.

Simple is the gold standard.

8-5-1 Terms

When you use a technical term instead of plain English, many jurors neither understand it (even when you have repeatedly explained it) nor use it in deliberations. Some jurors are uncomfortable using technical terms even when they understand them. And when jurors use technical terms, other jurors misunderstand.

Good teachers speak only plain English. Don't force your favorable jurors to argue your case in a nearly foreign language.

8-5-2 Details

Avoid details—throughout trial, and especially in closings. Jurors make no decisions based on details they hear in closing. Sometimes they think they do, but in fact they don't. You must do what they do: focus on the broad issues. A trial might be a mosaic, but jurors work only with the big picture. The problem with details is that they blur the big picture. Blurred pictures help the defense, not you.

---

2. *See* David Ball, Artemis Malekpour, and Debra Miller, Focus Groups: How to Do Your Own Jury Research (Trial Guides 2008).

8-5-3 Time

Jurors wanna go home. They wanna decide the case and go home as fast as possible.

So during closing, jurors are impatient. They fatalistically assume that you're going to blab forever, but they don't want you to. They think they don't need you to. They are almost always right. Every unnecessary word you speak, every wasted moment while you search for something you should have had at your fingertips, every pointless repetition, every single thing you do that they think you could have done more efficiently, makes them more impatient and less happy with you.

That said, **don't talk fast**. No one loves a fast-talking lawyer. In most areas of the country, speaking at roughly 150 words per minute is the limit if you want jurors to digest what you say. In some places (such as parts of the South) or with jurors for whom English is a recently learned language, your limit is about 120 words per minute.

Learning to change your natural speaking rate can be difficult, but it is necessary. It's one of those things most attorneys totally ignore without ever realizing how much harm they're doing to themselves. You can get help from the speech coach at a university theater department—and every college speech coach always needs a little extra money.

8-6 Why Are You Saying That?

Make sure you know exactly why you are saying what you're saying. Keep this note on your table throughout trial:

> **How can jurors use the current point in trial?**

Apply that note throughout trial, especially in closing.

8-7 Help Jurors Respond to the Folks at Home

Some jurors are reluctant to give much money if they anticipate criticism afterward by folks at home or work or others in the community. This is particularly true when jurors think a case is likely to get publicity or be talked about afterward. *Jurors know that no one will criticize them for giving too little.*

To offset this, tell them what to say to the folks at home: "When this case is over, if someone asks you, 'Why in the world did you decide to give all that money to that lady?' just tell them, '_____.'"

Fill in the blank with your *ABC* for that issue. For example: "The truck driver broke two easy safety rules; now a member of the community is crippled forever."

8-8 ESSENTIALS FOR CLOSING

8-8-1 Structure

Every opening and closing needs a clear structure. Good structure for opening (chapter five) has little leeway for alteration. But you have a lot of leeway in closing, because jurors already know the case. That doesn't mean you can drop into a wandering, stream-of-consciousness blather. Be certain that 1) you have a structure, 2) the jurors can perceive the structure, and 3) you do not wander outside the structure.

But unlike opening, there is no optimal structure.

The essentials detailed below largely derive from opening, but without Parts One or Two—the "Primary Rules" and the "Story of What the Defendant Did."

8-8-2 First Words

Do not start closing by wasting the power of primacy. Save your thank-you and "gee, you worked hard listening," etc., for the end of closing—or omit it altogether. And please, spare us at both beginning and end your "how privileged I've been to represent Marilyn"—even if you really have been. Few lawyers can say such a thing without sounding insincere.

And especially never start an opening or closing with: "Nothing I have to say is evidence." Not even in law school! Please.

When you start your closing, get right to the point. Be useful. Start being useful with your third word:

1) Good 2) morning. [That's the maximum allowable blather!]

3) Folks, in a little while you'll go into the deliberation room, and you'll have three jobs . . . , etc. (*See* section 8-3, p. 216.)

Remember that unlike opening, you can sequence the parts of closing in a variety of ways—so the order of the parts below can be changed.

8-8-3 Who We Are Suing and Why: The Safety Rules the Defendant(s) Violated

Please remember we're suing _____ for # reasons.

A. (A brief reminder sentence or two):

> The first reason we're suing Dr. Akroyd is because she violated the safety rule that says _____. She violated it by _____. The proof she violated it is _____.

B. (*A brief reminder sentence or two*): Summarize what was wrong with doing that and how it caused harm.

C. (*A brief reminder sentence or two*): Summarize what the defendant should have done instead.

8-8-4 Undermining (Liability and Damages)

In closing, unlike opening, omit the phrase, "it had to be determined whether" (*see* "How to Undermine," p. 146).

Instead, remind jurors that you considered each of these points before coming to trial; the defense did not spring them on you.

> You've heard the defense claim that_____. So if someone brings that up in deliberations remind them that . . . [*plug in your **ABCs**].

For example:

> You've heard the defense say Dr. Akroyd had good reason to think it was a urinary tract infection. So if someone brings that up in deliberations, remind them that no matter what Dr. Akroyd was justified in thinking, and even if her thinking had been right, she was still *required to consider cancer—and required either to rule it out or treat it.*

Do not rehash, do not "marshal the evidence," do not consider this your last chance to persuade. Do not re-explain the entire differential diagnosis process. Your troops are in the armory assembling their weapons for battle. So get to the point.

Do this for every liability point—including causation—you need to undermine. But be concise and *brief* because the jurors have already heard it.

Be especially careful to undermine each defense theme ("doctors can't see into the future") and each defense one-liner ("accidents happen"). Don't let

Closing

defense themes and one-liners get into deliberations without you giving your favorable jurors the *ABCs* to undermine them.

Be just as careful to deal with defense-favoring themes that the defense itself may not have brought up—such as, "She should have gotten a second opinion." This is another reason to do focus groups.

8-8-5 *Massaging the Negligence Instructions*

This part of closing must be done thoroughly in every closing. See detailed instructions in section 8-10, p. 231.

8-8-6 *Massage the Harms Instructions*

This is similar to massaging negligence instructions (*see* section 8-10, p. 231*ff.*). As you show jurors how to apply facts to law about each damages element, show how each client harm fits the instruction.

Write each figure on an enlarged replica of the verdict form.

8-8-7 *Arguments*

As you show jurors how to apply facts to damages laws, argue for why jurors should allow the amount you are calling for. This is one of the best places to use the damages arguments described later in this chapter, as well as those in *Reptile*.

Be sure to include the Harms-and-Losses-Only template (*see* section 3-13, p. 75).

If your client has previous harms or other harms the defendant did not cause, distinguish them from harms for which you are seeking compensation. Provide a two-column chart with the unrelated harms on the left and the harms the defendant caused on the right.

Unrelated Harms	Harms Caused By Defendant

Or you can use an "in-the-box/out-of-the-box" diagram.

Remind jurors that their job is to fix what can be fixed, help what cannot be entirely fixed, and make up for whatever can neither be fixed nor helped (*see* Fundamental Eight, p. 28).

8-8-8 *Story*

Closing is when to tell a strong story about your client's life as the injury was or is affecting her. Unlike in opening, your story in closing can take a wide variety of formats.

First Person Story

Since 1973, I have been urging attorneys to tell a first-person story in closing—as if your client, dead or alive, is speaking. (*Never use a first-person story in opening; see* "First Person Stories," p. 135.) Gerry Spence's Trial Lawyers College now does a great job of teaching first-person storytelling, even in the weekend-only sessions. Many closings have been made extraordinarily powerful by first-person stories. In a recent case, the impact of one such story was enough to make a juror fall ill (unfortunately resulting in a mistrial). So as with any powerful tool, use this one carefully. If you have a juror who has been through a similar experience (as in the mistried case), you could be putting her through another awful experience.

Caveat: *Never* use a first-person story without thoroughly testing it first in front of several focus groups. I have heard many jurors complain after trial that they really liked the plaintff's attorney until he told a first-person story—which the entire jury considered demeaning to their intelligence and a pathetic attempt to get sympathy. In one such case, it was the entire topic of discussion for an hour until the insulted jury unanimously voted for a defense verdict.

Other Story Methods

There are countless other ways to tell good stories. And a good story is always far better than just providing a list of facts about what your client's life is (or was) due to the harm.

One magnificent way to learn how to use any kind of story is by means of Jim Perdue's *Winning with Stories*.[3] He provides great advice and example after example.

Also see two Eric Oliver books: *Facts Can't Speak for Themselves*[4] and *Persuasive Communications*.[5] He helps you understand how to make your stories communicate.

And see SunWolf's *Jury Practical Dynamics 2*.[6]

Don't Be Tempted

As you learn different methods of telling stories in closing, you'll be tempted to use those methods in your openings. DON'T. Do your opening the way chapter five tells you. In opening, the story of what the *defendant* did is the only way to lay in the necessary learning + persuasion framework.

---

3. Texas Bar 2007.
4. NITA 2005.
5. TrialGuides 2009.
6. LexisNexis 2007.

Closing

Neither first-person stories nor any other kind can do that, and they always court considerable risk. Only once you get to closing does the whole universe of storytelling approaches serve your needs. (You might even want to look at how theater and film stories work: see *Backward and Forwards*, the standard text on how stories work in plays and films.[7])

Remember: as in closing itself, your stories must be structured, and the structure must be carefully thought out, concise, and clear to jurors.

8-9 Minimum Life-Care Plan in Closing

I learned this technique from Atlanta's Don Keenan. He was not my dear friend at the time, so I stole it from him. Now he's my dear friend, so I'm just borrowing it.

Either way, it's now yours.

If your minimum life-care plan (or your informal list of needs) has been properly presented in testimony (*see* section 6-15, p. 189), **show in closing how reducing the amount—by even a little—will hurt**. Otherwise some jurors will think of the plan as intangible and easily lower its value. Since minimum life-care money is usually a major component of your economic damages total, and since your economic damages total is often the benchmark on which jurors will base their noneconomics decision, you must **protect your minimum life-care figure**. It's actually easy.

Prepare a line-item chart of every life-care category. List each category by name (no explanation; the jurors already heard that). Show the cost of each category. Show the chart—hand out copies as well—so each juror can read along as you talk about it.

Suppose, for example, the list begins as follows:

Speech therapy	Six years	$13,500
Leg braces	Lifetime	24,567
Pain medication	Lifetime	57,400
Etc.		
Etc.		
TOTAL		$3,527,450

Display the list, and say:

> It's ultimately up to you to decide the right amount. Here's how:
>
> > In deliberations, if there's something on the life-care plan you all agree John should not have, cross it off. It's up to you.

---

7. David Ball (Southern Illinois University Press 1983).

Cross off any item you all agree he should not get. And subtract the cost of that item from the total down here. That way John gets what you think he should get, and he does not get anything you think he should not get.

For example, if you all decide he does not need the leg therapy, just cross it off—like this—and deduct its cost from the bottom.

With this approach—if you have removed from the life-care plan every item that might seem unnecessary or luxurious, if you have made sure every price has been justified, and if your life-care planner has explained the dire consequences of removing or diminishing each category—you are likely to get your entire life-care plan figure.

This method powerfully arms your favorable jurors.

Without this method, an unfavorable juror who wants to lower the minimum life-care figure easily leads even your most favorable jurors into negotiating over it. She just says, "Boy, three and a half million is a lot, but I'd go with half." So your minimum figure quickly becomes the ceiling as your favorable jurors degenerate into negotiating. The only question: How low will they go?

But when your favorable jurors understand the importance of the minimum figure, they're unlikely to agree to negotiate. Instead, they'll say, "Show us what you want to take out of that life-care plan. If we all agree, we'll see how low it takes us." They say this because you've shown them the consequences of taking *anything* out of the minimum life-care plan. They'll find little if any of it to be unnecessary.

And they'll regard the low-ball juror as unreasonable.

In fact, the use of this method often means the jurors will barely discuss the life-care plan before deciding to fully fund it.

Caveat: This method works only if you carefully follow the life-care plan suggestions detailed in section 6-15, p. 189.

8-9-1 Life Expectancy

(*See also* "Life Expectancy," p. 155.)

Point out in closing that **your client has the right to be taken care of no matter how long she lives**. She is not likely to die right on schedule according to life expectancy. She and her family have the right, and good grounds, to hope for a longer life, just like everyone else. And she has the right to the money she needs to take care of her injuries *no matter how long she might live*. The defendant who hurt her should shoulder the gamble.

The defendant willingly gambled with her safety in the first place, or she'd never have been hurt. Now they are trying to gamble with her safety again—if she lives longer than some table of *averages* says she *might*, she'll be without the very care and safety the defendant has made necessary. The defense claims they should fund only the "maybe" number of years she has left; this terrifies your client and her family. What happens when the money runs out? She has a 50/50 chance (greater with younger clients) of living longer, and a good chance of living decades longer.

But this time the gamble should be at the expense of the defense. If they pay enough for her *maximum possible* life expectancy and she dies sooner, the extra money is the most the defense has gambled. And that amount, no matter how much it is, is trivial compared to the gamble the defendant wants the jury to make your client take: essential care or no essential care. Your client did not ask to be in this position; the defendant put her there. So when it comes to a life expectancy gamble, the defendant, not the plaintiff, should own the risk.

Your client is worried right now about running out of money if she outlives her average life expectancy. Find out and show the spread beyond that age—such as, "57 percent live longer than the average, 40 percent live more than ten years longer, 30 percent live fifteen years longer, 15 percent live twenty-five years longer, and 5 percent live longer than that." Argue that she has the right not to have to lie awake at night worrying what she will do for money if she lives longer than the chart or the defense says—especially because if that happens, she'll be old enough to have the most desperate need of the money.

Point out that we all worry about running out of money someday, but unlike everyone else, your client can no longer do anything about it.

Make the jurors see how outrageous it is for the defense to pressure them to provide *less* money on the grounds that the plaintiff will die soon due to the condition she's in. *She's in that condition because the defendant's negligence put her there.* So for each year she now has to contemplate that the defendant has taken away, she is entitled to emotional suffering money for her shortened life expectancy. The emotional harm of that contemplation is worth more per year than her care would cost if she lived.

> The defense wants you to provide only enough money to care for Sally for a few years. At least they admit she should get something. But the defense wants Sally to die soon because it's cheaper that way.

> Sally is in terror over the possibility that she heard in this courtroom that she might lose twenty years of life because of the defendant. The defense created that terror to protect their money.
>
> The pain of that terror is far more serious than the cost of care for those same twenty years. So by arguing an early death for Sally, the defense is admitting that a much higher verdict is required. How much higher?
>
> You can figure out the *minimum* value of Sally's anguish over possibly losing each year the defendant says they've taken away from her. Look at the cost of the minimum life-care plan for that twenty years. It's $4 million. Twenty years of Sally's life is obviously worth many times the cost of care for those years.
>
> So let's figure it out: If Sally does die at fifty-two instead of seventy-two, the verdict should include the $4 million the minimum life-care calls for, multiplied by three or four—because loss of life is many times worse than the cost of any minimum life-care plan. So it's at least $12 million for those twenty years, or as much as $16 million or more.

If you have caps on noneconomic damages, add:

> But what is important is for you to simply fund the minimum life-care plan in a way that will cover her care when it turns out that she lives those twenty years after all. In fact, you should fund it for twenty years beyond that—for a total of $_____, because she may very well live that long.

You might also want to argue that by giving the defendants a break by deducting life-care money because they shortened her life, jurors would be encouraging future defendants to hurt their victims badly enough to do the same thing:

> Do we really want to teach anyone that they can save money just by making sure that when they hurt someone, they're better off causing enough damage to kill them young?

8-9-2 Senior Citizens and Life Expectancy

Many older jurors have seen their contemporaries die younger than life expectancy. That can lead older jurors to think that life expectancy is less than the average on the charts; after all, most of the exceptions they have seen—their own contemporaries—died early. Judicial notice of the chart does not persuade them. Instead, have an expert explain the step-by-step empirical process by which the chart arrives at its averages. This will give your favorable jurors a way in deliberations to deal with the recalcitrant juror on this topic.

8-9-3 Bottom-Line Figure

Defense jurors often argue that a fraction of the life-care figure would be enough to invest to provide an ample annual income to fund everything. Explain that that has already been taken into account: the bottom-line figure is the amount that, together with all the interest it can earn, will run out on the projected date. And argue that such factors as the '09 financial debacle and the unpredictability of future inflation make it a huge gamble for your client to have to depend on the life-care figure being as low as you are asking for. Again, it is the defendant's turn to gamble.

8-10 MASSAGING THE JURY INSTRUCTIONS AND QUESTIONS

One of your more important tasks in closing is to "massage" the jury instructions. That simply means to explain them in ways that help you.

Deliberating jurors don't know any law. Much of what they think they know is wrong in ways that can devastate your case. Sending written instructions into deliberations helps, but not much.

Written or spoken, the language of the instructions is usually impenetrable. Even with clear language, there's too much to absorb. Jurors have no way of sorting the important from the unimportant. Due to the boring and confusing barrage of instructions, many jurors end up remembering and understanding less law after they've heard and read the instructions than before.

This hurts you more than it does the defense. For example, few jurors mistakenly think money should be allowed just because someone was hurt. When they express that in deliberations, others correct them. But most jurors—including favorable ones—believe it is OK to factor rising insurance rates and other immaterial factors into the size of the verdicts.

As a result, when your favorable jurors do not know the important laws, opposition jurors easily hijack the case by using non-law. In a recent case, the judge used the word "malice" in connection with gross negligence. The word, of course, was buried in the massive stew of instructions. Result: During deliberations, defense-leaning jurors reminded the others that the judge had said "malice"—and "why would she have said it unless it meant that the jury had to find malice to decide there had been negligence?" Since plaintiff's counsel had not massaged the instructions, an eight-figure compensation verdict—which the jurors had already decided—plummeted to zero!

I wonder how that attorney explained that to his client.

So do two things: First, in closing, **explain the law and verdict issues**.

Second, make the jurors **comfortable with enforcing the law**. For example, teach them to call for the judge when there is disagreement over the law or when a juror refuses to follow the law.

A few judges don't want to be put in this position, because avoiding the dilemma is more important to them than upholding the law. Great example, ain't they?

If you have such a judge, you can at least tell your jurors that **they have the right to be on a jury that has reached its decisions within the law and not by violating the law**—so they don't need to violate their own standards by giving into another juror who is pressuring them to not follow the law and their sacred oath.

Fortunately, only a few judges have a problem being called in if a juror is trying to violate the law. If those few judges understood that roughly half of every jury pool is comfortable ignoring what judges tell them, those judges would have the self-respect to make sure their law is followed.

8-10-1 How to Massage

When your charge conference ends, select the instructions you need the jurors to get right. In most cases, this includes the definition of negligence and the damages elements. And there are often others. It may be essential, for example, that jurors clearly understand the exceptions to the sudden emergency doctrine, the logic of the last clear chance instruction, or the law on aggravating preexisting conditions—a thoroughly misleading phrase to jurors.

Put the essential words of each important instruction on a separate projection slide or piece of butcher paper. One instruction per page or slide—and only the part of the instruction you need to explain. For example:

> Negligence is the failure to use that level of care an ordinarily careful person would use in the same circumstance.

You may think that this simplest of instructions is clear. It's not. It's not clear even to most lawyers, who think it means "average" care. But "ordinary" and "average" are not synonyms. "Ordinary" means what everyone does—*nothing unusual*. In the instruction, "ordinarily careful" means doing what a person *being careful* would do. It does not mean what a person *not* being careful would do. Duh, eh? By definition, **a person being ordinarily careful does not needlessly endanger anyone**. "Average" conduct has nothing to do with it. It's A or F. Ninety-five percent of the drivers on the freeway speed; that may be "ordinary," but it is not ordinary *care*.

Same with "reasonable" care, in which "reasonable" means "based on reason" and not "moderate." There is no such thing as "reasonable care" that needlessly endangers, because by definition needless endangerment is not care of *any* kind.

A misstatement of law to a jury is extremely serious. Yet out of ignorance, plaintiff's lawyers allow the defense to confuse "ordinary" with "average" and "reasonable" with "moderate." Don't expect jurors—or even judges—to do better on their own. Chances are the judge has never thought about the vast difference between "ordinary behavior" and "ordinary care." The jurors certainly won't if you don't tell them. And the most persuasive way is this: **There is no such thing as care of any kind that needlessly endangers. As soon as anything needlessly endangers, it is no longer care.**

The defense does not get to redefine the English language.

To make sure jurors use the law correctly, massage the instructions as outlined below. As with opening statement, you must follow the template. It's not a list of suggestions—it's the optimal way to teach jurors the law and how to apply the facts to the law. Not much leeway here.

So:

First: *Show* the essential part of the first important instruction.

Second: *Repeat* its words aloud, preferably without looking at them. Jurors like to think you know the law.

Third: *Explain* the instruction in plain English. Practice doing this in advance or you will not do it clearly.

Fourth: Apply the facts to the instruction. Once you are sure the jurors understand the instruction, explain how the evidence applies to that instruction. Instead of alienating jurors by marshaling the evidence in a vacuum, show them how to apply the relevant evidence—which they already know—to the law you have just explained.

Do all four for an instruction, then go on to the next instruction.

8-10-2 Misconceptions about Law

Be particularly careful about misconceptions that can hurt you. For example:

Intervention

Many jurors believe that if the negligence is not intentional, there should be no money for pain and suffering. Some jurors believe that if the disease killed the patient, they cannot blame the doctor. This belief arises when you do not explain that ***failure to intervene* causes needless endangerment**, and the doctor must not allow needless danger—meaning harm she can prevent. Preventing harm requires intervention. Intervention is virtually the only reason the medical field exists.

Cause

The lay meaning of "cause" is different from the legal meaning. Layperson "cause" = to *make* something happen. Legal "cause" = to make *or allow* something to happen. That's a world of difference. So if one of the causes of death is that cancer was *allowed* to kill the patient when intervention would have saved the patient, that needless allowing of death makes the death the doctor's fault. Seems obvious? Don't count on it; explain it.

Breaking the Law

Another common juror misconception is that "because the defendant broke no laws, we can't blame him." Explain that negligence *is* breaking the law because *the law requires care*. The negligence law covers needless endangerment when more specific laws or rules have not been written. This is because the legislature knows it cannot cover every single specific kind of carelessness. Lack of a specific law does not give anyone license to be needlessly dangerous. Needless endangerment is against the law.

You can—and should—get the defense to agree to this. "Mr. Truck Driver, are you allowed to do something that needlessly endangers the public just because there's no specific law or regulation against it?"

Omitting Compensation

Jurors are also usually unaware that once they decide the defendant caused a particular element of damages, they *must* determine a dollar amount that equals the level of that specific harm. Make sure they understand this. They can decide how much money equals the harm, but omitting compensation altogether for a particular harm is illegal. If they think the harm exists, that automatically puts it over zero. Explain this after you have massaged each of the damages-elements instruction. And say:

> If during deliberations someone says they don't think emotional suffering should be compensated, remind them that they took an oath to follow the law, and no one has the right to make you be on a jury that makes decisions outside the law.[8]

If you allow jurors to go into deliberations with misconceptions about the law, you are to blame when those misconceptions hurt you. Massaging prevents the misconceptions. Even if a juror or two still has some misconceptions, you have armed your favorable jurors to correct them by saying: "During deliberations, if anyone says it was not the doctor's fault because he didn't cause the cancer, remind them that the doctor's duty is to intervene, or he is at fault." (*See* section 8-4, "Teaching Your Favorable Jurors How To Win (Arming Them)," pp. 218*ff*.)

8-11 LANGUAGE

When massaging the instructions, relate the lay language you've used throughout trial to the language in the instructions. **Do not use the language of the law until you massage the instructions in closing.** Early in trial jurors have too much new information coming at them, so they don't learn new words very well, especially not legal words. Jurors (and everyone else) best learn vocabulary when they learn a concept first, *then* the label for it—long after they know what it means. This is how the brain learns language in the first place. Babies know what Mama *is* before they know the word for her.

So, for example, don't say "preponderance" or "burden" in voir dire, opening, or testimony. Just say, "more likely right than wrong" or something similar (*see* section 3-2-1, pp. 63*ff*.). In closing, when massaging the elements, you'll say, "'Preponderance' just means what we've been talking about all through trial: 'More likely right than wrong.'" And bingo! They've got it.

8-12 INTANGIBLES ARGUMENT: RATIO TO TANGIBLE LOSSES

Depending on the case, this can be effective: near the end of closing, show a line-item chart that includes every element of damages the instructions mention.

---

8. Some instructions say that the jury may *in its discretion* award money. In this situation, they are not required to allow anything. But if your instructions use this wording, make sure it reflects the actual law. Surprisingly often, instructions are dead wrong.

Past medical expenses $_____

Past care $_____

Future care $_____

Past lost income $_____

Future lost income $_____

Subtotal[9]

$_____

Past loss of use of leg $_____

Future loss of use of leg $_____

Past physical pain $_____

Future physical pain $_____

Past emotional suffering $_____

Future emotional suffering $_____

Past loss of life's pleasures $_____

Future loss of life's pleasures $_____

Subtotal

$_____

Total

$_____

---

9. Use the subtotal and total lines only if jurors will be required to provide them.

Separate economic from noneconomic losses as shown (but do not label them as such). This results in a chart that graphically, not merely textually, shows the many areas of damages the jury is supposed to compensate for. Often the result is that the noneconomic visually outweigh the economic damages, which is a good proportion to show.

Do not itemize to the point of trivialization. Each line should be for a significant, substantial harm. If a hand has been harmed, do not make each finger a line item.

In preparing the lists before trial, leave the amounts blank so in closing you can fill in figures as you talk through them—at least for those you are allowed to fill in.

Uncover each line only as you get to it. This keeps jurors with you as you work down the chart. Otherwise, they read ahead without paying attention to what you are saying.

To use the list, start at the top, briefly justify the amount for each item, and write the figure in. Take your time writing each digit and **write neatly and large. No scrawling.** If you are normally a scrawler, practice writing numbers clearly. Scrawling means sloppiness or tentativeness, and you want these figures to look strong and emphatic. Making self-deprecating jokes about your pathetic handwriting just makes it more pathetic.

When you finish with the economic damages items, write in their subtotal. (In many jurisdictions this is as far as you can go with figures, because you cannot specify amounts for noneconomics. In such circumstances, this method is even more important.)

Once you give the economic damages subtotal, say this:

> This $_____ all goes to other people for John's care and to making John even with where he would have been if none of this had ever happened. Not one cent goes to John for the greatest harm in this case: what this did to his life. His human losses. To do justice, to balance the scales, fill in the blanks on these next lines.

If you are allowed to fill in those lines, do so, explaining why your figures are appropriate. If you are not allowed, tell the jurors to look at how much greater these human losses are than the medical bills and lost wages. "It's many times worse to lose your leg than your job, so the amount that goes on this line [*loss of use of leg*] should be many times the amount on this line up here [*future lost income*]."

If you cannot talk about proportionality, use your hands: Left hand palm down at waist level as you say the medical figure. Right hand palm up shoulder high or more for noneconomics when you say, "This is the kind of case that requires a substantial amount of money to balance the harm."

If the jury can take notes, watch to see if they write down your figures. It's a great sign.

8-13 HOLISTIC DAMAGES

When the amount you want for noneconomic damages is vastly greater than the economic damages, itemizing *or even asking for* economic damages can be counterproductive. If, say, the total economic damages is $250,000, but the noneconomic harms justify a $10 million verdict, the relatively minor economic damages can drag your verdict down.

This is why noted Los Angeles attorney R. Rex Parris often makes no economic damages claim. It's a matter of sacrificing a tiny amount in order to promote the large amount.

In some cases, an expert can explain why medical and care costs are so low—because medical science has been able to do very little to help. That helps show the seriousness of the harm. But consider giving up your claim for the medical and care costs so that they do not drive down your noneconomic verdict.

8-14 SCALES: CALCULATING THE INTANGIBLE AMOUNTS

Either in voir dire or opening, you should have promised jurors that you'd teach them how to determine the amounts for noneconomic damages. (*See* section 4-5-5, p. 91.) The method you will now teach in closing helps jurors arrive at a figure; it also arms your favorable jurors with a concrete way to fight for the amount they want to allow.

First, explain that the value of each noneconomic harm[10] **is based on three factors**:

How Bad? (e.g., How Much Does It Hurt?)

Where on the scale from mild to horrendous does the intensity of each harm lie? Pain, for example, can be minor, medium, or extremely bad.

How Long?

Pain can last from a few moments all the way up to permanent.

---

10. Just a reminder: Never use the terms "economic damages" or "noneconomic damages."

How Interfering? (How Much Does It Prevent the Plaintiff from Doing?)

Where on the scale of disability does each harm lie? A disability can interfere with functioning anywhere from hardly at all up through total incapacity.

Usually the jury instruction mentions the first two: ". . . compensation for pain and suffering in accordance with severity [*how bad*] and duration [*how long*]." Sometimes you get all three. But even if the instruction mentions none of them, this method works.

Once you explain the basic principle, provide an example. If physical pain is one of the harms, explain that the amount of money for pain is based on how bad, how long, and how interfering the pain is:

> For example, folks, if negligence hurts someone's arm and the pain is low, not too bad, there should be money to make up for that pain—but not much. "Not too bad" means low on the scale. That'd be the kind of case in which I'd have to ask you for a verdict of a few thousand dollars [*or "a very small amount," if you can't specify figures*] over the medical costs and lost income.

The figures I use here are for illustration. Choose your own.

> Now let's move up the scale: If the pain is worse, if it's the kind of hurting a person can't put out of their mind, maybe bad enough to even keep him from doing certain things, keeps him awake nights even when he takes all the medications they give him, then it takes more money to make up for the pain. That would make it the kind of case in which I'd have to ask you for a verdict into the tens of thousands of dollars [*Or "a fairly large amount," if you can't specify figures*] beyond medical costs and lost income, maybe even a hundred thousand if the pain was bad enough.
>
> Now let's go up the scale another step to "high." What happens when the pain is so bad it takes over everything? Nothing makes it go away, the person can't do anything—the kind of searing, constant pain they call "the window into Hell." That high up the scale, a few thousand or even a few hundred thousand cannot make up for it. In that kind of case, I would have to ask you for a verdict of more like five or six hundred thousand dollars, closer to a million, over and above medical and lost income costs. [*or, "In a case like that, I would have to ask you for a verdict of a great deal of money, in the same proportion as the pain."*]

Now, you know that the pain in John's arm is well into that high scale. That *makes this the kind of case in which I have to ask you* to allow $_____ for the intensity of pain in John's arm.[11]

The pain in his leg is not that bad, thank God, so it goes on the middle scale.

So all you have to do is add the middle-scale amount for his leg to the high-scale amount for his arm, and the total is your figure for the pain's intensity. [*If permitted, do the math—on a chart.*]

Note how this turns a single line item for pain into two line items.

Now what about the length of time the pain lasts?

Pain that lasts for a short time—a few weeks, maybe a month or two—is low on the scale. Takes just a little to make up for it. So that'd be the kind of case in which I'd have to ask for maybe a thousand or two beyond medical and income costs, ten or twenty or thirty thousand if it was high on the pain scale, too.

But what if it lasts for two or three years? Then that thirty thousand is not enough, because the pain has intruded on a big part of the person's life. That would make it the kind of case in which I'd be forced to ask for a few hundred thousand dollars, maybe a million, depending how long.

But at the top of the scale? Not just for a few weeks or a few years, but the rest of the person's life? Thirty years or more? Living every day, every hour with this pain? Getting worse with time, as arthritis and other problems set in to make it hurt more? Then we go higher on the scale. We're beyond making up for it with just a few hundred thousand or even a million dollars. Now the person can't even lie there at night and take comfort in hope—the one thing we cling to when we have nothing else—the hope that "Someday this pain will be gone." John cannot have that hope, because he knows the pain will never be gone. It will only get worse.

---

11. There is no damages phrase more important that "that makes this *the kind of case in which I have to ask you* to allow $_____ ." But when saying it, do not sound reluctant. Your tone should reflect your deep desire to ask for that amount *because* of the kind of case it is. I was remiss in not pointing this out in this book's previous edition. Fortunately, the National Jury Project's Susan Macpherson reported to me something I had not heard happen—lawyers sound glum and reluctant about having to ask for money! As if they were unwillingly forced. **Asking a jury to allow a proper dollar verdict is your most important task.** *Never* **do it reluctantly.**

> That puts it at the top of the high scale.
>
> So this is the kind of case in which I have to ask for at least $2 million dollars beyond medical and income costs for *how long* the pain will last.
>
> You add that to the amount for how much it hurts.

Do that for them on paper.

> Finally, how much does the pain *interfere* with things a person normally does? Just a little? If the person can do all but a few things he used to do, then it does not take much to make up for it. Say, just a limp, but he can still walk and run; that's maybe a few thousand—ten, maybe twenty thousand.
>
> But if there are lots of things the pain keeps him from doing, things that had been important parts of his life, that made his life worth living and now they're taken away, it takes more money. If it's too painful to work around the house or in the yard, if he can't walk without assistance or ride in a car more than a few minutes because of the pain, if he can't pick up his little girl, that's a major intrusion. That's the middle of the scale, which puts it in the range of a half million dollars, maybe more.
>
> Up at the top of the scale is the kind of case in which the pain is so bad that the person can't do anything. Everything his body used to be able to do, now someone else has to do for him. In this case, we're at the top of the high scale, where it takes a few million dollars to make up for what he can't do anymore. Add that to the amount for how bad it hurts and to the amount for how long it lasts.

Do the math on paper.

Use this method for each important pain, emotional or cognitive problem, disability, immobility, isolation, etc.[12]

8-14-1 Wrongful Death

The Scales also work for wrongful death. Death is the ultimate long-term harm: very top of the high scale. Being deprived of a father's guidance for a few years is a midscale loss; when the deprivation is permanent, it's the top of the scale.

---

12. *See* Fundamental Four, p. 7, on lack of mobility, which is usually a more effective damages factor than pain.

With this technique, you need never again be reduced to the lamest assertion attorneys ever use: "No one can give you a way to figure out how much money to give for pain or suffering. I cannot do that. Not even the judge can give you a way. You have to figure it out yourself." This translates into, "It's illegitimate."

Instead, in voir dire (or opening, if necessary), promise to give them, at the end of trial, the way to figure it out. Then in closing, give them The Scales.

8-14-2 Lesser Harm

When the harm is only middlingly painful, or is not permanent, or interferes with only a moderate amount of activity, The Scales work just as well.

> A small amount of harm is a small amount of money, a medium amount of harm is a medium amount of money, and a large amount of harm is a large amount of money. This case is in the middle. So it's the kind of case in which I have to ask you for more than the ten or fifteen thousand a small amount of harm would require. But it's not one of those cases where the pain is so bad I'd have to ask for many hundreds of thousands or even into the millions. This is in between, somewhere in the range of two or three hundred thousand dollars.

This method does not necessarily send jurors rushing into deliberations to use The Scales. They might not use them at all. But when a low-balling juror says—and he will—"I think $10,000 is enough," The Scales explanation has armed your favorable jurors to say: "No, not $10,000; they told us that was for cases where the pain was much less. This is one of the hundred-thousand-dollar cases."

Keep in mind that your primary goal in closing is to arm your favorable jurors so they can win the case for you. The Scales go a long way in doing that.

8-15 Admit Some Fault

With a persuasive comparative negligence argument against you, it can be best to acknowledge that some jurors may think it fair to assign some blame to your client. Give a suggested range:

> Someone might think some of the fault was John's. If everyone does, you can show how much of the fault you think was John's by giving it a percentage. You might think 5 or 10 percent, maybe even as high as 15 percent. Whatever you all agree on, write it on this line.

Jurors appreciate the honesty. And this tells your favorable jurors the range to argue for, if need be.

It also provides a benchmark that helps anchor the percentage jurors are likely to consider. It's best to do this during your second closing so that the defense cannot come back and give a higher percentage.

Often, you can proportionalize the amount of fault as being in the same ratio as the proportion of *what your client knew versus what the defendant knew* about the situation's potential for danger, as well as *how much time each had to avoid the danger*. The doctor knew—for years—all about the possible consequences. Mary did not even know 10 percent as much, and she found it out on the spur of the moment with no time to reflect on it—so the limit of her responsibility is well under 10 percent.

Also, there is a difference between apportioning blame for the event and blame for the harm. Analyze carefully to make sure you are presenting it the best way for your case. Your level of negligence might be trivial compared to mine, but maybe my enormous degree of negligence caused only a broken arm. Yours killed the guy.

8-16 Comparative Fault: Double-Dipping

In some cases, jurors are asked to apportion fault and then give an absolute figure for the total value of the damages. The judge then decreases the jury's dollar figure by the percentage they assigned for comparative fault.

To prevent double-dipping against you, explain in closing that the judge is the one who will reduce the jury's damages figure by the comparative negligence percentage. If you don't, the jurors might double-dip against you. First they will assign, say, 25 percent comparative fault. Then they decide on a $100,000 total figure, but they erroneously deduct the 25 percent and enter $75,000. The judge will lower the $75,000 by another 25 percent, so what should have been a $75,000 verdict ends up being $56,000. That's a $19,000 penalty for not explaining how it's supposed to work. It happens frequently.

Walk jurors through the correct process. Even if the dollar line(s) is below the apportionment line, tell them (and show how) to decide the absolute dollar amount(s) first.

> First, you decide the value of the harms and losses, no matter who caused them. You write that amount here.
>
> Then come up here to these lines. They ask you to assign percentages of fault to each line. So let's say that you think John was 5 percent to blame—write 5 percent on this line.

The judge will reduce this dollar line by 5 percent. Not you—it the judge's job.

Adjust this according to the format of your verdict form.

8-17 Proportions: The Damages Circle

Draw a pie chart on butcher paper.

Segment a pie slice to represent medical expenses. Cut another wedge for lost wages. Write the figure for each loss in its wedge.

Your cuts for economic losses should total far less than half the circle.

Explain that the whole circle represents all the money needed to fix what can be fixed, help what can be helped, and make up for whatever cannot be fixed or helped. The circle represents the total amount to achieve justice.

The circle is particularly useful where you cannot suggest specific figures for intangible losses. It visually proportionalizes the dollar amount of the intangibles to the dollar amount of the tangibles. Most important, the jurors can draw this circle for themselves in deliberations. Suggest that they do so.

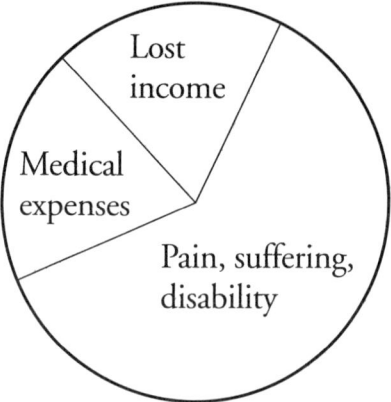

8-18 How Do You Decide on Appropriate Amounts?

Many attorneys are afraid to ask too little and are more afraid to ask too much.

Some try to gauge the "worth" of a case by comparing it to similar cases. But no two cases are alike, even when all the issues and evidence are similar. If nothing else, the parties, the jury, and the lawyers are different. Further, the other cases may not have been presented as well as you will be prepared to.

So how do you know how much you can ask for without creating a rebound effect to a lower verdict than it would have been, and without asking for less than they would have considered if you'd asked for more?

The only good way is by means of focus groups. You should be doing focus groups anyway, even for small cases, because there is no better way to learn how to present your case in court.

For larger cases, use a trial consultant to conduct your focus group. For smaller cases, you can do your own focus groups for comparatively little money. But do them properly or you will mislead yourself.[13]

A focus group won't reliably predict how much you're likely to get, but it can show you the ranges that real jurors will consider reasonable versus unreasonable. If a number of focus jurors individually decide that one hundred thousand is within a reasonable range, then jurors will probably not find you out of line for asking that much and a good margin more.

Ask your real jury for a margin higher than the highest amount the focus jurors found to be within a reasonable range. And be sure to explain that it's only a suggested amount—they can give more if they wish. Otherwise, they often believe they are allowed to give no more than you asked for.

8-19 Jurors' Weekends and Other Treasures

Be on the lookout for things the jurors themselves treasure that parallel what your client has lost. You can discover these things in voir dire, but you can also use what you know about people in the region. What do your jurors find valuable, and how do those things relate to what your client lost?

As Kentucky's Gary Johnson taught me years ago, for example, in areas where many people work at difficult, dangerous, extremely unpleasant jobs, such as in the West Virginia and eastern Kentucky coal mines, working folk live for their weekends. Knowing this, argue: "John has lost all his weekends. And he's lost that longer weekend called retirement, because his pain won't let him travel, work in the garden, play with his grandkids, or relax on the porch. John's pain won't give him a day off, ever."

This analogy works because it is personal to those jurors.

Jurors shield themselves emotionally from your client's catastrophic losses. By putting the harm in terms the jurors identify with, you keep them from walling themselves off.

If you have jurors with young children—jurors who showed themselves in voir dire to be strongly family-centered folks—emphasize your client's harms

---

13. *See* DAVID BALL, ARTEMIS MALEKPOUR, & DEBRA MILLER, FOCUS GROUPS: HOW TO DO YOUR OWN JURY RESEARCH (DVD) (Trial Guides 2008).

as they apply to his involvement with his kids and their welfare. Do not just show your client's feelings about being cut off from family involvements. Show how his kids feel about losing quality time and activities with Dad. And show how his knowledge that his kids feel bad about it exacerbates his own pain.

In other words, without being manipulative, clever, or condescending, tailor some of your damages arguments to things the jurors treasure. They'll feel your client's harms more directly. Nothing turns intangible to tangible as effectively as making it personal.

8-20 THE FIRST THING YOU THINK

When the phone call we all dread comes in the middle of a night, and it's about a loved one, that she's been hurt, the first thing you think is not, "Oh my, I wonder how much her medical expenses are going to be," or "I wonder how much salary she'll lose." Our first thoughts, our *only* thoughts, are about the important things: "Is she alive? Is she OK? Is she in pain? Will she get better? Where is she?"

Explain to jurors that these concerns are the real measures of harm.

8-21 TWO FUTURES

The more you show that money will make a difference, the more likely you are to get the money. (*See* Fundamental Seven, p. 24.) Georgia's Don Keenan asks jurors to look with him down the next fifty (or however many) years—in each of two directions.

> Look this way—the way with no money—and you see a bleak future. Cold institutional care for Shawna, separated from her mom, getting whatever care an overworked orderly can spare the time to give her in whatever kind of facility that year's state tax budget allows. The bleakness of an impersonal thing they call a "facility" full of strangers with their own problems.
>
> But look the other way—the way built on the verdict you provide—and we see Shawna surrounded by family; loved, cherished, given the best and most attentive care . . . .

In every case involving future harm—including most wrongful death cases where the family's pain will not easily heal—draw the "two futures" picture.

And make sure they understand how long fifty years is. For example, as of this writing in 2010 it's back to 1960—*before* JFK, just after *Sputnik*, etc.

Closing

In punitive damages cases, show a list of past victims next to a similar list of blank lines. In the future without a proper verdict, the blank lines will be filled in with the names of more victims. In the other future—created by a sufficient punitive damages figure—the blanks stay blank. No more victims.

Whether for compensation or punitive damages, the "two futures" argument gives jurors what they need to provide a good verdict—an awareness of the worthwhileness of a significant verdict. That is always a prime motivator of good verdicts.

8-22 Safety

One of the most worthwhile purposes of a good verdict is helping keep your client safe. In fact, jurors can get angry at the defendant when you point out that her refusal to meet her ttresponsibility has forced your client to live at needless risk since the injury. (No money for night care, so he's vulnerable to intruders; no money for emergency egress, so he's in danger if there's a fire; etc.)

Use a safety expert to explain the dangers your disabled client is in. Life-care planners don't spot them all. Even if they do, the presence of a safety expert makes a powerful statement in itself. And make sure your life-care planner factors in every potential safety issue.

For example, planners for paraplegics often include fire exits leading out of every room in the house. But they often forget about reworking the outside landscaping in a way that allows the paraplegic to quickly distance his wheelchair far enough from the house to be out of danger. A good safety expert will spot this quickly and suggest many other danger issues. This can add considerably to the money you can ask for—and that jurors tend to provide, since it has to do with safety.

8-23 Judo Law and "The Gift of Malingering"

Kentucky attorney and jury researcher Gary Johnson is the nation's expert at "Judo Law." He explains:

> When the defense has something bad, don't go on the defensive. That knee-jerk reaction is almost always wrong. Go into your office, lock the door, turn off the phone, and sit down and think. Think about it until you figure out how to turn it around 180 degrees and use it against them, so that it hits them harder than they can throw it at you.[14]

---

14. For a close look into Gary Johnson's extensive repertoire of superb trial tactics, see Gary Johnson & David Ball, Winning the Unwinnable Case (DVD) (Trial Guides 2007).

Florida criminal defense attorney Roy Black teaches the same thing, and I've seen him do it: look at the worst thing against you and figure out how to make it work for you.

Gary Johnson calls this Judo Law because it works like judo—taking what your opponent thrusts at you and turning its full force unexpectedly back against him.

For example, Judo Law will make you grateful for defense accusations of malingering, pain exaggeration, and anything else that portrays your client as dishonest. If your client will likely be credible to the jury, defense implications that she is being dishonest—along with her spouse and her physicians when they corroborate what she says about the level of her harm—give you the opportunity to use an extremely powerful damages argument:

> It was not enough for the defendants to cause so much physical harm, mental harm, and emotional harm. Now they have taken away the one thing they'd left intact: Sally's good name. To protect their money, they attacked her good name *in public* on the permanent record that will come out of this trial. They called Sally a liar: "Sally Robb is lying about her pain; Sally Robb is lying that she had to give up the job she loved; Sally Robb is lying that she cannot walk across a room without help." The defense has engraved this indelibly onto the permanent public record—a record that everyone can read, that everyone can see for all time. It's the record that Sally's kids will one day see—and they will, because when they're older they'll want to know about Mom's trial. The media can put it on the news. It's now part of the community: the accusation that Sally came in here, put her hand on the Bible, looked you in the eye, and lied to get money.
>
> They're trying to wreck her good name. Not because there's anything wrong with her name, but to protect their money.
>
> But there's good news: Unlike most of the harms in this case, you can *fix* this one. One hundred percent. How? **The instant your verdict is read aloud, Sally can get her good name back.** From the moment of your verdict, *if* it's for the full and fair amount, the community will know that the neutral jury that heard all the testimony saw that Sally was telling the truth.

By whatever amount the verdict is less than the full amount, that's the amount of dishonesty that will forever be attached to Sally's name. People who were not here will conclude you did not believe her—or her husband, or children, or doctors—when she said how badly she was hurt.

You need not ask for money for the damage to her name (though in some circumstances you can and should; a person's good name is not necessarily privileged fair game to a defense attorney). The point is that **her name will be restored if the jury provides the full amount for the harms resulting from the defendant's negligence**. This is a restorative argument: pay for the "usual" harms and her name is restored.

This argument provides a worthwhile, immediate purpose for noneconomic damages. Jurors who are uncomfortable providing much money for lost quality of life (because money does no good) will be more comfortable providing that money to restore Sally's good name. And once you have firmly established the total dollar figure you are seeking, that figure becomes the amount required to restore it.

Often the defense uses mini-versions of malingering claims. "Her pharmacy records show that half the time she did not take her pain medications." Here, too, apply Judo Law. Instead of getting defensive, you can often find a way to use it yourself to support your case:

> To keep her job she had to quit taking pain pills during the day so her head would be clear enough to keep her safe at work. So to earn a living, she has to be in bad pain five days a week. Only at home can she take her pain pills—by which time she's so exhausted from contending with the pain all day at work that she can't do anything but rest to recover enough to start all over the next morning. With the pain right back where it was.

This turns her into a fighter who won't quit—as opposed to the liar the defense claimed she is.[15]

8-23-1 Videos Cause Harm

Defense attorneys love their spy cameras. They say, "Aha! Look! She went *swimming*! Look at that! She's faking. Look at her splashing around with her kids. Obviously she's better than she claims."

---

15. *See* Rick Friedman, Polarizing the Case (Trial Guides 2007). If your client is not likely to be credible, please see supplement I, p. 481, for ways to prevent the defense from claiming that your client is malingering or exaggerating. Such claims are based on junk science, because there is no way to prove malingering or symptom magnification. *See also* Dorothy Sims, Exposing Deceptive Defense Doctors (James 2008) and the extremely important work of Michael Freeman (http://www.trialguides.com/authors/michael-freeman).

Apply Judo Law

The video of her swimming with her kids actually proves she has refused to give in—even though she knew her efforts to make sure her kids could have a normal day with Mom every so often would have her flat on her back in pain for days.

Show that the price she paid for weeding that garden or washing the car or swimming with her kids was agonizing pain and exhaustion. But does she get up and do it again the day after that? You bet.

The Dark Side—Stalking, Intimidation, Fear, and Shame

There is a dark side when the defense sends out its creeps with video gear to lurk in vans and under bushes *stalking* your client. Don't take this lying down. Trailing your client with cameras, secretly invading her privacy, peering in at the house and the school and the car may do no harm while it's happening—but when your client finds out, the feelings can be awful. Just ask her. That is harm piled upon the original harm: the intense and frightening feelings of deep violation and intrusion; fears that the stalking creeps could have been (and may still be) dangerous. The insecurity of knowing you are that vulnerable. The worry about what they might do with extra copies of the videos—the ones they didn't turn over to the defense attorney.

First the defendant drags your client into this nightmare by injuring her. Then he makes matters worse by refusing to be responsible for what he did. Now, when she's at her most vulnerable, he exposes her to yet greater fear and danger by getting some unknown creeps to stalk her with cameras.

If they hid in bushes to video her in the park with her children, if they hid in vans to take videos of her coming out of her ob-gyn's office, how does she know they did not aim their camera through the bathroom window to see if she could really toilet herself or shower unassisted? And who knows who has those videos? Will they show up on the Internet? Surely the creeps who do this kind of work are not so trustworthy that they heed the court's instruction to turn everything over.

You need not prove these "silly" thoughts true. The beyond-reasonable-doubt truth is that a normal person would have such thoughts, and they cut deep. They are real and deeply disturbing to a client already struggling with the consequences of serious injuries.

Clients rarely tell you about these feelings because they feel silly. Make her comfortable. Ask how she felt when she first learned about the creeps stalking her. Anger, sure—but then what? Shame? Humiliation? Terror?

Ask Dad how he felt when they found out that some unnamed guys sat in vans following his child around—even to school and back. Is the kid still scared about it? And what do those pretty bushes in the front yard now mean to the parents who just learned some goons with cameras concealed themselves in those bushes while videoing the house?

Ask your client if she worries about what personal—and irrelevant—things the creeps saw that they either did not video—or worse, did not turn over as the rules require.

Were They Seen?

If your client thinks she ever spotted the creeps, point out to the jury that **the only way these professionals ever let themselves be seen is if they want to be seen. So: "Did they let themselves be seen as a way to intimidate her into backing out of the lawsuit?"** Being stalked is threatening because you never know who the stalkers are or when they will be there or what they will do when there's no one around to help you. And these stalkers and the people who hire them know that a little bit of threat against a person or a person's child can make the person back out of the case.

The best source for how these creeps caused harm is to talk in depth with the client who was surveilled. This extra research can provide a foundation for developing a strong anger case against the defense. And it's not much of a stretch that the cause of this additional emotional harm was the initial negligence. So ask for extra money to compensate for it. A few hefty verdicts like that around the country and maybe these creeps who creep into this line of slime-work will creep back out.

8-24 VAGUE LANGUAGE

Always, but most especially in closing, **avoid vague or confusing language**. Be concrete. Pay special attention to the following:

8-24-1 *Nouns v. Pronouns*

No pronouns ("his," "hers," "him," "it," "she," "he," etc.) in closings. Pronouns wreak havoc with meaning: "Right after he lifted his leg against the hydrant, the policeman grabbed the dog's collar and he suddenly bit him on his butt." When you know what you mean and the listener does not, pronouns are a grave danger. Get completely out of the pronoun habit. Use nouns. Nouns clarify. And the less you use pronouns, the more often you weld the defendant's name to the wrongdoing. "He cut without looking" is less effective than "*Dr. Cornelius* cut without looking."

8-24-2 Verbs

In closing (but not in opening's story of what the defendant did) use strong, specific verbs. "Slams into" is better than "hits" or "collides." (In opening be more moderate; you don't yet have the standing for using the advocacy of strong language.)

8-25 PEOPLE CARE V. MONEY CARE

Folks, let's compare the level of care Snape Movie Palace used to protect the public in their parking lot with the care Snape is using to protect its $5 million here today. Here in trial, Snape uses the level of care people use when protecting something important to them, the way Snape's $5 million is important to Snape.

Which is why Snape has been so much more careful here in court than Snape was in their parking lot, where there was nothing to protect but the public.

How careful would Snape have been if Snape's $5 million in fifty-dollar bills had been sitting out in the parking lot that night? Would Snape have left blown-out bulbs in its security fixtures? Only one security guard to cover all four sides of Snape's building? No replacement when the guard took bathroom breaks? No guard in that dark lot for twenty minutes at a time? In deliberations, ask yourselves how many guards Snape would have hired to protect Snape's $5 million. How many cameras? How many lights? How long would Snape have left that dark lot unwatched?

Compare Snape's care in the lot to Snape's care in front of you: Snape did not hire an inexperienced guard to protect their $5 million. Snape hired Ron Jarrel, one of the state's most experienced and skilled defense attorneys. Snape did not leave Mr. Jarrel alone the way they left the parking lot guard alone. *Snape spent more money on Ms. Krueger, their hired opinion witness, to come talk to you for half a day than Snape spent on security in that parking lot for six months.*

Snape has two *working* video cameras covering less than 150 square feet around the money safe in the box office. But only one working camera to cover more 18,000 square feet of parking lot, and that camera couldn't even see 70 percent of it. Do the math: that means Snape was 250 times more careful with box-office receipts than with public safety.

Closing   253

> Snape even had a rule that there always had to be at least two people in the ticket office to protect Snape's money. There was an alarm system anyone in the ticket office could set off with their knee. And the alarm system was always in working order, because Snape checked it every week. Not once a year like Snape's parking lot cameras.
>
> A few minutes ago, Mr. Jarrel told you, "This is not a $5 million case." Folks, he means it. Mr. Jarrel speaks for Snape. Snape means it. Snape believes that the human well-being they took from Eddie isn't worth very much. That's their standard.
>
> They want you to apply the same standard—that public safety, human well-being, is not a big deal. Not in their parking lot, and not—Snape hopes—to you.

Simply contrast the care with which the defendants protect their money to the care with which they protected the public. In a med-mal case with bad medical records, compare those bad records to the neat, meticulous record keeping they used for billing, and the boxes and boxes of carefully maintained documents the defense has brought to trial to protect their $10 million.

American railroads spend a fraction of the money on public safety as they do on protecting their equipment and yards. They monitor the yards with expensive surveillance cameras and surveillance systems. But train engines have no simple video cameras for engineers to see blind spots in front of their high-speed trains.

Care-versus-*care* analysis lets you contrast the defendant's high-level care of themselves and their money with the low-level care they gave to public safety.

8-26 CLOSING: QUICKIES

8-26-1 *The Judge's Proportion of Time*

To support the legitimacy of money for noneconomic damages, point out (when true) that the judge will spend more time instructing on noneconomic damages than on economic damages "because the law places so much importance on *properly* making up for those losses with money, and because these decisions require careful consideration of all the harms."

8-26-2 *Help Her Be Helpful Again*

If your client had been a charitable, helping person before she was hurt and now can no longer be, a major "loss" is the pleasure she took in helping others. If she can no longer carry meals to the elderly, or raise money for a charity, or visit the sick, or do anything else she used to do to help, ask the jury to:

> Help her help people again. She cannot cook and carry those twenty meals a week anymore, but you can give back her inner satisfaction of knowing those folks are being well fed—if you include in your verdict the money for her to hire folks to buy and deliver the food. That way, her help continues.

Your client is eligible to have every loss replaced. Money that helps her regain the joy of helping others is legitimate compensation.

8-26-3 Law's Purpose; Jury's Purpose

"The purpose of the law is to balance the harm. The purpose of the jury is to figure out what it will take to balance the harm."

8-26-4 Taking Money from a Good Cause

If the defense argues that taking too much verdict money from the defendant will hurt a worthwhile organization such as a hospital, it should open the door to your citing how much insurance the hospital has, or at least to the fact that the verdict won't cost the hospital a dime. The defense is not allowed to defraud the jury just because something is not in evidence.

And in closing, point out that "There is no evidence that the defendant will have to pay any of this verdict, no matter how large it is."

8-26-5 Too Much?

"If that much money seems too much for one person, it's only because all that harm is too much to do to one person."

Chapter Nine

Public Respect and Trust: Restore It and Deserve It[1]

Talk doesn't cook rice.

—Chinese proverb

There is no effective weapon against the persuasive power of **selfless good works.**

—David Ball

9-1 The Problem

The jury pool is poisoned. A third of jury-eligible Americans hate and fear plaintiff's lawyers. This is because of what they think you *do*. They "know" you endanger their well-being: their jobs, their money, their health care, their families, their religion. They "know" you make your "exorbitant" living through *trickery* and *sham cases*. They "know" you happily and greedily profit from the misery of others. They "know" that when there's no misery, you and your clients invent some.

This affects cases of every size in every venue. And in legislatures across the country, public opinion lets legislatures slowly but certainly wipe out your profession.

The tort-"reform" campaign—carefully planned and executed—was unchallenged until just a few years ago. Result: a third of Americans now firmly believe that trial lawyers are a serious public menace.

That third is growing into half.

---

[1]. Adapted from an article originally (bravely) published in *TrialBriefs* (North Carolina Academy for Justice).

And there is no equally firm group of the opposite mind. Hardly anyone loves what you do.

For reasons that our public words, facts, and arguments can only make worse, you have no level playing fields in either the legislatures or courts.

As with every big-lie campaign, tort "reform" relies on grains of truth: Some greedy trial lawyers *do* misuse their power. Some verdicts *are* outlandish and harmful. Most trial lawyers and their organizations *do* support liberal politicians and judges who threaten the core values—including religious values—of many Americans. Medical liability insurance, personal insurance, as well as all kinds of products and services, have indeed gotten more expensive. Your fault!

Now, international corporations are preparing to spend nearly unlimited funds to kill you off.

Without fixing public opinion, our political activities and legislative lobbying are ultimately doomed. Legislators know they gain no voters for helping you and lose none for hurting you.

But it is too late to use words and messages and "the real facts." They make things worse. You cannot sit down, tell people the real truth, and thereby get them to believe you. People who think you're evil don't change just because you say, "Hey, I'm good, and here are some facts to prove it." That just makes people see you as hypocritical, which is more hateful than evil. If you don't believe me, imagine the most evil person you know is trying to "word" you into thinking he's good. With every word, you'll hate him more. And you won't buy any of his "facts" unless you see them for yourself. Simply put, it is too late for words because our side is too poisoned for our words to be believed.

Instead of words/messages/"facts," for the sake of your individual cases as well as legislation, you must ***show, not tell*** the public what you really are: a decent human being who cares about other people and not just money.

We must especially avoid the usual shallow, self-serving platitudes. For example: *"We're here for the little guy."* Tort-"reformed" citizen response? "Yeah, you love it when a little guy gets hurt *because you make lots of money.*"

Or, *"We're here to protect families."* Tort-"reformed" translation? "Yeah. *Your* families. Not ours. You undermine our health care, our jobs, our financial well-being, and even our God."

Or, *"We're here for justice."* Tort-"reformed" translation: "You love justice because you make a fortune from it."

You can lose your case by just starting your opening with, "Ladies and gentlemen, *we are here for justice.*" Tort-"reformed" translation? *"Aha! One of those greedy lawyers we've been warned about."*

In our younger years, most of us believed this: "If I could just sit down and explain to the other side what is wrong with their point of view, they would see the truth in what I say." Remember when you thought that?

Not even Gandhi, Jesus, or Martin Luther King Jr.—among history's most effective deployers of words—relied on words alone. They knew better. They knew they needed acts—even miracles—to persuade.

Fortunately, we don't need miracles. We have an easy, inexpensive, honest, worthy, and long-proven way to regain respect. In your circumstances, it is the only option. Trial lawyers can easily get public gratitude and find themselves among the nation's most-loved professions. The only hard part, I have found, is convincing plaintiff's lawyers and their organizations to do it.

Your fate and your profession's are in your own hands. Stop complaining about "bad jurors" and "rotten politicians." Just do what needs to be done. Here's how.

9-2 THE FOOLPROOF SOLUTION

So what can you do to unpoison the public mind? How do you regain the ground lost to the decades-long campaign against you?

First: *Shaddup!*

Please! No more "messages" and "communications" and "war-room" emissions. Words alone have never once in history rehabilitated a destroyed reputation. So: shhh!

Then start *doing things* that help others—but in a very particular way: **Help others in ways that do not simultaneously help you. Regularly, publically, and selflessly commit altruism.**

Good works. Blanket the nation with your good works. Not your lawyer works, but your no-revenue-producing good works. Use the things you have learned in your profession to step out of your lawyer's costume and into your good works costume.

Selfless good works is the most fundamental and universally accepted principle of persuasion. They trump everything else. Words alone to fix a bad reputation *ALWAYS* make the reputation worse.

In playwriting and screenwriting, the foolproof method of selfless good works is called "Saving the cat."[2] The principle—you easily persuade an audience that a character is good by *showing* the character *doing* something *selfless or disadvantageous* to himself that *helps someone else*. It works in real life even better than in the movies. (It's the opposite of kicking the puppy.)

How can I call this foolproof? Because I know it from Shakespeare, from marketing experts, from psychologists, from neuroscientists, from *Reptile*, from history. And from those many individual attorneys already doing it.

Selfless good works is even the prime ingredient of classical oratory, where the focus is always on deeds and never on words—no matter how oratorically soaring the words. Re-read Mark Antony's "oration"—how he turned the angry Roman crowd that had been cheering Caesar's assassination. Mark Antony turned the crowd not by the power of words, but by pointing out what Caesar had *done*.

Even Jesus needed deeds, not just words. And his words almost always were about acts, not concepts or "facts."

If Jesus isn't a strong enough example, look at Walmart: When Walmart's reputation sank to the point where it affected sales, Walmart did not mount more sales campaigns. Instead, Walmart started *doing good things*, such as improving employee health benefits. And who was *first* to show up in New Orleans after Hurricane Katrina? Walmart! With three huge eighteen-wheelers loaded with fresh water.

And now that heartless corporation that made its employees go without health care has further mended its bad reputation by giving out four-dollar prescriptions.

When Mideast terrorists found that their violence was alienating their own supporters, the terrorists started programs of medical help, schools, and other social services. The terrorists knew better than to rely on words.

Of course, effective persuasion uses words. But without *deeds*, words are useless. You can't win a case by stamping your foot and saying, "My client is right so give us money!" Neither can you change the minds of tort-"reformed" jurors or politicians by stamping your foot and saying, "Trial lawyers are good, so trust us!"

We don't need to match the increasing tens of millions the insurance companies, chambers of commerce, and national and international corporations continue spending to wipe out trial lawyers. All we have to do is replace our pathetic campaign of words/arguments/"facts" with good *selfless* works. That will outweigh every million the other side can spend.

---

2. *See* Blake Snyder, Save the Cat (Michael Wiese Productions 2005).

There is no effective weapon against the power of selfless good works.

9-3 Does It Work?

Come back with me to the early 1990s. An Atlanta attorney—Don Keenan—is doing some playground injury cases for kids mangled or killed because half-ton dead branches eventually fall, or because jagged pieces of metal fence poke out young eyes, or because of any other of a number of common and commonly ignored playground dangers.

Don Keenan wins his cases, so he's doing right by these kids. But in the dark of night, he thinks, "Do I really want to some day lie on my deathbed knowing that all I've been is the guy who comes around afterward to clean up? Just the garbage man?"

Don decides it's not enough.

He thinks, *Why not keep kids from getting hurt in the first place?*

Now *there's* an act against a trial lawyer's self-interest! Prevent the very kind of harm that provides his cases!

Don prints up a playground safety checklist. One little page. About one cent per copy.

He distributes them all over the place—grocery stores, kids' clothing stores, malls. So parents can take the checklist to their kids' playgrounds and check off every safety-required item.

No dead overhanging branches.

No missing rubber safety tips.

No jagged fences.

No broken pavement.

Etc.

Any item on the list that a parent could not check off was to be reported to the principal, then the school superintendent, then—if still necessary—the news media.

In this easy way, Don protected innumerable kids. And he *showed* he was a caring person. He never stood around proclaiming such counterproductive, self-serving, hollow words as, "I care! I care! Watch me care!"

Instead, he *acted*. Deeds, not words.

To this day he continues to act—*in ways that do not simultaneously enrich himself.*

Because, as every child knows, "saving the cat" does not help your reputation when you're paid to save the cat.

Over the years, Don continued protecting kids. His Keenan's Kids Foundation has become a major public force in protecting children. His 2006 book—*365 Ways to Keep Kids Safe*—carries his work even farther. His annual public exposures of dangerous toys save countless lives.

Did Don's good deeds help him as a trial attorney? Well, when he sets foot in trial, there is no tort "reform." Jurors know—or quickly find out online—that Don Keenan is the guy who protects kids. So when jurors see him here protecting the kid in this particular case, they know he's doing what he always does: protecting kids who need protecting.

Every trial lawyer in America could get to an equivalent status. But most think they are too busy to deal with that kind of thing or that they are not "big enough" to make a difference, not even to their personal reputations much less the profession.

But they can.

Not every trial lawyer can start a public service foundation as Keenan did—though if you give a damn you can easily band together with a few other lawyers and do it. Not every lawyer can write child-safety books that Oprah orders her audience to read, though you can fill your Web site with safety tips instead of those embarrassing marketing claims about how good a lawyer you are. *Every* trial attorney can find good and selfless works to do. And even without Oprah's help, you can easily and inexpensively show your community your good works and ask the community to help with them. You can also let the community know how someone can benefit from whatever you are doing or get involved in helping to do it.

And as you'll see below, you can turn your Web site into a help center instead of a marketing center. That way, when jurors look you up, they'll see you actually doing good work instead of bragging about what a great winner you are (which makes them suspicious of you: if they think you're a great winner it's easy for suspicious jurors to think you win by technique, not justice).

9-4 THE SPECIFICS

A few years ago I was explaining the "good works" principle to a seminar for the Consumer Attorneys Association of Los Angeles. They had chosen that name despite its exclusion of most of their own members' concerns (most clients are not hurt by being consumers), but it was a good-faith—if naïve—attempt to find a quick solution to the ravages of tort "reform."

Speaking to them, pleading to them, I told them to quit diddling around with name changes and instead "Go do good, *selfless* works!" Change not your name, but the world and how your profession is regarded.

A lawyer raised his hand to ask, "What good is there we can do?"

He was not kidding. This poor soul lives in the middle of L.A., a city with problems on every block, yet could not think of any good that needed doing. Well, in case he's reading this: ***"Simply go do the good thing nearest you!"***[3] Keenan was doing playground cases, so he did the thing nearest him by helping protect playground kids before they got hurt.

It's an easy club to join: *Do what's nearest.* What's in *your* world that you can help make safer, better, or easier for people—and that you can help without simultaneously profiting from it?

Here's a sampling of what trial lawyers and their enlightened organizations have done so far:

9-4-1 2006—Oklahoma

Dangerous heat wave. People dying from the heat. A trial lawyer goes to buy a window air conditioner. Buys two. Goes home. Calls a social agency to get the name of someone in danger of dying from the heat. That evening the TV news features the lawyer and a lawyer buddy installing the air conditioner.

Cut to:

Elderly man in the same room saying, "I have heard of this kind of thing happening to other people. I never thought it would happen to me." He goes on to explain how the heat nearly killed him the night before, but now . . . and he begins to cry.

Among TV history's most powerful TV moments.

Two days later:

Members of the trial lawyers' academy in Oklahoma chip in enough to buy dozens of air conditioners. They install them where needed all over the state. Result #1: lives saved. Result #2: great news headlines extolling trial lawyers.

---

3. "Do the duty which lieth nearest to thee! Thy second duty will already have become clearer." Thomas Carlyle.

In Oklahoma, the term "Trial Lawyer" now has new respect and affection, because the trial lawyers called their air-conditioner program "***Trial Lawyers Are Cool.***"

9-4-2 2006—Connecticut

A Connecticut Trial Lawyers Association press release announces that a dozen Connecticut plaintiff's *trial lawyers* are standing by to provide *free* legal assistance to veterans in need of help with the government agencies that are supposed to help veterans. For days, this is a leading news story in New York and throughout New England.

And lots of veterans are being helped.

9-4-3 Years Ago—Midwest

A Midwestern town runs out of money for Fourth of July fireworks. A trial lawyer steps in. To this day he personally pays the few thousand a year for the fireworks. He dresses up as Uncle Sam and gives the Fourth of July speech. Everyone loves it. He's become a town hero and institution. Do you think tort "reform" hurts him when he goes to trial? Nope.

9-4-5 Web Sites

Smart trial lawyers are turning their Web sites to good-works use. Rather than the usual ultra-transparent greedy brag sites such as the *"We-are-great-lawyers-who-will-win-your-case"* site, or the *"Look-at-my-picture-don't-I-look-professional!"* site, or the *"Here's-me-in-my-library-of-books-I-haven't-opened-in-a-decade"* site, or the *"Here's-my-great-victories-where-I-got-juries-to-give-wads-of-money-that-other-lawyers-wouldn't-have-gotten"* site, smart lawyers are now transforming their Web sites into **help centers**.

How? By using the Web site to help people. So when jurors look you up during trial—as they will no matter what the judge says—they'll see that you're about caring and good works, not marketing and greed.

Fill your Web site with lists of online and local injury support groups, books to help victims cope,[4] books to keep people safe,[5] and other help resources. Facts people need to know. Your legal-services peddling should be a subordinate page on your site that viewers reach by a small, secondary link. If they need you, they'll find you.

---

4. Such as *Fighting Back, the Rocky Bleier Story*—which has helped countless badly injured folks deal with their agony.
5. Such as *365 Ways to Keep Kids Safe* (Balloon Press) and Pal Malone's *The Life You Save* (Da Capo Lifelong Books).

In Atlanta, the Gary Martin Hayes Law Firm runs Keep Georgia Safe (keepgeorgiasafe.org), providing safety education and crime prevention training to the community. The firm also has run public service ads against drunk driving (and Mr. Hayes then served as an officer for MADD). This and similar efforts show, not just tell, that he's about safety rather than greed.

In northeastern Pennsylvania, the law firm of Hourigan, Kluger, & Quinn has established HKQ Kids (hkqkids.org), an active and well-known community force in protecting children. Also take a look at keenanskidsfoundation.com. These are models that virtually any attorney or small group of attorneys can replicate in their own community and even extend onto the national scene, as does Keenan's Kids.

Go to waiting.com to see what Wisconsin's Gordon S. Johnson Jr. has done to create a helping Web site. A person in need of help and information not about legal services, but how to deal with having a family member in a coma, searches on line for "coma." Within the first page and a half of search results, waiting.com pops up, leading the searcher to an extraordinary site. It's extraordinary because it provides help, services, and guidance about understanding and dealing with coma. It offers legal services almost secondarily.

When someone in that position needs an attorney, Mr. Johnson will obviously be high on their list—but the site is not about that. So when jurors on one of his cases look him up online, they see waiting.com, clarifying what kind of person he is—not the heartless, greedy threat painted by tort "reform" that we can't talk our way out of, but the decent human being providing valuable help for free.

9-5 A Potpourri of Good Works

You don't need the list that follows. On your own, you can figure out plenty of good works you can do. But this list will gear up your thinking.

Many firms give out free bike-rider helmets. That's kind of easy: buy stuff and give it away. So don't brag about it—it's a start, but you can and should do better. Providing money is nice, but **to make a difference in how people think about you, provide your own personal time and effort, not just your money**. Otherwise you come across as just a rich lawyer throwing your money around.

One rural western firm supplies a staff person every afternoon to serve as school crossing guide.

A North Carolina firm invites the public (via posters and holiday events listings) to join its staff stuffing holiday stockings for overseas service men and women; the firm and its co-sponsors provide a nice supper for the stuffers.

Your firm can provide free legal services to help local social-help agencies or start-up schools.

You can serve on a school's or agency's board—and publicly seek support for it.

You can run an "emergency assistance" hotline on your Web site—where people in need can post their needs and people interested in helping can review the site often to see how they can help.

You can find ways to help senior citizens, or the homeless, or food banks, or other areas of community need.

You can run a December holidays table at a local mall to collect presents or cash for kids.

You can bolster public safety by providing taxi tokens to tavern drunks for free cabs home.

You can team with other lawyers to do safety checks of public and business facilities. Report the results on your Web site or in a newspaper column. Or you can provide checklists so people can do their own safety checks of playgrounds, malls, parking lots, etc.

You can become an actively involved supporter and fund-raiser for a worthwhile—and non-controversial—local charity.

You can teach English to immigrants—free. Advertise to attract attendees. Learn how to teach by Googling TEFL ("Teaching English as a Foreign Language"). You can become an expert in just a few hours.

Teach adult literacy classes.

Tutor kids or any other group that needs tutoring.

Provide continuing help to kids with illnesses, disabilities, or permanent injuries. (For an inspiring example, see this chapter's Epilogue.) Team up with a local hospital. Provide help for social workers who deal with these problems. Underwrite in-hospital entertainment for kids or do the entertainment yourself, if you are entertaining enough to entertain kids (reading stories, etc.). Sponsor in-hospital pet-visitation programs or therapy-animal programs.

Help raise money to sponsor or coach a local Special Olympics team. Arrange free tickets to cultural and sports activities for families that can't afford them; better yet, arrange the events themselves, because just paying for the tickets just makes you a rich lawyer. Become a visible advocate for social agencies—MADD, YM/WCA, shelters, etc.

Post on your Web site (with proper attribution) the fact that hundreds of people needlessly die every day in American hospitals due to safety rule violations. Provide a list of ways people can protect themselves and their loved ones while in the hospital.

Choose any area of public danger. Explain the danger and give safety advice. For example, post safety tips on cars—new and used—for such things as child passenger safety. Some popular used cars have rear-seat belts that do not properly protect children.

Some hospitals offer free tutoring on how to properly set up and install the infant car seat. Hospitals do this before mother and baby leave for home. You can do it on your Web site.

Post a list of streets dangerous for bicycles in your community.

Be openly available for free legal help when disaster—flood, hurricane, etc.—strikes. Organize twenty-five lawyers across your state to show up at disaster sites with the Red Cross or other state disaster relief officials to offer FREE help. One state's trial lawyers' academy has already launched this program. Their purpose is to help folks—free—with insurance claims and other legal matters that emerge from the disaster. Show people you are there to help soothe one of their greatest worries in such situations. Don't turn any of it into a profit-making case.

Get involved with the Bob Woodruff Family Foundation or others to help support the overwhelming number of returning brain-injured veterans.

Team up with two or three other trial attorneys to write a regular legal-advice column in a local minority-reader newspaper. (Great for marketing, and you'll provide an essential service.)

Team up with two or three other attorneys to do a weekly drive-time radio show for a local station. Cover topics such as local trials and verdicts, guidance on how to stay safe in various situations (*e.g.*, in hospital), legislative matters that can affect individuals, legal advice people need to know, etc. Don't blow your own horn; instead, *help* people. Don't even give out your phone number; if they want you, they'll look it up.

Adopt a highway. Keep it spotless.

Help your local children's Guardian ad Litem program or Friends of the G.A.L. They need help, your help will change young lives, and you might get into heaven.

If you advertise, your ads should be helpful, not just marketing pleas. For example: "We do not want to see you as a defendant in court, so please: *Don't text while driving.*" Or, "If you speed in a school zone and hurt a child, we will come after you in trial. So slow down."

If you buy the back page of the phone book, fully half your ad should contain emergency numbers or some other useful service. For a small ad inside the phone book, include a line or two that supports a local cause or delivers a selfless message: "Support Mothers Against Drunk Driving." Or, "Make trial lawyers obsolete: Do everything safely." Or, "Safety First. We already have plenty of business."

Always remember that your *time* and money, not just your money, is the key.

9-6 Rejecting Cases

Stop creating tort-"reformed" jurors. Chances are high you do it all the time. That's because there's a good way to reject cases—and a bad way. The bad way is how it's almost always done. The good way requires a little more than just the usual "no, we can't take your case"—but you have to do it. If you don't start doing it, you are neither a useful force in dealing with tort "reform" —nor are you a decent person.

Keep in mind that when you have to turn away a case in the usual way, you are compounding the harm the defendant apparently did. There is no way you can wriggle out of that accusation, because it is virtually always true. And the person you turned away always feels it.

So do it the good way: send folks away with some real help.

For example, when rejecting a potential client, provide her with contact information and descriptive information about no-cost and low-cost support and assistance groups for folks with her kinds of injuries. Include local and online social and community services as well as national resources for folks who have been harmed in the same way.

Ask your clients and past clients for ideas: What has helped them? Relay those ideas to folks you cannot take as clients.

In other words, stop claiming you are here to help the public when you constantly turn most of them away without even trying to help. You are in a position to provide a lot of help, and you must.

Ask your experts—doctors, psychologists, and grief counselors—for ideas. Collect pamphlets, reading recommendations, and other resources. Describe available videos at the local library. Have your staff person compile all this.

Have your most empathetic staff person *unhurriedly* review it all with the person you have to reject as a client.

Every would-be client comes to you for help. So when you can't take the case, *you have no moral right to have wasted their time and then give nothing in return.* You need to stop making people in fear and pain come "audition" for you and then send them away as if they are worthless. **Stop, please, the ghastly practice of turning people out without helping them**—as if their fear, pain, anger, and loss are beneath your notice unless they can profit you.

When you turn away supplicants without helping them in some way, you have made them fruitlessly grovel. That makes enemies. If there's a God, he will be one of them. No religion in the world—except the religion of greed—says it's okay to turn away people in need.

With each rejectee, you create a small and powerfully vocal cadre *in your own community* that now "*knows*" you are about nothing but greed. The cadre includes the rejected client, his family and friends, and everyone he ever talks to about what you did.

How many such cadres have you created so far?

Most trial attorneys—*each one on his or her own*—have thus transformed hundreds and thousands of folks who were not initially tort "reformed" into some of our most virulent tort-"reform" jurors. How do I know? Because I have talked in depth to lots of them. By the time they get onto your jury, you'll have forgotten their names. But they'll remember you.

9-7 ORGANIZATIONS

Urge *and help* your state trial lawyers organizations and AAJ to do good, self-less works. Not as minor activities, but as one of their major activities. Not as a note tucked away in a subpage of their Web site or in some subcommittee, but as one of the organization's *principle* raisons-d'etre. If our organizations want to help us regain respect, they have to take this next step.

They will whine, "We can't afford it!" "We don't have time!" Nah. How much time and money did it take the Connecticut Trial Lawyers to send out a press release about helping veterans? How long did it take the Oklahoma folks to e-mail members to get money for air conditioners? Ten minutes or twenty? So when some state organization claims they "don't have the time or resources to pursue this good works concept," I know what they are really saying: "We like the status quo."

Well, next time you lose a case or get too low a verdict, it will partly be because of the status quo.

Of course, when your organization says they can't afford it, they probably mean it—because they have never seriously considered how to do it. Tell them to either put it on their radar or take you off their membership radar.

Bar associations all over the country are involved in disaster and other kinds of assistance. So are a very few trial lawyer organizations, though none do enough. The fact that trial lawyers organizations do little or nothing is shameful—and it contributes heavily to the lack of respect and trust our side has.

> The fallout from the way many attorneys turn away people they can't accept as clients, combined with the failure of most trial lawyer organizations to lift an active finger to do or facilitate good works, is a one-two combination punch that does us as much harm as the tort-"reform" movement itself.

9-8 SHOW THE WORLD

An outstanding attorney in one of America's great law firms heard me teach all of the above.

"No!" she said. "My firm has done good works for years—and we still cannot win a case!"

She gave me their annual report of all their good works. Amazing. **But the public knew nothing about them.** Among Jesus's first recorded words are these: "Neither do men light a candle and put it under a bushel, but on a candlestick; and it giveth light unto all that are in the house."

Counselor, your selfless good works are your candle. We have a huge house to light.

Today, that same firm lists its good works on its Web site. (It should be the site's main page, with everything else on subpages. It's not, but it's a start.)

Your moral, invincible, foolproof solution is your visible, selfless, good work. Good works are the only way to regain the lost ground of forty years of tort-"reform" attacks.

How do you make your good works visible in the community without bragging about them? Simply invite the public to help you with their effort and time.

9-9 Epilogue

Come back with me a few years to an AAJ conference in Puerto Rico.

The hotel lobby.

A lawyer I don't know confronts me. "Ball!" he hollers. "You ruined my life!"

Feeling I need no more of this conversation, I start backing away.

But he grabs me. "Dammit, Ball, you told us to do good works. *Near-at-hand* works."

I look for an escape route.

He continues, still yelling at me: "I do cases for kids who are serious burn victims. I know that the hardest thing—beyond even the pain—is the disfigurement, awful for a kid to grow up with. So I started a summer camp for them. They spend close time with others in the same boat. They gain confidence. They learn how others handle it. The damn idea grew like kudzu!

"Now I got five burn camps! Takes half my time! One camp is in Israel for Arab kids, Christian kids, Jewish kids—now my summer vacation requires a passport! I don't earn a cent from it! What the hell?!?"

Is he gonna punch me out?

Then he—New Jersey attorney Sam Davis[6]—says, ***"And I have never been happier in my life."***

Sam has shown us the gold standard. Thank God for Sam! If enough trial lawyers get to that level, tort "reform" will devolve to a barely believable historical oddity.

But if we rely on the blather of words and "communications," if we don't do what this chapter says to do, soon there will be few if any plaintiff's lawyers. Because the poisoned third of the public will grow to half, and when it does, your work will be outlawed.

So get busy.

Or get a book on how to do some other field of law.

---

6. *See* http://www.burnadvocates.org. And send Sam money to help support the burn camps.

SUPPLEMENT A

JURY VOIR DIRE

Supplement A presumes that you have reasonable voir dire leeway (time, range of questions, attorney-conducted, etc.). If not, never neglect to seek improvements, as discussed just below in section A.

Even without sufficient voir dire leeway, study this section carefully. It contains much of use even for the most limited voir dires.

Your best guides to jury selection: *Blue's Guide to Jury Selection*, by Lisa A. Blue and Robert B. Hirschhorn, two excellent lawyers who are consistently of enormous help and inspiration to their colleagues. And *Jurywork* by the National Jury Project—a "bible" of the jury consulting profession. The guidance below provides important auxiliary offerings and focal points.

A-1 THE LAW

The Law Can Help

"The voir dire examination of jurors . . . [is] to enable counsel to exercise intelligently the peremptory challenges allowed by law."[1] Most venues have a similar case. But even without it, the judge who resists has some agenda other than justice.

You can also find assurances of a "fair jury." Such assurances cannot be fulfilled without enough voir dire time and the leeway to go beyond "will-you-follow-the-law?" questions.

The Law Can Help If You Know It

Too few plaintiff's attorneys know and bring to trial the necessary law. Judicial discretion is not as broad as many judicials think. Go armed with whatever you can find to allow sufficient voir dire time, particular kinds of important questions, written juror questionnaires, and other improvements.

Don't spring your improvement requests at the last minute. Give the judge time to contemplate the issue when she's not simultaneously worrying about a dozen other things—such as whether she has enough prospective jurors to allow for the extras your request might require.

The Law Can Help If You Use It

One of the most overblown attorney's fears is that you might "offend" a judge by pursuing what you need to represent your client—such as necessary voir-dire leeway. But respectful, concisely written, plain English, well-documented, and timely briefs do not offend.

Lawyers often excuse their failure to seek important voir dire improvements by telling me: "Oh, you don't know our judges around here," as if they're in a specially designated bad-judge zone. "Even asking for an improvement like that will get her mad." But all good trial consultants have seen many of even the "worst" of judges entertain and grant well-crafted motions for voir dire improvements.[2] And the only times a sane judge will get annoyed is when the motion is last minute, or sloppy, or ill-informed, or insultingly critical of the judge's usual practice.

---

1. *State v. Brown,* 280 S.E.2d 31, 32 (N.C. Ct. App. 1981).

2. Of enormous help in seeking improvements (and in much else): LISA BLUE AND ROBERT HIRSCHHORN'S BLUE'S GUIDE TO JURY SELECTION (2004) and JURYWORK. Both contain excellent ideas for voir dire improvements, guidance and sample motions for requesting them, and other important aids.

When seeking voir dire improvements, show the judge why they are necessary *in this particular case* as opposed to most others. For example: "This particular case is too unusually complex and detailed for me to be able to anticipate every possible topic I might need to follow up on in voir dire, so I have no way of submitting those follow-up questions to you without flooding you with voir dire questions. That's one reason I need attorney-conducted voir dire." Or, "This particular case deals with unusually personal matters—such as intimate sexual practices and attitudes that people usually keep private. Unlike open-court voir dire, a written questionnaire will provide confidentiality and thus encourage jurors to answer candidly." You can find "unique" things like this in most kinds of cases. By including one or more in your motion, you enable the judge to say yes without seeming to set a personal precedent for similar requests in the future. (So when someone later says, "But judge, you let _____ do it," she can respond, "Yes, but that was for a very particular set of circumstances.")

A-2 RULE #1

Rule #1 for jury selection—otherwise known as Ball's rule—is "Shut up and listen." In voir dire, if more than 10 percent of the words are yours, you are hurting yourself. So shut up.

You almost certainly did not choose law school by being the kind of person who listens well when you don't have to. So you have some self-training to do. In voir dire, lend the jurors your ears, not your mouth.

A-3 OPEN-ENDED QUESTIONS

Rule #1, "Shut up and listen," is simple and effective. It's also a challenge. It requires, among other things, that your questions be short, open-ended, and designed to elicit a lot of talking.

So ask short, open-ended questions.

Then shut up and listen. You'll get more information.

And at home, your family will start to like you.

Open-ended questions are those that cannot be answered in only a word or phrase. ("Please tell me about . . ." instead of "Do you . . ."; "What's your workday like?" instead of "What kind of work do you do?" or the transparently sexist "Do you work outside the home?") Unlike closed-ended questions, open-ended questions contain no implicit limitation on the answer's length. The closed-ended "Do you know we only have to prove that what we say is more likely true than not true?" limits the response to one word, or a grunt, or nothing. The open-ended "How do you feel about it being so easy on us?" does not. (Some judges take umbrage at hearing you say "feel." With such a judge, substitute the word "think": "What do you think about it being so easy on us?")

Remember: You cannot make good jury selection decisions based on one-word answers. That is why closed-ended voir dire questions are inept.

Why, What, How, Tell Me

Open-ended questions start one way, closed-ended another.

OPEN-ENDED questions start with:

Why[3]   Tell me why

What   Tell me what

How   Tell me how

Tell me about that

CLOSED-ENDED questions are not merely those that ask for a yes or no answer. They also invite one-word or single-phrase answers. They start with:

When	Was
Where	Were
Is	Do
Are	Did
How many	

Starting with "when," "where," "is," "are," "was," "were," "do," "did," or "how many" is the most common cause of violating Rule #1. The only thing worse is the ghastly, "I take it by your silence that . . . ," a question that elicits no information of any kind whatsoever and offends jurors by putting words into their mouths.

Limited Uses of Closed-Ended Questions

There are only three legitimate uses of closed-ended questions in voir dire:

1. To introduce a new topic about which you will immediately ask open-ended follow-ups. *Example:* The closed-ended "Who here has safety rules at work?" followed by open-ended questions such as, "Mr. Jones, tell me about the safety rules at your printing

---

3. "Why?" and "Tell me why" are open-ended, but somewhat confrontational. They tend to make listeners defend what they've already said instead of elaborating on it. "Tell me about that" is more productive. *See* chapter 3, p. 65.

plant," and "How do you feel about having to follow those rules?" and "What happens when someone breaks those rules?" and so on.

2. The second use of closed-ended questions is to nudge quiet jurors into a response mode. Get them to raise their hands. ("Who here has ever been through jury selection?"[4]) This chips away at their reluctance to participate.

3. The third use of closed-ended questions is during the final steps of a cause challenge, as covered below.

Aside from those three uses, save your closed-ended questions for cross-examination and for housebreaking pets. (On the other hand, the answer to the closed-ended "And isn't it true, Fluffy, that you did this?" is "Woof." Just think of all you'd learn if you asked instead the open-ended "Fluffy, tell me about this.")

A-4 THE ALL-PURPOSE FOLLOW-UP QUESTIONS

You learn little of value until the third follow-up question. When you ask a question like "Who here has ever been in a wreck?" some hands go up. You duly note the names—and then move on to a different topic! Yet having been in a wreck does not make anyone a good juror or a bad one. It's always a toss-up.

The only reason to ask a question on any new topic ("Who's ever been in a wreck?") is to follow up on the answer. Here is the gold-standard all-purpose follow-up question:

Please tell me about it.

After they tell you about it, say,

Please tell me about *that*. [*Or Eric Oliver's "What else?"*]

And then,

Thank you. And please tell me a little about that.

So:

Q: Who here has been in a wreck?

---

4. I hate to spend so much of my career invoking Eric Oliver, but the dawg is smart. He points out that "Who here . . ." has an individual personal quality to it, while "How many of you . . ." has the opposite.

Hands go up. Someone at your table notes the names because you have nothing to write with, since you know that taking notes during voir dire hinders communication. You call on a juror whose hand is up:

Q: Please tell me about it.

You could have asked:

Were you hurt?

Or

Whose fault was it?

Or

How did it happen?

But being smart, you said, "Please tell me about it."

This hands control to the juror, which is where both of you want it. He can pick any subtopic he wants. His unprompted choice will reveal something about his attitude toward the wreck. He might say, "This guy just slammed into me" (i.e., the wreck was *someone else's fault*). He might say, "Worst thing I was ever involved in in my life" (i.e., the *seriousness* of the wreck is his most salient connection to it). It might be how badly he was injured. (So he'll *compare* that to the one in this case.) It might be what his injuries later kept him from doing. (Ditto.) It might be how he sued or got sued or decided not to sue or prayed he wouldn't be sued. It might be what happened to his insurance rates—or any of a number of other subtopics. By your saying, "Tell me about it," you let him select his most salient subtopic. For example:

A: Well, they blamed me, but it wasn't my fault. The jerk hit me.

So this juror knows the sting of being falsely accused. That means there's some chance he will identify with the defendant. Not necessarily, but follow up to find out:

Q: Tell me about that.

A: Well, people always blame someone else, and that's what he did. I was just driving along, and . . . .

"People always blame someone else" is not a bias likely to help your cause. So this was important information to unearth. You would probably not have unearthed it if you'd chosen his subtopic by asking, say, "Did you get hurt?"

In response to "tell me about it," a juror might say,

A: Totaled my car. But I walked away without a scratch.

Probably not a good plaintiff's juror for a slow-speed rear-ender case. How likely is he to believe a low-speed impact leaving barely a dent could hurt anyone? But don't decide too soon. Keep going:

Q: I'm glad you weren't hurt, but tell me about it.

A: It was luck. I've seen plenty of wrecks with hardly any car damage where the driver got clobbered.

That's what a follow-up question does for you. And the only follow-up question you ever need is "Tell me about it." By giving up control over the choice of subtopic and letting the juror control the direction of the conversation, you learn things you might not otherwise even suspect enough to ask about.

If, after a number of "tell me about it's" and "what else's" you've not gotten to a subtopic you need to hear about, go ahead and ask. "What kind of car were you in?"—or whatever else might be important to you. But if you give the juror a chance to mention it *unprompted*, you'll know that it's something truly on his mind—rather than something off his radar that he's talking about only because you prompted it.

Here's another example of leaving the choice of subtopic up to the juror:

Q: Who here has—or knows anyone who has—ever been injured by using any kind of manufactured product?

Juror Jones raises her hand.

Q: Please tell me about it.

A: I cut my hand on a power screwdriver.[5]

Q: Tell me about it.

Instead of "Tell me about it" you could have asked, "Tell me about what happened." But you don't know that *what happened* was the most important thing to this juror. It might be what a piece of junk the product was, how mad she was at Sears for selling it, how she should not have been using a power tool she knew nothing about, or . . . the possibilities are endless. In this instance, she said:

A: The handle came loose.

Q: Tell me about that.

---

5. Pay attention to the wording. Someone or other—probably that damned Eric Oliver again—teaches that it's not what you say, it's how you say it. "I cut my hand on a power screwdriver" places blame differently than "A power screwdriver cut my hand."

A: The metal underneath the handle sliced my hand. I wasn't looking.

Q: Tell me about that.

A: I had to keep my eyes on the wood so I wouldn't scratch it.

Or:

Q: Who here has—or knows anyone who has—ever been injured by using any kind of manufactured product?

Juror Jones raises her hand.

Q: Please tell me about it.

A: The handle came loose.

Q: Tell me about it.

A: It was a piece of junk. First time I use it the handle comes loose. I brought it back, and they said I used it wrong. But they gave me my money back. I told them not to put it back on the shelf. I bet they did.

Useful? And you'd never have gotten there if you had controlled the choice of subtopic.

If you ask "Tell me about that" a few times and still do not learn some specific thing you want to know, such as whether she filed a claim, go into more leading but still open-ended follow-ups, such as "What did you do about it?" But don't start with those specifics.

A-5 DEMOGRAPHICS: THE ERROR

Very rarely can you safely deselect jurors based on demographics: race, age, nationality, occupation, or any other demographic grouping. Not all GenXers (or members of any other generation) think alike, so the "cohort" approach to jury selection is dangerous. Nor do all Jews or African Americans or middle-aged guys with beards or any other group think alike. Ignorance of this sort runs rampant among racists and others who judge individuals on the basis of their demographic grouping. Don't bring it into jury selection. All teachers are not bad for your case, nor are all middle-aged black women good for it. Demographics is not only lazy, but dangerous—because it does not work.

However, demographics can help you spot certain shared life experiences that might shape values, attitudes, or feelings. Inner-city African Americans are likely to have experienced first-hand—or know and trust others who have experienced—police misconduct. That can make some of them—by no means all—more likely to believe that police misconduct occurred in your particular case. But even that belief does not tell you how any particular juror is likely to decide an issue in the case, because some will believe that police misconduct happens no matter what its victim has done, and others will believe that people can easily avoid being its victims. Note how far we are from the demographic itself.

The American Society of Trial Consultants, consisting of more than a third of America's "professional" trial consultants, recently widely advised exercising strikes based on the demographic of church affiliation. Might as well base strikes on the weather on the moon.

> ### QUOTE OF SHAME
>
> From "How Attorneys Can Use Religion to Be More Effective at Trial" (American Society of Trial Consultants' The Jury Expert, 7/08).
>
> > If the potential juror is Jewish, she may be more lenient to the defendant across many issues. In death penalty cases, prosecutors should remove Catholics and defense attorneys should remove Protestant potential jurors.
>
> ASTC even provided a nifty chart instructing when to strike or keep Protestants, Catholics, and Jews! It's a useful chart for KKK meetings—but not jury selection.

A-6 THE WORST ROLE MODEL: THE DEFENSE

Over the course of your career, most of the jury-trial advocacy you likely see is what defense attorneys do. Defense attorneys are a wretched model for you. Baby ducks who follow monkeys will grow up into something interesting, but not useful ducks.

You cannot model your work on anything defense lawyers do. This is partly because your work and your techniques need to be significantly better than theirs, and partly because defense attorneys have a different set of tasks. Of course you need to know what the defense is going to do in voir dire (*see, e.g.*, p. 280, section A-8, "Inoculation") and throughout trial. But never mimic any defense attorney's methods and approaches. A baseball batter does not hit home runs by modeling his work on the center fielder's.

A-7 Poisoning the Jury

Old-school "wisdom" (read "myth") holds that asking certain questions endangers your case because those questions might elicit bad answers that will poison the jurors. So a juror saying, "I hate money for pain and suffering, and here's why!" will affect other jurors.

Relax. Forget all about it. Jurors in voir dire do not affect each other's thinking. Even if they did, would you prefer to wait for it to happen in deliberations when you can't do anything about it?

I recently guided a death-penalty voir dire. Counsel wanted an individually sequestered voir dire. Good idea in some situations, but counsel wanted it for the wrong reasons. Good reasons might include the fear that in a group voir dire bad pretrial publicity might come to light or that you often learn more when questioning a juror out of the others' hearing. But the attorney's unfounded worry was the fear that in a group voir dire, pro-death-penalty jurors would poison the minds of anti-DPers or middle-of-the-roaders. But jurors don't think, "Thank God for Juror Number Seven! I always thought the death penalty should be used sparingly—but now I see the light! Hallelujah and hang 'em all!"

Jurors do not modify attitudes, biases, or opinions just because some other juror (or counsel) offers a different one. In fact, hearing others say things they disagree with makes most jurors cling more firmly to their own viewpoints.

An opinion is not a death pill. An attitude is not a potion. Get the jurors talking. Get them to say things that show how bad they will be for you as jurors. That is the highest purpose of jury selection's voir dire.

A-8 Inoculation: Anticipating Defense Poison Questions

> **Building the Resources**
>
> My firm is collecting defense poison questions and inoculations based on this section's guidelines. Please help. Send ball@nc.rr.com any poison questions used against you, and if you have any, the inoculation questions you used. Let us know how they worked.

Defense Poison Questions

The defense frequently asks some questions intended not to gather information, but to poison jurors with conclusions against your case. Unethical as this is, and no matter what a juror's answer, the question itself creates an incomplete or false "fact" in the juror's mind. That false or incomplete "fact" is the poison: it makes the juror think something bad—often dispositively bad—about your case.

A poison question's "something bad" is always simple, so it can be lethal. As an easy short cut through the otherwise hard work of decision making, the poison keeps some jurors from hearing much of your opening; their minds are already more or less made up. For example, when the defense asks, "Who here thinks it's OK to drive under the influence of alcohol?" some jurors think, "Aha! The guy who's suing was driving drunk! My mind's made up, and I don't need to listen any more." So they barely hear and even less believe your eventual explanation that your client's drinking made no difference.

In other words, the poison takes on far more weight than it deserves, and the weight does not easily come off.

Some defense poison questions are based on flat-out lies. Some contain a grain of truth, but are still lies or in some other way create an unfair bias against your client. A few poison questions are honest representations of a defense position, but require an answer more involved than you can provide in voir dire.

POISON Q: Have you ever known a student or employee who pretended to be sick in order to get out of school or work? How do you feel about people who do that? How do you feel about people who do it to get a jury to give them money?

False Fact: The plaintiff is pretending to be too injured to work.

POISON Q: Do any of you know people who pretend to be in more pain than they really are?

False Fact: The plaintiff is pretending to be in more pain than she really is.

POISON Q: How many of you think an injured person should get money to stay out of work for as long as he feels like it?

False Fact: The plaintiff could go back to work, but prefers to get money so she doesn't have to go back.

POISON Q: Anyone here think that just because something went wrong during childbirth that a doctor should automatically be sued for a lot of money?

False Fact: The plaintiff is suing for something the doctor could not prevent.

POISON Q: How many of you think it's OK to use marijuana?

Grain of truth: Your client has used marijuana. Now the anti-illegal-drug bias is firmly in place, no matter what connection marijuana had to the case.

POISON Q: Anyone here ever signed a medical consent form?

Grain of Truth: Your client signed a consent form.

Lie: That it covers negligence.

POISON Q: How many of you know that the Ford Explorer follows every federal guideline?

Truth: Ford followed every federal regulation.

Lie: That lets Ford off the hook.

POISON Q: Who here has ever kept something important from their own doctor? Do you know anyone who has? How do you feel about someone who does it?

Harm: Jurors thinking 1) your client hid something that was 2) material.

Primacy of hostile belief (section 4-2-1, p. 82) can kill. So don't allow it.

To Win or Not to Win?

To *win* the battle surrounding a poison issue, you usually need a more complex response than you can credibly (or allowably) provide in voir dire. And you'd need to ask jurors—if only implicitly—to believe your response. But voir dire is too early for a plaintiff's attorney to ask for belief (*see* section 5-2-1, pp. 112*ff*, on premature advocacy).

Besides, trying to win the poison issue in voir dire undermines your ability to spot and remove jurors who will be susceptible to the poison no matter what.

You need to take advance measures. Choose and craft your inoculation serum carefully.

"Tit for Tat?"

You could ask your own poison questions: "How many of you know people who text while driving?" (which the defendant did) or "Who here thinks it's OK for a construction foreman to use marijuana on the job?" (which your client's supervisor did). But even when such questions poison jurors against the defendant, they don't inoculate against the upcoming defense poison questions. Instead, they are more likely to raise more suspicions about you and your case than about the defense. *Remember:* Most effective defense tactics are counterproductive in your hands.

So a "tit-for-tat" approach is not the answer. Instead—

A-9 INOCULATE

Preempt the defense poison. Ask a question that shows jurors that the poison issue has two sides. You need not *win* the issue in voir dire, and should not try—but you do need to *make sure the jurors won't accept the defense implication as true and conclusive.* It is enough to leave jurors with an open mind, because soon in opening you can dispose of the poison infection altogether.

How/When to Inoculate

You inoculate by asking a particular kind of *information-gathering* question **before** the defense asks its poison questions.

Inoculation means using a benign dose of something to create an immunity or resistance to a *later*, otherwise fatal dose of the same thing. It does not work retroactively. Inoculation against plague the day after you contract plague leaves you with plague—and can make it worse.

When you don't inoculate in advance, the smart defense lawyer will ask:

> One question Ms. Plaintiff's Counsel did not ask—and I can understand why she did not—is this: Who here thinks it's OK for patients to hide the truth from their own doctors?

This "proves" to jurors that you know that this topic is so bad for you that you're hiding it. But when you inoculate as instructed below, the poison is weakened or neutralized. You'll still have to kill it in opening, but you'll be talking to jurors whose minds are still open about it.

Gather Information

A good inoculation question not only blocks the poison from most jurors but also helps you spot jurors on whom no inoculation will work on that issue.

> **Anticipated poison:** How many of you think it's OK to drink and drive, then blame someone else for the wreck?[6]

Even without the last phrase, if that question is the first the jurors hear about alcohol, with some jurors you can have just lost the case. The damage is done because you'll seem to have hidden and thereby validated the bad news—possibly irremediably.

And since you never got to find out which prospective jurors are likely to be most susceptible to that particular poison—and they can be some of your otherwise best jurors—you can end up keeping them on the jury without knowing how dangerous they are. So ***Precede, Block, Spot:***

1. Inoculation questions must **precede** the defense poison.

2. Inoculation **blocks** the poison by showing there are two sides to the issue.

3. Inoculation helps you **spot** jurors who aren't likely to stay open to both sides of the poison issue.

A-10 CREATING INOCULATION QUESTIONS

1. Decide what you think the defense poison questions will be.

2. Frame your own questions to deal with the topic neutrally and get you some useful information.

Example: The poison of, "Your client was drinking."

1. **Anticipated defense poison Q:** Who here thinks it's OK to drink and drive?

2. **Inoculation:** If there's a car wreck and one of the drivers was drinking, some folks feel that the drinking driver is automatically at fault. Others feel, "maybe not, depending on the circumstances." Which are you a little closer to?

---

[6]. Or: "Who here thinks it's OK to drive when you're under the influence of a medication that affects your judgment and reaction time?"

Follow up—particularly with jurors not firmly in the second group—with "Tell me about that" and "Tell me more."

When the defense later asks its poison question about alcohol, most jurors will think, "Well, it depends on the circumstances." And you'll already have spotted the exceptions. Without inoculation, *most* jurors are likely to succumb to the poison.

Here are some examples of common poison questions and suggested inoculations:

Malingering

Anticipated defense poison: Have you ever known a student or employee who pretended to be sick in order to get out of school or work?

Inoculation: Who here has ever been accused of lying about being sick or exaggerating about how sick you are?

Not Telling Doctor Everything

Anticipated defense poison: Who here has ever kept something from their own doctor?

Inoculation: When you answer all the nurse's questions before you see the doctor, why do you think the nurse writes the answers down?

Or:

Inoculation: Some folks feel that it's up to the doctor to make sure he asks a patient everything necessary. Other folks feel that that makes it too hard on the doctor—that patients should know what the doctor needs to know, and tell him. Which folks are you a little closer to?

Consent Form

Anticipated defense poison: Anyone here ever sign a medical consent form for yourself or your child?

Inoculation: Some folks think that signing a medical consent form means they accept any harm that happens, no matter why it happens. Other folks think it just means harm that could not be avoided. Which are you a little closer to?

As always, follow up with "Tell me about that."

Federal Standards

> **Anticipated defense poison:** How many of you know that when Ford manufactured the Ford Explorer, they followed every single federal guideline?
>
> **Inoculation:** Some folks think that all a company has to do is to meet federal safety standards. Others feel that federal standards are not enough when the company could have done more. Which group are you a little closer to?

When you follow up this particular question, the judge might well intercede with "the law": that following federal standards does not get a company off the hook. This kills the poison for those jurors who are comfortable with that law, but *you must still detect jurors who aren't*. So ask:

> Some folks feel that the law's not quite fair, because it makes things too hard on the manufacturer—because a manufacturer should be able to rely on what the government approves. Other folks think the law is OK. Which are you a little closer to? [*Do not **justify** the position of thinking the law is OK.*]

And of course, follow up (tell me about that, etc.).

Whether or not the judge intervenes by explaining the law, throughout trial the defense will still emphasize that the defendant followed all federal standards—hoping you've let a juror through who feels that federal standards are enough. But if you inoculated, you probably spotted any such juror in voir dire and removed her.

Whether or not the judge intervenes, jurors' answers to your follow-up questions will neutralize the upcoming poison about Ford following all federal standards. In fact, with this as with many poison questions, if you handle this inoculation well, good defense attorneys will be too smart to later ask that poison question at all.

As with other poison topics, if you do not inoculate against "followed all federal standards," you may well trace your ultimate loss (or steeply diminished verdict) to the moment the defense asked about it.

Pain Exaggeration

> **Poison:** Does anyone think it's OK for someone to exaggerate their pain to get a jury to give them money?
>
> **Inoculation:** Some folks feel that most people will exaggerate their pain to get more money from a jury. Others don't think so. Which are you closer to? [*Then: "Please tell me about that," etc.*]

This inoculation topic feeds into Rick Friedman's essential method of dealing with accusations that your client is pretending or exaggerating (see his book *Polarizing the Case*).

Remember, you're not trying to *win* the poison issue in voir dire. You just want to keep the question open and find out which jurors won't.

You might also want to ask:

> **Inoculation:** Who here knows anyone who's ever been accused of exaggerating their pain when they were really telling the truth?[7]

Jurors who have been—or know someone who has been—unfairly accused of pain exaggeration can have strong feelings about it. When a hand goes up in response to the question, just ask the all-purpose follow-up, "Please tell me about it." Not "How did it feel?" because that seems (and is) manipulative in this context, as if you're trying to engineer the answer. "Tell me about it" leaves the nature and topic of the answer clearly and completely up to the juror. That's what voir dire is about.

Even if no prospective juror has—or knows anyone who has—been accused of exaggerating their pain, you have still inoculated. You have sounded a note of the injustice of being groundlessly accused of exaggerating.

A-11 WHICH INOCULATION?

How do you know in advance whether the defense is going to ask a particular poison question? Well, it makes no difference. Either way, you need to find out which jurors will most likely accept the defense's side of the issue. And since you can find that out with inoculation questions, go ahead and inoculate.[8]

For example, the defense may or may not introduce its usual *"no immediate pain means no long-term harm"* contention as poison in jury selection. Either way, you will already have asked,

---

7. Like many questions, the answer to this can expose some good jurors to a defense peremptory. This can hurt—you lose a good juror—or it can help you by deflecting a defense strike from another more harmful use. This is an on-the-scene judgment call.

8. When you're not sure whether the defense will use a particular poison issue anywhere in trial, you have to play the odds: Should you add potentially unnecessary poison by inoculating against something the defense might never mention anywhere in trial? Or is it worse to gamble on the defense using it in voir dire to poison without your having inoculated? This is always an issue—and case-specific judgment call.

Some folks think that when someone's in a crash, the pain always starts right away. Other folks think some pain won't show up for days. Which are you closer to?

Then follow up.

And along the way, as Kentucky's Gary Johnson points out, this elicits great "testimony" from the best fact "witnesses" you can have: jurors. When you follow up the question, jurors will tell you about their own experiences—or experiences of people they know and trust—with injuries that produced no pain for days, weeks, or even months. So you've 1) inoculated just in case the defense asks about it in voir dire, 2) learned which jurors don't think it can happen, and 3) provided credible and otherwise inadmissable "evidence" that it happens all the time.

Not bad for one little voir dire question!

> If you need inoculation for a topic not covered in this chapter, e-mail ball@nc.rr.com; David will try to help. Indicate if the request is time-sensitive.

A-12 "Why Is She Asking About That?"

The law may give you the right to ask questions, but jurors don't necessarily grant you that same right. Personal privacy is an increasing concern these days, especially when the privacy invasion is at the hands of the authorities—such as lawyers in court. And among tort-"reform" jurors, your invasion of privacy can approach the level of personal threat.

At a minimum, some jurors will resent questions for which they see no purpose in your asking.

So early in voir dire, explain you are *required* to ask questions.

Assure them that all your questions are necessary, but the necessity of some won't be apparent until later in trial. And you're not allowed to explain it at this point.

Don't say that you'll try not to be intrusive. It's counterproductive—like a dentist saying, "I'll try not to hurt you." It's also a lie: you will indeed be intrusive because they, not you, will define "intrusive." Even "what's your name?" is intrusive when someone thinks you have no right to ask.

And claiming that you won't be intrusive gets some people defensive and shuts them down.

During voir dire, don't explain why a question is necessary, such as by saying, "This case is about a highway wreck, so I have to ask about your experience with highway wrecks." They will figure out the connection for themselves.

So:

> Folks, during this process I'm required to ask some questions. You'll see the reasons for some, but not others, and I'm not allowed to explain at this point. But as trial goes on you'll see why I asked them.

A-13 HOME

"Where do you live?" is often a threateningly intrusive question. Many jurors don't want all those strangers in the courtroom to know how to find them. When you or the judge asks where they live, it should be a general approximation—"What part of the city do you live in?"—rather than anything that can be interpreted as a request for their specific address.

Even better is to ask the question in a way that gets jurors talking: "Tell me a little about the part of the city you live in."

A-14 GET THE WHOLE ANSWER

No matter the kind of question, never assume that a juror has given you all the answer she has to give. After she tells you all about the wreck she was in, ask what other wrecks she's been in or seen. And when she tells you about another one, ask about any more. Keep the information flowing until you verify that there's no more information.

This is important not just with experiences, but with opinions and attitudes as well. Once a juror has said all he has to say about his distrust of lawyers, ask what else he does not like about the civil justice system. "What else?" is a great question.

This is extremely important, because when a juror has multiple experiences or opinions/attitudes relevant to a question, she'll often start with those she's more comfortable with—which means they are probably the least useful for you to hear.

A-15 INTERRUPTING

Never interrupt a juror.

Time pressure often makes you interrupt and commit other sins that will eventually send you straight to communicator hell. Don't succumb.

A-16 REWORDING

Another communication sin you'll commit under the pressure of time: rewording a juror's answer.

Never do it.

Rewording answers makes that juror and others less likely to say much else. Rewording is also arrogantly rude; it creates resentment, not rapport—as if you're saying, "You're too stupid to speak your own confused, inarticulate mind so you need someone with a brain—*me*—to help."

When even the smartest attorneys reword an answer, they usually get it wrong. That makes others see you not only as arrogant, but as an arrogant dummy. Oddly, the smarter you are, the greater the chances you'll reword inaccurately.

And the poor juror will usually go along with your inaccurate rewording, so now you've 1) insulted her and 2) misled yourself.

Rule of thumb: You are almost never smart enough to know what someone else is trying to say.

Further: When a juror is struggling—unaided—to word her thoughts, you will likely be admitted far deeper into her thoughts than when you jump in and reword. And as always, listening silently shows respect for the juror, which is one of the most important things you can do.

In jury selection—and in life—let people speak for themselves. You're not the only talking biped in the room. When a juror does not make herself clear, ask her to say it again or to say it another way.

The only time to reword answers is in the end-stage of pursuing a challenge for cause. ("So I understand that if you become a juror, you won't be able to set your hatred of plaintiff's lawyers aside?" "No I won't, because you keep rewording my answers, you jerk!")

Testimony

As bad as rewording the responses of a prospective juror is rewording witness answers. On cross or direct it often masks the real answer, and displays you as manipulative. (*See* section 7-6, p. 213, on controlling too visibly on cross.)

A-17 GET THEM TALKING

Your hardest voir dire task can be just getting folks to talk.

The easiest solution is to start with the most talkative jurors. They will show other jurors what is expected and make the others more comfortable in doing it.

"But," you say, "at the start of voir dire, how do you know who the most talkative jurors might be?"

Watch them as they congregate in the hall before jury call in the morning. Some will be talking, some listening. If you cannot go to observe them, send someone to do it.

If voir dire starts in the afternoon, eat lunch where the jurors eat and observe who talks. I know you're busy with other things, but at this point nothing is more important than learning about the prospective jurors.

If you have no opportunity to observe before voir dire, watch as they are ushered into the courtroom. Even a small remark or gesture can reveal a juror who is comfortable talking. The juror holding the door for others, or who seems outer-directed by looking around at other people, or even who thanks whoever held the door for them, can prove to be talkative.

Once prospective jurors are seated, note which ones seem comfortable being there or who seem interested in the process.

Jurors who seem intimidated, uncomfortable, or distanced are rarely talkative at first, so start with others. Talkative jurors might lean slightly forward as the judge introduces voir dire. Talkers might be among those who seem most comfortable during the judge's remarks and may seem most aware of and interested in the other jurors. Talkers may even be among those who most comfortably and audibly respond to your "good morning."

It's worth the effort to find the talkers, because your questioning a talkative juror eases the path for everyone else to talk comfortably.

Talkative jurors are more likely to be the leaders in deliberations, so there is double benefit to spotting them. You cannot afford leaders on the jury who seem likely to be even mildly against your case, because leaders can sway an entire jury. And leaders tend not to be swayable. (*See* section A-22, "Identifying Leaders," p. 304.)

If you mistakenly start with a juror who turns out not to be talkative, ask two or three questions, temporarily abandon that juror, and move on to someone else.

Once you get a talkative juror, stay with him for a while. The questions suggested below will maximize that juror's talking. The more that juror talks freely, the easier it will be to get other jurors talking, because you will have established a conversational standard with that first talkative juror. You can reinforce it by going next to another talkative juror.

But it's really hard to get people talking if you're the one being talkative. This is an easy trap throughout voir dire, especially at the beginning. With every question you ask, remind yourself of Rule #1: "Shut up and listen." Please post this prominently on your bathroom mirror in permanent marker:

The only one who likes to hear you talk is *you*. Everyone else is pretending.

After all, the amount you learn by talking is zero.

You can't *talk* jurors into talking. A few verbal nudges might help, but there's a lot more you can easily do. Most of it requires that you listen, not talk. Unfortunately, listening is harder than talking. That's why it's rare.

Most prospective jurors are uncomfortable talking to you, especially in front of strangers in the formal setting of court. Remember how bad and constricted you felt the first time you went to court as an attorney? In jury selection, many jurors feel worse.

Few attorneys are blessed with the kind of personality and presence that spontaneously make jurors eager to talk with them. To make matters worse, you are likely to be nervous at the start of trial. That nervousness makes jurors even less willing to talk with you, because no one is comfortable talking to a nervous person.

Jurors are further discouraged from readily talking to you because your business clothes and your lawyerly demeanor—a horrible thing to possess—make you seem to occupy a more powerful position. Few people are comfortable saying anything they fear that a higher-up might disagree with or find of little value.

Some jurors simply don't like being asked questions. Others mask their nervousness by means of sullenness or a veil of silence or terseness.

Court's an intimidating place. Someone in a black robe, for God's sake, is staring down at them from on high and has ordered them to tell the truth or else! This is not an easy crowd to get talking.

So start voir dire with questions specifically designed to get jurors talking: ask about them and their own lives. Forget your case for a while. When you start with questions that can be difficult to answer, many jurors talk less throughout voir dire. Begin with their jobs, families, backgrounds, values learned from parents and taught to their children, and plans for the future.

Do not ask, "What do you do for a living?" That closed-ended question gets one-word answers: "Astrophysicist." When you ask about their workday, jurors respond more fully. So:

Tell me about your job; what is your workday like?

Ask how they spend their non-working time. In addition to making jurors more comfortable in talking, it also provides clues to how they might respond to case issues. Here's a nearly sure-fire way to get a juror warmed up to talking:

> What makes you good at your job? [*or*, What makes you a good parent?]

Even quiet jurors can be eager to answer this. It gives them the opportunity to establish themselves within the otherwise dehumanizing "you're-a-lowly-cog!" feeling they get in court. Jurors will remember that you were the one who provided that favor.

Even normally quiet jurors can be so eager to respond to "What makes you good at your job?" that I've seen some get angry because counsel forgot to ask them despite having asked it of others.

If you're not rushed for time, you can find out a lot—and send some recalcitrant jurors to babbling away—by asking:

> What kinds of things make some people not so good at your kind of work?

And:

> What do you like about your work?
>
> What don't you like?

Remember to follow up with "Please tell me about that." Even though this is just the "get-'em-talking" part, you'll often learn as much about them now as throughout the rest of voir dire. For example, the characteristic of liking people—which not all jurors share—is revealed when a juror says that her favorite thing about her job "is the people." So even when a juror says, "I don't like anything about my job," ask:

> Q: Is there anything other than the money that you'd miss if you left that job? Tell me about that.
>
> A: The people, I guess. I'd really miss the people.
>
> Q: Tell me about that.
>
> A: Blah blah blah.

> Q: Please tell me more.
>
> A: Blah blah blah blah.
>
> Q: When some people stop working at a job, they go back from time to time to visit. Others would never want to do that. Which are you a little closer to?

Etc.

And ask:

> If you could choose, what kind of work would you do instead? Tell me about that.

Work History

Be sure to get a complete work history. The past ten years is not enough. The juror might have been a doctor until twenty years ago when he got sued too often to remain in practice. One of the most important shaping influences in someone's life can be the work they do and have done, even decades ago. Fifty years ago I drove a taxi. Other than the Peace Corps, it was my most shaping influence in terms of attitudes and beliefs.

If a judge resists your asking so much about jobs, remind her that one of your most important case issues is, for example, lost earnings/earning capacity as well as the loss of the on-the-job companionship that goes to emotional suffering. So what can be more relevant than the ways in which jurors think and feel about their own job situations?

If you have reason to think that the judge might limit your time on this or anything else, find out in advance. Don't get caught having to redesign your voir dire in the midst of conducting it. By finding out the judge's limits ahead of time, you can plan for them and move for improvements (*see* section 4-1, p. 79). (Further, it is always a good idea to follow Don Keenan's advice and prepare an abbreviated voir dire, just in case.)

Other Good "Get 'Em Talking" Questions

> Other than religion and honesty, what are the two most important things you learned from your parents? Tell me about that. Please tell me more about that.
>
> Other than religion and honesty, what are the two most important things you want your children to have learned from you? Tell me about that. Please tell me more about that.[9]

---

9. "Other than religion and honesty" is necessary or you won't hear much else from many jurors.

Where'd you go to school? Tell me about that.

What did you specialize in? Tell me about that.

What kind of work did you end up doing that school helped prepare you for?[10] Tell me about that.

Then move on to "What do you spend your time doing?" questions:

Tell me what you do when you're not at work?

What're your evenings like?

What're your Saturdays like?

What're your Sundays like?

Adjust those questions according to their work schedule.

Lower the Barriers

Aside from the specifics of your questions, all you do—including your tone, body language, choice of words, clothes you wear, and comments—should be designed to make jurors comfortable talking. So:

Never disagree or argue.

Never make jurors feel as if they're taking a test or in a contest. Say over and over that there are no rules, no expectations, no right and no wrong responses. "The only right answer is what is right to you."

Never be friendlier to jurors who answer in ways you like.

Never seem to approve of the content of answers you like.

Do not succumb to the amateurishly transparent manipulation of following up for the purpose of leading a juror into saying "good" things in the hope that they'll make other jurors see the light. That actually hardens the views of jurors who don't happen to agree with the point. And it shows that you are a manipulator—exactly what they expected you to be, and now you have confirmed it.

Always "honor the answers," as Gerry Spence teaches. Don't listen to an answer and then just move on to someone or something else without reacting. Even a nod tells the juror you thought enough of what he said to have absorbed it. Here's an unfortunate "oh my" moment that can result when you ignore this:

---

10. Be alert for prospective jurors who seem to have failed to fulfill their dreams: the pre-med student years later working in a gas station; the sixty-year-old actor still waiting tables; the defense attorney you beat once too often; etc. Unfulfilled dreams can make people cynical, a juror characteristic that usually goes in your negative column.

Q: Mrs. Hicks, you know someone who was killed in a wreck?

A: My husband.

Q: OK, good, and Mrs. Ehle, you had your hand up, too?

Counsel made Mrs. Hicks feel small and unimportant by not respecting her. This shows callousness and a low level of listening. It raises the barrier to prospective jurors talking because counsel seems to be a total jerk. It happened because counsel was more intent on getting facts than on being a human being. That's a deadly reversal of priorities.

Jurors are not there as your servants or employees. It's the other way around.

Don't go overboard. A good response to Mrs. Hicks would have been, "I'm sorry to hear that." But in fact you need to know more about her husband's death, so ask, "Would you mind my asking a few questions about it?"

Even when an answer has little importance, *acknowledge* the answer. You're not entitled to it.

Word Questions in Ways that Lower the Bad Response Barrier

Good wording lowers the barrier to jurors telling you "bad" things. Instead of, "What **major** problems would you have with money for pain and suffering?" ask, "What problems—**even small ones**—would you have including money for pain and suffering?" Otherwise, a juror may truthfully say she has no *major* problems and not mention the lesser problems you need to know about.

Another way to lower the barrier is to make the jurors feel that having "bad" responses is perfectly acceptable. You can't do that with a terrible question like, "Will the fact that you were in a wreck make it impossible for you to be a fair juror in a case about a wreck?" That creates a barrier to your getting any answer except no, and it won't be a reliable no. The question's wording makes the juror feel that no is the proper response. So he's likely to say no regardless of what he thinks. Many jurors are uncomfortable saying anything you might disapprove of. So make them comfortable in doing it or you'll miss their most important information. Ask: "Anyone who's been in that kind of wreck might have some problems being a juror in this kind of case. What do you think?" This gives her permission to tell you—and makes her more comfortable telling it.

Some People

The most useful way to lower barriers to bad answers is the "some folks/other folks" format: **"Some folks think *X*; others think *Y*. Which might you be closer to, even a little?"**

For example:

> Q: Mrs. Smith, some folks don't put much confidence in how the FDA checks drug safety. Other folks think the FDA does well. Which group do you think you might be closer to, even a little?

If you have to ask the entire group instead of an individual:

> Q: Some folks don't put much confidence in how the FDA checks drug safety. Other folks think the FDA does very well. Who here might be a little closer to the first group? To the second group? In the middle?

This gives every juror permission to give you "bad" answers. And with every response that indicates a possible tilt against your case, or a possible disconnect with the law, the judge will be hard-pressed to justify barring you from following up with each such juror.

Here's how the "some/other people" questions work:

> Q: Ms. Jones, some folks have a little trouble allowing money for pain and suffering because money can't make the pain go away. Other folks think money for pain and suffering is OK.[11] Which group do you think you might be closer to, even a little?
>
> A: Maybe the first. A little.
>
> Q: Please tell me about that.

On some carefully selected questions, you can go even farther in giving permission:

> Q: Ms. Johnson, some people would have a little trouble allowing money for pain and suffering because money can't make the pain go away. That's why my mother would never do it. Other people think money for pain and suffering is OK. [*You might get an objection re: "my mother." Usually not. Try it. The objection won't hurt you.*]

---

11. Do not say, "Some people think it's OK, *and that they would listen to the judge when he says to later."* That bullies jurors into good answers whether they mean it or not, so you learn nothing, make the juror feel manipulated, and diminish your chances of frank answers even on other questions.

This makes it very easy for jurors to reveal problems with money for pain and suffering, or whatever the question is about. Some will really let you have it. So you can ask:

Who agrees with Mr. Elmwitz?

And you're again off and running with another juror who is now comfortable talking.

"I feel the same way he does." Never settle for that answer. At a minimum, ask:

I need to hear it in your words, so please tell me about it.

Other Dos and Don'ts

DO:

- Be friendly. Not ingratiating; just friendly.

- Be human. Not the "lawyer man" or "lawyer woman" or other super—but actually sub—human you might be accustomed to acting out in court. Be the human you are in a normal real-life situation—unless, of course, you're always a stiff, formal, authority-displaying, invulnerable, perfection-showing, or mask-wearing semblance of a real person.[12] Do not be formal or "professional" or lawyerly. Relax. This is a layperson jury, not a professional firing squad.

- Be sensitive to juror discomfort, including jurors who seem confident.

DO NOT:

- Do not wear power clothes in voir dire. No dark blue or black suits. Jurors are more comfortably forthcoming to men wearing sport jacket, tie, and slacks. Women should avoid severely formal clothing. In voir dire, both sexes should avoid power clothing and power colors.

- Do not write down what jurors say; have someone else do it.

- Do not wear those silly half-reading spectacles that make you peer over the rims at people. It looks snooty. Jurors talk less when they think you are snooty.

---

12. If you have trouble being a normal person—if you have to hide your human self behind your cardboard lawyer self—several excellent, easygoing consultants can help you. Chief among them are Joshua Karton (Santa Monica, CA). In Maryland near D.C.: Gillian Drake. And a stint with TLC (the Gerry Spence college) even for only a weekend can be of enormous benefit.

- Do not act as if you are more important than the jurors.
- Do not try to impress jurors.

Legalese

To make jurors comfortable, speak plain English. There is never a time—not in voir dire or any other time in jury trial or bench trial or in your career or in your life after law school—when you should speak or write legalese. Legalese means saying "*prior*" instead of "*before*," "*subsequent*" instead of "*after*," "*find*" instead of "*decide*," "*action*" instead of "*lawsuit*." It means using defense-lawyer-like syntax ("The house was painted by Mr. Jones" instead of "Mr. Jones painted the house").

Lawyerly language keeps jurors from understanding and wanting to please you. It also makes them reluctant to talk to you as much as they otherwise would.

As Raleigh attorney and law professor Donald Beskind points out, and as even Justice Scalia now pleads that you do, you should avoid legal syntax and legal language even when writing briefs or motions. Clarity is easily digested, most credible, and helps create respect and rapport. Legal language makes you seem like a scared 1L student.

Legal language is also a Reptilian menace.

And hey, don't talk like a lawyer at home, either. Have some respect for your family. **No one who respects his listener speaks legalese.**

Some have said (actually it was me) that the first rule of conducting jury voir dire is to shut up and listen, and *talk the way you talked before you went to law school.*

The Really Silent Type: Non-Talking Prospective Jurors

When a jurors stops answering after just a word or two, prod gently:

Q: Tell me just a bit more.

Do not say, "Can you tell me just a little more?" because the easy answer is "No," or "Not exactly," or some other equivalent of "Leave me alone." With a juror unwilling to speak much of anything, you might say:

Q: Help me out: I really need to hear just a little more.

This kind of juror wants to be left alone. In a gentle and polite way, you need to make him less comfortable trying to remain silent than giving in and talking to you. You do this throughout voir dire by:

– re-reminding jurors that there are no right answers.

- moving a little closer to the recalcitrant juror so she feels she's talking just to you, not the entire room.

- requesting that voir dire be conducted in small groups—twelve or fewer—with the judge, counsel from both sides, and the court reporter sitting near the jury so the whole thing seems less formal and intimidating. You might even request moving the proceedings to a smaller room. Trials are meant to be public events, but not jury voir dire.

When the court reporter or the judge can't hear, go to the bench and explain that when people are asked to speak more loudly than their normal volume, many become self-conscious and they focus on their discomfort rather than on their answers. This shuts them down. A judge's "Speak up!" does not change human nature. So enlist the judge's *real* help: get a smaller room or seat counsel and the judge very near the jury, etc.

Once you ask what a juror's thoughts are, let him talk. Do not interrupt. Do not argue. Show no signs of disapproval or disagreement or impatience. Keep quiet. Listen. Nod slowly. Colorado trial consultant Mary Ryan points out that a lot of good information is lost simply because lawyers nod curtly—an impatient move that tells the juror to shut up. So nod slowly. Gesture for more. And follow up whatever the juror says by asking, "What else?" or "Please tell me more."

Practice

Try asking someone ten questions in a row, all with some variation of "tell me about that," such as, "What else about that?" "Say a little more on that, please?" Etc.

Then go into advanced practice: Ask someone twenty open-ended follow-ups in a row. Keep working at it until you can do it comfortably without backsliding into a closed-ended question such as "Did you . . . ?" I bet you will—until you practice.

Then gather a half-dozen people and practice on them as a group, as if they were a jury. Use one person's answer as the basis for follow-up questions, first to that person and then to the others. This is a basic method of good voir dire.

A-18 ENJOYMENT V. CONTROL

The National Jury Project's Diane Wiley points out that it's hard to do jury voir dire well unless you enjoy it. When you don't, jurors spot it. That makes them less likely to talk openly with you. It can also distance them from you throughout trial.

But how can anyone enjoy voir dire? It's unpredictable. It's uncontrollable. You get no discovery. God knows what these people will *say*! No matter how much you prepare, there's no telling how things will go. You don't get to impeach jurors; they can say anything they want, and who knows what it will be, and there's nothing you can—or should—do about it.

All this can make you so uncomfortable that you try to control prospective jurors as if they are witnesses on cross-examination. Don't. You get useful information from jurors only when you altogether stop trying to control what they say. Of course, being the kind of person who chose to go to law school, you probably don't enjoy giving up control. So you may have some self-counseling to do. Your spouse and kids can probably help, or at least eagerly give you a ride to the necessary counseling.

There is nothing more interesting and valuable—and thus enjoyable—than hearing what real people have to say. When the waiter at my favorite restaurant brings my dinner, he says, "Enjoy." From here on, as you read this section, as you prepare your jury voir dires, and as you conduct them, "Enjoy!" Otherwise it will be ineffective, and you can't send it back to the kitchen.

A-19 VOIR DIRE: TO SEE SPEAKING

"Voir dire" means "to see speaking." Some people think it means "to speak the truth," which it does not. Even if it did, you don't get to a juror's truths when you are talking. You learn nothing about them, and they learn terrible things about you: that you talk too much, that you are trying to manipulate them, and that they should avoid being influenced by you as much as possible.

That's why Rule #1 is so important.

I know that in law school you did all the listening you could stand and that you vowed never to do any listening again. I also know "advocate" means "to speak." But please, not in jury voir dire.

In fact, *listening* in voir dire—even the required 90 percent of the time—is not enough. You must listen with real interest. Your follow-up questions and the tone in which you ask them must show real interest in how the juror might answer.

Rapport

Overt attempts to create rapport backfire. Jurors don't trust a lawyer who kisses the rapport part of their bodies.

But rapport is easy: simply listen carefully to what jurors say.

Human beings feel rapport with anyone who genuinely and carefully listens to them. You need not—and should not—wear rapport on your sleeve or say ingratiating things or share little off-the-cuff (and easily backfirable) jokes. Just listen attentively and respond appropriately. This shows the listener that you care about her. That's what rapport is. Try it at home.

In the 1950s, high school girls were taught to develop rapport with boys by being good listeners, even when a boy blathered on about some topic of no interest whatever: his car's camshaft or how far the coach made him run at football practice. Those 1950s girls knew the way to a boy's heart: listen with interest. It worked on us. It works with jurors. When you listen with interest, the listener is yours.

And they talk to you more.

And the rapport makes jurors want to see the evidence in a good light for your side.

A-20 CONDITIONING

Do Not Inform or Persuade.

You cannot follow Rule #1 ("Shut up and listen") if you use voir dire to inform or attempt to persuade ("condition") jurors. This is one of many times that ethics and good strategy overlap. Informing and persuading should be your primary goals throughout trial—except in jury voir dire. Jurors in voir dire quickly infer which way you want information to flow. If they think you want information flowing from you to them, they talk less and only pretend to listen.

A-21 WHEN THE JUDGE STOPS YOU

With any question, the judge might say: "Hold on. What does that have to do with anything? Ask something else." This is often because the judge does not see the information-seeking relevance of the question. When she says something is irrelevant, often she means that given her necessarily limited knowledge of the case and her few seconds of considering this particular question, she has not spotted its relevance. She might not be a mean person who cackles in delight when she foils your plans. It's possible she's just trying to be a good judge. As a good judge, she's willing to be informed—especially in advance of trial—about what makes things relevant.

So if you anticipate that a judge might not see the information-seeking relevance of, say, "Tell me what makes you good at your job," simply tell her. For example:

> Judge, my client was hurt in ways that keep him from his job. We are claiming damages for it. I do not want jurors whose own experiences make them think there are no special abilities necessary to doing a job. Such jurors would be candidates for me to challenge peremptorily, and this question helps me learn who they are.

If nothing else, alerting the judge in this way can make her more lenient next time you receive an objection to a voir dire question and she has to rule quickly. Thus, for every voir dire question you plan to ask, be prepared to articulate your case-related, information-seeking reason to ask it.

Often, the judge needs a reminder (and maybe a memorandum of law) that voir dire is not solely for seeking information for cause challenges (as in, "Can you follow the law?"). Voir dire is also for gathering information on which to base an intelligent exercise of peremptory strikes. When a judge rejects your question and says, "Just ask them if they can follow the law," respectfully remind the judge that if a juror cannot follow or is even substantially impaired (*Wainwright v. Witt*, 469 U.S. 412 [1985] Holding 1) from following the law, that goes not to peremptory, but cause challenge. Thus, being limited to asking whether a juror can follow the law keeps you from being able to discharge your obligation of gathering information upon which to intelligently base peremptory challenges. It reduces you to making peremptory challenge choices based mainly on demographics, which can easily run counter to *Batson* and its progeny.

The converse of the good-at-your-job question can elicit attitudes relevant to most malpractice cases:

> Mr. Jones, you're a plumber. Are there some good plumbers and some not so good?

That is your one closed-ended question on the topic. It is solely to open a new topic. When Mr. Jones says, "Yes," open it up with "Please tell me about it." The information-seeking purpose is to find out how disturbed this prospective juror is by carelessness, sloppiness, low standards, and so forth. You also want to know how he feels about those qualities in his own kind of work, because they are an important part of the life experience he is likely to draw on when deciding the case.

And the question yields far more. Simply from the tone in which the juror answers it, you can learn how strongly he or she feels about incompetence and carelessness.

A-22 IDENTIFYING LEADERS

Leaders are jurors who strongly influence other jurors during deliberations. A leader favorable to your side is obviously helpful. An unfavorable leader—even just one—can cost you the case or reduce damages by a factor of ten or more.

Once you spot a leader, try to remove her unless she is *very* likely to be favorable. You can gamble on nonleaders, but not on leaders. Take no chances.

You decide whether a juror will be a leader in the following ways.

Ask

Come right out and ask prospective jurors to tell you the particular situations in which other people tend to regard them as leaders. Follow up with "Please tell me about that."

Then ask them to tell you the particular situations in which other people tend to regard them as followers. Follow up with "Tell me about that."

With both of these questions (and with most other voir dire questions), don't make the blunder of settling just for the first answer you get. "People tend to regard me as leader when we do sports." Follow that up, and then ask: "In what other situations do people tend to think of you as a leader?" Don't move on to another juror while this one might have more answers.

Look at Occupation

A leader in the workplace is a likely jury leader. Managers, teachers, supervisors, administrators, bosses, and organizers are among those likely to be jury leaders. As you learn each juror's occupation, consider what human relationships are involved on the job. Is leadership part of the job? How many people are under her? How often is she in decision-making situations? What is her level of responsibility and decision making? How much coordinating does she do? Does she lead any groups that are charged with making decisions? How much do other people listen to her? What does she say about herself as a leader?

Job Expertise

A taxi driver may have no particular leadership qualities. But other jurors might take her as a reliable and thus a neutral, persuasive authority on matters such as dangerous nighttime neighborhoods. An office clerk might be regarded as authoritative when it comes to business machines. This kind of authority gives an otherwise nonleader a leader's weight and status on that particular topic.

Other Experiences and Activities

Beyond occupation, other life experiences and activities can create single-topic leaders who become disproportionately influential on those topics—even if they do not try to influence others. It's a matter of how other jurors will regard them. A juror who has had extensive surgery can become influential on the medical issues in your case. A juror who cares for an invalid at home can be considered an authority on home care. Even a juror who was bonked in the head by a baseball thirty years ago might be regarded by his fellow jurors as an insightful expert on post-concussion behavior ("I got slammed and walked away just fine").

Volunteers and people with special training can also be single-topic leaders. For example, a library volunteer knows not only about books, but about working with the public. So in case-related matters concerning working with the public, jurors may defer to that library volunteer's opinions. Even someone who has merely taken a Red Cross CPR course can be a strong influence on the jury's choice of which expert cardiologist to believe.

A juror with previous jury experience sometimes carries more weight than first-timers. She is also a more likely choice for foreperson. While the position of foreperson is rarely as influential as some lawyers think, a foreperson with previous jury service often is. She "knows how it's done." Even if she does not become foreperson in this case, her previous juror experience can endow her with some leadership power—especially early in deliberations, which can be a critical time.

Leadership Attributes

Articulate people, especially those who talk easily and effectively, are often leaders because deliberations are mainly a speaking event. Jurors who fully and confidently answer your open-ended questions are often leaders. (But the converse is not necessarily true: relatively silent jurors in voir dire may still be leaders.)

People with charisma, or who are very well-known, are often jury leaders because other jurors tend to defer to them.

People who are popular are often jury leaders even when they do not try to be. They are popular because they are well liked, so other jurors try to please them.

Celebrities, including local celebrities, tend to be leaders.

People in high-status professions, such as doctors, tend to be leaders.

People who easily offer opinions tend to be jury leaders, if they listen as readily as they speak. Loud-mouthed know-it-alls make a lot of noise, but are not usually leaders. However, they can be mulishly stubborn jerks and sometimes take positions just to be contrary to others (see below). They make unanimity or near-unanimity harder to achieve.

Jurors allow themselves to be led by fair discussion-coordinators who are good listeners. Jurors want to follow a respectful person who has the self-confidence not to bully and who will prevent others from bullying. Such a democratic leader can hold great power in deliberations because other jurors allow themselves to be coordinated by her, and many can eventually gravitate toward her opinions.

Problem solvers become jury leaders, as do take-charge people.

Organizers are leaders, but not necessarily opinion leaders. Because they are interested primarily in leading the progress of a group's activity (such as making a difficult decision), they are likely to be consensus makers and lead the way to compromise verdicts.

If you have the principal burdens, be wary of prospective jurors who take stands in voir dire that seem intentionally different from other jurors' stands. This can indicate a common personality type that seeks stature or pleasure by confronting, challenging, or resisting the majority just for the sake of doing so. Such ornery jurors can cause dissension and ill feelings, dividing the jury.

Subtle Signs of a Leader

Many leadership signs are subtle. When jurors are returning to the box after a recess, followers tend to sit and look straight ahead. Leaders often look around to see what's going on in the room or if everyone is back in their seats.

During voir dire recesses, observe how jurors behave with each other. Those who talk most may be leaders. Also be on the lookout for people who take the initiative in such simple matters as seating arrangements, holding doors, even pushing the elevator button. Have an associate hang around the hallway to observe which jurors seem to be leading such decision-making processes as where to go for lunch.

Leadership Is a Comparative Quality

Someone can be a leader even if she does not seem likely to lead someone like you. A juror deferential to you might exert considerable control over other sorts of people. In a room of lieutenants, the general is boss. But a roomful of sergeants heeds the lieutenant. So consider the makeup of the jury as a whole before concluding whether or not someone is a leader.

Also consider gender and race. For example, can the woman who is a potential leader on your behalf hold sway over the particular men who will be on the jury? Will the white Mississippi redneck let himself be led by the Black guy?

A-23 Depth of Attitude/Opinion/Belief

The fact that a juror says he believes something does not mean he believes it deeply. We all have attitudes, opinions, and beliefs that run deep, but most run shallow and barely influence what we do—including how we decide cases.

This is why so much professional opinion polling is wrong. It is easy to think something is deep-seated when it is actually shallow and even transitory, and so can easily be neutralized or reversed by other factors.

For example, many jurors say they favor damages caps. Early research suggested that this means they'd enforce a low damages verdict and even be difficult on liability. But it soon became clear that for *most* jurors there is no correlation between what they say in advance about caps and whether they are good liability or damages jurors. This is because *most* jurors who say they are for caps hold that opinion so shallowly that it easily dissipates as trial goes on. In fact, many—not all—will turn out to be unusually strong on liability and unusually generous on damages. In voir dire, you have no way of knowing whether or not the stance on caps will give way to a strong plaintiff-oriented stance—except by determining where on the scale from strong to weak the stance lies. You must do this before deciding how much to weigh that juror's stance.

The same is true for every attitude, opinion, and belief a juror directly tells you about.

In a recent case, a juror said she was a *very* (italics hers) *conservative Republican* (italics hers) who *firmly* (italics hers) believed in damages caps!" (Exclamation point hers.) She said that a million dollars was plenty for anything no matter what. "No matter what!"

She also said, "Oh yes, your Honor, of course I will follow the law as you give it to me." Easily fooled, the judge refused to remove her for cause. Having no peremptories left, we were stuck with her.

Fortunately, we needed only nine of twelve jurors to win.

As it turned out, the verdict came quickly, and it was large. Astonishingly, it was *unanimous* (italics mine)! In interviewing jurors later, we learned that our conservative Republican caps lady had pushed for a very different scale of damages than everyone else. Everyone else wanted to allow a few million dollars. The caps lady? Twenty million dollars.

Her attitude about caps had been shallow enough to be dislodged by the way she felt about the case. This is common when using Reptilian advocacy methods, but it sometimes happened even before that.

So you cannot assume that a juror deeply believes anything he says he believes or that it will have any effect on his decision making. Shallow beliefs are context-oriented—i.e., they shift as the context shifts.

Go Beneath the Words

If you ask a juror how deeply she believes something, her answer—no matter how certain she is about it—will be unreliable because she doesn't actually know.

So you must go beneath the words. Ironically, you do this by getting the juror to talk about the topic as much as you can get her to do. Once you've asked, "Tell me about it" three or four times, you'll usually be able to gauge whether a stance is fiercely and deeply held, or shallow enough to dissipate in light of the case. This will keep you from wasting a lot of peremptories.

Caveat: Promises

It is dangerous to elicit promises or agreements from jurors. Don't ask them to make deals with you ("Will you promise us to . . . ?"). Jurors resent being asked to assure you of anything in advance.

And deals jurors make in jury selection aren't worth the breath it takes to make them.

Supplement A

A-24 THE LAST SIX QUESTIONS

At the end of every jury selection ask the following six questions.

Before doing that, if the jurors do not yet know anything about the case, give them a fifty-word thumbnail sketch.[13]

First Three General Questions

Ask number one of the final six:

> Given the kind of person you are—and your attitudes, your life experiences, opinions, everything about you—what is there about you that might help you, even a little, to be a juror on this kind of case? Other than your ability to be fair and listen to both sides?

Do not say ". . . to be a good juror . . ."; just "to be a juror."

Because this is a positive kind of question, it often gets answers that negative questions ("what's wrong with you?") miss. Example: "My background in engineering will help because I'll be able to tell why the ceiling fell down." Now you can decide if this self-proclaimed expert is dangerous for you. So ask, "Tell me about that," and so forth. From another juror you might hear, as I once did, "I read a lot, and I probably know more than most professionals about the problems with highway design." Or, "Our neighbors are physicians, and we've talked a lot about how hard it is to do that kind of work, so I'll be very qualified to gauge what the doctor did in this case."

The question is effective because, as in the above examples, it often does not occur to a prospective juror that there might be anything *wrong* with his answer; he thinks it's good. But depending on which side you're on, it could be disastrous to let such persons on the jury.

Ask this question first of the most articulate and thoughtful of the prospective jurors. Ask follow-ups. This will get information you need and

---

13. Up to this point, the less the prospective jurors know about the case, the better. The more they know, the more easily they can shade their voir dire answers to get either on or off the jury, as they prefer. Unfortunately, some judges want you to give a "mini-opening" before voir dire starts. This is an enormous disadvantage to you if you fall into making or even implying any accusations, because it is too early for you to do that without creating suspicion (*see* section 5-2-1, p. 112). When a judge forces you to do a mini-opening, keep it 100 percent neutral, such as:

> This case is about someone who was hurt while using a manufactured product. Over the course of trial you'll hear each side tell you their point of view about why it happened and how much harm it caused.

Meticulously prepare your mini-opening so that you don't slide even slightly into anything accusatory or adversarial.

simultaneously give other jurors time to think about the question so they will more likely have a useful answer when you get to them.

Be sure to include the last sentence: "Other than your ability to be fair and listen to both sides." Otherwise everyone's answer will be, "I can be fair and listen to both sides."

Then ask #2, the other side of the coin:

> Given the kind of person you are, your attitudes, life experiences, opinions, everything about you, what is there about you that you think might make it just a little bit *harder* for you to be a juror on this kind of case?

Don't say "make you a bad juror." And be sure to say "just a little bit."

Even if the judge has already filtered out prospective jurors for hardship,[14] some will say they will find it hard to be a juror because they have a schedule conflict or some other logistical problem. Sometimes it's the upcoming death of that same poor grandmother who died six times while the juror was in college. Other times you might hear about a real hardship problem. Either way, get yourself out of it. Explain that you are not allowed to deal with that; the judge has to—unless, of course, this is a juror you want to get rid of. In that case, lead the juror into saying that she will not be able to concentrate on the evidence because she'll be worried about the problem.

Many jurors will have no useful responses to either final question numbers one or two. But some will, resulting in important information that even the most thorough of voir dires would have missed.

Then go to #3:

> What else is there—anything at all—that you would want me to know about you if you were me trying to decide who will be on the jury? Any little thing. Even if you're not sure it makes any difference?

Again, this often gets nothing useful. Occasionally it's a bombshell.

Jurors' Rights Questions

These are your final three questions:

---

14. Inexplicably, some judges do not ask about hardship until after the attorneys have questioned everyone. This wastes everyone's time and can make voir dire drag on endlessly while you start all over to fill slots you thought were long filled. Always petition to have the judge do hardship cause hearings first.

Dr. Sunwolf (her real and entire name), the brilliant attorney, jury consultant, and communications scholar, helped to originate the questions from which the following questions have been adapted.

Ask these as group questions. First:

> Jurors have some important rights. You'll need to know these rights so you can use them when necessary.
>
> First, you have the right to hear all the testimony.[15] Every word. So when you don't hear something a witness says, will you all be comfortable raising your hand and telling the judge, "Your honor, I did not hear what the witness just said"? Will you all do that?

Unless a juror says no, there's no need to follow this up. If a juror says no, it will probably be because she's uncomfortable having to interrupt. This is a pretty good clue that that juror is not a leader (*see* section A-22, p. 304). And it gives you the opportunity to say that the testimony is so important that we all have to be sure she hears it all—so even if she's uncomfortable, would she be OK "poking the next juror to tell the judge there was something you couldn't hear."

The second jurors' rights question:[16]

> When trial ends and you go home, you'll have the right to have been on a jury that followed the law that the judge will give you. No one—not even the judge, and certainly not another juror—has any right to do anything that puts you in the position of having been on a jury whose verdict violated your personal oath or affirmation as a juror.
>
> In other words: as a juror, you have the right to keep your integrity 100 percent intact.
>
> This is the most important thing for you to keep in mind the whole time.
>
> And here's my question.

---

15. Say "testimony," not "evidence." Many jurors think evidence means stuff you show them, not what a witness says.

16. As you ask this question, stand in the vicinity of a courtroom Bible. If you're afraid to look too spiritual, just being near the Bible gets jurors to notice it without your pointing it out or even seeming to stand near it for a purpose. The vast majority of jurors have strong enough religious beliefs to want to avoid violating an oath or affirmation when God might so clearly be looking, as the aura of courtroom might make more likely—and when it comes to God, few jurors will take any unnecessary chances.

This is extremely important, so emphasize it by pausing briefly to look around to get everyone's attention. And deliver the following slowly:

> At trial's end, the judge will tell you the law.
>
> You're under oath or affirmation to follow those laws.
>
> So during deliberations, when another juror wants the jury to do something outside the judge's law, will you be willing to say, **"I won't do that, and you don't have the right to ask me to"**?[17]

Follow up:

> If that juror continues to try, you don't have to argue with that juror. All you have to do is tell the judge that there's a juror who wants you to ignore the law. Everyone willing to do that?

Then:

> Will you do your best to *remember* your absolute right to be on a jury that follows the law?

And here's your final question:

> And finally: Will you agree to follow the law yourself?

No need to ask follow-ups for any of this unless a juror has trouble with it.

Remember that few judges are willing to "explain" the law. But they are generally willing, when necessary, to re-admonish that everyone must follow the law and not urge others to ignore or violate it.

A-25 CHALLENGING FOR CAUSE

Michigan Trial Consultant Eric Oliver says that jury voir dire's primary purpose is to pursue challenges for cause. It's an easily acquired skill. Lawyers who have not mastered it waste endless peremptories and so are needlessly forced to seat dangerous jurors.

The four steps in the process are:

---

17. In a very few venues, jurors (in the noble tradition of Zenger) are allowed to decide not to apply the law. But even in those venues, no one is likely to object to your saying that jurors must follow the law. And within those venues, generally no one is allowed to tell jurors that they can ignore the law. On this matter, the courts generally allow judges and lawyers to lie by saying the law must be followed—even when the state constitution says otherwise. It's a judicial power grab.

1. Know the law

Counsel, I tell thee this gently in thine ear: With astonishing frequency, even the best of counsel think they know the law about jury selection when in fact they don't. For example, in one state, over the course of two years I watched three otherwise good lawyers damage their clients by needlessly losing between five and ten easy cause-dismissal motions when the judges "rehabilitated" by asking "Can you follow the law?" This was professional negligence by counsel because it was reversible error, and they did not know enough to object. I frequently see equally serious blunders due solely to counsel incorrectly thinking she knew the law.

Another example: The expectation that a juror "can" follow the law is usually not the law. In Federal venues, for example, a prospective juror who is merely "substantially impaired" from following the law *must* be excused for cause. [*Wainwright v. Witt*, 496 U.S. 412 (1985).] Further, the "substantial impairment" need not be shown with "unmistakable clarity." So a strong suspicion that a juror would have "substantial" (i.e., having a real effect on) problem following the law must be dismissed. You can't argue to have the judge follow that law if you don't know it.

2. Know the judge

Know in advance how the judge makes cause dismissal decisions. Be prepared to work within them. And be prepared to lodge effective objections when those limitations and rulings are not legitimate. Preserve your objections, including your ultimate objection to seating the jury; use all your peremptories so the appellate court can consider the issue; etc. Be polite, but do not go passive.[18]

If you skillfully lay the groundwork for a cause challenge, this cursory (or even a thorough) rehabilitation is less likely to succeed.

3. Start with open-ended questions

What do you do when you spot something that might support a challenge for cause? First, ask many open-ended questions about it:

---

18. The most egregious kind of abdication of a judge's sworn duty is the use of a juror's "I can follow the law" as reason to deny a cause challenge. Every judge knows "I can follow the law" or "I will follow the law" are not sufficiently credible as a basis for anything. Yet judges often throw justice and the system's integrity to the lions on that shaky basis. It's like leaving a safe unlocked because people out on the sidewalk say they won't rob it. After all, if "Yes, I'll follow the law" is a sane disposition of a cause challenge, then a not-guilty criminal plea must result in a directed defense verdict. One reason the public has so little respect for the justice system is that they have so often seen judges pretend that this kind of judicial abuse is legitimate. It is, in fact, disgraceful.

We have many tools to deal with these awful voir dire practices by judges. These tools are found within state and federal constitutions, case law, and other existing requirements that call for and guarantee the fairest possible jury.

Tell me about that.

Tell me more about that.

Tell me more about *that*.

What have you read about it?

What have you heard about that?

How do you feel about it?

Why do you think _____ happens so much?

How strongly do you feel about it?

Tell me about that.

You want to elicit extensive responses to open-ended questions because judges are supposed to rule on the totality (the "universe") of what a juror says, not merely on any single phrase such as "I can follow the law." The more the *unled* juror says that shows bias, the more the totality leans towards a cause dismissal.

And the more you get the juror to nail down his bias with certainty and emphasis, the greater her reluctance later when the judge or your opponent tries to rehabilitate her.

During the process, never be or sound hostile or negative. Be friendly, understanding, and even admiring of the forcefulness with which the prospective juror clings to his belief. Make the juror feel that it is a "badge of honor," as Texas trial consultant Robert Hirschhorn puts it, to be honest and forthright enough to speak up.

Complete your series of open-ended questions with:

You have a right to your opinion, don't you?

Tell me about that.

4. Shift to closed-ended questions

After eliciting all you can with open-ended questions, shift to closed-ended. But be careful. With closed-ended questioning, it's easy to slide into a hostile tone. Pay extra attention to remaining friendly and gentle. The nicer you are, the more likely the juror will go where you want. So:

How long have you felt this way?

So it's safe to assume that you're not likely to suddenly change your mind in the next few days [weeks]?

And you would not want to set your belief aside?

Setting it aside would be hard?

You obviously know your own mind, so I assume you're not going to set it aside just because someone comes along and tells you to set it aside?

And that's OK; no one has the right to make you set it aside. Not even the judge. So even if the judge told you you'd have to set it aside to be a juror, you'd find it difficult, right?

Not likely that you'd set it aside?

It's so unlikely that it would be dishonest for you to swear that you'll set it aside?

So you could not honestly swear that you'd set it aside even if the judge told you you'd have to, in order to follow the law?

What you're doing is attempting to take the juror through a "rehabilitation" while he's still under your control. If he backs off, you've lost nothing since the juror would surely have backed off as soon as the judge or your opponent started rehabilitating.

And remember this: rehabilitation means getting a juror to contradict himself. So argue as follows: While "rehabilitation" might be the common practice in your venue, a juror's contradiction makes it permanently uncertain which of the answers is true. That uncertainty makes the juror unfit to serve, because it means he cannot be trusted to follow the law. Moreover, the more trustworthy thing such a juror says is what he said *unled*—i.e., what he told you.

A-26 PRETRIAL REHEARSAL

The best trial techniques, even once mastered, are ineffective unless you are fresh at doing them. That is why many of the best and most experienced lawyers do a practice voir dire before every trial.

Not more than three evenings before voir dire, preferably the night before, gather eight or ten strangers and spend a few hours practicing on them the voir dire you will do in court. This helps you hit the ground running when you do it in court. It makes you more confident, secure, and relaxed—and thus more credible. It makes you more comfortable with the necessity of listening. And that creates better rapport.

Best of all, when you start your jury voir dire in trial, it will seem like the second day—because you have just done it the night before in your office.

This is why actors rehearse and athletes scrimmage. In fact, the better and more experienced they are, the more they practice and rehearse. If attorneys scrimmaged everything they do in trial, that *alone* would raise the quality of trial practice in America to unrecognizable heights.

But few will do it—so you can gain an enormous advantage over them. Practice, practice, and practice. And then practice some more. Michael Jordan did not get good by reading about basketball. And he did not get better by skipping practice. Even at the height of his career he came back to Chapel Hill to spend hours and days in what had been his college gym practicing the basics. His greatest brilliance was realizing the necessity of endless practice from beginning to end of his playing career.

Your voir dire practice session will even make the judge like you more, because you will waste less time finding your feet as you get started with voir dire in court.

An advanced practice session will also let you safely try new methods—such as getting prospective jurors deliberating right in front of you. This is the pinnacle of good voir dire.

Mr. Jones, what do you think about that? [*i.e., what Mr. Smith just said.*]

When Mr. Jones has answered, go back to Mr. Smith:

Mr. Smith, what about that?

Then involve other jurors.

Ms. Johnson, which way of thinking are you closer to?

Tell me about that.

Done well, you'll start them "deliberating." As if they're auditioning for the part of juror. You'll not only hear what they feel about the topic and how strongly they feel it; you'll also see who is articulate and persuasive, who might be a leader, who folds, how well informed each juror is, and what kind of language they use when talking about the topic.

You'll also see how each juror interacts with the others—which is of the utmost importance in deliberations. Does she bully? Respect what others say? Does she listen—or just talk? Does she try to find common ground or just emphasize how her opinion differs? Does she pair up with others? Group with others? Enlist others? Does she need to be right no matter what anyone else says? Does she talk in moderate terms or extreme? Etc.

Supplement A

When I tell you to practice the night before trial starts, you might say, "Don't you realize how busy I am?" Yeah, I do. Do *you* realize how important a well-run jury selection is?

If you don't have time to practice jury voir dire the night before trial, you lack the resources to do your job right; you are short-shrifting your client. Complaining that you have no time to practice something as crucial as jury voir dire is the same as saying you don't have the staff to handle the complex case you have taken.

A-27 JUDGE-APPROVED QUESTIONS; JUDGE-CONDUCTED VOIR DIRE

In some jurisdictions, you have to submit jury voir dire questions for the judge to approve. Keep in mind that the judge rarely knows the case well and never knows the case from your point of view. So help the judge see the appropriateness and need for each question you submit. Explain:

- How each submitted question will identify biases and attitudes necessary to intelligently exercise your challenges.
- How those biases and attitudes can affect juror decision making.
- How some such biases and attitudes might be appropriate for a cause dismissal, and others would be appropriate to consider for a peremptory dismissal.

To give the judge reason to include each question you offer, submit your questions this way:

#7

"Who has ever had to use crutches?"

and

"Who knows anyone who has ever had to use crutches?"

Follow up by asking, "Please tell me about that."

Purpose. Plaintiff had a hard time on crutches for six weeks. Prospective jurors who've had easy time or know someone who did will likely undervalue Plaintiff's ordeal. So we must learn who used crutches and their difficulty with them.

Challenge Basis. In follow-up questioning, juror might say, "I had no trouble with crutches and can't see how anyone would." If follow-up shows difficulty for her in compensating, we will ask the Court for cause dismissal.

This provides the judge justification for allowing the question and sensitizes the judge to your challenge concerns.

When submitting questions for the judge to ask, include the follow-up questions he should also ask. For example, if the initial question is "Who here has ever missed more than a few weeks of work because of an injury?" follow up with:

> Please tell me about that.
>
> How long were you (or the person you know) out of work?
>
> Tell me about that.
>
> How much income did you (or the person you know) lose?
>
> How did you (or the person you know) feel about missing that much work?
>
> Tell me about that.
>
> What difficulties were there when you (or the person you know) returned to work?

And so forth.

Some judges ask no follow-ups; others ask as many as you provide and more. Judges are more likely to ask when you provide the follow-up questions. Follow-ups help judges better understand the purpose of the initial question and can help the judge be a more useful information-gatherer for you. What you're doing, of course, is teaching the judge how to effectively ask good voir dire questions. Suggesting the exact wording for the question makes his job easier, so he's more likely to ask them.

Supplement B

Story for Opening Statements

B-1 Storytelling

Narrative story is the foundation of movies, plays, and novels. It used to be the foundation of poetry, centuries back when everyone loved poetry. But once poets got too big for their britches and started omitting story, their mass audience minusculized. Let that be a warning to you—not just about poetry, but trials, too. Both require stories unless you're content with reaching only a minority of your listeners.

Tell a story in a bar and everyone listens. Tell storyless poems in a bar and, perhaps deservedly, you probably get beat up.

Similarly, tell a story in trial and everyone listens. Conduct storyless trials and, deservedly for sure, you get beat up.

Why?

Because story provides pleasure. Pleasure motivates the closest—and most sympathetic—possible listening. As a result, human beings are story gluttons.

Even better: The brain's hardwiring instantly and fully absorbs story. Once absorbed, the story becomes the framework that in turn absorbs and stores everything else on the topic. So your simple narrative story of what the defendant did (*see* section 5-5-2, pp. 124*ff.*) becomes, automatically and autonomically, the jurors' well-organized storage structure—like well-organized bookshelves—for everything else they later hear about your case—the science, the arguments, the laws, the personalities, and all else. The key word is *later*. Do not mix the science, the arguments, the laws, the personalities, the accusations, or anything else, into your opening-statement story of *what the defendant did*.

The unique power of story as an information bin is why a ninth-grade kid who can't pass a third-grade history exam has almost perfect recall and understanding of even the most information-packed of movies. Once a story is embedded, everything else falls into place.

So the story of what the defendant did must come early in opening.

Providing story first and all the rest afterward is our single most effective way of conveying information. It is the product of eons of evolution, and one of our most precious survival mechanisms. Don't waste this resource.

Many kinds of stories are essential to your case, including the story of what the defendant did, the stories that your witnesses—especially your damages fact witnesses—tell to frame their testimony, and stories of what your client's life is like now.[1] The advice below applies specifically to the story necessary in opening: the story of what the defendant did. Your goal is to match the nature of this story to the brain's precise hardwiring for accepting and housing story. That means:

Simplicity.

You need not be a gifted storyteller. Simply apply the following principles. And apply them simply.

One Fact Per Sentence

Provide a simple narrative of what the defendant did. "Simple narrative" means one fact per sentence. Do not say: "The truck driver drove through the red light, skidded across the center line, and hit an oncoming car head-on." That not simple; it's three separate facts. Three facts requires three sentences:

> Truck driver Wyatt drives through the red light.
>
> Truck driver Wyatt skids across the center line.
>
> Truck driver Wyatt hits an oncoming car.

This simplicity creates emphasis, directness, and crystal clarity.

Present Tense

Use the present tense. The brain does not directly register past or future tense. It has to translate past and future tense to present tense before storing it. Simplify by cutting out that needless step. That keeps the brain more attentive to the story itself.

---

1. *CAVEAT:* See Supplement F, pp. 391*ff.* for warnings about careless use of first-person narratives ("I wake up in the morning, and it hurts to climb out of bed . . .," etc.)

Past tense distances the listener. Present tense is immediate. What happened is always less important that what is happening now.

So instead of: "He drove through the red light," simply say, "He drives through the red light."

Get into present tense at the start of the story by saying:

> Please come back with me to June 12, 2008. We **are** in downtown Rochester. Acme Corporation's truck driver **is** headed West on . . . .

Chronological Order

The brain's sense of time developed in only one direction: forward. So in storytelling, *any* violation of strict chronology is deeply confusing. This is why almost every novel, movie, and play adheres to strict chronological sequence. It is the *only* simple sequence, and *simple* is the first story commandment.[2]

Be particularly wary of telling a story that uses the "V" structure. In the "V" structure, you tell the jury what one defendant did through the day up until 8:00 p.m. that evening; then you say, "Now let's leave him there and go back to the morning to see what the other defendant did." Not even Hollywood's most skilled screenwriters can do this in a clear way; it *always* adds unnecessary confusion. So never use it on jurors, unless in voir dire you discover that they can all quickly tell you their phone numbers backward. That would mean they're from a different planet than Earth.

Actions

A story is not comprised of facts, descriptions, accusations, or explanations. Leave those things out. You need the story's **actions** in place *first,* before you start laying in anything else. So as you tell the opening's story of what the defendant did, omit what he did not do, why he did or didn't do something, what it meant, and everything else that is not a simple statement of what he did.

---

2. The ancients began stories "*in medias res,*" meaning in the middle, and then referred back to past events as the present unfolded. This works for Greek epics and tragedies. It does not work for lawyers, trials, movies, plays, or most novels. What's the difference? Because the ancient Greek audience knew the plot in advance, so there was no confusion. Jurors don't know your story in advance.

Actions Only

So what is an action?

Simple: For our purposes, **an action is a) something someone *does* that b) an observer** *can seen or hear him do. Can you—or a camera—see it or hear someone doing it?*

So for our purposes, thinking, for example, is not an action. No one can see it or hear it. Being hungry is not an action; it is invisible. But you can see someone eating, so while *hunger* is not an action, *eating* is.

An explanation is not action. Explaining is an action, but the explanation itself is not. So in your opening story you can say:

The boss explains how the engine works.

But do not, at this point, explain how the engine works.

I cannot say this too many times: Your story in opening is nothing more than a present-tense narrative of *what the defendant did*, action by action.

Each action is a separate thing the defendant did.

Each action is described by an active, not passive, verb. ("The painter paints the house," not "The house is painted by the painter.")

The grammatical *subject* of every sentence (the noun) in the opening story should be the name of the defendant (not the pronoun). The predicate of every sentence (the verb) should be an action of the defendant's. (It is called the predicate precisely because it means "say it first.")

If you mix any other information in with the defendant's actions, you will ruin—perhaps permanently—your story's ability to be the framework into which each juror can file everything else. So don't say, "The car was a 2001 Chrysler." That sentence presents a fact, state of being, a description—but not an action. If you can easily slip the fact into an action sentence, you can get away with it—such as, "Joe Defendant starts his 2001 Chrysler." But do this no more than a few times or your story will be full of information no one can keep track of—which is the opposite of simple.

So every sentence of the opening story should roughly follow this pattern:

Joe Defendant does _____.

Then end that sentence and start the next one:

Joe Defendant does _____.

So:

Joe Defendant washes his car.

Supplement B

>Joe Defendant rinses off the soap.
>
>Joe Defendant drinks from the hose.
>
>Joe Defendant takes his pill.
>
>Joe Defendant sits down.
>
>Joe Defendant dials 911.

Etc.

People Listen to Actions

They listen less to descriptions, states of being, and explanations. This is the basic principle of plays and movies. Well, not many French movies. But movies and plays that most Americans can sit through.

Move Forward in Time

Every sentence of your story must move forward in time—be the movement a split second forward or a century forward. If the time at the end of the sentence is the same as the time was at the beginning, the story has stopped—so jurors tend to stop listening. If a sentence does not progress the story forward in time, leave it out for now.

Short Sentences

Use only short, simple sentences. No compound or complex sentences. Simple sentences are easier to listen to. So no semicolons. Very few commas. In opening, jurors are nervous about whether they can learn all they have to. They want a guide who will help them. From the first words of your initial story, show them (don't just tell them) that you are that guide.

Importance of Each Action

Do not hurry through one action to get to the next. Give each action its own importance. That does not mean to make every action seem to be of *equal* importance. But every action important enough to be in the story should be important enough not to rush through or subordinate as if it makes no difference.

Read this next story aloud as though every separate point has importance:

>Come back with me to seven o'clock this morning.//
>
>My alarm rings.//
>
>I wake up.//

I roll out of bed.//

I open the curtains.//

I look out.//

I see snow falling.//

I take a shower.//

I go downstairs.//

I drink some coffee.//

I read the *Times*.//

I put on my coat.//

I go outside.//

I scrape the windshield.//

This looks stilted on the page. But spoken aloud in such a way as to give each event some importance, it will be listened to. It is in the structure and rhythm to which the brain is by far the most receptive. Note the use of present tense. Note the brevity and simplicity. Note that every sentence contains a new action and forwards us in time. Note the lack of description and explanation. *Note the absence of anything that cannot be seen or heard.*

You can fit in some descriptive material. But be sparing:

My alarm rings.//

I wake up **slowly.**//

I roll out of my bed.//

I open the **red** curtains.//

I look out.//

I see **heavy** snow falling.//

I take a **hot** shower.//

I go downstairs.//

I drink some coffee.//

I read the *Times*.//

I put on my **winter** coat.//

I go outside.//

I scrape **heavy ice off** the windshield.//

So you can get a good amount of information in, but don't overdo it; include only what is essential to furthering the story.

Few lawyers can effectively convey both the story (events) and the explanatory details (information) at once. Almost all who think they can are dead wrong. This is because **listeners layer in only one new level at a time: first the actions (what someone did), and—later—the explanations, omissions, thoughts, feelings, and so forth.**

Practice this method whenever you tell stories, not just to jurors. If you have children, they will appreciate it. If you have no children, get a friend to listen.

Selectivity and Starting Point

Start your story with the first relevant thing the defendant did. This means you have to look for it in discovery. The story did not necessarily start when the truck came through the red light. It started earlier, when the driver glanced away from the road. Or it started even earlier, when the company hired this driver.

Remember that the earliest things a listener hears in a story can be what the listener goes on to think the whole story is about. This makes the listener hear everything that follows in the light of the beginning. Thus, starting with the wrong action can weaken your whole story.

Select the events the jury needs in order to understand what happened *in the way you want them to understand it.* Delay events that hurt you. Do not conceal them; deal with them later in opening.

This sounds easy, but you can fall into a trap by talking too early about the things your client did, no matter how proper or laudatory they were. Jurors tend to attach blame to the first actions they hear about. In this way, innocent actions will turn damning. This is a basic principle of dramatic storytelling. If I watch a character early in a play or movie while I am thinking there is some chance, however small, that he may be up to no good, I will tend to see even his most innocent actions as wrongful.

This happens in trial when you tell jurors what your client did before they know all about what the defendant did. This is because as soon as jurors start hearing about what happened, they start assigning blame—but they tend to assign blame only to the events they hear about. So limit the actions to those the defendant did. Your story needs to be solely about what the *defendant* did. Leave your client out—except as the eventual passive receiver of harm.

So if the doctor failed to diagnose your client's cancer, do not start by telling us what your client did ("Jane calls the doctor for an appointment.... Jane goes to see him on January 8 . . ., etc.") That makes jurors start by thinking about why Jane chose that doctor, why Jane did not ask for a second opinion, why she waited until January 8. By the time you get to the first thing the doctor did, jurors have already nailed some blame on your client.

Instead, start by telling us what the doctor did: "Dr. Smith sees a patient. Dr. Smith examines her. Dr. Smith orders a test. Dr. Smith sends it to the lab. Dr. Smith looks at the result. Dr. Smith . . . ." That way, jurors begin by thinking about what the doctor—not Jane—did wrong.

Even things that have nothing to do with your client can deflect and diminish defendant blame.

For example, take a premises liability case: An assault in a motel room. Three vicious prison escapees attack an elderly couple in the couple's room. Do NOT start the story this way:

> It's 3:00 a.m. January 12, 2008. Three Central Prison inmates shoot a prison guard through the head. The prisoners escape over the prison wall. They run. They get to a stoplight at an intersection. They surround a gray Buick. They pull the elderly driver out. She struggles against them. They shoot her in the chest. They drive off in her Buick. They lose their pursuers. They park in the dark behind the C'mon Inn Motel. They shove open the door to Room 123. John and Jane, my clients, wake in terror. The escapees demand money. One of them beats John while . . . .

That is good storytelling. The jury will listen. They will get the full horror of what the escapees did to John and Jane. Jurors will get the point: these bad guys were really bad.

This would be fine, except your case is not about the escapees. It is about a motel owner who installed flimsy doors and who never told guests of previous break-ins.

Starting the story with the escapees leads jurors to blame the escapees instead of the owner. Juror shock and anger will be directed at the prison escapees. By the time you finally get to the real story of your case—what the motel owner did—the jurors will be irrevocably blaming the escapees. You'll have created your own competition.

Here is a better beginning for the plaintiff:

> It's January 12, 2008.
>
> The owner of the C'mon Inn Motel goes to a hardware store.
>
> The motel owner looks at a selection of locks.

The motel owner buys the cheapest one.

The motel owner goes back to his motel.

The motel owner installs the $3.00 locks.

The motel owner installs one on the door of room 123.

Two months later.

Nine in the evening.

The motel owner is working the desk.

The motel owner listens as an elderly couple asks, "We saw your sign that says it's safe; is it really?"

The motel owner says, "Absolutely."

That night in room 123, the elderly couple is beaten and robbed.

By shining your narrative light on the actions of the motel owner at the beginning of your story, you make jurors blame the owner instead of the escapees. The escapees are not in the story so they are not on the jurors' minds. So you do not deflect the blame from where you need it.

Added benefit: this kind of storytelling makes the defendant's negligence seem to lead inevitably to the harm.

Always ask yourself what your beginning would lead jurors to think if it were all they were going to hear. What does it make the jurors focus on? This is always a necessary test for you to run, because you know the whole story, so you already know what your focus is. But your focus is not your jurors' focus. You have to make your story create the focus you want.

"Would Not Happen to Me"

Here's another reason to keep the initial focus off your client. When a juror hears that something bad has happened, she wants to believe that it would never happen to her. So she makes herself believe in some comforting ways that separate herself from the plaintiff.

For example, in the motel case, jurors say to themselves, "Oh, that would not have happened to me because I would never have stayed in a motel room that faced the back lot."

In a medical negligence case, jurors say, "Oh, that would not have happened to me because I would have gone for a second opinion." (Jurors commonly say this even though they have never in their lives sought a second opinion!)

In a products liability case: "Oh, that would not have happened to me because I'd never have bought that kind of car." Or, "If I'd been driving, the car would not have rolled because I'm a better driver." So now it's your client's fault instead of the defendant's!

When a juror thinks this way, he tells other jurors: "The plaintiffs never should have stayed in that kind of room!" or "She should have gotten a second opinion!" or "It's his own fault for buying that kind of car!" or "She should have known how to drive that kind of car." And because this kind of thinking is common and unavoidable human nature—we all do it—these remarks carry weight with other jurors.

Because of this comforting psychological mechanism, jurors commonly rely on even the flimsiest of reasons to persuade themselves that this kind of harm would never have happened to them, because they would not have done what the plaintiff did.

So always limit your initial opening story to the defendant's actions ("The motel owner chooses a $3.00 lock"). Everything else undermines the effectiveness of the story.

Supplement C

The Ball Opening: A Guided Template

The "Ball Opening" relies on—and is partly developed from—the earlier work of a long string of consultants and lawyers, starting with the National Jury Project's groundbreaking Diane Wiley. So "Ball's Opening" should really be called the "Ball-&-Sources Opening."

Bullet 1: Once you understand and master every step of the annotated sample below, you'll quickly and easily adapt it to any kind of case.

Bullet 2: To understand each step of Ball's Opening and how best to do it, carefully study chapter 5 and use this supplement as your guide. This opening structure is neither a cookbook recipe nor a monkey-see-monkey-do set of gimmicks. It is a sophisticated weapon that requires skilled deployment. You will not do it well if your understanding of it is shallow.

Bullet 3: Note the economy of language: not a word more than necessary. This is the "Karate" principle: the fewer words, the greater impact per word. (It's the opposite of the usual practice in law: you could cut *most* of the words in almost any lawbook or motion or opening without losing a bit of meaning.)

Bullet 4: The boldface headings are to guide you. Don't say them to the jury. But stay strictly within them.

Bullet 5: Is it really necessary to follow the template exactly? Yes. Do not assume a change is OK just because you think it's OK; you'll almost certainly be wrong. This template carefully, wisely plants the structure of your case into the jurors' minds in the clearest, most persuasive, and most lasting possible way. It steers you clear of almost every hidden danger lawyers routinely stumble into because they've not done the extended research it takes to find those dangers. So what feels good to you probably won't be. When you tell me, "But I could see they responded well to the change I made," you probably did not read the conscious or subconscious minds of some of the more troublesome jurors.

Bullet 6: Don't worry about the length of the opening below. I'm trying to provide enough for you to see how to do each part. The matter of your own opening's length is a different issue. (The general rule on length: judge willing, you can go as long as jurors listen, and jurors listen for as long as they think you're saying things they need to hear. *See* section 5-17, p. 175.)

> **Bullet 7: BULLET POINTS.** *Never* show a text bullet point to introduce a *new* topic. Never. No matter who else you have seen show introductory bullet points, she's screwing up. Don't be a bullet-point lemming. Don't do it in front of a jury, or when teaching, at a business meeting or mediation conference, when preparing athletes for play or soldiers for battle (the Pentagon has finally learned this!), arguing with your spouse, or telling your kids a bedtime story. When presenting new material, if you want to use bullet points, show each one *after* you've finished explaining that point; use the bullet point as a sum-up, not introductory, label. Especially in opening, introductory bullet points yank the jurors' attention off you. Introductory bullet points do not work the way paragraph and section headings do in a book. Once a *listener* sees an introductory bullet point, he subconsciously thinks he's gotten the main point so does not listen carefully.

Bullet 8: Attorneys who have mastered this opening tell me that putting it together clarifies and enhances the entire case—not only for the jurors, but for the attorney. And even the judge. It becomes your controlling matrix from which everything else proceeds. Unlike the movie *Matrix*, this opening makes everything crystal clear—again, for you as well as for the jurors. It becomes your mission control center from early trial preparation through the end of closing. As such, it is your ultimate application of logic and reason to the totally subconscious, nonlogical process of juror decision making.

In the template I have broken up the lines so you can see where to take *very brief* pauses so that jurors can follow each phrase you say. This requires that you omit any phrases that jurors do not need to hear. It also requires that you play this as a teacher, not an advocate.

Opening Template

TEXT

I. Primary rule(s) the defendant violated.

Good morning. **(1)**

A driver

is never allowed

to needlessly endanger the public. **(2)**

Before changing lanes,

a driver must make sure the new lane is clear.

If he does not,

and as a result hurts someone,

the driver is responsible for the harm. **(3)**

NOTES

1. Say "Good morning." Don't sound like an undertaker; sound friendly. Mean it. Be pleased to see them, but don't grin. Leave them a very brief moment to respond. Have someone at your table note their reactions during that moment. Cool reactions might mean you have some bridges to build during trial.

2. Tone here is important. Don't sound like Moses coming down from the mountain. Sound like you're just reminding us of something we already know. Don't sound portentous or important. Or like a moral persuader. The rule is not a pronouncement. Just inform us of the first (the umbrella) rule. We'll all agree with it. You won't need to persuade us. And a well-selected second rule will be received in the same way, unless it is about an unfamiliar topic.

When you must use a rule that jurors won't automatically understand and agree with, give it within the framework of a) an authority and b) the umbrella ("needless danger") rule: "Two expert scientists from the Omega Nuclear Research Center in Lansing will be here to explain to us that in making a new universe, the maker must create the same number of positive particles as negative ones. When a universe maker does not do that, she needlessly endangers the public. So she'd be responsible for any harm her violation causes." At this point in opening, it's enough for you to teach jurors the rule and the consequences of violating it. That accomplishes your goal: for jurors to spot the violation on their own as you tell the story of what the defendant did.

You'll explain later why positive and negative particles have to be in balance.

3. At the start of opening, two rules is plenty. The rest come later. Some cases need three at the start of opening, but never more than three. One or two rules will sit saliently in jurors' heads as you tell the story of what the defendant did, so jurors will spot the rule violation for themselves. Three makes that less likely. Four makes it impossible.

TEXT

II. STORY OF WHAT THE DEFENDANT DID. (4)

Now please let me tell you the story of what happened in this case. (5)

Interstate 95

through Rocky Mount.

July afternoon.

Recent rain. (6)

Sarah Prince drives south, past mile marker 173. (7)

NOTES

4. The line breaks in the text indicate very brief breaks—not quite a pause, but just enough for jurors to digest one bit at a time. This is particularly important at the start of opening. If you run too much together, jurors won't hear it well no matter how simple it is.

5. "Story." Yes, you must say "story." For incontrovertible reasons, "story" is an irresistible Reptilian force. It makes jurors—even the worst—listen carefully. Weirdly, some advocacy advisors teach that "story" can mean only "fiction." This is based on no research and no understanding of how contextual language works. It's like saying that devout Christians stop believing in Jesus when the minister tells the story of Christmas. Walter Cronkite spent decades telling Americans "news stories"; not one listener ever thought he meant fiction. The "story" of the birds and the bees does not make anyone think there's really no such thing as sex. Trust jurors to know what you mean when you say "story." And you'll cull its myriad benefits. See supplement B and *Reptile*.

6. At the start of the story, you can use a very few pieces of static information to "set the scene." So "Interstate 95 through Rocky Mount. – July afternoon. – Recent rain" is okay. Do not use more.

7. This is a subtle point: If you just say, "Ms. Prince drives south," it meets all the story requirements (supplement B) except one: each sentence must move the action forward in time. For inescapable neurological reasons, we listen far more carefully to a story sentence that takes us forward in time. "Ms. Prince drives south" does not do that. But adding "past mile marker 173" does—it takes us from the moment before she's at marker 173 to the moment after. So for the listener, the mile marker serves as a time marker. I know this must seem trivial to you, but it's the basis of all good storytelling because it profoundly interlocks with the way the brain works. Here's proof: In your mind's eye, picture someone "driving south." Now see her driving south past a mile marker. There's a lot more movement, so there's a lot more listening.

TEXT

Ms. Prince **(8)**

enters a number on her cell phone. **(9)**

Ms. Prince tells someone on the phone, "I'm doing all I can to get there on time." **(10)**

Ms. Prince sees a slightly slower car ahead of her.

    SHOW: diagram

Ms. Prince speeds up as she cuts one lane left. **(11)**

    Pause. (12)

NOTES

8. Remember: The grammatical subject of every sentence is the defendant's name. This is crucial to keeping juror attention where you want it and off of everyone else, especially your client.

9. This early in opening, don't say anything like "Not looking at the road is dangerous." Such a statement is premature advocacy (section 5-2-1, pp. 112ff.) because it's an opinion, not an event. So it does not belong in this kind of story.

That said, framing the statement as a rule does not constitute premature advocacy. "A driver must look at the road" is not an opinion; it's a rule. It still does not belong in your story, but you can use it before the story so jurors will spot the violation in the story when you say, "Ms. Prince looks down at her phone." This persuades jurors without telling them what to think.

10. You could add: "She puts the phone away." But this is not the defense's story; it's yours. Let the defense seem defensive later by making them say, "Oh, she wasn't really on the phone anymore!" That gives you double-dip mention of driving-while-phoning. That helps regardless of when she did it; it violates a safety rule that jurors want other people to follow. Jurors won't approve of a violation or the violator just because she stopped violating the rule before hurting someone by means of some other rule violation.

11. Don't make overtly persuasive or emphatic word choices in the story of what the defendant did; that's premature advocacy (*see* section 5-2-1, pp. 112ff.). So don't say, "She shot [or zipped or careened] into the left lane." Find something somewhat milder, but still effective: "She cut into the left lane." "Cut" is better than "She changed lanes to the left," but does not quite cross into premature advocacy.

12. This pause gives jurors time to realize that the rule they've just heard (driver must look before changing lanes) has been violated. You must not say "she did not look." In the story of what the defendant did, never mention something she didn't do. You want jurors to figure it out for themselves. They're more likely to hold onto their own conclusions than yours. And we can't see someone not doing something, so leave defendants' omissions out of the story. If you have the information, you can say: "Ms. Prince looked down at her radio. She sped up and cut into the right lane." All these things can be seen. So they are not advocacy, and they fit story criteria.

TEXT

SHOW: diagram

Ms. Prince hits a pickup truck in the left lane.

Ms. Prince knocks it into a tree in the median. **(13)**

SHOW: diagram

Ms. Prince stops on the right shoulder.

Ms. Prince calls her office.

Ms. Prince says she'll be a little late. **(14)**

Another motorist calls 911. **(15)**

The pickup truck's driver, Norman Wyeth, now has permanent brain damage. **(16)**

At my table is Alison Wyeth, Norm's wife. **(17) (18)**

I'm their lawyer. **(19) (20)**

NOTES

13. As in the previous note, do not say, "She does not see a pickup truck in the lane to her left." It's an omission.

14. Always find out what the defendant did right after the negligent act. It can be damning.

15. At the end of the story you can—for the first time—tell us what someone other than the defendant has done, as long as it's not your client and as long as it makes a powerful point.

16. Note how unnecessary are the usual words, "because of the wreck." Remember, the fewer your words, the more jurors register each one. That's a major reason why less is more in everything from the wording of a phrase all the way up through the length of your case.

17. The jury will look at her. So tell her in advance to listen carefully to your opening. Don't tell her how to respond, but just to listen carefully.

18. Keep your brain-damaged client out of court as much as possible. *See* section 6-18, p. 194.

19. There is some blithering nonsense floating around that people are less offended by the word "attorney" than by the term "lawyer." Or vice-versa. If you believe either, will you also buy the bridge I have for sale in Brooklyn?

20. No need to say that you're their lawyer, or who's at your table, if the jurors already know it from jury voir dire.

TEXT

III. Who are we suing and why?—The safety rules the defendant(s) violated.

We're suing Sarah Prince for violating two highway-safety rules. **(21)**

A. First rule-violating act

First, Ms. Prince violated the rule to look before changing lanes.

Ms. Prince admits not knowing the truck was there until she hit it.

Ms. Prince admits she did not look. **(22)**

Ms. Prince admits she'd have seen the pickup if she'd been looking. **(23)**

She says she's more likely right than wrong **(24)**

that she'd have seen it—and that beyond that, she's certain that if she'd looked, she'd have seen it. **(25)**

Ms. Prince admits she knew at the time that changing lanes without looking is dangerous. **(26)**

B. What's dangerous in general about violating this rule? **(27)**

(28) State Trooper Lamont Boswith investigated this wreck.

He'll explain to us **(29)** that changing lanes without looking is among the most common causes of injuries and fatalities. He'll say he's more likely right than wrong about that, and beyond that, he's certain.

NOTES

21. You should be allowed to call a rule "a rule" when a witness will later refer to it that way. For purposes of whether you can say it in opening, it makes no difference whether the defense agrees that it's a rule. (*See* Fundamental Five, p. 10, on rules.)

22. This tells jurors how you know that she violated the rule. Don't ask jurors just to take your word for it—or anything else. It's too early for that. Instead, make yourself the messenger and tell them how you know that what you're saying is true. This is essential throughout opening. Even the best of trial advocates lose important ground when they ask for trust too soon.

23. This also tells jurors how you know she violated the rule.

24. The phrase "more likely right than wrong," etc., is part of your preponderance method. *See* section 3-1, pp. 61*ff*.

25. *See* section 3-4, p. 67, and section 3-5, p. 68, on maintaining your preponderance theme in opening.

26. This can take you into punitives; *see Reptile,* p. 71.

27. In this question, do not say a word about your case. Wait for Part C. It can be hard to delay talking about your case, but for the rule to carry full effect, you must.

28. At this point I have stopped indicating where to take brief pauses. But you still should not revert to high-speed tying together all your phrases.

29. Never say, "explain to you." Include yourself: "to us." This helps unify you with the jurors. Someone smart taught me this, but I don't remember who.

TEXT

He calls changing lanes without looking "blindsiding"—because when you're looking at the road ahead, you're not going to spot someone suddenly cutting into you from alongside. **(30)**

B1. Tentacles of danger (31)

Trooper Lamont explains that blindsiding is a menace on every kind of road, not just freeways: a blind lane change on a local street at low speeds can send another driver into other vehicles, pedestrians, or even kids in a front yard.

Trooper Lamont and others in the case will say that *every driver must be sure the space he's moving into is clear*—whether the space is in front or alongside. Or even behind, when backing up. *Before a driver moves into any new space, she is 100 percent responsible for making sure it's clear.*

In other words, I have to make sure you're not where I want to go. And as Trooper Lamont will say, it's enough for a witness in trial to be more likely right than wrong—but a driver has to be *certain* that before moving into a new space, there's no one already there. **(32)**

C. How did the violation in this case cause harm?

Ms. Prince wanted to go where Norm already was. But because she did not look she never saw him—so she knocked Norm off the road. **(33)**

Dr. Jonathan Cranning, who studies highway wrecks **(34)** and runs NC State University's neutral Highway Research Institute, has a long career both

NOTES

30. Depending on venue, you don't necessarily violate the Golden Rule restriction by placing the juror (as "you") into the shoes of your client, except on the topic of damages, as in, "How much would you want if this had happened to you?" In many venues, you can say things like, "What would you do in that situation on the highway?" But do your own due diligence on this.

31. This is where you relate the specifics of this case rule to the specifics of the lives of your jurors and their families. *See* "The Why-We're-Suing Paradigm," pp. 139–140, and *Reptile*.

32. This reinforces your preponderance theme and emphasizes—by contrast—the only acceptable level of care the defendant was allowed to have exercised. And it does not undermine the witness's credibility since she will say, "beyond being more likely than right, I'm certain." *See* chapter 3, section 3-5, pp. 68–69.

33. As a general rule, do not change terms during trial. Norm's "pickup" is always a "pickup"; don't call it a pickup now and a Ford later. No matter how clear you think the shift is, to some jurors it won't be. This is partly because jurors hear only some of the words you say, so easily get lost or confused.

34. Do not use the word "accident," as in "accident reconstructionist." Remember that every act of negligence derives from a choice to violate a rule, and there is nothing accidental about a choice. Jurors tend to forgive people for accidental behavior, but not for making choices dangerous to others. *See* Fundamental Five, p. 10, as well as *Reptile*.

TEXT

as a full professor and as an onsite working engineer. **(35)** He'll show us police photos of the pickup's tire marks across the median and into the tree. He'll explain that they show that Norm did a skillful job trying to regain control and slow down. But the slick wet grass and soft dirt made it impossible. So the pickup hit the tree at nearly full speed. Dr. Cranning will say that he's more likely right than wrong about this—and that beyond that, it all lies within that degree of expert certainty that's based on reason.

The full force of the impact with the tree slammed Norm's head back against his door pillar.

D. What should the defendant have done instead?

Ms. Prince should have followed the safety rule requiring drivers to look before changing lanes.

E. How would that have helped?

If Ms. Prince had looked, she'd have known to stay out of Norm's lane. So instead of swerving into him, she'd have taken her foot off the gas for a moment or just tapped her brake. Either would have been enough to stay safely behind the slower car up ahead. **(36)**

Repeat the same sequence for each violated rule:

A. Second rule-violating act

Ms. Prince also violated the safety rule that requires drivers to signal before changing lanes.

The drivers behind Ms. Prince saw that she did not signal before changing lanes. **(37)** They'll both testify to being more likely right than wrong about this, and beyond that they are certain.

They're also certain that Ms. Prince did not signal when she pulled over to the right shoulder to stop. And once stopped, she did not turn on her emergency flashers. **(38)**

NOTES

35. A combination of academic and field experience is important to jurors.

36. This is another place where lawyers love to add the unnecessary, by saying something like, "But she was in too much of a hurry!" When you present your case as clearly as this opening does, you don't need to say she was in a hurry. Jurors figure it out, making it truer to them, more important, and less dislodgable. And the emotional connection will be stronger.

If you have facts that tell us she was in a hurry, tell them to us in the story: "Ms. Prince calls her office saying she's doing everything she can to get there on time." This says she's in a hurry without inserting you in the process. It's more credible, more respectful of juror intelligence, and helps you maintain rapport.

37. Again: Don't ask jurors to take your word about anything. Always explain how you know that the defendant broke the rule—as with, "the two drivers saw . . . ."

38. Though these two acts of negligence caused no harm, they show a pattern of not signaling. Patterns are strong evidence.

TEXT

B. What's dangerous in general about violating this rule?

Trooper Boswith will explain how dangerous it is to turn or to change lanes without first signaling your *intention* far enough in advance for the rest of us to take any necessary safety measures, such as swerving and blowing the horn.

B1. Tentacles of danger

Signaling creates the *"safety cushion of time"* we must provide to others before doing anything they might need to know about.

For example, a pedestrian needs to know if a car is going to turn the corner into the pedestrian's crosswalk. The pedestrian needs to know—while she still has time to get out of the way or get out of the crosswalk. Otherwise, by the time the car turns, it can be too late.

Trooper Boswith will also explain that signaling provides others with a second layer of safety: signal lights quickly attract our attention, so we're more likely to see what we need to see. That's why signal lights are safer than old-fashioned hand signals, which were less likely to be noticed.

This principle is so important that even large, bright-yellow school buses have to flash bright warning lights long before they begin to stop. That's to attract everyone's attention to the fact that a school bus is getting ready to stop, making everything safer for the rest of us driving and for the kids getting on and off the bus.

In every situation, the driver who does not signal creates an unnecessary danger zone for everyone else.

We'll hear testimony from Mr. Anthony deMara. Mr. deMara teaches driver's education at Pineville High. He'll bring us the statistics he shows students. His statistics show how many tens of thousands of people—including pedestrians—are maimed and killed every year because others violated the rule requiring signals before changing lanes or turning.

Mr. deMara will teach us what he teaches his students: The only time you are allowed to change lanes or turn without signaling is in an extreme emergency when there's no time.

He'll explain that unannounced driving moves are surprises, and surprises on the road are a menace. He'll explain that what he teaches is all more likely right than wrong, and that beyond that it lies within that degree of driver-safety certainty that is based on reason.

NOTES

TEXT

You might be thinking that all this is obvious. But the part that is not so obvious is how many people are maimed and killed every year because others violate these obvious rules.

C. How did this violation cause harm?

In this case, by violating the signaling rule, Ms. Prince blindsided Norman. He had no way to know she was coming.

D. What should she have done instead?

Ms. Prince should have followed the rule to signal before changing lanes.

E. How would that have helped?

The signal light could have attracted Norm's attention. That would have given him time to slow down out of her path, or blow his horn, or swerve left. So she would not have hit him.

The third reason we're suing Ms. Prince is that she's refused to meet her full responsibility for Norm's permanent brain damage. **(39)**

IV. UNDERMINE NEGLIGENCE DEFENSES (40)

Before coming to trial, we had to determine several things. **(41)**

NOTES

39. Some judges won't like this, thinking that it's a reference to negotiations. But it goes to damages: your client's suffering has been made worse by the defendant's failure to pay the right (and needed) amount, so this has to do with emotional damages.

40. There are usually more things to undermine than I have here, but by now you should get the point. And remember that some defenses originate with the jurors, not defense counsel. For example, a medical malpractice defense won't likely argue that the plaintiff should have gotten a second opinion—as in, "Gee folks, just take a look at this dumb schnook, my client! Anyone whose doctor looked like this would surely have gotten a second opinion!" But jurors often blame the plaintiff for not getting a second opinion, so you need to deal with it in this section. Focus groups and one-on-one discussions with people who are not lawyers will reveal other kinds of juror-originated, defense-favoring points you need to counter. Example: when jurors in a car-wreck case hear nothing about seat belts, they usually assume that your client was not wearing his. They make this assumption despite the judge telling them that they must not consider it. So if your client was wearing a belt, find a way to tell them.

41. Remember not to say that this comes from the defense. You must create the impression that you took care of these concerns before the defense ever got involved.

TEXT

For example, did Ms. Prince have to cut into the left instantly to avoid hitting the car ahead of her? After all, if she had no choice, we'd not be here suing her.

So we asked the witnesses and the trooper.

The drivers behind Ms. Prince testify that the car ahead of Ms. Prince was going just a little slower and was more than three hundred feet away. They say they are more likely right than wrong about this, and beyond that are certain. Ms. Prince agrees. Trooper Boswith says this gave Ms. Prince plenty of time to signal and change lanes safely or to slow down. So Ms. Prince had no reason to cut left quickly, much less cut left without looking or signaling.

We also had to determine whether Norm was speeding. Again, we asked the witnesses. They say that Norm and Ms. Prince were going the same speed—the speed limit—until Ms. Prince sped up and cut over. And yes, those witnesses will testify that they are more likely right than wrong about this, and beyond that are certain. **(42)** So it was determined for sure that Norm was not speeding. **(43)**

We also had to determine whether Norm should have been able to regain control before hitting the tree. Dr. Cranning, the expert on wrecks, will explain that tires spinning at highway speed on a median of wet grass and soft ground are almost impossible to control or slow down. Dr. Cranning will explain that not even professional race drivers would have been able to do it. Once someone has been knocked into a wet median, it's usually a matter of luck whether they'll hit something or even go all the way into the oncoming lanes.

Dr. Cranning will also testify that being knocked out of control puts a driver in a sudden dangerous emergency situation—and that no driver does his best in those situations because he's terrified and has only a split second to decide what to do.

And he'll say he's more likely right than wrong about that—and, beyond that, it's all within that degree of certainty that's based on reason.

V. Causation and damages

A. Introduction (44)

Your verdict form will ask how much money the verdict should be. To figure that out, you take only one thing into account: the level of the harms and losses the defendant caused.

NOTES

42. This wording is awkward—intentionally so. You want it to attract attention. It's an important boilerplate imprint that maintains your preponderance theme.

43. Of course this tells us that Prince was not speeding. And it implies Norm might have been hanging out in the left lane when he should not have been. But those are less important considerations than dealing with the possibility that Norm had been speeding—not just because speeding would make him partly at fault, but also because speeding would have made the force of the impact partly his force. That could lower the verdict. (This is a typical example of how very carefully you need to weigh what you say in opening.)

44. There are different ways to word this introduction, as long as you include the necessary elements: a) Harm and losses only, b) no sympathy, c) explanation why they're going to hear about the harms and losses. You might also want to introduce "fix, help, make up for" in this section. (*See* Fundamental Eight, p. 28.)

TEXT

Nothing else.

You are not allowed to raise or lower a verdict because of anything like sympathy for either side—or because the right amount of money seems like too much for one person—or whether the proper amount might raise the prices of things we all have to buy—or anything else but the level of the harms and losses the defendant caused.

In other words, how much will it take to *fix* the harms and losses that can be fixed, *help* the harms and losses that cannot **(45)** be completely fixed, and

make up for harms and losses that can neither be fixed nor helped? **(46)**

Mr. Defense Attorney agrees: in deciding money, harms and losses the defendant caused are the only consideration.

Judge Maxim will instruct you that it's the law.

So I have to show you those harms and losses. Not for sympathy. The time for sympathy is long past. **(47)** We're here for you to fix, help, and make up for.

So here's what we'll show you about the harms and losses:

B. Mechanism of harm (How did the negligent act cause each injury?)

The wreck killed millions of Norm's brain cells. **(48) (49)** All the harms and losses in this case come from the number of brain cells the impact killed.

The impact slammed Norm's head against the door pillar.

SHOW: simple diagram of head impact

The entire force carried directly into Norm's skull, where it smashed his brain against the skull's hard, boney inside wall. Here's what his doctors will show us: **(50)**

SHOW: simple diagram of brain mashing against inside of skull

Supplement C

NOTES

45. A minor but sometimes important point: Don't say "can't"; say "cannot." The acoustics of a courtroom as well as the ears of aging jurors can make "can't" sound like "can." When a word's contracted form carries the same root sound as the uncontracted form (is, isn't), don't use the contraction: doesn't, isn't, wouldn't, shouldn't, aren't, etc. But when the contracted form's root sounds different, there won't be any confusion: will/won't, etc. (For more on important language issues, see my *Theater Tips and Strategies for Jury Trials*, Third Edition, 2001, pp. 21ff. (NITA).

46. Note the repetition of "harms and losses" in this section. In almost every other situation, I am the first to insist that you do not keep repeating yourself. But this section is an important step in reinforcing your "harms and losses only" theme. So long as you don't uselessly repeat yourself in other places, the rare repetition will help you here.

47. This will not keep jurors from feeling sympathy. It won't even keep them from acting on sympathy. But it powerfully makes the point that nothing can be factored into the money decision except the harms and losses.

48. For purposes of this sample opening, I include only brain damage. Repeat the process for every other kind of injury.

49. CAVEAT: This step-by-step explanation is just for purposes of illustration. Before relying on its content for any particular case, consult your expert.

50. Remember to cite your witnesses, fact and expert, rather than ask jurors to take your word for anything in opening.

TEXT

Dr. Ruth Rinaldi is an award-winning neuropsychiatrist. She runs the Brain Studies Institute at Manhattan's Pauling Medical Center. We brought her in as an independent, neutral expert to study and report on what happened to Norm. Dr. Rinaldi will explain that the human skull cannot protect brain cells against sixty-mile-per-hour impacts. And she'll show us that the impact killed Norm's brain cells in three different ways.

First: the force of the impact itself:

SHOW: simple diagram of brain squashing against inside of skull (51)

This impact and crushing killed millions of brain cells. Brain cells are unimaginably tiny, because it takes so many for the brain to do its work.

Second, Dr. Rinaldi will explain that the impact violently twisted Norm's head [**use your own head to show it**]. (52) Dr. Cranning, the expert on wrecks, will show us that Norm's head went from zero twist speed almost instantly to more than fifty miles per hour of twisting [**illustrate the zero-to-high-speed change with your hand**]. Dr. Rinaldi will explain that with so great a sudden skull acceleration, the brain takes a moment to catch up. During that moment, the skull twists much faster than the brain, so the skull scrapes its jagged inside wall against the soft outside of the brain.

SHOW: simple diagram (53)

This scratched at, stretched apart, and scraped millions more brain cells into useless, dead shreds. Like a coarse metal file scrapes a piece of wood down into tiny fragments of sawdust.

Third, millions more cells were killed by bleeding inside the brain. The bleeding came from broken tissue and cells in the skull. Dr. Rinaldi—and Norm's own doctors—will show the actual pictures of the bleeding in Norm's skull. Here's a diagram of how it happens.

SHOW: simple diagram of blood pooling

Brain bleeding kills brain cells because the blood has no place to go and collects into pools and drowns the cells it touches.

NOTES

51. In general, most medical illustrations are far too complex for jury or judge use. You need simple line drawings, strictly limited to only the graphic information that makes the point you are trying to show. So, for example, with this exhibit, you want jurors to see no more than a brain compressing into the inside of the skull. You don't want a bunch of colors, textures, other details, terms (Latin or English), or anything else other than the fact that something soft is banging into something hard. If a graphics designer or company cannot do this simply, get rid of them. You don't want illustrations that look like medical book illustrations. Jurors are not medical students and won't spend hours studying an illustration loaded with stuff they know they don't need.

52. For example, your simple mime of banging a steel rod into your lower leg can make jurors squirm, creating empathy far better than the best of illustrations.

53. Sometimes it's best to use a motion exhibit, such as an animation of torque injury. Use slow motion to show how the skull is forced to turn so quickly that the brain takes an instant to catch up and is scraped against the skull wall. The cost of animation has fallen steeply, so if you can find an honest animation company, this will be more affordable than you might think.

TEXT

And as the pools of blood get larger, they press hard against the brain and crush more brain cells to death. Again, in the millions.

SHOW: simple diagram or simple animation (54)

Every doctor in the case will tell us that the more dead brain cells, the more the brain loses its abilities. **(55)**

Dr. Rinaldi will explain that the brain cells are literally killed. They cannot heal and come back to life. Cell death is permanent. And no new cells grow to take their place. **(56)**

So Norm's brain will always have to make do as best it can despite so many dead cells.

Dr. Rinaldi will show the consequences. When some of the body's muscles die, the body cannot do its job as well. The same is true of the brain when brain cells die: the brain can no longer do many of its jobs. Each lost job ability in the brain is called a brain "*deficit.*" **(57)**

For one example of a brain deficit, a person might no longer be able to recognize faces of people he's known all his life.

When too many cells of another kind are destroyed, the brain can no longer interpret light signals from the eye, so the person is blind even though her eyes are in perfect shape.

When certain cells deep enough in the brain are destroyed, the brain can no longer regulate breathing, so the person will die from lack of oxygen—even if the lungs are in perfect shape. **(58)**

Everything a person thinks, feels, does, remembers, or decides requires living brain cells. When too many cells are killed, the brain cannot shift that work to other cells. It's like removing the memory chips from a computer: no memory chip, no memory. The human brain is a billion times more complex, but the principle is the same: destroy enough cells that do a particular job and the brain can no longer do that job well—or even at all.

NOTES

54. By now you should see the effectiveness of step-by-step explanations of the mechanism of the harm—the incremental journey from impact (or whatever) to each deficit/loss. It's a strong hedge against defense causation denials. When jurors have a clear mental picture of the step-by-step mechanism, they are far more likely to believe that it happened.

55. There are more ways that brain cells are killed, but by now you see how each functions as one of the steps leading from impact to deficit. It's the same step-by-step process with every kind of injury. With a broken arm, for example, you'd walk the jury step-by-step from impact through each layer of skin to breaking the broken bone and consequent pain, disability, etc.

56. Notice how rarely I have used pronouns. Pronoun use is among the most common causes of juror confusion. "He","him", "they," "theirs," "hers," etc., are always clear to the speaker, but often not to the listener.

57. Note that we have taken another step here.

58. To explain the general concept of "brain deficits" (or anything else), begin with examples that do not apply to this case. Once you layer in that understanding, then layer in the specifics of this case. Teaching in layers is essential.

TEXT

C. Personal consequence of each injury

Let's look at Norm's permanent brain deficits. Five are particularly serious. They're his main harms, so you need to know how bad they are in order to calculate your verdict. **(59)**

First, **short-term-memory deficit.** Norm's brain remembers almost nothing new. If you ask Norm what his dad gave him for his ninth birthday, Norm can tell you all about the red Schwinn bike. But ask Norm what his dad said at dinner last night, and Norm can't remember his father was there.

Tell Norm a joke and if he gets it, he'll laugh. Tell him the same joke tomorrow and he'll laugh again, as if he's never heard it before. Because as far as his brain knows, he never has.

Aside from jokes, loss of short-term memory is bad. It's dangerous. Short-term memory is one of the brain's most important abilities.

Now, Norm is no quitter. **(60)** Every morning at the kitchen table he works on memory exercises. Over the past three years his hard work has paid off a little. When he started, he'd look at the front page newspaper headlines for a few minutes, then turn the page over, wait a minute—and be able to remember none of them. It was like trying to fill a water bucket with a big hole in the bottom.

SHOW: newspaper front page; let jurors view it for a moment; close it.

Remember any?

Now, because Norm has worked hard for three years, he can usually recall one, sometimes two.

But never three, no matter how hard he tries or how long he looks. And an hour later he's forgotten the one or two he initially remembered.

You can teach him a new task today—such as a simple computer program—and sometimes he'll get it. But in a few hours he'll have forgotten—not just how to do it, but that you ever tried to teach it to him. He no longer has enough short-term memory cells to process new information.

What does this do to a person? It's not just about jokes and newspaper headlines. It's about meeting new people. It's about remembering what pills to take or where he left his reminder list of medications. It's about remembering safety instructions or remembering that he turned the stove on so it needs to be turned off when he's done cooking. It's about locking the door at night—or anything else that requires remembering anything new.

Supplement C

NOTES

59. Up to this point, you've told us what happens in general when too many brain cells die: you've taken us step-by-step from impact to brain deficits. This generalized explanation comes before focusing on your client's deficits. Again: layering.

60. One of your client's most positive and important characteristics is his refusal to throw in the towel. Americans love people who refuse to quit even in the face of great adversity. And your showing us how he tries tells us: what the client can do, not just what he can't. *See* Fundamental Ten, p. 40.

TEXT

And if the short-term memory cannot learn anything new, nothing gets to the long-term memory.

Norm won't ever again remember a new client's name at work. He won't know what new products have come in. And he sure won't remember where he put them.

It's not just about work. **(61)** Try watching a movie sometime when you have no memory. Fifteen minutes into a movie, Norm cannot remember the beginning: what happened, who are these people? So movies make no sense anymore. Norm and Alison used to love going out to the movies together. He still wants to go with her so she can enjoy. But Alison knows he sits there bored and frustrated because he can never remember enough to follow the plot. Same with books and news stories.

Even if Norm's short-term memory loss were his only deficit, it would be enough to intrude on every minute of his life and everything he does. But he has four other brain deficits just as severe.

One of those is that he can't do anything more than the simplest of tasks. The **brain cells that take people through the steps of most tasks are missing** in Norm. Watch.

SHOW: video of Norm trying to shelve some products from his job. Then:

As Dr. Rinaldi will explain, Norm cannot connect the dots. The task is simple: put the boxes on the floor with the similar boxes on the shelves. But even so simple a task requires many steps in the brain, and those steps require the very cells that are now dead.

If someone yells "fire" in the middle of the night, Norm would wake up and probably know which way the door or window is—just the way he knows where the blue boxes are on the shelf. But he would not be able to connect the dots and execute the process of getting out of the house.

So Norm can never be left alone, not daytime or night, because there's no way to know when there'll be an emergency. Dr. Bryan Waters, an expert at developing caretaking plans for brain-damaged people, will explain that leaving Norm alone is worse than leaving a three-year-old alone. Not that Norm always has the mind of a three-year-old—but he does when it comes to making decisions and executing tasks necessary to common safety. In a

NOTES

61. Extend the effects of the deficits beyond the workplace.

TEXT

fire, a three-year-old would probably be able to take the steps to get out of the house. Norm certainly would not. **(62) (63)**

A month ago at breakfast, Norm spilled some orange juice. Alison came into the kitchen to see what had happened. Norm was barefoot and standing on broken shards of glass. He knew this had something to do with a towel. His feet were bleeding. He knew he'd spilled juice. He knew there was broken glass. He knew his feet were cut. But he could not connect the dots to do anything. **(64)**

He was humiliated, shamed, in front of his own wife, even though Alison understood.

This is what happens when drivers on the highway don't look where they're going. **(65)**

. . . . **(66)**

NOTES

62. Injuries that impair your client's safety are resonant with jurors—especially if you offer safety measures that can help. Any kind of mobility or decision making or visual/aural impairment can create safety concerns. Look for them carefully. Get help from experts (not necessarily your witnesses) in finding them. (Treating doctors will miss most of them.) And show how money can provide ways to eliminate or minimize those dangers.

63. Cahoots Caveat: Some life-care planners sell the very services they prescribe! That lets the defense start its opening with, "Good morning. In this case, the guy claiming Mr. Smith needs 10 million for care items is the same guy who sells all those care items. That tells you everything you need to know about this case. Thank you for listening." This undermines your life-care planner, your case, and—especially—you.

Also, some life-care planners belong to lawyer's groups that—as the defense likes to say—"teach plaintiff's attorneys how to get lots of money out of juries." Even if jurors don't believe this right away, they'll later confirm it online. Life-care planners (and other experts-for-hire) join and teach at such groups to market their expert-witness wares. So stay sane when choosing life-care planners and every other kind of expert. And stay ethical. There's nothing ethical about an expert testifying for her own benefit, and jurors know it. (Be alert for similar situations on the defense side. Does their IME teach defense seminars? Etc.)

64. Vignette illustrations like this little story are one of the engines of your damages case because they crystallize each harm in Reptilian ways. These little stories are memorable and credible, especially when you present many of them from different witnesses. Stories trump generalities. In opening, provide two or three damages vignettes and lots more during testimony.

65. The harms and losses in your case serve as examplars of what violating the safety rules does. This spreads the tentacles of danger (*see* chapter 5, p. 142, fn 8, and *Reptile*), thus motivating jurors to hold the defendant to her full responsibility.

66. You'd continue here with Norm's other kinds of brain deficits and how they affect him.

TEXT

Undermining a damages issue (67)

Brain damage is called "invisible damage." It's like high blood pressure—no way for anyone to know whether or not it's there without accurate tests and other investigative measures. You'll hear from the experts who did those tests on Norm.

The invisibility of brain damage is a problem for other reasons. The invisibility is one of the worst harms in this case. It's the cause of the constant humiliation Norm has to deal with. So it's driven him into near-isolation—just like it does most people with brain damage.

Here's why: Norm *looks* fine. He can walk in here and out of here; he can even talk to you, and you'd probably think nothing's wrong with him. Should we not be able to tell by seeing and hearing that he has brain damage? Could this mean that the damage is not as bad as the brain doctors tell us?

We asked Norm's doctors, and we asked independent brain expert Dr. Rinaldi. They'll explain that on the surface, most people with brain damage look and sound perfectly normal. If you don't happen to see them trying to do something they cannot do, or remembering something that is gone from their minds, you would not notice any problem.

That's why brain damage can never be diagnosed just by looking or listening. Almost every person with this level of brain damage will look and sound fine.

As Dr. Rinaldi will explain, it's not like a broken leg. When someone has a broken leg, no one expects him to run. But brain damage is invisible, so people still expect you to do normal things. For example, last year Norm was out for a walk with an out-of-town friend who was visiting. They were a ten-minute walk from the house and turned to start back. The visitor asked, "Which way?"

Norm had lived ten minutes from there for eighteen years. But put on the spot, he could not get home.

This was humiliating even though his friend knew about the brain damage. With strangers it's far worse—the constant risk of being unable to handle some simple task or respond to some simple question. Deep humiliation is one of the worst feelings people can have—most of us can remember every time we were ever humiliated, all the way back to childhood. We do all we can to avoid being humiliated again. But for Norm, if he's out in public there's no way to avoid it. It's possible at any unpredictable moment. The only way he can prevent it is to avoid people altogether. Which is brutally hard on a person who loves being around people.

NOTES

67. Jurors never doubt that a wrongful-death victim is dead. But jurors easily and often doubt there's really brain damage or that it's as serious as you claim. The defense plays on this doubt. Your job is not merely to show that the defense is wrong, but that they know better. (You need to do this with every defense witness insofar as you can, and that's usually pretty far.) It turns the defense—not just the defendant—into a Reptilian danger.

TEXT

To avoid constant and unpredictably public humiliation, people with brain damage gradually take to staying home over the years, venturing out less as they have more and more humiliating experiences on the outside. Even at home, eventually these folks withdraw into their own bedrooms. Many end up spending theirs days sitting on their beds, blankly staring at afternoon TV—because every step beyond their own room represents a new danger of being humiliated.

So Norm has lost the companionship of his friends at work, because he can no longer do his job. He cannot get new work because every new job, no matter how routine, requires learning something new—which Norm cannot do with his short-term memory deficit.

And all this comes from the fact that most people with brain damage look and sound normal. You'll see when he takes the stand to testify, though if you know what to listen for, you might spot some disconnects. **(68)** To most people he'll seem normal. Dr. Rinaldi will explain this. It's like a person with cancer who can look completely healthy from the outside. **(69)** And she'll explain how she knows for certain that Norm is seriously brain damaged despite how he looks and sounds: she'll walk us through the tests, the signs and symptoms nobody can fake, and the relationship between the bleeding inside his skull and the location of the parts of his brain that don't work anymore—which there's no way anyone can fake.

Dr. Rinaldi will also explain the steps a doctor must take to see whether or not someone has brain damage and how much brain damage there is. One of the required steps is carefully placing yourself in a neutral frame of mind. Another is gathering all the available information. Dr. Rinaldi will show you that no one the defense is bringing to trial met those required steps. Dr. Rinaldi will explain that when you don't fully take those steps, you can come to whatever conclusion you want that serves your own agenda, so the conclusion is not valid. **(70)**

NOTES

68. If you allow jurors to feel smart by spotting brain damage, they'll be more likely to spot it.

69. Because your client looks and sounds OK, the defense knows that many jurors will conclude there's nothing wrong with his brain. So it's better for jurors never to see your client. As counterintuitive as this seems, it is true. You can usually get everything necessary into evidence without your client.

But if you need him to testify, or if the defense is going to call him, be sure to have made the "looks good" point in opening. And precede his testimony with your expert's—explaining how/why people look and sound OK despite brain damage, and how that very invisibility causes one of the worst harms in the case.

70. There are almost always other causation or damages issues you must undermine. I've included only enough here to show how. In brain-damage cases, the most common tend to be the failure of imaging to show any damage, and the common assumption—bolstered by what jurors can find online—that brain damage eventually heals on its own when other parts of the brain take up the lost abilities. (Regarding the immense problem of what jurors find online, and what to do about it, see supplement H, "Virtual Reality."

TEXT

VI. "Before." (71)

After all is said and done, you're here to see the difference between Norm before the wreck and Norm now. To determine the level of harms and losses, you compare before with now.

At this point you now know what he's like today. So what about before?

Here's a job evaluation note from Norm's file. His boss wrote it, and he'll be here to tell us even more.

[Take the letter from a manilla file and read it aloud; do not show it.] (72)

"Norman Wyeth is outstanding. He loves to work with our customers. He remembers everything about them—birthdays, kids, problems they had from their last visit. He's our fastest guy solving problems around the shop. He never runs out of energy. If every employee was like Norm we'd double our sales with half the staff."

That's a before-and-after difference. Because now Norm cannot work.

How about money? One of the losses is money—lost job income, lost money for care. Norm and Alison are deep in debt. But before? Their credit rating was near-perfect. The house was 85 percent paid for. They'd saved a whole lot for their kids' college. Now it's all gone for Norm's care. The house is mortgaged to the hilt. And since they're in debt, they cannot get the loan they need to pay for more care.

That's a before-and-after difference.

What about Norm's quality of life? We'll hear from many folks who knew Norm when he was his old self: high-energy guy, loved being around people, always smiling, always a source of help and strength for everyone. You'll see more photos like this—

SHOW: simple collage of photos showing Norm in family, high-energy, people-centered situations (73)

That's Norman before.

Rice Brewster lives across the street from Norm and Alison. She'll tell us about the time Alison decided the front yard needed redoing and that Norm was just the guy to do it. Rice said that for a solid month, Norm was out there after work every day, all day on weekends, even after dark—digging and planting and trimming and laying in sidewalk. Rice will tell us that the neighborhood kids would stand there and watch the "crazy guy who never stopped!"

NOTES

71. You can place "fixes/helps/make up for" before or after the "Before" section.

72. Removing a real paper from an actual file ("job file," get it?) and reading it aloud will make it more memorable than just putting it up for jurors to read themselves.

73. In some venues you can't show exhibits in opening. But you can accomplish the same thing with just a few vignettes about the old Norm from your fact witnesses, especially nonfamily.

TEXT

And when the work was done, Rice will tell us, Norm still was out there all the time taking care of it, making sure every leaf was in place, power-mowing and power-trimming and fussing. But now he just sits on the porch, wishing he could get up and do things—but he can't. He's not allowed near power equipment. He never has energy. **(74)** And most of the yard tasks involve steps his brain can't keep track of. Rice remembers the time she saw Norm watching a helpful neighbor trim Norm's bushes, and Norm stood there writing down the simple steps. "It broke my heart," she'll tell us.

VII. What can the jury do about it?

So we're all in this room for three reasons: to fix, help, make up for.

First, we're here for you to determine how much money it will take to fix everything that can be fixed. For example, verdict money for Norm's medical and care costs will *fix* those financial losses. And verdict money to replace lost income *fixes* that loss. Verdict money for improvements to make Norm's home safe for someone with brain damage *fixes* the loss of those costs. **(75)**

Second, we're here for you to decide how much it will take to *help* the harms and losses that can be helped, but not completely fixed. For example, Norm cannot drive anymore. **(76)** Nothing can completely fix that. But it can be helped with verdict money to cover taxis or a part-time driver and the necessary companion to go with him when he needs to—or even just wants to—go someplace when Alison is at work. **(77)** Remember, it's dangerous for Norm to go anywhere alone. **(78)** And he knows he's less likely to be humiliated by something if someone goes out with him.

Finally, we're here for you to decide how much it will take to match the level of the worst harms in the case: the things that cannot be fixed and cannot be helped. For example, nothing can bring back Norm's short-term memory. Nothing can help him be able to read a book again, or enjoy a movie, or help one of his kids with homework. The quality of Norm's life is the most important part of this kind of case.

NOTES

74. One of the deficits you'd have included earlier in opening is the huge amount of energy that brain damage uses up, leading to near-exhaustion much of the time and the inability to do many things that would be easy for other people. I omitted it because there are already enough deficits to have made my teaching point for you.

75. Expand on this: What other potential fixes are there? Why necessary? What happens if they are not provided?

76. When your brain-damaged client insists on driving, you must put a stop to it. You can't claim executive deficits, inability to react in emergencies, etc., and then loose that menace on the community. And there's no such thing as driving only where it's safe, such as to and from his neighborhood store. An emergency can arise anyplace. In deliberations, jurors looking for reasons to disbelieve the level of deficits (and everything else about you and your case) will go back over and over to "but he's driving!" Your argument that it's his last vestige of independence will create resentment, not support. Jurors care about their own safety a lot more than your client's independence.

77. Generally, provide two or three examples of harms that can be helped.

78. Safety helps are important.

TEXT

So we'll show you what cannot be fixed so that you can determine how much it takes to match it. We'll show you how to do the calculation, because yes, you can put a dollar value on it. **(79)**

For the rest of Norm's life, he and Alison will live every moment with what happened. This is not like a broken leg that heals. This harm goes on harming.

Norm and Alison are great folks. You'll see that they fight the good fight every day. They make the best of everything. In their quiet way, they are heroes.

My job is to show you what's behind the heroism.

By the end of this case, you'll see that the evidence, the facts, the truths, make this the kind of case **(80)** where I'll have to come back at the end and ask for a very large verdict. It will be so large that when I tell it to you now, it will shock you. But as you'll see, the amount of harm is shocking, too. So I'll have no choice. You'll see why this is the kind of case in which I'll have to ask for a total verdict of $25 million. **(81) (82)**

NOTES

79. *See* section 8-14, pp. 238*ff.*, "Scales."

80. "Why this is the kind of case" in exactly those words can be the most important words you say in trial. For good reason I won't explain why. You have to trust me.

81. There's a lot of debate about whether or not to provide a dollar figure—and when to do it. But it's a silly debate. You absolutely should provide it, and this is the first place to do it. *See* section 5-5-7, p. 163*ff.*

82. In venues where you cannot specify a figure, say it this way:

> By the end of this case, you'll see that the evidence, the facts, the truths, make this the kind of case in which I'll have to come back later and ask for a verdict so large that it will shock anyone who's not heard how much harm the wreck did. Part of that verdict will be_____ [economic damages figure]. All of that goes to other people for Norm's care and to replace Norm's lost income so he'll be financially even with where he'd have been if this had never happened. But in this kind of case, that's the small part of the verdict. Because it's for the smallest part of the harm. The larger part is what the wreck has done to Norm's life. As you'll know by the end, the harm it has done is overwhelmingly significant. So I'll have to come back and ask for an overwhelmingly significant verdict.

TEXT

Thank you. **(83)**

NOTES

You should be allowed this kind of argument even where you are not allowed to proportionalize economic versus noneconomic damages. If not, try this:

> By the end of the case, you'll see that the evidence, the facts, the truths, make this the kind of case in which I'll have to come back later and ask for a verdict so large that it will shock anyone who's not heard how much harm the wreck did. Part of that amount will be _____ [economic damages figure]. That all goes to other people for Norm's care and to replace Norm's lost income so he'll be financially even with where he'd have been if this had never happened. But that's only one part of the verdict. The more important part is what the wreck did to the rest of Norm's life. And that is overwhelmingly significant. So I'll have to come back and ask you for an overwhelmingly significant verdict.

When your economic figure is small compared to what the total verdict ought to be, consider not asking for the economic amount, because it can create a low-scale anchor. In that situation, and when barred from asking for a specific total figure, say something like:

> By the end of the case, you'll see that the evidence, the facts, the truths, make this the kind of case in which I'll have to come back later and ask for a verdict so large that it will shock anyone who has not heard how much harm the wreck did. You'll know what kind of case it is because you'll know what the wreck did to the rest of Norm's life. And that is overwhelmingly significant. So I'll have to come back and ask you to allow an overwhelmingly significant verdict.

83. Sit down. Because you went to law school, the Devil will sore tempt you to continue. Don't.

Supplement D

Sample Opening

CAVEAT: The material in this sample opening is just for purposes of illustration. Before relying on its content for any particular case, consult your expert.

I. Primary rule(s) the defendant violated.

A driver is never allowed to needlessly endanger the public.

A driver must look where he's going and see what's there to be seen. If he does not, and as a result hurts someone, he's responsible for the harm.

II. Story of what the defendant did.

Now please let me tell you the story of what happened in this case.

Come back with me to July 2007.

South of Fayetteville.

Interstate 95.

Midafternoon. Light traffic. Dry road.

Carolyn Snopes is driving south in her Ford Explorer.

Ms. Snopes is in the right lane.

Ms. Snopes is going 72 miles per hour.

Ms. Snopes drives around a curve and into a straightaway.

Ms. Snopes drives 700 feet down the straightaway.

Ms. Snopes lets her Ford Explorer drift to the left edge of the right lane.

   SHOW on diagram.

Ms. Snopes collides into the back left corner of a Nissan that was driving the speed limit in the right lane.

Ms. Snopes slams on her brake.

Ms. Snopes watches the Sentra go out of control and into the center median and into a tree.

Ms. Snopes stops on the right shoulder.

Ms. Snopes calls her husband.

Ms. Snopes waits in her car for the police to arrive.

The crash leaves the Nissan's driver with a broken shoulder and other injuries. He is Benjamin Compson. You met him during jury selection.

III. WHO WE ARE SUING AND WHY: THE SAFETY RULES THE DEFENDANT(S) VIOLATED

We're suing Ms. Snopes for violating two public-safety rules.

A. Rule-violating act. (i. What did she do? ii. How do we know she did it?)

i. First, she violated the public-safety rule requiring her to watch the road at all times.

ii. Ms. Snopes admits she did not see the Nissan until she hit it.

B. What's dangerous *in general* about violating this rule (and *who says so*)?

Ms. Snopes herself will tell us the dangers of taking your eyes off the road. She'll explain that there's no way to tell what you might hit—a car or someone walking by the side of the road or a state trooper at a traffic stop, or that you could easily drift into the next lane and hit anyone there from the side. Walter Stezack, East Central High's certified driving instructor, will show the numbers: that not looking at the road causes more than 80 percent of road and interstate highway fatalities every year, as well as almost every serious pedestrian injury and death.[1] Mr. Stezack will explain that a driver who takes his or her eyes off the road is needlessly endangering everyone anywhere in the area.

C. How did violation cause harm in this case (and *who says so*)?

In this case, the police report shows that Ms. Snopes had 700 feet to see Ben's Nissan. But she took her eyes off the road so long that she did not see Ben until she felt and heard the impact. The police report shows that by hitting Ben off-center on the left, she pushed the back end of his Nissan to the right, like this. That started him into a spin across the lane to his left, onto the median, and into the tree.

---

1. These statistics are offered only as examples; do not rely on their accuracy.

D. What should the defendant have done instead?

Ms. Snopes should have followed the rule that drivers must keep their eyes on the road at all times.

E. How would that have helped (and *who says so*)?

Ms. Snopes will testify that if she had been looking and seen Ben's Nissan, she'd either have slowed down before she hit him or pulled into the left lane to pass him.

IV. UNDERMINE NEGLIGENCE DEFENSES.

Before coming to trial, several things had to be determined.

First, it had to be determined whether Ben was a cause of the crash for going slower than a safe interstate highway speed. So we checked the police report. It reports Ben's speed was 65, the speed limit. Ben confirms this. And during trial we'll hear testimony from Bill Faulkner, who was driving in the left lane a ways behind Ben. Mr. Faulkner will tell us that he and Ben had been going the same speed for a few minutes before the crash, and that their speed was right around 65. So it was determined that Ben was not going too slow.

Second, it had to be determined whether Ben caused the wreck himself by suddenly slowing down so abruptly in a vehicle with no brake lights—so that even a driver who was paying attention coming up behind would have hit him. After all, if Ben had done something that made it impossible for a driver behind to avoid hitting him, we would not be here suing Ms. Snopes.

So first we asked Mr. Faulkner if Ben slowed down. Mr. Faulkner will tell us that he was watching closely because he saw Ms. Snopes coming up behind too fast—and that Ben never slowed down at all. Mr. Faulkner also says that Ben's right brake light came on after the crash a few times as Ben was trying to regain control.

We also asked an expert mechanic to see if Ben's brake lights were working. Henry Joad, the service manager at the Honda Nissan Service Center in Fayetteville, will be here to tell us that he checked the Nissan and saw that the rear right brake light was working, but that the left one had been broken when Ms. Snopes hit Ben. But Mr. Joad reports that the left-bulb filament was intact, so it would have been working before the crash.

So it was determined that Ben did not slow down abruptly, because if he had, Mr. Faulkner would have seen it and Ben's brake lights would have come on.

The third thing that had to be determined was whether the crash impact might have been so minor that Ben could easily have maintained control if he had not oversteered right afterward.

So we asked the state trooper about this. North Carolina State Trooper Tom Sutpen explains that even professional drivers would have trouble regaining control when hit from behind at an angle. Trooper Sutpen will also tell us that in high-speed chases, the way they send the fleeing car out of control is to have a pursuit car tap the fleeing car gently from a rear angle—but nowhere near as hard as Ms. Snopes hit Ben. Trooper Sutpen will explain that no matter what the driver does, the car will go out of control because it starts the rear wheels sliding sideways too fast for anyone but a professional to get back control. It's not the same as just sliding on water or ice, because the gentle tap adds extra force to the slide that the driver cannot overcome. So it was determined that there was nothing Ben could have done to keep from hitting the tree.

V. Causation and damages.

A. Introduction to harms and losses.

In this kind of case, the verdict form asks how much money the verdict should be. To answer, you can factor in only two things: the *harms* and the *losses* Ms. Snopes caused.

So we'll have to show you those harms and losses. We won't be showing them to get sympathy—the time for sympathy is long past. Sympathy—either for Ben or for Ms. Snopes—is not allowed to move the verdict up or down. Nor is any worry about whether the amount necessary to match the harms and losses might seem like too much money for one person, or whether it can make the pain and disability go away, or whether it might raise or lower prices of things we all need to buy. Or any other consideration—except for the level of the harms and losses.

Mr. [*Defense Attorney*] agrees with this, and her honor will explain that it's the law.

So here are those harms and losses:

For the remainder of the opening, see the previous supplement section.

SUPPLEMENT E

DIFFERENTIAL DIAGNOSIS IN MED MAL OPENING[1]

This sample is for a case in which every step of the differential diagnosis has been violated. The sample is easily adapted to any failure-to-recognize or failure-to-diagnose or failure-to-take-proper-measures case.

When your case is about a violation of only one of the steps, you can be less detailed in the other steps, but don't omit them. The context of the violated step is important. So, for example, if the doctor did not rule out something he'd put onto his differential list, you need not spend much time on how possible causes get onto the list, since that's not in dispute.

The defense runs scared when you center a failure to diagnose case on differential diagnosis, because it wipes out such bogus claims as "The doctor was reasonable in thinking the problem was an infection instead of cancer because it had all the well-known signs of infection." So in depositions and trial you will encounter such pathetic escape attempts as: "Well, differential diagnosis is just an academic exercise that is not used in the real world," or "No one does that any more." Your own experts will tell you that a full differential is always required. A doctor's choice not to use every step *always* needlessly endangers the patient. So if you're lucky the defense expert may allow it—but the jury won't and neither will the law, because *there is no such thing as a standard of care (or even ordinary care) that needlessly endangers.*

This is one of very few situations in which the rules in Part One of your opening should take longer than a minute.

You need not use the exact wording suggested below, but if you change it, make sure that your changes 1) improve it, 2) do not take more words, and 3) are no less simple and clear.

(Line breaks = very brief pauses or breaks.)

---

[1]. The sample in this section is taken from an opening by Miami's Darryl Lewis, a partner at Searcy Denney Scarola Barnhart & Shipley in Miami. He's one of the best trial advocates and teachers I know.

Good morning.

[RULE][2]

Everyone on both sides of this case

will testify that they agree

with medicine's main safety requirement:

"A physician

is never allowed

to needlessly endanger

a patient."[3]

One of the most dangerous ways

a doctor can needlessly endanger

is to violate any step

of a Differential[4]

Diagnosis.

When a doctor violates any step of a differential diagnosis

and as a result needlessly harms a patient

the doctor is responsible for the harm.

So let's begin with what Differential Diagnosis means.

It's really simple.[5]

During trial, we'll hear from two expert physicians:

---

2. As explained in supplement C, in most cases, two rules for the start of opening are plenty. Three is absolute maximum. You'll get the others in later in opening (see below).

3. You can explain later that "needlessly endangering a patient" violates the Hippocratic oath to do no harm—because "needlessly endangering a patient" is the most likely way to do harm.

4. This is a strange word to jurors, so pronounce it clearly and distinctly, especially the first time you use it. (There is almost never a reason to use any other technical words in trial. The fewer you use, the more the jurors can focus on the important ones: "differential diagnosis.")

5. Assure jurors that they will be able to understand everything. Then make certain that you make it clear and keep it clear. No big words, no long sentences. *See* section 5-10, pp. 171–172.

Supplement E

Dr. Franklin Schneider, who runs the heart center at Central Medical University and teaches heart medicine at Northern State Medical School.

And Dr. Rebecca Aaron. She teaches family medicine and treats patients at the Metropolitan Medical Pavilion in San Francisco.[6]

> *I have stopped indicating your brief pauses, but don't speed up. Jurors can't process hearing something new as rapidly as you might want to speak it.*
>
> *Early in opening, avoid qualitative adjectives such as "outstanding expert." Stay neutral in every way. No advocacy until you get to "why we're suing," below.*

They'll explain Differential Diagnosis.[7]

They'll tell us that in every case, every doctor must use every step of a differential diagnosis for every patient with any kind of abnormal signs or symptoms.

The patient can be male or female, young or old, in good or bad physical condition. If the patient has abnormal signs or symptoms of any kind, every doctor must do every step of the differential every time. No exceptions.

The purpose of a differential diagnosis is to look for the cause of a patient's signs or symptoms—without needlessly endangering the patient by missing any possible cause.

A differential diagnosis makes it impossible for a doctor to ignore a possible cause that she should have seen. So as the experts will tell you, a doctor who does not do the full differential is playing Russian Roulette with his patient.

So how does differential diagnosis work?

Step one: Gather information. Once a doctor sees that a patient has any abnormal symptoms, the next thing the doctor must do is to make a symptoms list. That means to find out every symptom the patient has, and put each one onto a symptom list.

The doctor can do the symptom list in her head or write it down—as long as she does it.

SHOW: blank symptom list [not a slide; use a board]

---

6. No need to dwell here on credentials. Just mention one or two of the best for each expert.

7. As you explain, be certain you do so from a neutral point of view. You can explain how important it is, but make absolutely no implication that the defendant did anything wrong. This is extremely important. *See* p. 127 on premature advocacy. The tiniest implication by word or tone or facial expression that you're accusing the doctor of anything is likely to seriously undermine your opening.

So if a patient reports lower right abdomen pain, the next thing the doctor must do[8] is put "lower right abdomen pain" on the symptom list.[9]

SHOW: put "lower right abdomen pain" on the symptom list.

The next thing the doctor must do is find out every other symptom the patient has. As she finds each new symptom, she must add it to the symptom list. So if the patient tells the doctor he has some fatigue, the next thing the doctor must do is add "fatigue" to the symptom list.

SHOW: add "fatigue" to the symptom list.

That's step one: gather symptoms.

SLIDE: Bullet point—"Step One: Gather and List Symptoms"[10]

Now. Let's say a patient comes in to the doctor with two symptoms: abdomen pain and fatigue.

Once the doctor lists those symptoms, the next thing the doctor must do is to list *every possible cause* of the symptoms. They go on the "differential suspect list." There can be one cause or many.

Every possible cause goes on the *suspect list*. The doctor must not leave any out, not even if she thinks it's a very unlikely cause. The experts will explain that very unlikely causes kill people all the time. So leaving out *any* possible suspect cause needlessly endangers patients.

Just like in a criminal case: If there are eight possible suspects in a shooting, the police must list all eight. They cannot guess about leaving one out just because one seems less likely than the others.

So when there are symptoms of lower right abdomen pain and fatigue, the next thing the doctor must do is to list every possible cause for it.

The *suspect causes* include possible stomach gas, possible pulled muscle, possible appendicitis, and possible tumor. The doctor can do the suspect list in her head or on paper. But she must do it. So:

---

8. Please pay special attention to the phrase, "the next thing." By using the same phrase in the upcoming story of what the doctor actually did, jurors will spot the doctor's omissions without your having to point them out—which is how you need it to happen. *See* p. 127 explaining why you should not explicitly cite defendant omissions in your opening's story of what the defendant did.

9. Use an example that does not apply to your case. You are teaching the principle, and it is best to do that without referring to the specifics of your case.

10. Never show a bullet point before you explain any new point orally. Use the bullet point to label what you have just explained.

Supplement E

SHOW:[11] SUSPECTED CAUSES of Abdomen Pain and Fatigue

1. Possible stomach gas

2. Possible pulled muscle

3. Possible appendicitis

4. Possible tumor

There are others, but this will be enough to explain how it works.

Most important: she must include every possible suspect cause.

SLIDE: add (do not replace) "Step Two: List Suspect Possible Causes."

The next thing the doctor is required to do is to *prioritize* the list of suspects. That means to put every *urgently dangerous* cause at the top.

An urgent danger is a possible cause that can quickly and severely injure the patient.

"Appendicitis" can quickly injure. If nothing is done about an supplement and so it bursts, severe infection can result and cause permanent harm. So the doctor must put "appendicitis" at the top of the list.[12]

SHOW: move "Possible appendicitis" from #3 to #1, and star "appendicitis":

SUSPECTED CAUSES of Abdomen Pain and Fatigue

1. Possible appendicitis***

2. Possible stomach gas

3. Possible pulled muscle

4. Possible tumor

"Tumor" is also a danger. It is also time sensitive, but less urgent than appendicitis. So "tumor" goes below "appendicitis." Tumor is more urgent than stomach gas and pulled muscle. So it goes above them.

SHOW: move "Possible tumor" from #4 to #2, so we have:

SUSPECTED CAUSES of Abdomen Pain and Fatigue

---

11. If you are not allowed to use exhibits in closing write this "in air"—use gesture to indicate each line item.

12. You need not discuss urgent possible causes when there were none. But there can be time-sensitive dangers, and you treat them the same way.

1. Possible appendicitis***

2. Possible tumor*

3. Possible stomach gas

4. Possible pulled muscle

And that's step three:

SHOW: add Step Three to the board: "List and Prioritize Possible Causes"

Once the doctor has done this list, what's the next thing she must do? That's step four:

Rule out or *treat* every danger *before it can harm [kill]* if it turns out to be the real one.

So the doctor must act very quickly to treat or rule out appendicitis. That's why it has three stars.

The doctor has more time to treat or rule out tumor, but he cannot delay long enough for the tumor to be able to injure or kill.

In other words, the next thing the doctor must do is treat or rule out.

"Rule out" means to use tests and other scientific methods before crossing off a possible suspect cause. Guessing one away is never allowed. The doctor must never rule out on the basis of "probably not."

Nor is the doctor allowed to just pick the likely cause and ignore the unlikely ones. Even when an urgent possible danger is *un*likely, the doctor still must handle it as if it's real and about to happen.

So in the abdomen pain case, no matter how likely a pulled muscle might be, the doctor must still proceed as if appendicitis is the real cause. The doctor cannot guess away any possible urgent cause.

Even if the doctor *proves* that the cause of the abdominal pain is a pulled muscle, she still must proceed as if the other causes are also real. This is because the presence of one cause does not rule out any others. A patient can have a pulled muscle and appendicitis at the same time.

Think of it this way: If you smell smoke in the house, one suspect cause could be that the neighbor is burning leaves. Another suspect cause could be that the house is on fire. Even if you actually see that the neighbor is burning leaves, that does not rule out the possibility that there's a fire in the house.

So that's step four. Treat or rule out.

Supplement E

SHOW: add Step Four: "Treat or Rule Out"

With me so far? Good. You can now answer the most important question medical students must be able to answer before they are allowed to call themselves doctors. You know how doctors do a differential diagnosis.

IF a doctor does not follow every differential diagnosis step,

and as a result he injures [kills] a patient,

the doctor is responsible for the injury [death].

[STORY OF WHAT THE DEFENDANT DID]

Now let me tell you the story of what happened in this case.

April 14, 2008. Clinic of gynecologist Arlen Malina.

Dr. Malina listens as a patient describes a symptom: that when she lies down, her heart races.

In the record, Dr. Smith reads that a test has showed another symptom: overactive thyroid—a gland right here.

SHOW: touch your neck where the gland is.

Dr. Malina learns of another symptom: irregular menstrual cycles.

Dr. Malina sees another symptom: the patient's eyes bulge.

The next thing that Dr. Malina does is to tell the patient that overactive thyroid is caused by "approaching menopause."

Dr. Malina hears the patient ask, "What about my heart racing?"

Dr. Malina says, "Don't worry about it."

The next thing Dr. Malina does is to prescribe Premphase, a hormone replacement drug for treating menopause.

Then Dr. Malina orders another thyroid test.

Four days later,[13] April 18th, Dr. Malina gets the new thyroid test results. He sees that the thyroid is overactive, producing too much hormone.

Nine days later, on April 27th, Dr. Malina's office takes a message from the patient reporting that the patient has new symptoms: abdominal swelling and bloating—swollen feet—and wants help.[14]

---

13. Always give the time lapse, not just the date. This helps jurors track time better.

14. Note that the patient is not named and that the grammatical subject of every sentence is the name of a defendant.

Three days later, May 1st. Dr. Malina sees the patient and her son.

Dr. Malina sees new symptoms: the patient has swollen legs. She's coughing. And she now has shortness of breath, extreme fatigue, and weakness all over.

Dr. Malina watches the patient's son press on her legs and ankles. Dr. Malina sees that they are so swollen that the son's fingers leave abnormal, deep indentations.[15]

Dr. Malina sees another symptom: a vein pulsing in the patient's neck.

Dr. Malina notes that he can see the blood moving through her veins.

Dr. Malina orders a heart test and a video of the inside of her abdomen.

Dr. Malina tells the patient to keep taking Premphase for menopause.

Next day, May 2nd. Dr. Malina returns the patient's call from five days earlier. He tells her to stop taking Premphase.

A week later, Dr. Malina's office receives the heart test results and the abdomen ultrasound video.

Same day, Dr. Malina gets a phone message from the patient about new symptoms: swelling all over her body and her abdomen is so full of fluid that it is rock hard. Dr. Malina sees that the patient is asking if her abdomen should be drained.

Next day, May 11th. Dr. Malina calls her back. Dr. Malina learns that she is still full of fluid, still extremely fatigued, still wants treatment. Dr. Malina says he'll look at her heart test and ultrasound results.

Next day, May 12th. Dr. Malina looks at the abdominal ultrasound and sees too much fluid along with rock-hard swelling.

Later that day, Dr. Malina learns that his patient is coughing, weak, cannot sleep, and vomiting, new symptoms.

The next thing Dr. Malina does is to tell her to take Premphase.

Three days later. May 15th. Early morning. The patient's daughter finds the patient in bed. No pulse. Calls 911.

At hospital, the patient dies.

Three days later: autopsy shows every organ in the patient's body is swollen, congested, full of fluid: her heart, liver, lungs, spleen, kidneys, abdomen, and even her brain. Her feet, ankles, legs, abdomen, face: all badly swollen. Heart twice the normal size.

---

15. This was a fact the defense denied. But this is our story. You'll deal later with the denial.

The patient's name was Lillian Cramden. Her symptoms had all been caused by congestive heart failure.[16]

Two days after his patient dies, Dr. Malina reads the heart-test results that had been waiting for him in his office for five days. He sees that her heart had needed immediate treatment.

[WHY WE ARE HERE (OR "Who we are suing and why")]

Now let me explain why we are here.

We are suing Dr. Malina for six reasons.[17]

[REASON ONE]

a. [*State the first rule violation for which you are suing*]

The first reason we are suing Dr. Malina is that he violated the patient-safety rule requiring him to list every possible cause of Lilian's symptoms.[18] He admits he never put congestive heart failure on his list of possible suspect causes. Instead he assumed that her symptoms were from menopause, even though some of her symptoms had nothing to do with menopause, and all her symptoms had to do with congestive heart failure. The experts will explain to us that all of Lilian's symptoms were among the most common symptoms of congestive heart failure.

b. [*What is wrong—in general—with the violation?*]

The experts will tell us that a doctor cannot read a crystal ball to tell how a case will turn out in the future. So he must use the full differential diagnosis to be sure he won't needlessly miss anything in the present. The experts will tell us that not doing a full differential diagnosis is like playing Russian Roulette with patients. Sooner or later the doctor is certain to seriously injure or kill someone. This is true in every kind of case with every kind of patient.

Please refer to the Template in supplement C for the rest.

---

16. One of the most persuasive things you can do as the opening progresses and during testimony is to show the step-by-step mechanics of how each symptom was caused by the real cause. So in this case you'd show how congestive heart failure led to fatigue, swelling, racing heart, and so on.

17. Here is the paradigm for each reason you are suing (*see* pp. 139*ff.* for the full explanation).
    a. State the action or omission for which you are suing. Do not explain or elaborate.
    b. Anchor what is wrong *in general*—not in this case—with that action or omission.
    c. What harm did it do in this case?
    d. What should the defendant have done instead?
    e. What good would that have done?

18. If a judge won't let you talk about rules, just say, "We are here because Dr. Malina chose not to _____."

SUPPLEMENT F

SAMPLE FIRST-PERSON STORY FOR CLOSING

A first-person story is one you tell in the words of your client. For example, to tell us that he crossed the street, instead of saying, "He crossed the street," you say, "*I* cross the street." In other words, for the duration of the story you pretend to be your client.

A first-person story can convey movingly how it felt or feels to be your client in the circumstances created by the defendant.

An actor invented first-person storytelling 2,600 years ago. It has been used off and on in trials since before 1950. It's popularity waxes and wanes because its success ranges from excellent to awful, and it's hard to know in advance. But like Longfellow's curly-forehead girl, as horrid as the result can be, when the technique works it's very good. Many variables make the difference. Unlike most of what I teach, the lawyer's personal nature is one of them.

You should try the technique—but only after testing and retesting your proposed first-person story in a *well-run* focus group. Cases have been lost or had their verdicts slashed because of untested or badly tested first-person stories.

SYMPATHY BID

There are ways in which a first-person story can produce horrid results. To many jurors, first-person stories seem outright bids for sympathy. Some jurors have reported that the technique's play for sympathy so offended them that it was a main deliberation topic. "All through the case everyone'd said we're not to use sympathy, but then the attorney did it with that story. He was cheating."

Here's a real transcript[1] of a juror's typical and corroborated response:

---

1. This interview was conducted by one of the best: Consultant Nurhan Karakas, Tacoma, WA.

Juror: And I can tell you this, that the last, during the closing arguments. When Mr. Ranhosky [*the plaintiff's attorney*] put on his little show and he acted as if he was speaking for the client. Nobody liked that. It's like he was making it seem like we are all a bunch of stupid people or whatever. That's what most people felt about it.

Interviewer: Tell me more about that.

Juror : Nobody really liked that.

Interviewer: What did he do?

Juror: When he said that, he was talking to us as if he was—I can't remember the little boy's name now.

Interviewer: Bryan.

Juror: Bryan, yes.

Interviewer: What did the other jurors think of that?

Juror: Everybody felt insulted by this.

Interviewer: How come?

Juror: Because it made it seem like that the attorney was playing on our intelligence. Our intelligence—he insulted us.

Interviewer: How was he doing that? Tell me more.

Juror: It was—it just like it was something that not—to not look at the facts, but instead like "You've got to think about me." He was acting as if he was the little boy. Everybody looked at that as a sympathy show and playing on our intelligence. So it was offensive. That didn't go well with the jury.

Interviewer: How long did you guys talk about that?

Juror: It was the first thing that we started talking about. I can't tell you how long, but it was the first thing. Everybody pretty much had the same feelings about it.

This awful reaction happens only rarely. But rarely is too often. So while I encourage you to use first-person stories, **first test it.**

Some of Gerry Spence's Trial Lawyers College instructors are among the technique's best teachers. Hopefully they agree that this technique carries so much force that you must test before using.

Below is an example that has been used successfully. But even if you use it nearly verbatim, you still must test it coming from you. Phoenix's brilliant James J. Leonard has graciously allowed me to include it.

Mr. C, Mr. M, and Mr. F are, as you'll see, what the plaintiff calls her chemo medications made necessary by the defendant doctor's failure to diagnose cancer. The jury already knew that "Mr. C" is Cytotoxan, "Mr. M" is Methotrexate, and "Mr. F" is 5FU (Fluorouracil).

Mr. C—Mr. M—and Mr. F

Briiinnnng! Time to get up. Not much to say about any sleep last night. Then again, never do sleep the night before the days when I have to go box with Mr. C, Mr. M, and Mr. F.

Frank's downstairs making noise. He knows not to worry about breakfast this morning, no coffee, nothing.

Get in my sweats, go downstairs, get in the car. Beautiful day out today. Shame I won't be enjoying it.

Take our ride from home to the health care center. Perhaps today I will find the answer to one of life's great mysteries: why on the trip to the doctor's office where Mr. C, Mr. M, and Mr. F await, are the lights always green and the trip is so fast—while the same trip back home all the lights are red and the whole trip is nothing but slow?

Then again, maybe this will be a lucky day. Maybe my tests will be so bad that I will not keep my date with Mr. C, Mr. M, and Mr. F.

There's the doctor's office. Just to see the place makes me physically ill.

Through the door, look around quickly. All I see are a lot of sick people. Take my seat, avoid looking at all the sunken eyes around me.

Comes the call: Annette! Time for blood tests.

Into the hallway. End of hall. Take my seat. Chairs are like those we used to have in grade school, with a nice arm rest.

Here come the blood suckers. Nice people, I'm sure, but I can't think of them any other way. My lousy veins: ouch—ouch—ouch!

Hmm. All in all not so bad today. Took them only four sticks to get a needle in and get the blood they need to test.

Back to the hallway and my chair.

Next up: the chest film. This is the biggie. To see if the cells have started spreading. Like into my lungs.

I wait.

Finally—"Annette, your turn." Time for the photo shoot. Hunch those shoulders forward! Right face and lift those arms!

Back to my third-grade chair. Wait for Dr. Jones. This is the wait that drives me crazy. Has the cancer spread?

Metastasized?

Every month, that wait.

"Annette, the doctor is ready." I go in.

This is when the fog always hits. I can barely hear what he's saying. "What's that? What's that?" Oh, it hasn't spread to my lungs so I will dance with Mr. C, Mr. M, and Mr. F again for another round.

It's round eight.

Down the hallway to the treatment room. Two big brown chairs with the large arm rest. Not buying one to decorate the house. Lousy brown color. Arm out. A few pokes. The needle is in.

This is when I always want to just get up and say, "Oh, forget it. Let me live my life without this."

Needle in the vein and I get that hot flash all over my body. And that metallic taste in my mouth. Mr. C, Mr. M, and Mr. F are coming on board for the ride.

Maybe Mr. C won't be so mean today. Maybe Mr. M will be nicer.

Starting to feel sick already. Come on, Frank, stop talking with the ladies at the desk and let's get in the car and get home. Maybe even Mr. F . . .

Again on the trip home, the car has the amazing ability to hit the red lights.

Please, Mr. F—just this one time . . . just once . . . be nice, be OK . . .

Ah, no such luck.

> Get home, quick upstairs, start to puke. Heave, heave, heave, until nothing's left and then it's dry. But it doesn't stop. Mr. C, Mr. M, and Mr. F, when will you ever stop?

Then Jim dropped out of the first-person narration:

> Some of you might remember that during jury selection I asked if you were a boxing fan. I asked because if you are, you've often heard about "the fight of the year," "the fight of the decade," "the fight of the century." Well, Annette is in real fight—not for a championship. For her life.
>
> The first round told her what every other round would be like. Mr. C, Mr. M, and Mr. F come around every month, month after month. And after every round, Annette asks the same question: "Can I get up off the stool one more time, can I go out for one more round?"
>
> Every time Annette has taken the challenge. She's gotten up. She's gone on with the fight. Every time she looks Mr. C, Mr. M, and Mr. F, looks them square in the eye, and tells them, "Bring it on! I want to live."
>
> "Give me life."

That's quite a bit more effective than saying, "The chemo pills made her feel sick." *Just remember to test it first.*

SUPPLEMENT G

PITFALLS: A PRIMER FOR THE NEW LAWYER; A REMINDER FOR THE NOT-SO-NEW

By Artemis Malekpour, MHA, JD[1]

Jurors start out suspicious of you. Here's a typical and real deliberation dialogue from a mock trial I conducted. I am the moderator they discuss. They've been led to believe that this mock trial is really a kind of "mediation" resolution project.

Juror #1: . . . some lawyers do have principles. I think the moderator is a nice lady, and she's a lawyer.

Juror #2: And you notice she doesn't practice.

Juror #3: She tries to mediate.

Juror #1: (*responding to #2's comments*) I was thinking the same thing.

Juror #3: Lawyers with morals mediate.

Juror #1: She said "it all shows in my face" and I was thinking, "yeah, you couldn't get up in front of a jury and . . ."

Juror #2: . . . lie.

Juror #3: Basically, lawyers have to find the truth inside the lies that they can actually use to cover their client's butt, which is awful, I don't know how they do it.

Don't confirm their suspicions. As consultants and curious courtroom observers, my partners and I have witnessed some of the best attorneys have lapses in thought, judgment, or simple grace during trial. Moments—however brief or prolonged—where something the attorney will say or do inadvertently

---

1. Artemis Malekpour is David Ball's senior partner in the firm of Malekpour & Ball.

shoots himself in the foot or provokes a cringe from his audience. Or confirms the jurors' incoming biases about lawyers.

You may have seen this yourself, either with co-counsel, from across the aisle, or while watching other trials: those times where an attorney's actions or words trigger the jury's eyes to collectively roll or—even worse—minds to slam shut in frustration or disgust. Tough to advocate or persuade when no one's listening or folks no longer care.

While such gaffes and slip-ups can send a case into a tailspin, the more pressing issue is that many attorneys are unable to recognize the impending crash landing. Even as they relay the gory details to us postmortem, it's difficult for some attorneys to identify the pitfalls they encountered or appreciate the impact of their stumbles.

For many attorneys, these trial blunders are earned honestly. Indeed, they can typically be traced back to our time in the hallowed halls of law school. Beginning with our first steps, we learn how to think, talk, and even dress like lawyers. Our developing lawyerly persona is the basis on which we're judged—from first semester through the bar exam. For three years, we're surrounded by classmates competing to achieve that same image and graded by professors who long ago mastered the look and sound.

Kicker is—once a lawyer takes her trial skills into the "real world" with a jury, the graders of her work are no longer classmates or professors. Instead, it's the everyday Joe—or, more often, Joe the Plumber—who's evaluating you, deciding whether to pass or fail your work. What makes you a hit in law school and legal circles can sink you in the courtroom. And you don't even know what's landed you in such a deep hole, because everyone else in your bar association is doing the same thing.

So what are those pitfalls that sweep your legs out from under you in a jury trial?

THE WORDS YOU USE

Let's start with what you say. This section is long, as the potential pitfalls are many.

Somewhere along the line, perhaps as we were studying for the SAT or some other college entrance exam, we learned that the bigger the words we used, the smarter we would seem. To appear more scholarly to the masses, we expanded our vocabulary and number of syllables. The more obscure the word, the more intelligent we sounded.

By the time we landed in law school, we'd hit the jackpot—a brand new lexicon to master, with specialized words and meanings unique to the distinguished profession of law. Our own secret society of nomenclature.

- Exculpatory
- Foreseeability
- Defeasance
- Jurisprudence
- Testatrix
- Arrearages
- Estoppel

The mere utterance of each term can make a promising young attorney's toes curl with pleasure.

We discovered in our legal training that even words commonly used by the general public are twisted into uncommon phrases and meanings understood only by astute legal minds.

- Attractive nuisance
- Specific performance
- Criminal conversation
- Piercing the corporate veil
- Remainder subject to open
- Due process

Get your tongue around any one of these or—better yet—use them in a sentence. You couldn't seem brainier if you tried.

Unfortunately, contrary to the standard academic line of thinking, big words aren't impressive, at least not in the courtroom. Rather, they can make a lawyer seem elitist (not a great image to project on behalf of your client), out of touch, or attempting to hide something.

Normal people don't talk like that. When you are being judged by normal people, why speak abnormally?

Beyond being perceived as a snot or a snob with the funny talk, an attorney runs a huge risk that jurors won't understand the complex words or phrases being tossed around the courtroom. Or by the time a juror figures out a definition or meaning in his head, he's missed the next three things the attorney has said.

Here's an example that might not be obvious to you. Attorneys love to use this expression, and it never fails to make the Malekpour & Ball partners squirm in our seats.

Prior to

or its evil counterpart,

Subsequent.

These may seem like simple words, commonly heard even outside the legal community. You'll often notice people use these words when they want to sound sophisticated or proper: "Prior to delivery of the package, but subsequent to the thunderstorm . . ."

Yet even though these may seem like commonplace expressions, for some people, even if they know the phrase well or have heard it a million times, they still need to stop and think, "Wait—subsequent—does that mean before or after?" While a juror is processing that in her head, whatever else you have said in those next few seconds—likely the key information the juror needs in order to decide your way—has flown through one ear and out the other.

The real tragedy here: there are much easier words you can use to get the same point across. Ready for them?

Before

After

Guaranteed that everyone instantly knows what both words mean without a second's thought. So why make someone waste their mental energy, particularly when they've got bigger fish to fry, that is, trying to find fact in this lawsuit?

Even worse than a juror wasting precious time and effort trying to define a word in her head? The juror concluding that whatever the attorney is saying is *over* her head.

Typically, jurors don't raise their hands in the middle of trial to request the plain meaning translation of a difficult word. More often, jurors just decide there's no reason to listen until someone starts speaking regular English again. Even the most skilled trial attorney can't win a case when the audience has tuned him out.

Worst of all is when jurors assume they know what you mean when they don't.

Hedonistic damages

To a layperson, you may have just said something naughty.

Defense expert

Now you've just acknowledged that their side's hired gun knows what he's talking about.

In both cases, you've probably perked up at least a few jurors' ears. Unfortunately, it's for the wrong reasons.

Unexpectedly, you've left your jurors with an impression you did not intend, and you may not even realize what you've done. Rather than take that risk, consider the impact and potential meanings your words may have with jurors. Choose what you say carefully so there's no chance of your words and meaning getting lost in a juror's self-translation.

The trap of this pitfall isn't limited to just legalese or the words you say when speaking to jurors. You must also be careful with the language you use with witnesses, particularly experts. Whether it be a medical malpractice case where you're questioning a doctor, or a tire failure case with the reconstructionist or engineer on the stand, avoid using their language, no matter how fluent you've become in it.

Counterposed vectors

Hemodynamic balance

Hypertension

Brachycardia

Moments of force

Learning terminology so you can communicate with an expert doesn't help if neither of you communicate well with jurors. Use nothing but regular speak for your gallery of regular folk so that they understand instantly. Teach your witnesses to do the same. The money you pay your experts can be squandered if their explanation confuses, misleads, or makes no sense to your audience. Worse yet, even after you have defined the jargon and without your knowledge, jurors may still apply the normal lay meaning to the jargon—which can often be harmfully at odds with what you intend to convey:

Positive results (sounds great, but not if it's a biopsy).

Negative results (sounds bad, but not if it's a biopsy).

Instead, use:

Bad results

or

Good results

as the case may be.

Further: when a pregnancy test shows someone is pregnant, is that positive or negative? Good or bad? Use words that convey the actual meaning: "The pregnancy test showed she was not pregnant" is crystal clear. "The pregnancy test was negative" can lead jurors to think the opposite of what you're actually saying—which creates enormous confusion when you later talk about the pregnancy.

If your witness keeps using technicalese, correct her each time.

Jurors do not learn more than a word or two of vocabulary. Why make the jurors' job tougher than it already is? Particularly when you want them to like you, your client, or at least your case.

Challenge yourself to find the simple way to express something. Ask someone who has not been bitten by the big-word bug what he would say to describe something. Google the term or phrase if need be to uncover the plain meaning or straightforward definition that the general population will understand.

It's not about talking down to the jurors or treating them as if they were stupid. They'll pick up on that in a heartbeat and resent you for it (and with good reason).

It's about using universal language that we all know, no matter where we are or what we've done in our lives.

Of course, with every rule, there is an exception. Or, perhaps, a footnote.

Even using simple language can get a lawyer in trouble. Consider the following word choices:

Accident versus *wreck*

Mistake versus *negligence*

Ran into versus *crashed*

Failures versus *choices*

Prove versus *more likely right than wrong*

As we learned in high-school English class, words have both a denotation (that is, literal meaning) and connotation (that is, idea or feeling). Consider early on—before you even go to trial—what sentiment you want your words to convey in telling your story. How do you want your jurors to react?

Will jurors shrug that "the defendant just made a mistake"? Or was the defendant negligent?

Will jurors dismiss your claim because it was "just an accident"? Or did the defendant cause a wreck?

Did the doctor "simply fail to run a test"? Or did the doctor choose to ignore the patient's symptoms?

Do you need to "prove" your case (which, to jurors, often means "be certain" or "100 percent sure")? Or do you just need to show that you're more likely right than wrong?

How you describe is just as important as what you describe.[2] The power of words should not be underestimated. Our minds paint their own pictures of what happened as we listen to a story. We make assumptions and fill in gaps based on what we hear and how it's told to us. Words that do not communicate clearly invite greater gaps, leaving jurors to fill in more and more on their own. As a result, jurors can end up deliberating a case that's very different from the one you thought you presented.

Depending on how long you've been in your law practice or immersed in the legal language, there's a good chance you've lost the ability to judge your words and what they can mean to the general public. So every opportunity you get, practice communicating with people not involved in your case or the practice of law. A group of fourteen-year-olds will do. Do they understand what you're saying? What image does your story create in their heads? How do they react to what you tell them? What conclusions do they make?

The simple-words rule applies as early as jury selection. No prospective juror wants to look stupid because he didn't understand your question. Striving to appear smart at the expense of a juror is an awful way to begin trial. The classic example: "We have the *burden* of *preponderance*. How do you feel about that?" Trust me, most of them have no idea what you just asked, and many won't admit it. They'll just say, "Fine." But you won't be fine with the burden they think you have by trial's end.

What You Do With Your Words

Even when you use simple words, how you deliver them can mean everything in the world. A common pitfall we see at trial: the message of what's said is not received because of how the messenger said it.

I recently ran across an example of this while judging a moot court competition at my law school. It had been a while since I'd been involved in any sort of oral arguments, so I made sure I knew the case issues and both sides' positions before I arrived.

First group of the night, petitioners first up. I was impressed with how well both students knew their stuff. But they spoke so quickly as they delivered their road map and arguments, it truly felt like my head might explode.

---

2. *See* Eric Oliver, Facts Can't Speak for Themselves (NITA 2005).

My fellow judge on the panel—an incredibly bright law professor—then got in the game, hurling questions at the students at the same seemingly ridiculous pace. Arguments were flung back and forth in such rapid fire that what I knew about the case going in was completely annihilated. Trying to wipe the wide-eyed look off my face as I stifled a giggle, I thought to myself, "Ah yes, I remember—law school."

I spent the next four hours in a time warp, teetering between trying to restore just enough of my pricey law school training to keep up with the evening's discussion, but not enough to do myself any lasting damage, lest my partner Ball kill me for returning to them talking like a lawyer.

What's habit and conventional in law school can end up biting you in the butt once you're in the real world. When you speak too quickly at trial, you make it tough for jurors, or even your own witnesses or client, to follow.

Slow down.

Take a breath.

Pause briefly at the end of each thought.

Take time to process your words.

Take time to pronounce your words.

Keep a calm, steady pace. It will help you think as much as it will help jurors and your client understand. And it will avoid the appearance that—in the words of my mother—you have a hot potato in your mouth. You can still look smart if you take your time to deliver your words.

A great model of this is President Barack Obama, with his deliberate pacing of his words. Even among those who disagree with what he says, there's little argument that President Obama's style and controlled delivery effectively display an intelligence and confidence that, in turn, allow the message to be heard.

How to Keep Those Words Organized

An organized presentation of your case helps foster clarity in communication. Too often, attorneys get trapped in their own quagmire of thoughts, and the jurors are the ones at the end left trying to dig their way out of the mess.

Here's the scenario: you walk into a room as someone is in the middle of telling a story. Try as you might to catch up or figure out what you missed, often you have no idea what the heck they're talking about. When the next twenty minutes of conversation center around that story, that can leave you out of the loop and frustrated.

Even more infuriating: you're there for the beginning of the story, right through to the end. Yet you still don't understand what happened because the story jumped all around. There appears to be no rhyme or reason in the telling of the tale. You're given the end before you even know all the players, or you can't keep the timeline straight in your head. The puzzled look you throw at the storyteller is dismissed with a "Oh, I guess you had to be there." Meanwhile, you're thinking, "That didn't make a lick of sense—reminder not to listen to what that clown has to say ever again."

Now put yourself in the courtroom, but this time, step into your jurors' shoes and take in the scene from their perspective. When jurors walk in, they have no idea what they're about to hear. Most of them are prepared to listen to a tale of some sort, but—in the majority of cases—the jurors have not had the chance to preview the back of the book jacket to know what this tale is about. They're starting at the title cover, waiting for someone to turn to page one.

Meanwhile you, their narrator, have been living with the story, immersed in every detail, for months, even years. By the time you arrive in the courtroom, you're ready to close the final chapter and put your story to rest. But, for your jurors, they still don't know the characters, and they have yet to see the plot.

Your opening is the first opportunity jurors will have to hear that story you've been waiting so long to tell them. The format of the delivery is crucial. You must organize your thoughts and sequence your story logically so that jurors can easily follow. Otherwise your jury may lose their way or their interest.

Stream-of-consciousness openings hardly ever work. As you're telling your story to a new audience, recognize that you are creating a memory framework in their heads. Each component must have an order to it for the structure to hold together.

You already have established a strong framework in your own mind. So your stream of consciousness can wander all over and still easily bring you back home. Jurors cannot do this when there's no framework yet built. Carpentry 101: without the walls, a door or roof makes no sense.

You must give jurors the necessary building blocks in an order that will logically fit as they work their way from the ground up. You can't plop them in the middle of Chapter 12, halfway through the fifth sentence of the third paragraph, and expect them to know where they are.

When your case is well organized in your opening, jurors can drop in and out of the story at any point during trial and easily find their way back—because they're already rooted with a clear understanding of what's happened.

When you bounce around in your story during opening, you leave jurors behind with no basic comprehension of the facts or arguments to return to . . . unless the defense provides them with a version. This is one reason why you need to tell the story in ways that make jurors listen to it, remember it, and keep them from disbelieving it as you go.[3]

Simple words, good delivery, and proper story are among the essential ingredients for meeting the essential goal:

K(eep)

I(t)

S(imple)

S(irs and Ladies)

The more complicated your case is, the less likely jurors are to find for the plaintiff. They shift to the defense because it's safer: siding with the defense doesn't seem to change anything, so jurors don't have to feel that weighty responsibility. One of the most common reasons for a defense verdict: the jurors just didn't "get it" [that is, your case]. So they felt in no position to pass judgment against the defendant based on something they didn't quite understand or know enough about. Jurors would rather leave things as they are than make uninformed changes. Frankly, can you blame them for not taking that risk?

Too Much Information

Another pitfall for attorneys: throwing too much information at their juries.

Attorneys must digest a lot of information as they prepare each case. They gain a great deal of knowledge about specified fields and topics as they work through discovery. And commonly, as attorneys take on the same types of cases over the years, they soon become experts in their own right. They often thrive on the details they learn and the wisdom they've acquired.

By the time of trial, an attorney is eager to share all that information with everyone in the courtroom—if only to show how well he's done his homework on behalf of his client. One of the hardest jobs he now has is sorting the important from the unimportant. But often this critical task gets overlooked.

Telling jurors everything you've learned only adds to the mayhem and madness of their task. Just as big words aren't impressive or appreciated, neither is TMI (too much information).

---

3. *See* pp. 119*ff.* and supplement C, p. 329.

Just imagine that you're putting together a puzzle. All of a sudden you realize there are these extra pieces that you don't know what to do with.

If there are too many extras, you may get overwhelmed, or lose interest. Depending on how frustrated you get, you may decide to discard the puzzle entirely.

That's what jurors are doing with your case—they're putting together a puzzle. If they get too many pieces, or pieces that don't seem to fit anywhere, jurors get angry with the person handing them the pieces. Jurors learn not to take any more pieces from that person, and they no longer trust the puzzle pieces they've already been given.

Jurors don't need to hear all the mechanics or minutia of a case, those extra pieces of the puzzle. Simply, what's the rule and how did the defendant break it? Then what harm did it do? Build from that into how violating those rules endangers everyone, and then undermine the defenses with the smallest possible amount of detail. More is less, especially when it comes to verdict size.

Give jurors only the pieces of information they need to know to make decisions. Don't pass along "stuff" that you think is just good for them to know—or good for them to know you know. Otherwise, as jurors tell us all the time, they just start ignoring you.

Remember that every item of information—no matter how clear you think its import is—is subject to juror distortion into "information" that hurts you. Too Much Information paves the path to losses and low verdicts. Lazy lawyers provide it. Responsible ones take the time and energy to sort the useful from the remainder.

Further, when something is important for jurors to know, make sure they understand why: how does this piece of information fit the puzzle and help your case? Otherwise, jurors aren't likely to pay much attention, even as you continue into more useful information. Once they adjust their listening down, it does not easily come back up.

So in a medical malpractice case, give jurors just enough medicine to understand the rules the doctor broke. You don't need jurors walking into the deliberations room with a medical degree.

Indeed, too much knowledge in their hands can be dangerous. "This is so complicated that I just can't blame the doctor even if he did make a mistake."

Simplicity = clarity. Too much information = mud.

Too Much Repetition

Repetition is NOT the way to understanding.

Do I need to repeat that?

Attorneys often believe that they can get jurors to listen to or understand what they are talking about by repeating it over and over again.

In post-trial interviews, we've learned that repetition is one of the jurors' biggest peeves. It drives jurors crazy to hear an attorney go over the same information multiple times. Eventually, the words all become "yada yada yada" to their ears.

For the sake of their sanity, jurors will often choose to tune the attorney out. But what they really want to do, they often tell us, is scream: "Hey, Mr. Attorney—we got it the first twenty times you told us. We're not idiots!! And you're a jerk for thinking we are!"

Sometimes an attorney's need to continue repeating herself is understandable, but there are still limits. It's understandable when the repeated points are crucial. But not ad nauseam. Give the jurors credit for having heard you the first few times, and then stop.

Oddly, attorneys do the most repeating of things that are absolutely pointless to repeat. In cases where the wreck took place within one moment, attorneys still yammer out the time, day, date, and year over and over and over—despite their total irrelevance! This is mindless, and the jurors know it. It is a legalese holdover from the nineteenth century when attorneys writing documents were paid by the word. Stop doing it. Repeat the crucial points with restraint and omit the pointless stuff like unnecessary dates and everything else that falls into the category of "yada yada."

Often, attorneys repeat themselves because they do not like the way they said something the first time. This failure of preparation undermines your credibility. And it makes some jurors see you as a hypocrite when you later try to keep a witness on cross from repeating what he said in a slightly different way. So when you find yourself repeating and rewording in trial (or in oral motions), use it as a sign that you need more advance practice to keep from sounding like a bumbler.

Certainly there are themes you want to reinforce all through trial. Rules, preponderance—you want these concepts kept foremost in jurors' minds so that every piece of evidence they get, jurors then filter and gauge through these recurring themes.

But parroting information in front of a jury doesn't help anyone, and jurors can begin to resent it as a waste of their (little paid) time.

How to Make It Memorable with Less Repetition

If you want jurors to remember something, find a way other than repetition. Use your voice, your hands, your physical placement in the courtroom to anchor the point in jurors' minds.

For example, when you're giving a rule, maintain the same cadence and pattern in your speech each time you say the rule. Hit the same pause marks. Be consistent in the rise and fall of your voice. Deliver it from the same spot in the courtroom. Use the same hand gesture.

When you're talking about what the defendant did, maybe you walk over to the defense table, standing in the same spot near the defendant each time.

When discussing your client's injuries, indicate the part on your body where the harm was done and use that same gesture each time. So if there's brain damage, whenever you mention the mechanism of impact you might consider grasping the top of your head with both hands and pretend to give it a violent shake.

Every time you deal with preponderance, hold your hands as the Ball method teaches[4] to show the balancing scales.

A note here on the Ball preponderance method to avoid an unintended pitfall: the tip of the scale should be slight, with the right and left hands tucked close together to clearly indicate the level of proof needed. We often see well-meaning attorneys get sloppy with this, with their hands so far apart they don't make the intended point of just the tiny height difference. Jurors believe the burden is indicated by the distance between the hands, so it makes the burden seem very high. You know what you mean when you do "the hands," but chances are jurors haven't read Ball. So palms up is not enough; they need to be near each other.

You can make your facts and arguments stick in jurors' minds by using deliberate movements rather than repetitive words. Jurors copy what they see, so the act or gesture gets into deliberations. It helps you send your jurors into the jury room armed with memorable tools they can easily use.

That's far better than having them no longer listen to you during trial because you endlessly repeated everything from the crucial to irrelevant junk.

HONOR THY JURORS AND THEIR ANSWERS

Another area steeped in possible pitfalls and stumbling opportunities is jury selection. Before you even present your case, you can find yourself in hot

---

4. *See* page 3-2-2, pp. 63*ff.*

water with jurors because of how you interact with and react to them in voir dire.

Voir dire is often not an attorney's favorite part of trial. In fact, for some trial attorneys, it's what they dread most and what they feel least comfortable doing.

There will often be times during voir dire that you'll hear things you don't particularly like.

"Society these days is sue-happy."

"I think people don't take enough personal responsibility for their own actions."

"I wouldn't give a dime to anybody for so-called pain and suffering."

"I believe lawyers are scum."

The urge to turn each comment into a debate or chance to persuade may be strong—after all, you didn't go to law school for nothing. But for the sake of your case and your client, nip that urge in the bud. You do yourself no favors by taking on a juror in voir dire.

Instead, respect whatever jurors tell you, even if it's bad for your side. Remember, you want to get all that out now rather than get burned by it later on.

Respect does not mean you must agree with what a juror has said. It's not necessary to nod your approval. But you can nod to show that you're paying attention and appreciating what the juror has to say.

Respect by allowing a juror to finish a thought without interrupting. Respect by turning your body and head toward the juror to give your full attention rather than drawing back or turning away. Respect by acknowledging that the juror has a valid viewpoint, even if it opposes yours. Respect by thanking the juror for being honest.

> You never really understand a person until you consider things from his point of view—until you climb inside of his skin and walk around in it. —*Atticus Finch*[5]

Respect that each juror's opinions are shaped by his or her different background and experiences, just as yours have been. Respect that there may be other jurors on the panel who see things as this juror does and will be watching intently to see how you respond.

So don't argue or debate. Voir dire is not the time to "inform" or "educate" your audience. You don't have to agree with what your jury pool tells you.

---

5. Harper Lee, To Kill a Mockingbird (New York: Warner Books, Inc., 1960).

Simply respect the answers you get. As Gerry Spence teaches, honor a juror's feelings, even if you don't like the juror's answer.

Really listen to what your potential jurors have to say, in ways similar to those described below.

If you're familiar with the David Ball method, this should be obvious to you by now. "Of course, I want to hear what jurors have to say. I know that's going to help me pick which jurors will be good for my case or [more likely these days] deselect who's bad."

But this goes beyond simply hearing the content of their answers. It goes to the human activity of listening in the way a caring person listens. So certainly you should be thinking about your case as you conduct voir dire. Just don't forget to be human about it.

How?

For starters, try as best as you can to return to those days before you became a lawyer.

If a friend had told you back then that they'd been badly hurt in a car wreck, how would you have reacted? Not just what you'd have said, but what you'd have felt and acted. This does not mean you have to feel for every juror the way you would have about your friend, but humans are caring even with strangers.

If someone back then had told you they'd just lost a family member to, say, cancer, what would you have said to them? How would you have said it? How carefully would you have listened—even to the information you had no need for?

As an attorney and good student of Ball, you know you want to learn more. That entails being interested in the person talking, not just the information being delivered. So pay real attention—and don't hide behind that all-too-common flat affect facial mask many lawyers retreat behind. Come out and—as Spence and his folks teach—"be in the moment." Just like real life, not like some artificial courtroom world.

And ask questions that get at real information rather than just leading jurors to the specifics of what you think you want to know. So:

"Tell me about that."

Remember that in that jury box, you're talking with people who don't yet give a flip about your case. In voir dire, they just care what happened to them. Completely understandable. And important to keep in mind.

You always want to follow up with someone's answer, but be socially appropriate and considerate in how you do it.

If a potential juror tells you that someone smashed into them on the freeway three years ago, or that a loved one was misdiagnosed by a family practitioner and died, don't immediately ask if they sued. That's a typical lawyer's response. Indeed, that's the way many jurors expect you to react—as the vulture of an ambulance chaser they think you are and that your knee-jerk "did you sue anyone?" seems to confirm.

Be the unexpected.

If someone says they were hurt in a slip and fall, or their spouse was killed by a defective product, tell them first how sorry you are to hear that. Be sincere with your words. Acknowledge their loss and feelings, and recognize that the experience may still be painful for them. That takes just a few well-chosen words, not a speech. Then ease them into a follow-up: "If you don't mind, as much as you're able, please tell me a little about that . . ."

Always let the juror dictate where the conversation goes. Explore the issue as far as you're able, but always be mindful of how comfortable the juror is talking about it. When the juror's given you all she's willing to give, tell her you appreciate her sharing that information with you.

Don't press or push anyone on your panel, even if you intend to get rid of them. I once watched a plaintiff's attorney being relentless in his questioning. The poor juror barely held herself together as the attorney grilled her about a tragic event in her life. The judge finally intervened and (mercifully) dismissed the juror.

From the back of the courtroom, I watched the excused juror leave. The second her hand hit the door, her face collapsed, and, as she escaped into the hallway, she burst into tears.

Meanwhile, the attorney—unlike everyone else in the room, including the jurors—was oblivious to the damage he had just inflicted. He was just pleased to have booted her. But the victimized look on that juror's face remains forever imprinted in my brain. The experience will likely never leave her. And it was certainly in the jury's mind as the trial progressed. The attorney had made them his enemies. He turned them completely against his case before he even had a chance to give his opening.

I felt the same as the jurors did—even though I'd walked into the courtroom inclined to be on the plaintiff's side. Imagine what a display like this does to neutral or hostile jurors!

Even the most compassionate of attorneys can inadvertently come across as inconsiderate or unfeeling in their single-minded focus and determination to pick a favorable jury. And even upon reflection afterward, most attorneys don't understand how their questions or the way they responded to jurors might have been inappropriate.

Case in point: At a seminar many months ago, a former partner Debra Miller described an awkward exchange she had once witnessed between an attorney and juror. The case was about toxic fumes. A prospective juror told of a loved one who had been dangerously exposed to a poisonous gas. Without skipping a beat, the attorney's response: "For how long?"

The seminar's roomful of attorneys sat quietly. Then they kind of looked around at each other. Puzzled. As if to say, "So what?" A few chuckled a nervous little laugh, assuming there was a punch line there that they had just missed. Hard to believe they had not gotten the point—but it was clear that the seminar participants, just as that attorney, were unable to figure out what was wrong with that follow-up.

For a layperson, it would have been obvious: "How could the first thing out of your mouth not have been, 'I'm so sorry to hear that,' or 'I hope your loved one is OK'?!"

But when attorneys are in their one-track legal minds, focused solely on the trial above everything else, the automatic thinking when they hear something is: "How does this affect my case?"

In that instant, as I watched these brilliant attorneys struggle to see the problem, it dawned on me just how detached the legal community can be from the real world.

In the pursuit of justice, all our thinking and concern turns to "just us." At that point, no matter how worthwhile your case, you have left behind the essential of being human. And that seriously undermines your ability to be a decent trial attorney.[6]

Sure, your voir dire questions must be information-seeking. You're in court, not at a dinner party. But in the words of George Costanza: "You know, we're living in a society! We're supposed to act in a civilized way."

Don't feed into that stereotype of a vulture-circling, ambulance-chasing plaintiff's lawyer. Don't check your manners or your humanity at the courtroom door. Honor your jurors; honor their answers. You'll be amazed at how much good that will do for all involved.

---

6. If "being human" in trial tends to escape you, there's good help. The Trial Lawyers College (TLC, which runs the Spence "Ranch" and other programs) does superb work in this area. One of TLC's best instructors, the brilliant trial advocacy trainer Joshua Karton (Los Angeles), can bring you a long way in a few private sessions. You can arrange an individual or a multi-firm workshop with him in your area. In addition, AAJ runs programs in which these folks sometimes appear. Pursuing their kind of work may well be the most worthwhile thing you've ever done—both as an attorney and as a human being.

KNOW WHO YOUR AUDIENCE IS

A snag that some attorneys hit once jury selection is over: they lose sight of the people they need to persuade.

Attorneys typically don't take advantage of all the resources readily available these days to tell them more about their jury pool. And what little attorneys may be able to find out about their jurors during the selection process gets forgotten or neglected as the trial moves forward.

In this day and age of Facebook, My Space, and Twitter, people share a great deal of themselves with the public. Every group or organization seems to have their own Web site, and there are countless blogs and forums for people to post every thought and idea that pops in their heads.

So there's a decent chance you can learn a lot about your jurors—in some cases, even before you meet them in the courtroom. And what you find on the Internet may be more revealing than the answers you get from them during voir dire.

Once the Court tells you who your prospective jurors will be, Google every name on that list. Do this even if you don't get the list until just before voir dire starts; if possible, have two or three people ready to fire up their laptops and begin a search.

If you have more advance notice, assign a member of your trial team to the primary task of researching the names on the jury list. You never know what's out there on the World Wide Web that can facilitate the path to jury selection and keep you from making unnecessarily dreadful choices.

If you appoint a member of your staff, choose someone who has time to do a thorough job searching for information on each juror. Simply typing in a name doesn't always work. You need to be creative to narrow or refine your search, as not everyone goes by their given name, and a common name like Jane Smith produces 24,100,000 hits. Your researcher needs to know the little tricks of the trade and must have the persistence to keep searching, no matter how many dead ends he may run into.

The gold standard is to use a professional who understands the kinds of things you need to know and has the research skills to find them quickly.[7]

Even when you get the jury list at the last minute, and you have only a half hour for jury selection, have someone doing as much Googling as can be done in the time you have—especially with the "gray area" jurors.

Then when you've completed jury selection, Google the seated jurors in detail. You need to know everything you can find about the jurors who will

---

7. *See, e.g.*, www.itk-research.com.

be hearing the case. This is especially important when jury selection was too brief for you to find out much. So find out afterward, because knowing about your jurors helps you know how to try your case and makes any settlement decisions a lot safer for you.

Knowing who your jurors are gives you a better gauge during trial of what parts of your case might connect with them, what analogies will resonate with them (particularly in terms of safety rules and community concerns), and what might offend them. The humor or analogy or reference that scores you points in Jersey might draw raised eyebrows or disapproving looks as you travel south. Better that you learn this by doing your homework on the Internet than from the hostile glares in the jury box.

UNCOVER WHAT YOUR AUDIENCE MAY FIND

Googling is not limited to knowing who your audience is. You also need to find out what your technologically savvy audience knows (or may discover).

A common problem attorneys now face: there's an endless amount of information that a juror has access to outside the bounds of a courtroom that never gets filtered through the lawyers or judge.

These days, no longer can anyone believe that a verdict will be based solely on what judges, lawyers, and witnesses tell a jury. It can be based *mostly* on what jurors do not learn at trial. You need to know what that is.

> I don't believe I have to be loyal to one side or the other. I'm simply asking questions.—*Juror #11*[8]

Jurors often come into a courtroom believing that neither side is telling the truth. And during trial they hear little that gives them an easy and trustworthy answer. So jurors search for the "truth" online. Result: Cases sunk by what they find.

Don't think it won't happen to you. It will. No matter how many instructions and stern warnings judges give, jurors can't—and don't want to—stop themselves from looking. With laptops, netbooks, iPhones, Blackberries, and similar search-friendly mobile gadgets so readily accessible, it's quick and easy for jurors to seek out information on the Web. And there's no way to prevent or monitor that.

So we're in a different world. You *must* know everything that's out there that a juror might find; you can't deal with it if you don't know about it. So you must Google everything in your case: you, your law firm, your clients, their family members, the defense clients and families, witnesses for both sides, every issue, the injuries in the case, the experts and the topics they

---

8. Sidney Lumet, Director, *Twelve Angry Men* (1957).

testify about . . . every bit of your case that jurors could possibly research, you need to know about.

You need to do this thoroughly and immediately upon accepting a case and continue to monitor through its final disposition, even if your case is not high profile or has no chance of catching the media's or public's attention.

Example: You claim your client has migraines—like daggers stabbing into his eye sockets. Part of his claim is that the pain keeps him from working. But a picture on his cousin's Facebook page shows him having a grand old time tailgating with pals before a football game. Bye-bye verdict money!

Or what about that online ad for a migraine "cure"? Bye-bye verdict money—without you ever even knowing that a snake-oil ad did you in.

Jurors don't automatically trust what they hear in court, but they easily trust what they find on the Internet, because it seems "neutral." Usually, they don't bother to check the accuracy of what they've found. So don't gamble or bury your head in the sand. Take the time and effort to uncover what jurors might find.[9]

FOLLOW WHERE YOUR AUDIENCE GOES

One of the most interesting aspects of trial is cross-examination. That's when things have the potential to really get juicy, causing the ears of even the most bored juror to perk up. Because that's the truest test of a case—when the person asking the questions and person answering disagree.

It's in these head-to-head match-ups when jurors feel they are better able to determine which side makes more sense to them, and those riding the fence find themselves nudged in one direction or the other.

But cross-examination is also where attorneys can unwittingly do themselves a lot of damage—not because of what is said (which obviously can have its own ramifications), but how it comes across.

You can lose your biggest advocate on the jury because of how you conduct yourself during cross-examination.

As they're preparing for trial, many attorneys will tell us, "I can't wait to get my hands on the defense's _____ on cross. I'm going to tear him into shreds in front of the jury." This may very well be the moment you most anticipate and relish at trial. Especially if the witness was particularly nasty or uncooperative when you took his deposition.

Word to the wise: when you get your turn on cross, don't go in with guns a-blazing. Your game plan should not be to bully or thrash a witness, even if

---

9. For more detailed information and help with this, see supplement H, "Virtual Reality."

that's a fun or seemingly justified thing to do. Take your cue from the jury before you attack.

Remember that jurors don't have the history you do with the witnesses. Jurors don't know what's happened before trial or even what happens during contentious moments during the trial (when they get sent out of the room so the parties can duke it out in their absence). Beyond that, jurors don't have the investment you and your client do in the case. So their potential for outrage is significantly lower and not as easy to ignite.

If you begin a cross-examination at full tilt, ready to tear into the witness, jurors will likely recoil—sometimes visibly—from what they perceive to be a hostile, unwarranted attack. Instead of appreciating your brilliance in trapping the defense witness in a lie or moment of hypocrisy, all the jurors will think is: "Why is that lawyer being so mean?" Result: Jurors begin to feel sorry for that witness, ignoring or excusing whatever the witness has to say or has done. And they start hating you.

Follow your audience—let them get mad at or disgusted with the witness before you do. Once you sense the jurors are ticked off with the person on the stand, that's your cue to unleash the hounds.

No one likes a bully. We do value people standing up for themselves or striking against a danger.

Allow jurors to see the threat or evil before you pounce.[10] Better yet, don't pounce.

A FLARE FOR THE DRAMATIC

The desire to conjure up drama in the courtroom can needlessly trip an attorney up in a variety of ways.

For a majority of your jurors, your trial is probably their first time ever stepping into a courtroom or hearing a real case. Juror familiarity with the legal system is often limited to what they see on TV or in movies. But that's not real. Not every case is an episode of *Law and Order* or *The Practice*. Don't try to make it one.

You want to be passionate about your case, but your passion must be genuine. We see too many scripted tears, manufactured attempts at heated confrontations, and feigned displays of righteous indignation. The general public has become increasingly more desensitized and dubious of seemingly staged emotional outbursts.

---

10. For more help with this, *see* section 7-6, pp. 213–14.

Jurors spot a phony a mile away. If you think I'm exaggerating, conduct a focus group. Find out for yourself how much wool many jurors will expect you to try to pull over their eyes.

And be careful in seeming to seek juror sympathy. If you keep a photo of your clients' dead child at the corner of the plaintiffs' table, jurors can be turned off by what they see as a shameless attempt to tug on their heartstrings. What might have been a reminder to you of who you're fighting for could seem to jurors like a cheap gimmick for their benefit.

No matter how credible you think you come across, you're a plaintiff's attorney, so jurors will doubt your motives and judge your actions very critically. The first suspected sign of a sham and you've lost at least some of them.

This is partly because jurors are being self-protective—they don't want to be tagged as idiots falling for what they think are your contrived maneuvers or legal shenanigans. The reputation of jurors took a hit with the verdict in *State of California v. Orenthal James Simpson*. What that trial left in its aftermath was the notion that attorneys seek to put stupid or naïve people on juries to easily wheedle them into a verdict that defies logic and evidence. If a juror has the bad fortune to be picked to serve, she's going to do her darnedest to make sure the attorneys don't use their wiles to make her into a fool as well.

But the other part of that can also be that jurors don't want to think of themselves as cold hearted jerks for siding against someone who has been injured or killed. So to justify a defense verdict, jurors love to find ways to fault you for using cheap ploys to gain their sympathies.

Judges instruct that jurors must not base their decision on sympathy. So most jurors resent you for trying to elicit it. That's another reason it's important to explain to jurors why you're showing them or telling them something: so they don't presume you're just trying to pull a fast one over on them by appealing to their sentimental side.[11]

That's also why it's important to do focus groups: so you can see what jurors' reactions will be to your exhibits and evidence. You may have put together what you believe to be a powerful day-in-the-life or video montage of your client. But—*most* of the time—jurors make their own assumptions based on what they notice in the video that you never spotted.

Example: You see the home as a humble, simple dwelling in need of modifications for your young plaintiff now paralyzed.

Jurors see a framed picture of a soldier and American flag, strategically placed in the background as a brazen appeal to the jury's sense of patriotism.

---

11. *See* section 5-5-5-A, p. 149.

Or they hear the trailing sound of a really annoying fight in the next room between mom and another child. Or, as we've seen more than once, they spot expensive cars visible through a window out in the driveway—including, once, the lawyer's own Lexus!

But even with something as seemingly innocuous—and even real—as the soldier's photo, if the jurors take it as an appeal to their patriotism, they think they've seen through your cynical little ploy. In this true-story illustration, focus group jurors—not the lawyers—caught the problem before it had a chance to do damage at trial.

Another true example:

The lawyer saw an adorable shot of a mother bathing her little girl in the kitchen sink. The shot is playful, loving—shows how much these good parents care for their darling daughter, how dedicated they have always been to her well being, how devastated they must now surely be by what's happened in this case. The lawyer loved it.

But some jurors saw a naked little girl, carelessly plopped in reaching distance of a butcher's knife, with idiot mom ten feet behind the counter, recklessly out of the grasp of her child—this child now being exploited in front of a jury (and any potential pedophile) by her parents and lawyers for the sake of what "must" be a get-rich-quick scheme.

Same photo—two different interpretations. The jurors' version may never have dawned on you. It's an innocent photograph of a little kid, for Pete's sake! You can find it in any family album, and anyone would think it was cute. How absurd that someone could think otherwise!

But it's easy from even a well-meaning juror's point of view, because a lawsuit is a game changer, and every minor detail is subject to scrutiny and criticism.

You can easily miss these deadly traps. So even if you do a careful post-mortem after a bad verdict, you might never find out the real reason you lost at trial.

So never assume or guess what jurors' reactions will be. Do focus groups so you can know.

And never try to manipulate the jurors' feelings. Well-run focus groups will tell you when you're doing that. (Improperly-run focus groups won't and can even delude you into thinking that the dangerous thing you're doing is working fine.)

TECHNOLOGICAL OVERLOAD

Visual aids are powerful tools when used properly. Often jurors find it easier to comprehend and recall something if they are able to see it, rather than just hear or read it.

My partners have penned an article[12] that extensively covers the art of visual communication. Yet we still see the same problems arising at trial.

We're in a multimedia world, so to keep up with the times, attorneys feel they need to power up when they go to court. And some just love gadgets. With ELMOs, PowerPoints, and video technology, there are often more surge protectors and power cords on the floor than people in the room.

But in your quest to be trendy and cater to an electronics-driven society, beware of relying on too much technology. As we've all experienced, the best equipment in the world often crashes when we're most counting on it. And the best lawyers in the country appear woefully incompetent with the flick of a switch that doesn't do its job. Bright lights and big pictures don't always impress, and there's a huge risk of overkill.

My first introduction to PowerPoint came while I was getting my graduate degree in Healthcare Administration. Several of our courses required presentations, and PowerPoint was the format we were taught to use. Made sense, I thought, for the business types to use it in boardrooms. But in the courtroom? That I did not anticipate, at least not with the frequency I've seen. Did I miss that class in law school?

Because attorneys have little training in PowerPoint, they usually use it badly. They muck up the slides with a whole lot of words filling the screen. Jurors can miss the message of what they're seeing because they're too busy reading.

And many attorneys use bullet points to introduce new topics, a long-discredited method of trying to communicate. Bullet points are banned in much of the corporate world, and virtually never seen on TV commercials—because everyone who understands how to communicate knows that bullet points impair the communication of any new topic.

If you must do PowerPoint, don't get trigger-happy with those bullet points. When there is a laundry list of bullet points in front of us, our eyes tend to scan through haphazardly rather than really focus on each line and every word. We don't bother—nor do we care—to read everything on the page because we feel that it's too much information for us to absorb.

---

12. "The Basics of Visual Communication in the Courtroom (Avoiding the Common Traps)" by David Ball and Debra Miller. I'm happy to send it to you: request from artemis@consultmmb.com.

Or we read ahead rather than listen to each point you're trying to make. Even if your bullet list is short, once jurors have finished reading and you're still talking, jurors will listen less carefully or never tune back in to what you're saying because they feel they've already gotten the gist from what you've given them on the screen. So uncover each bullet point one at a time, to make sure your audience stays with you.

Make one point per slide and lose all the rest. As with everything in trial, simplicity goes a long way to understanding.

Show the bullet point only after you have explained the topic. Talk to the jurors about what you want them to know (with a blank screen behind you), then pop up a bullet point that succinctly summarizes what you just said. Lawyers often do this in reverse, as they see the bullet points as a way around having to use notes in front of a jury. The goal of a PowerPoint should be to assist the jurors in their learning and retention, not serve as a favor to the lawyer as he's presenting.[13]

Even if your exhibits are limited to poster boards, keep in mind that you can still overwhelm a jury. Yes, some people learn more visually, while others are auditory learners. But trying to appeal to both senses simultaneously can create a distraction for many as they try to look, read, and listen all at the same time. No one can review or read a new exhibit and simultaneously listen to what the lawyer is saying. Allow time for the jurors to see the exhibit.

And this sounds silly to have to say, but the fact is that many lawyers still stand right between the exhibit and the jury, or talk while looking at the exhibit instead of the jury, or place the exhibit where some jurors can't clearly see it, or pay no attention to how the glossy surface is reflecting light in a way that keeps half the jurors from seeing the exhibit's content. For that reason, please avoid the blunder of using glossy-surfaced exhibits. You're looking for juror impact, not a Kodachrome moment.

Another common problem we see: You show jurors an exhibit. Let's say it's a photo of the wreckage from your case. You give jurors a chance to look at it. Then you start speaking again. Maybe you've even moved on to a new point. But you've left that exhibit up on the screen or easel. Guess where your jurors' eyes (and minds) still are: on that picture. They're not hearing a word you say. So when you're done with the exhibit, put it away. If it's a poster board, turn it over. If you're using slides, black out the screen. Once you've removed the visual from their eyes, the jurors' attention will return to you.

---

13. For more tips on how to use PowerPoint properly, see CLIFF ATKINSON, BEYOND BULLET POINTS: USING MICROSOFT POWERPOINT TO CREATE PRESENTATIONS THAT INFORM, MOTIVATE, AND INSPIRE (Microsoft Press 2005).

Exception: Sometimes you have one exhibit that is the "logo" for the case—it is powerful and evocative, such as the photo of the half-empty beer can on the floor of the defendant's car. In that situation, leave it up all the time, and during the defense case have it in plain sight, but turned away from the jury so it's never out of their awareness.[14]

As with videos, be careful that your exhibits don't mean one thing to you, but something different to some jurors. If your client fell from a balcony, you may decide to bring in the railing to show how poorly it was constructed or maintained. But a jury may see an obvious danger that no one in their right mind would have leaned against.

As with all your exhibits, test them out in front of nonlawyers who are not involved in your case. Find out what others think before you commit to using something in trial. It can spare you a stumble when it really matters.

One final point on visual aids: if you're about to show the jury something disturbing, whether it be pictures or video or anything else, resist the shock factor. Warn them first. Jurors will appreciate the head's up. And while a few may cover their eyes, it's almost guaranteed that even they will take a peek. In fact, if given a warning, jurors are likely to pay more attention to what they're about to see. How many times have you heard a news or sportscaster say, "We must warn you, what you're about to see may be disturbing to some viewers," and you're suddenly on the edge of your seat?

But remember, visuals are not always better than words. *Most* day-in-the-life videos lower verdicts. This is because words can put an image in our heads better than videos (particularly if you do a good job describing the trauma or harm). Explaining how your client's arm got caught up in the blades of a faulty lawn mower may be more effective than showing the scars, depending on the degree of injuries.

Discussing the effort it takes your client to simply get out of bed or go to the bathroom may be more compelling than having your client demonstrate these tasks on video. Or you may find that the time it takes your client to complete such a simple maneuver may be a powerful statement by itself (which is why you won't do your case or client any favors by fast-forwarding through the process for the sake of holding your jurors' attention, even if you have a clock running alongside to show how long it's actually taking). So think whether you need a visual or whether the jurors' imaginations will do your damages case more justice.

---

14. *See* BALL, THEATER TIPS AND STRATEGIES at 125.

Who's That at the End of Your Table?

Remember your client? The reason you came to trial? Not just her name, but her physical presence. Seems silly to ask, but you'd be surprised. A pitfall that topples many: attorneys can be so focused on trying their case, keeping organized and on top of everything at their table, that they often forget to interact with the most important entity at the table, their clients.

If you care about your client—and hopefully you do or else you should consider a career change —let the jurors see that. Make sure they know you like your client so they are more open to liking her as well. This is true in both civil and, with only a few exceptions, criminal cases.

How many times have you formed an impression based solely on what you first see? Whether it's something that you take the time to notice or something that just strikes you as odd or interesting, with that first gander, you think you've got a person or situation summed up.

Once that opinion has been formed, it's hard to shake, particularly when it's negative. From that point on, everything you learn about that person or thing is tainted by those initial shades of disapproval or distaste, usually fueling the unfavorable image in your mind, even irrationally so. No matter how much good you later learn, it's difficult to root out the bad.

Jurors start off the trial very curious about your client and case. After all, that's the reason why they are there. They begin to take stock of what's before them as soon as they walk in: who's the guy suing or on trial, what's happened to bring him (and them) here, is he a good guy or someone they just know they're going to hate? How strong of a case does he have, and are they going to care what happens to him?

Don't let that first impression that jurors have of your case be you disregarding your client. No matter how busy or stressed you become, do not ignore the person who brought you into that courtroom.

Get your client's input, beginning with jury selection. Your client or one of his family members may get a bad vibe or nasty look from a prospective juror that you missed. Call me crazy, but that seems like an important thing you might want to know before entrusting that juror to make a decision that could affect your client's life.

With that said, I'm not advising you to turn jury selection over to your client or his family. They don't have the skills, knowledge, or experience to know what makes a good or bad juror. Their opinion is just one more piece of information to incorporate into the mix when it comes down to making your decisions about who to strike.

And depending on the case, you will need to be selective with how much information about the jurors you share with your client or his family. For instance, in a violent criminal trial, you don't want your client or his family reading jurors' responses to written questionnaires.

Continue to check in with your client throughout the course of the trial. Jurors are watching at all times. If they see you treat your client as immaterial or dispensable, they're likely to follow suit. Why should they care about your client if they believe you don't?

When you have the opportunity, spend the lunchtime period with your client. Too often, attorneys use that moment to catch up with other aspects in the case and neglect the central part. How many times have you been guilty of wolfing down half your sandwich before you ask, "Where's my client right now?" You may be expecting your paralegal to keep tabs on your client's whereabouts, but it's important for you to stay on top of that as well. Include your client in your lunch plans when appropriate. Don't always delegate someone else to take care of your client. Show that you care as well.

When you're not able to spend time with your client, make sure someone on your staff is. Whether it's walking in together, sitting next to one another, or talking together during the breaks, always make sure that someone from your office is interacting positively with your client. The last thing you want is jurors to see that you have left your client to fend for herself or sent her retreating to warmer faces in the peanut gallery any time there's a break in the action because she's feeling snubbed by her legal team.

Just as you should be aware yourself, give a stern warning to your client before trial begins (and reiterate throughout its course) that she's always being watched—starting the instant she leaves home. Same with the family.

Be wary of how your client comes across to jurors. If your client claims his leg is injured, but then sprints to catch an elevator before the doors close, jurors will see. If he claims to have emotional suffering, but then yucks it up with his family during the lunch break, jurors will see. If he claims to be out of work and struggling to make ends meet, but gets dropped off at the courthouse steps each morning in a Mercedes, well . . . you get the point. More than one case has been lost because of what jurors saw when they glanced outside through the jury-room window.

Paying attention to your client becomes especially challenging when you're dealing with a spouse or, even worse, ex(es). It's important that they get along or at least behave in each other's presence once they are in the public's view. To foster at least the appearance of a united front, be sure that you don't neglect or exclude one or the other in your conversations or even in how you sit at the plaintiffs' table. What can sometimes occur on an all-male legal team is that the ex-husband will sit beside the attorneys, while the ex-wife gets regulated to the end of the table. The sentiment that projects to the jury, particularly the women on your panel, is that the ex-wife is being frozen out or disrespected. This seemingly inconsequential point can heavily color how some jurors see you and your case.

SETTING THE MOOD

Human beings have a need to feel safe and secure in their surroundings. They also need that sense of belonging, to feel connected to something or someone.

The members of your jury are no different. They become no less human as they slide through the metal detectors at the courthouse doors. But with so much on their plates, attorneys sometimes take for granted how important it is to make sure these basic needs of their prospective fact finders get met. Attorneys make the mistake of treating the trial as a process, when their jurors are viewing it as an event.

Jurors usually find the courtroom a strange, intimidating place. Imagine walking into a situation where everyone seems to know the rules but you, and they all seem to belong but you. All eyes are on you to do something, but you're not sure what or how.

If you've ever been in that position, remember now how you felt when you encountered your first friendly face. To this day, you may still have warm memories when you think of that first person who was nice to you.

As a plaintiff's attorney, you have that opportunity to make the new kids on the block feel at ease. Once they enter the jury box, you are typically the first person to speak directly to each of them and (hopefully) engage them in conversation. Take advantage of that moment. Make a concerted effort to get each juror feeling relaxed in this new environment. You want your jurors to be comfortable with you and the process in general. If you can get them to feel safe with you, they're more likely to trust what you say to them.

This does not mean you should go out of your way—or out of your comfort zone—in being friendly to jurors. No one likes a butt-kisser, in or out of court. You want to come across sincere in your warmth so that jurors get a real sense that you actually do like them, appreciate them, and want them to feel at home. If this is not in your nature (and indeed, it's not in everyone's), consider turning jury selection over to co-counsel if he has a friendlier disposition. While you may feel it's important for you to connect with the jurors right off the bat, it does you no good if that initial interaction is forced or fake. Better that the jurors' first experience with the plaintiff's side be positive than leaving them feeling as if they need to shower after dealing with a slimeball of an attorney. (If this is an area where you need improvement, consider doing a practice voir dire—or several—before you head to trial.)

There are attorneys out there who strut into court like they own the joint. We've all seen them, and maybe some of us have wanted to be them. But while a certain amount of ego is good, even healthy, leave it at home. No one likes a lawyer who acts superior to anyone—especially not to the jurors.

No matter how many years you've been practicing law, always be aware of how you come across to others who don't know you or have a preconceived notion of your kind. You may be the greatest thing since sliced bread, but showing that is pure arrogance. Hubris is a color that suits no one well.

REALITY CHECK

We've worked with many wonderful, caring attorneys over the years. Their compassion and commitment to their clients serve as motivation to us to continue to join in the battle for those fighting for justice. But as much as we admire those qualities of a good plaintiff's attorney—caring, concerned, dedicated, tenacious, crusading, honorable, steadfast, passionate—sometimes these same traits can skew judgments when trying a case, preparing for a case, or even taking a case.

The injustice you may see in a potential client's circumstances may not be viewed the same by others. You may believe your plaintiff to be a good guy, but others may be turned off by his personality or even his laugh. The harm done to him you value in the millions, while everyone else doesn't understand what the big deal is.

Good facts in your mind could be bad facts to someone else. What's unimportant to you could be another's tipping or turning point.

We see it in every focus group we do—something overlooked or discounted by the attorney becomes a big deal in the eyes of a jury. In a recent medical malpractice case, there was one mention of a bed being broken down during labor and delivery. Never even crossed the attorney's minds that this minor detail would be significant. Turned out to be a huge point for the jurors that helped flip several to the plaintiff's side.

In another session, the plaintiff's attorney wanted to emphasize the relationship his client had with her son, to show that she was someone who was cared for and would be taken care of properly if they had the money to do so. Jurors immediately saw the son as money-grubbing and manipulative, trying to control his mother so that he could profit from what happened to her. Some jurors even suggested that the son might "get rid of" mom as soon as he got his hands on the verdict money. Each juror claimed to feel badly for the mother's injuries, but used the son as a reason why she should receive nothing.

Know what your problems are before heading into trial. Focus groups are an excellent way to identify the trouble spots in your case—not what *you* think they are, but what regular folk who haven't been entrenched in the file for months or years believe they are.

Sometimes the resources aren't there to do a focus group. Or maybe you haven't even taken the case yet. Look around, both inside and outside your office. You've got a vast number of opinions, different experiences, and points of view all around you. Ask your secretaries, paralegals, family members, neighbors, even your mail carrier. Better yet: go to the mall, a restaurant, the park and talk to strangers. Describe the case—minus party names—in a nutshell (good practice for keeping it simple). Then find out what they think. Get them to tell you more about that (good practice for voir dire). Learn all you can about your case before it becomes your case or before it becomes another loss.

Supplement H

Virtual Reality: How Jurors Finding Information Online Can Swing Your Case

Adapted from an article by

Lauren Havens, MSLS

In-the-Know Research, LLC

www.itk-research.com

lauren@itk-research.com

What You Don't Know Might Kill You

The online version of a city newspaper reports a severe-injury highway wreck with contested blame. Another report states that a civil trial will soon begin. Following the second report are readers' comments. One reader comments that he knew the plaintiff and claims he was a drug user and heavy drinker, so the wreck was "undoubtedly" the plaintiff's fault.

In fact, the plaintiff was neither a drinker nor a drug user, which would have been easy to prove to a jury. However, since the plaintiff's counsel had no idea there was such a comment online, it never occurred to her to bring it up in trial.

A juror on the case did a quick search on Google, found the comment, and conveyed the damaging information to the other jurors. On that basis the "hidden" fact caused a defense verdict. To this day the plaintiff's counsel probably has no idea why.

You can't fight what you don't know. This was an instance of how the online view of reality can easily warp a case.

Another perspective of reality found online, this time something true: a jury consultant, David Ball's partner Artemis Malekpour, discovered that the grown children of the dead parents in a wrongful-death case ran an organization that would have been found immoral and despicable by 95 percent of the venue's population. Ms. Malekpour discovered this with just a few minutes of searching Google. Next morning she notified her client, the plaintiff's counsel. Fortunately, the case had settled the previous evening, well into eight figures. Had the defense known what was easily accessible online, and what the jurors would have gone home and found online on the first evening of trial (or that the defense could have found a way to get into evidence), the defense would never have settled and at trial would have been hit with no more than a small verdict.

In a third case, a particular medical treatment would have prevented serious harm to a hospital patient. The plaintiff had strong proof and a strong chance of vanquishing the defense expert. One juror went home and found—online—a seemingly neutral and reliable source. It reported a virtual reality that the defense expert would not be able to say, since it could easily be shown to be false: that the treatment was highly experimental, dangerous, and almost never successful. But when the juror has seen it and you don't know about it, you don't bother to show that it's false. Virtual reality trumps true reality every time because virtual reality seems to jurors to be from a neutral source.

In a fourth case, the plaintiff's expert engineer never bothered to tell counsel that his engineering license in that state had been suspended. Yet a juror found that information online.

In a fifth case, a juror read somewhere online that there has to be a loss of consciousness for there to be brain damage. This bogus information agrees with the defense position. Since it's online, the juror regards it as neutral, and the result is a verdict reflecting no brain damage.

Jurors don't even have to go home to access information online. Mobile devices can get to the same online information, and bailiffs follow jurors neither home nor to the bathroom stall.

Legal minds can try to figure out how to deal with this easily available information, but they will fail to find a way to keep it out of trials. They will fail because technology moves faster than legal changes. No judge can intimidate jurors into abandoning their beloved computers and mobile devices. Short of sequestering jurors without mobile devices, access to online information is now a permanent, problematic part of what jurors regard as "evidence"—and often the most important part.

We have already seen juries make their decisions based not merely on facts and law, but on the virtual reality depicted online. This information revolution is only beginning. It will continue to evolve.

You can't fix the accessibility problem, but you must find out what's out there in the virtual world that relates to your case: people, "facts," the science,

Supplement H

and more. You can't grapple with what you don't realize is out there, and when the defense knows about it (or has planted it), or a juror finds it, you can be dead in the water without even knowing you've left land.

No one knows the current extent of the problem; the practice is almost entirely covert. However, anyone who has interviewed jurors after trial, or who knows human nature, realizes that the problem is significant and growing.

After all, many jurors care a lot less about the judge's orders than they do about making the right decision. They don't trust either side as much as what they consider to be the "neutrality" of the virtual world.

WHY YOU SHOULD DO THE RESEARCH

Jurors go online to find what they can about the parties and their families, witnesses, lawyers on both sides, matters of fact and science, standards in contention, and virtually everything else they can think of connected with the trial. What they find could be true, false, legally irrelevant yet damaging; it could be planted by the defense, some organization with an agenda, or just someone's kid. Your expert may have something on his Web site that could hurt you, such as "I have helped lawyers win even the weakest of cases." (Yes, one did. True story!)

The defense thoroughly searches for what jurors will find. What follows will show you how to do your own search better than the defense, except when they have the research professionally done.

There are two kinds of information that are particularly important:

1. Things jurors might discover that you need to know to protect your case

2. Things you can use against the defense.

WHAT YOU SHOULD RESEARCH

Put yourself in the shoes of a persistent, clever juror who is trying to find everything he can to help him persuade other jurors against you and your arguments. The juror will first look for everything he can find out about your client, your client's family, your fact and expert witnesses, your firm,[1] and everyone else who could possibly have something out there that would make you or your case look bad.

---

1. Be wary about what's on your firm's Web site. Most attorneys' sites are intended to market services, which means that your site may be the last thing you want jurors to see.

The juror will then try to find out if he can invalidate or validate the rules, standards, facts, science, statistics, and everything else you've presented. Even when the juror isn't hostile, he will likely seek information that confirms what he already believes and that he finds more comfortable to believe in. It's more comfortable for a juror who smokes to believe that smoking won't hurt *him*, that *he* won't get lung cancer, and that the expert witness giving testimony is really just overhyping the facts or even lying. If WebMD has an article that disagrees with statements you made in court and you don't know about it, you won't know that in trial you might have to find a way to explain why the point made by that article isn't true. You might as well stay home in the first place if you aren't going to search for this kind of contradictory information, because without making the arguments necessary to win over the juror who goes to WebMD (and other sites) for his medical information, all of your efforts can easily come to nothing.

Jurors can be hostile and want to crash your case. The hostile juror will intentionally seek out alternatives to your claims about the facts, science, the law, and almost anything else you say. You need to know what he'll find so you can deal with it. If you claim that your client sustained a brain injury, the juror will research brain injuries to answer questions like: Is brain damage (or RSD, or whatever) really permanent? Can a particular impact cause the claimed injury? Can the particular injury really disable a person?

Even the friendly juror can turn against you because of what she finds online.

So you have to research every aspect of the case that could cross a juror's mind. Remember that what you don't know can kill your case.

WHEN TO DO THE RESEARCH

When feasible, do your first round of thorough research to help you decide whether to accept the case. You don't want to work up a case and then find something online that makes the case unwinnable.

Before you sign any experts to the case, research them. Don't end the case before it starts by letting someone testify who has damaging information online, like a YouTube video capturing him yelling obscenities or making statements in an interview that contradict what he'll be claiming for this case.

Do the next round of online research as you learn more about the case and who the witnesses and jurors will be.

Within no more than a week of trial, conduct another thorough search to find anything that has cropped up since the first thorough search. If you do this more than a week or two in advance, you'll miss recent items, including items that the insurance company, defense, or defense-oriented professional and advocacy organizations plant for jurors to find. It's a nasty, but easy and deadly maneuver.

When you don't have the time or resources to be so thorough, at least research the potential client and family before you accept the case. Then do as much research as possible in the last few weeks before trial.

When deciding how to spend your very limited time in preparing for the trial, remember that even one bad finding can kill your case if you don't know about it.

WHO SHOULD DO THE RESEARCH?

Your goal is to find all that a purposeful, search-experienced juror might find. Do not assume that you know how to do this as well as some jurors do. A young juror who has grown up with a computer mouse in hand can be a far better searcher. However, don't assume that age is everything; for many senior citizens with time on their hands, online searching has replaced bingo as a source of entertainment.

Being able to perform good online research doesn't just come with knowing how to work a computer. Good researching skills require training, practice, and knowledge of how to find particular kinds of information. If you're like most people, this kind of research is not within your skill set, at least not yet. It may seem easy, but performing good online research takes more than just going to Google; it takes knowing where and how to find different kinds of information. You'll need to find and search a wide variety of sites.

If you do this work yourself or assign it to a staff person in your office, you must not allow a cursory job. The results of the research might be minor in many cases, but sooner or later—and not much later—it will be serious enough to ruin a case.

You're in a race with whichever jurors might have time, energy, and know-how to do this right. They won't find just your political contributions, which can take less than ten seconds. They'll also find an endless array of other details about your life—some true, some false, some about someone else with your name who seems like you. And that's just on the topic of *you*.

When a case has a lot at stake and you cannot afford to gamble, you need a professional who knows the kinds of things to alert you to. For smaller cases, your own efforts will be far better than nothing, as long as your efforts are well-informed—which is partly this paper's purpose. Nonprofessionals are much more likely than professionals to miss important things, but doing no research at all will miss a whole lot more.

How Long Does It Take?

Average time to adequately research an individual varies widely. A professional researcher needs roughly an hour to an hour and a half for each individual. Multiply that by 150 percent when a bright, well-instructed nonprofessional does it.

Jurors: For prospective jurors, a professional researcher can do a sweep for major pieces of information in as little as fifteen to twenty minutes per juror, though more time is safer. Allow a nonprofessional half again that much. Research on specific prospective jurors takes less time than everything else. This is because you can be relatively specific about what you are looking for, as compared to the open-ended challenge of researching the trial's cast of characters and topics. Think of the online research of prospective jurors as an in-depth, improved version of the old-fashioned "drive-by," which was rarely worth the time. Online research can reveal a lot more than a look at someone's front yard: family and financial situations, political and often church affiliations, criminal and professional organization records, and on and on.

Once the jury is seated, you should conduct more open-ended, thorough research about each juror. You need to find out everything you can about your seated jurors. You might even find something that shows that a hostile juror materially lied in jury selection to get on the jury. Carefully researching each seated juror is always important, but it is particularly important when you had little or no jury selection time. So allow roughly an hour to ninety minutes per seated juror when a professional does it, and half again that time when your staff person does it.

As important as this stage is, you don't want to do it yourself once trial has started.

How Do You Do It?

There are a few tools you need to begin.

Time

Set aside a block of uninterrupted time for researching. If you keep needing to answer phone calls or are otherwise distracted, the research will suffer. Be patient. The results of the research are well worth the time you put into it.

Internet Access and a Search Engine

A search engine searches the Web and finds Web pages that are relevant to your search terms. Each search engine will produce search results that are unique to that search engine.

General search engines include Google.com, Yahoo.com, Bing.com, and Altavista.com. These search engines will search all file formats that their Web crawlers have located on the Web. Web crawlers are computer programs that browse the Web in a methodical manner and allow indexing of the pages by the search engine.

Format-specific search engines include SlideFinder.net, which only searches PowerPoint slides. In general search engines, you can also specify a particular format to search for by using the Advanced Search function. File type options include Adobe PDF (.pdf), Microsoft Word (.doc), and Shockwave Flash (.swf).

Topic-specific search engines include Novoseek.com, which is a biomedical search engine. Using a topic-specific search engine will produce results narrowly specific to the topic, but it may not be where jurors look. So you may find results that are more applicable to the case at a general search engine even though the topic-specific search engine produces more informative results on the actual topic.

A Way to Take Notes

When you find information during your search, don't try to memorize it. You can copy important text and paste it into a program like Microsoft Word or Notepad. You can also use pencil and paper. Whatever your preference for taking notes, keep track of what you find and even where.

If you're performing an initial search into a possible juror or expert, you may want to revisit certain sites later, after the person has been assigned to the trial or as the trial draws near. If a juror updates his Facebook status or his Twitter account during the trial to say, "This sucker's going down!" you want to know about it.

The remainder of this supplement is in two parts:

Part A explains how to find information about *topics and concepts* that are in or are related to the case: the science, the medicine, similar situations, comparative verdict sizes, etc. Do not limit yourself to topics the defense may bring up. You need to know what the jurors will find and use.

Part B explains how to find online information about *people:* the parties, attorneys, witnesses, jurors, and everyone else involved.

Throughout this supplement are **In Practice** sections. They illustrate some of the research results for a sample case, a virtual-world research project. All of the people, businesses, and brands discussed are based on real examples, but the names have been changed.

The information and details in this article are representative samples. They do not constitute an exhaustive list of the information that was found.

In Practice:

Here are the skeleton facts of the case: Plaintiff Caleb Winters was driving his Penn Tumbler, an SUV, on an interstate in North Carolina. A Roadwell tire blew, and the Tumbler rolled over. Caleb was left with brain damage. No one else was hurt.

Winters is suing Roadwell, and Roadwell is blaming Penn.

PART A: RESEARCHING TOPICS OF THE CASE

Getting Started

Research the topics and ideas critical to the case separately from researching the people involved.

Jurors will look up information on topics discussed in the courtroom. Maybe they want clarification on what they heard. Maybe they're trying to figure out who's being deceptive. You need to know what they're going to find, whether it's true or not.

Time Involved

As with researching people, researching topics can vary in how much time is required. Sometimes you won't know how much research is necessary until you start the research.

Set aside at least three hours per topic, and you should be able to cover a lot of ground. You may need to do more research once those three hours are up, but you should have a much better idea of how much more time you need by then.

STEP 1: LIST EVERY TOPIC OR ITEM RELEVANT TO THE CASE

Start with those items, and as you research those and continue to think about the trial, you'll start to think of additional items that could prove useful to look into. To get you started, consider:

- What materials are involved?
    - *Ex:* Faulty brakes that led to a car crash
- Were companies or brands involved?
    - *Ex:* Nike or Coca Cola

- What Rules of the Road methods are we are depending on, and what is out there that could undermine our contentions about them?
    - *Ex:* A doctor violated a code of ethics that resulted in the patient's death.
    - *Ex:* A physician must do every step of a differential diagnosis.
- Is there disagreement about either of these that a juror may find?
- Are there different terms or concepts that won't be familiar to the jurors?
    - *Ex:* The chemical aspartame
- What is the accuracy of our positions on the science or other assertions that we are making?
    - *Ex:* Can someone really be hurt badly in a seven mph crash with little or no car damage?
    - *Ex:* Can early detection of a particular kind of cancer make any difference to long-term outcome?

In Practice:

Item 1—Tires and tire recalls

The item most central to this case is the issue of the tires, which were blamed for the accident. The tires become the first item we want to look into.

Item 2—Roadwell

Item 3—Penn and Penn Tumblers

We are suing Roadwell, the tire manufacturer, and Roadwell is suing Penn, the car manufacturer. These two companies and the information they are distributing will be items to research.

Item 4—Tire blowouts

We claim that badly designed tires caused the wreck. However, when they blew out, was there something that the driver could or should have done? We may be saying that the normal driver cannot handle a car during a blowout, but there could be something online that says "every driver has to know this." As a "ncutral" assertion, the online remark will most often trump your expert.

Item 5—Closed-head injury and brain damage

Due to the wreck, the plaintiff sustained a closed-head injury. This has a specific medical definition that the jurors are not likely to be familiar with. When jurors look for more information, what will they find on WebMD or a less reliable place that contradicts what we will be saying in the courtroom?

We can be claiming brain damage when the plaintiff did not actually hit his head, but instead received the damage via a contrecoup injury. A juror may find this site: http://www.braininjury.com/injured.html. The first page of the site talks about boxers and bowling balls hitting people. A juror may come to the conclusion that that level of impact is necessary for brain damage and that our claims are false. The site also sounds like no one can really tell if brain damage is permanent. Jurors are unlikely to read carefully, so a site like this can fill their heads with dangerous "facts" that can sink a case.

STEP 2: GO FIRST TO SITES THAT SEEM AUTHORITATIVE TO JURORS

These sites include WebMD, medical centers, government agencies, professional associations, companies, and any other organization that seems to offer authoritative information. These sites are helpful when they agree with you, but can cost you the case when they disagree or even seem to the careless reader to disagree.

If you are unsure if there are any authoritative sources, Step 3 below may help you find authoritative sources to consult.

Authoritative sites can be produced by:

A. The Government and News Organizations

You may have already looked into the laws and regulations relevant to the case. However, what will the juror find? The information online about a case may not be up-to-date or accurate. Also, the law in one state can be radically different in another, and some Web sites do not differentiate.

If the defendant in this case has made a point to provide information online about all of the cases that they have won in the past, jurors may think that they are in the right. Roadwell could have won ten cases out of a thousand, but if those ten cases are easy to find online and the ones that Roadwell lost are almost impossible to find, you need to know that.

Consider how easily you're able to find regulations or cases and how accessible they are for the average citizen and the juror. How clear is the information you find? Is it provided in a way that the average consumer can understand?

Government information can be found on several levels.

(i) Federal

If you're unsure of which agencies may have information that is relevant to your topics, enter search terms into a search engine like Google that specifies government sites.

Ex: "tire recalls" site: .gov

By indicating that you only want search results from sites that end in ".gov," you limit the search results to just government sites. If you only want educational sites, such as those affiliated with universities, you can specify that the site address end in ".edu."

You can also go to www.usa.gov to find government information. This will search a wide range of agencies and government levels, including some state sites.

In Practice:

Item 1—Tires and tire recalls

There are several federal regulatory agencies that could provide information relevant to the case.

- The National Highway Traffic Safety Administration (http://www.nhtsa.gov/) provides recall information relating to vehicles and equipment at http://www.recalls.gov/nhtsa.html. Additionally, www.recalls.gov is a site provided by the government for recalls of all consumer items, but since we are just looking for recalls relating to tires, the NHTSA section of the site is the area we need to look at right now.

- Safercar (http://www.safercar.gov/). The "tire recalls" area of recalls.gov redirected us to this site, which provides consumer information for safe driving; auto ratings; and recalls, auto and tire.

- The U.S. Department of Transportation's Federal Motor Carrier Safety Administration (http://www.fmcsa.dot.gov/) provides federal tire regulations, with which manufacturers must comply.

A lack of information or regulations can be just as informative as finding what you are looking for. We were unable to find information regarding the tire manufacturer's responsibility versus the consumer's responsibility.

Once a manufacturer sells a tire to the consumer, to what degree is the consumer responsible for the condition of the tire? If the consumer does not keep tire pressure at exactly the levels recommended by the tire manufacturer, is it the consumer's fault if the tire blows out? Make sure you're fighting only the defense and not the Internet.

Some of these questions will be answered, or attempted to be answered, during the course of the trial. However, consider how the juror will view these regulations—or lack of regulations—as well as how difficult any regulatory information is to find or how easily it is misunderstood when jurors find it online.

Item 2—Roadwell

Federal information about Roadwell is primarily limited to recall information. However, since the federal government does not clarify the relationship between the manufacturer and the consumer, this alerts us to look for what information the manufacturers, Roadwell and Penn, may be distributing that makes claims about the manufacturer-consumer relationship. Specifically, does Roadwell claim that responsibility passes to the consumer when items are purchased? Since there isn't government information to contradict claims like that, jurors may find the manufacturer's claims and assume that the manufacturer has the right to pass on that responsibility—regardless of the law in your venue. This is something that needs further investigation.

Item 4—Tire blowouts

In addition to providing information about tires, The National Highway Traffic Safety Administration (http://www.nhtsa.gov/) provides information on its site about research the agency has done into tire blowouts and car accidents.

Documents throughout the site mention that underinflation is often the cause of a tire blowout. The site is not so clear on exactly how underinflated a tire has to be before a blowout becomes a real risk. If the difference in tire pressure is only slightly under that of the manufacturer's recommendation, does that push the blame for the blowout onto the driver? Finding this indicates that we should search for what Roadwell has to say about responsibility for tire blowouts and underinflated tires.

One document on the NHTSA site states that while tire blowouts account for about 0.1 percent of crashes, the tire blowouts are generally caused by faulty tires. Severe underinflation of the tires could potentially cause problems. The emphasis on *severe* in the text of this document may help undermine the defense's potential argument that the crash was the result of underinflated tires. However, if Roadwell claims that the tires on the plaintiff's Penn were within the range of "severe underinflation," jurors may find that the fault was on the plaintiff, not the manufacturer. So another item we need to find out is what range Roadwell has claimed constitutes "severe underinflation."

The NHTSA does have recommendations for how to handle a vehicle if a tire blows out, and the Safercar site (http://www.safercar.gov/) also has instructions for how to safely maneuver the car if a tire blows out. The mere presence of such instructions can put more responsibility on your client ("she should have known") than you anticipate.

If the tire blew and the plaintiff had a few seconds to react before the vehicle rolled over, jurors may think he was responsible for the accident. People tend to think that they could have handled a situation better, so if the plaintiff did not take an action that he should have—as recommended on http://www.safercar.gov/—jurors may think to themselves that they would have known what to do and so would have handled the situation better, resulting in a less damaging wreck. If they come to that conclusion, you may have just lost the case. Even if you win, the verdict will be far smaller.

Item 5—Closed-head injury and brain damage

The National Library of Medicine and the National Institute of Health are two excellent medical authorities. They provide resources that will be very beneficial for this case:

- MedlinePlus (http://medlineplus.gov/) provides medical information in easy-to-understand language. It is intended for use by nonscientists and so may be one of the resources that jurors turn to most during this trial to learn more about the issues being discussed.

  In a MedlinePlus article on types of head injury, a juror could find the following about an open-head injury: "This usually happens when you move at high speed, such as going through the windshield during a car accident." Since the article mentions an open-head injury resulting from car accident but not a closed-head injury, jurors may come to the conclusion that only open-head injuries can happen during a car wreck.

- The National Institute of Neurological Disorders and Stroke (http://www.ninds.nih.gov/) provides in-depth information that is more scientific in its language than MedlinePlus. This site provides information that is particularly useful for detailing what kind of long-term effects could result from a brain injury, including Alzheimer's. This can help you, but it can also hurt you if you have not mentioned them in trial: jurors might think you don't know things you ought to.

  The MedlinePlus article on traumatic brain injuries links to an article available from the National Institute of Neurological Disorders and Stroke. This article is on traumatic brain injuries and may mislead some jurors: "Traumatic Brain Injury: Hope through Research." The title makes it seem as though the organization had found a way to alleviate the problems associated with traumatic brain injuries like the closed-head injury in this case. The article itself describes research that is being done, but does not allude to brain injury damage being curable. The article actually has an excellent section on the long-term effects of such an injury. If jurors look here for information, though, will they take the much more positive perspective of the title of the article, or will they read for more information and find the more sobering details?

There have been many popular literature articles in sources like *Reader's Digest* that spread misinformation about how the damaged brain can "compensate" in ways that restore normal functions. This common misconception is a real danger that attorneys must deal with in trial.

- PubMed (www.pubmed.gov) is a service of the National Library of Medicine and the National Institute of Health. This database contains scientific literature that may be too technical for most members of the public to understand. Since it is a medical resource that is easy to find when searching online, however, we looked at what was available that a juror might find and "understand." For example, using an MRI to detect abnormalities resulting from closed-head injuries has been found to be more sensitive than performing a CT scan. If the plaintiff underwent a CT scan instead of an MRI, maybe the assessment of the brain damage isn't right. So if you've said that your client's brain injury does not show on imaging, but you have done only a CT scan, the juror may think you avoided doing an MRI or more advanced scan out of fear that there will be no visible damage.

(ii) State

Some states have more information online than others.

In Practice:

Item 1—Tires and tire recalls and Item 3—Penn and Penn Tumblers

Penn did recall parts from the Penn Tumbler involved in this case. If the defense tries to say that the wreck was caused by that defect and not by the tires, we have the information necessary to defend against that claim: the plaintiff had the defective parts fixed prior to the accident. If you did not know about the recall, you would not think to make this important point, because it is relevant only to someone who knows about the recall—i.e., the juror and not you.

Item 2—Roadwell and Item 3—Penn and Penn Tumblers

Searches in state government Web sites for Roadwell and Penn allow us to locate state court documents and local news reports related to other cases in which the companies were involved. How will jurors regard them? The searches turn up a lot of court cases involving these companies. If the plaintiff knew about these previous court cases and bought the products despite the concerns these cases raise about them, doesn't he share some responsibility for the accident? "We all know these things roll over, so . . . ."

Both Roadwell and Penn are also involved with the national and state parks. Roadwell donated 10,000 acres to the state of Tennessee for a wilderness preserve. Are there any jurors from Tennessee or particularly fond of hiking? A large gift like this may make people more likely to believe that a company did not intend harm with the tires it produced. "If Roadwell made such a generous donation to Tennessee, surely Roadwell cares about the community, is a good corporate citizen, and didn't mean to do anything wrong." You can deal with this, but only if you know about it.

Are there jurors who have a fondness for these companies because of the donations that they have made? These donations may be more problematic if the case was taking place in Michigan, Pennsylvania, or Tennessee, where the companies have made significant contributions. Still, North Carolina citizens who are jurors in this case may still be influenced by the companies even if no significant contribution was made locally. When researching potential jurors, look for any who are from or spent significant time in the states where Roadwell and Penn are most visible in the communities. You can find out in jury voir dire; when you find one, ask them about their view of the company as a corporate citizen: Good? Bad?

Item 5—Closed-head injury and brain damage

The Brain Injury Association of America (BIAA) has charters in forty states, including North Carolina, the location of the trial. Though not a government association itself, BIAA works with government agencies and commercial entities. The organization provides services for individuals who have had a brain injury and advocates for brain injury victims.

Because it is not a trial-neutral group, if your medical expert belongs to the BIAA, jurors will perceive him as being partisan, not a neutral expert, which can be problematic.

One of the sponsors of the Brain Injury Association of North Carolina (BIANC) is the legal firm that the plaintiff's counsel works for. Because of this sponsorship, the defense may claim that information presented by the plaintiff is tainted. To prevent this, any information from the Brain Injury Association should be confirmed through additional, authoritative sources.

(iii) Local

Local government sites vary widely in what's available online. Urban areas tend to have more information online than more rural areas. If you're working with a more rural audience, check out resources provided by nearby urban areas that may supplement local information.

The information found on local sites will highlight news that is important to that community in addition to providing local news stories that are not available on larger, more national sites. If a local news site features national reports about the recession and other stories about local layoffs, the community is hurting and may be influenced if the defendant provides many of the local jobs.

In Practice:

Item 5—Closed-head injury and brain damage

By searching local news sources, we found that two teenagers recently sustained severe brain damage after a bicycle accident. Duke University and local churches were part of a local effort to help the families of the boys pay the medical bills. News coverage of the boys' recovery notes that though their brain damage was significant, there does appear to be some healing. This may lead to the belief by some jurors that the plaintiff may heal from his brain injury.

The UNC School of Medicine and the Duke School of Medicine have a lot of information available on brain injuries. However, while anyone can search the school's Web site and find abstracts of relevant documents, access to the documents themselves is restricted to individuals affiliated with the schools. People could go to the medical library at either school for information since such libraries often allow members of the public to use the library collection. This would require that the individual physically travel to the library. The information gathered from the libraries is less likely to be biased or false.

Though the libraries are available to the public, most people will not find it convenient to travel to the libraries for research. Instead, they are likely to rely on information publicly available online, which can be very difficult to distinguish as being authoritative or misleading.

B. Associations and Professional Organizations

These can include professional organizations that license individuals, like medical boards, or groups that advocate within a field for particular standards and practices.

In Practice:

Item 3—Penn and Penn Tumblers

The United Auto Workers has members working for Penn. Most of the information on the union's site relates to their financial negotiations for Penn workers.

The United Auto Workers and Penn joined forces for an interesting maneuver. They formed the National Joint Committee on Health and Safety (NJCHS), which provided money to researchers to do certain kinds of studies and to report the results (aka supported studies). Several of the researchers involved in this venture have a well-documented history of receiving money from companies without disclosing that information before publishing the results of their work. When a researcher takes money from oil, tobacco, and auto companies to produce reports that show that workers at those companies, or consumers of those products, are not being harmed by exposure to the products, the research is likely biased and not in the best interest of the public.

Are any researchers involved in supported studies also serving as experts in this case? When one is, linking him to supported studies and showing how the studies are misleading will undermine his credibility.

This is the kind of information the plaintiff in our case can use to demonstrate a history of intentional harm. It also helps to show that the evidence the defense provides is flawed because companies influenced researchers to report particular kinds of results.

If jurors find these studies, and our legal team does not reveal that the studies were performed with a particular agenda in mind, jurors may rely on their inaccurate conclusions.

Item 4—Tire blowouts

The Tire Industry Association produces guidance on tire manufacturing. The group published Passenger and Light Truck Tire Conditions Manual (2005), which would help consumers gain knowledge about how to maintain tires and discusses issues like how to handle a tire blowout. However, the manual is not provided online or for free. The manual costs close to $300, which puts it out of range for most consumers. While this manual does provide information on standards for the tire industry, it is not reasonable to expect that consumers would have access to this information, which means that consumers should not be expected to obey any "standard" way to handle a tire blowout described in this manual.

Item 5—Closed-head injury and brain damage

There is a Brain Injury Association with a branch in North Carolina. The Web site for the North Carolina branch provides information on brain injuries, resources for additional information, links to government information, and even provides a free online course to help those in North Carolina who provide services to those with brain injuries.

This is the kind of Web site that we want jurors to go to. If you mention it in trial for some legitimate purpose, such as by asking in voir dire if a prospective juror has been to that site, jurors may go there. It is, of course, unethical to motivate jurors to go there. But if you have a legitimate reason for asking the question, you should be on safe ground. It is legitimate to probe into what jurors know and where they have looked. Just make sure none of your experts are associated with this group (*see* ii. State, Item 5, above).

C. Companies Responsible for the Product or Service

In Practice:

Item 1—Tires and tire recalls and Item 2—Roadwell

Roadwell maintains a Web site that provides information about Roadwell products. The SB380 tire that was on the plaintiff's Penn Tumbler was recalled in 2008, but the Roadwell Web site still states: "Whatever the season, whatever the road surface, count on the SB380 to deliver performance on demand." There is no recall notice on the page with the item description. Is this negligent of the company?

There is recall information, including the SB380 recall, on other pages within the Web site, but they are more difficult to find. Can a consumer be reasonably expected to be aware of the recall if there is no notice on the item description page?

If the defense argues that the plaintiff should have known about the recall and taken appropriate actions, we need to demonstrate how difficult this information is to find. We also need to find what other ways Roadwell may have distributed recall information, such as through a mailing list to consumers who signed up voluntarily or were automatically enrolled when the product was purchased.

Item 3—Penn and Penn Tumblers

Penn also maintains a Web site that provides information about the company and its products. Included on the site is information for owners of the vehicles. There is some recall information available to users who enter their truck's VIN into a provided field. There is also an owner's guide for each vehicle, and in the guide for the Penn Tumbler, there is a very large warning that utility vehicles like the Penn Tumbler are more susceptible to rollovers than other vehicles.

Penn will want to argue that consumer information like this moves the responsibility for the wreck to the consumer. It also allows Roadwell to argue that Penn, rather than Roadwell, was responsible because Penn's vehicle rolled over easily.

D. Web Sites that Jurors May Think Are Authoritative, Whether They Actually Are or Not

These kinds of sites can include medical resources sponsored by drug companies or other sites that appear to provide legitimate information, but have some kind of bias or ulterior motive—or that are just based on ignorance.

In Practice:

Item 5—Closed-head injury and brain damage

WebMD (www.webmd.com) is a commercial site with its own agenda, but many people go to this site before going anywhere else for medical information because they believe it to be a neutral information source. Unfortunately, some information on WebMD is faulty, and the article on concussions—which was one of the top results when we searched the site for closed-head injuries—is a bit troubling. The article states that concussions do not include injuries where there is bleeding under the skull or into the brain. This contrasts with an entry in the Mayo Clinic Web site, which discusses bleeding around the brain. Confusion on any medical topic is more likely to help the defense than the plaintiff, so with contradictory information out there, you have some clarifying to do.

The Mayo Clinic (www.mayoclinic.com) is a not-for-profit organization, and the Web site is another popular source of medical information. In addition to providing information online, the Mayo Clinic provides medical services at several locations in the United States. The Mayo Clinic is one of the resources that MedlinePlus refers users to, so the referrals from MedlinePlus have the government's seal of approval, which WebMD does not.

Jurors may not be able to tell the difference between a Web site with more accurate information, like the Mayo Clinic, and one with the potential for less accurate information, like WebMD. Finding the differences now, before the trial starts and jurors find this information, will prepare you to defend against the inaccuracies that jurors may find.

STEP 3: FOR EACH ITEM, CONDUCT A BROAD SEARCH

As with the initial search for individuals, begin with a broad search and catch any large information pieces. You don't have to conduct a search for each individual item you noted in Step 1, but keep those items in mind as you start to formulate your searches. You may need to search for synonyms of those items, broaden or narrow the search topic, or even combine multiple items within the same search.

In Practice:

Searching for "tires" would result in too large a search. Instead, we did an initial search for *Roadwell Penn Tumbler tire recalls*. This combined the concepts of Roadwell, Penn, and tire recalls. Be flexible in how you search. Combining concepts may lead to the discovery of previous incidents or items that are relevant to your current case.

As you search each item, keep these questions in mind:

A. What and How Much Information Is Available?

If a company ceased production on a sewing machine, have they removed the user's manual from the Web site or are they still supporting customers who bought the machine before production ceased?

In Practice:

Item 1—Tires and tire recalls

We found news articles and documents relating to the large series of recalls and suits over Roadwell tires on Penn automobiles. The legal team has hopefully already examined these documents, but such documents are also easy for jurors to find. If Roadwell and Penn have publicized the cases that they won while the ones they lost are more difficult to find, it may appear to jurors that the companies won a majority of the cases. Even if that isn't true, it could influence jurors in this case.

When researching, we need to pay attention not just to the cases that we found, but to how they are portrayed, whether they are continuing, if people are still paying attention to the trials and their aftermath, and what kinds of comments people posted (and continue to post) to the Web sites. The comments around the time of the cases were very angry, but there has been very little since the cases were resolved. If they were so easily forgotten, jurors may have forgotten as well. Be alert throughout the trial for doors the companies open to letting this information in.

B. Who or What Is Providing the Information and Why?

Be alert for intentions, biases, and attempts to deceive or persuade. Even without the intention to deceive, information on a Web site may be incorrect or skewed.

This is *extremely* important. If you're trying to prove that a drug company knew a drug was not safe, there may be claims being distributed from apparently neutral sources that the drug is safe. The pharmaceutical company may be behind the dissemination of the information, paying researchers to report favorable assessments—and don't think insurance companies are above such shenanigans.

In Practice:

Item 1—Tires and tire recalls and Item 2—Roadwell

Sadly, one of the main Web sites that posted information about the 2,000 recalls seems to have been created by a "McLitigator" group, a group of attorneys hoping to take advantage of the publicity about the danger of the recalled tires from Roadwell. By creating a Web site that tracked and publicized the coverage of recalled tires from this company, they encouraged people who had Penn cars and/or Roadwell tires to come hire them. If you're not a part of one of these firms, let the jurors know in jury selection.

Item 1—Tires and tire recalls and
Item 4—Tire blowouts

Other Web sites provide information on blowouts, how to avoid them, and how to handle them when they occur. Some of these sites are provided by less-than-scrupulous or just unsophisticated plaintiff's teams. These sites are badly disguised infomercials, purporting to provide safety information. Well-designed sites, on the other hand, can provide good information without appearing to troll (*see* section 9-4-5, p. 262).

Item 2—Roadwell

The warranty information for Roadwell tires includes safety information—but the warranty can be found only online. The warranty assumes that once the consumer has accepted the tires, the consumer is entirely responsible for their condition. The consumer must "properly maintain" the tires according to the inflation levels stated in the warranty. If he does not, the consumer is responsible in the event of a tire blowout. There is no range of recommended inflation levels, but rather a specific psi. This means that the slightest variation can result in a claim that the consumer did not "properly maintain" the tires.

The defense can use the well-documented warnings and warranty instructions to argue that the poor tire maintenance moved the responsibility for the accident from Roadwell to the plaintiff. In many situations, this kind of information shows up only online. You need to know it's there in order to know you have to counter it. Did the company provide the information to protect the consumer or the company?

Item 5—Closed-head injury and brain damage

One of the first search results in a broad search for *closed-head injury* is a Web site sponsored by a plaintiff's legal team. The site seems to be providing medical information, but since it is sponsored by a law firm, the information may appear to be biased. The site also provides information on how to take legal action, so jurors may think that all plaintiff's attorneys—including you—are out to take advantage of other people's misfortunes. If your evidence mirrors the wording on these sites, jurors who see the resemblance can mistrust you for it.[2]

---

2. As chapter nine points out, helpful information on your Web site can help establish your credibility as a decent person. But when the information seems mainly to serve the purpose of helping you get cases, it has the opposite effect.

STEP 4: NARROW THE SEARCH BY FOLLOWING LEADS DISCOVERED DURING THE BROADER SEARCH IN STEP 2

In Practice:

Item 1—Tires and tire recalls and Item 2—Roadwell

After finding that there had been a series of cases in 2000 relating to Roadwell tires, we looked for continued coverage and recalls. We found that the tire on the plaintiff's car had been recalled and that there have been several suits over that tire model. Though the recalls are posted on official recall sites, they are not covered on Web sites that consumers often frequent like CNN.com or local news sites. The consumer would have to go to a site that focuses on recall information, which is far outside the range of daily activities for the average consumer. If we can show how difficult it was to find such recall information, we can make jurors realize how unreasonable it is to expect the plaintiff to have been aware that an issue even existed. And you can show how easy it would have been for the company to have gotten that information into the consumer's hands more directly.

Although the recall Web sites are out of the way for the average consumer, the customer could sign up at the point of sale for a service that would notify him or her of any recalls. We cannot find online whether a particular individual signed up for this service, but if the defense can show that the plaintiff was offered the opportunity to sign up and refused to do so, it may be very unfavorable for us. Once you know this, you know enough to get your client to explain that he never knew about it. If you don't know about it, in deliberations a juror who found it online will say, "He was supposed to sign up…." Etc.

STEP 5: SEARCH POPULAR SITES THAT JURORS WILL GO TO

Jurors won't just be going to authoritative sites. Many popular sites have dubious information, but since these are places where jurors will get information, you need to know what's on those sites.

While searching, keep in mind that it isn't just news or other information that you find that could be important to the case. The comments that users post to articles can give you information about how people feel about the topic.

A. News Sites

- National or worldwide news sources
    - *Ex:* CNN.com or BBC.com

- Local or regional news sources
    - *Ex*: Local paper or television station's Web site

Be alert to differences in how items are reported on a nationwide scale and on the local level. News sources and editorials in San Francisco will have very different tones when discussing gay marriage than in a conservative community in the South. For example, a conservative community may focus on how much controversy there is about the issue and include quotes from local religious leaders who are against gay marriage. A more liberal community may have less of a religious focus and highlight pending legislation and the efforts of local organizations that support gay marriage rights.

In Practice:

Item 1—Tires and tire recalls

When we searched news sources for the Raleigh/Durham area in North Carolina, where this case will take place, one of the first results was about how a recent series of recalls would mean layoffs at a local Penn plant. Safety may be very important to each individual, but financial security should also be kept in mind when working with members of this community. A juror may side with the defense because he thinks his community would be hurt by a multi-million-dollar verdict against the company.

Item 3—Penn and Penn Tumblers

Penn has been in the news a lot in the past couple of years since the company turned to the government for financial assistance during the economic recession. The chief executive officer of Penn flew in a private plane to Washington, DC, to ask for government bailout money in November 2008. The company received a lot of bad publicity at that time that jurors will likely still remember. The news stories are also still in the top results when searching for company information. If the juror had forgotten about that bad publicity, she will be easily reminded if she searches online.

B. YouTube

In Practice:

Item 5—Closed-head injury and brain damage

There are many videos on YouTube relating to brain injuries. Many are medical in nature, and some have specific audiences like attorneys or people without a medical background. Some of the videos provide false information, like how brain damage isn't permanent and the patient can improve by "being positive." You need to know exactly what these videos say so you can counter it, when necessary, in trial.

C. Wikipedia

In Practice:

Item 2—Roadwell and Item 3—Penn and Penn Tumblers

When we examine the Wikipedia article on Roadwell, we find something very interesting. The article contains absolutely no information about any recalls. In fact, it's written like an ad for Roadwell and doesn't contain negative information about the company, links to court cases, or negative consumer reports.

There is an article in Wikipedia for "Roadwell and Granger tire controversy." Granger is a small tire maker that Roadwell owned during the recalls. Even though Roadwell was the parent company during the recalls, Roadwell's name is scarce in the article. By playing up the controversy and shifting blame from Roadwell to Granger, Roadwell maintains an untainted name, even though the two were part of the same company.

Item 5—Closed-head injury and brain damage

When searching for information on closed-head injuries, we find an article on head injuries on Wikipedia. This article is really troubling and could lead to misconceptions by the jurors. It states that if someone sustains a brain injury and does not have an abnormality of the brain already, that person should fully recover. The only long-term effect listed is: "persons who sustain head trauma resulting in unconsciousness for an hour or more have twice the risk of developing Alzheimer's disease later in life." You need to assume that jurors will read and believe this article.

The Wikipedia article "traumatic brain injury" is more informative, but the language in that article is more difficult to understand because of so many medical terms. That makes the article mentioned just above far more dangerous to you.

D. Social Networking Sites Such as Facebook and MySpace

In Practice:

Item 2—Roadwell and Item 3—Penn and Penn Tumblers

The Facebook profiles for Penn and Roadwell present another reason to research potential jurors before the case begins. Each company has several Facebook profiles, and there are hundreds of fans of each company and their vehicles. By maintaining a positive social presence online, Penn and Roadwell may be wooing a certain part of the population, a part of the population that could be on the jury. Don't let them on yours.

E. Local Government Web Sites

You may have already found this kind of information in Step 2, but use this as an opportunity to make sure you searched these sites well. Here you're not necessarily looking for government ordinances or regulations. Instead, look for news, events, or other kinds of information that would be updated regularly.

Some local governments will e-mail information to people if they sign up for updates via an RSS feed (usually through an option on the main page). When you take on a case, you may consider signing up for the RSS feed from the local government site.

STEP 6: SEARCH LOCATION-SPECIFIC RESOURCES

Some sites and information may be available only to the local population. Don't miss these resources if you're researching from a state or municipality different from that of the potential jurors. These sites contain more of the kinds of information discussed above, and given who sponsors these kinds of sites, the information can seem far more credible than on other sites—making it all the more important that you know about it. In other words, it's not just a matter of what jurors find, but where they find it.

Location-specific resources include the following.

A. Libraries

Libraries are one of the most important location-specific resources. Public libraries often have online catalogs that people can search, regardless of whether the individual has access to the library itself. By searching the catalog, you can get an idea of whether the library has print resources that would be useful to jurors during the trial.

Libraries usually have restricted access to electronic resources due to licensing agreements with the providers of the resources. If you have a library card, you can access the resources. If you do not have a library card, you may not be able to see all of the resources, but by searching the library's Web site and even calling the library for more information, you can get some idea of what is available to people in the area. The library can often provide a wealth of information, so do not discount its importance.

In Practice:

This case takes place in North Carolina; the accident occurred in North Carolina, and jurors will be residents of the state. We need to know what resources are available to North Carolina residents that would not be available to other people. In addition to checking publicly available resources like CNN.com, people may access these location-specific resources, which can often provide more information than what is publicly available. Instead of being limited to viewing only a few free news stories from *The Wall Street Journal*, for instance, residents may have access to the complete archives because the local library has a subscription.

North Carolina residents can access NCLive, which allows access to *The Wall Street Journal* and other newspapers, encyclopedias, and databases. Access to NCLive is provided by the state library system, and all residents with a card to a public library in the state can access NCLive.

Item 1—Tires and tire recalls and Item 2—Roadwell

NCLive has many news stories about Roadwell tire recalls. This sets the stage for highlighting Roadwell's history of ignoring widely known defects, which endangers the public and makes each juror aware that this company is looking out for itself at the expense of the people. NCLive also has stories that detail how the Tumbler vehicle in particular is known for having trouble with its tires and that a few years ago Penn temporarily cut its ties with Roadwell because of the recalls and suits that were occurring.

If the trial was taking place in another state, jurors may not be able to access this information. Not all states provide services like NCLive, and where similar services are available, the resources are different. Just like the resource collections available at multi-campus universities, the items selected for inclusion differ drastically from one location to another.

Item 5—Closed-head injury and brain damage

While conducting a search of *The Wall Street Journal*, which is available through NCLive, we find an article that reports that researchers are increasingly finding decreased functioning due to brain injuries that did not show up until years after the initial injury. Run this by your expert as potential material for trial. While a Google search may find this or similar articles, access to NCLive ensures that the user can see the full text of the article. The full article is not always available when conducting a search in Google or other free sites.

B. Historical Societies or Collections

These may be found on chamber of commerce Web sites or can be listed on the local library's site.

C. Museums

These, too, can often be found on the Web site for the chamber of commerce, but they can also be found by searching Google and specifying the geographic location.

In addition to its regular exhibits, the museum may also offer online exhibits and have an in-house library or archives.

In Practice:

Item 3—Penn and Penn Tumblers

Thankfully, this case is not taking place in Michigan, where Penn has its headquarters. The George Penn Museum in Michigan is one way that the Penn company tries to promote a positive image of an all-American company that has the public good at heart. You need to find and study Penn's public face online so you deal appropriately with it in trial. Some companies establish philanthropic foundations jurors can learn about online. You need to know about them. Sometimes you can even find that what the company did as a defendant conflicts with the foundation's goals.

D. Public Colleges and Universities

Like local public libraries, colleges and universities can provide a wealth of resources to the local population. If the college or university is public, any citizen of the state can use its resources in the libraries. Due to licensing restrictions, only people affiliated with the university can access electronic resources off-campus, so jurors would need to physically go to the library to access its electronic resources. Even on campus, some electronic resources are restricted to people within particular departments.

Search the library catalog to see what is available even if you cannot access the item itself. The catalog record can provide information about the resource.

Also, libraries at universities often have more financial resources than local public libraries, so they may also have online exhibits available as part of their public service initiatives.

If you search these sites from your own computer, do not think that access is blocked to jurors just because it's blocked to you. Public universities have a mission to serve the public, not just students, so public computers are provided on campus for members of the public to use, and many non-student jurors will have access from off-campus because they are affiliated with the university.

In Practice:

Item 1—Tires and tire recalls and Item 2—Roadwell

The Southern Historical Collection at a local university contains transcripts of hearings and other documents about Roadwell. Many of the documents can only be accessed by going to the library on campus, but some items are available online.

Item 5—Closed-head injury and brain damage

A search of the library catalog for the University of North Carolina at Chapel Hill led us to resources from the Rancho Los Amigos Medical Center, one of the most prominent centers for rehabilitation. The center published easily understood information on brain damage (http://www.rancho.org/patient_education/bi.pdf) that would be very useful to jurors. That clarity, plus the dual endorsement of the very credible center and the equally credible university, can give this information extraordinary weight with jurors. If it conflicts with what you're offering, you can be in trouble. Many jurors will give credence to virtually anything listed in a university library's catalogue, mistakenly thinking that university libraries screen for truth. This is one reason jurors go to such catalogues in the first place. Ignore what they can find at your peril.

STEP 7: USE FOCUS GROUPS TO PURSUE TOPIC-SPECIFIC RESOURCES

Ultimately, the question is this: "What topics are jurors likely to research for themselves? At the top of the list are the most in-dispute topics in trial, such as the medicine, the science, statistics, and the technology. But you'll never guess them all. This leads to what has now become one of the most important reasons for doing focus groups.

When you do a focus group, allow the focus-jurors plenty of opportunity to ask what more they'd like to know. You can be pretty sure that your real jurors will want to know the same things, many of which you will not have anticipated. So you'll know what they're likely to research online. You need to get there first.

PART B: RESEARCHING INDIVIDUALS

Getting Started

In general, topics are harder to research than people because there is no clear-cut, concise list of topic resources, but you can look up your name and anyone else's using pretty much the same resources.

Do not research individuals and topics at once. Separating them reduces the chance that you will get sidetracked.

The steps below show you how to get as much people-information as possible in the shortest possible time.

In Practice:

More about the case: Research the medical and tire experts.

When searching for this information, if you find a great page on the topic of brain damage, don't go there now. Make a note of it for later; don't do both at the same time. Even the best of researchers misses important information when trying to research both people and topics at once.

Remember, we are not looking for information that will be apparent during the trial. We are mainly seeking **intrusive information**, true or false, that can hurt us. We're also looking for useful information that the defense has withheld or that they are not aware of, such as how the defense expert engineer has lost his license in another state.

When time is limited, do at least a quick search of your own experts for any online traps such as someone slamming your medical expert on Craigslist (www.craigslist.org) or a site like RateMDs (www.ratemds.com).

STEP 1: LIST INDIVIDUALS CRITICAL TO THE CASE

Make sure you know who is important to the case so that you know who you need to research. When you know how much work you have ahead of you, you have a finish line to work toward.

You may find it is easier to research in groups or simply go person by person.

In Practice:

The people we need to research for this case:

Plaintiff's side

        Plaintiff—Caleb Winters

        Plaintiff's lead counsel—Bob Jones

        Plaintiff's co-counsel—Sam Waters

        Plaintiff's first brain damage expert—Daphne Cash

        Plaintiff's second brain damage expert—James Wagner

        Plaintiff's tire expert—Cameron Frank

Defense's side (Roadwell)

    Defense attorney—Frank Garron

    Defense's brain damage expert—Larry Kane

    Defense's tire expert—Matt Nisco

It is often easier to research people in a similar grouping—such as medical experts—one after another since many of the resources are specific to particular groups. So we do all of the research for medical experts before moving on to the tire experts, for whom we check a different set of resources.

This strategy may not work for you, but you may want to try it, especially until you become familiar with how to do this kind of research.

STEP 2: SEE IF THE INDIVIDUAL HAS A PERSONAL OR BUSINESS WEB SITE

You can usually find these sites by searching for the person's name and geographic location.

Ex: "Frank Garron Raleigh"

Information found on these sites is provided by that individual, so it has his or her seal of approval. This doesn't mean that the information reflects well on the individual. There can be some pretty embarrassing—and harmful—information on the site.

The statements on the site and how the site looks can make an impression on jurors. It can also give you ideas of what additional searches to perform.

In Practice:

Plaintiff's first brain damage expert—Daphne Cash

Oh, goodness. The plaintiff's brain damage expert, Daphne Cash, has a Web site that is positively flamboyant. It's bright pink, like a certain medicine, and there's a lot of flash and sparkle.

Daphne is a TV personality, a celebrity psychiatrist, so the flamboyance makes some sense. She is likely to be recognized by the jurors since she has appeared on television shows and has written popular books.

You've almost certainly seen her site before doing this research, and you know what she's like; otherwise, you wouldn't have hired her. Take a second look, though, with fresh eyes. A woman like this might be brilliant on the stand, but what will the jurors think when they see a site like this? Will they be prejudiced against her before she even gets the chance to speak?

Even if you've worked with Daphne before and researched her then, research her again for this case. Daphne makes a lot of television appearances and public comments, so you need to make sure that nothing embarrassing has appeared since the last time you researched her. For example, Daphne recently made public demeaning comments about a woman who gave birth to multiple babies: "Only animals have litters."

This kind of problem should show you the wisdom of researching each potential expert before signing her up.

Plaintiff's second brain damage expert—James Wagner

Again, you've probably already seen this site and know something about James Wagner. However, take a second look, and try to think about how a juror would see this site. If there are no inappropriate comments on the site, what else does the site tell the juror about this guy's credentials? Wagner's site makes a positive impression on people trying to figure out if he really knows what he's talking about. While Daphne's site portrays a dramatic personality, his site is entirely professional.

* * *

Business networking and personal social Web sites, like LinkedIn and Facebook, may have links to the expert's publications or things that he recommends. When they are relevant to the case, you need to find out what the documents say. You don't need to read everything the person has written word-for-word, but review everything to be sure there are no land mines. (For more information on publications, *see* Step 9: Miscellaneous, B Publications.)

In Practice:

Plaintiff's second brain damage expert witness—James Wagner

Research every potential witness. Research every expert before committing to having him in the case. Some of the online information about James Wagner could destroy his credibility, so if we find the information before signing him on, we can make a more informed decision about whether to take on that risk.

James Wagner posted on his Web site some of the articles that he has written. In one, he states that his teacher and mentor was prominent psychiatrist Richard Walker. Not being familiar with this individual, we looked up Walker and found that he had been an expert witness during a rather famous trial. Walker had helped to defend a man who murdered a member of one of America's most prominent political families.

Some jurors could turn against Wagner for this. If the mentor he brags about was willing to testify on the behalf of an "obviously" guilty man, might Wagner be just as "misleading" for money? This is especially dangerous when there are seemingly credible online comments about the defense in the earlier case having hired "liars" to get their client off.

If these items had been found after Wagner had been signed to the case, all we could do is defend against it. If we find the information and still decide to sign him to the case, we can prepare for what jurors may find. We might even be able to remove any damaging items before jurors have the chance to find them. Since Wagner had posted this comment on his own Web site, he can probably remove the comment before we sign him to the case.

STEP 3: USE A SEARCH ENGINE TO DO A BROAD SEARCH FOR THE INDIVIDUAL'S NAME TO SEE WHAT IS IMMEDIATELY VISIBLE ABOUT THAT PERSON

For example, enter into the search engine Google (with the quotation marks): "James Wagner"

Performing the search with the quotation marks searches for the phrase exactly as it is entered. Such a search will not find results with a middle initial (James I. Wagner) or a nickname (James "Jimmy" Wagner).

Repeat the search without the quotations to see any results that might include a middle initial, which the search with quotations would not have caught.

Then search with a full middle name.

You may consider adding additional terms to help narrow the results to the individual that you're looking for, such as including the state in which the person works. Keep in mind, though, that the jurors may not think to do that initially. So if you start that way, you might miss things that the juror's more general search would have found.

In Practice:

Plaintiff's second brain damage expert—James Wagner

When we were searching for James Wagner without quotations, we also found results on his son. Finding information on family members can be useful. James Jr. works for an animal wellness company. This company does not handle human medical issues or do brain imaging work for animals. If it had, however, James Senior may be seen as having a vested interest in giving testimony that would help his son. We're safe this time, but the next case may not be free of such conflicts.

If we think that jurors could be confused between James Senior and James Junior, we could bring up the difference during voir dire. If James Junior can edit the online profile, which some companies do not allow on the company Web site, we could insert information to clarify that James Senior is an expert in the field, not James Junior.

A. Watch for People with the Same Name as the Individual You're Searching For

Jurors may mistake the individual involved with the trial with one of these false hits, so be alert for them.

In Practice:

Plaintiff's lead counsel—Bob Jones

Although there is a lot of information available about Bob Jones online, his name is so common that a multitude of the wrong Bob Joneses hide a lot of true hits for the Bob Jones in your case. Adding geographic information or other relevant terms to the search helps narrow the results to the Bob Jones we're looking for.

> *Ex: Bob Jones North Carolina*
>
> *Ex: Bob Jones (attorney OR law)*

Bob seems to be an upstanding citizen, and the false hits that turn up in a broad search like this are thankfully not problematic for the case. The false hits are for a Presbyterian minister from the nineteenth century and for a famous musician. There are others, like an artist, but these account for the bulk of the results. If the false results were mainly associated with people like serial rapists or dirty politicians, there could be problems.

There are potential problems to be aware of: When we enter the attorney's name into Google, the first result is for a law firm, but not the law firm that our Bob Jones works for. There is also a listing of an attorney named Bob Jones who was disbarred for stealing client's money. In voir dire, you'd want to assure jurors it's not you—but you would not know you had to if you didn't know this information was easily available.

B. Watch for Biases or Conflicts of Interest

These could be biases that the individual already seems to have, or they could be outside factors that could seem to affect his truthfulness on the stand.

In Practice:

Roadwell's tire expert—Matt Nisco

Matt Nisco has reason to favor Roadwell. He has worked for several tire companies, including Roadwell. He served on a task force set up by Roadwell to examine what health risks workers may have been exposed to while working in the company's factories. Although the United Auto Workers were involved in that study, the conclusions of the research were heavily in favor of Roadwell, who paid for the research. That can undermine Nisco's credibility. So don't rely on a juror finding it; elicit it yourself in trial.

STEP 4: SEARCH FOR FINANCIAL INFORMATION

It can be useful to know about a witness's unusually extravagant lifestyle. For example, a defense expert maintains a lavish home with a four-car garage, swimming pool, and huge estate that can all be viewed in Google Earth. Those pictures make it easy to impeach him when he makes his usual bogus claim of being in court for the sake of truth instead of further riches.[3] Try not to hire experts who can be similarly trapped. All a juror needs is the expert's home address, and she can probably find good pictures of the lavish home.

Look up the tax records for the residential addresses, which can usually be found by searching for the individual's name on the county's tax site. Not all counties have electronic records available, but many do. Accessing records that are not freely available online could require the kind of resources that only a professional researcher would have or require actions offline like making phone calls or physically going to an office. So you don't need to worry that a juror might find them.

Business tax records will not provide much information about the individual's finances unless he is an owner or a shareholder in an S-corporation. Yet it can be revealing to see where the business is or what it looks like from the satellite and street views of Google maps. While you can use Google Earth to view areas as well, you must download the Google Earth application before being able to use it, so first be sure your computer can handle it; not all of them can. The satellite view from Google maps can be accessed more quickly, and it requires no downloads. Also, most addresses in Google maps can be viewed from a "street view," which shows what the address looks like if standing by or driving along the road, and this view shows more detail than the Google Earth view. You may try using both viewing applications, but since the maps view is easier to access, jurors are more likely to see them than Google Earth images.

In Practice:

Defense's brain damage expert—Larry Kane

---

3. *See also* DAVID BALL, REPTILE: THE 2009 MANUAL OF THE PLAINTIFF'S REVOLUTION (Balloon Press 2009).

Larry Kane has a business address in California that appeared perfectly legit until we went to Google maps and viewed the satellite image of the area. It was in the middle of a large residential area and had a very large swimming pool. We searched for information on the property and found that it was zoned residential. We also found that a few years ago Mr. Kane had requested that the property be split into two parcels, presumably so that he could sell one. The piece of property, which he claims as his "office," comprises more than 5,000 square feet and is valued at over $700,000. The swimming pool is listed as 800 square feet. A jury may see his calling the property his office as a very shady practice.

Kane has made a point of saying that money isn't the reason that he's a witness in cases like this and that he doesn't really know how much he's being paid for it because his secretary takes care of that little issue. However, the information about his property shows that he cares very much about money. The companies he works for pay very well, and his testimony has helped win their cases. This fact may go a long way to undermine his credibility if we can show that his desire for a paycheck makes him less than honest on the stand.

Plaintiff's lead counsel—Bob Jones

Remember how the plaintiff's lead counsel has a really common name? Even in the county property records there is another Bob Jones. That Bob Jones isn't doing too badly, either, and he owns a boat in addition to residential property. If a juror sees entries for "Bob Jones," he could easily come to the conclusion that the plaintiff's lead counsel Bob Jones owns a residence worth $750,000, another residence worth about $1,200,000, and a yacht. He had none of that the day he got out of prison twelve years ago. That much wealth visible in records could be a problem even if it doesn't all belong to our guy. When you know about confusing details like this, clarify it in trial. In voir dire: "Does anyone know the Bob Jones who owns a mansion in Hilton Head?" Etc.

Plaintiff—Caleb Winters

Before you agree to take on a case, research the client. When we view Caleb Winters's house from the street view in Google maps, we see a Corvette and a Mazda sports car in the driveway. Other sources show that he's an organizer of a road-racing club. This could lead to a juror's serious suspicion that Caleb, not the tires, caused the wreck. Caleb may not have told you any of this before you decided to take on the case.

* * *

Search for miscellaneous financial information.

This can include seeing what school a son or daughter is attending, what contributions have been made to community efforts or to the university from which the individual graduated. If the person's CV or Facebook profile mentions an alma mater, try searching the school's Web site for his or her name.

Political contributions are discussed in Step 6.

In Practice:

Plaintiff's co-counsel—Sam Waters

Sam went to law school at North Carolina Central University. He has been active with the school since his graduation and has made several financial contributions.

Defense attorney—Frank Garron

Frank went to law school at the University of North Carolina at Chapel Hill. He has made donations to the school and has served on boards there. He is quoted in one of the school's publications as stating his reason for practicing law is to "stand up for individual rights." He looks like a genuine guy to jurors who find that information.

However, when was the last time Frank "stood up for individual rights"? The information we find initially indicates that for the past few years he has been working for large companies, not individuals. We look for more information about his activity in the past few years. Although Frank has worked for some large corporations, he has also worked on smaller cases defending individuals.

Though we followed a lead and it didn't pan out in this case, sometimes it does. Check every credential carefully. The most frequently faked credentials tend to be the early ones: degrees not finished or an article improperly claimed. People tend to forget to remove their old lies later in their careers, when they no longer need them.

STEP 5: SEARCH FOR CRIMINAL RECORDS, BOTH STATE AND FEDERAL

For expert witnesses, this should be a quick search just to cover your bases. For the plaintiff(s), defendant(s), fact and character witnesses, and individuals on the jury, it may take more time. Search for people with the same name in addition to the exact individual you know. A search for common names especially will turn up people who are not the individuals you are looking for, but are close enough that a juror may be confused as to who exactly the records refer to. False hits can be just as important as correct ones.

A Note on Online Criminal Background Check Services

There are online services that will search for criminal records. You do have to pay for the services. We do *not* recommend that you rely on these services. The records are not necessarily true; these services mainly search freely accessible databases like the ones mentioned below and can contain errors such as if individuals have the same name. Jurors are unlikely to pay for services, so to do what they're most likely to do, use the free services listed below.

However, a juror may already have blanket access to these services—through a friend, for example. This is not likely, but when you can't afford to miss anything, or have reason to suspect there might be something to find, go ahead and be thorough by using the fee-based search services.

Federal records (free) can be found through:

- The Federal Bureau of Prisons (http://www.bop.gov/iloc2/LocateInmate.jsp). This will find information on individuals incarcerated since 1982.

- The National Sex Offender Registry (http://www.fbi.gov/hq/cid/cac/registry.htm).

In Practice:

Defense's tire expert—Matt Nisco

There is a Matt Nisco listed as a registered sex offender in South Carolina. It is not the Matt Nisco in this case, the defense tire expert, but jurors may find and mistake him for the other one. Jurors aren't likely to notice or even know the expert's middle initial, which is a different initial from the other Matt.

* * *

In very few cases, a Freedom of Information Act request to the U.S. Parole Commission (http://www.justice.gov/uspc/foia.htm) may be useful. Significant time, often weeks or months, can be involved with this kind of request, so its use should be limited to when you have reason to believe that the individual does have a record not noted elsewhere. Instructions are available on the Web site if you do pursue this option.

State and county records vary from state to state as to how much information can be found online. Some departments that have information include:

- Department of Corrections
- Department of Crime Control & Safety

- State Bureau of Investigation
- Office of the Sheriff

STEP 6: SEARCH FOR POLITICAL AND MILITARY INFORMATION

Finding out which political party a person associates with may not seem particularly useful. However, any of the information you find while researching, including political information, can provide a clue to the next step. It can also reveal aspects of the person's personality.

There are two basic kinds of political information to search for: contributions and party affiliation. Consider this information in light of other information about the juror. The fact that a person is a registered Democrat may be unimportant on its own. However, consider that piece in light of what else you know. If that individual regularly contributes to Republican campaigns but is a registered Democrat, what's going on there?

Affiliation

If possible, check voter registration records for party affiliation. These are often available through the Web site for the Board of Elections for the county in which the individual lives.

Contributions

Want to know what political contributions the person has made? Check out the Federal Election Commission's database (http://www.fec.gov/finance/disclosure/norindsea.shtml). Political contributions have to be reported, and the data provided here is more accurate than performing a quick search in Google. While most political party contributions don't tell you much, a contribution to a controversial or unusual candidate can tell you a lot. For example, a prospective juror who gives money to Ron Paul, Al Sharpton, or Dennis Kucinich is likely to have some associated values and attitudes that can impact how she reacts to your case.

Military Experience

Service records are generally kept confidential. The military does not currently provide a searchable database of formerly active individuals, but there are some commercial sites that could reveal information. If you use those sites, be wary of any results you find since they are not necessarily validated by the government or military.

Some people include military information in their CVs. Sometimes the information was falsified. You can try to verify service by searching for what the individual may have been doing instead, like going to college. This is one kind of information that you may have to verify by a lack of other information.

In Practice:

Plaintiff's lead counsel—Bob Jones

An article on a local news site reports that an individual with the same name and in the same state was dishonorably discharged. Because of this, we need to know whether the attorney on our side was in the service or not. We find that he did serve in the military during Vietnam. The confusion is easily cleared up in jury selection.

STEP 7: CHECK OUT YOUTUBE AND SOCIAL SITES LIKE FACEBOOK, MYSPACE, LINKEDIN

Like the individual's personal or business Web site, these sites allow individuals to post information about themselves, and they're the places where they're most likely to let foolish information be visible to the public. Hopefully your expert witness won't post a profile picture on Facebook of himself drunk at a party, but others involved in the trial may not think to remove such damaging pictures or information. Check the Facebook profiles for the individual's children. In one case, a kid referred to his lawyer dad as a "shark." So, Counsel, do you know where your child is? Better find out—he might be on Facebook writing about you!

Social sites can also provide information not found elsewhere, such as the individual's interests and affiliations. If the individual you're researching has tight privacy settings, you may not be able to see their full profile, but some information is generally available for the public to view, such as who their friends and associates are.

An expert witness may post a video online that records him or her making statements that would be helpful for the current case. Videos on YouTube may be posted with or without the permission of the people in the video, so you may find some revealing information. Searching by the person's name is usually the easiest way to find relevant videos. That way you'll also find damaging videos of people with the same name.

In Practice:

Plaintiff—Caleb Winters

The plaintiff worked in the drama department of a major university for a long time. There are videos on YouTube of the productions in which he collaborated, and some of them are extremely homoerotic. He has also written extensively on gay topics. You may need to screen prospective jurors for anti-gay attitudes.

Plaintiff's first brain damage expert witness—Daphne Cash

Daphne is a public figure, and there are many videos of her on YouTube that give you and the jurors a chance to see her in action. In contrast to the crass, off-putting commercialism of her Web site, the way she handles herself in the videos conveys a professional, assuring demeanor. While videos on the Internet can hurt cases, the videos of Daphne could really help this case by helping to establish her as someone with credibility.

On a negative note, Daphne also made demeaning comments that were caught on camera. The comments were specifically about a celebrity mother, but they came across as anti-working mother. The comments came off as extremely catty, not at all the comments of a professional psychiatrist. Jurors may be offended by these comments and by other left-wing comments Daphne has made.

STEP 8: TRY TO LOCATE RELIGIOUS INFORMATION

You can't always find religious information. Some religious affiliations will be on the individual's personal or business Web site or it could be on a social site like Facebook.

Some churches have online directories. News articles and event photos can also provide this information.

This information is more or less important depending on the kind of case, much like the military service information. When religious information is important, find out before doing the online research whether the judge will let you ask about religious information in a pretrial written juror questionnaire or oral voir dire. Also, many jurors will tell you where they go to church when you ask what they do with their "nonworking hours and weekends."

When religion is important, make sure that before jury voir dire you do the research necessary to find out the nature of every church in the venue. Is the prospective juror a snake-handler or a Unitarian?

Make sure to check what is online about the religious affiliations of all individuals in the case whether it seems relevant or not. Do this before you hire experts. There can always be something harmful online. In many American communities, you may be gambling by hiring an expert who belongs to or teaches in a very unpopular church, other house of worship, or even a cult.

In Practice:

Plaintiff's lead counsel—Bob Jones

Bob Jones is a member of a local nondenominational Christian church. He provides this information in his biography on his firm's Web site. This seems innocent. However, the church is involved with regular demonstrations outside local abortion clinics. Even if jurors don't see the original newspaper articles about the demonstrations, the news organizations have electronic archives that provide access to articles from the past few years. A very simple search of the news organizations' Web sites revealed multiple articles about the church's demonstrations.

Some news sites provide free access to current articles, but charge for access to older ones. Even if a juror doesn't want to pay to see the full article, the headline may contain enough information that the juror will seek additional information elsewhere or will just draw conclusions from that. Article headlines in this case were very explicit about how the church members' demonstrations have occasionally bordered on violence. Belonging to many other nondenominational churches would not be a problem, but this church has a very solid reputation as being confrontational in a way that could be good or bad for the plaintiff, depending on the political and religious views of the jury.

STEP 9: MISCELLANEOUS

Depending on the individual, you'll need to search for additional things. You won't need to find this information for everyone. Whether you need to do these searches depends largely on the kind of work that the person does. Searches you may want to run include the following.

Licenses or Other Credentials

These can be medical, building, teaching, or other professional licenses. Go to the organization or agency that grants these credentials, like the American Bar Association or the state medical board. Make sure that the person has an operating license, and see if it was ever revoked. How to find this information will vary by the kind of license that the individual has, so you may need to check a variety of Web sites. Do not assume that being licensed in forty-nine states means things are as they should be in the fiftieth.

In Practice:

Defense's tire expert—Matt Nisco

When looking into the licenses for Matt Nisco, we have to go to several Web sites for information. He claims to be licensed in several states, so we check the Web site of each state he mentions. The Web site for the Michigan Department of Energy, Labor, and Economic Growth allows users to check a variety of professional licenses, including accountancy, cosmetology, and security guard. Here, we found that Nisco's Professional Engineer license had been suspended in 1985—and why, which can be very useful.

Plaintiff's first brain damage expert witness—Daphne Cash

We looked into Daphne Cash's education and found something that a juror may really have a problem with. She was born and raised in New England, but she went to medical school in Grenada. Was she not good enough to get into a medical school in America? A juror may think that a degree from a foreign medical school isn't as good as one from a proper American school, so she probably doesn't know what she's actually talking about, especially considering how flamboyant her Web site is. This can have a significant effect on jurors.

A. Ratings and Popularity

Doctors and teachers often receive online feedback from patients and students. Sites like RateMDs (www.ratemds.com) allow patients to post comments about their experiences. Sample comments include: "Doctor thought my eighteen-year-old daughter, who had a kidney stone, was just there to get drugs." Rate My Teacher (www.ratemyteachers.com) included this review about a high school teacher: "She will make fun of students and make small comments to bring down one's self esteem."

Being able to post anonymous comments may make someone feel more comfortable giving a well-earned bad review. It could also make it easier for someone to lie. Real reviewers and people with an agenda may be posting comments. Jurors won't be able to tell the difference.

Nondisclosure agreements for patients are not uncommon, and if a patient signs one when receiving medical services, the patient can be prevented from posting a public review on sites like Angie's List (www.angieslist.com). While those agreements do not prevent a patient from suing for medical malpractice, the patient may be prevented from posting public comments about his or her experience with the doctor.

In Practice:

Since some of the expert witnesses in this case are practicing doctors, we checked out their ratings. Though there was nothing particularly telling about the ratings in this case, patients can divulge details about the doctor's personality, professionalism, waiting times, billing issues, or whether the patient felt like the doctor actually cared. Watch the dates of when the comments were posted. If they were posted recently, the comments may have been planted to project a particular image of the doctor for jurors to find. If your client is a doctor, or if you have medical experts, they may have a lot of recent negative comments. You may be able to have the comments removed before the trial begins and jurors see them.

In this case, since many of Daphne Cash's patients are celebrities, they may not want to post reviews that could reveal they've been to her for help. According to Daphne's medical license, she spends half of her time with patients, so either she lies about how much time she spends helping people, or she is more active with patients than she initially appears. So when she's on the stand, get her to talk about her work with patients. That will help counter her very public, celebrity image that may undermine her with some jurors. Jurors like experts with continuing real-world experience and not just academic, media, or testifying experience.

B. Publications

You may have already found some publications on the individual's Web site. This is not the only place jurors can find what that witness has published. To find out what a juror might know, you should also check journal archives and news sources.

Look for items that the person wrote besides full articles. If your expert wrote an editorial a few years ago about how great a certain medical procedure is, his credibility is undermined if he's currently testifying about the negative consequences of that procedure. The expert is unlikely to list the editorial on his CV as something he authored, but it will turn up if a juror does a broad search. It may not matter to jurors that the expert wrote the editorial before more research showed the negative effects of the procedure. All the juror will know is that he said one thing a few years ago and is now contradicting himself under oath.

In addition to reviewing the article content, look at the citations. Are they legitimate citations, or were they made up? Even prestigious journals have been known to falsify data or leave unchecked citations in articles that prove false when a juror follows it up. Few jurors will go that far, but once in a while one will—and so you should, not only to make sure that the rare juror does not find something that makes your expert look very bad, but to find anything you can use against a defense expert.

Feedback

You're probably already accustomed to finding documents that people involved in the trial have written. Take another look, though. Did your expert witness write articles or books? If they published books, check out the listing on Amazon's Web site, or another bookseller, and see what people have said about it. If the person wrote articles, you may also be able to find reader comments about them.

In Practice:

Plaintiff—Caleb Winters

The plaintiff, Caleb Winters, is a former professor at a major university. He worked in the drama department and wrote several books about acting and the theater.

The books he wrote are about gay characters in plays and how some characters (and playwrights) who are thought of as straight are really gay.

Before jurors even see the plaintiff, they can find through a very simple search that the plaintiff does not try to hide his sexual preference and lifestyle. Some jurors will see the books as promoting a deviant lifestyle encouraging homosexuality.

Very unfortunately for this plaintiff, there is another gay man with the name Caleb Winters, even the same middle initial and around the same age. A name does not have to be common for someone else to have it.

This other Caleb and his partner live on a large piece of property in New England and invite gay men to use the area as a mountain retreat. This other is also an artist who draws only naked men.

The very public lifestyle that this other Caleb entertains can be a problem for our plaintiff. Many jurors believe homosexuality is an abomination to God that can lead to the divine destruction of the community. The jurors don't have to be extremely conservative to have a problem with the lifestyle that they find when they do a search for "Caleb Winters." Our plaintiff may be gay and open about his sexuality, but the other Caleb has a much more in-your-face online presence that seems to recruit others to homosexuality. The two Caleb's were extremely difficult for us to distinguish, but jurors can get interested and follow every lead without ever realizing there's a distinction to be made.

In this case, the "real" Caleb—the plaintiff—happens to be gay. If he were not, the problem would still exist because it's so easy for jurors to find his online presence and assume he's the plaintiff.

Plaintiff's second brain damage expert witness—James Wagner

James Wagner, one of the plaintiff's brain damage experts, has written several books about brain injuries. They have excellent ratings on Amazon and seem to sell very well. When jurors find this, it will help establish Wagner as a credible source on brain injuries even before he takes the stand.

Finding that easily accessible online feedback about the expert is a plus when deciding whether to use him.

Plaintiff's first brain damage expert witness—Daphne Cash

Daphne's books have been met with very mixed reviews, and some of the comments are more than a little negative. One reviewer said that Daphne should be jailed and, "If you're in this book's target audience, you are already far too dim to comprehend just why this book is so lousy." The reviewer is from North Carolina, where the trial is taking place.

Finding these kinds of negative reviews is why you need to research the individual before signing him or her to the case. If you've already signed Daphne to the case before you find these reviews, you can only cope with the situation. If you know about it beforehand, you can avert it entirely.

C. Soapbox or Informative

Some people just write articles so they can voice their opinions. Are the publications more opinionated or are they intended more to get information out there?

Finding published material and reader comments about it on Amazon, Barnes & Noble, and other such sites is one of the easiest searches a juror can run. Though nothing like this was found in our working case since medical experts rarely criticize one another in public print, there was an incident in a nonmedical field with books a witness had written. The books are sold on Amazon and are written for a professional audience. While their ratings seem great at 4.5 stars, there is something odd about the comments. Most readers like the books and rate them well, but a handful of readers have written scathing reviews. Oddly enough, the bad reviews are all from people in California, where the expert lives. This could be an attempt by his competitors to discredit him; it could be plants from the opposition in this case or other cases. Or it could be the only "true" reviews from people who know him best.

In Practice:

Defense's brain damage expert witness—Larry Kane

While researching the medical expert witnesses, we found that Larry Kane, the defense's brain damage expert witness, published only short articles that seem to be intended to damage potential competitors' credibility.

Kane badmouths researchers and those working in academia, people who are often put on the stand as expert witnesses ("Academicians may be good researchers, but terrible teachers"). You could use his opinion to undermine other defense experts, if they are mainly academicians. Kane even writes that *only* those who are primarily expert witnesses or have significant experience testifying are capable of being good witnesses. It's very obvious that he wrote the articles as marketing in order to promote his expert witness business.

D. Work on Previous Cases

You may already be familiar with how an individual has assisted with previous cases, but what are your jurors finding? Jurors will not find or read the summaries of all of the cases the individual has worked on, but they can easily find some of them. You may also find information that surprises you, such as cases that embarrass the person or that could undermine the person's current work.

In Practice:

Defense's brain damage expert witness—Larry Kane

Larry Kane has worked on a lot of cases. He was pretty involved with the tobacco cases in the 1980s and 1990s. He even testified before Congress. The statements he made during these cases, as well as the side that he was trying to help (big tobacco), is good for us and not so good for him anymore.

Kane doesn't mention these cases on his Web site or in the wealth of information he provides online. He worked for the tobacco companies, heartily defending them and denying many of the health consequences of smoking. Several times he testified that nicotine was not addictive, that people who stop smoking don't go through real withdrawals like people with *real* addictions.

Since Kane made these statements, the public sentiment has turned increasingly against tobacco. While tobacco farmers may like that he tried to defend their livelihood, many other Americans will see his comments as deceptive and intending to harm their health. He's a psychiatrist and is supposed to help people, but in these cases, his goal seemed more motivated by getting money from big tobacco than in working for the best interests of the people. Knowing this, he may have minimized his tobacco activities in his CV—but once you get the details for yourself, you have some potentially great impeachment and undermining material. "You're the same Dr. Kane who testified under oath that tobacco is not addictive?" and, "That was what the tobacco companies paying your bill wanted you to say?"

Plaintiff's first brain damage expert witness—Daphne Cash

Daphne has been involved in some high-profile cases that could work in our favor. She worked with a famous case in which a woman in a coma had the plug pulled. Daphne served as an expert witness for the family that was fighting not to have the plug pulled on this woman, who was unable to survive without the assistance of medical equipment. This will help establish how she fights for life and the rights of the individual. On the other hand, it will deeply offend jurors on the other side of this issue. Before signing her on, you need to assume jurors will know or learn about it and consider how much it might affect jurors in your venue.

START RESEARCHING!

As you can see, research doesn't just mean going to Google. Relevant information can be found in a variety of resources and can vary highly from case to case.

Performing good, thorough research will take time, but it will help ensure that once you get into the courtroom, you won't be blindsided by outside factors. If you cannot do the research yourself and know that you're doing it well, distribute the research to others assisting with the case. In cases of high importance, particularly longer cases during which jurors will have far more time to go online, consider using a professional researcher. You never know where a juror's wander through the Internet will lead him. So when jurors have ample wandering time or reason, you want to make sure that your side got there first so you know what to do about everything the jurors can find.

If you have questions about anything in this article, please contact:

Lauren Havens at lauren@itk-research.com.

ADDENDUM: WHAT'S *ACTUALLY* ONLINE THAT DAMAGES YOUR ARGUMENT

We conducted an online search for material that supports the defense's argument that the plaintiff could not have sustained brain damage from a low-speed rear-end car accident. Unfortunately, there's a lot out there that will kill your case if jurors find it and tell the other jurors about it.

The easiest way to get a quick idea of what's available online about a topic is to do a simple search in a search engine like Google or Bing.

From the Google search box, there are a variety of keywords and phrases that jurors may use and that you should try, too, for this or any other case.

How to Conduct a Simple Search

The simplest search is just to list several common words and phrases in the search box:

Ex: car accident brain injury

The search engine finds Web pages that contain all of those words, but in no particular order on the page.

For this case: *car accident, brain injury, brain, brain damage, car, vehicle, injury, damage, low-speed, low-speed accident, rear-end collision, rear-end, collision, long-term effects, physical therapy.*

Consider synonyms and words that may be associated or that a juror would think of. In court you may talk about "sustaining a traumatic brain injury," but will a juror search for that or for *"getting hurt on the head"* or *"head injury"*?

For this case: *Traumatic brain injury, head injury, brain damage, head damage, concussion, whiplash, hurt head, physical damage.*

Use quotations to locate pages with an exact phrase: *"injuries sustained from a rear-end car accident."*

This found a lot of results about the kinds of brain damage that could occur from a variety of car accidents, not just the low-speed ones discussed in court. Plus, they're really not turning up the information that I, the juror, want to find that will refute your arguments.

Find results that have an exact phrase, but also have other words on the page: *"injuries sustained from a rear-end" car accident brain damage.*

The results of this search came primarily from sites hosted by law firms or sites that direct the reader to find a lawyer if he has been in such an accident. Since the juror is going to disregard these sites as biased in favor of the plaintiff anyway, these sites are going to be disregarded, at best. At worst, they're going to anger the juror against you even more since he'll see an entire industry that is trying to make money off the pain of others.

To get rid of results hosted by lawyers or legal firms, exclude results with those words: *car accident brain damage –legal –law.*

Don't forget about variations of words, including plurals, possessives, or spelling variations (even common misspellings). For example, "*injury*" will prompt different results than "*injuries.*"

Searching Medical Sources

Since the juror is looking for information on a medical condition, he would not just use Google but would seek out sources tailored to providing medical information. The juror would not just want an overview of a condition. He wants to see facts from the scientific community.

This means that he will find, whether he searches for them specifically or not, scientific papers that were originally published in respected sources, not just posted on a blog or personal Web site by a rogue scientist. Some of these papers were found using the searches noted above in Google.

One medical resource that a juror may search is PubMed (http://www.ncbi.nlm.nih.gov/pubmed/), which provides abstracts and often full-text papers that were published in respected scientific journals. Many papers supporting the defense's arguments were easy to find here.

An Absence of Evidence

The search for evidence that physical harm is unlikely to occur in a low-speed car accident is a bit tricky. The presence of a possible medical condition (the plaintiff's position) is easier to support with evidence than it is to provide evidence that the condition does not exist (the defense's argument). Proving an absence of something is just harder to do.

So, jurors are likely to initially encounter a great deal of information about the medical condition that the plaintiff claims to have, but that will not stop a juror from finding information contrary to your arguments. It may take a few search attempts before the juror realizes that just searching *car accident brain damage* will not yield the information that he wants.

While it may not be popular to try to prove the absence of a deity, one of the classic cases of "absence of evidence is not evidence of absence," there is a definite incentive for insurance companies or others to find evidence for the absence of physical harm in low-speed accidents. Where there is an interested party, there is the possibility for biased information.

Since insurance companies really want to convince people of a particular truth, they don't disseminate information just randomly on the Internet; they pay professional researchers to do research and report the results in respected journals. Other businesses with a certain interest do the same thing, like when a manufacturing company pays researchers to find that workers encounter no physical harm from handling chemicals in the manufacturing plant.

Researchers' articles are searchable in PubMed and elsewhere on the Internet as a result of the journals' publication process. Since people—scientists and the public—respect the science reported in those respected journals, other researchers relied on the reports and referenced them in their own studies, which further distributed the information and increased the impact of the pyramid effect in this case.

The Pyramid Effect

This brings up the pyramid effect. Once a juror finds one page or article that fits his needs, that document or how he searched to find that item is likely to lead to additional sources. Articles especially are likely to do this because they cite other articles that the juror will then access.

Once the juror gets started on this path of finding an article and then finding other articles cited in the first, it's easy for the juror to get tunnel vision, forgetting that there are contrary opinions. Articles are cited in papers not because the author disagrees with those articles (generally), but because those articles support the author's current work.

Once the juror finds a few articles that claim that low-speed collisions almost never cause physical damage, it starts to look like the defense has a solid case. The juror may not search for evidence supporting your case. You have to show him that what he found supporting the defense is erroneous, but you have to find these items before you know what you're fighting.

Damaging Quotes Found

"No test subject reported having discomfort symptoms during or immediately after any of the test collisions."

When test subjects did finally have discomfort, "No treatment or therapy was needed and none of the test participants had any further symptoms that related to their test exposures for greater than eighteen months following the testing."

"An identifiable threshold exists and has been documented that relates velocity at impact to injury potential. The threshold of injury is above that of vehicle damage."

"There is a direct correlation between the severity of impact forces and the probability of developing chronic symptoms."

"Most people recover from head injuries and have no lasting effects."

Supplement H

A chart with the results of crash tests on human subjects, the speed of the collision, and any symptoms. These were low-speed collisions, and the chart would be really damaging if the defense used this in court without the plaintiff's counsel being aware of the limitations of the study or having other studies to back up their side.

"The impacts resulted in no injury to any of the human volunteers, and no objective changes in the condition of their cervical or lumbar spines. The results indicate a minimum injury tolerance to low speed rear-end impacts for males and females."

"Proponents of this pathology argue that the quest for compensation generates malingering. Litigants might remain "sick" because of the "rewards" they are given or are likely to obtain by remaining hyper-disabled by the compensation system."

"The likelihood of significant injury arising from a low-speed rear-impact collision is the subject of scholarly debate." This makes it sound as though it's not really clear if significant injury can arise from such an impact. "The most severe symptom reported in these tests was minor neck pain lasting one week."

"Most claim adjusters have a general understanding that low-velocity rear-end accident scenarios do not produce significant injuries and at best might produce some short term transient muscle stiffness and perhaps mild aches and pains. However, most claim adjusters do not have an understanding, biomechanically, that their intuitive sense regarding minimal injury potential is actually supported by scientific biomechanical engineering principles and tests."

"Indy race car drivers have been subjected to 80 g's without permanent injury."

"The prevalence of chronic neck pain in the general population is the same as the risk of late whiplash following an acute whiplash injury."

"The 'limit of harmlessness' for stresses arising from rear-end impacts with regard to the velocity changes lies between [6.2 mph] and [9.4 mph]."

"Symptoms commonly attributed to whiplash injuries following low-speed motor vehicle accidents, particularly chronic neck pain, are psychogenic."

"It is highly unlikely or impossible to injure the temporomandibular joint in a whiplash-type motor vehicle accident injury."

"The likelihood of transient acute neck and shoulder muscle strain injury and possible mild compressive irritation of the posterior neck may increase" at a delta V of 5 mph.

A low back injury is "quite unlikely as a result of a low velocity rear-end collision."

"A 10-mph rear-end impact for an unsuspecting occupant was within human tolerance for injury."

"Whiplash injuries, particularly late whiplash, are less common in countries where no remuneration exists for the injuries and their long-term sequelae, or where awareness of the injury is not thought to be widespread."

"Specific actions or movements common to daily living or sports and recreational activities don't cause injury, yet involve forces similar to, or higher than, those produced in whiplash injuries."

"Acute whiplash injuries do not cause, or are unlikely to cause, chronic pain."

"A rear impact with a change on velocity of [5 mph] or less is within tolerance for a reasonably healthy occupant."

"How much force is necessary to cause permanent brain damage is under study, and hence still unclear."

"The collision that usually causes the least amount of damage is called a low speed impact crash. A low impact crash is generally defined as one that takes place at speeds under 10 miles per hour (mph)."

"Many times, the term 'litigation neurosis' is used to describe those who complain of persistent symptoms in what seems to be a minor accident." Catchy term, isn't it? If a juror found this term, he's likely to search for it and find a lot more information. Litigation neurosis has been the verdict in several court cases that the juror may read about.

"How many times have we heard 'I was only going a few miles an hour' or 'I had just started forward at the red light when I hit them.' They are only after the money. How can they say they are injured that severely?"

Supplement I

What Is a Defense Expert Really Allowed to Say?

Defense experts often testify—explicitly or by subtle innuendo—well beyond the limits of their expertise, the facts, and science.

> For further essential help dealing with this stunningly ubiquitous problem, see section 7-4, pp. 210ff., as well as chapter twelve of *Reptile*, along with the brilliant work of Michael Freeman (forensictrauma@gmail.com), Dorothy Clay Sims in *Exposing Deceptive Defense Doctors*, and Rick Friedman in *Polarizing the Case*.

In 2004, I asked one of the smartest attorneys I know (and my valued friend) Virginia attorney Roger T. Creager (The Creager Law Firm, Richmond, Virginia) to let me include one of his motions in this book. Roger has used the arguments in the motion below in many traumatic brain injury cases. He usually schedules a pretrial hearing on the evidentiary issues raised by the report or deposition testimony of the defense neuropsychologist. Many of these issues may need to be raised again during trial so the judge can rule more precisely.

Almost every time Roger has used the arguments in the motion below, the judge has imposed numerous significant limitations on defense neuropsychologist testimony.

The admissibility of "malingering testimony" has not been fully addressed by the Virginia Supreme Court, and the handling of such testimony has not been uniform in the Virginia trial courts. In *Rose v. Jaques*, 597 S.E.2d 64, 74 (Va. 2004), the Virginia Supreme Court upheld a trial court ruling excluding all of a defense neuropsychologist's profered testimony regarding malingering. But the Supreme Court did not fully address the general admissibility of such testimony. The Court simply held that the record on appeal was insufficient to establish that the neuropsychologist had actually formed any opinion regarding malingering by the plaintiff. The Court noted that the expert's report stated that he was unable to offer a "formal diagnosis of malingering." *Id.*

Supplement I

STATE OF VIRGINIA

IN THE CIRCUIT COURT OF THE COUNTY OF
CHESTERFIELD

PAUL R. SMITH,[1]	)
Plaintiff.	)
v.	) Law No.: CL02-1074
TAE KWON KICK, INC.,	)
d/b/a TAE KWON KICK Classes	)
and/or	)
A.J. Lou's Tae Kwon City,	)
and	)
JENNIFER L. WEBB,	)
Defendants.	)

MEMORANDUM IN SUPPORT OF MOTION TO
LIMIT TESTIMONY OF JOHN O. THOMAS, PhD

PROCEDURAL BACKGROUND AND FACTS

The Plaintiff, Paul R. Smith (Smith), has been diagnosed by both his treating medical doctors with a traumatic brain injury resulting from injuries sustained when he was kicked in the head during a Tae Kwon Do class on May 15, 2001, by Jennifer L. Webb (Webb), the instructor at a facility owned and operated by Tae Kwon Kick Classes, Inc. (Tae Kwon Kick). Webb is very experienced in Tae Kwon Do, which is similar to Karate, and holds a Black Belt in this form of martial arts. It is indisputable that a Tae Kwon Do kick from an experienced Black Belt can, if delivered to the head, cause serious injury or even death.

Webb was doing a "no-contact" demonstration of a kick during a Tae Kwon Do class in which Smith was a student. At Webb's direction, Smith was bent forward in a helpless position with his head towards Webb. Rather than stopping her kick short of Smith's head, however, Webb negligently caused or allowed her foot to violently strike Smith in the head. Because students involved in such demonstrations always would "play act" as though they are actually kicked, nothing seemed unusual when Smith fell backward

---

1. All party names in this motion, with the exception of the names of the attorneys and law firms, have been changed.

onto his buttocks. Smith felt something squish in the back of his neck, and felt funny, but he thought he would be all right. In the following days, however, Smith had pain and stiffness in his neck, as well as difficulty concentrating and sleeping.

When his problems did not get better but instead worsened, Smith sought professional help from his primary care physician, Cole A. Jacobson, MD, on May 17, 2001, just two days after the kick. On May 23, 2001, he returned with difficulties that included a "foggy" feeling, severe neck pain, and headaches. His scalp was tender, and he had pain and spasms in his neck. He was evaluated as having possibly sustained a concussion.

A subsequent computerized tomography (CT) scan ordered by Dr. Jacobson's office was normal as was a Magnetic Resonance Imaging (MRI) scan that was eventually also done, but this is often the case with mild brain injuries since CT and MRI scans cannot detect injuries and changes at the cellular level. On June 19, 2001, Dr. Jacobson saw Smith for continuing problems in mental functioning he had experienced since the kick to the head. Dr. Jacobson referred Smith to Elizabeth A. Acosta, MD, a nationally-recognized neuropsychiatrist, who specializes in the evaluation, treatment, and care of persons suspected of having sustained a brain injury.

On June 20, 2001, Dr. Acosta performed a comprehensive evaluation of Smith. Dr. Acosta's medical diagnosis was that Smith had sustained a concussion on May 15, 2001. Dr. Jacobson had already previously arrived independently at the opinion that Smith had sustained a brain injury. Dr. Jacobson testified in his deposition that there is "[n]o question in my mind that he had a significant brain injury before I referred him to Dr. Acosta." October 21, 2003, Deposition of Cole A. Jacobson at 46. Dr. Acosta further diagnosed Smith with Post-Concussive Syndrome and Adjustment Disorder with anxiety, all caused by the original concussion from the Tae Kwon Do kick on May 15, 2001. Dr. Acosta and other specialists (occupational therapist, speech-language pathologist, physical therapist, massage therapist) have treated Smith for these conditions with medications and therapies over the more than two years since June 20, 2001.

More than two years after Smith's injury, the Defendant hired a psychologist, John O. Thomas, PhD (Thomas), to perform a neuropsychological evaluation of Smith. Thomas is not a medical doctor. Moreover, although he is referred to as a neuropsychologist, the license Thomas holds from the Commonwealth of Virginia is simply that of a psychologist. Virginia does not issue any special license or certification for neuropsychology. A neuropsychological evaluation consists of administering and scoring numerous tests, almost all of which are written tests, and a few of which are verbal. A neuropsychologist is not qualified to practice medicine or to perform any physical examination or medical evaluation of a person, and is not qualified or licensed to prescribe medications.

What a neuropsychologist is qualified to do is give certain tests of mental functioning and then score the results by comparing them to normative data, thereby indicating whether each set of test results falls within the High Average, Average, or Normal, Low Average, Borderline Impaired, or Impaired ranges. Thomas has in fact given tests to Smith, has scored them, and has determined the range for each set of test results. A copy of Thomas's report with all attachments is attached hereto as Exhibit A (hereinafter referred to as "Thomas's Report"). Page 15 of Thomas's Report summarizes the scoring of Smith's test results, and is attached hereto as Exhibit B. These results show that Smith's performance fell within the Impaired or Low Average ranges in numerous areas of functioning. This represents a change as compared with his pre-injury functioning, inasmuch as even Thomas admits that Smith's mental functioning prior to the Tae Kwon Do class on May 15, 2001, would have been at least in the Average range (Thomas's Report at 6).

Smith has no objection to Thomas testifying to the scored results of his testing, as set forth in Exhibit B. The contents of Thomas's Report makes clear, however, that Thomas intends to use the scoring of his test results, which is the only proper subject of his testimony, as a mere "jumping off" point. Thomas's Report reveals that he intends to go beyond the proper subjects of his testimony, and use innuendo, implication, pejorative word-selection, and other techniques to attempt to disparage, undermine, and damage the Plaintiff's case in numerous ways which, if allowed at trial, would violate Virginia evidence law. Smith has therefore filed a Motion in Limine asking the Court to rule that Thomas's testimony will be limited at trial in accordance with the evidentiary requirements and restrictions imposed by Virginia law.

ARGUMENT

Although Thomas is employed at the Medical College of Virginia, he is not a medical doctor. Thomas is licensed by the Commonwealth of Virginia only as a psychologist. He is not an "MD," but rather is a "PhD."

It is equally clear that although defense experts like Thomas are sometimes referred to by defense counsel as performing an "independent" examination, Thomas is not remotely independent in this case. He never was involved in any treatment of Smith. No treating health-care provider ever sought his assistance. He is a well-known defense expert regularly retained in litigation settings and is a witness who earns a great deal of his living testifying for hire for defendants. In this case, the defense hired Thomas, paid him for his work on this case, and will pay him for his testimony at trial. Thomas has never spent a moment on this case that was independent as is the case with the treating doctors. By the time Thomas was hired to assist the defense, this matter was already in litigation and it was clear to him from the moment that he was hired that the defense hoped to prove that Smith did not suffer from impairments caused by a brain injury.

Yet, there is nothing that Thomas can do to change the actual results of his testing, which are adverse to the defense. The tests were given and Smith provided his answers. The results were scored, by comparison to normative data, and fell within various ranges. Smith's performance was impaired in numerous areas. These matters, which are the only scientifically based topics of Thomas's testimony, are established and unchangeable, and they are adverse to the defense.

Because of his obvious bias, it is perhaps not surprising that Thomas's Report does not properly confine itself to relating the test results and the normative scores. Instead, in manifest efforts to convey his belief that Smith's impairments are not the result of a brain injury, Thomas goes far beyond his field and ranges into comments which are not based on any real science, constitute medical opinions, are subjective in nature, involve marshaling of hearsay medical records entries not properly admitted through Thomas and about which Thomas is unqualified to comment, amount to argument in the guise of expert testimony, are tantamount to comments on credibility, and are otherwise improper.

Before turning to the details of these evidentiary problems as revealed in Thomas's Report, it is useful to revisit the numerous basic principles of Virginia evidence law applicable to expert testimony. If expert testimony violates any of these principles, it is inadmissible.

In civil cases, expert testimony is admissible only when the testimony complies with all of the following requirements:

(1) Only a medical doctor can testify regarding diagnosis and causation of brain injuries.[2] In *John v. Im*, the Virginia Supreme Court held that because a psychologist is not a medical doctor he is not qualified to testify regarding issues of diagnosis and causation of brain injuries. The Court held:

> We also hold that the trial court properly excluded Nash's opinion testimony that John [the plaintiff] sustained a mild traumatic brain injury as a result of the automobile accident. An opinion concerning the causation of a particular physical human injury is a component of a diagnosis, which is part of the practice of medicine. *Combs v. Norfolk & W. Ry. Co.*, 256 Va. 490, 496, 507 S.E.2d 355, 358 (1998). Nash was a licensed

---

2. See *Combs v. Norfolk and Western Rwy. Co.*, 256 Va. 490, 495–497, 507 S.E.2d 355, 358–359 (1998); *John v. Im*, 263 Va. 315, 559 S.E.2d 694 (2002).

psychologist, not a medical doctor. Therefore, since Nash was not a medical doctor, he was not qualified to state an expert medical opinion regarding the cause of John's injury. See *id.* at 496–97, 507 S.E.2d at 359.

John v. Im, 263 Va. 315, 321–322, 559 S.E.2d 694 (2002) (footnote omitted) (emphasis added).

(2) Expert testimony must provide expert assistance which is necessary to help the trier of fact in understanding the evidence.[3]

Expert testimony which is merely argumentative or concerns matters about which the jury should be allowed to reach their own conclusions violates this principle.

(3) Expert testimony must be based on a fully adequate foundation.[4]

(4) Expert testimony must not be speculative in any way or founded on assumptions or beliefs that lack a fully sufficient factual basis.[5]

(5) There must not be any "missing variables" that the expert has failed to fully consider (or is not qualified to fully consider).[6]

(6) Hearsay and other inadmissible types of evidence cannot be included in the expert's testimony on direct examination.[7]

---

3. *See* Code §§ 8.01-401.1 and -401.3; *Keesee v. Donigan*, 259 Va. 157, 161, 524 S.E.2d 645, 647 (2000); *Tittsworth v. Robinson*, 252 Va. 151, 154, 475 S.E.2d 261, 263 (1996); *Chapman v. City of Virginia Beach*, 252 Va. 186, 191, 475 S.E.2d 798 (1996) (reversible error to admit expert testimony which did not assist the jury but rather concerned issues within the range of common experience).

4. *See, e.g., Tarmac Mid-Atlantic, Inc. v. Smiley Block Co.*, 250 Va. 161, 166, 458 S.E.2d 462, 465 (1995).

5. *See Keesee*, 259 Va. at 161, 524 S.E.2d at 648; *Tittsworth*, 252 Va. at 154, 475 S.E.2d at 263; *Tarmac*, 250 Va. at 166, 458 S.E.2d at 466.

6. ITT *Hartford v. Virginia Financial Assoc.*, 258 Va. 193, 201, 520 S.E.2d 355, 359 (1999); *Tittsworth*, 252 Va. at 154, 475 S.E.2d at 263; *Tarmac*, 250 Va. at 166, 458 S.E.2d at 466.

7. *See* Virginia Code Section 8.01-401.1 (hearsay data may be brought out on cross-examination). In *Meade v. Belcher*, 212 Va. 796, 188 S.E.2d 211 (1972), the Virginia Supreme Court held that a doctor should not have been permitted to give an opinion which was based upon medical records which were not introduced as evidence in the case. Section 8.01-401.1 was enacted to allow an opinion to be based upon hearsay, such as hearsay medical records, but the statute does not alter the evidentiary prohibition against the introduction of the hearsay itself in direct testimony. An expert must also be precluded from testifying regarding the opinions, conclusions, or observations of others. See *McMunn v. Tatum*, 237 Va. 558, 379 S.E.2d 908 (1989) (expert may not testify to hearsay opinions of others); *CSX Transportation v. Casale*, 247 Va. 180, 441 S.E.2d 212 (1994) (same).

(7) Only expert opinions formed and held to a reasonable degree of scientific certainty are admissible.[8] Expert testimony which amounts to subjective thoughts and impressions masquerading as science should not be allowed into evidence. This is particularly true in view of the danger that jurors may place great weight on experts who have impressive academic credentials and are often very experienced and skilled witnesses, and cross-examination may well prove to be inadequate to undo the damage done by such faulty testimony.

(8) Purportedly "scientific" evidence will not be admitted unless it is actually based upon scientific methodology or testing that produces results that are sufficiently scientifically reliable to be admissible as evidence.[9]

(9) The expert must be qualified to give each opinion and each item of testimony he intends to offer.[10]

(10) Expert testimony must not invade the province of the jury.[11]

(11) Issues relating to determining credibility and weighing the evidence are reserved for the jury.[12]

(12) Expert testimony should never suggest or imply that there is a scientific way to determine whether a party or witness is telling the truth.[13] The Court has held that "in reality, in our system of justice, the jury decides what is true and what is not."[14]

---

8. *Spruill v. Commonwealth*, 221 Va. 475, 479, 271 S.E.2d 419 (1980); Virginia Code § 8.01-399(C) ("Only diagnosis offered to a reasonable degree of medical probability shall be admissible at trial").

9. *See Satcher v. Commonwealth*, 244 Va. 220, 244, 421 S.E.2d 821, 835 (1992), cert. denied, 507 U.S. 933 (1993); *Spencer v. Commonwealth*, 240 Va. 78, 97–98, 393 S.E.2d 609, 621, cert. denied, 498 U.S. 908 (1990); *John v. Im*, 263 Va. 315, 322, 559 S.E.2d 694, 697 (2002).

10. *Swiney v. Overby*, 237 Va. 231, 233, 377 S.E.2d 372, 374 (1989). *See CSX Transportation, Inc. v. Casale*, 250 Va. 359, 365, 463 S.E.2d 445, 448 (1995).

11. *See Velazquez v. Commonwealth*, 263 Va. 95, 104, 557 S.E.2d 213, 219 (2002); *Virginia Power v. Dungee*, 258 Va. 235, 259, 520 S.E.2d 164, 178 (1999); *David A. Parker Enterprises v. Templeton*, 251 Va. 235, 467 S.E.2d 488 (1996); *Brown v. Corbin*, 244 Va. 528, 531, 423 S.E.2d 176, 178 (1992); *Grasty v. Tanner*, 206 Va. 723, 146 S.E.2d 252 (1966). The Virginia Supreme Court has continued to apply this rule despite the enactment in 1993 of special statutory provisions relating to expert testimony regarding ultimate issues. *See* Virginia Code § 8.01-401.3; *David A. Parker Enterprises v. Templeton*, 251 Va. 235, 467 S.E.2d 488 (1996).

12. *Lenz v. Commonwealth*, 261 Va. 451, 469, 544 S.E.2d 299, 301 (2001) ("It was the province of the jury to assess the credibility of the witnesses"); *Kimberlin v. PM Transport, Inc.*, 264 Va. 261, 266, 563 S.E.2d 665, 667 (2002) ("a jury should weigh the evidence, [and] determine the credibility of the witnesses").

13. "The mention of polygraphs in the presence of the jury impermissibly suggests that there is a scientific way to find the truth where in reality, in our system of justice, the jury decides what is true and what is not." *Robinson v. Commonwealth*, 231 Va. 142, 156, 341 S.E.2d 159, 167 (1986).

14. *Id.*

(13) Expert testimony must not be repetitive or cumulative.[15] Often, when expert testimony is challenged as inadmissible, the proponent of the evidence will argue that any flaws and problems in the evidence can be brought out on cross-examination, and thus there is no need to exclude the evidence. Thus, trial courts may be tempted to allow questionable expert testimony into evidence on the theory that its weaknesses can be exposed on cross-examination and the jury can then determine what weight should be given to it.

This approach is not permitted under Virginia law.[16] Rather, the Virginia Supreme Court has made clear that the trial court must always act as the "gatekeeper" charged with the responsibility of limiting expert testimony to its proper bounds.[17] It is "for the trial court, not the jury, to decide whether the foundation had been laid for the introduction of" the expert testimony.[18] The admissibility of expert testimony presents a "strictly legal question" for decision by the Court.[19] If the proffered expert opinions are not admissible, the jurors should never hear them. Moreover, it unnecessarily lengthens and

---

15. *See, e.g., Harrison v. Commonwealth*, 244 Va. 576, 585, 423 S.E.2d 160 (1992).

16. In *CSX Transportation, Inc. v. Casale*, 250 Va. 359, 463 S.E.2d 445 (1995), the Virginia Supreme Court cited a Fourth Circuit Court of Appeals decision **reversing** a trial judge who "held that if an expert does not have an adequate basis for his opinion, it is for counsel to bring out the deficiencies on cross-examination and for the jury to decide what weight, if any, the opinion should be given." 250 Va. 359, 367, 463 S.E.2d 445, 450 (1995). The Virginia Supreme Court quoted with approval the following language from the Fourth Circuit's decision: It was an abuse of discretion for the trial court to admit [the expert's] testimony . . . . The court may not abdicate its responsibility to ensure that only properly admitted evidence is considered by the jury. Expert opinion evidence based on assumptions not supported by the record should be excluded. *Id.* (quoting *Tyger Constr. Co. v. Pensacola Constr. Co.*, 29 F.3d 137 (4th Cir. 1994), cert. denied, 513 U.S. 1080 (1995)).

17. In cases where numerous aspects of the proposed expert testimony are challenged as inadmissible, the "gatekeeper" role of the trial court becomes particularly active and demanding. For example, if the court has already excluded five other forms of opinion offered by the same expert, the court may begin to feel that at some point fairness dictates that the expert be allowed to state at least some part of his opinions. In these situations, however, the trial court must bear in mind that each and every aspect of the expert's opinions which does not full meet the requirements of Virginia evidence law must be excluded, even if this means that the expert will be allowed to offer few, if any, opinions at trial. It is not the fault of the opponent of the evidence or of the Court that most or all of proffered opinions of the expert are inadmissible. In these situations, the trial court must serve as a "floodwall" against the steady flow of inadmissible expert opinions which would improperly prejudice the jurors. The party offering the expert testimony must show that it fully complies with Virginia law regarding admissibility of such evidence. Any and all such testimony which does not satisfy the admissibility requirements must be excluded as a matter of law.

18. *CSX Transportation, Inc. v. Casale*, 250 Va. at 367, 463 S.E.2d at 449.

19. "In summary, the question before the trial court was one of the admissibility of evidence, not its weight—a strictly legal question." *CSX Transportation, Inc. v. Casale*, 250 Va. at 367, 463 S.E.2d at 450.

complicates the trial to allow direct testimony and cross-examination of experts regarding opinions which ought to have been excluded.

Indeed, if cross-examination were sufficient to overcome the effect of inadmissible expert testimony, there would be no need for the numerous decisions of the Virginia Supreme Court carefully limiting the nature and scope of expert testimony that may properly be admitted into evidence. Particularly in the case of testimony from a highly-educated, articulate, persuasive, experienced, extensively credentialed expert hired and paid by a party, there is every reason to believe that cross-examination will be insufficient to correct the harm done by allowing the jurors to hear expert testimony which ought to have been excluded. Hence, the Virginia Supreme Court has again and again held that trial courts committed reversible error by allowing into evidence expert testimony which failed to satisfy even just one of the numerous evidentiary requirements which must be met prior to admission of such evidence.[20]

The mere fact that a witness is qualified to testify as an expert does not relieve the trial court of its duty to act as the "gatekeeper." Rather, the court must make the required threshold admissibility determinations as to each and every aspect of an expert's testimony which is challenged. "Qualification of an expert witness does not insure admission of his every statement and opinion."[21]

Application of the evidentiary standards reviewed above to the opinions and statements contained in Thomas's Report demonstrates that Thomas's intended testimony would, if allowed, violate numerous principles of Virginia law, and should be limited in accordance with the foregoing principles.

Some examples will illustrate the numerous evidentiary problems with Thomas's expected testimony. Because these problems are subtle, insidious, and pervade Thomas's Report, identification of them requires a detailed examination of his Report. The evidentiary problems identified below based

---

20. *See, e.g., Keesee v. Donigan,* supra (trial court committed reversible error in an automobile crash negligence case in allowing an accident reconstruction expert to testify concerning "average" driver perception and reaction times absent evidence that a party fell within the average range; expert testimony cannot be based upon assumptions without evidentiary foundation); *Tittsworth v. Robinson,* supra (trial court erred in admitting expert testimony regarding forces of collision and causation of injuries where experts failed to consider all pertinent variables and relied upon results of dissimilar tests); *CSX Transportation v. Casale,* 247 Va. 180, 441 S.E.2d 212 (1994) (new trial was required because trial court erred in allowing expert testimony which included hearsay introducing a new and different diagnosis into the case); *Chapman v. City of Virginia Beach,* 252 Va. 186, 191, 475 S.E.2d 798 (1996) (case remanded for new trial because trial court erred in admitting testimony by a "human factors psychologist" that the physical properties, configuration, and unsecured condition of a gate section created a hazard and that it was reasonably foreseeable that a child's head could become entrapped in it; this testimony did not assist the jury but rather concerned issues within the range of common experience).

21. *Swiney v. Overby,* 237 Va. 231, 233, 377 S.E.2d 372, 374 (1989). See *CSX Transportation, Inc. v. Casale,* 250 Va. 359, 365, 463 S.E.2d 445, 449 (1995).

on statements in Thomas's Report are representative, but not complete or exhaustive. Numerous other instances of the same evidentiary problems appear in Thomas's Report.[22]

A good place to begin a review of Thomas's Report is his ultimate opinion in this case. Thomas's "bottom line" opinion is set forth as follows: "In summary, comprehensive evaluation did not substantiate a diagnosis of brain injury. Instead, a psychological disorder unrelated to the 2001 incident offers the best explanation for the unusual pattern of symptoms and test results." Thomas Report at 13 (emphasis added).

Thomas thus makes clear that he intends to opine, both directly and indirectly, on whether Smith suffered a brain injury in the May 15, 2001, incident and whether a brain injury was and is the cause of Smith's symptoms and impairments as indicated by Thomas's testing. Yet, this is exactly what Thomas is not permitted to do under Virginia law since he is not a medical doctor. In this regard, it is important to note that the *Im* case, cited above, did not establish a new rule of evidence in Virginia. Rather, the *Im* case simply applied long-established principles which had been summarized several years earlier. In 1998, the Virginia Supreme Court held that the diagnosis of injuries and determination of the cause of injuries were matters generally reserved for expert testimony only from medical doctors. The Court held:

> On appeal, Combs argues that the trial court erred in allowing Schneck [a biomechanical engineer] to give an opinion regarding the cause of Combs's ruptured disk.... Combs objects, however, to Schneck's testimony concerning the cause of Combs's ruptured disc, arguing that only a licensed, medical doctor is qualified to render such an opinion.
>
> In response, N&W contends that since the study of biomechanics includes the application of scientific and engineering principles to determine forces exerted on the human body, Schneck was qualified to state an expert opinion regarding the cause of Combs's injury. N&W also asserts that Schneck's entire testimony was admissible to rebut Michael Shinnick's testimony concerning the forces placed on Combs's spine at the time of his injury. We disagree with N&W.
>
> The issue whether a witness is qualified to render an expert opinion is a question submitted to the sound discretion of the trial court. *Poliquin v. Daniels*, 254 Va. 51, 57, 486 S.E.2d 530,

---

22. The defense will presumably argue that Thomas does not necessarily intend to testify to each and every matter set forth in his Report. Perhaps that will prove to be true, but it will nevertheless benefit the parties, the Court, and Thomas to address the numerous evidentiary issues raised by Thomas's Report before Thomas is called to testify.

534 (1997); *King v. Sowers*, 252 Va. 71, 78, 471 S.E.2d 481, 485 (1996); *Tazewell Oil Co. v. United Va. Bank*, 243 Va. 94, 110, 413 S.E.2d 611, 620 (1992). The record must show that the proffered expert witness has sufficient knowledge, skill, or experience to render him competent to testify as an expert on the subject matter of the inquiry. *King*, 252 Va. at 78, 471 S.E.2d at 485; *Griffett v. Ryan*, 247 Va. 465, 469, 443 S.E.2d 149, 152 (1994); *Noll v. Rahal*, 219 Va. 795, 800, 250 S.E.2d 741, 744 (1979). The fact that a witness is an expert in one field does not make him an expert in another field, even though the two fields are closely related. *Tazewell Oil Co.*, 243 Va. at 110, 413 S.E.2d at 620; *VEPCO v. Lado*, 220 Va. 997, 1005, 266 S.E.2d 431, 436 (1980).

The practice of medicine includes the diagnosis and treatment of human physical ailments, conditions, diseases, pain, and infirmities. *See* Code § 54.1-2900. The term "diagnose" is defined as "to determine the type and cause of a health condition on the basis of signs and symptoms of the patient." Mosby's Medical Dictionary 480 (5th ed. 1998). Thus, the question of causation of a human injury is a component part of a diagnosis, which in turn is part of the practice of medicine.

Schneck was qualified at trial as an expert in the field of biomechanical engineering and he was competent to render an opinion on the compression forces placed on Combs's spine at the time of the incident. However, Schneck was not a medical doctor and, thus, was not qualified to state an expert medical opinion regarding what factors cause a human disc to rupture and whether Combs's twisting movement to catch the toilet could have ruptured his disc.

Combs v. Norfolk and Western Rwy. Co., 256 Va. 490, 495–497, 507 S.E.2d 355, 358–359 (1998) (emphasis added).

The Virginia Supreme Court has repeatedly reaffirmed the rule of law it applied in *Combs* and *Im*. Thus, for example, in *N&W Railway Company v. Keeling*, 265 Va. 228, 576 S.E.2d 452 (2003), the Virginia Supreme Court held that the trial court properly refused to allow an expert in biomechanical engineering with a specialization in vestibular mechanics to give testimony which would result in him directly or indirectly conveying his opinions regarding the cause of plaintiff's injuries.

In this case, Thomas's "Diagnostic Impression" is that Smith's problems are not caused by real physical injuries, including injuries to the brain, but instead are the result of Hypochondriasis. See Thomas's Report at 13. In other words, according to Thomas, the problems are not the result of real physical injuries but rather are all in Smith's head (i.e., are "somatic"). This testimony, if allowed, would transgress almost all the principles of Virginia evidence law reviewed above. Thomas is not a medical doctor and therefore is not qualified to testify that Smith has suffered or has not suffered injuries to his body (including his brain). A diagnosis of Hypochondriasis necessarily depends upon a determination that real physical injuries are not involved. "The essential feature of Hypochondriasis is preoccupation with fears of having, or the idea that one has, a serious disease based on a misinterpretation of one or more bodily signs or symptoms. . . . Repeated physical examinations, diagnostic tests, and reassurance from the physician do little to allay the concern about bodily diseases or affliction." Diagnostic and Statistical Manual of Mental Disorders—IV, 300.7 at page 504 (copy attached as Exhibit C).

Clearly, this "opinion" depends entirely on a medical determination, i.e., whether Smith did in fact sustain injuries to his brain and neck on May 15, 2001. If he did sustain such injuries and his difficulties are caused by those injuries, then he could not properly be diagnosed as a hypochondriac. Thus, for Thomas to say that Smith suffers from Hypochondriasis is the equivalent of Thomas testifying regarding the medical diagnostic and causation issues in this case, which he cannot properly be allowed to do.[23]

Moreover, it is clear that Thomas is not only undertaking to improperly address medical issues, he is also undertaking to comment on the credibility and reliability of Smith's treating health-care providers who are medical doctors. Smith's treating doctors will testify that he did sustain a brain injury and that his continuing difficulties are the result of his brain injury. Thus, Thomas, who is not even a medical doctor, has taken it upon himself to conclude that the diagnosis of Smith's treating medical doctors cannot be believed, and that Smith should have known that his treating doctors' diagnosis was wrong. All of this is very far beyond Thomas's limited role in this case, would violate the principles reviewed above, and should not be allowed.

---

23. The defense may argue that Thomas should be allowed to testify to a diagnosis of Hypochondriasis based upon the examination and report of Megan Brooke, MD, a defense expert who is a medical doctor. The fact of the matter, however, is that the diagnosis of Hypochondriasis necessarily involves a medical determination. It should be made, if at all, by a medical doctor. Importantly, Dr. Brooke did not make a diagnosis of Hyponchondriasis in her report. See Report of Megan Brooke, MD (attached as Exhibit D). The defense should not be allowed to get this type of diagnosis, which depends upon medical determinations regarding the physical injuries sustained, into evidence through the "back door" of Thomas's testimony. Moreover, it is clear that if Thomas is allowed into the diagnostic territory at all, he will inevitably (and improperly) convey his opinion that Smith did not sustain a traumatic brain injury that caused his continuing impairments. The camel's head should not be allowed into the tent, or the rest will soon follow.

It is important to note that the defense has already hired an expert who is a medical doctor, specifically Megan Brooke, MD, and has paid Dr. Brooke to exam Smith and review his medical records. Under Virginia law, Dr. Brooke will be permitted at trial to give her opinions (subject to the constraints of Virginia evidence law) regarding the nature and extent of injuries Smith suffered on May 15, 2001, and the nature and extent of the symptoms and impairments caused by those injuries. Dr. Brooke has issued a report in this case, and it is clear that she will not be bashful about supporting the defense position: For example, Dr. Brooke states in her report:

> While I do believe he had significant musculoskeletal discomfort and associated difficulty in sleeping, concentration and functioning for the first 6–8 weeks following this injury, I do not believe that his current difficulties in functioning are related to a traumatic brain injury. Even if one wishes to believe that Mr. Smith did suffer a Grade I mild brain injury (concussion), there is no way that his current extreme difficulties in areas ranging from photophobia to emotional stability to cognitive limitations could be related to this.

Report of Megan Brooke, MD (attached as Exhibit D), at unnumbered page 4.

Limiting Thomas's opinions to the testing and scoring thereof will therefore not deprive the defense of a "fair fight" at trial. The defense has hired a medical doctor who will give opinions favorable to the defense. The medical doctors in this case disagree about the nature and extent of the brain injuries and impairments caused by the kick on May 15, 2001. These medical experts can testify regarding their opinions and the manner in which they arrived at them, and the jury can then weigh, consider, and evaluate their testimony and credibility. As in *Keeling*, other experts who are medical doctors are expected to testify about the medical issues which Thomas attempts to address in his Report, and there is no need to allow Thomas to improperly enter into this area of testimony.

It is critically important, however, that the defense not be allowed to inject Thomas into this battle which is properly reserved only for the medical doctors. Thomas should testify regarding the areas of impaired functioning indicated by his testing of Smith. Thomas should not be allowed, however, to say anything which suggests or implies his beliefs regarding whether a brain injury is or is not the cause of those areas of impaired functioning. The defense also should not be allowed to improperly bolster and corroborate Dr. Brooke's opinions by having Thomas roam far afield of the actual results of his testing (i.e., Smith's performances fell within the impaired, low average, average, and high average ranges). It is clear that Thomas, if given the chance, will convey to the jury that he concurs in Brooke's opinion that Smith did not suffer a brain injury that caused his continuing impairments. Because Thomas is not a medical doctor, however, it is extremely important that Thomas be prevented from conveying his opinions on this issue in any way.

Moreover, what Thomas cannot properly do directly, he also should not be allowed to do indirectly, by innuendo and implication. Thomas's report is replete with instances where he subtly but plainly conveys "in so many words" his opinion that Smith did not sustain a brain injury sufficiently serious to cause the impairments and symptoms he has demonstrated.[24] Thomas relates, for example, that Smith "wore unusual attire" to his testing sessions. Thomas Report at 2. Clearly, Thomas is not being called as an expert on clothing. Moreover, this comment is highly subjective. What seems "unusual" to Thomas may seem ordinary or at least not "unusual" to someone else. In a similar vein, Thomas charges that Smith wore "Hollywood style sunglasses (though indoors in a darkened room), large earplugs, and a Panama hat throughout the examination." Thomas Report at 2. Once again, Thomas is not being offered as a clothing expert. He is also not a medical expert on light and sound sensitivity caused by brain injury. Moreover, none of Thomas's editorializing about Smith's attire is "scientific." Thomas used no light or sound meter, took no measurements regarding the positioning,

---

24. The decision in *Keeling*, supra, demonstrates that a trial court should not allow testimony which even indirectly violates the prohibition against medical testimony by nondoctors. In *Keeling*, the defense called a biomechanical engineering expert to testify regarding the relationship between blood pressure and cerebral spinal fluid pressure in the area of the inner ear and middle ear. The plaintiff suffered a perilymphatic fistula (an opening between the inner ear and middle ear that allows perilymph fluid to permeate the middle ear from the inner ear) which he contended resulted when he blew into a testing mechanism as part of pulmonary function tests given by his employer. The defense expert's testimony did not directly state opinions regarding the diagnosis and cause of the plaintiff's condition. The plaintiff contended, however, that the defense expert should not be allowed to give testimony which, in effect, intruded into the area of testimony reserved for medical doctors. The plaintiff argued that it would violate *Comb*s and *Im* for the defense expert to testify that such fistulas are "usually" the result of an infection or something that causes the tissue or the bone to deteriorate. Such testimony obviously would have conveyed the expert's opinion or impression that the fistula in question was probably caused by an infection or bone deterioration, and was probably not caused by the pulmonary function test. The trial court excluded the testimony, and the Virginia Supreme Court affirmed. On appeal, the defense also argued that the trial court also erred in refusing to allow other proffered testimony which purportedly did not address the issue of causation at all. The defense argued that the testimony would have been limited to answering questions about pressure in the inner ear. The Virginia Supreme Court held that, even though the defense's "subsequent proffer did not include questions as to the cause of the fistula," the trial court nevertheless properly excluded this expert testimony too because the trial court concluded that the defense did not intend to limit its questions to pressure in the inner ear and the proffered testimony involved opinions based on both medical and biomechanical matters. 265 Va. at 235. *Thus, the teaching of the* Keeling *decision is that where the substantial import and effect of expert testimony will be likely to address, even partially or indirectly, the issues reserved for medical doctors, the testimony should be excluded.*

direction, and other characteristics of the light and sound sources, and performed no tests regarding the effectiveness of Smith's sunglasses, earplugs, and hat in reducing light and sound.

More importantly, Smith's attire is not "unusual" if, as his treating medical doctor, Dr. Acosta, will testify, he suffers from light and sound sensitivity caused by a mild traumatic brain injury. In that case, the measures which Smith has taken would be quite "ordinary" measures which are widely used to address problems caused by a brain injury. Thomas's statements quite clearly convey his own opinion that Smith did not suffer a lasting brain injury and impairments resulting therefrom. Thomas has chosen words which subtly but obviously convey a negative impression—Thomas is clearly signaling that he disbelieves the medical opinion of Dr. Acosta that Smith sustained a brain injury causing light and sound sensitivity.

Under Virginia law, however, Thomas is not qualified and not permitted to testify directly as to his opinions on whether Smith sustained a brain injury, or has light and sound sensitivity or other impairments as a result of a brain injury. See *John v. Im*, 263 Va. 315, 559 S.E.2d 694 (2002). Moreover, these matters have not been and could not be addressed by him in any scientific way. He should not be allowed to signal his inadmissible opinions indirectly in subtle but nevertheless effective ways.

In Thomas's "Impressions"[25] at Paragraph 1 he states that the "[m]edical records did not provide evidence that Mr. Smith sustained a neurological injury (e.g., no evidence of altered mental status, normal neurological examination) as a consequence of the May 2001 incident." Thomas Report at 11. Later, Thomas asserts that "[t]he severity, diversity, and intensity of cognitive symptoms reported by Mr. Smith is far in excess of expectations given the nature of his accident." Thomas Report at 12. Thomas is not qualified to review the medical records and testify regarding these medical issues as to the presence, absence, or extent of injuries, including injuries to the brain. See *John v. Im*, supra.

Many of Thomas's "Impressions" consist of marshaling and argumentatively presenting the medical records (e.g. the "[m]edical records did not provide evidence that Mr. Smith sustained a neurological injury"), and reciting secondhand and with approval the report of another defense expert, Megan Brooke, MD. See, e.g., Thomas Report at Paragraphs 1, 2 [first], 2 [second]. Indeed, Thomas has compiled a six-page Supplement I which consists of a secondhand review and excerpting of Smith's medical records. These matters

---

25. Even Thomas's own terminology in his Report occasionally unwittingly reveals that much of what he says is not any type of scientific finding or conclusion, arrived at with any degree of certainty, but rather is merely an "impression" or belief misleadingly presented in the garb of science.

are not proper subjects of Thomas's testimony. Even where an expert is permitted to offer an opinion which is based in part upon hearsay data and information, he is not permitted to testify to the actual hearsay data and information on direct examination. See Virginia Code Section 8.01-401.1 (providing that hearsay data may be brought out on cross-examination). Prior to the enactment of Section 8.01-401.1, an expert could not even give his opinion if it was based in part on inadmissible hearsay. See *Meade v. Belcher*, 212 Va. 796, 188 S.E.2d 211 (1972) (doctor should not have been permitted to give an opinion which was based upon medical records which were not introduced as evidence in the case). The statute allows the expert to give his opinion even though it is based in part on inadmissible hearsay, but it does not alter the long-standing prohibition against hearsay.[26]

Thus, Thomas should be precluded from testifying regarding hearsay contents of medical records, and he should also be precluded from testifying regarding the opinions, conclusions, or observations of others, such as the other defense expert, Megan Brooke, MD. See *McMunn v. Tatum*, 237 Va. 558, 379 S.E.2d 908 (1989) (expert may not testify to hearsay opinions of others); *CSX Transportation v. Casale*, 247 Va. 180, 441 S.E.2d 212 (1994) (same).

Thomas also should be barred from testifying regarding the medical records or the medical opinions of Dr. Brooke, Dr. Acosta, or Dr. Jacobson, on the additional independent ground that Thomas is not a medical doctor, and he therefore has no proper role to serve in commenting upon or testifying regarding these matters. Thomas also should not be allowed to testify regarding any alleged previous loss of consciousness or brain injury in a sleigh-riding accident when Smith was a child. Because Thomas cannot diagnose the presence or absence of a brain injury, testimony regarding previous alleged brain injuries is also irrelevant to Thomas's testimony in this case and beyond his expertise.

In order to introduce any portion of the medical records, the defense would have to authenticate the records properly, and then bring the entries involved within an exception to the hearsay rule. Often, medical records involve multiple layers of hearsay, and thus cannot be admitted into evidence unless the proponent of the evidence establishes that each level of hearsay falls within an exception to the hearsay rule. The contents of medical records and the opinions of other defense experts, if admissible, should be introduced in a proper manner through other witnesses, and not in a back-door, cumulative, repetitive, argumentative, hearsay fashion through Thomas.

---

26. The decision in *May v. Caruso*, 264 Va. 358, 568 S.E.2d 690 (2002), establishes additional grounds on which the medical records entries listed by Thomas should be excluded. Such entries often are cumulative, do not assist the jury in weighing and evaluating the testimony of the medical experts, and can potentially overwhelm and confuse the jury.

In Paragraph 3 of his "Impressions," Thomas asserts that "[c]omprehensive neuropsychological evaluation of this 52-year-old man revealed an abnormal profile of results with impaired-range performances within several areas assessed: auditory attention and concentration; visual and verbal learning; hypothesis testing, visuoperception." Thomas Report at 12. Thomas's actual test results, therefore, demonstrated impaired functioning by Smith.

Rather than confine himself to the actual results of his testing, however, Thomas then attempts, in effect, to undermine his own test results, and thereby cast doubt and suspicion on Smith. Thomas states:

> For example, on a test of verbal learning, Mr. Smith did not benefit from additional exposure to word list items over a number of trials as most other people; he recalled as many words after Trial 3 as he did after Trial 5. Additionally, he also recalled more numbers in reverse sequence (6) than he did during the forward sequence (5) on test of auditory attention. This result is unusual, given the fact that adequate attention to the forward trial is necessary for satisfactory performance on the backward trial. The severity of observed cognitive deficits indicated by quantitative testing is greater than expected for most persons with a severe brain injury.

Thomas Report at 12 (emphasis in original).[27]

Thomas wants to say, in so many words, that Smith did not do as well on the testing as Thomas thought he should do, that he should have done better, etc. Yet the very purpose of the testing was to test and measure Smith's performance in various areas of functioning. If the tests are a scientifically reliable measure of mental functioning, then Thomas should testify to the ranges into which Smith's performances fell, and should say no more. If the tests are not a scientifically reliable measure of functioning, then Thomas has no scientifically reliable testimony at all to offer. Either way, his editorializing about what he expected and about his impressions and beliefs about Smith's performance is unscientific, unreliable, and inadmissible.

Clearly, what Thomas intends to do is not only to testify that the results of his testing indicate areas of impaired performance, but to then suggest and imply that these results are not to be believed, that these measured

---

27. Thomas's quoted opinions are very similar to the opinions that were excluded in *Keeling*. In that case, the biomechanical engineer testified that a fistula is "usually" caused by an infection or bone or tissue deterioration. The Supreme Court held that this testimony was improper. Thomas's quoted opinion asserts, in effect, that severe symptoms and impairments like those suffered by Smith are not usually caused by brain injuries. In both cases, the opinions are equally improper since their practical effect is to indicate the nonmedical expert's beliefs regarding what caused the plaintiff's condition and impairments.

impairments are not caused by a brain injury, but rather are exaggerated and made up by Smith.

Thomas persists in this vein:

> Our experience has been that persons presenting with similar patterns of very severe impairment require close supervision and assistance with daily living activities within a structured living environment (e.g., skilled nursing facility). Nevertheless, the patient is functioning independently in most activities of daily living and drives.

Thomas Report at 12.

Once again, Thomas is essentially saying that the performance impairments of Smith cannot be believed. He is also testifying about matters as to which he lacks personal knowledge, lacks a sufficient foundation, and has not performed any scientific inquiry. Thomas did actually not perform any detailed or scientific study of the extent to which Smith "is functioning independently in most activities of daily living and drives," or of the degree to which Smith is actually successful in these activities.

Thomas also asserts in a subjective manner that Smith "did not evidence difficulties with carrying out instructions[.]" Thomas Report at 5. Yet, the actual results of Thomas's own testing showed that Smith's "recall of a set of instructions was within the Impaired range immediately following presentation" and that "[f]ollowing a second presentation and a 10-minute delay" his performance was "in the Low Average range." Thomas Report at 6. Thomas should be confined to testimony which is scientifically based and is relating the actual results of his testing.

Another example of improper comment and innuendo by Thomas lies in his commentary regarding a test of recall of 15 items. Thomas indicates that Smith recalled 11 of 15 items and four of five sets. He then editorializes: "Patients with a severe brain injury often obtain perfect or near perfect scores on this measure." Thomas Report at 6. The clear implication is that Smith's results are so poor that Smith must not have been doing his best, that the impairments must be exaggerated, and perhaps even are the result of malingering. Yet, neuropsychological experts agree that their field of expertise does not include any scientifically reliable method of determining whether someone is malingering or faking a brain injury. See infra. Moreover, under Virginia law only a medical doctor is qualified to testify to opinions regarding whether impairments are caused by a brain injury. See *John v. Im*, supra.

Thomas concedes that Smith's overall performance on a test of verbal learning "was in the Impaired range[.]" Thomas Report at 6. Not content to leave it at that, however, Thomas wants to testify not only regarding the scoring of the scientific test results, he wants to editorialize that "[a]n abnormal learning curve was observed. Most people recall an increasing number of words after each consecutive trial. Mr. Smith, however, recalled as many words after Trial 3 as Trial 5 (8 words)." Thomas Report at 6. It is apparent, however, that Smith did recall an increasing number of words after Trial 1, Trial 2, and Trial 3. Figure 1 to Thomas's Report shows that Smith scored as follows: Trial 1—4 correct, Trial 2—5 correct, Trial 3—8 correct, Trial 4—9 correct, Trial 5—8 correct. In other words, just like the normative group, Smith's results improved after each trial on the first four trials. The only place where Smith's pattern of results deviated from the normative pattern was that after Trial 4 his score fell by one.

Thomas has thus "cherry-picked" the test data in a manner that seems to support his own subjective, unscientific belief that Smith's impairments are not the legitimate result of a brain injury, and to imply that Smith's pattern of performance is somehow suspicious-looking. Yet, this is not the proper or scientifically reliable function of neuropsychological testing. This type of minute variation in a few isolated test responses (out of the hundreds and hundreds of responses given) is simply not a sufficient basis for any scientifically reliable opinions regarding Smith and his impairments. That this is true is obvious from the fact that Thomas has given such extensive tests over a two-day period, and then scored the results by major categories against a vast body of normative data. Thomas should be confined to testifying to overall results of his testing and the scoring of his test results since this is the only area which neuropsychological testing has achieved any scientific reliability. Yet another reason Thomas should not be allowed to testify to the minute details of individual test results is that these individual results constitute hearsay test data which may be explored on cross-examination, but cannot be brought out on direct examination. See Virginia Code § 8.01-401.1.

Moreover Thomas's own data shows that not all test subjects improve their performance from Trial 4 to Trial 5. This is evident from the fact that the normative group results go from an average of about 11.3 to an average of about 12.0 on Trial 5. This is indicated by Figure 1 attached to Thomas's Report, which plots the normative group results at approximately 11.3 on Trial 4 and 12.0 on Trial 5. The normative group test results thus do not increase by an entire point (1.0) from Trial 4 to Trial 5. The only way that the normative score could have increased by less than a full point is if at least some members of the normative group did not increase their performance at all from Trial 4 to Trial 5, or perhaps even declined in their performance. If everyone had improved their score by one or more, the average score of the normative group would have gone up by at least one point. Thus, even within the normative group there were some people who did not improve their score after Trial 4.[28]

It is unsound and improper for Thomas to create the impression that Smith's results are "suspect" or "fishy" when he does not have a scientific basis for arriving at that opinion. Moreover, if Thomas believes his test results are not trustworthy or scientifically accurate, then he should say so, in which case his results would very likely have to be excluded completely. He should not be allowed, however, to have it both ways, i.e., to testify to results of neuropsychological testing, and yet at the same time suggest and imply that the test results are "suspect" (not a reliable indication of the functioning they are designed to measure and purport to measure) and instead mean something entirely different (that the measured impairments are not the result of a brain injury but rather are all in Smith's head).[29]

Thomas also comments on the Minnesota Multiphasic Personality Inventory-2 test results that "[p]sychological distress was suggested by the patient's response style. Such individuals often "cry for help" and report a number of physical problems. Somatic complaints such as headache, body pain, dizziness, nausea, and fatigue are common." Thomas Report at 10. Once again, Thomas has gone far beyond the proper bounds of his testimony. Because Thomas is not a medical doctor, he is not qualified to offer any opinions which directly or indirectly convey his views regarding whether Smith's headache, body pain, dizziness, nausea, and fatigue are the results of real physical injuries to his brain and neck or are somatic, i.e., not the result of real physical injuries. An individual who has real physical injuries and reports a

---

28. This attack on Thomas's opinions using a careful review of his own data may very possibly invite the observation, "Well, that can be brought out on cross-examination." As noted earlier, however, where expert testimony is not based on a scientific foundation, is not reliable to a reasonable degree of certainty, and violates other evidentiary requirements, it must be excluded and cannot be allowed into evidence subject to cross-examination. Cross-examination is simply not an adequate remedy for the introduction of inadmissible testimony.

29. Once again, the requirements of scientific reliability and a reasonable degree of scientific certainty must be rigorously applied to each link in the opinion-making process. Thus, for example, in *Santen v. Tuthill*, 265 Va. 492, 578 S.E.2d 788 (2003), the Virginia Supreme Court held that even though a preliminary breath test may be a generally reliable method of testing blood alcohol level, testimony regarding such test results was inadmissible since there was no evidence to show specifically that the particular machine used had been regularly calibrated to make certain that it was accurate. Similarly, Thomas should not be allowed to testify regarding any purported "unusual learning curve" purportedly indicated by one or two responses since there is no evidence to show that any scientifically reliable and verifiable process or methodology enables a neuropsychologist to arrive at any opinion based on such extremely limited data with any degree of scientific certainty. Figure 1 should be excluded because it purports to depict this "unusual learning curve," because it does not support any scientifically-based opinion, because it will distract and confuse the jury, because it violates the prohibition against the introduction of hearsay test data on direct examination, and because its improper prejudicial effect outweighs any probative value it may have.

number of physical problems is not manifesting somatic symptoms or manifesting some type of psychological tendency toward "cry for help" behavior, but rather is simply telling the truth about his injuries. Because Thomas is not qualified to offer diagnostic opinions regarding the nature and extent of the actual physical injuries to Smith, he should not be allowed to give any testimony which suggests that Smith's reports of symptoms are somatic rather than the result of real injuries.[30]

Similarly, Thomas should not be permitted to testify that Smith's report that his speech is not "the same as always" is an example of "Mental Confusion and Deviant Thinking" (Thomas Report at 10). If Smith has sustained a traumatic brain injury, then his speech is almost certainly not the same as always. This item is therefore indicative of "mental confusion and deviant thinking" only if one assumes, as Thomas has, that Smith did not in fact sustain a brain injury. Yet, Thomas is not qualified to make that determination. The same is true of virtually all of the items highlighted by Thomas under the headings at the bottom of page 10 and the top of page 11 ("Somatic Symptoms, Mental Confusion and Deviant Thinking/Belief, Anxiety and Worry, Depression, Sexual Concern, Beck Depression Inventory"). These items are common symptoms of brain injury, and are noteworthy as examples of somatic symptoms, mental confusion, deviant thinking, etc., only if one assumes that Smith did not in fact sustain a brain injury, a determination which Thomas is not qualified to make.

Thomas should also be precluded from giving any testimony which suggests or implies that Smith has not done his best on the testing or has somehow exaggerated his problems. This is the obvious implication of many of Thomas's statements and the innuendo and "spin" he places on certain isolated details of the test results which he clearly views with suspicion and disbelief. Yet, the truth, which is widely recognized even in the field of neuropsychology, is that there is no scientific way by which a neuropsychologist can determine that a test subject is not doing his best, is not performing up to his true capabilities, is exaggerating his symptoms, or is faking or malingering. This type of testimony should not be allowed because it is not scientifically reliable, is unduly subjective, involves numerous assumptions and "missing variables," invades the province of the jury, and violates numerous other principles of Virginia evidence law. See "Role of Defense Neuropsychologists Should Be Limited Under Virginia Evidence Law," Vol. 14, Number 4, *The Journal of the Virginia Trial Lawyers Association* (Fall 2002). [A copy of the cited article is attached hereto as Exhibit E, and the arguments made and authorities cited therein are hereby incorporated herein by reference.]

---

30. Figure 4 should be excluded on the same grounds asserted in the preceding footnote with respect to Figure 1, and for the additional reasons discussed in the text.

Neuropsychological testing and opinions regarding test-taking motivation, use of "best efforts," exaggeration, malingering, and similar matters have not achieved scientific reliability, but rather are riddled with problems, uncertainties, and inaccuracies. Research that has directly examined the capacity of neuropsychologists to detect exaggeration of impairments and malingering "has provided little basis for confidence in their success."[31] There is little or no evidence that the subjective opinions of neuropsychologists regarding exaggeration of impairments and malingering are reliable.[32] A 1994 study indicated that even neuropsychologists who performed comprehensive assessments including face-to-face contact with examinees still had problems accurately detecting malingering.[33] Clinicians with extensive experience did no better than those with limited experience.[34] Additionally, "there is no credentialing or related process that provides a direct and representative assessment of a neuropsychologist's capacity to detect malingering."[35]

These studies indicate that neuropsychological methods and tests for detecting malingering have not achieved anything that even approaches scientific reliability. Indeed, in the clinical and forensic context, assertions that malingering opinions are reliable are almost entirely speculative since, "[i]n many, if not most, instances, the clinician does not receive feedback on the accuracy of positive or negative identifications of malingering."[36]

Just last year, a Virginia Circuit Court applied the evidentiary principles reviewed above to testimony of two defense neuropsychologists (one of whom was Thomas himself) and carefully limited their testimony in accordance with the evidentiary requirements set forth herein. In ruling on a Motion in Limine prior to a jury trial in mid-2002, Fairfax Circuit Court Jane Marum Roush held that the neuropsychological experts "will not, in direct testimony, opine that the plaintiff is lying, faking, malingering, or not credible."[37] Judge Routher further stated from the bench that no expert

---

31. David Faust & Margaret A. Ackley, "Did You Think It Was Going To Be Easy? Some Methodological Suggestions for the Investigation and Development of Malingering Detection Techniques," in Cecil R. Reynolds (ed.), *Detection of Malingering During Head Injury Litigation* at 1 (1998).

32. David Faust & Margaret A. Ackley, supra, at 3. Neuropsychologists Faust and Ackley survey the limited neuropsychological literature and studies regarding "malingering," and additional citations to the materials that support the problems and concerns discussed in the text of this article can be found in their article.

33. Id. at 2.

34. Id. at 3.

35. Id. at 21.

36. Id. at 5.

37. *Batzel v. Gault*, Law No. 195596, Order entered April 12, 2002 (Fairfax Circuit Court 2002) (copy attached hereto as Exhibit F).

would be permitted to state opinions that amounted to "any variation" of these opinions.[38] Additionally, Judge Roush stated from the bench that any reference to "secondary gain" would "invad[e] a province of the jury."[39] At trial, Fairfax Circuit Court Judge Gaylord L. Finch amplified the Court's earlier Order to preclude the defense neuropsychologists from giving any opinions or testimony that the plaintiff did not use his "best efforts" on their testing, was "not trying," "exaggerated his symptoms," or produced results that were "worse than you might have expected." The Court ruled that all of these variations were also inadmissible under Virginia law, and limited the testimony of the defense neuropsychologists accordingly.[40]

It is of no consequence that Thomas's Report does not explicitly use the words "faking," "exaggerating," "not doing his best," "malingering," or similar words. Thomas has nevertheless signaled his beliefs, impressions, and suspicions along these same or similar lines. Any version of this type of testimony should not be allowed at trial because this testimony, in effect, amounts to offering opinions which are subjective, unscientific, unreliable, and violate numerous principles of Virginia evidence law. See article attached as Exhibit E and authorities cited therein.

CONCLUSION

Therefore, the Plaintiff requests that the Court enter its Order ruling that Thomas's testimony at trial shall be limited in accordance with the principles of Virginia evidence law set forth herein. A sketch Order is submitted herewith.

---

38. *Batzel v. Gault*, Law No. 195596 (Fairfax Circuit Court 2002), Transcript of April 12, 2002 Hearing at 32 (copy attached hereto as Exhibit G).

39. *Batzel v. Gault*, Law No. 195596 (Fairfax Circuit Court 2002), Transcript of April 12, 2002 Hearing at 21 (copy attached as Exhibit G).

40. *Batzel v. Gault*, Law No. 195596 (Fairfax Circuit Court 2002), Transcript of May 2, 2002 Trial Proceedings at 3-4 (copy attached as Exhibit H).

INDEX

A

AAJ (American Association for Justice) 267, 269, 413
ABA (American Bar Association) 81, 122, 469
accessing information online. *See* searching online sites
accidents. *See* inadvertent wrongdoing
Ackley, Margaret A. 503
Acme Trucking, First National Bank and Bobby Smith v. 39
actions in storytelling 126–127, 321–325
active voice 126, 170, 252
Adobe PDF (.pdf) 435
affidavits, expert 195, 219
"after" stories about plaintiffs. *See* "before" and "after" stories about plaintiffs
aggravate (word usage) 160
Altavista.com search engine 435
American Association for Justice (AAJ) 267, 269, 413
American Bar Association (ABA) 81, 122, 469
The American Jury (Kalven and Zeisel) 111
American Jury Project report (ABA) 122
American Society of Trial Consultants (ASTC) 279
analogy, explanation by 139
anchoring noneconomic damages
 about 29–30
 during closing arguments 243
 obstacles to 55–56, 58
anger
 affecting verdict size 18–19
 displayed by plaintiff's counsel 20
Angie's List site 470
appeals
 disputing note-barring for jurors 219
 offer of proof in 81–82
appearance (dress)
 plaintiffs 169, 194
 plaintiff's counsel 175

arming jurors 70, 217–221, 225, 228
ASTC (American Society of Trial Consultants) 279
Atkinson, Cliff 421
attitudes and beliefs of jurors
 bored with testimony 180
 about compensating multiple survivors 105
 fear of not understanding 171–172
 identifying during voir dire 307–308
 identifying what jurors treasure 245–246
 about impossible cases 104
 juror perceptions. *See* juror perceptions
 about paid experts 105
 persistence of belief 82–83
 personality traits and. *See* personality traits of jurors
 plaintiff's first witness and 181
 primacy of belief 82, 111, 223
 showing motivations to jurors 172–173
 speaking in front of a group 217
 about tort "reform" 86–87
 unfulfilled dreams and 295
 willingness to help others 98–99
 work history shaping 294
 would not happen to me 327–328
attorneys. *See* defense counsel; plaintiff's counsel
attribution in life-care plans 157–158
authoritative sites 438–439
award (word usage) 76–77, 84

B

Backward Analysis technique 124
Backward and Forwards (Ball) 124, 227
Bailey, F. Lee 20
Ball, David
 Backward and Forwards 124, 227
 "The Basics of Visual Communication in the Courtroom" 420
 Focus Groups 101, 221, 245

505

on good works 269–270
on good works principle 255, 260–261
Reptile. *See Reptile* (Ball and Keenan)
Theater Tips and Strategies for Jury Trials 37, 124, 176, 353, 422
Winning the Unwinnable Case 247
Ball Opening. *See* Opening Statement Template
Ball's rule 273, 292, 302, 411
bar associations 268
baseline, identifying for jurors 88
"The Basics of Visual Communication in the Courtroom" (Ball and Miller) 420
Batson v. Kentucky 94
Batzel v. Gault 503
"before" and "after" stories about plaintiffs
in direct examination 185, 186–187
in opening statements 161–163, 166, 368–370
"before comes after" sequence 163
behavior
defendant. *See* defendant conduct
driving by plaintiffs 38, 197, 371
in-trial impressions regarding 35–36
irrelevant considerations regarding 35
out-of-court 37–39, 198
self-deceptive beliefs about 35
Belcher, Meade v. 487, 497
beliefs of jurors. *See* attitudes and beliefs of jurors
Beskind, Donald H.
on avoiding legalese 299
on client's point of view 8
on controlling witnesses 213–214
on doctor's apologies 17
on juror's use of emotion 98
on redemption stories 33
on vignettes 186
Beyond Bullet Points (Atkinson) 421
"beyond reasonable doubt" concept. *See* Preponderance Template
BIAA (Brain Injury Association of America) 443
BIANC (Brain Injury Association of North Carolina) 443, 445

biases
of jurors against plaintiffs 79, 130, 205
searching online for 461–462
Bing.com search engine 435
Black, Roy 248
Bleier, Rocky 262
Blue, Lisa A. 81, 271, 272
Blue's Guide to Jury Selection (Blue and Hirschhorn) 81, 271, 272
Bob Woodruff Family Foundation 265
Bogusarian maladies 211–212
boil-downs 70
Brain Injury Association of America (BIAA) 443
Brain Injury Association of North Carolina (BIANC) 443, 445
brain injury cases
bogus online information about 430
caregiver considerations 57
causation and damages example 150
court appearances and 36, 194, 196
Creager motion for 481–504
danger for client from 7
driving restrictions and 371
hitchhiking defense experts on 207
researching online sites 441–444
Breit, Jeffrey 58
Brown, North Carolina v. 272
Brown v. Corbin 488
bullet points
in opening statements 174, 330, 384
primer for new lawyers on 420–421
burnadvocates.org site 269
business networking sites 38, 467–468

C

California v. Orenthal James Simpson 418
caps, verdict size 93, 230
caregivers
Caretaker/Noncaretaker scale 96–98
identifying in jury pool 56
unpaid 56–59
untrained 26, 57–59
Caretaker/Noncaretaker scale 96–98
CaringBridge.org site 38

Carlyle, Thomas 261
Carroll Towing Co., United States v. 15
Caruso, May v. 497
Casale, CSX Transportation, Inc. v. 487, 488, 489, 490, 497
case managers in life-care plans 157
causation and damages
    domino mechanism for 150–151
    fix-help-make up for damages framework 154–158
    on harms and losses 149–150
    hitchhiking defense experts in 206–209
    information needed for jurors 180
    on mechanism of harm 150–151
    opening statements on 149–161, 350–366
    personal consequences of injuries 152
    undermining defense on 152–154, 166, 224–225
    word usage 234
    in wrongful death cases 151
causation experts 31
cause challenges 312–315
cause dismissals 65–66, 105, 313
challenges for cause 312–315
Chapman v. City of Virginia Beach 487, 490
charitable organizations
    Caretaker/Noncaretaker scale and 97
    worthwhileness of money and 58–59
child witnesses 104
chronological sequence in storytelling 124, 321
circle, damages 244
City of Virginia Beach, Chapman v. 487, 490
clarity in speaking 114, 119–121, 171
clients in trial
    appearance (dress) of 169, 194
    "before" and "after" stories about 161–163, 166, 185, 186–187, 368–370
    being stalked 251
    client characteristics 33
    client's point of view. *See* client's point of view
    court appearances by 36, 194–196
    direct examination for 183
    driving restrictions for 38, 197, 371
    exaggerated symptoms accusation against 22, 154, 247–251
    fighting spirit of 40–41
    interim deprivation of 159–160
    juror perceptions about 33–41, 79, 130, 194–195, 205, 423–425
    life expectancy of 155–156, 209–210, 228–231
    malingering accusation against 22, 154, 247–251, 481–504
    money falling into the wrong hands and 39–40
    normal behavior of 35–36
    out-of-court behavior 37–39
    play-the-hand-you're-dealt jurors and 49
    preparing for trial 36–37
    primer for new lawyers on 423–425
    seat belt usage 166–167
    smoking by 37, 145
    stereotypes 33–34, 167–169
    subordinate during storytelling 130–133
    vignettes about 33, 163, 169
    as visual exhibits 36
client's point of view
    about degree of harms and losses 32
    first-person narrative and 7
    isolation and lack of mobility 7
    learning the harm from 7–9, 152
    showing dangers 7
closed-ended questions 84, 274, 314
closing arguments
    about 215–216
    active voice in 252
    arming jurors during 217–221, 225, 228
    avoiding double-dipping in 243–244
    citing hitchhiking of defense experts 209
    comparative fault in 242–245
    on compensation 225, 235–238
    on economic damages 237
    evaluating points to make during 222
    first-person narrative in 7, 135, 226, 391

on first thing you think 246
first words in 223
fix-help-make up for damages framework in 30
on harms and losses 254
Harms-and-Losses-Only template in 225
Harms-and-Losses-Only Template in 75–78
help jurors respond to community 222–223
on intangible losses 231–234, 235–238
on judge's proportion of time 253
KISS principle in 221–222
length of 222
on life-care plans 227–231
on life expectancy 228–231
making defendant face responsibility 20, 247
making jurors listen to 217
making notes for 216
massaging jury instructions 225, 231–235
on noneconomic damages 237
people care versus money care 252–253
Preponderance Template in 69–71
pronouns in 133
storytelling in 225–227
structure of 223
suggested defendant motivations in 19
teaching law during 70
time spent on harm and losses 4
on two futures 246–247
undermining defense in 205, 224–225
on verdict size 225, 235–238, 254
when to write 216
Why-We're-Suing paradigm 224
word usage in 93, 231, 251
CNN.com site 453
collateral-source doors
fix-help-make up for damages framework and 28
opening by mentioning past care 26
opening during voir dire 88
opening in closing arguments 20
opening in opening statements 158
opening when questioning defendant conduct 17
Combs v. Norfolk and Western Rwy. Co. 486, 492, 495
Commonwealth of Virginia, Harrison v. 489
Commonwealth of Virginia, Lenz v. 488
Commonwealth of Virginia, Robinson v. 488
Commonwealth of Virginia, Satcher v. 488
Commonwealth of Virginia, Spencer v. 488
Commonwealth of Virginia, Spruill v. 488
Commonwealth of Virginia, Velazquez v. 488
community losses
from injuries 31
noneconomic damages and 59
play-the-hand-you're-dealt jurors and 49
community-safety approach 30, 142, 197
comparative negligence 242–245
compensation. *See also* verdict size
beyond life expectancy 156, 228–231
calculating for wrongful death cases 241–242
closing arguments on 225, 235–238
defining 54–55, 75–76
for interim deprivation 160–161
Judo Law and 248–249
misconceptions about 234–235
for multiple survivors 105
Why-We're-Suing paradigm on 144
complexity in trials 179
compromise, juror 46
concepts and topics, researching online. *See* topics and concepts, researching online
conflicts of interest, researching 461
Connecticut Trial Lawyers Association 262
consent forms 148, 285
conservatorships 40
consortium, loss of 57, 173
Consumer Attorneys Association of Los Angeles 260–261
Content/Malcontent scale 100–101
Corbin, Brown v. 488
cost considerations in life-care plans 158, 227–228
Costanza, George 413
Craigslist site 457

Index

Creager, Roger T. 210, 481–504
credentialing, researching 469–470
criminal records, researching 464–466
crocodile tears from defendants 21–22
Cronkite, Walter 112, 335
cross-examination
    controlling witnesses in 213–214
    of first witness 181
    hitchhiking defense experts in 206–209
    litigation syndrome 211–212
    primer for new lawyers on 416–417
    rules for analysis 205–206
    undermining defense counsel in 205, 209–210
CSX Transportation, Inc. v. Casale 487, 488, 489, 490, 497

D

damages
    causation and. *See* causation and damages
    economic. *See* economic damages
    noneconomic. *See* noneconomic damages
damages circle 244
damages-only cases, opening statements for 164–169
danger
    from bogus information on online sites 39
    client injuries and 7
    in family-provided care 57–58
    life-care plans and 155, 157
    needless. *See* needless danger
    play-the-hand-you're-dealt jurors and 49
    safety rule violations and 12, 14–17
    tentacles of danger 142, 342, 346
    in untrained caregivers 26
    Why-We're-Suing paradigm on 139–144
Daniels, Poliquin v. 491
David A. Parker Enterprises v. Templeton 488
Davis, Sam 269
day-in-the-life videos 191–194, 418–419
death cases. *See* wrongful death cases
death penalty cases 280
debriefing focus groups 101
defendant conduct
    after negligent act 17–20, 135–136
    in attacks on clients 22
    as choices made 23
    community losses and 31
    direct examination on 181
    exposing motivations behind 18–19, 172–173
    facing responsibility for 17, 20, 56, 159–160, 247
    harm upon harm in 18
    lack of remorse in 21–22
    last-minute stipulated negligence 21, 165
    mechanism of harm on 150–151
    opening statements on 113, 124–138, 165
    as outrageous conduct 14–17
    play-the-hand-you're-dealt jurors and 49
    punishment and 51
    safety rule violations in 10–14
    starting point in stories 134, 325–327
    as unusual behavior 35
    Why-We're-Suing paradigm on 139–144, 340–348
defense counsel
    advantages from voir dire limitations 79
    claiming exaggeration of symptoms by client 22, 154, 247–251
    claiming malingering by client 22, 154, 247–251, 481–504
    defense poison questions 280–288
    on earlier deficits 160–161
    hitchhiking defense experts from 206–209
    jurors perception about 19
    jury nullification plea 55
    on Opening Statement Template 115
    plaintiff expert discrediting 200–204
    on plaintiff's court appearance 36, 195
    on plaintiff's life expectancy 155–156, 209–210, 229–231
    planting bogus information 39
    as role models 279
    Rules of the Road targeting 11–14
    time spent on harm and losses 4
    undermining in closing arguments 224–225

undermining in cross-examination 205, 209–210
undermining in opening statements 145–148, 152–154, 166
defense poison questions 280–288
deliberations
   arming jurors for 70, 217–221, 225, 228
   dialogue excerpt from 397
   information needed for 180
   instructions about 217
   jurors' rights during 66–67, 71, 77–78
   misconceptions about law and 235
   note-taking jurors and 219, 221
   perceptions about harms and losses and 108
   personality traits and 100
   poisoning other jurors 91
   preponderance during 70
deliberations focus groups 101
delivery. *See* speaking
demeanor
   during hitchhiking 207–209
   of jurors 90
   during opening statements 176
demographic jury selection 94–95, 278–279
Department of Transportation 439
depositions
   preparing clients for 36–37
   uncovering false remorse during 22
   undermining 153
depression, expert testimony about 206–208
Detection of Malingering During Head Injury Litigation (Reynolds) 503
differential diagnosis 207, 211, 381–391
directed defense verdicts 313
direct examination
   about 179–180
   day-in-the-life videos in 191–194
   for plaintiffs 183
   on harms and losses 188
   on intangible losses 187
   questions in 180, 182–183
   rules discussed in 179

   show-and-tell demonstrations in 190, 199–200
   storytelling in 185–186
   witnesses and testimony in 182–204
   word usage in 235
disability counselors 166, 188
discovery
   about degree of harms and losses 32
   expert witnesses and 202
   looking for motivations during 173–174
   TMI during 114
discussion focus groups 101
Dispossessed (Insider/Dispossessed scale) 99–100
divine punishment 50
.doc file format (Microsoft Word) 435
Donigan, Keesee v. 487, 490
double-dipping, comparative fault and 243–244
Drake, Gillian 37, 298
driving by plaintiffs 38, 197, 371
drug usage by plaintiffs 145
Duke School of Medicine 444
Dungee, Virginia Power v. 488

E

economic damages
   cautions using term 24
   closing arguments on 237
   comparing noneconomic and 55–56
   holistic damages and 238
   life-care plans and. *See* life-care plans
   negative anchoring for 29–30
   voir dire questions about 88, 90
economists 156
egregious conduct. *See* defendant conduct; outrageous defendant conduct
emotional suffering
   community losses and 31
   defendant conduct adding to 17
   Emotion/Non-Emotion scale and 98–99
   fix-help-make up for damages framework on 30
   last-minute stipulated negligence and 21, 165

Index

from loss of services 58
from plaintiff court appearance 196
secret video taping and 250
Emotion/Non-Emotion scale 98–99
ending stories 134
epidemiologists 210
event-only storytelling 126–127, 321–325
exaggerated symptoms accusations
    against plaintiff 22, 154, 247–251
    inoculation questions against 285–287
expert affidavits 195, 219
expert witnesses
    in direct examination 180, 200–204
    on family members as unpaid caregivers 57
    fraudulent opinions and 212
    on harms and losses 4, 7–9, 32, 47, 106
    high-school teachers as 198–200
    hitchhiking defense 206–209
    on liability 191
    on life-care plans 189–191
    on life expectancy 210
    on litigation syndrome 211–212
    online research about 39
    as paid experts 105, 199
    phrasing words about 145
    researching criminal records on 464–466
    researching licenses and credentials of 469
    researching ratings and popularity 470–471
    researching work on previous cases 474–475
    on time estimates in intangible losses 31
    undermining defense by 146–147, 153, 205
    validating rules 122
    Why-We're-Suing paradigm on 139, 142, 144–145
Exposing Deceptive Defense Doctors (Sims) 22, 69, 154, 210, 249, 481
eye contact in opening statements 176

F

Facebook site 38, 414, 435, 452, 467–468
Facts Can't Speak for Themselves (Oliver) 226, 403
facts in storytelling 126, 320
fact witnesses
    online research and 38
    proportioning time with 4
    on safety rule violations 139
    undermining defense with 147
failure to diagnose cases 123
fair-trade value (compensation) 54, 75
Faison, William O. 166
false remorse 21–22
family and friends
    direct examination of 184
    instructions on juror communication with 44
    in-trial impressions about 36
    money falling into wrong hands of 39–40
    out-of-court behavior 37–39
    as unpaid caregivers 56–58
    as untrained caregivers 26
    as visual exhibits 36
Faust, David 503
Federal Motor Carrier Safety Administration 439
federal standards
    on criminal records 465
    inoculation questions and 286–287
    on warning labels 18–19, 172
financial information, researching 462–464
First National Bank and Bobby Smith v. Acme Trucking 39
first-person narrative in closing arguments 7, 135, 226, 391
first thing you think 246
first witness for plaintiff in direct examination 180–181
first words
    in closing arguments 223
    in opening statements 119
fix-help-make up for damages framework
    community losses 30–31
    fix aspect in 28, 39
    help aspect in 28, 29–30
    make up for aspect in 28, 30–31
    online research and 39

opening statements on 154–161
focus groups
    limitations of 44
    predicting verdict sizes 245
    primer for new lawyers on 418–419, 426–427
    researching topic-specific resources 456
    spotting personality traits in 100
    testing day-in-the-life videos on 192
    testing first-person story on 226
    testing videos on 162
Focus Groups (Ball, Miller, and Malekpour) 101, 221, 245
follow-up questions
    all-purpose 65, 72, 85, 89, 107, 275–278
    in direct examination 182
    motion for voir-dire improvements on 81
foreperson (juries) 305
Freedom of Information Act 465
Freeman, Michael 210, 249, 481
Friedman, Rick
    Polarizing the Case 22, 69, 154, 210, 249, 481
    Rules of the Road. See Rules of the Road methodology
Friends of the G.A.L. 265
frivolous cases 87, 105
future care costs 158

G

gathering information. *See* information gathering
Gault, Batzel v. 503
Georgia, good works in 263
geriatric specialists 106, 157
Ghandi, Mohandas 46
God's will jurors 50
Golden Rule prohibitions 152, 343
good works principle 253–255, 257–270
Google.com search engines 435. *See also* searching online sites
Google Earth 38, 462
government organizations 438–444, 453

government standards
    on criminal records 465
    inoculation questions and 286–287
    on warning labels 18–19, 172
Grasty v. Tanner 488
Grief and Loss (Hall and Tecala) 106, 188
grief counselors
    about 188
    about harms and losses 32, 106
Griffett v. Ryan 492
Guardian ad Litem program 265
guardianships 40

H

Hall, Robert T. 32, 106, 188
hand language 63, 237–238, 409
"Hand Rule" 15
hardship cause hearings 310
harms and losses
    as basis for verdict size 26
    calculating 72–78, 234–235
    causation and damages on 149–150, 150–151
    closing arguments on 225, 235–238, 254
    defining compensation for 54, 75–76
    determining lesser harm 242
    direct examination on 181, 183, 188
    fix-help-make up for damages framework on 29–31
    Harms and Losses Lists 106–109
    harm upon harm in 18, 250
    improper factors to consider 73
    intangible losses 183, 187
    intervention and 234
    juror perceptions about 47–48
    learning extent of 7–9
    from loss of services 58
    massaging jury instructions 225
    noneconomic damages and 56
    noneconomic harm 7
    show fighting spirit during 40–41
    specialists reporting on 32, 106
    stipulated negligence and 21, 165
    stories illustrating depth of 93
    time spent on 4–5, 83, 253

verdicts and degree of 32
   as visual exhibits 36
   Why-We're-Suing paradigm on 140, 143, 165
   witnesses on 185, 188
Harms and Losses Lists 106–109
Harms-and-Losses-Only Template
   about 71–72
   in closing arguments 75–78, 225
   in opening statements 74
   in plaintiff's testimony 75–76
   in voir dire 72–74
harms consultants 32, 47, 106
harm upon harm 18, 250
Harrison v. Commonwealth of Virginia 489
Havens, Lauren 429–480
Hayes, Gary Martin 263
hedonistic (word usage) 93
high-school teachers 198–200, 470–471
Hippocratic oath 382
Hirschhorn, Robert B. 81, 271, 272
historical societies as location-specific resources 454
hitchhiking in cross-examination 206–209
hkqkids.org site 263
holistic damages 238
hollow advocacy 186
Hourigan, Kluger, & Quinn law firm 263

I

illegal immigrants 145, 167–168
Im, John v. 486–487, 488, 491, 492, 495, 496, 499
important, jurors feeling 42–43
inadvertent wrongdoing
   juror perceptions about 23, 102–103
   safety rule violations and 10–11
In Control/Not-in-Control scale 101–102
individuals, researching online. *See* people, researching online
inferences from evidence 198
information gathering
   about degree of harms and losses 32
   for inoculation questions 284
   online research. *See* searching online sites

   during voir dire 43, 83–85
inoculating against defense poison questions 283–288
Insider/Dispossessed scale 99–100
intangible losses
   calculating 159–160
   closing arguments on 31, 235–238
   direct examination on 187
   opening statements on 159–160
interim deprivation of plaintiff 159–160
intervention 234
intrusive information. *See* people, researching online
isolation as noneconomic harm 7, 196
ITT Hartford v. Virginia Financial Assoc. 487

J

Jaques, Rose v. 481
Jew, Rodney 156
Johnson, Gary C.
   on identifying what jurors treasure 245
   on inoculation questions 288
   on Judo Law 247–248
   on making jury feel importance of cases 42–43
   on verdict size 10
   on word usage 84
   Winning the Unwinnable Case 247
Johnson, Gordon S., Jr. 263
John v. Im 486–487, 488, 491, 492, 495, 496, 499
Jordan, Michael 1, 316
The Journal of the Virginia Trial Lawyers Association 502
judges
   appealing decisions of 81–82
   cause dismissals 65–66, 105, 313
   forcing plaintiff presence at trial 196–197
   instructions regarding peremptories 85
   involvement in voir dire 302–303, 317–318
   judge-approved questions 317–318
   mini-opening by 99, 309
   on note-taking by jurors 219

pre-instruction on the law 122
proportion of time on instructions 253
rehabilitating jurors 80–81, 313
time limitations for voir dire 79–80, 294
Judo Law 247–251
juror perceptions
    about allowing noneconomic damages 87–93
    attitudes and beliefs. *See* attitudes and beliefs of jurors
    about child witnesses 104, 188
    compromise and 46
    about controlling witnesses 213–214
    about danger levels and safety rules 14–17
    from day-in-the-life videos 192, 193
    about defendant conduct 10–22
    about defense counsel 19
    about degree of harms and losses 32
    about economists 156
    of first-person narrative 135
    about fix-help-make up for damages framework 28–31
    about God's will 50
    about harms and losses 4–5, 47–48
    about hollow advocacy 186
    about importance of cases 42–43
    about inadvertent wrongdoing 23, 102–103
    initial impressions about cases 82–83
    juror self-protection and 3
    from online research 38–39
    opening statements and 111
    about pain and suffering 7, 47–48
    persistence mechanism and 82–83
    personality traits and. *See* personality traits of jurors
    about plaintiffs 33–41, 79, 130, 194–195, 205, 423–425
    about plaintiff's counsel 6, 19–20, 63, 112–113, 425–426
    play-the-hand-you're-dealt 49
    poisoning other jurors 1–2, 73, 91, 255, 280–289
    about preponderance 64
    primacy mechanism and 82
    primer for new lawyers on 417–419
    about punitive verdicts 51
    about reactions to verdict 44–45
    seeing from client's point of view 7–9
    from self-deceptive beliefs 35
    shaping during voir dire 83–85
    about smoking 37
    tolerance for pain 93
    about tort "reform" 85–87
    verdict size based on 10, 18–20, 23–24
    about who gets the money 33–41
    about worthwhileness of money 24–27
jurors' rights questions
    Harms and Losses Only Template and 77–78
    Preponderance Template and 66–67, 71
    voir dire and 109, 310–312
jury consultants 89, 311
jury instructions and requirements
    arming jurors for deliberations 70, 217–221, 225, 228
    calculating compensation 53–54, 72–78, 91, 159–160, 164, 238–242
    in closing arguments 217–221, 222–223, 225
    on comparative fault 242–245
    Harms and Losses Lists 106–109
    judge's proportion of time on 253
    jurors' rights and 66–67, 71, 77–78
    massaging 225, 231–235
    note-taking by jurors 219, 221, 238
    pre-instruction on the law 122
    Preponderance Template and 61–72
    rehabilitation and 80–81, 313
    voir dire questions and 90
    word usage in 235
jury nullification 55
Jury Practical Dynamics 2 (Wolf) 226
jury selection
    based on demographics 94–95, 278–279
    primer for new lawyers on 409–413
    religion and 102, 279
    voir dire and. *See* voir dire

Jury Trial Innovations (National Center for State Courts) 81
Jurywork (National Jury Project) 81, 271

K

Kalven, Harry, Jr. 111
Karakas, Nurhan 391
Karton, Joshua
   about 8, 37, 298, 413
   on goal of storytelling 129
Keeling, N&W Railway Company v. 492, 495, 498
Keenan, Donald H.
   on client preparation 37
   on good works 259–260
   on lawyers and knowledge 114
   on life-care plans 227
   on two futures 246
   on witness preparation 183
   Reptile. See Reptile (Ball and Keenan)
keepgeorgiasafe.org site 263
Keesee v. Donigan 487, 490
Kentucky, Batson v. 94
Kimberlin v. PM Transport, Inc. 488
King v. Sowers 492
KISS principle
   in closing arguments 221–222
   in opening statements 124–125
   primer for new lawyers on 406
Klieman, Rikki 36, 182

L

lack of mobility
   as damages factor 241
   danger and 7
   as noneconomic harm 7
lack of remorse in defendant conduct 21–22
Lado, VEPCO v. 492
Landlubber-Passenger (Ship Captain/Landlubber-Passenger scale) 101–102
Langer, Steve 115
language. *See* word usage
leaders, jurors as 97, 103, 291, 304–307
leading questions 80–81, 313

learning the harm
   from client's point of view 7–9, 152
   hollow advocacy and 186
legal jargon
   avoiding in questioning 299–300
   boil-downs replacing 70
   cautions against 29
   primer for new lawyers on 398–403
length of opening statements 175–176
length of stories 134
Lenz v. Commonwealth of Virginia 488
Leonard, James J. 393
Levine, Moe 183
Lewis, Darryl 381
liability
   determining number of witnesses 185
   hitchhiking defense experts on 207–209
   inadvertent wrongdoing and 102
   juror compromise and 46
   premises liability cases 131–133
   Preponderance Template on 61, 71
   product 16
   undermining defense on 224–225
   when to focus on 5
   witnesses on 188, 191
libraries as location-specific resources 453
licensing, researching 469–470
life-care plans
   attribution in 157–158
   case managers in 157
   closing arguments on 227–231
   cost considerations in 158, 227–228
   direct examination on 189–191
   empirical evidence in 157
   geriatric specialists and 157
   investigating extent of harms 7–9
   life expectancy in 155–156, 228–231
   minimum 154–155, 189–191, 227–231
   opening statements on 154–155
   substantiating high figures in 46
   unnecessary frills in 25
   word usage in 154, 158
life expectancy of plaintiffs 155–156, 209–210, 228–231
The Life You Save (Malone) 262

lighting
    for day-in-the-life videos 193
    for opening statements 177
    primer for new lawyers on 420
LinkedIn site 38, 467–468
litigation syndrome 211–212
loss of consortium 57, 173
loss of services claim 58
Lumet, Sidney 415

M

Macpherson, Susan
    on identifying caregivers in jury pool 56
    on arming jurors 220
    on instructions to jurors 44
    on juror emotion 99
    on noneconomic damages 30
    on play-the-hand-you're-dealt jurors 49
    on stereotypes 34, 168, 169
    on tone when asking for money 240
    on word usage 70
MADD (Mothers Against Drunk Driving) 263, 266
Malcontent (Content/Malcontent scale) 100–101
Malekpour, Artemis
    about 397
    Focus Groups 101, 221, 245
    on seat belt usage 167
    primer for new lawyers 397–427
    searching online sites 429–430
malingering accusations
    against plaintiffs 22, 154, 247–251
    inoculation questions against 285
    Virginia case example 481–504
Malone, Pat
    The Life You Save 262
    Rules of the Road. See Rules of the Road methodology
marshaling evidence 215–216, 224
massaging jury instructions 225, 231–235
Mayo Clinic site 447
May v. Caruso 497
McDonald's coffee case 87
McLean, Don 216

McMunn v. Tatum 487, 497
Meade v. Belcher 487, 497
mediations
    day-in-the-life videos at 194–195
    dialogue excerpt from 397
medical malpractice cases
    comparing people care versus money care 253
    investigating extent of harms 7–9
    jury selection in 44, 81
    medical information for jurors in 179
    mock trials for 167
    opening statements in 135, 381–391
    storytelling in 327
    tort "reform" and 2
    undermining defense in 148, 153
MedlinePlus site 441
Microsoft Word (.doc) 435
military experience, researching 466–467
Miller, Debra
    "The Basics of Visual Communication in the Courtroom" 420
    Focus Groups 101, 221, 245
    on voir dire experience 413
minimum life-care plans
    closing arguments on 227–231
    direct examination on 189–191
    opening statements on 154
mini-opening 99, 309
mini-stories. *See* vignettes
Minnesota Multiphasic Personality Inventory 501
mobility (lack of)
    as damages factor 241
    danger and 7
    as noneconomic harm 7
mock trials 167, 397
momentum, beliefs and 82–83
money
    as common motivation 172
    falling into wrong hands 39–40
    in fix-help-make up for damages framework 28
    getting along fine without 26–27, 58
    other sources of 26

recipients of 33–41
as unnecessary 25
verdict size. *See* verdict size
witnesses on 188
worthwhileness of. *See* worthwhileness of money
"more likely right than wrong" concept. *See* Preponderance Template
Mothers Against Drunk Driving (MADD) 263, 266
motions for voir-dire improvements 80–81
motions in limine 55
motivations
    for defendant conduct 18–19, 172–173
    in helping others 98–99
    juror perceptions and 47
    omitting in storytelling 128
    of paid experts 199
museums as location-specific resources 454
must-believe motivations 19
MySpace site 414, 452, 467–468

N

National Highway Traffic Safety Administration (NHTSA) 439–440
National Institute of Neurological Disorders and Stroke 441
National Institutes of Health 441
National Joint Committee on Health and Safety (NJCHS) 444
National Jury Project
    on arming jurors 220
    on clarity in speaking 114
    on enjoying voir dire 301
    on instructions to jurors 44
    on juror emotion 99
    Jurywork 81, 271
    on open-ended questions 84
    on stereotypes 34, 168
    on tone when asking for money 240
    on worthwhileness of money 24
National Library of Medicine 441
NCLive site 454
needless danger
    breaking the law and 234

failure to intervene and 234
from family-provided care 58
levels of danger axiom 14–15
ordinary care and 15, 233
others do it defense 16
police officers and 122
product liability and 16
reasonable care and 15, 233
Rules of the Road on 12–14
standard of care and 13–14
Why-We're-Suing paradigm on 142
negative anchoring for economic damages 29–30
negative stereotypes 34, 167–168
negligence
    as outrageous conduct 14–17
    as breaking the law 234
    comparative 242–245
    defendant conduct after the act 17–20, 135–136
    defined 232
    hitchhiking defense experts in 206–209
    inadvertent wrongdoing and 103
    information needed for jurors 180
    massaging instructions in closing arguments 225
    mechanism of harm on 150–151
    minimal harms and losses and 5
    needless danger and. *See* needless danger
    Rules of the Road on 11–14
    safety rule violations and 11–14, 119, 138–145
    undermining defenses for 145–148, 348–350
    Why-We're-Suing paradigm on 165
    word usage 231
New Jersey, good works in 269
news organizations 438–444, 450–451
NHTSA (National Highway Traffic Safety Administration) 439–440
NJCHS (National Joint Committee on Health and Safety) 444
Noll v. Rahal 492
Noncaretakers (Caretaker/Noncaretaker scale) 96–98

nondisclosure agreements 470
noneconomic damages
   anchoring 29–30, 55–56, 58, 243
   calculating 53–54, 91, 164, 238–242
   caps on 230
   charitable foundations and 58–59
   closing arguments on 237
   comparing economic and 55–56
   defining compensation in 54–55, 76–77
   fix-help-make up for damages
      framework for 28–31
   harms and losses and 56
   Judo Law and 249
   jury nullification plea and 55
   as legal jargon 29
   opening statements on 164–165
   voir dire questions 87–93
   worthwhileness of money and 24, 53
noneconomic harm
   isolation as 7, 196
   lack of mobility as 7, 241
   physical pain and 7
   word usage 238
Non-Emotion (Emotion/Non-Emotion scale) 98–99
Norfolk and Western Rwy. Co., Combs v. 486, 492, 495
normal behavior. *See* behavior
North Carolina, good works in 264
North Carolina v. Brown 272
notes and note-taking
   closing arguments and 216
   jurors and 219, 221, 238
   online searches and 435–436
   opening statements and 111, 177
   voir dire and 85
Not-in-Control (In Control/Not-in-Control scale) 101–102
Novoseek.com search engine 435
nullification, jury 55
N&W Railway Company v. Keeling 492, 495, 498

O

Obama, Barack 404
objections in limine 55
offer of proof 81–82
Oklahoma, good works in 261
Oliver, Eric
   on closed-ended questions 275
   on de-selecting jurors 45
   Facts Can't Speak for Themselves 226, 403
   on follow-up questions 72
   on how you say things xxxv, 277
   Persuasive Communications 226
   on voir dire 312
Olivier, Laurence 173
online sites
   good works on 262–263, 268
   primer for new lawyers on 414–415
   searching. *See* searching online sites
open-ended questions 84–85, 273–275, 313
opening statements
   about 111–112
   appearance (dress) during 175
   "before" and "after" stories about
      plaintiffs 161–163, 166, 368–370
   beware of the unknown during 166–169
   bullet points in 174, 330, 384
   on causation and damages 149–161, 350–366
   credibility with jury and 112–113
   for damages-only cases 164–169
   on defendant conduct 113, 124–138, 165, 172–173
   enunciating during 173–174
   eye contact in 176
   on family-provided care 57, 58
   first person narrative and 7
   first words in 119, 223
   fix-help-make up for damages
      framework 30, 154–161
   Harms-and-Losses-Only Template in 74
   hollow advocacy in 186
   juror fear of not understanding 171–172
   jurors listening intently to 169–171
   KISS principle in 124–125
   length of 175–176

Index 519

on life expectancy of plaintiffs 155–156
lighting for 177
on loss of consortium 173
loss of personal image 166
in medical malpractice cases 135, 381–391
movement in 176
on noneconomic damages 164–165
notes and 111, 177
Preponderance Template in 67–68, 156
primer for new lawyers on 405–406
promising calculation method 242
pronouns in 133, 357
rehearsing 176–177
rules discussed in 119–123, 129–130, 137–144, 164, 382
sample opening 377–380
storytelling in 119–120, 124–138, 226–227, 319–328
structure of 113–114
template. *See* Opening Statement Template
time spent on harm and losses 4
undermining defenses 145–148, 152–154, 166, 348–350
on verdict size 93, 164
vignettes in 163, 169, 363
Why-We're-Suing paradigm in 138–145, 165, 340–348, 389
word usage in 160, 235, 384
Opening Statement Template
about 114–116, 329–330
errors made using 123
part I: primary rules 119–124, 164–165, 332
part II: story of what the defendant did 124–138, 165, 334–338
part III: who we are suing and why 138–145, 165–166, 340–348
part IV: undermine 145–148, 166, 348–350
part V: causation and damages 149–161, 166, 350–366
part VI: "before" part of story 161–163, 166, 368–370
part VII: what the jury can do about it 163–164, 166, 370–374
Optimist/Pessimist scale 96
ordinary care, needless danger and 15, 233
Orenthal James Simpson, California v. 418
organizations
good works and 267–268
government 438–444, 453
news 438–444, 450–451
professional 444–446
organized presentations 404–406
others do it defense 16
outrageous defendant conduct
after initial act 17–22, 135–136
defining negligence as 14–17
outside reasons (word usage) 77–78
Overby, Swiney v. 488, 490

P

pain and suffering
as tort-"reform" buzzwords 84
client fighting spirit during 40–41
community losses and 31
defendant's conduct adding to 17
from depression 207–208
fix-help-make up for damages framework on 29
hitchhiking defense experts on 207
intervention and 234
juror perceptions about 7, 47–48
jury nullification plea and 55
last-minute stipulated negligence and 21, 165
learning the harm in 8
noneconomic harm and 7
painting bleak picture of 24
personal consequences of injuries 152
sources of money and 26
voir dire questions about 84, 89, 90
worthwhileness of money and 59
pain counselors and specialists
in direct examination 188
on loss of personal image 166
reporting on harms and losses 32, 106

paradigm for Why-We're-Suing
   in closing arguments 224
   in opening statements 138–145, 165, 340–348, 389
Parris, R. Rex 57, 238
Passenger and Light Truck Tire Conditions Manual 445
passive voice 171
past care costs 158
patterns as evidence 345
pauses in speaking 119–121
.pdf file format (Adobe PDF) 435
Pellicer v. St. Barnabas Hospital 81
Pennsylvania, good works in 263
Pensacola Constr. Co., Tyger Constr. Co. v. 489
people, researching online
   about 435
   getting started 456–457
   pyramid effect and 478
   step 1: listing individuals critical to case 457–458
   step 2: checking if people have web sites 458–460
   step 3: search engines to broaden name search 460–462
   step 4: searching for financial information 462–464
   step 5: searching for criminal records 464–466
   step 6: searching for political and military experience 466–467
   step 7: checking out YouTube and social networking sites 467–468
   step 8: locating religious information 468–469
   step 9: searching for miscellaneous information 469–475
Perdue, Jim 226
peremptories during jury selection
   cause challenges and appeals 79
   for disabled or injured jurors 47
   judge instructions regarding 85
   noneconomic damages questions 90
persistence of belief 82–83
personal image, loss of 166

personal injury cases 79, 259
personality traits of jurors
   Caretaker/Noncaretaker scale 96–98
   Content/Malcontent scale 100–101
   Emotion/Non-Emotion scale 98–99
   In Control/Not-in-Control scale 101–102
   Insider/Dispossessed scale 99–100
   leadership 97, 103, 291, 304–307
   Optimist/Pessimist scale 96
   religious fundamentalists 102
   Ship Captain/Landlubber-Passenger scale 101–102
personal privacy and voir dire 288–289
Persuasive Communications (Oliver) 226
Pessimists (Optimist/Pessimist scale) 96
pitfalls for lawyers. *See* primer for new lawyers
plaintiffs. *See* clients in trial
plaintiff's counsel. *See also* primer for new lawyers
   behavior outside courtroom 198
   displaying anger 20
   good works principle 255–270
   juror perceptions about 6, 19–20, 63, 112–113, 425–426
   online research about 38–39
   rejecting cases 266–267
   seeing from client's point of view 8, 152
   time spent on harm and losses 4
play-the-hand-you're-dealt jurors 49
PM Transport, Inc., Kimberlin v. 488
point of view in storytelling 128–129
poisoning jurors
   tort-"reformed" comments 1–2, 255
   during voir dire 73, 91, 280–289
poison questions 280–289
Polarizing the Case (Friedman) 22, 69, 154, 210, 249, 481
police officers
   needless danger and 122
   police misconduct defense 95
Poliquin v. Daniels 491
political experience, researching 466–467
positive stereotypes 34
Precede-Block-Spot inoculation 284

premature advocacy
    defined 111, 112
    Harms and Losses Lists 106
    in storytelling 127
premises liability cases 131–133
preparation for trial
    preparing child witnesses 105
    preparing clients 36–37, 183
Preponderance Template
    about 61–63
    in closing arguments 69–71
    in defense testimony 69
    legal jargon and 63
    in opening statements 67–68, 156
    in plaintiff's testimony 68–69
    preponderance formula 63
    in voir dire 63, 64–67
presentations, organized 404–406
present tense in storytelling 125, 320
primacy of belief
    closing arguments and 223
    defined 82
    opening statements and 111
primer for new lawyers
    about 397–398
    on Ball rule 411
    on bullet points 420–421
    on cross-examination 416–417
    on focus groups 418–419, 426–427
    on juror perceptions 417–419
    on jury selection 409–413
    on KISS principle 406
    on legal jargon 398–403
    on lighting 420
    on online sites 414–415
    on setting the mood 425–426
    on TMI 406–407
    on opening statements 405–406
    on organized presentations 404–406
    on plaintiffs 423–425
    reality check for lawyers 426–427
    on repetition and understanding 408–409
    on speaking 403–404
    on sympathy bids 418
    on videos 418–420
    on visual aids 420–422
    on voir dire 409–413
    on word usage 398–403
    on World Wide Web 414–415
Principles for Juries & Jury Trials (ABA) 81
products liability cases 16, 328
professional organizations 444–447
pronouns
    in closing arguments 251
    in opening statements 133, 357
    in storytelling 133
proportion of time on harms and losses 4–5, 83, 253
prove or proof (word usage) 64, 66
publications, researching 471
public colleges and universities as location-specific resources 455
public policy
    life expectancy defense and 155
    of respect for judicial system 80–81
public respect and trust
    foolproof solution 257–259
    good works principle examples 259–263
    for judicial system 80–81, 313
    problem with 255–257
    rejecting cases 266–267
PubMed site 442, 477–478
punishment
    divine 50
    inadvertent wrongdoing and 103–104
    jury nullification and 55
    punitive nature of 51
punitive damages cases 51, 247
pyramid effect 478

Q

questions
    child witnesses and 105
    closed-ended 84, 274, 314
    in closing arguments 231–235
    controlling witnesses with 213–214
    defense poison questions 280–288
    in direct examination 180, 182–183
    do and don't tips 298–299

encouraging bad answers to 89
follow-up. *See* follow-up questions
get-'em-talking 292–300
judge-approved 317–318
leading 80–81, 313
lowering bad response barrier with 296
about noneconomic damages 87–93
open-ended 84–85, 273–275, 313
poisoning jurors 280–289
"some people" 297–298
about tolerance for pain 93
about tort "reform" 85–87
about verdict size caps 93
in voir dire 83–86, 309
quiet jurors 293–294, 299–300

R

Rahal, Noll v. 492
RateMDs site 457, 470
reasonable care, needless danger and 15, 233
"reasonable man" standard 15
redemption stories 33
rehabilitation, juror 80–81, 313
rehabilitation therapists 48
rehearsing
    opening statements 176–177
    voir dire 300, 315–317
religion
    on divine punishment 50
    jury selection and 102, 279
    searching online for 468–469
remorse lacking in defendant conduct 21–22
repetition and understanding 408–409
Reptile (Ball and Keenan)
    about 114
    client preparation 37, 183
    client's carelessness 15
    community resources 26, 49
    community-safety approach 30
    damages arguments 225
    damages-only cases 164
    expert witnesses 202, 481
    fix, help, make up for framework 28
    good works 258
    harms and losses 5
    inadvertence 103
    isolation and mobility 7
    juror self-protection 3
    negative stereotypes 34
    opening statements 151, 154
    religious matters 50, 102
    repentance 160
    rules 121, 139, 185
    searching for financial information 462
    settlement conferences 194
    small cases 42
    stipulated negligence 21
    tort "reform" 130
    trial methods 46
    worthwhileness of money 25, 59
ReptileKeenanBall.com site xliii, 37, 183
researching online sites. *See* searching online sites
respect. *See* public respect and trust
responsibility for conduct
    closing arguments on 247
    making defendant face 20, 56
    opening statements on 159–160
    refusal to face 17
reward, compensation and 54
rewording
    jurors 290–291
    witness testimony 290
Reynolds, Cecil R. 503
Robinson, Tittsworth v. 487, 490
Robinson v. Commonwealth of Virginia 488
Romeo and Juliet (play) 161–162
Rose v. Jaques 481
RSS feeds 453
rules
    discussed in cross-examination 205–206
    discussed in direct examination 179
    discussed in opening statements 119–123, 129–132, 137–144, 164, 382
Rules of the Road methodology
    on applying the rules 11–12, 121, 202
    on inadvertence 103
    on needless danger 12
    on only permissible choice 12–14
    on rules 139

Index

on safest choice 12–14
on umbrella rule for every case 12
rule violations. *See* safety rule violations
Ryan, Griffett v. 492
Ryan, Mary 300

S

"safe enough" choice 13–14
Safercar site 439, 440
safest choice, needless danger and 12–14
safety rule violations
    community losses and 31
    danger and 12, 14–22
    defendant conduct showing 10–14
    harms and losses and 5
    inadvertent wrongdoing and 10–11, 23, 103–104
    negligence and 11–14, 119, 138–145
    Opening Statement Template on 119
    personal consequences of injuries 152
    phrasing wording for 144
    Rules of the Road on 11–14
    umbrella rule for 12
Santen v. Tuthill 501
Satcher v. Commonwealth of Virginia 488
Save the Cat (Snyder) 258
scales (calculating intangible amounts) 238–242
scales for personality traits
    Caretaker/Noncaretaker scale 96–98
    Content/Malcontent scale 100–101
    Emotion/Non-Emotion scale 98–99
    In Control/Not-in-Control scale 101–102
    Insider/Dispossessed scale 99–100
    Optimist/Pessimist scale 96
    Ship Captain/Landlubber-Passenger scale 101–102
Scalia, Antonin 299
scene-setting in storytelling 133
search engines 434–435
searching online sites
    absence of evidence and 477
    examples of information found 38–39, 429–431, 478–480
    getting started 475–477
    how long it takes to research 434
    how to research 434–436
    about people 435, 456–475
    primer for new lawyers on 414–415
    about topics and concepts 435, 436–456
    what to research 431–432
    when to research 432–433
    who should research 433
    why to research 431
Searcy Denney Scarola Barnhart & Shipley law firm 381
seat belt usage by plaintiffs 166–167
self-deceptive beliefs of jurors 35
self-protection, juror 3
senior citizens and life expectancy 230
sensory input in storytelling 126–127
sequence
    "before comes after" 163
    for closing arguments 223
    of witnesses in direct examination 188
settlement conferences 194–195
severe-injury cases 186
Ship Captain/Landlubber-Passenger scale 101–102
shock factor warnings 422
Shockwave Flash (.swf) 435
show-and-tell demonstrations 190, 199–200
Simpson, O. J. 95, 418
Sims, Dorothy
    Exposing Deceptive Defense Doctors 22, 69, 154, 210, 249, 481
    on malingering testimony 154
simultaneous events in storytelling 125
SlideFinder.net search engine 435
Smiley Block Co., Tarmac Mid-Atlantic, Inc. v. 487
smoking by plaintiffs 37, 145
Snyder, Blake 258
social networking sites 38, 414, 435, 452, 467–468
social workers 32, 106
"some people" question format 297–298
Sowers, King v. 492
speaking. *See also* storytelling
    clarity in 114, 119–121, 171

getting jurors to talk 290–300
juror fears about 217
jurors listening intently to 169–171
movement while 176
pauses in 119–121
primer for new lawyers on 403–404
slowly 222
succinctness in 170–171
Spence, Gerry
on honoring jurors' feelings 411
on honoring the answers 295
Trial Lawyers College 8, 136, 226, 298, 392
Spencer v. Commonwealth of Virginia 488
Spruill v. Commonwealth of Virginia 488
stalking plaintiffs 251
standard of care
on depression 207–208
differential diagnosis and 207
needless danger and 13–14
starting point in stories 134, 325–327
St. Barnabas Hospital, Pellicer v. 81
stereotypes 33–34, 167–169
stipulated negligence 21–22, 165
storytelling
about defendant conduct 124–138
actions in 126–127, 321–325
active voice in 126, 170, 252
Backward Analysis technique 124
"before" and "after" stories about plaintiffs 161–163, 166, 368–370
chronological sequence in 124, 321
in closing arguments 225–227
day-in-the-life videos 191–194
defendant's name in 125
in direct examination 185–186
effective elements of 132–133
ending stories 134
events in 126–127, 321–325
facts in 126, 320
first-person narrative in 7, 135, 226, 391
illustrating depth of losses 93
importance of sentences in 134
length of stories 134
omissions in 127

one fact per sentence 126, 320
in opening statements 119–120, 124–138, 226–227, 319–328
point of view in 128–129
premature advocacy and 127
present tense in 125, 320
pronouns in 133
redemption stories 33
sensory input in 126–127
setting the scene in 133
short sentences in 125, 323
simultaneous events in 125
starting point for stories 134, 325–327
structuring stories 227
subordinate client during 130–133
time considerations in 124–126, 323
video camera perspective in 127–129
vignettes. *See* vignettes
word usage in 119
would not happen to me beliefs and 327–328
striking jurors. *See* peremptories during jury selection
succinctness in speaking 170–171
suffering. *See* emotional suffering; pain and suffering
Sunwolf, Dr. 66, 226, 311
.swf file format (Shockwave Flash) 435
Swiney v. Overby 488, 490
sympathy bids
child witnesses and 104
first-person stories and 226, 391–393
primer for new lawyers on 418
showing harms and losses 147, 150, 352, 380
videos and 162, 192

T

Tanner, Grasty v. 488
Tarmac Mid-Atlantic, Inc. v. Smiley Block Co. 487
Tatum, McMunn v. 487, 497
Tazewell Oil Co. v. United Va. Bank 492
Teaching English as a Foreign Language (TEFL) 264

Tecala, Mila Ruiz 32, 106, 188
TEFL (Teaching English as a Foreign Language) 264
Teitel, Ernie
   on case overviews 99
   on charitable foundations 59
   on child witnesses 188
   on day-in-the-life videos 194
   on informing and advocating 112
   on jurors attitudes about impossible cases 104
   on learning the harm 8, 152
   on life-care planning experts 7
Templeton, David A. Parker Enterprises v. 488
tentacles of danger 142, 342, 346
testimony, witness. *See* witnesses and testimony
Theater Tips and Strategies for Jury Trials (Ball) 37, 124, 176, 353, 422
Thomas, Clarence 35
time considerations
   closing arguments and 222
   as component in intangible losses 31
   judge's proportion of time on instructions 253
   searching online sites 434, 436
   spent on harms and losses 4–7
   in storytelling 124–126, 323
   in voir dire 4, 80, 83, 289–290, 294
   writing closing arguments 216
Tire Industry Association 445
"tit-for-tat" approach 283
Tittsworth v. Robinson 487, 490
TMI (Too Much Information)
   in closing arguments 221
   in direct examination 179
   in opening statements 113–114, 130
   primer for new lawyers on 406–407
tone
   of jurors 90
   of plaintiff's counsel 112
   when asking for money 240
   when controlling witnesses 214–215
Too Much Information (TMI)
   in closing arguments 221
   in direct examination 179
   in opening statements 113–114, 130
   primer for new lawyers on 406–407
topics and concepts, researching online
   about 435
   getting started 436
   step 1: listing every topic relevant to case 436–438
   step 2: visiting authoritative sites 438–447
   step 3: conducting broad searches 447–449
   step 4: narrowing searches from lead discovered 450
   step 5: searching popular sites 450–453
   step 6: searching location-specific resources 453–456
   step 7: focus groups pursuing topic-specific resources 456
   time involved 436
tort "reform"
   fighting 2
   fraudulent opinions and 212
   frivolous-case questions 87
   Harms-and-Losses-Only Template on 72–73
   juror feeling of importance and 42
   jury biases against plaintiff and 79, 130
   jury nullification plea and 55
   preponderance and 71
   Preponderance Template and 64
   voir dire questions about 85–87
Transportation, Department of 439
traumatic brain injury cases. *See* brain injury cases
trial consultants. *See also* specific types of consultants
   about 298
   on all-purpose follow-up question 72
   conducting focus groups 245
   on demographic jury selection 95
   on de-selecting jurors 45
   on jurors' rights questions 66–67
   on note-taking by jurors 219
Trial Lawyers College 8, 136, 226, 298, 392, 413

trial lawyers organizations 267
trials
   complexity in 179
   fighting tort "reform" in 2
   goal of xli
trust. *See* public respect and trust
trust accounts 39–40
Tuthill, Santen v. 501
Twelve Angry Men (film) 415
Twitter site 414, 435
two futures argument 246–247
Tyger Constr. Co. v. Pensacola Constr. Co. 489

U

umbrella rule for every case 12
UNC School of Medicine 444
undermining defenses
   in closing arguments 224
   in cross-examination 205, 209–210
   in opening statements 145–148, 152–154, 166, 348–350
understanding, repetition and 408–409
United Auto Workers 444–445
United States v. Carroll Towing Co. 15
United Va. Bank, Tazewell Oil Co. v. 492
universities as location-specific resources 455
University of Minnesota Law School 136
unpacking focus groups 101
U.S. Parole Commission 465

V

Velazquez v. Commonwealth of Virginia 488
VEPCO v. Lado 492
verdict size
   anticipation of criticism for 222–223
   based on coming back for more money 27–28
   based on harms and losses 26
   calculating for noneconomic damages 53–54, 91
   calculating for wrongful death cases 241–242
   calculating harms and losses 72–78
   caps on 93, 230
   client preparation and 37
   closing arguments on 225, 235–238, 254
   defendant conduct and 10, 18–20
   degree of harms and losses and 32
   family as unpaid caregivers and 56–58
   fix-help-make up for damages framework and 28–31
   focus groups predicting 245
   God's-will jurors and 50
   Harms-and-Losses-Only Template and 71–78
   inadvertent wrongdoing and 23, 102
   in-trial impressions and 36
   Judo Law and 248–249
   juror compromise and 46
   juror feeling of importance and 43
   money falling into wrong hands and 40
   opening statements on 161, 164
   plaintiff court appearance and 194
   play-the-hand-you're-dealt jurors and 49
   Preponderance Template on 71
   punitive 51
   self-deceptive beliefs and 35
   sneaking in during voir dire 93
   worthwhileness of money and 24
videos
   day-in-the-life 191–194, 418–419
   in direct examination 180
   focus-group testing 162
   Judo Law and 249–251
   primer for new lawyers on 418–420
   storytelling perspective about 127–129
vignettes
   about client characteristics 33
   in direct examination 185
   in opening statements 163, 169, 363
Virginia court cases. *See beginning with* Commonwealth of Virginia
Virginia Financial Assoc., ITT Hartford v. 487
Virginia Power v. Dungee 488
virtual reality. *See* searching online sites
visual aids
   while arming jurors 221
   clients as 36
   demonstrating causation and damages 151
   in intangibles argument 235–238

for life-care plan testimony 190
massaging jury instructions 232
primer for new lawyers on 420–422
show-and-tell demonstrations 199–200
show-and-tell demonstrations in 190
voir dire
all-purpose follow-up question in 65, 72, 85, 89, 107, 275–278
asking about verdict size caps 93
asking questions during 83–86
Ball's rule and 273, 292, 301, 302
cause dismissals 65–66
challenges for cause 312–315
about child witnesses 104, 105
closed-ended questions in 274
creating rapport 302
defense counsels as models 279
defined 301
demographic errors and 278–279
discovering personality traits during 95–102
encouraging bad answers during 89
enjoyment versus control 301
explaining importance of cases during 42–43
fighting limitations 79–82
finding out juror background during 44
fix-help-make up for damages framework in 30
getting jurors talking 290–300
getting whole answer in 289
Harms and Losses Lists in 107–109
Harms-and-Losses-Only Template in 72–74
identifying attitudes and beliefs of jurors 307–308
identifying baselines for jurors 88
identifying caregivers during 56
identifying leaders during 304–307
identifying tort-"reformed" jurors 85–87
information gathering during 83–85
interrupting jurors 289
judge involvement in 302–303, 317–318
juror personality traits 95–102

jurors' first impressions during 82–83
jurors' rights questions and 109, 310–312
last six questions to ask 309
law on 272–273
on life-care plans 190
about life expectancy 210
motions for improvements to 80–81
on noneconomic damages 53–54, 87–93
offer of proof in 81–82
open-ended questions in 273–275
peremptories in 47, 79, 85
personal privacy and 288–289
poisoning the jury during 280–289
Preponderance Template in 62–67
primer for new lawyers on 409–413
promising calculation method 242
rehabilitation during 80–81, 313
rehearsing 315–317
rewording jurors 290–291
sneaking in verdict size amount 93
taking notes during 85
time considerations in 4, 80, 83, 289–290, 294
about tolerance for pain 93
word usage in 84–85, 235
volunteer work 305–306

W

Wainwright v. Witt 66, 303, 313
waiting.com site 263
Walmart 258
warning labels 18–19, 172
WebMD site 432, 438, 447
welfare mom 167
Why-We're-Suing paradigm
in closing arguments 224
in opening statements 138–145, 165, 340–348, 389
Wikipedia site 39, 452
Wiley, Diane
on clarity in speaking 114
on enjoying voir dire 301
on open-ended questions 84

Winning the Unwinnable Case (Johnson and Ball) 247
Winning with Stories (Perdue) 226
Wisconsin, good works in 263
witnesses and testimony
    child witnesses 104
    in direct examination 180–204
    expert witnesses. *See* expert witnesses
    fact witnesses. *See* fact witnesses
    Harms-and-Losses-Only Template for 75–76
    hitchhiking 206–209
    jurors bored with 180
    Preponderance Template for 68–69
    rewording 290
    sequence of 188
Witt, Wainwright v. 66, 303, 313
Woodruff, Bob 265
word usage
    for aggravate 160
    avoiding legalese 299–300
    in closing arguments 93, 231, 251
    for damages phrase 240
    in direct examination 235
    during deliberations 76–77, 77–78, 217–221
    for inadvertence 103
    jurors and 88
    in jury instructions 235
    KISS principle in 221, 406
    in life-care plans 154, 158
    misconception about legal terms 234–235
    on undermining defenses 146–148
    in opening statements 160, 235, 384
    Preponderance Template on 63, 70–71
    primer for new lawyers on 398–403
    on rule violations 144
    tort "reform" and 84
    in voir dire 84–85, 235
    when explaining rules 76
work history of jurors 294–295, 304
World Wide Web
    good works on 262–263, 268
    primer for new lawyers on 414–415
    searching. *See* searching online sites
worthwhileness of money
    charitable foundations and 58–59
    future medical inventions and 25
    necessity and 25
    noneconomic damages and 24, 53
    other sources of money and 26
    plaintiffs surviving without money and 26
    unclear purpose and 25
    witnesses as source of 186–187
wrongful death cases
    calculating compensation for 241–242
    child witnesses in 188
    demonstrating causation and damages in 151
    grief counselors in 106
    learning the harm 8
    multiple survivors in 105
    negligence in 148
    vignettes in 186
    voir dire for 79, 89

Y

Yahoo.com search engine 435
YouTube site 451, 467–468

Z

Zauzig, Chuck 66, 217
Zeisel, Hans 111

About the Author

David Ball, PhD, is widely acknowledged as America's most influential trial consultant. A founding partner of Malekpour & Ball Consulting, he has worked on hundreds of civil and criminal cases, providing focus groups and mock trials; guidance in jury selection, case analysis, and presentation; and highly developed negligence, causation, and damages strategies.

With Don Keenan, Ball also wrote the bestselling *Reptile: The 2009 Manual of the Plaintiff's Revolution*. Additionally, Ball wrote *Theater Tips and Strategies for Jury Trials* (NITA), now in its third edition. Along with Artemis Malekpour and Debra Miller, Ball created the Trial Guides DVD *Focus Groups: How to Do Your Own Jury Research*, and teamed up with Gary C. Johnson to produce the CD and DVD set *Winning the Unwinnable Case* (Trial Guides).

Ball has long been one of the nation's most in-demand CLE teachers. He and partner Artemis Malekpour advise plaintiff and criminal-defense attorneys, as well as commercial litigators, on cases of every size and in every venue. He can be reached at ball@nc.rr.com.

BOOKS, CDS, AND DVDS BY DAVID BALL

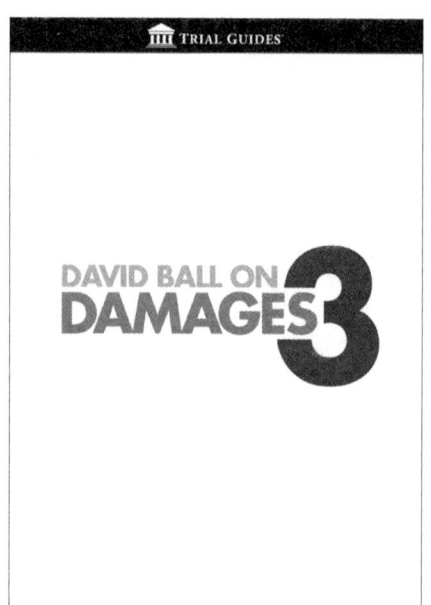

DAVID BALL ON DAMAGES 3 (AUDIOBOOK)

David Ball on Damages 3 is also available as an audiobook (twelve CD set).

THEATER TIPS AND STRATEGIES FOR JURY TRIALS

This practical guide helps you navigate the changes that occur in jury trials and refine your approach to jury persuasion. Based on both research and the experiences of lawyers and trial consultants across the country, *Theater Tips and Strategies for Jury Trials* presents techniques of the stage and screen you can use to win in the courtroom.

Focus Groups: How to Do Your Own Jury Research

In this DVD, David Ball, Artemis Malekpour, and Debra Miller explain step-by-step how to set up, conduct, and analyze your own high-quality focus groups for a fraction of the cost of hiring a consultant.

Winning the Unwinnable Case

This CD and DVD set reveals the inspiring story of how one of the United States' best trial attorneys, Gary C. Johnson, prevailed in a nearly impossible case. Learn how to deal with some of the most common problems encountered in nearly every personal injury case.

OPENING TEMPLATE

　　I. Primary rule(s) the defendant violated

　　II. Story of what the defendant did

TEMPLATE FOR OPENING

　　III. Who we are suing and why: the safety rules the defendant(s) violated

　　　　(From here on, cite experts and other witnesses for everything you say. Make yourself the messenger, not the source.)

　　　　A. What was the rule-violating act?

　　　　B. Without referring to your specific case, tell us what's dangerous in general about violating this rule.

　　　　C. How did the defendant's violation of this rule cause harm in this case?

　　　　D. What should the defendant have done instead of violating the rule?

　　　　E. How would that have helped?

　　IV. Undermine negligence defenses

　　V. Causation and damages

　　　　A. Introduction to harms and losses

　　　　B. Mechanism of harm
　　　　　　(How did the negligent act cause each injury?)

　　　　C. Personal consequences of each injury

　　　　D. Fixes and helps (treatments, and so on)

　　　　E. What cannot be fixed or helped

　　VI. "Before"

　　VII. What can the jury do about it?